THE UNITED NATIONS SERIES

ROBERT J. KERNER, GENERAL EDITOR

SATHER PROFESSOR OF HISTORY IN THE
UNIVERSITY OF CALIFORNIA

❖

CZECHOSLOVAKIA
EDITED BY ROBERT J. KERNER

THE NETHERLANDS
EDITED BY BARTHOLOMEW LANDHEER

POLAND
EDITED BY BERNADOTTE E. SCHMITT

BELGIUM
EDITED BY JAN-ALBERT GORIS

CHINA
EDITED BY HARLEY FARNSWORTH MacNAIR

❖

Other volumes in preparation

Chapters by

Florence Ayscough, Derk Bodde,
Pearl S. Buck, Chan Wing-tsit,
Ch'en Meng-chia, Chiang Yee,
A. Kaiming Chiu, Homer H. Dubs,
Esson M. Gale, L. Carrington Goodrich,
Clarence Herbert Hamilton, Han Yü-shan,
Alice Tisdale Hobart, Lewis Hodous,
Robert E. Hosack, Hsiung Shih-i,
Hu Shih, Kenneth Scott Latourette,
Li Choh-ming,
Paul Myron Anthony Linebarger,
Harley Farnsworth MacNair,
Franz H. Michael, Henry Killam Murphy,
Dryden Linsley Phelps,
Francis Lister Hawks Pott,
David Nelson Rowe, John K. Shryock,
Agnes Smedley, Têng Ssŭ-yü,
Wang Chi-chen, William Charles White,
Karl August Wittfogel, Wu Ching-ch'ao

CHINA

Edited by

HARLEY FARNSWORTH MacNAIR

Professor of Far Eastern History and Institutions in the University of Chicago

UNIVERSITY OF CALIFORNIA PRESS
BERKELEY AND LOS ANGELES · 1946

UNIVERSITY OF CALIFORNIA PRESS

BERKELEY AND LOS ANGELES

CALIFORNIA

⟡

CAMBRIDGE UNIVERSITY PRESS

LONDON, ENGLAND

PRINTED IN THE UNITED STATES OF AMERICA

BY THE UNIVERSITY OF CALIFORNIA PRESS

TO THE MEMORY OF
SUN YAT-SEN THE IDEALIST

TO THE GENERALISSIMO
CHIANG KAI-SHEK THE STATESMAN

AND TO THE GENIUSES
AND THE BLUE-CLAD "COMMON PEOPLE"
WHO THROUGH THE AGES HAVE CREATED THE
GREATNESS WHICH IS CHINA

The United Nations Series

THE UNITED NATIONS SERIES *is dedicated to the task of mutual understanding among the Allies of the Second World War and to the achievement of successful coöpera- tion in the peace. The University of California offered the first vol- umes of this series as a part of its contribution to the war effort of this state and nation and of the nations united in the greatest con- flict known to history; it offers the later volumes, of which this is the first, to the peace effort; and it heartily thanks the editors of the respective volumes and their collaborators for their devoted service and for their efforts to present an honest, sincere, and objective appraisal of the United Nations.*

ROBERT J. KERNER
General Editor

Editor's Preface

CONCERNING NO OTHER COUNTRY *have the policies of the "Great" Powers and expressions
of public opinion clashed more in the past
hundred years than with respect to China.
Greed and ignorance within and without that state go far to explain
such clashes. This is not the place, however, in which to utter praise
or adverse criticism of the land, the people, and the cultural institutions under consideration. But since critics, reviewers, and other
potential readers often wish to be told at the outset "what the book
is about," it is fitting to set forth briefly the objectives of* China.

*The aims of the United Nations Series as a whole are clearly indi-
cated in the Note by the General Editor. The specific aims and objectives of the present volume are, it is hoped, made clear by the
Table of Contents. The Editor's aim was to persuade several of the
most distinguished authorities available, during a period of war,
to present the most recent scholarly information concerning a
people whose culture has developed through many thousands of
years, and in whose homeland occurred the outbreak of what is
popularly, if erroneously, known as the Second World War. It was
necessary and especially desirable that this volume should be the
product of international coöperation such as may be hoped for in
all phases of life in the postwar world. The nationality of the coöp-
erating scholars was not, however, a matter of prime importance.
What was particularly intended was that each contributor should
be outstandingly qualified to handle the subject undertaken. It
is believed that these aims have been attained.*

*No less true than trite is it to remark that present-day China, like
other countries, can be comprehended only in the light of its past—
hence the space allotted to the multitudinous aspects of the devel-*

*opment of the Chinese people, their culture, outstanding person-
alities, and institutions through the ages. No less desirable was it
that the portrayal should be realistic rather than sentimental. The
Republic of China, like the United States of America, has gone
beyond the stage in which it needs to adopt an apologetic attitude
or to resent objective criticism. Without becoming bumptious or
chauvinistic, the Chinese, including their rulers, are able to bear
criticism, favorable or unfavorable, to weigh advice, and to act
upon that which is impartial and sensible. The story of the Middle
Country, past and present—its religious and secular systems of
thought, leading institutions, arts, economic development, military
and political conditions—is presented to the best of the abilities
of those who have graciously given here of their time and knowledge as part of their contribution to the war and peace efforts of
the United Nations.*

*To all who have helped in the production of this work, the
Editor wishes to express sincere thanks and gratitude. He and the
General Editor alone know how many have aided, positively and
negatively, by participation and nonparticipation, by advice and
suggestion. At times the rehearsal of a drama or a radio broadcast
is as interesting as the finished production. It would be an exaggeration to say that the volume of correspondence which lies back
of this book equals in value the book itself, but it may be divulged
that it all but equals it in interest. In bound form, these letters will
be one of the most treasured items in the Editor's library, and,
although seen by few, will constitute a valuable commentary on
human nature, historiography, and bookmaking.*

*To Professor Homer H. Dubs, especial thanks are expressed for
the care he has taken in making clear to the uninitiated the pronunciation (within parentheses in several chapters) of many Chinese
terms. The Wade-Giles system of transliteration has been used
throughout the volume, with the exception of a few place names
for which Government Post Office spelling has become common,
and a few individual names, especially Cantonese, for which variant spellings have become well known. Unfortunately, the Wade-
Giles system sometimes gives an erroneous impression of sounds as
pronounced by the Chinese. In an attempt to prevent mispronun-
ciation by Occidentals who do not speak Chinese, Messrs. Homer*

H. Dubs and Charles Sidney Gardner have worked out a modification of the Wade-Giles system of transliteration.

To Professors Chan Wing-tsit, Têng Ssŭ-yü, and Ch'en Meng-chia, most sincere appreciation is expressed for the way in which they came to the rescue when others, who had promised to handle certain topics, belatedly found it impossible to carry out their plans.

A heavy debt of gratitude to Professor Kerner is cordially acknowledged for his enactment, on several occasions, of a role not greatly dissimilar to that undertaken by dentists and midwives. Without his courteously gentle but magnetic proclivities, the United Nations volume on China might easily have lacked that unity and relative completeness which it possesses.

Finally, to two friends, Mr. James William Christopher, M.A., the Editor's graduate assistant, and Mr. C. C. Shih, Ph.D., a former student, go the said Editor's deep appreciation and gratitude for valuable literary criticism and for aid in a variety of ways in the final preparation of typescript for the Press.

HARLEY FARNSWORTH MACNAIR

The House of the Wu-t'ung Trees
5533 Woodlawn Avenue
Chicago 37, Illinois
March 9, 1946

Contents

Lecturer in History, University of California, Los Angeles; delegate of China to the Congress of Education, Geneva, Switzerland, 1929; associate director, rural education, National Association, Mass Education Movement, China, 1929–1931; Professor of History and Government, 1933–1938, and chairman of department, 1937–1938, St. John's University, Shanghai; research commissioner, Economic Research Department, Central Bank of China, Chungking, 1940–1941; translator of the *San-tzŭ Ching;* author of "The Meaning of Experience in the Philosophy of John Dewey" (unpublished doctoral dissertation, Boston University); "The Coming Order in Eastern Asia," in *Global Politics* (ed. by R. H. Fitzgibbon, 1944); "Research Movements and Institutions," chap. v in *China Christian Year Book, 1937;* several syllabi on China; and contributor to various periodicals.

Associate Professor of Chinese, University of Pennsylvania; Ph.D., University of Leiden, 1937; with Office of War Information, Washington, D.C.; formerly with Far Eastern Section, Research and

Analysis, Office of Strategic Services, Washington, D.C.; student of
Chinese, Peiping, 1931–1937; traveling fellow, Harvard-Yenching
Institute, 1931–1935; translator of *Annual Customs and Festivals
in Peking as Recorded in the Yen-ching Sui-shih-chi by Tun Li-
ch'en* (1936); *A History of Chinese Philosophy,* by Fung Yu-lan
(1937–), Vol. I; author of *China's First Unifier: A Study of the Ch'in
Dynasty as Seen in the Life of Li Ssŭ* (1938); *Statesman, Patriot, and
General in Ancient China* (1940); *China's Gifts to the West* (1942);
and of numerous sinological articles.

CHAPTER III

Some Revelations of Recent Excavations .   .
By WILLIAM CHARLES WHITE, D.D.

Professor of Chinese Archaeology, University of Toronto; Keeper
of the East Asiatic Collection, Royal Ontario Museum, Honorary
Lecturer in the History of Missions, Trinity College, Toronto, and
Lecturer in Missions, Wycliffe College, Toronto, since 1934; Cana-
dian Church missionary to Fukien, 1897–1909; first (Anglican)
Bishop of Honan, 1909–1934; adviser in Canada, China Interna-
tional Famine Relief Commission, 1934; holder of numerous deco-
rations from the Chinese government, 1915–1925; recipient of the
Gold Medal of the Red Cross Society of China (1923); co-author of
*Chinese Jews: A Compilation of Matters Relating to the Jews of
K'aifeng Fu* (1942), in 3 vols.; author of *Tombs of Old Lo-yang*
(1934); *Tomb Tile Pictures of Ancient China* (1939); *An Album of
Chinese Bamboos* (1939); *Chinese Temple Frescoes* (1940); and of
numerous articles and reports.

PART TWO: HISTORICAL AND POLITICAL
DEVELOPMENT

CHAPTER IV

Antiquity: To the Fall of Shang (ca. 1028 B.C.)
By L. CARRINGTON GOODRICH, Ph.D.

Associate Professor of Chinese History, Columbia University; sometime Instructor in English, Peking Union Medical College; sometime
assistant resident director, China Medical Board, Rockefeller Foundation, Peking; member, American Council of Learned Societies;
member, Advisory Committee, Biographical Directory of American
Scholars; member, American Oriental Society; co-author of *A Syllabus of the History of Chinese Civilization and Culture* (1929); author
of *The Literary Inquisition of Ch'ien-Lung* (1935); *A Short History
of the Chinese People* (1943).

Contents

The Greatness of Chou (ca. 1027–ca. 221 B.C.)

By Ch'en Meng-chia, LL.B., M.A.

Professor of Archaeology and Palaeography, National Southwest Associated Universities, Kunming, Yünnan; LL.B., National Central University of China, Nanking; M.A., Yenching University, Peking; Research Professor, Research Institute of Chinese Studies, National Tsing Hua University; Research Associate, Department of Oriental Languages and Literatures, University of Chicago, 1944–; author of "The Sacrificial Systems as Found in Ancient Inscriptions of Shang and Chou," in *Yenching Journal of Chinese Studies*, No. 19 (June, 1936); "Myths and Witchcraft during the Shang Period," *ibid.*, No. 20 (December, 1936); "A Study of Hu of King Yü Han," *ibid.*, No. 21 (June, 1937); "A Study of Kao Mei, Chiao-she and Tsu-miao," in *Tsing Hua Journal*, Vol. 12, No. 3 (July, 1937); "The Origin of Wu-Hsing, or the Doctrine of the Five Elements," in *Yenching Journal of Chinese Studies*, No. 24 (December, 1938); "The Names of the Kings of Shang," *ibid.*, No. 27 (June, 1940); "The Seat of Learning and the Site of Heaven-Worship in Ancient China," in *Tsing Hua Journal*, Vol. 13, No. 1 (April, 1941); "Notes on Archaic Chinese," *ibid.*, Vol. 13, No. 2 (July, 1943); *Chinese Bronzes in Foreign Collections, with an Outline in English* (published by National Library of Peiping, Shanghai, Commercial Press, 1941); "The Authorship of Ku-wen Shang-shu," in *Quarterly Bulletin of Chinese Bibliography* (Chinese edition; National Library of Peiping), N.S., Vol. 4, No. 3 (December, 1943); "A Study of the Ancient Bamboo Books Discovered in the Ching Dynasty," *ibid.*, Vol. 5, No. 2 (December, 1944).

CHAPTER VI

From the Fall of Chou to the Fall of T'ang (ca. 221 B.C.–A.D. 906) . . . . . .

By Têng Ssŭ-yü, Ph.D.

Assistant Professor of Chinese History and Language, University of Chicago; director, Chinese Language and Area Studies, Army Specialized Training Program, University of Chicago; Fellow, Harvard-Yenching Institute, 1938–1941; editor-in-chief, *Historical Annual*, Yenching University, Peking, 1933–1935; joint editor, *Newspaper Chinese by the Inductive Method* (1943); co-author of *An Annotated Bibliography of Selected Chinese Reference Works* (1936); *Translations of Text Selections and Exercises in Newspaper Chinese by the Inductive Method* (1943); author of the *T'ai-p'ing Kuang-chi Yin-te* (An Index to the T'ai-p'ing Kuang-chi) (in Chinese; 1934); *A History of the Chinese Examination System* (in Chinese; 1936); *Chang Hsi and the Treaty of Nanking, 1842* (1944); and of numerous historical articles in Chinese and English, includ-

Associate Professor and acting chairman, Far Eastern Department, University of Washington; sometime student, universities of Freiburg (Ph.D., 1933), Hamburg, and Berlin, and Orientalische Seminar, Berlin; pre-Hitlerian attaché, Foreign Office, Berlin; professorial member, faculty of National Chekiang University, Hangchow, and "On the March" into interior after Japanese invasion, 1934–1938; Research Associate and Lathrope Fellow, Walter Hines Page School of International Relations, Johns Hopkins University, 1939–1942; author of *Der Streit um die Mandschurei* (1933); *The Origin of Manchu Rule in China: Frontier and Bureaucracy as Interacting Forces in the Chinese Empire* (1942); *Our Peace with Japan* (1945); and of numerous articles.

Director, Chinese History Project, Columbia University, since 1934; former director, Institute of Social Research, Frankfort-on-the-Main; member, Institute of Pacific Relations, American Oriental Society, and American Geographical Society; editor-in-chief, *History of Chinese Society* (1945); author of *Die ökonomische Bedeutung der agrikolen und industriellen Produktivkräfte Chinas* (1930); *Wirtschaft und Gesellschaft Chinas: Versuch der wissenschaftlichen Analyse einer grossen asiatischen Agrargesellschaft* (1931–); *The Foundations and Stages of Chinese Economic History* (1935); *New Light on Chinese Society: An Investigation of China's Socioeconomic Structure* (Institute of Pacific Relations, 1938); "The Society of Prehistoric China," in *Studies in Philosophy and Social Science* (formerly *Zeitschrift für Sozialforschung*), Vol. VIII (1939); and of other articles in learned journals.

Contents

1931–1937, President, 1945–, Peking National University; chairman, Translating and Editing Committee, China Foundation for Promotion of Education and Culture, Peiping, 1931–1938; invited by British government to serve on Advisory Committee on British China Indemnity, 1925; chairman, Shanghai Conference of Institute of Pacific Relations, 1931; corresponding member and councilor, Academia Sinica; honorary member, American Academy of Arts and Sciences; organizer and editor, *The Endeavor* (Peking weekly paper), 1922; editor, *Independent Critic* (Peiping); co-author of *China's Own Critics* (1931); *Studies in Political Science and Sociology* (1941); author of more than a hundred poems; author of, among many others, "Suggestions for the Reform of Chinese Literature," in *La Jeunesse* and *Chinese Students Quarterly* (1916), which formed first manifesto of the literary revolution in China, and "A Constructive Revolution in Chinese Literature," in *La Jeunesse* (April, 1918); *Chung-kuo Chieh-hsüeh Shih Ta-keng* (Outline of the History of Chinese Philosophy) (1918); *Essays on the Rights of Man* (1920, 1924, 1930; in 12 vols.); *The Development of the Logical Method in Ancient China* (1922); *History of Living Chinese Literature* (1928); *An Anthology of Chinese Songs* (1928); *Philosophy of Tai Chen* (1928); *The Life and Works of the Monk Shen Hui* (1930); *The Chinese Renaissance* (1934); and of numerous works in Chinese.

CHAPTER XIV

Folk Religion 231

By LEWIS HODOUS, D.D.

Professor of History and Philosophy of Religion, Hartford Theological Seminary, 1928–1941; head, Chinese Department, Kennedy School of Missions, since 1917; President, Foochow Union Theological School, 1914–1917; served with Chinese Red Cross during Revolution, 1911; joint editor, *Careers for Students of Chinese Language and Civilization* (1933); co-author of *A Dictionary of Chinese Buddhist Terms* (1937); author of *Buddhism and Buddhists in China* (1924); *Folkways in China* (1929).

CHAPTER XV

Confucianism 245

By JOHN K. SHRYOCK, Ph.D.

Dean of the (Episcopal) Convocation of North Philadelphia, since 1942; Canon, Cathedral Church of Christ, since 1940; Far Eastern editor, *Journal of the American Oriental Society*, 1929–1941; attended Nanking Language School, 1917; teacher and headmaster, St. Paul's School, Anking, 1917–1926; lecturer, University of Pennsylvania, 1927–1933; trustee, Central China College, 1935; translator and editor, *The Study of Human Abilities: The Jên Wu Chih of Liu Shao* (1937); co-author of *The Black Magic in China Known as*

PART FOUR: THE ARTS, LITERATURE, AND EDUCATION

Contents

Contents

Society, and International P.E.N. Club; author of *Pioneering Where the World Is Old* (1917); *By the City of the Long Sand: A Tale of New China* (1926); *Within the Walls of Nanking* (with Proem by Florence Ayscough; 1928); *River Supreme* (1929); *Oil for the Lamps of China* (1933); *Yang and Yin* (1936); *Their Own Country* (1940); *The Cup and the Sword* (1942); *The Peacock Sheds His Tail* (1945); and contributor to various periodicals.

Modern Education 427

By Francis Lister Hawks Pott, D.D., S.T.D.

President, St. John's University, Shanghai, 1888–1941; President Emeritus since 1941; decorated, Order of Chiaho, second class; translator of religious, scientific, and biographical works into Chinese; author of *The Outbreak in China* (1900); *A Sketch of Chinese History* (1903); *The Emergency in China* (1913); *Lessons in the Shanghai Dialect* (1913); *A Short History of Shanghai* (1928); and of numerous articles and reports.

China's Examination System and the West   441
By Têng Ssǔ-yü, Ph.D.

PART FIVE: ECONOMICS AND RECONSTRUCTION

Economic Development 455

By Wu Ching-ch'ao, Ph.D.

Chief secretary, Chinese War Production Board; Professor of Sociology, University of Nanking, 1928–1931, and National Tsing Hua University, 1931–1935; senior secretary, Executive Yüan of National Government of China, 1935–1937; senior secretary, Ministry of Economic Affairs, 1938–1944; author of "Economic Reconstruction and Planning: Wartime and Post-war," in *Voices from Unoccupied China* (ed. by H. F. MacNair; 1944); and of articles in various learned journals.

Agriculture 466

By A. Kaiming Chiu

Librarian, Harvard-Yenching Institute, Harvard University; Fellow, Brookings Institute, Washington, D.C.; member, Academia Sinica; honorary consultant, Chinese Government Directorate of

Statistics; sometime Research Fellow, Peiping Research Institute of
Social Sciences; Lecturer in Economics, National Tsing Hua University, Peking; Professor of Economics, National University of Peking;
co-author of *An Economic Survey of 184 Farms in Shentse County,
Hopei Province* (1936); author of "Recent Statistical Surveys of Chinese Rural Economy, 1912–1932" (unpublished doctoral dissertation, Harvard University, 1938); and of articles in learned journals.

CHAPTER XXXIII

Professor of Economics, National Southwest Associated Universities,
Kunming; Ph.D., University of California, 1936; acting research
director, Nankai Institute of Economics, Nankai University; editor,
Nankai Social and Economic Quarterly; served in the United States
with the Chinese Government Commission for Postwar Study, and
as technical expert, Chinese delegation, United Nations Monetary
and Financial Conference, 1944; with C.N.R.R.A., 1945–; author of
"International Trade under Silver Exchange: China, 1888–1935"
(unpublished doctoral dissertation, University of California); and
of numerous articles in the Chinese and English languages.

Research Associate (Associate Professor), Institute of International
Studies, and Research Associate, Department of Foreign Area Studies, Yale University; Fellow in History, University of Chicago, 1933–
1935; Fellow in Humanities for the study of Far Eastern languages
and history, General Education Board, Harvard University, 1935–
1937; Rockefeller Foundation Fellow for the study of the Chinese
language and history, Peking, 1937–1938; Lecturer in Far Eastern
Affairs, School of Public and International Affairs, Princeton University, 1938–1943; research analyst, Special Defense Unit, Department of Justice, and research analyst, Experimental Division for
Study of Wartime Communications, Library of Congress, 1941; special research technician in China, and special assistant to the
United States ambassador in Chungking, 1941–1942, under the
Office of the Coördinator of Information; co-author of *American
Constitutional History* (1933); author of "A Comparison of the
Background of the Monroe Doctrine with That of the Open Door
Policy" (unpublished doctoral dissertation, University of Chicago,
1935); *China among the Powers* (1945); and of various reports and
articles related to field of Far Eastern studies.

Contents

List of Illustrations

[xxix]

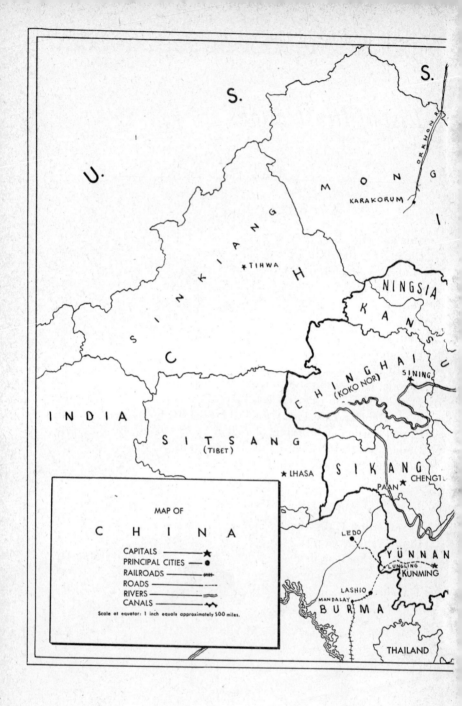

MAP OF

C H I N A

CAPITALS ───────★
PRINCIPAL CITIES ──●
RAILROADS ───────┼┼┼┼
ROADS ──────────
RIVERS ─────────
CANALS ─────────

Scale at equator: 1 inch equals approximately 500 miles.

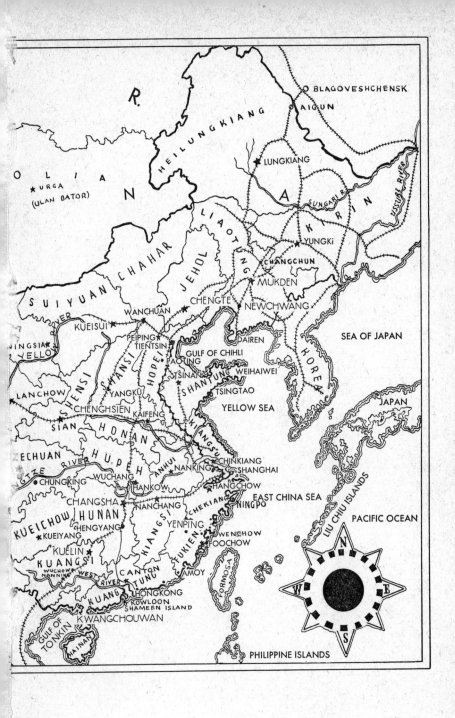

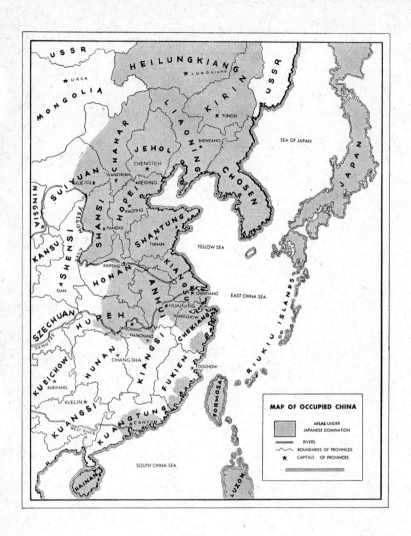

MAP OF OCCUPIED CHINA

AREAS UNDER
JAPANESE DOMINATION

RIVERS

BOUNDARIES OF PROVINCES

★ CAPITALS OF PROVINCES

CHINESE NATIONAL ANTHEM

San Min Chu I

ORIGINAL

TRANSLATION BY
TU TING-HSIU

三民主義
吾黨所宗
以建民國
以進大同

咨爾多士
為民前鋒
夙夜匪懈
主義是從

矢勤矢勇
必信必忠
一心一德
貫徹始終

San Min Chu I
Our aim shall be
To found a free land;
World peace be our stand.

Lead on, comrades;
Vanguards ye are!
Hold fast your aim
By sun and star!

Be earnest and brave
Your country to save.
One heart, one soul;
One mind, one goal!

Part One

BACKGROUND

CHAPTER I

Molding Forces

BY HAN YÜ-SHAN

IT IS NOT BY ACCIDENT that China was one of the United Nations engaged in fighting for the democratic way of life. China's molding forces constitute part of the world's democratic heritage. Instead of advocating man's conquest of Nature, the early sages believed that harmony with Nature would bring enduring satisfaction. Confucius is said to have crystallized this thought in his doctrine of *T'ien Jên Hsiang-yü* (t'ien ren siang-yü), Heaven and Man in Partnership. He taught that when the ways of Nature are sincerely valued, man participates in the creative process of the universe and can lead a meaningful existence.

For more than thirty centuries China had a government consisting of six ministries. How assiduously attempts were made to harmonize these institutions with Nature can be seen at a glance:

Ministry of Heaven:
  In charge of all important affairs of
    state,
  since Heaven covers all

Ministry of Earth:
  In charge of revenue and education,
  since Earth supplies and educates

Ministry of Spring:
  In charge of ceremonies and rites,
  since Spring is the return to life
  and the occasion for festivities

Ministry of Summer:
  In charge of military affairs,
  since Summer implies "the fire of
    discipline"

Ministry of Autumn:
  In charge of justice,
  since Autumn is the time for
    reaping
  what has been sown; and for the
    separation
  of the tares from the wheat

Ministry of Winter:
  In charge of public works such
    as the
  building of dikes and granaries,
  since Winter is the time when
    farmers
  have leisure to work for the state

[3]

Observation of Nature inspired Lao Tzŭ (lao dz) to develop his philosophy of *wu-wei,* or effortlessness—the highest principle of government. Nature speaks not; nevertheless, the ongoing of the seasons achieves the nurture of the ten thousand things of creation. Therefore the best government is the one which interferes least with the people. This laissez-faire principle did not entirely agree with the realistic golden mean of Confucius, who sublimated it by introducing a theory of government by real men. The moral qualities of a sage are expected to inspire the people to bring themselves into a natural and harmonious relationship.

Confucius developed a program for human beings based upon heavenly principles. Chief of these was his theory of government for the people—a reiteration of an ancient idea called the Mandate of Heaven: "Heaven sees as the people see; Heaven hears as the people hear." A similar ancient dictum, which Confucius emphasized, was: "To gag the voice of the people is more dangerous than to dam the flow of a river. The wise engineer of the river deepens its basin and facilitates its flow. The wise ruler encourages men to speak out freely." This lesson from Nature is said to have been expounded by Confucius (551–479 B.C.) and later by his disciple Mencius (372–289 or 390–305 B.C.). In the *Hsaio Ching* (Classic of Filial Piety) Confucius is reported to have said: "If an emperor has seven outspoken ministers, he cannot lose his empire in spite of his misdeeds . . . therefore, in the face of wrong or of unrighteousness, it is the duty of the son to oppose his father and the duty of the minister to oppose his sovereign." Mencius went a step further: "In case a ruler treats his people as if they were grass and dirt, the people should regard him as a bandit and an enemy." These ideas were popularized in proverbs.

No inspiration from Nature has had more powerful influence for the continuity of the race than the Confucian "mountain-river" theory. (See chap. xxii, below.) "The virtuous," the Sage is reported to have said, "find delight in mountains; the wise, in rivers. The wise are active and the virtuous are tranquil. The wise are joyful; the virtuous are long-lived." Each completes the other. There is consummation of joy wherever the individual becomes the key or the focal point of harmony between Nature and man, the infinite and the finite, the permanent and the transitory. Hope can be found in a precarious world, freedom can be achieved through discipline, and music can be heard in silence. Continuity between the local and the cosmic is achieved only through free expression of the spirit and attainment of discipline. In aesthetics the free mind has the capacity to arrest local beauty and transform it into cosmic significance. In ethics, life is made purposeful by striving for the mountainlike solidity of personal integrity and, at the same time, for the riverlike fluency of the power of assimilation.

The ideal of harmony with Nature is almost uniquely Chinese. It is basic in the language, art, politics, and ethics of China. Nature is the soul of Chinese inspiration. This molding force inspires and sustains China today. The great faith, expressed again and again by the nation's leaders, in ultimate moral as well as military victory comes from a people willing to pay the price of victory. The Chinese know from the experience of thousands of years that true and final triumph belongs to the morally strong—not to barbarous violators, Occidental or Oriental, of the fundamental rights of man.

◇   ◇   ◇

Closely akin to Nature is the second of the great molders of Chinese thought and conduct, namely, agelong reverence for the fathers and the mothers of the race.

Men naturally pay special regard to their parents. It was the unusual emphasis placed by the sages of China upon this instinct as a potential molder of conduct and a unifier of society that helped to determine the type of life and institutions which is uniquely Chinese. Religion, ethics, education, art, and the conduct of affairs both great and small have been inextricably bound by this one emphasis. It is a motivation of profound importance from child-hood to the grave for every member of the Chinese race.

The child learns that he is not an isolated individual, but an in-dispensable link between his forefathers and his own children to come. It is his duty to bring honor to his forefathers and to open a way for his descendants. To the adult, bringing honor to his fore-fathers has never consisted merely in ceremonies of ancestor wor-ship. By becoming a master calligrapher, an artist, a statesman, a loyal friend, a patriotic subject, a brave defender, a faithful servant, an honest merchant, a hard-working farmer—by persevering in his efforts to gain knowledge and virtue, and by putting these into practice to the best of his ability in any walk of life—he becomes a filial son. The satisfaction provided by this principle is as boundless as it is aged: it prescribes a way which can be understood by the least important member of society, a way which gives every individual a destiny to be fulfilled. There has been no double standard for the masses and the privileged. Every man has responsibility in proportion to his capacity.

The democratic factor in the "filial way" can easily be seen, since it is the norm. The principle has been buttressed by the sayings attributed to Confucius: "In the face of wrong or of unrighteousness it is the duty of the son to oppose his father." Relationship is not the pivotal point: the moral law is the common denominator. To a mind like Confucius' there could be no slavish obedience to parents and rulers when a question of right and wrong was involved.

On the subject of ancestral rites a quotation from Harold E. Gorst[1] is timely:

> For two hundred years people have unceasingly squabbled about the signification of the ancestral cult. Some have maintained that the Chinese actually worship the ghosts of their forefathers, and that the kowtow before an ancestral table is an act of idolatry. Others, on the contrary, have asserted that there is no more idolatry in bowing to the shade of a great-grandfather or burning a paper coat to hide his nakedness in the next world, than there is in the Christian custom of placing flowers on a grave, or hanging up a photograph of the departed on the wall of your chamber. It is interesting, perhaps not uninstructive, to note that the latter view is shared by the cultured Chinese. When Archdeacon Moule explained to a Chinese official the missionaries' objection to the ancestral rites, the latter replied: "Sir, you are mistaken. Ancestral worship is not idolatrous. It has not the high significance which you imagine. It implies merely a reverential and affectionate rite in memory of the departed, whom we desire to serve in their absence as though they were still present with us."

Ancestral worship in China implies a living faith. Before the shrines of their ancestors, husband and wife have composed their differences, since harmony is indispensable to the filial home. Studying in the ancestral halls or bowing before the tablets of their ancestors, sons who have entered the "gateway of Confucius"—as the educational world was long called—have felt they must work

---

[1] For notes to chapter i see page 521.

for something far beyond mere personal fulfillment. Many a ruler of China has refused humiliating conditions offered by an enemy, with the exclamation, "How could I dare to face my ancestors if I submitted to such a thing?" And in recent years countless Chinese have been more concerned about the moral judgment of future generations on their conduct of the war than they have been concerned about saving themselves.

Among the concrete benefits which come to the individual from the system of filial piety is that of "group insurance." Each child bearing the family name has his birthright, the right to the advantages of education and whatever assets the family possesses. Each aged person counts on as much comfort in his declining years as the family can possibly give. Modern Chinese have criticized this practice for its tendency to encourage weakness and dependency and for its exploitation of the younger generation by the aged. Yet it has had great moral and political influence throughout the centuries in developing social fraternity and security.

⋄   ⋄   ⋄

A third pillar of Chinese society was the civil service examination system.[2] (See chap. xxx, below.) For centuries this constituted the main avenue to officialdom. It was developed under the Earlier Han dynasty, a little before the beginning of the Christian era, and was in force until its abolition, in 1905, by the Empress Dowager Tz'ü-hsi.

The young student was known as a *hsüeh-sheng* (a learning-to-live person). Education was called *chiao-yü* (jiao-yü) (cultural nurture), and the examination system was based upon the assumption of the necessity for personal culture if one was to administer for the state. But from the term *hsüeh-sheng* it will be noted that the ideal conception of culture was not the dry-bones affair which the examination cells too often suggested.

Mastery of learning meant discipline. Education was considered the means by which men could win honor through writings, noble deeds, and service to the state. The making of a fortune held no such possibilities of prestige, but through education a man's immediate family, his ancestral line, his village, even his province— if the honor was exceptional—would receive praise and renown.

Contemplation of Nature supplied the foundation of Chinese characters, in a language that conditioned many aspects of the Chinese heritage: literature, art, and moral concepts. From such pictographs as those of the sun, the moon, mountain, and river came ideographs for morning—the sun peeping above the horizon—and evening—the setting sun, larger in size, and seen through tall grass. When imitative, indicative, and logical compounds were insufficient, phonetic compounds were created. Written characters were not subject to radical change, but served to bring unity and continuity. An educated Chinese can still read the classics of two thousand years ago. Moreover, Chinese and Japanese, though having different spoken languages, may communicate with each other through the written characters which the Japanese adopted more than fifteen hundred years ago.

To the Chinese, written characters have always been regarded as among the greatest of gifts. Not only scholars but the least privileged among the masses consider them sacred. Characters are said to "make Heaven rejoice and Hades tremble"; they "capture the rhythm of the universe" and put men in tune with its music.[3] (See chap. xxi, below.) A character scroll written by a great scholar is treasured above gold. Prior to modern times, banknotes carried poems. Sacrificial vessels were inscribed with eulogies, and common vessels with proverbs. (See chap. v, below.) Indeed, characters have exalted the nation, for to the Chinese they mean beauty and power and inspiration. To become a great calligraphist is not easy, but it is a joyous pursuit, comparable to that of becoming a master painter.

Even an infant perceived the joy in the faces around him when he was able to recognize his first characters. He won favors continually by adding to them. Rarely did he understand the meaning of the sounds which brought him reward, and throughout childhood he had to strain continually to grasp the ideas they represented.

But imagine the occasion on which a learned man is summoned to determine the most auspicious day for the five- or six-year-old to enter the "gateway of Confucius." Consider the feast which marks the day of decision, the fine clothes prepared by the parents, the special acts of veneration before the ancestral tablets, the discipline of the child for holding the sticks of incense to be burned at school! Finally, watch him, on the great day, trudging off in his finery, the San-tzŭ Ching (san-dz jing), or Three-Character Classic— a primer of knowledge studied by every schoolboy for more than seven hundred years—in a neatly tied cloth cover in one hand and a small teapot in the other. His father or his mother accompanies him, carrying the bundle of incense which he is to burn before the portrait of Confucius.

The initiation begins: the boy is met at the door by one of the older students, who takes him to the teacher; the teacher orders the students to stand on either side of the classroom facing one another. The neophyte now places his incense in the burner and carefully lights it. Then he performs the ceremony of Nine Prostrations before the portrait above the table. Three times he almost touches his head to the floor, then rises to repeat these kowtows twice. There is no whispering or giggling from the older students: the more poised and dignified the novice, the greater is their admiration. He completes the ceremony and turns to his teacher to prostrate himself three times; finally, he bows deeply three times to his fellow students.

Now the child is ready to receive instruction. For the first time he is addressed by his new name. Heretofore he has had a "milk" name only. The new name is a "book" name, selected with reference to the boy's condition, prospects, and studies, or some event connected with his life.[4] Both the "milk" name and the "book" name follow him through life.

With all eyes upon him, the little hsüeh-sheng is addressed somewhat as follows: "Now, Yü-shan, you are a disciple of Confucius, the greatest teacher of all generations under Heaven. You must no longer walk like a crab, sidewise. You must walk forward with rhythmical control, focusing your attention on what is ahead of you, not gazing to right or left to distract your attention. When you meet your father and mother upon arriving at home, you must bow deeply to them. This you must do to all older people as occasion requires. These things will help you to remember that the older and the younger have their proper precedence. All that you do must be done carefully and with propriety, so that you will be sensible of what it means to be a gentleman. You understand that this opportunity for study comes only through the self-denial of your parents."

And so the boy was initiated. The first words of the *San-tzŭ Ching* became the first lesson of his formal education:

> In men at birth, Nature is basically good:
> Nature is similar; through learning, a difference results.

Far beyond him as most of the passages were, he loved and respected this classic, and discovered more of its meaning as he grew older.

In this early education every tool and process had significance: for example, a boy's ink stick was decorated with characters and symbols; his inkstone was so made as to provoke his wonder and admiration; his skill in grinding his own ink was noted by his teacher.

In preparation for the imperial examinations—as the civil service examinations were sometimes called—in the four or five years after initiation into the literary life, students memorized the *San-tzŭ Ching* (Three-Character Classic), the *Pai Chia Hsing* (One Hundred Surnames—actually there are more than four hundred), the *Ch'ien-tzŭ Wên* (Thousand-Character Essay), the Four Books: the *Lun Yü* (Analects, or Dialogues, of Confucius), the *Ta Hsüeh* (Great Learning), the *Chung Yung* (Doctrine of the Mean), the *Mêng Tzŭ* (Works of Mencius); the Five Classics: the *Shu Ching* (Book of Documents, or Book of History), the *Shih Ching* (Book of Poetry, or Book of Songs), the *I* (or *Yi*) *Ching* (Book of Changes), the *Li Chi* (Book of Rites), the *Ch'un Ch'iu* (Spring and Autumn Annals). Every day the students practiced calligraphy and the composition of essays and poems. This amount of work may seem impossible, but it was standard.

After he had mastered this body of learning to the satisfaction of his teachers and had passed a test given by the county magistrate, the *hsüeh-sheng* was ready to go up for his first official trial in the great examination system.

The first test was known as the hsien, or county, examination. An average of two thousand students competed in each county. Shut up for a night and a day in his cell, the candidate was required to compose two essays and a poem. The first of the two sessions eliminated poorly prepared students. About one per cent were selected for beauty of penmanship, grace of diction, and understanding of the classics. These twenty-odd students—"flowers of talent"—were awarded the first degree, *hsiu-ts'ai* (budding genius).

The *hsiu-ts'ai* found themselves in an advantageous situation: they were accorded prestige and respect by all and were welcomed in local affairs where learning was especially required. They were exempted from payment of taxes and from liability to corporal punishment. Residing within the magistrate's area, they were outside his jurisdiction; they could not be punished unless they had first been tried by the educational commissioner and their degree had been taken away.

The second stage in the official tests was the provincial examination, which was held every third year, except when extra opportunities were offered in celebration of such auspicious events as the birth of a prince or the holding of a jubilee. About fifty thousand *hsiu-ts'ai* matriculated in the school of learning each year. They were permitted to study in the district academies, where they spent three years of exacting discipline in preparation for the provincial examination. In the course of this period two further siftings took place. The higher group, called *ling-sheng* (salaried student), received a subsidy.

The provincial examination consisted of three sessions conducted by imperial examiners. Each session lasted three days. In the name of the emperor the chief examiner called upon the spirits to inspire or disturb the minds of the candidates according to their deserts. As he intoned this prayer, many firecrackers were set off. Thus the examination began. Locked in his cell, the student faced the stern necessity of three days of utmost concentration.

In the first session he was required to produce three essays: one on a subject from the Analects, one from the *Chung Yung* (Doctrine of the Mean), and one from the *Mêng Tzǔ* (Works of Mencius). He must also compose a poem of eight couplets. In the second session the candidate wrote five essays, one from each of the Five Classics; and in the third session, five essays on the art of government, supporting his statements with reference to great historic ideas. His originality was shown in his application of these ideas to the problems given.

The foregoing requirements were to test the candidate's reading and the depth of his learning. Calligraphy was not counted on this occasion. Each paper was marked with a cipher copied by an official clerk; thus no examiner could discover the candidate's identity.

The number of contestants in different provinces ranged from three thousand to seventeen thousand; consequently, the quota varied from fifty-two to one hundred eighty-four persons to be

EXAMINATION HALLS

selected for the second degree, *chü-jên* (jü-ren) (promoted man). Each *chü-jên* was honored at an elaborate banquet, and received a gown and an official cap with a gilded button; also twenty taels of silver, so that he might erect flagpoles over the gate of his family residence and a wooden tablet above the door to inform all passers-by that this family had produced a *chü-jên*.

The third and highest examination was the palace examination, held triennially at the national capital. In the spring following the giving of the provincial examination the holders of the *chü-jên* degree traveled to the capital from every corner of the empire at the expense of the provincial treasuries. To help them test their knowledge a preliminary examination was held, which was similar to the provincial examination. The palace examination was usually given several weeks later. It had one session only. The problem consisted in writing an essay on a current political problem: irrigation, colonization, river conservation, unification of currency, organization of militia, programs for education. Here calligraphy reappeared as an important factor in determining the results of the examination; forms must be rigidly observed. The number of successful competitors this time would be about three hundred fifty. The degree was *chin-shih* (dzin-shzh) (achieved scholar).

The top three scholars received special honors; a third of the *chin-shih* became members of the highest literary institution, the Hanlin Academy (forest of scholars). The remaining scholars were classified in three grades of the *chin-shih*.

The successful one in the final contest, the great palace examination, was called *chuang-yüan* (juang-yüan), model scholar of the empire. Fine embroidered clothes, as well as a banquet, were given him by the emperor. He was now an acknowledged superior among ten thousand contending scholars, with solid prospects of an official position from which he might rise step by step to the highest offices in the empire.

Parallel to civil service examinations were military examinations conducted after much the same pattern. Held by county, province, and capital, they conferred the same degrees but with the character for "military" added to each. Skill in archery and great physical strength were the most important attainments in these contests.

In the county examination the candidate for the first degree obtained, from a scholar holding the degree of *hsiu-ts'ai*, a document certifying various particulars concerning himself. Thus he was guaranteed by a man of literary standing. He then came before the magistrate at an appointed time.

Candidates appeared at three sessions to compete in shooting arrows while standing and while riding a horse, in the use of large swords, and in lifting heavy stones. Great strength and skill were necessary to bend the bows, to handle the stones, and to brandish the swords.

The most worthy competitors were selected for similar tests given by a literary chancellor, in addition to a written test which consisted in copying from memory a military treatise. The chancellor could graduate a quota of these military men equal to the number of literary graduates.

Provincial and national examinations followed the same general pattern, but demanded relatively greater strength and skill. Successful competitors in national examinations were assured of employment in the imperial armed forces.

Literary or civil officials superintended all military examinations. Bearers of military degrees were not only limited in employment, but also had little social prestige: military *chin-shih* were not admitted to the Hanlin Academy.

The twenty-century-old civil service examination system conditioned innumerable important phases in the life of China. It is apparent, however, that the system could not have developed apart from the conditions peculiar to China under the empire. The system examined about two million candidates for literary degrees every year, and passed only two or three per cent to the first degree; thus it skimmed the cream of the country to serve the state. The scholars represented every corner of the empire with its diversity of needs. Some came from the homes of farmers and knew from experience the problems of the majority of the people. They could, therefore, act as a definite check on the monarch. Finally, the system may be said to have given the most powerful of motivations for implanting the kind of cultural nurture in which the Chinese people believed: the cultivation of disciplined personality, service to the state, and the production of great writings, calligraphy, and paintings. (See chap. ii.)

⋄ ⋄ ⋄

Another unique factor in the Chinese heritage is the significance given to history: the mechanics of historiography and the interpretation of history constitute some of the oldest and most basic forces in achieving a reasonable way of life. According to tradition, the office of historian was among the first political institutions; it was initiated by the legendary Yellow Emperor (or Lord) (2697–2597 B.C.). The function of the court historian was twofold: to record and transcribe great principles and events, and to advise upon the conduct of rulers and to judge them. An examination of the *Shu Ching* (Book of History) and the *Ch'un Ch'iu* (Spring and Autumn Annals), the latter a history of the years 722–481 B.C., said to have been written by Confucius, will illustrate both functions.

In ancient times the rulers of China were expected to make tours of inspection every five years to examine the work of local officials, listen to the petitions of the people, and make declarations to them. The tours were recorded by court historians, for future reference. Hence the historians could—and often did—record the misdeeds of their lords.

The compilation of a national history was a function of certain scholars in the imperial government, but these writings were not open to imperial inspection. The final editing and publication of a dynastic history came only after the dynasty had fallen. This gave historians an opportunity to recount the misdeeds of a dynasty for the warning of future generations, and bore perpetual witness to the fact that no one can escape history.

The institution of historians dates back to very ancient times. Many scholars, conscious of their high mission, braved the wrath of despotic rulers to lay the foundations of a great tradition. Ts'ui Chu (ju), a commander of the palace guard of the sixth century B.C., killed the Prince of Ch'i (tsi) for having deprived him of a fascinating beauty—widow of the Lord of T'ang, a magistrate. The official historian put this chapter of infamies on record. Ts'ui Chu took the tablet from the state archives and executed the historian. A brother of the historian renewed the record—and suffered death also. A second brother of the historian then presented himself, pen in hand, to repeat the tale and seal it with his blood. With this the tyrant's heart was touched: he spared the life of the third historian and allowed his own condemnation to stand. The right of historians to tell the truth about the monarch became such a fiercely guarded tradition that even the most tyrannical rulers feared to punish the censor or the historian.

Members of the Hanlin Academy were in charge of the literary enterprises of the empire; a majority of the censors were appointed from among them. The censorate was so powerful an institution that its members were free to speak on all matters concerning public welfare; particularly were they frank in political criticism.

If history is the expression of national life—a tissue resembling that of a living organism uniting past and present—there is no better way to measure the achievement of the Chinese people than by their regard for history. In China today the constitution in-

cludes the rights of petition, impeachment, and auditing; these
show how contemporary China studies the experiences of the past
with an eye to present-day needs. Modern scholars imbued with
the old learning are best fitted to guide their country through the
present period of confusion. Generalissimo Chiang (jiang) owes
quite as much to his classical learning as he does to his modern
training.   ◇   ◇   ◇

Finally, as a molding force in Chinese life, the use of proverbs by
the people should be considered. China is a land of proverbs. Their
terse and forcible language satisfies the realistic and humorous
temperament of the people. They express the deep-lying Chinese
sense of family honor and respect for older people. Proverbs contribute to peace in the communal life of the family: they induce
self-denial, control, and discipline. They have enhanced the basic
belief in the social and political proprieties by which Chinese
society has evolved. Though there are many dialects, the country
is blessed by characters which are understood in their written form
wherever the people can read. The language, spoken and written,
is adapted to the creation of epigrammatic expression. Rich and
poor, learned and unlearned, have thought and spoken in proverbs
so much that these constitute a second language. The term "ignorant coolie" is a misnomer, for the average laborer in China is a
reservoir of proverbs, the expressions of wise and tested experience.
Children learn to quote proverbs to support their ideas and conduct. Indeed, the Chinese have produced enough proverbs in their
history to constitute a clear mirror of their manners, customs,
opinions, and beliefs.
   A few examples will illustrate the wisdom of this folk language
of the Chinese heritage:

No tribulation, no sainthood.
Without having tasted extreme bitterness, one cannot fully appreciate the
meaning of sweetness.
Unwilling to climb the mountain, how can you expect to see the landscape?
A little impatience ruins a great program.
One moment of patience prevents sorrow for one hundred days.
Forbearance is the best treasure of a household.
The contented alone know what happiness is.
Sow melons, reap melons; sow beans, reap beans.

Learning is like rowing upstream: if you do not advance, you fall back.

An iron bar may be made into a needle—provided you work long enough.

Live to old age, learn to old age.

Generals and statesmen are not grown from seed; hard struggle by every youth is the vital need.

When you have the goods, you do not need to worry about a customer.

Distance proves the strength of a horse; time shows the heart of a man.

To make a friend in a year's time may be difficult; to lose a friend in an hour may be easy.

To face together a common enemy is easy; to share profit is difficult.

If one word escapes your mouth, four horses cannot catch up with it.

When two people are of the same mind, their strength can break iron.

Do not lace your shoes in a melon patch, nor adjust your hat under plum trees.

When you ride on a donkey, do not see only the man in the sedan chair ahead of you: look also at the fellow coming along on foot behind you.

If one shows respect for his parents at home, he does not need to burn incense in a far-off temple.

Filial piety moves Heaven and Earth.

According to Bacon, "the genius, wit, and spirit of a nation are discovered in its proverbs." If this be true, how great are "the genius, wit, and spirit" of the Chinese nation!

CHAPTER II

Dominant Ideas

BY DERK BODDE

THE CHINESE have been less concerned with the world of the supernatural than with the worlds of nature and of man. They are not a people for whom religious ideas and activities constitute an all-important and absorbing part of life—this despite the fact that there are nominally more Buddhists in China than in any other country in the world. Buddhism entered China from the outside. Before its impact, in the first century of the Christian era, China produced no thinker who could be classed as a religious leader, with the doubtful exception of the philosopher Mo Tzŭ (480–390 B.C.). It is ethics (especially Confucian ethics), and not religion of a formal, organized type, that has provided the spiritual basis of Chinese civilization.[1]

The prevailing attitude of sophisticated Chinese toward the supernatural is perhaps best summed up by Confucius (551–479 B.C.). Once, when asked by a disciple about the meaning of death, he replied, "Not yet understanding life, how can you understand death?"[2] Later thinkers have generally tended to adopt a skeptical attitude toward the unknown. Most of them, when expressing themselves on the subject, have denied the possibility of personal immortality.[3] This attitude marks a difference of fundamental importance between China and most other major civilizations, in which a church and a priesthood have played dominant roles.

The preceding remarks do not mean that before the coming of Buddhism there were no religious manifestations in China. What is important is that from the beginnings of Chinese history the most

---

[1] For notes to chapter ii see pages 521–523.

vital and sincere form of religious feeling was that expressed in the worship of departed ancestors.[4] This has been of decisive importance, for ancestor worship is a form of religion that can appeal to, and be performed by, only the immediate family groups concerned. Therefore it could not develop into a national or an international organized faith similar to Christianity or other world religions.

Side by side with the ancestral cult, various objects and forces of nature were also worshiped, such as sacred mountains, rivers, and the life-giving soil. These, however, were generally conceived of in abstract rather than personified terms, and even the supreme Chinese divinity, T'ien, or Heaven, rapidly lost its anthropomorphic qualities and became a purely abstract ethical power. There was no elaborate pantheon or mythology in ancient China.[5] Likewise there was no priesthood, because the worship of the divine forces was performed not by the common people or by a priestly class but almost entirely by the ruler, who, as the "Son of Heaven," acted as intermediary between the world of the supernatural and the world of man. A pantheon, a mythology, and a priesthood are all comparatively late phenomena in China, connected either with Buddhism or with the religious and popularized form of Taoism (see chap. xvii), which developed, in part, as an imitation of the formal aspects of Buddhism.

In later times the innumerable divinities of Buddhism and Taoism found a ready welcome among the Chinese masses, but this testifies more to the highly eclectic nature of the Chinese mind than to any strongly religious feeling. Because of this eclecticism the Chinese, like the Hindus, have been remarkably free from religious bigotry. The few persecutions have usually been directed not against religious ideas but against religion as a social and political institution threatening the security of the state.

Another fundamental difference between Chinese civilization and that of the Near East and of India is that in early China there was no idea of divine retribution after death. The concept of rewards and punishments meted out in heaven or hell during a life hereafter is utterly alien to Chinese thought, and appears in China only with Buddhism.[6] The early Chinese did, however, believe in a celestial realm known as T'ien, or Heaven, and a nether region known as Huang Ch'üan, the Yellow Springs, but apparently they

conceived of them only in the vaguest terms, and certainly never as
abodes of the blest and of the damned. Each human being was
supposed to have two souls: the *p'o,* or anima, produced at the time
of conception, and the *hun,* or animus, which was joined to the *p'o*
at the moment of birth. After death the *hun* ascended to heaven;
the *p'o* remained in the tomb with the corpse for three years, after
which it descended to the Yellow Springs.

◇　◇　◇

If the supernatural world has held a lesser place in Chinese than
in most other civilizations, the reverse is true of the world of nature.
For the Chinese, the world of nature with its mountains, forests,
storms, and mists has been no mere picturesque backdrop against
which human events are staged. The world of man and that of
nature constitute one great indivisible unity. Man is not the supremely important creature he seems to Westerners; he is but a
vital part of the universe as a whole. This feeling may have originated in the overwhelmingly agrarian character of Chinese civilization and its dependence upon the regular succession of the forces
of nature. It is a feeling which permeates a great part of Chinese
philosophy, art, and literature.

In Taoism, the philosophy which has best expressed this mystic
awareness of universal unity, many striking anticipations are found
of the ideas propounded in the West by Rousseau some two thousand years later. Like Rousseau, the Chinese Taoists said that
human moral standards are artificial and hence invalid, that the
appurtenances of civilization are corrupting, and that, therefore,
man must cast off these trammels and return to nature. Yet Taoist
naturalism differs fundamentally from Occidental romanticism,
in spite of certain remarkable superficial resemblances.

In the first place, it avoided the latter's sentimentality, emotional excess, and emphasis upon love between man and woman.
In the second place, romanticism has countenanced the breaking
of moral restraints in the name of spontaneity and originality.
Taoism also did away with human moral standards, but replaced
them by a higher standard, that of the *Tao,* or Way, the first cosmic
principle of the universe, from which the Taoist school takes its
name. Man, said the Taoists, must subordinate himself to the *Tao,*

that is, to nature. This is to be done not by a facile surrender to one's emotions but by a process of self-discipline (through meditation and other means) that will result in lessening of desire and consequent calm and contentment amid the simplicities of the natural life. In the final stage the Taoist devotee aims at achieving a state of union with the surrounding universe in which he is so completely freed from the bonds of human emotion that neither joy nor sorrow, life nor death, can affect him. In this respect Taoism remains in accord with the general tendency of all Oriental mysticism.

Taoist subordination of the self to the universe also differs importantly from another current of modern Occidental thought. In the West, happiness is to be found by harnessing the forces of nature to the will of man and thus increasing the means for man's material enjoyment. In China, the sage traditionally has been one who adjusts himself to the universe as he finds it and thus gains what he considers true happiness: contentment in simplicity. This widely accepted concept goes far to explain why the Chinese, whether educated or illiterate, can remain cheerful and even happy under poverty and privations which would be intolerable to a Westerner. It explains, also, why the Chinese, though they developed remarkably scientific techniques in the compilation of dictionaries, histories, encyclopedias, and other scholarly works, failed to apply these techniques to the world of nature and thus failed to create a physical science.[7]

Yet this prevailing attitude toward the physical universe—an attitude perhaps best summed up in Wordsworth's phrase as a "wise passiveness"—has not prevented the Chinese from attempting to classify and systematize natural phenomena. In simplest terms, the Chinese theory of cosmogony may be summarized as follows:

Lying behind the physical universe is an impersonal first cause or prime mover known as the *Tao*, or the Way, from which all being has evolved. *Tao* manifests itself in the form of two all-inclusive principles: *yang*, the principle of activity, heat, light, dryness, hardness, masculinity; and *yin*, the principle of quiescence, cold, darkness, humidity, softness, femininity. Through the eternal interaction of these principles the five primary elements come into existence: fire (the essence of *yang*), water (the essence of *yin*), and earth, wood, and metal (combinations of *yang* and *yin*). These elements combine and recombine to produce all things in the universe, including heaven (sky, atmosphere, stars), which is preponderantly *yang,* and earth (soil, plants, animals), which is preponderantly *yin.* The Chinese have compiled lists of categories in fives, such as the five colors, five smells, five tastes, five tones, five internal organs, as correlatives of the five elements.[8]

The splitting up of the world into sets of fives is typical of the rationalistic Chinese mind, which tries to find order and plan in all things and therefore has taken particular delight in inventing numerical categories.[9] The theory of *yin* and *yang*, the five elements, and their correlatives has for more than two thousand years been the basis of Chinese medicine, alchemy, astronomy, and naturalistic speculation. Although it represents an attempt to use the scientific method, it has not led to a true physical science because, being based upon arbitrary analogies, it disregards direct observation of nature.

In connection with this theory of cosmogony it is important to make a clear differentiation between the Chinese dualistic system based upon interplay of the *yin* and *yang* principles, and the superficially similar dualisms of light and darkness, good and evil, which are found in the Near East and in the Occidental world. The latter dualisms are based upon the concept of mutual antagonism between two conflicting members and the consequent necessity of conquering evil so that good may eventually triumph. They are often closely connected with religion.

Yin-yang dualism is based not upon mutual opposition but upon mutual harmony. The feminine *yin* and the masculine *yang* are equally essential for the existence of the universe. Each is complementary to the other; neither is necessarily superior or inferior from a moral point of view. This concept is a striking manifestation of the Chinese tendency to find in all things an underlying harmony and unity, rather than struggle and chaos. In it the Chinese seem to have come closer to the ideas lying behind much of modern science than have Westerners with their traditional good-versus-evil type of dualism.

The third of the three categories mentioned, that of the world of man, comprises the heart of Chinese philosophical speculation. How to get along equably with one's fellow men: this is the problem that Confucianism set itself to answer—as Taoism posed for itself the problem of how man can adjust himself to the outer universe. From early times the Chinese have realized that, unless this central problem of human relationship can be solved, material power and progress serve but to increase the afflictions of mankind. A realistic and pragmatic people, the Chinese launched their frontal attack upon this vital question, and in so doing produced many works on ethical and political philosophy, which, however, did not always attain their pragmatic goal. They sometimes fell into the common error of assuming that morality can be realized automatically, through the preaching of lofty doctrines, without regard for the practical difficulties that lie in the way of realization of these doctrines. This is, perhaps, the most serious indictment of Confucianism (see chap. xv), but it is far from universally true: many Confucian thinkers were not mere philosophers in an ivory tower but men of affairs, active in government, who directly concerned themselves with political programs that would serve to carry their ideals into operation.

The Chinese rejected both the abstruse metaphysical speculations of the Hindu and the explorations into logic that have been one of the major contributions of Occidental philosophy. This practical concern with the immediate exigencies of human life helps to explain why the Chinese, although they have contributed to the world many inventions of the highest practical value—paper, printing, porcelain, and the mariner's compass,—have not developed a theoretical natural science.

Connected with their intense preoccupation with human affairs is the Chinese feeling for time—the feeling that human affairs should be fitted into a temporal framework. The result has been the accumulation of a tremendous and unbroken body of historical literature extending over more than three thousand years. This history has served a distinctly moral purpose, since by studying the past one might learn how to conduct oneself in the present and future. Hence the writing of history was not left to the whims of a few historically minded individuals. From the founding of the Han empire, in the third century B.C., one of the first duties of a new dynasty was to compile the history of the preceding dynasty; often there was appointed for the purpose a large board of government-supported scholars who were set to work upon the historical archives. The resulting dynastic histories are not limited to bald narration of political events, but include valuable essays on economics, law, water-control works, astronomy, bibliography, geography, and many other topics, as well as biographies of hundreds of illustrious individuals. This temporal-mindedness of the Chinese marks another sharp division between them and the Hindus.[10]

◇　◇　◇

What was the nature of the society that the Chinese took such pains to record? Confucianism aimed at teaching each individual to take his place with the least possible friction in his own social group and to perform his allotted duties so as to bring the greatest benefit to the group as a whole. The basic and most important unit of Chinese society was the family or clan, to which the individual owed his first allegiance, and which he served, first, by sacrificing to departed ancestors; second, by caring for the elder generation still living; and third, by rearing descendants of his own to carry on the family line. In return, the family acted as a protective group of mutual aid, shielding the individual from an often hostile world. Through its cohesiveness it succeeded in maintaining the fabric of Chinese life and culture even in times of almost complete social and political collapse. Because of the stress upon family in China there has been a correspondingly limited development of nationalistic feeling, except in a vague cultural sense, and little of that fiery patriotism which is so much exalted in the West.

Beyond the family lay the state, which was regarded as merely an enlargement of the family unit. The term *kuo chia,* "nation," literally translated, means "national family," and it was common for the emperor to refer to himself as *min chih fu mu,* "the parent of the people." Each person occupied a definite position and was held responsible for the performance of stated duties. Yet, paternalistic though it was, the system did not (in theory, at least) operate solely for the benefit of a ruling class. If inferiors were expected to serve superiors with loyalty, superiors were equally bound by certain definite obligations to their inferiors. Confucianism stressed the reciprocal nature of these duties and obligations. It also emphasized that the primary duty of the ruler is to give good government to his people: to do this, he must himself set a high moral standard and must select with care the officials who serve under him. It thus attached great importance to the power of personal example of men in public life and the need for their moral self-cultivation.

Owing to the development of an intensive agricultural economy (see chap. xxxii) stimulated by a widespread government-fostered system of irrigation works, it was possible for a large population to subsist upon a comparatively small amount of land. The empire spread to huge proportions and developed into a complex bureaucracy employing an army of officials. Yet despite its size and inclusive character the Chinese state remained sufficiently flexible for social change and individual initiative. It aimed at moral suasion rather than legalistic compulsion, and rejected the somewhat cold and mechanical type of government, based on law, which has been a cornerstone of Occidental civilization. Legal codes existed, but they were subject to individual judgment and interpretation, based upon the body of traditional experience and morality known as *li*.

It was therefore possible in Chinese society, especially in times of political change, for determined men to work their way to high positions—a feat accomplished by several founders of dynasties who rose from humble origins. Women, similarly, although they held an inferior position before the law, frequently exercised great power within and beyond their family group. Thus China has produced a goodly number of female painters, poets, historians, and rulers. There was extremely little in Chinese society that suggested any permanent stratification of social groups.

The moral basis for society was the belief, shared by the majority of Chinese thinkers, that man is by nature fundamentally good, that there is no such thing as original sin, and hence that any person, even the lowliest, is potentially capable of becoming a sage.[11] Evil, according to the Chinese view, does not exist as a positive force; it is simply the result of a temporary deflection from the essential harmony of the universe. With these concepts go the optimism, the good humor, and the will to live that are marked characteristics of so many Chinese. The Indian dictum that life is suffering was inconceivable to the Chinese mind; even with the coming of Buddhism it never succeeded in gaining general acceptance.

Because they believed that all men can be taught morality the people of the Middle Kingdom placed an importance hardly paralleled elsewhere upon the value of learning. Wisdom, one of their five cardinal virtues, meant an understanding of right and wrong and of moral principles generally. Hence the stress upon the classics, which the Chinese regarded as containing deep moral truths; upon history as an instrument whereby man may be taught to avoid the mistakes of his forefathers; and, eventually, upon all humanistic scholarship.

This led to the creation of the most distinctive feature of Chinese government, the famed examination system. Until recent times, other countries—with few exceptions—have been ruled by a hereditary aristocracy, a priesthood, a military hierarchy, or a rich merchant class. But in China, since the period of the Western Han dynasty (206 B.C.–A.D. 9), entry into the bureaucracy that governed the country was limited to those who succeeded in passing a series of strict government examinations based upon thorough knowledge of the classics. Service in the bureaucracy was the highest attainable goal.

Such at least was the theory. In practice the system operated best in periods of strong political unity; in times of strife or dynastic change it tended to break down. Moreover, it contained manifest defects, such as undue stress upon memory, and the fact that the wealthy enjoyed superior opportunities to acquire the education that would make success possible. Another weakness of the governmental system under the empire was the inadequate payment of officials, who were thus tempted to increase their income dishonestly. The same tendency was strengthened by an unfortunate feature of the family system: a successful member was under moral obligations to support his less prosperous relatives. These defects, however, apply more to the bureaucratic system as a whole than to the examinations per se, and were partly compensated by an intricate and ingenious system of checks and balances designed to reduce the abuse of office to a minimum. Considering the size and geography of China, its government has operated with relative efficiency over a long period of time and with less corruption than most Westerners have believed.

Prior to their abolition in 1905, the examinations, when properly administered, provided an impartial and purely intellectual test that each candidate had to pass, through his own efforts, in order to enter the coveted ranks of the scholar-officials. Likewise, the examinations were open to all members of society, with trifling exceptions. Little wonder, therefore, that Voltaire,[12] comparing this system with European political conditions in his day, declared: "One need not be obsessed with the merits of the Chinese to recognize that the organization of their empire is in truth the best that the world has ever seen, and moreover the only one founded on paternal authority."

A corollary to respect for learning has been a corresponding dislike of violence and strife. Reason, arbitration, and compromise are (in theory, if not always in practice) the instruments for settling disputes in China, and the man who resorts to force shows that he is in the wrong. China has had its share of strife, yet a large anthology could be compiled of essays and poems lamenting the sufferings and horrors of war. The poor but worthy scholar has been the typical hero of Chinese literature. There has been little of the glorification of military genius so characteristic of the West. Prior to the outbreak of the Fifth Sino-Japanese War (1937–1945) the prevailing attitude toward the soldier was best summed up in the proverb, "Good iron is not beaten into nails; a good man does not become a soldier."[13]

A basic concept underlying the Chinese theory of government is the "right of revolution." According to this theory—before 1912— the ruler, being the "Son of Heaven," enjoys divine sanction for his rule through a celestial Mandate, or Decree, which is conferred on him by Heaven. As long as he rules in the interests of the people he cannot legally be overthrown. Bad government, however, is displeasing to Heaven, which then indicates its dissatisfaction through such inauspicious natural phenomena as droughts, floods, or earthquakes. If these warnings go unheeded, heavenly disapproval is further manifested in the form of popular revolts, which may culminate even in the ruler's dethronement and the founding of a new dynasty. Success in such revolts means that Heaven has withdrawn

its Mandate from the evil ruler and has passed it on to a new line.
This theory originated in China before the first millennium B.C.
It was elaborated by later writers—notably Mencius—and is perpetuated in the modern term for revolution, *ko ming*, which literally means "changing the Decree." Together with the influence
of the nonhereditary scholar class, it has acted as a strong check
upon abuse of power by the sovereign, and thus has given to China
an ideological preparation for democratic institutions which, there
is reason to hope, will enable it in future to assume its rightful
place among the world's great democracies.

✧   ✧   ✧

It is impossible to overstress the fundamental oneness and harmony
of the Chinese *Weltanschauung*. The Chinese mind sees no real distinction between the world of the supernatural, the world of nature, and the world of man. They are bound up in an all-embracing
unity. "All things are complete within me," proclaims the Confucian, Mencius (372–289 or 390–305 B.C.),[14] thus echoing the sentiment of the Taoist, Chuang Tzŭ (*ca.* 365–*ca.* 290 B.C.), who says,
"Heaven and Earth came into being with me together, and with
me, all things are one."[15]

Applied to social relationships, these concepts manifest themselves in the emphasis of Chinese writers upon restraint, tolerance,
equanimity, and pursuit of the golden mean. "Let the states of
equilibrium and harmony exist in perfection, and a happy order
will prevail throughout Heaven and Earth, while all things will
be nourished and prosper." So says the *Chung Yung* (Doctrine of
the Mean), one of the works formerly memorized in the traditional
system of education.[16]

The world has been convulsed by a terrifying struggle. Now that
the major military phases of that struggle are over, it behooves the
West, in justice and in self-defense, to learn and to act upon these
principles in the world that emerges. If civilization is to survive,
Occidentals and Orientals must coöperate as never before. The
world must be one—a world in which all creeds and races, Eastern
and Western, live on a basis of justice, equality, and brotherhood.

CHAPTER III

Some Revelations
of Recent Excavations

BY WILLIAM CHARLES WHITE

S INCE THE TURN OF THE CENTURY, treasures have
been unearthed which have thrown a flood of
light upon the rich cultures of ancient China.
The colorfulness and wide range of the arts
and crafts of the Ch'ing (1644–1912) and Ming (1368–April 25,
1644) periods have been eclipsed by the purity and simplicity of
newly discovered Northern Sung (960–1127) and T'ang (618–906)
wares. Yet these have had to share honors with the wealth of
archaeological data of pre-Christian eras. The Chan Kuo, period
of the Warring (or Contending) States (*ca.* 480–*ca.* 222 B.C.), and the
Ch'in (255 [221]–207 B.C.) have been enriched with exquisite inlays
and low-relief decorations of bronze and jade which Westerners
attributed formerly to the two Han dynasties (206 B.C.–A.D. 220);
and the Shang (tradl. 1766–1122 B.C.) has quite overshadowed the
Early, or Western, Chou (jou) period (tradl. 1122–770 B.C.).

Museums and art collections have not yet caught up in their
classifications with these revolutionary discoveries. Many a bronze
is still labeled Chou or "probably Chou" which should be marked
Shang or Shang-Chou overlap, and much Eastern Chou or Warring States material is still spoken of as "Scythian style" and is
retained in the Han period. Material and data have piled up too
rapidly for collectors to take adequate stock of facts and to adjust
classifications.

The outstanding archaeological discoveries in recent years have
been connected with An-yang, in northern Honan, known as the
"Waste of Yin." Here was discovered what may have been the site

of the last capital of the Shang dynasty. (See chap. v, below.) Treasures of the highest significance have been brought to light. At first
the finds were casual and occasional; then, for a few years, scientific excavation was carried out by the Academia Sinica. In 1937
war with Japan halted such activities. Preliminary reports of early
excavations have been published, but most of the recovered material remains to be examined, classified, and made known.[1]

All archaeological discoveries have a flavor of romance, but it
would be difficult to find a story so thrilling and so fraught with
historical implications as that connected with An-yang. The story
begins in 1899 with the discovery of the Oracle Bones, called for
a time "Dragon Bones," when they were sold in drug shops for
medicinal purposes. Wang I-jung, a distinguished Hanlin paleog-
rapher and libationer in the Confucian sacrifices, purchased two
collections of inscribed bones, in 1900, from Peking merchant
speculators. In the same (Boxer) year, when the imperial court fled
from the capital, he took his own life. In 1902 Wang's son sold the
collection to the scholar Liu O (T'ieh-yün), who greatly enlarged
it and in 1903, in the first book on the subject, published reproductions of more than a thousand of the inscriptions. Whence the
bones came was unknown except that they were from the province
of Honan. Not until 1914 was the site definitely located at the village of Hsiao-t'un, a little west of An-yang.

The Oracle Bones are mostly fragments of animal scapulae and
plastra of tortoises. In ancient times they were used at court for
divination, and then were stored as archives. Thousands of fragments are in collections outside China, but in China itself a great
quantity, amassed by the Honan Provincial Museum and the
Academia Sinica, remains to be examined. The script was incised
with small, sharp cutting tools, whether of bronze, of jade, or of
rodents' teeth is not clear. A few pieces have been found with brush
writing. (See chap. xxi, below). Some inscriptions were deeply incised and inlaid with turquoise. The inscriptions are not easily
deciphered; few paleographers are able to unravel the meaning.
Nevertheless, a great deal has been learned about the life, customs,
and beliefs of the Shang people. The bones are contemporary documents; the effect of their discovery has been to take some three or

---

[1] For notes to chapter iii see page 523.

more centuries from the twilight of tradition and bring them into the category of authenticated history—which is by no means to say that every problem in the Shang period has been cleared up.

Chinese records contain chronological lists of early rulers—lists hitherto accepted as traditional. An authentic chronology of the Shang kings is now being worked out. Names and relationships of historical personages inscribed on the Shang bones verify statements recorded in the *Chu Shu Chi Nien* (Bamboo Books, or Bamboo Annals) and the *Shu Ching* (Book of Documents, or Classic of History).[2]

Shang culture contained basic elements of the arts, crafts, religious beliefs, and social institutions which have carried through the succeeding three thousand years of China's history. The underlying theistic faith of the Shang people, their sense of immortality as revealed in ancestral worship, their desire for orderliness in government and life, and their unwavering loyalty to family solidarity are exemplified both in the bone inscriptions and in the ceremonial objects which have been unearthed at An-yang.

In addition to carved bone, shell, and ivory, jade held an important place in Shang culture. Pendants, beads, and symbols, exquisitely carved in forms of animals, birds, and fish, have been found, as well as larger objects: marble sculptures, ceremonial axes, weapons, and various implements.

Of supreme importance were, and are, the bronzes of Shang. In dignity of form, delicacy of design, and technical excellence they have never been surpassed. There was an astonishing variety of shapes and styles in bronze ceremonial vessels and other objects. The aesthetic aspect was not lacking; apart from decorative designs in low relief, the use of turquoise inlay and lacquer filling was not uncommon. No gold and silver objects or inlays have yet been found, and iron apparently was not used. Shang weapons were mostly of bronze, and included dagger axes, bows and arrows, spears and javelins, and knives. But there seem to have been no daggers or swords.

One of the unanswered questions with respect to this high culture is why several of its phases apparently terminated when the Shang was replaced by the Chou dynasty. To the present, no inscribed bones from Early Chou times have been discovered, although inscribed bronzes are numerous, and it is known that the tortoise shell was consulted as an oracle by Chou diviners. The white pottery of Shang is not found in Chou, or in later, times. Chou, and all later, bronzes lack the style and refinement of Shang bronzes. Sculpture also disappeared. Although small jade objects were made in the Early Chou period, there seems to have been little sculpture of importance until near the end of the Chou, when a fresh style of jade work far surpassed that of Shang.

◇   ◇   ◇

In the year 770 B.C. the Chou court was moved to the district of Lo, later known as Lo-yang, in Honan. Thus began the period known as that of the Eastern Chou (770–256 B.C.), which included the period of the Warring States (ca. 480–ca. 222 B.C.).

Confucius was born in 551 and died in 479 B.C. Although the classics attributed to his authorship are history and contain much information in regard to historical events, social institutions, and philosophical ideas, authentic antiquities and archaeological data of this period are, for the most part, unknown or undetermined.

This lack has been rectified somewhat by acquisitions made in the last twenty years. The story of the recovery of these treasures is a romance of archaeology. Most of them were found within the domain of Chung-chou (jung-jou), the "Middle Kingdom," which actually was the state of Chou. In the north were finds at Li-yü, in Shansi; in the south was the cultural material common to the Huai River Valley of Honan and Anhui, which centered in Shou-chou.

The more important material was that uncovered in the heart of the Chou state. The tomb at Hsin-chêng (sin-jeng) was vouched for by the late Carl W. Bishop of the Smithsonian Institution. Most of the Hsin-chêng finds went to the Honan Provincial Museum at K'ai-feng, though many came into Western collections.

Royal tombs were discovered in the foothills of the Mang Mountains, near Chin-ts'un (Golden Village), in western Honan. This village is on the site of "Old Lo-yang," the capital of Eastern Chou from 509 to 255 B.C.—the classical age of China.

In the summer of 1928 heavy rains caused a sinking of the soil which suggested the existence of a tomb.[3] After boring tests had been made and two exploratory shafts had been sunk, it was found

necessary to excavate the whole tomb. It was exceptionally deep—
forty-seven feet—and thirty-five feet square. On its south side a
ramp ten feet wide led to the surface more than two hundred feet
above. On each side of the ramp were parallel trenches—called
"horse pits" (*ma-k'êng*) by the local inhabitants—in which chariot
parts and skeletal remains of horses were found. In the center of
the floor of the excavation was a tomb chamber, constructed of
heavy squared timbers. It was hexagonal in shape, more than
twenty feet across, and about seven feet high. The roof was made
of two overcrossing layers of large fir timbers. Above these were six
layers, each a foot thick, of charcoal and pebblestone alternately.

The space above the chamber, thirty-five feet or more, was filled
in with ordinary soil to the surface of the ground. There was but
one coffin in the tomb. It contained lime and fragments of bone—
and the most exquisitely carved jade objects known in China. Some
of the best pieces are now in the Freer Gallery in Washington, D.C.
In the Nelson Gallery at Kansas City is a jade disk, with dragons
carved on its circumference, which probably came from the Chin-
ts'un treasures.

Tombs similar to the one excavated at Chin-ts'un were discovered near by at Lo-yang. These yielded objects of the greatest significance: many types of chariot fittings and horse trappings, an
abundance of tomb furniture and implements, and a large number
of bronze ritual vessels—many bearing inscriptions—as well as stone
and lacquer objects. An astonishing discovery, also, was glass, in
many forms—in particular, some well-made beads of eye design,
similar to those of the sixth century B.C., from Egypt and the
Mediterranean. The only difference between the two types was
that spectrum analysis revealed barium in the Chinese beads but
none in the Egyptian.[4] Gold, silver, turquoise, and lacquer were
widely used for decorative inlays, and jade plaques and pendants
of superb quality and workmanship were abundant.[5] Bronze mir-
rors, swords, and daggers appear for the first time; stone chimes,
more refined in shape than those of the Shang period, were relatively common; and bronze bells, much more finely decorated than
those of Shang or Early Chou times, were found in great variety.

Most of these objects had been accepted as probably Eastern
Han (A.D. 25–220) until inscribed bells discovered in the tombs

provided a definitely historical basis. This group is now known as the Piao (biao) bells. There were two sets, one with a long, and the other with a shorter, historical inscription. The former bears the date of the twenty-second year of the reigning king, but does not give his name. Reference is made to a "Chief of Han" who recognized the "Duke of Chin" (dzin) as overlord. Both were subordinate to the "Son of Heaven," king of the central state of Chou. These inscriptions definitely place the bells in the Eastern Chou period, not later than 403 B.C., when the Chin state was divided into the three feudal states of Han, Wei, and Chao (jao). These were destroyed in 230, 225, and 222 B.C., respectively.

Eliminating the later Chou kings who ruled less than twenty-two years, only three rulers remain: King Ling, which would date the bells in the year 550 B.C.; King Wei-lieh, which gives the year 403 B.C.; and King An, which gives the year 379 B.C. The last must be ruled out on historical grounds; either of the other two dates may be accepted as a possibility. Since these dates are well within the limits of the classical period, they definitely establish that the objects in the Lo-yang tombs belong to the classical age.

In general, classical forms and styles of decoration are lighter and more delicate than those of any preceding period. The animal style is still common, but it takes on greater variety of form and more life and freedom than earlier types. Its character is similar to that known as Scythian; so it has been spoken of as "Scythian style" or "so-called Ch'in." This style may have originated outside China, but it is more likely that it was based upon earlier forms, Chinese in origin, which were carried westward and later returned to China, imbued with the lighter Scythian-style elements. This lighter style must have found congenial soil for development in the intellectual and literary atmosphere of the classical period.

◇   ◇   ◇

The excavations of Stein, Pelliot, Hedin, LeCoq, and others, along the caravan routes linking China with the West,[6] resulted in rich finds of paintings, inscriptions, sculptures, and silks which prove the existence of earlier contacts with Persia and Greece. The area in Chinese Turkestan providing the greatest quantity of important material is the Tun-huang (dun-huang) oasis in western Kansu.

Here are the Caves of the Thousand Buddhas, the Valley of Ten Thousand Buddhas, and other ancient shrines—an archaeologist's paradise. Sir Aurel Stein, first to explore this area thoroughly, made the most of his opportunity. Today a wealth of information is available in his records. The period covered by the more important discoveries along these routes is that from the Han to the end of the T'ang (A.D. 906). These finds have been supplemented by the uncovering of much T'ang dynasty material, particularly in Honan.

Before railways were constructed, the main arteries of travel wound over the same routes for untold centuries, leaving the graves untouched. With the advent of railways, particularly that of the Lung-hai, which parallels the Yellow River from east to west across the province of Honan, innumerable graves were unearthed and thousands of glazed pottery figurines lay scattered along the route of the new railway. These figurines were not valued by the Chinese; they are not even mentioned in early Chinese books, yet some of them must have appeared through the centuries. European construction engineers, recognizing their possible value as works of art and certainly as of antiquarian interest, sent some of the figurines to Europe, where they were at first received with suspicion. But, when it was definitely ascertained that they belonged to the T'ang age, their value was recognized and a demand was created.

Today they constitute valuable source material for the study of costumes and equipment of racial groups and social classes of the Sui and T'ang dynasties (A.D. 589–906), and of earlier centuries. This material is not found in quantity in Chinese collections. In those of Europe, North America, and Japan it still remains an almost untouched field for comparative study of the culture of the T'ang and preceding dynasties.

◇ ◇ ◇

It is now agreed that the finest porcelain in the world was made by Chinese under the Sung dynasty (A.D. 960–1279), especially in the Northern Sung period (A.D. 960–1127), when the court was at Pien (bien), or K'ai-feng, in Honan. The kilns of greatest importance were near the capital, but throughout the province, particularly north and southwest of K'ai-feng, excellent porcelain was made. Because of invasion from the north the court was transferred to

Hangchow (hang-jou), in the province of Chekiang (je-jiang), in the period of the Southern Sung (1127–1279). (See chap. vii, below.) The manufacture of porcelain, however, was not disrupted, and the refinement of imperial porcelain continued.

Among the most noted wares of both periods was the Yüeh, made in Yu-yao hsien, east of Hangchow. In the main this porcelain belongs to the celadon group, but the green is more gray or olive in tone than the green of the most highly prized celadon. Kiln sites with much waste have been found at this place. Some of the many fragments of Yüeh vessels are incised with a year date, most frequently A.D. 978. This particular Yüeh ware has only recently been located and defined.[7]

Other important varieties of porcelain, some of which had been recorded in Chinese literature but not identified, have lately received confirmation from kiln sites found in Honan, in Kiangsi (jiang-si), Chekiang, and Fukien (fu-jien).

The best of these Sung porcelains, besides the Yüeh ware mentioned above, are the Kuan (guan), the Ko (go), and the Jü (ru), the Lung-ch'üan, or celadon, and the Ying-ch'ing (ying-tsing), or shadow blue. Other varieties which have long been known are the Chien (jien), the Pai-ting (ba-ding) of different varieties, the Chün (jün), the Tz'ǔ-chou (tz-jou), and the Kuang (guang).

The beauties of Sung porcelains cannot adequately be described. Their delicate curves and delightful proportions, their tints of soft dove gray or bluish green or shadow-blue white, their velvety unctuousness of crystalline glaze—all have been combined to produce incomparable works of art. Small wonder that the Ch'ien-lung emperor (1736–1796), gazing into the limpid depths of a small Kuan bowl, saw the spirit of a muse. What he wrote in the spring of 1777, and commanded to be etched in that enchanted pool, ran something like this:

> Kuan ware first did win renown
> When the Court of Sung crossed to the South.
> Made solely for imperial use,
> Ministers nor people dared to gaze thereon.
> Six hundred years or more have passed since then,
> Yet two Kuan vessels, rare as stars at dawn,
> May still be found in market-square or temple-court,
> On sale as curios!

A great day for archaeology is dawning in China. When the world returns to normal it may be expected that the revelations of the last four decades will be a powerful stimulus to the quest for further knowledge of China's ancient culture. It has long been known that the civilization of China is of great antiquity and that the unbroken sequence of its development is unparalleled in history, but without the evidence of recent discoveries none could have believed that its past was so glorious. The warp and woof of Chinese history have taken on increasingly brilliant coloring and have exhibited a more integrated design as the pattern unfolds. Yet recent finds are but tokens of the treasures yet to be revealed.

The agelong practices of reverencing ancestors and of depositing with the dead the objects which surrounded them in life have led to the preservation of many relics in the earth; and the inhibitions restraining the Chinese from the sacrilege of tampering with tombs have made for the safe custody of these objects through the centuries. Not that tombs were never surreptitiously opened and looted, but the law of the land and the public conscience were always against such practices.

Now times have changed and inhibitions have been lifted. Though respect for the old and reverence for ancestors will continue, the scientific mind of new China will demand that the buried past be called upon to make its contribution of knowledge and wisdom, of truth and beauty, for the perfecting of the greater China which is being fashioned through suffering, sacrifice, and discipline. The spirit of adventure will inspire exploration of the wonders which still lie hidden on sites of many a capital, palace, and shrine of the Celestial Empire, and will capture and restore, for all mankind, further evidence of China's invincible greatness.

Part Two

HISTORICAL
AND POLITICAL
DEVELOPMENT

CHAPTER IV

Antiquity: To the Fall of Shang (ca. 1028 B.C.)

BY L. CARRINGTON GOODRICH

WHEN FRIEDRICH HIRTH wrote *The Ancient History of China,* in 1908, he started with a discussion of China's mythological and legendary past. This was standard practice, although Hirth exhibited a healthy skepticism. In 1912, when Berthold Laufer published *Jade: A Study in Chinese Archaeology and Religion,* he expressed doubt that China had ever had a neolithic stage. Herbert A. Giles, writing of Chinese characters, asserted, in the preface to the first edition of his *Chinese-English Dictionary* (1892): "There does not remain to us one single specimen of an inscription of a pictorial or pictographic nature, and it seems improbable that such ever existed." Marcel Granet, in *La Civilisation chinoise* (1929), cast doubt on the findings of the Oracle Bones of An-yang.

Thanks, however, to the imagination, persistence, and scientific skill of numbers of investigators, and to the financial backing of governments, foundations, other agencies, and individuals, much is now known about many of these matters. The panorama of China's prehistory has been rolled far back. But it is not alone in prehistory that knowledge has been deepened. Archaeologists and epigraphists have added half a millennium to the nearer historical period and have contributed many important facts to the once almost purely literary story of China's antiquity. The writings of students of metallurgy, zoölogy, botany, agriculture, anthropology, and kindred sciences have all played their part in presenting a more fully developed picture of the beginnings of the Chinese people. Furthermore, discoveries throughout the ancient world have thrown light not only on the sources of China's civilization but also on parallel movements in other cultures. There are many gaps yet to be filled—in fact, Chinese archaeologists had an abundance of material awaiting the termination of the war to be published,—but remarkable advances have been made in recent decades along many lines. It is but fair to add that the scholars mentioned above helped to prepare the way, and would have been among the first to rejoice in the recent accretions to knowledge.

Between September, 1935, and March, 1936, an artesian well 2,840 feet in depth was sunk in the city of Tientsin (tien-dzin) on the plain of northern China. Many wells had been dug in this region, but none of more than a quarter this depth. At the lowest point and at frequent intervals between were found small bivalved shells (*Lutraria,* common in tributary waters of the Hwang Ho, i.e., Yellow River) and small snails with flat, coiled shells (*Planorbis,* often noticed at margins of springs and lakes near by). The sand in which they were discovered had once been the top layer of the Yellow River delta, where snails and bivalved mollusks lived under essentially the same environment as that of their modern descendants. The digging of this well demonstrated, as no previous excavation had done, how much the rock floor of this part of the Asiatic continent has sunk, and what an immense load of silt and sand the Hwang Ho has carried down and spread over the sinking plain in order to keep the ancient home of the Chinese above sea level. The Yellow River, then, has been not merely "China's sorrow"; it has been also China's blessing!

✧ ✧ ✧

While the ancient home of the Chinese was in process of building, hominids, that is, prehumans, and a large variety of animals, most of them now strange to this region, were roaming the plain and the hilly barrier. This is known from evidence at Chou-k'ou-tien (jou-kou-dien), about twenty-five miles southwest of Peking (beijing). There is every reason to agree with J. G. Andersson,[1] one of the early discoverers of this site, that probably ten similar localities merely await the pickax of the paleontologist. In any case, the data

----

[1] For notes to chapter iv see pages 523–524.

are well authenticated. Thousands of fossilized bones unearthed here were found, not in the bed of a stream, dissociated from their mates, but together, embedded in the limestone rock. The geology of each stratum and each cave of Dragon Bone Hill is well known, and the remains of the fauna and flora taken to the laboratories of the Geological Survey in Peking have been studied almost as carefully as the teeth and skulls of the hominids.

These hominids lived long before any representative of human evolution thus far discovered in Europe, perhaps several hundred thousand years ago. According to Dr. Franz Weidenreich,[2] chief authority on their remains, Peking man, or *Sinanthropus Pekinensis*, and Java man, or *Pithecanthropus erectus*, resemble each other, and both may conceivably have descended from a primitive hominid in the southern part of China. At all events, the earliest forms of mankind have been discovered on the eastern periphery of the Eurasian continent. *Ex oriente lux!*

A point made by the late Dr. Davidson Black of Peking,[3] and questioned by Dr. Weidenreich,[4] opens up opportunities for debate as fresh discoveries are made. Black believed, with Haeckel, in a common dispersal center of humanity, and thought, with Osborne and others, that it was in the central Asian plateau. Weidenreich, arguing for polycentric evolution, points out that Mongoloid man, including modern Chinese, shares much in common with *Sinanthropus*, whereas in most other races of mankind these characteristics are rare. The hominid's shovel-shaped teeth are found among eastern Asiatics and Amerindians, but are not common elsewhere. The hindmost bone of the skull, sometimes called the Inca bone, is independent in Peking man, in modern Chinese, and in eight per cent of the men belonging to the ancient Inca civilization; it is rare, however, among Europeans. These and at least three other characteristics seem to prove his point.

The cranial capacity of *Sinanthropus* varied between 850 cubic centimeters and 1,220 cubic centimeters, as against 1,350 cubic centimeters in Recent man. He had apparently arrived at erect posture, as he knew how to hunt, was acquainted with fire, and was skilled in the fashioning of simple tools and their uses; consequently, he did not rely on his hands for locomotion. Ten fragments of spine and limb bones confirm this, and, adds Weidenreich, they are more nearly human in appearance than the dozens of teeth and several skulls found at Chou-k'ou-tien and studied in his laboratory. *Sinanthropus* subsisted probably in considerable measure on meat, and may well have been cannibalistic, but he ate other things also. The evidence is in the deep layers of ash found piled against the walls of caves in which his own remains were found; they included charred bones of horse, bison, rhinoceros, and other game animals which have no descendants on the Yellow River plain today, together with thousands of fragments of hackberry seeds. Peking man, says the Abbé Breuil,[5] also split the bones of large mammals to obtain marrow, made implements of bone and deerhorn, and worked the brain cases of deer to make drinking cups. Dr. Dubois (discoverer of *Pithecanthropus*) and Dr. Black thought, too, that Peking man and his kind were capable of articulate speech,[6] an opinion which Weidenreich shares.[7]

◇ ◇ ◇

In the course of time, perhaps several hundred thousand years, *Homo sapiens* evolved from this hominid, and the remains of his bones and his workshops and habitations were strewn over a wide area. They have been found, since 1923, in northwestern China, Inner Mongolia, Kirin (ji-lin) province, and even at an upper cave in Chou-k'ou-tien itself. Russian explorers have also reported paleolithic sites along the Angara River as far as seventy-five miles north of Irkutsk, Siberia, and at a spot near Baisun, Uzbekistan, formerly Russian Turkestan.[8] These sites are characterized also by finds of fossilized fauna and flora of an older age, perhaps middle Pleistocene, and of implements made by human hands. At Sjara Osso Gol in Inner Mongolia, for instance, French paleontologists discovered, seventy meters below the level of the Ordos plain, where no hard rock occurs, "remarkably small" stone implements, together with bones of such animals as the camel and the antelope. In September, 1934, the Japanese mission to Kirin reported the find, at Ku-hsiang-tun (gu-hsiang-dun), of carved bones of mammoth, cow, water buffalo, deer, horse, mouse, monkey, hare, musk deer, wolf, tiger, hyena, and bear. Most noteworthy were the artificially sharpened tusks of the mammoth. There were drinking horns made of spines, and kitchen knives of bone.

Similarly, in the upper cave at Dragon Bone Hill, the Chinese found, along with three complete and four incomplete human skulls, the skeletal remains of wild animal life much more closely ancestral to present-day fauna than that associated with *Sinanthropus*. With these remains were artifacts showing a more highly developed craftsmanship: a needle broken at the eye, a stone, three shells, and a considerable number of animal teeth, all evidently perforated for human adornment; also fragments of mother of pearl and pieces of iron ore, which latter may have been worked for its red powder. These finds suggested to W. C. Pei that there must have been long-range communication, as the shells are similar to those found 200 kilometers away on the coast, and the iron ore was probably obtained from Lungkuan, 150 kilometers to the north, a place separated from Chou-k'ou-tien by high mountain ranges. In all likelihood, a considerable population of men and beasts inhabited a wide stretch from the Yellow Sea to innermost Asia, and the indications are that they enjoyed a milder climate than at present obtains in this area.

The Pleistocene was a period of repeated glaciation in Europe and the eastern part of North America. In eastern Asia, however, there was no widespread glaciation. The glacial shield (averaging 1600 meters in western Europe) thinned out to 700 meters over the Urals and 500 meters over Taimir. This enormous area of ice generated winds of great velocity—drying winds which fled to a warmer region and helped to desiccate the Tarim and Gobi plains.[9] These winds picked up vast amounts of clay and rock flour in central Asia and deposited them farther to the east. In all probability this induced man to migrate, for his remains seem to be found only at the base or top of the primary loess. Possibly it was at this time that the first men started to trek to Alaska. That they were descendants of Mongoloid man appears a settled fact today. Among many evidences, N. C. Nelson[10] has noted Alaskan stone implements of the same type as those he had picked up in the Gobi. The first period of migration could not have taken place more than twenty thousand, and may have occurred around ten thousand, years ago. From that time on, as Hrdlička well expressed it, "The Asiatics came in dribbles."

Not all men, however, sought refuge in North America. Some

began to people the islands of Japan—the modern Ainus are probably descendants of these; others fled to the pleasanter climate of
central and southern China; still others went as far afield as Mela-
nesia. The loessification of northeastern Asia was an event of first
importance; it provided a soil which has modified the face of China
and given man a productive surface which he early learned was
good. In due course, man returned to the Yellow River Valley and
again started fishing its tributaries, hunting in the hills and under-
brush, and testing the richness of the surface loess. How long ago
this occurred is not known; one site north of the Wei River,
Pao-chi (bao-ji) hsien in west-central Shensi, reputedly the oldest,
is reckoned at approximately 6000 B.C. Other sites are less ancient
by some three or four millennia.

◇ ◇ ◇

By the time man again settled in the areas covered by loess he had
made advances in the art of living. He now could fashion better
tools of stone, bone, wood, and shell; he lived with his fellows in
small communities; he began to acquire knowledge of root and
leaf crops; and he probably fished and hunted with better success.
The Pao-chi hsien find suggests that man by the sixth millennium
B.C. had domesticated the pig; before long he domesticated the dog.
He knew how to manufacture a coarse kind of pottery, which he
fashioned into rather long vessels with pointed bottoms, and he
used a stone-bladed hoe for cultivation.

By the third millennium B.C. he was harvesting millet and possibly wheat and dry rice. He lived in circular pit dwellings which
had plastered walls and an entrance at the top. He may have grown
hemp. The existence of spindle whorls of clay and stone shows that
he and his wife—for women had an important part in all forms of
production[11]—knew how to spin thread. Pottery impressions suggest the weaving of cloth, mats, and baskets. For defense and attack
he had axes, knives, balls (for a pellet bow or sling?), and bow and
arrows. Arrow points of stone, bone, and shell have been found.
For decoration these early people used hairpins, rings of many sizes
and shapes, shell (necklaces and pendants?), and possibly cinnabar
to daub their bodies. For amusement or other purposes there were
whistles.

Most of the pottery unearthed is a handmade ware, usually gray in color, fashioned in a wide variety of shapes. A minor but highly interesting group of vessels was in all likelihood wheel-made, "buff to red-brown in color, with a surface susceptible of taking a high burnish. It is frequently decorated with geometric designs painted on in black, red, and white; often a white slip is used."[12] As late Stone Age sites have been found over a wide area in eastern Asia, it is to be noted that this type of ware occurs only at sites in the north and in eastern Turkestan. Not one authentic fragment has been reported in the Yangtze (yang-dz) Valley and farther south. This suggests that it is an intrusion from the west, and that workmen skilled in the making of painted ware may have penetrated China via Turkestan, into Honan and elsewhere.

The Swedish archaeologist Folke Bergman, however, has issued a timely warning[13] that the discoveries of polychrome pottery in Iran, Baluchistan, India, Russian Turkestan, northern China, Jehol, and Inner Mongolia have not simplified the question of connection between east and west. "Vase painting," he says, "is a rather complicated phenomenon. It presupposes a highly developed ceramic art with skilled workmen well acquainted with the fabrication of hard-burnt wares; furthermore, knowledge of the production of certain colours, and familiarity with the brush." He thinks the art must have evolved in a single center in chalcolithic times. But where? Might it have been not in western Asia but in the Tarim basin of central Asia?

Trade appears to have been little developed in this remote period. As the late Carl W. Bishop[14] remarked, "Communities must have been very nearly self-containing; probably for each the world was bounded by its own visible horizon." It is not until the first knowledge of copper (the chalcolithic period) that cowries are found in the transit provinces of Kansu (gan-su) and Sinkiang (sin-jiang). The shells may have come from as far away as the Maldive Islands.

The human material of the painted pottery stage has been little studied. A group of bones from Manchuria was investigated and reported on by Dr. Davidson Black,[15] who wrote on some of the diseases from which these people suffered: dental caries, alveolar disease, intercostal neuralgia, sciatica, and lumbago. One disease—

syphilis—is conspicuously absent, indicating that the scientists who
look for its origin not in the Old World but in the New are probably right. The teeth in this find showed such extensive and frequently uneven wear as to suggest that the people chewed much
that was gritty. Dr. Black also held that the remains of the 120
bodies recovered from chalcolithic (?) sites in Kansu were probably
proto-Chinese; they exhibit only unimportant differences from
the measurements of modern Chinese living in the Yellow River
delta.

The last division of the Neolithic or late Stone Age is characterized by a new type of pottery, a black wheel-made ware, much of
it thin and lustrous. Associated with it in the seventy sites thus far
uncovered, mostly in eastern China in Shantung (shan-dung),
Anhui, Honan, and Chekiang (je-jiang), are many evidences of
advances in human culture. Those who made this pottery were
plainsfolk who lived in villages averaging 300 by 300 meters in
size, often surrounded by walls. Their homes were circular pits,
the floors of which were about 4 meters across, with a hearth in the
center. A few had oblong stoves.

Fundamentally, these plainsfolk were farmers, and they built
their settlements close to streams where the soil was rich. Included
in their diet were meat, game, fish, and shellfish. Judging by the
remains in their rubbish heaps, they had added cattle, sheep, and
horses to the older domesticated animals, the pig and the dog. They
manufactured new types of jars, including some with covers; many
of these rested on three hollow legs. Although continuing to make
many of the tools and decorations earlier mentioned, they made
special use of shells. They also used clay to model doll-like vessels,
rattles, and other toys. To forecast the future they practiced scapuli-
mancy—divination by means of reading the cracks formed by exposing the scapula of an animal to fire. The dead they buried face
down.[16]

The boundary dates of this period are thought to be plus or
minus 2000 B.C. Bronze, wheeled vehicles, and writing soon appeared. Indeed, although some features of the black pottery stage
were peculiar to the period, the majority continued and were
developed by succeeding generations living in approximately the
same region.

Traditionally, Chinese history begins with the Hsia, an era sketchily treated by historians. If a Hsia dynasty existed it was probably when man in the Yellow River Valley first experimented with bronze in the making of tools, weapons, and vessels, extended the use of the wheel, made his first tentative essays at pictographs, and discovered the use of the silkworm.

Exact dates for Hsia and Shang still constitute a matter for conjecture. In recent years many have been critical of the traditional dating (Hsia, 2205–1766 B.C.; Shang, 1766–1122 B.C.) and have preferred the less-known chronology of the Bamboo Books (Hsia, 1994–1524 B.C.; Shang, 1523–1028 B.C.). It is interesting, however, to note that the latest scholarly pronouncement from China favors, for the Shang, dates closely approximating the traditional, 1751– 1122 B.C.[17] Chinese historians are apparently moving through the same cycle as Western historians, who, after discarding much of the core of the historical traditions of early Israel, Homeric Greece, royal and early republican Rome, and Arthurian England, are now beginning to accept the basic historicity of the Old Testament, the *Iliad,* and other early records.[18]

It is possible that the first decades or even centuries of the Hsia period coincided with the last phase of the Stone Age. If so, the ruling group may have governed the territory characterized by black pottery sites. Indeed, some years before 1928, when the first black pottery site was discovered twenty-five miles east of Tsinan (dzi-nan), Shantung, the late well-known scholar, Wang Kuo-wei (guo-wei), concluded that the Hsia people had occupied eastern Honan and western Shantung. Fu Ssǔ-nien (sz-nien) puts the territory farther to the west: Honan, southern Shansi, and part of Shensi. If Fu be correct, the hypothesis that the Hsia and black pottery stages coincide breaks down, and it must be surmised that these were another ruling group who played their part in clearing the land, developing agriculture, and making ready for a still more advanced regime.   ◇   ◇   ◇

Whether the Shang dynasty began to dominate the Yellow River plain in 1751 B.C. or in 1523 B.C., little is known concerning the first part of its history. The reigning family and the court are said to have occupied several capitals in the initial period, until they settled, some years after 1400 B.C., at a place near modern An-yang, Honan province, on the banks of the Huan River, a tributary of the Yellow River which then flowed near by.[19] With this city as governmental center the royal house ruled over an area which contracted and expanded according to the fortunes of war. How far its writ carried is open to debate. Possibly it ruled at times from the mountainous barrier north of Peking to the Yangtze in the south and from the coastline westward to Kansu. At other times, however, it must have shrunk dangerously close to the region of the court, for the capital was subject to occasional raids.

Information concerning the Shang people and their culture scarcely extends beyond the court, since it is this area only—the city and the great royal cemetery—which has been excavated. Knowledge of triumphal tours abroad, receipt of tribute from outside peoples, and defense of the capital is derived from the laconic records here exhumed. No comparable records have been unearthed at any other point, although a number of bronzes, apparently of Shang date, have been found elsewhere.

Nine kings appear to have ruled here. In addition to leadership in war they were responsible to the people for the actions of nature, and probably mediated with the Unseen by performance of a ritual dictated by a priestly caste. Assisting the kings and priests were numbers of civil and military officers. The capital alone required a considerable bureaucracy.

The king worshiped Ti (di), who was possibly an ancestral deity, and other lesser divinities. It is known that he frequently consulted the oracle since the questions asked of the diviners and their replies were engraved on animal bones and tortoise shells, materials durable enough to be preserved. The subjects of the king's interest included inquiries concerning male and female royal ancestors and the ceremonies paid to their manes, the harvesting of millet, invasion of enemy territory, hunting excursions, and prevention of calamities caused by storms and floods.

Animals used in sacrifice by burning, drowning, or interment were, in order of importance, cattle, sheep or goats, swine, and dogs.[20] Less commonly, horses and human victims—probably captives—were sacrificed. To what degree officials and common people joined in the sacrifices and in other religious observances is unknown; members of the aristocracy doubtless went through somewhat similar ceremonies. There were temples for sacrifices to ancestors; sacrifices to spirits, called *shên,* were made both indoors and in the open air.

The time unit of the Shang was a week of ten days. The next larger unit was a cycle lasting six weeks or sixty days, although there was also a month or moon of thirty (sometimes twenty-nine) days. A year commonly lasted six cycles, but frequently it had to be corrected by the addition of one week, two weeks, one moon, or even two. The Shang people, who knew the principle of lunation, kept their calendar fairly accurate by frequent adjustments. By a careful study of all published oracle records bearing dates of the month, Dr. Wittfogel[21] has ascertained that the Shang people observed the proper seasons for planting and harvesting, cattle breeding, and hunting. He has deduced, from these and other data, that they enjoyed a somewhat more temperate climate than do modern inhabitants of An-yang.

Autumn and winter were the seasons for war. Raids and counter-raids seem to have been the order of the day—at least for the king and his nobles and their slaves. The court needed tribute from near and far which armed force alone could exact. Armies were small: three to five thousand men in all. The well-born, protected by helmets and possibly by leathern armor strengthened by wood and bone, fought in horse-drawn chariots accompanied by men on foot. For attack they used spears and halberds of bronze, and the composite bow which shot arrows tipped with points of bronze, bone, and stone.

The main industry of the common folk was farming. Their chief crop, which they both cooked and brewed, was millet. They turned up the soil with spades, foot plows, hoes, and mattocks shod with stone and shell. Irrigation, as necessary here as in the west of Asia, and reclamation of marshland were widely practiced. Animal husbandry was probably second in their economy; they made large use of pigs, dogs, sheep, goats, cattle, and horses. The sheep were not sheared, however, nor were the cows milked. Hunting as an industry and a pastime probably took place in the hills near by. Warriors needed furs for raiment, hides for protection, plumes for helmets, and ivory and horn for various uses.

In the city were many artisans and craftsmen who built and furnished homes, palaces, government buildings, temples, and tumuli, and who otherwise served the well-to-do. There were merchants also, men who dealt in goods brought from a distance—for example, salt, sea shells, and metals. The origin of some of the raw materials used—copper, tin, lead, antimony for the making of bronze—is still a mystery. A history compiled about 100 B.C. declares, "The kingdom of Ch'ang-sha [about 600 miles to the south] produces raw lead and tin." But did the Shang people know this? Sir Percival Yetts[22] notes that the local histories of recent date record an ancient tradition that copper, tin, and other metals were mined only some thirteen miles away; but again, how old and how well informed is this tradition?

Craftsmen turned out objects of high artistic merit. Using hemp for cloth, they also wove silk. A few pieces of silk wrapped around knife handles have been preserved, but they are so much weathered that their artistry cannot be judged. Stone, bone, and ivory were skillfully carved, and surfaces were often inlaid with turquoise or mother of pearl. Houses, mainly of wood, with roofs supported by stone-based pillars, stood on platforms of pounded earth. Nothing but the bases is left by which one may assay their splendor. For palaces, shrines, and tombs, handsome vessels fashioned in white pottery and in bronze were made for the living and the dead. Many of these vessels have survived to reflect the glory of the court and the honor paid to the deceased.

Of utmost importance was, and is, their knowledge of writing. This appears on animal bones, shells of now extinct tortoises, and, to a minor extent, on bronze vessels, a few weapons, pieces of pottery, and jade. It is assumed that writing was done on perishable materials such as wood, bamboo, and silk. Whence came this writing? Was it autochthonous? There are numbers of pictographs which have parallels elsewhere. Miss Helen Chapin,[23] for example, has drawn attention to the similarity between a pictograph on a Sumerian chariot wheel, dated by Wooley *circa* 3500 B.C., and the Shang character for chariot. This may prove only that the human mind sometimes works in like fashion in different regions. Further evidence is necessary before these questions can be answered.

Thus far, about 2,500 signs have been recovered; of these more than half have been identified. They reveal a not immature script, often recognizably similar to the writing of today—though marked changes have occurred, in part through use of different writing materials, but also as accompaniments of a maturing civilization. As Erkes has remarked,[24] since so much of the writing on bones thus far published concerns divination, the content is rather stereotyped. But discovery of archival records and other matter may well show that the Shang Chinese had a flourishing literature based on a fairly flexible tongue.[25]

The dynasty ended with a crash. A people from the western marches, probably in alliance with other disaffected or hostile tribes—all doubtless as Chinese as the Shang but living on a lower cultural level,—moved into the central and lower Yellow River Valley, and in a generation or so utterly destroyed the capital city and the supremacy of Shang. Remnants of the royal family and their adherents were scattered far and wide (Korea traces its legendary beginnings to one such group), but some who escaped liquidation were allowed to remain in central China, where they continued their ancient rituals and customs for several centuries. Thus some of the heritage of knowledge and skill of this bright era, soon to be followed by a dark period in civilization, was spread abroad and conserved for the future.

CHAPTER V

The Greatness of Chou
(ca. 1027-ca. 221 B.C.)

BY CH'EN MENG-CHIA

THE CHOU is the longest dynastic period in Chinese history. It began with a group of feudal states clustered around and centered in the royal house. Two and a half centuries later, Chou had been reduced in power to the position of a nominal kingship; the real forces of government were held by feudal lords. Although the Chou originated in a western border area, the dynastic cultural pattern was eventually Chinese as handed down from the Shang. Into this pattern the Chou gradually absorbed other border states and tribes which originally were non-Chinese. At first the political organization was limited to the nobility, but in time the common man was admitted to governing power. Finally, archaeological researches indicate that the culture at the beginning of the Chou age, in the eleventh century B.C., made extensive use of bronze and that toward the close of the dynasty this shifted to iron. The Five Hegemonies of the Ch'un Ch'iu—Spring and Autumn—period (722–481 B.C.) and the leadership of the Seven States, among a host of lesser powers, in the Chan Kuo, or era of the Contending States (ca. 480–ca. 222 B.C.), were symbols of the collapse of Chou power and forerunners of the unification achieved in the Ch'in-Han period.

Unfortunately, source materials for a detailed history of the Chou are not available. Except for the Chou Records and the Chronological Tables, the earliest historian, Ssŭ-ma Ch'ien (ca. 145–ca. 87 B.C.), in his *Shih Chi* (Historical Record), gave no information for this period. Ssŭ-ma's uncritical use of so-called pre-Han sources and his conjectural filling of gaps renders necessary a reconstruction of Chou history. For this, two main sources exist: first, inscriptions on bronze vessels, which often supply accurate and detailed records for the periods with which they are concerned; and second, the known pre-Han documents, when critically treated. It is not surprising that the results yielded are often at variance with traditional history.

The Chou tribe was originally at the great bend of the Yellow River, in what is now northern Shansi. Later the tribal leaders established their power in the Wei Valley of present-day Shensi. Tradition makes Hou Chi, God of Millet, the first Chou ancestor. The character for *chou* represents a square field divided into quarters on which plants are marked. It is therefore a major probability that the Chou tribe practiced an agricultural economy.

Concerning the Oracle Bones of Shang Wu-ting's time, in the second half of the thirteenth century B.C., the records state that "Shang attacked Chou." A fragment of another record contains part of a sentence beginning, "Order the Marquis of Chou . . ." The *Chu Shu Chi Nien,* or Bamboo Annals, report: "At the time of King Wu-i of Shang, King Chi of Chou came to court. King T'ai-ting of Shang ordered King Chi to be Master of the Shepherds, and later killed him. At the time of King Ti-i of Shang, the Chou people attacked Shang." In the *Shih Ching*—Book of Poetry, or Book of Songs—is found the statement, "T'ai Wang attacked Shang." T'ai Wang was the father of King Chi, who had been slain by the Shang. From this, and considerations stated in the preceding paragraphs, two points of major importance stand out: first, that the Chou tribe was in the west, in Shensi; second, that, though Chou was vassal to Shang, there were occasional passages at arms between vassal and master.

Concerning Wên Wang (?–1027 B.C.) the *Shu Ching*—Classic, or Book, of History, or Book of Documents—declares, "Wên Wang exterminated the Yin [Shang] dynasty." The *Shih Ching* reaffirms this in a passage of similar content. In several places the *Shih Ching* and the *Shu Ching* declare that "Wên Wang received the Decree [of Heaven]." The *Shih Ching* further states that "Wên and Wu received the Decree [of Heaven]." Inscriptions on the bronzes of Western Chou say, "Wên and Wu received the Decree of Heaven."

The formula "received the Decree of Heaven" can be explained in at least two ways: it can mean "to be king by the order of Heaven," or it can mean "to succeed in possession of the kingdom." Either way, it denotes that Wên Wang, father of Wu Wang and Chou Kung, that is, the Duke of Chou, began the conquest of Shang.

From information supplied on Oracle Bones and Shang bronzes it is clear that Chou Hsin, the last king of Shang, had moved most of his troops eastward in order to attack the eastern barbarians. Successful in this venture, he was at a tactical disadvantage in meeting the assault of the Chou tribe, which came from the west, under Wu Wang, before the Shang armies could return. The last Shang king fell in battle. Wu Keng, heir to the Shang throne, was captured and placed under the guard of two of Wu Wang's brothers, Kuan and Ts'ai. Although he was now in possession of An-yang, the capital of Shang, Wu Wang yet feared the Shang armies in the east.

The political developments of the ensuing five years are of great importance. Again, the inscriptions from the bronzes of Western Chou are the chief sources of reconstruction. Two years after his conquest of Shang, Wu Wang died. His son Ch'êng succeeded him, but another of Wu Wang's brothers, Chou Kung, the traditional hero of this period, who is often incorrectly referred to as regent, held the real power among the Chou. Meanwhile, Kuan and Ts'ai had come to identify their interests with those of Shang and were ready to support it by action. The Shang army had induced the barbarians of both east and south to ally themselves with Shang and stand against Chou.

At this point Chou Kung, in three strategical moves, justified his later fame. History does not, however, admit for it the same reasons as are assigned by later tradition. Chou Kung's first step was to attack An-yang again, and then to execute his brother Kuan and the Shang heir, Wu Keng, and to exile Ts'ai. He placed his youngest brother, K'ang Hou, in power at the Shang capital and thus made one of the descendants of Shang a figurehead in the state of Sung. Second, Chou Kung moved his army eastward into territory yet strongly Shang. Here, in present-day Shantung province, he utterly defeated the Shang allies and pushed the remnant of the barbarians far eastward to the coast. Thus he cleared the way for

his son Po Ch'ing to become governor of this area. The result was
a mixture of eastern Shang and western Chou.

The state created in the east, and later called Lu, came to be
accepted as the archetype of Chinese culture. Its great philosophers
of a subsequent period, Confucius and Mencius, contrasted the
rule of Chou Kung with the confusion of their own times and considered him the heroic figure of classical antiquity.

Chou Kung's third move was to build a new capital at Lo-yang
(ca. 1020 B.C.) to stand guard toward the south and the east. The
old capital at Fêng continued to watch over the west. The Shang
people were compelled to migrate to Lo-yang, to be the more easily
watched by Chou Kung's second son, Chün Ch'en, who had been
appointed chief of the eastern capital. This exploit of Chou Kung
is referred to in the bronzes as the "second conquest of Shang"—
and thus it is known that the first must have been that gained by
Wu Wang.

The reign of Mu Wang (ca. 965–928 B.C.) brings to a close the
first half of Western Chou. After Mu Wang's reign the shapes and
styles of the bronzes are noticeably different, an indication of new
conditions. The inscriptions pertain to developments in the system
of officials and in ritual instead of the continuing echoes of war.
Several chapters in the Shu Ching (Book of Documents) purport
to belong to the Early, or Western, Chou period. By comparison
with inscriptions on the vessels of the time following Mu Wang,
however, it is clear that these chapters were compiled at a later
date than conservative scholars have generally held.

The inscriptions of the period of Mu Wang and the Bamboo
Annals continue the history of warfare. A small remainder of the
Shang are recorded as having joined a barbarian tribe living in the
northwest, the Kuei-fang, and then rebelling against Chou. This
uprising was quelled by Mu Wang. Further trouble requiring suppression is reported in the south. Under the Western Chin, when
the Bamboo Annals were unearthed, another book, called the
Biography of King Mu, supposedly written in the third century
B.C., was found. It describes the expeditions and travels of Mu
Wang in the western regions and was probably inspired by a
knowledge of the period when Mu was forced to suppress rebellion
in that quarter. The small bit of original history has been overlaid

with fiction, however, and the account of Mu Wang's exploits in
the west is greatly exaggerated.

Kung, I, and Hsiao—the three rulers who in turn succeeded
Mu Wang—held the kingdom peacefully for about seventy years.
Among the factors which may help to account for changes in the
bronzes in this period were the more settled conditions within the
Chou kingdom and at its borders. A further reflection of these
conditions is to be observed in the regulation of court rituals and
in the balance—both in the structure of the whole and the making
of separate strokes—which now becomes part of the characters.

A branch of the eastern barbarians, anciently settled in the area
of present-day Shantung, had migrated southward into the Huai
River Valley in the times between Shang and Chou. In the course
of the period covered by the three rulers following Mu Wang, the
barbarians—the so-called southern Huai—spread into the valleys
of the Yangtze and Han rivers. Their rebellions began under Chao
and Mu Wang. An inscription on a bronze bell relates that "Yi
Wang conquered the southern and eastern barbarians, thirty-six
states in all." From another inscription comes the information that
Li Wang also fought the southern barbarians, and history adds that
he was defeated. Li Wang's defeat and the continued pressure of
the southern Huai barbarians revealed his incapacity to rule under
difficulties. Li was then deposed, either by the feudal lords or
through an uprising of the people, and was exiled.

Following Yi Wang (ca. 887–858 B.C.) and Li Wang (ca. 857–842
B.C.) traditional history writes that the Duke of Chou and the Duke
of Shao assumed control in a manner similar to a regency. The
bronze inscriptions and the Bamboo Annals present the situation
somewhat differently by naming Kung Pe Ho (Kung was the name
of a fief, Pe was the rank, and Ho was the personal name) as
regent—or, more accurately, as usurper. Ho's control lasted for
fourteen years after the exile of Li Wang (842 B.C.), and is known
as the Kung Ho period (841–828 B.C.). The Shih Chi (Historical
Record) of Ssŭ-ma Ch'ien relates that Li Wang died and his son
Hsüan became ruler in the fourteenth year of Kung Ho.

All sources agree that Hsüan Wang was an exceptionally able
king throughout the forty-six years of his reign (827–782 B.C.). That
he was successful in his wars against the southern Huai barbarians

is recorded both on the bronzes and in the *Shih Ching* (Book of Songs). The Bamboo Annals extend the narrative and note six expeditions against the barbarians of the northwest. Three of these were led by the feudal lords of Ch'in and Chin, two states bordering on the frontier territory; these expeditions met with only one reverse. Two of the three expeditions led by the royal Chou were defeated. Clearly, the Chou kings were no longer capable of carrying on independent warfare against the barbarians. Moreover, border states such as Ch'in and Chin, which continually engaged in skirmishes to maintain their frontiers, were developing formidable military strength.

Yu Wang (781–771 B.C.), son of Hsüan, favored the issue of his concubine Pao-ssŭ and attempted to name him heir apparent, thereby replacing P'ing, his legal heir. The latter appealed to his mother's people, the Shen tribe, to support his claims. In a coalition with other western barbarians, the Shen killed Yu Wang and his concubine's son and placed P'ing on the throne.

◇　◇　◇

P'ing Wang, supported by the states of Lu and Hsü, moved eastward to set up his capital at Lo-yang. This change of capital marks the beginning of the period called the Eastern Chou.

During their rule from the western capital, Fêng, in the Wei River Valley, the Chou kings, on the whole, proved equal to the twofold task of controlling the feudal lords and maintaining a certain level of culture, as is shown in the uniformity of grammar and character usage on the bronze inscriptions. This uniformity was lost in the Eastern or Lo-yang period, when the kingship was nominal and control was held by the nobles. Inscriptions began to reflect local variations; heterogeneity replaced the uniform pattern of earlier centuries.

The decline of Chou is adumbrated by the rude behavior of the nobles. When P'ing Wang died (720 B.C.) the Duke of Lu did not attend the funeral ceremonies. In the course of the next two and a half decades P'ing's successor, Huan Wang, visited Lu five times in attempts at conciliation. Again, in battle against the state of Cheng, Huan Wang was wounded. The person of the king was no longer held in extraordinary honor.

In the seventh century B.C., Ch'i and Chin successively assumed the hegemony which supplanted that of Chou, although a nominal kingship was still maintained. Because the threat of barbarian expansion was increased by lack of central authority, the states were forced to act independently. In this process the larger ones swallowed the smaller. Finally, from among the most powerful there emerged a hegemon referred to as the *Pa*. The functions of the *Pa* were to repulse the increasingly troublesome barbarians and to enforce respect for the Chou sovereign. The institution of the *Pa* prevented another strong state from setting itself up as ruler in place of Chou. This delicate balancing of power and the traditional respect for kingship kept a member of the Chou on the throne.

Briefly summarized, the political system of the Ch'un Ch'iu (722–481 B.C.) was still aristocratic, since the nobles were of the royal family, and great effort was made to retain old forms and preserve traditions. This formulation of proper behavior ceased entirely at the end of the Ch'un Ch'iu with the rise to power of Wu and Yüeh—states which evolved from among the barbarians of the southeast.

In the Chou age there were three different attitudes toward the barbarian tribes. The vigorous power of Western Chou (*ca.* 1027–771 B.C.) sought to attack and conquer the border tribes; in the Ch'un Ch'iu—Spring and Autumn—period the states were forced to defend themselves against the growing strength of non-Chinese clans; finally, in the Chan Kuo, or era of the Contending States (480–222 B.C.), contacts with the barbarians were sought and assimilation was attempted. The influx of barbarians infused the Chinese pattern with new life and vigor, nor was the unique character of the firmly established Chinese states lost. Rather did Chinese culture gradually infiltrate the outlying tribes until they too became Chinese. Out of many states, large and small, developed seven which were the most powerful. Their strength was mainly derived from acceptance of the incoming barbarians, whereas the more conservative states, which rejected the new tribes, rapidly declined.

In the Ch'un Ch'iu period none of the rulers of the Chinese feudal states used the title Wang (king). Among the barbarian tribes the head of the state of Ch'u had been designated by this title since the beginning of Eastern Chou (770–256 B.C.), and when, in the Ch'un Ch'iu, this state entered the Chinese group, its leader still referred to himself as king. Toward the close of the Ch'un Ch'iu, in the sixth and fifth centuries B.C., the leaders of two barbarian states, Wu and Yüeh, which had just become part of the Chinese pattern, adopted the title Wang. In the second half of the fourth century B.C., in the Contending States era, the rulers of the Chinese states also began to use the title. The following table illustrates how rapidly the idea spread, once the barbarians had broken the Chinese rule of usage:

334 B.C. Both Ch'i and Wei reciprocally adopt the title.

325 B.C. Ch'in adopts the title.

323 B.C. Both Han and Yen adopt the title as they join a group of five states using it reciprocally. The five states were Wei, Chung Shan, Ch'in or Chao, Han, and Yen.

322 B.C. Six major states had already adopted the title Wang. These were Ch'u, Ch'i, Ch'in, Han, and Yen. The state of Chao probably adopted the title about this time, but the histories do not state the exact year.

Throughout the Chan Kuo, or Contending States, era (480–222 B.C.) changes took place which are of maximum importance to the history of later China. Hereditary succession to power ended and the high officers assumed both control and title. This was illustrated in the state of Ch'i, where the ruler, heretofore always a member of the Chiang clan, royal Chou on the maternal side, was ousted by his high officer, a member of an outside family named T'ien. In the state of Chin three high officers, Han, Chao, and Wei, dispossessed the king and divided the state into three parts, each under the rule of one of these officers. The state of Ch'in established two classes of administrative units, called chün (commandery) and hsien (district). The principles governing the ownership of land were now radically altered: for the first time, officials were given salaries by the crown and were not owners of the land, as in former days, but only overseers. As a result of these changes the common man who had ability could enter the service of a king as an administrator.

This brought about other developments. The scholars of the time began private teaching and thereby opened the way for the common people to receive an education and enter government service. This soon gave rise to a class of professional statesmen. Occasionally, a state would hire from the frontier areas a non-Chinese who was skilled in military matters and would put him in charge of army affairs. Thus was created a class of professional soldiers. Ambitious kings surrounded themselves with militarists and political philosophers, who were treated as honored guests. Appreciation of the value of public works is shown by the ambitious engineering projects undertaken by single states. Although the canal system for this period is not known, it may be pointed out that at the end of the Ch'un Ch'iu the King of Wu went to meet Chin at Huang-ch'i, in present-day Honan, by "linking the rivers and making canals." The Wei state, during the disruption of the Chan Kuo, built a highway which is mentioned in the *Shui Ching Chu* (Commentary on the Water Classic). A project in which many states participated was the building of barriers against the northern barbarians. These barriers were finally linked by Ch'in Shih Huang Ti to form the Great Wall.

The disunity prevalent during the era of the Contending States contained within itself the promise of unification. In time, the strongest state, Ch'in, imposed its will on the rest and welded the parts into a whole under a single ruler, Ch'in Shih Huang Ti, First Emperor of Ch'in. Much of the apparatus of government which enabled Ch'in to organize successfully had been developed in the preceding Chan Kuo period. Much of it was retained and amplified by the Han rulers. Some of it yet remains. Both in spite of and because of the furor of internal dissension, China was ready for unification.

◇   ◇   ◇

The last year of the last king of Chou, 256 B.C., is the end of the Chou dynasty. According to the Chronological Tables of the *Shih Chi* (Historical Record), from the removal of the capital eastward to Lo-yang until 256 B.C. is 515 years, the duration of Eastern Chou; this makes 771 B.C. the final year of Western Chou. Almost all the records are in fairly close agreement for this period, not only with regard to its total length but also for the years of each king's reign.

A difficult problem arises when the chronology of Western Chou is considered, for the *Shih Chi* contains no table, either for the length of individual reigns before the Kung Ho period (841–828

B.C.) or for the period as a whole. The chronology of Western Chou can be reconstructed only in piecemeal fashion. It is necessary to proceed backward from the year 771 B.C.

The validity of the Bamboo Annals has been variously tested, and they have been found trustworthy even in details. They were compiled in 297–296 B.C.; and, inasmuch as they are in agreement with the bronzes of Eastern Chou, materials of a much earlier date, they are to be preferred to the *Shih Chi* as a source for reconstructing Western Chou chronology. Moreover, the approximate dates given in early independent works for various periods are substantiated by the dates recorded in the Bamboo Annals. It is known that the first year of the Kung Ho period was 841 B.C.; and since Kung Ho held power for fourteen years, Hsüan Wang's first year must be 827 B.C. Prior to Hsüan, from Ch'êng Wang to Li Wang, there were eight generations. Assuming four generations to a century, this dates the beginning of the Chou dynasty *circa* 1027 B.C. According to the Bamboo Annals, Western Chou lasted 257 years; if the first year of P'ing Wang of Eastern Chou be taken as 770 B.C., then the first year of Western Chou is again 1027 B.C.

The Chou age may be conveniently divided into three periods: (1) that of the Western Chou (*ca.* 1027–771 B.C.); (2) that of the Feudal States (770–481 B.C.) to the end of the Ch'un Ch'iu (an overlap is made, however, because the Ch'un Ch'iu begins in 722 B.C.); and (3) that of the Chan Kuo, or era of Contending States (480–222 B.C.), a period which lasted thirty-four years after the last year of the last Chou king. Periods 2 and 3 comprise the so-called Eastern Chou. The total of years for the Chou dynasty is 772.

⋄   ⋄   ⋄

Cultural differences between Western and Eastern Chou are, in a general sense, of the same type as their political differences. There was no difference between Shang and Chou with regard to ancestor and nature worship. The development of ancestor worship in the Chou family tended to form a pattern of the family group which, when transferred to the state, had a certain practical political value.

Of the natural forces worshiped by the Shang the most powerful was called Shang-ti (*shang* means high), whose life was conceived of as similar to that of an ideal king. Shang-ti was thought of as having a court and high officials and direct relations with the king. Shang-ti's adoption by the Chou is known from the bronzes; inscriptions make it clear that "Shang-ti orders [something or someone]," and that after death members of the Chou family go to live at the court of Shang-ti.

At the same time the Chou were developing the idea of T'ien (sky) on the same plane with Shang-ti. The bronzes show that the two were at first interchangeable: some inscriptions record "the decree of Ti"; others record "the decree of T'ien." At a later date, T'ien superseded Shang-ti as the more powerful. Two essential notions concerning T'ien are obtained from the bronzes and the *Shu Ching* (Book of Documents): the first is, "Stand in awe of T'ien's might"; the second, "Respect illustrious virtue [*tê*]." These are fundamental in the attitude of Confucius (tradl. 551–479 B.C.) toward T'ien and the human person.

It is strange that no mention of *kuei* (ghost) is made until the Eastern Chou period, whereas *shên* (spirit) is recorded earlier. There are, then, two categories of such phenomena: one is the spirit of the deceased human being, called *kuei;* the other, called *shên*, includes hundreds of nonhuman spirits, and ghosts which were always disembodied.

Bronze inscriptions from the state of Ch'i, in the period of the Eastern Chou, record three expressions belonging to the same class of ideas: one concerns being "not old," that is, remaining young; another refers to "eternal life"; the third means "not to die." All three ideas are subjects of prayer, possibly addressed to T'ien, although it is not so stated in the inscriptions.

In the years following Confucius the intrinsic religious qualities involved in ancestor worship and in the ideas of both T'ien and Shang-ti were gradually dissipated until they were practiced only as forms by the intelligentsia, and held as minor, often misunderstood tenets by the common people. Henceforward until the coming of Buddhism there were no practices with a strictly religious content.

For the history of philosophic thought before the time of Confucius, documents are scarce and not well organized. Confucius made a deep study of his people's cultural heritage. The tradition

to which he returned time and again was the summation of Chou
culture as exemplified in the state of Lu. Both Mencius (372–289
or 390–305 B.C.) and Hsün Tzǔ (340–245? or 298–238 B.C.), as students of the Master, followed much of his teaching—shifting the
accent as each saw and understood the demands of his own time.
Confucius stressed aristocratic government and the regulation of
the common people. Mencius, however, emphasized the importance of the people, and Hsün Tzǔ developed a doctrine in which
the concept of law held first place.

As the barbarian states entered physically and culturally into the
Chinese world they made their strength felt not only in the political sphere but also in the realm of ideas. The culture of the
northern barbarians deeply influenced both Chin and Ch'in. Legal
structure and concepts of the function of law began to outweigh
other considerations. The background for this may possibly be
traced to the barbarian emphasis on military matters and discipline. It is believed that the philosophy of Mo Ti (or Mo Tzǔ), of
the fifth and fourth centuries B.C., was partly derived from such
influences.

The eastern barbarians, because they came from the coastal
regions, evolved ideas associated with years of observing the character of the ocean, and tended to concentrate on the importance
of change. The inland groups, never subjected to the sudden and
terrifying movements of a great body of water, had basic notions
of stability. These groups with their different horizons brought a
new cosmological picture into Chinese thinking. The attraction
of the ocean is illustrated by the number of visits made by Ch'in
Shih Huang Ti. Impressed by the instability of the sea and feeling
keenly the ephemeral quality of existence, the coastal peoples populated the sea with immortals who were always happy and who
were not subject to the vagaries of nature. This free fancy and
imaginative invention caught hold in Ch'i; it was of peculiar importance in the growth of concepts found in the thought of Chuang
Tzǔ and Lao Tzǔ.

Among the southern tribes the patterns of thought were conditioned by limitations imposed by geography and climate. Heavy
and at times almost continuous rainfall nurtured the conviction
that life was monotonous and drab. There was little or no cultiva-

tion, and horizons were cut short by dense jungle growths. Religious observances focused on myriads of ghosts and spirits. This influence was strongest in the state of Ch'u; though literary production was small, a dim and oppressive sense of the tragedy of life can be felt in the *Ch'u Tzŭ* (Songs of Ch'u).

Philosophical activity reached its apogee at the end of the Contending States era. The school of Mo Tzŭ, in developing and emphasizing the art of disputation, had a wide range of application in other schools. The tendency of the period, in philosophy as in politics, was toward unified presentation. The systematization which had started under the Eastern Chou was applied by the Taoists to the problem of ordering everything in a closed structure, under a single heading.

The *I Ching* (Book of Changes) was used from early times as a handbook of divination by means of the tortoise shell and milfoil. It is necessary to emphasize that this handbook had no philosophical content. The scholars of the Chan Kuo (480–222 B.C.) or later, however, composed a commentary on this work giving philosophical interpretations. The combined text and commentary were used to create a cosmological picture based on the idea of unity.

The early prose writings are mainly the inscriptions of the Western Chou bronzes and the *Shu Ching* (Book of Documents). The language of the bronzes, and often of the *Shu Ching*, maintains an economy in the use of characters which results in extreme terseness of style. Both are characterized by close adherence to the rules of syntax and, despite their brevity, a rich vocabulary. The contents were limited to the orders of the king and a bare statement of facts. The genuine text of the *Lun Yü* (Analects of Confucius) is clear and simple and continues the traditional brevity of earlier prose.

The writings of Mencius (372–289, or 390–305 B.C.) display more of a conscious striving for literary style. Descriptive passages and interesting anecdotes depart from the tradition of austere simplicity. The prose style of Chuang Tzŭ, a younger contemporary of Mencius, stands midway between that of Mencius and that of Han Fei Tzŭ (d. *ca.* 233 B.C.). The latter, writing at a time when the art of disputation was at its height, argued various points in his prose works, and so lengthened the paragraphs that a style more

nearly that of the essay resulted. Much the same is true of Hsün
Tzŭ (340–245?, or 298–238 B.C.). The monotonous styles of Han Fei
Tzŭ and Hsün Tzŭ did not recommend them as models to Han
scholars, who revived the style of the *Shu Ching*.

Inscriptions on the bronzes at the close of Western Chou, particularly those on bells, make use of rhyme schemes. There is little
doubt that early ballads were sung with rhymes, but the use of
rhyme schemes in the written language is of much later origin. The
Shih Ching (Book of Songs) has three parts: a series of ballads, a
class of songs called *ya,* and a group of odes. The latter two were
used in court ceremonies. The Odes of Chou can be divided into
two classes: the oldest have no rhymes and lack a pattern; the
second group has both rhyme and pattern, and cannot, by comparison with the bronzes, be dated before the close of Western
Chou. The entire content of the *Shih Ching* probably stems from
a Chinese source, for when it is compared with the earliest works
written in the Chinese language but outside the Chinese tradition,
sharp differences in style, form, and content are obvious. Writings
particularly valuable for such comparison are the *Ch'u Tzŭ,* or
Songs of Ch'u. Here terseness is missing in both sentence and
stanza, which are drawn out to great length. The repetitions characteristic of the *Shih Ching* are absent, and the tone of moderation
is replaced by imaginative fancy. The two works are obviously
products of separate groups. Since the *Shih Ching* is by far the
older it is generally agreed to be of the Chinese tradition.

The earliest-known written documents in the Chinese language
already show an advanced stage of development. The bronze inscriptions of Western Chou make use of a set of personal pronouns
with case and number distinctions. These gradually disappear in
the period of the Eastern Chou and are nonexistent in that of the
Han. The development of certain characters can be traced on the
bronzes as their usage varied; for example, *chih* appears first as a
demonstrative adjective, then as a sign of the genitive case, and
later as a pronoun of the third person singular. It is used in present-
day writing in all three senses—plus later additions. During the
slackening of central power under the Eastern Chou, slight differences in syntax can be detected on the bronze inscriptions, but the
main syntactical pattern never changes. Variations in the spoken

language created dialects of wide disparity, but the written language, because it was controlled by a central authority, has shown only insignificant changes in syntax.

Developments in the script of the Chou dynasty mirror faithfully the shifts in political control. Early Chou script is sharp and strong, tending to become more balanced and moderate in the age of the Western Chou. It is weakened and slanted in the Eastern Chou and the Ch'un Ch'iu periods. In the Contending States era it is unrestrained and artificial. Under the leadership of the Seven States the Ch'in state retained and preserved the traditional script of Western Chou, which was called Large Seal script, and when, at the end of the Chan Kuo, Ch'in unified the states, it adopted this script, calling it Small Seal, and enforced its general usage.

◇ ◇ ◇

The court system of ritual employed in the Chou age is obscure, but some knowledge of it may be gained from the bronzes. Royal audiences were usually granted at dawn and occasionally in the twilight before dawn. For this reason the Chinese character for "audience" had the original meaning of "early morning." The practice of holding audiences was continued for two and a half millennia, and ended only with the fall of the Ch'ing dynasty, in A.D. 1912.

Chou audiences took place usually in the royal residence or temple, although sometimes in the home or temple of a noble. The audience chamber was gained through a gate entering a courtyard at the north end of which was the *t'ai-shih*, or great room. Leading up to the *t'ai-shih* were steps on which the king stood facing south. At his right was the historian. The officers, standing at the left, were conducted by a high official, the *pin-hsiang*, or master of court ceremonies, who approached the king facing north. The orders for the day, previously written on bamboo slips, were announced by the historian and given to the officers, who made deep obeisance and withdrew.

This was the form of ceremony beginning with Mu Wang (*ca.* 965–928 B.C.) and continuing throughout the rest of the Chou age. The orders on the slips were considered of such importance that they were often cast as inscriptions on bronze vessels and were thus preserved for posterity. Likewise, they were compiled and edited to form the *Shu Ching* (Book of Documents). It is because of this preservation of early documents in their original form that the bronze inscriptions are considered more trustworthy than the *Shu Ching*.

The *pin-hsiang* was required to know the court ritual and thus was the only person capable of presenting others to the king. In the Chan Kuo era interstate relationships were, for the most part, carried on through the medium of such rituals; in consequence, great importance attached to the position of master of court ceremonies. It was the aim of Confucius to train his pupils so well in the ritual that they could fill this position. Since many affairs of state were carried on by the *pin-hsiang*, this office grew in importance until it became the chief one at court.

As an adjunct to the court ritual certain musical forms were used. It is probable that there were popular songs and dances, possibly with accompaniment, but these were not part of court ceremony and were looked upon as vulgar by Confucius. Bells, drums, and a small wind instrument made of clay, similar to the ocarina, were used. Many other musical instruments, however, are listed in the *Shih Ching* (Book of Songs). The purpose of the music was to set a rhythm for the performance of the ceremony. The officials in procession wore, hanging from their clothing, pieces of jade which were used to keep time with the bells. Small bells with clappers to provide rhythm were sometimes attached to sacrificial vessels. By the time of Confucius, reaction had set in against this simple traditional music, and the preference for music from the state of Ch'êng drew severe censure from the Master.*

◇   ◇   ◇

There are few data concerning economic history under the Chou, but indications of relative values may be gleaned from inscriptions listing gifts presented to nobles and officers by the king. A comparison of the bronzes of the first half of Western Chou with those of the second half reveals the fluctuation in values. Gifts common to both periods were jade, weapons, sacrificial wines, and salt. In

---

* The history of music in China poses a difficult problem: why, in a culture highly developed in all the other fine arts, is music always an importation?

the first half of Western Chou, articles mentioned as gifts were cowrie shells, red gold, bronze, various animals (such as deer, cattle, birds, and horses and chariots), and occasionally clothing. For the second half are listed cowrie shells, red gold, and bronze, but much less frequently; to gifts of horses and chariots, fittings are added; more gifts of clothing are recorded. Silks are found listed only for the later period.

The barbarians offered tribute of horses, cowries, metal, jade, and silks. An inscription of the second half of Western Chou reads, in part: "The Huai barbarians have been my tribute men for a long time. They dare not fail to offer tribute [and men for] service. . . . The king ordered that the market should be in a definite place, and must not be in the barbarians' territory. The feudal lords and the people must not pay tribute to the barbarians." Another inscription of the same period records exchange values in the bartering system: "One horse and one roll of silk are exchanged for five slaves."

The inconvenience of barter on a large scale led to the use of cowries, silks, and metal as money. The actual shift to a money economy did not take place until the Chan Kuo era. Development of a merchant class in the Ch'un Ch'iu period made this a necessity.

The basic material for agricultural implements and weapons in the Chan Kuo era is iron, in contrast to the earlier use of bronze. Art forms still employed bronze and had added silver. The technique of inlay, also, had been developed. Lacquered wares appear for the first time in the Chan Kuo period. Stone monuments and inscriptions had been used by the state of Ch'in since the time of Eastern Chou.

The calendar of the early Chou did not differ greatly from that of Shang, which was used for both harvests and sacrifices. In Chou times, however, the calendar was used for harvests only. The month was divided into parts corresponding to the phases of the moon. Under the Western Chou the feudal lords used the calendar of the royal house; under the Eastern Chou the inscriptions show that each state calculated its own dates for various events. Four seasons are used in the calendars of Eastern Chou. The earlier Western Chou records do not name the four seasons, which may possibly indicate a continuance of the Shang calendar of two seasons, spring and autumn. The political confusion of the Chan Kuo period was doubly confounded when both astrology and astronomy were used in calendrical systems. The result was a maze of complexes which has not only obscured the chronology of ancient history but has also complicated the study of philosophy.

The extremes of this age—the Western Chou at the beginning and the Chan Kuo at the end—display, for the first, a conservative calm, and, for the latter, disruption and complete confusion. It is clear, however, that the evolution was continuous, with no sudden breaks. The final unification under Ch'in was the logical outcome of developments beginning under the Shang and in the early days of Western Chou. The Chinese culture pattern had assimilated all newcomers, had drawn from their life and vigor, and yet had retained its own forceful character. Not until the advent of Buddhism was there a major shift—so firmly established was that quality known as "Chinese."

CHAPTER VI

From the Fall of Chou to the Fall of T'ang (ca. 221 B.C.-A.D. 906)

BY TÊNG SSŬ-YÜ

THE FEUDAL STATES were finally conquered and China was unified under the Ch'in dynasty in 221 B.C. That year marks the beginning of the empire which endured until A.D. 1912. The Ch'in state had modest beginnings. The progenitors of its people probably had in their veins a considerable amount of Tatar blood.[1] Its cultural and social organization was different from, and inferior to, that of contemporary states. The eventual success of Ch'in in unifying the country was due, in part, to its geographical position in Shensi and Kansu,[2] from which it could easily attack others while being itself difficult to attack; in part, to the ability of its statesmen, such as Duke Mu, Duke Hsiao, Shang Yang (Lord Shang),[3] Lü Pu-wei, Han Fei Tzǔ, and Li Ssǔ; and, in part, to the experience of its veterans, who were constantly at war with other states and with tribes on the frontier.

After completing unification in 221 B.C., the former Prince Chêng (b. 259 B.C.), king of Ch'in from 247 B.C., assumed the title Ch'in Shih Huang Ti—First Emperor of Ch'in. The territory of the empire was extended from the Yellow River basin to approximately its present limits. The name China was probably derived from Ch'in. Ch'in Shih Huang Ti hoped that his empire would be transmitted from himself "to the second emperor and so on for ten thousand generations."[4] But the imperial—in contrast to the royal—dynasty lasted only fifteen years (221–207 B.C.). Short-lived as it was, the Ch'in dynasty introduced important and far-reaching changes.

---

[1] For notes to chapter vi see page 525.

The first was the abolition of feudalism, which never again held full sway as it had under the Eastern Chou. The empire was divided into forty-two commanderies, which were subdivided into prefectures and towns. In the commanderies the emperor appointed administrators, military governors, and overseers. To disarm the feudal forces the First Emperor collected all weapons and had them melted down to make bells and bell supports—the reverse of the procedure of Peter the Great, who melted church bells to make guns.

The second important change was the standardization of the written language. This was the contribution of Li Ssŭ, chief counselor to Shih Huang Ti. Li standardized the variant forms of writing in one system which was made universal throughout the empire. Despite the many dialects and the political disunity of China, the written language has remained the same since the days of Ch'in. The universality and continuity of the written language have contributed immeasurably to the longevity and unity of Chinese culture.

The third important event was the construction of the Great Wall, some fifteen hundred miles long, through the labors of countless convicts. Shih Huang Ti's Wall was in reality a linking of earlier ramparts to form a barrier against the Turkish Hsiung-nu, or Huns. It survives as a monument to Chinese isolationism.

Ch'in Shih Huang Ti would have been a great hero in Chinese history had he been a benevolent ruler. In the years 220–219 B.C. he traveled extensively to observe whether the people were loyal to him, and also—since he was in terror of death—to search for the elixir of life. As in the Roman Empire, wide tree-lined roads were constructed for the emperor's travels, the movement of troops, and the development of commerce. While Shih Huang Ti traveled, a magnificent palace was built for him in Shensi, with a secret tunnel entrance to obviate the danger of assassination. Three attempts were made on his life, but in spite of such warnings he continued to play the tyrant. At the suggestion of Li Ssŭ he ordered the burning of a great number of books in 213—an early attempt, on a great scale, at control of thought. In the following year he is reported to have had more than four hundred sixty of the literati executed for daring to disapprove his methods and ideals. After the death of Ch'in Shih Huang Ti in 210, the country was disturbed by popular revolutions for nearly a decade.

Chinese traditional historiography has depicted Shih Huang Ti as an inhuman tyrant under whom the country suffered irremediable damage. The charge is true; nevertheless, he was an extremely able and farsighted statesman. His iron hand and harsh punishments may have been needed to unify the empire and encompass his other reforms.

The Ch'in period was one of unification: of the empire, of the written language, of measures and weights, and of thought. In addition, the foundations were laid for development of territory, nationhood, political system, and academic thought.[5]

❖   ❖   ❖

The Han dynasty is divided into two parts: the Western, or Former, Han (206 B.C.–A.D. 9), the capital of which was at Ch'ang-an (near modern Sian), and the Eastern Han (A.D. 25–220), with its capital at Lo-yang, Honan. Between the two dynasties Wang Mang established the Hsin dynasty (A.D. 9–23.)

The downfall of the Ch'in dynasty was hastened by the tyranny of the government, heavy taxation, forced labor, and the desire of the former feudal lords to restore the six states conquered by the Ch'in. There is a notable tendency throughout Chinese history for the people to revolt whenever government oppression becomes excessive. Thus the Han dynasty came to power as the result of a proletarian revolution. The leader who eventually succeeded was Liu Pang. Of peasant origin and little education but of imposing appearance, Liu had been chief of ten villages and in charge of escorting convicts to work on the tomb of Ch'in Shih Huang Ti. In the year 209 B.C. some of the convicts escaped on the way; others were set free by Liu himself. Soon uprisings broke out elsewhere, and the Ch'in dynasty was overthrown in 207. Thereafter the rebels fought among themselves for five years until, in 202, China was again united and at peace.

Enthroned in 202 as the first emperor of Han, Liu Pang is known to history by the posthumous title of Han Kao-tsu, the Great Ancestor, or founder, of Han. He had learned a lesson from the fact that the Ch'in central government had lacked the support of local governments in times of trouble. Therefore he appointed his most valued ministers as kings of the territories they had conquered; to others he assigned lesser rewards of marquisates. The form of the feudal system was thus temporarily restored. The kings were permitted to appoint their officials, except for a chief minister who was chosen by the central government. Privilege made the kings haughty and disloyal to the central government; some tried to revolt. Finally, all the generals and associates of Han Kao-tsu were either killed or expelled from the empire.

The emperor frequently conducted punitive expeditions in person. In 200 B.C. he was besieged for seven days in Shensi by the Hsiung-nu, who decades earlier had formed their first empire in Mongolia. The gift of an imperial princess as consort to their ruler—and other presents—secured peace until 166 B.C. Wounded in fighting rebels, Kao-tsu died in 195 B.C.

The successor to the first Han ruler was weak. Political power fell into the hands of Kao-tsu's widow, who in 188 B.C. became the Empress Lü, one of the three most powerful empresses of Chinese history (the others were Wu of the T'ang dynasty and Tz'ŭ-hsi of the Ch'ing, or Manchu, dynasty). The Empress Lü placed her brothers and other members of her family at the head of various armies and government bureaus. Thus the Lü family wielded authority in the central government until the death of the empress in 180.

The next ruler, Wên Ti (180–157 B.C.), was notable for his Taoistic theory of government. (See chap. xvii, below.) He did not trouble the people, but followed a policy of noninterference. Extremely frugal, he strove to maintain peace and prosperity and gave orders that his funeral ceremonies should not be elaborate. All this was in keeping with the simple needs of an agricultural society. To a certain extent Wên Ti fostered conservatism by copying the political and legal system of the Ch'in dynasty.

After a period of generally benevolent government, respect for law began to break down and in 154 B.C. several leading vassals revolted against Han Ching Ti (156–141 B.C.). Ching Ti, adopting the legalistic theory of government, resorted to severe punishments. The revolt was mercilessly suppressed and the people thereafter were governed by strict laws. It was in the reign of Ching Ti that

China was again really unified. Civil rather than military government was not achieved, however, until the reign of Wu Ti (140–87 B.C.).

Wu Ti—the Martial Emperor—is one of the most famous rulers in history. Enthroned at the age of seventeen, he was energetic in internal development and external expansion. In administration he initiated many political and social changes. Most important seems to have been a civil service system in which appointments were based partly on election, or recommendation by local officials, and partly on examination. This system (*ca.* 165–125 B.C.) was suggested by the scholar Tung Chung-shu, on whose advice Confucian theory became the guiding principle of government and Confucian scholars were given control of civil administration. Confucianism became a state cult in the second century B.C. (See chap. xv, below.) Feudalism was again abolished, this time by dividing each fief equally among the sons when a lord died; thus, after a few generations, no fief would be of great extent.

It was an age of expansion: Korea, Annam, and Sinkiang were brought under Chinese jurisdiction. Silk routes across Asia were established, and in the year 138 B.C. Chang Ch'ien was sent westward overland to make an alliance against the Hsiung-nu with the Yüeh-chih, an Indo-European people. Though he failed in his political and diplomatic objectives, Chang Ch'ien made known something of the greatness of Han China to western Asia, and in return brought back (*ca.* 126 B.C.) information concerning many states in which he had traveled or of which he had heard during his journey. He introduced the Chinese crossbow, the peach, and the apricot to the West, and carried back to the East the grape and alfalfa.

Han power reached its heyday in Wu Ti's reign of more than half a century. At the same time this period marked the beginning of a gradual decline of the dynasty as a result of the emperor's foreign wars and expensive public works. Also, Wu Ti was superstitious; in his later years much trouble was caused by his interest in sorcery and by the intrigues of eunuchs and of relatives of his concubines. The eunuchs and the families of imperial wives and concubines gradually became more and more powerful until finally the government of the Western Han was usurped by Wang Mang.

Wang Mang was a nephew of the mother of the Emperor Ch'êng

(32–7 B.C.). Through his family connections and his good conduct Wang Mang became grand minister at the age of thirty-eight and acting emperor at fifty-three. After three years of deliberate planning, aided by his lifelong practice of a virtuous mien to conceal his real cunning, Wang Mang made himself emperor (A.D. 9–23) without an armed revolution. He undertook political and social reforms, including the nationalization and equal distribution of land and the abolition of slavery. He also proclaimed six state controls, or monopolies: salt, wine, iron, mines and other natural resources, coinage, and the Five Equalizations, including banking and credit. The Five Equalizations were directed toward stabilizing prices of commodities in general use. The six monopolies of Wang Mang may be characterized as state socialism and his land policy as communistic. He frequently changed the currency system; he also restored feudalism. But his reforms failed in large part because he attempted too many changes at once, lacked the machinery and trained personnel to carry out his plans, and was an object of hatred to the imperial Liu family. The net result was the rise of banditry and insurgency throughout the empire. After a reign of approximately fourteen years Wang Mang met violent death at the hands of a rebel.

The dynastic history of the Western, or Former, Han depicts Wang Mang as a hypocrite. Some modern scholars, however, consider him one of the greatest statesmen China has ever produced.[6] Others regard him as a forger of Confucian classics, or consider the account of him in the *Han Shu* (History of Han) as "unprejudiced and justified."[7] These conflicting reports suggest that Wang Mang was a politician as well as a statesman, and that, usurper though he was, and somewhat of a hypocrite, he was one of the world's earliest utopians and social reformers.

◇ ◇ ◇

The Eastern, or Later, Han was a continuation of the Western, or Former, Han dynasty inasmuch as descendants of the Liu family overthrew Wang Mang and restored the legitimate house. The founder of Eastern Han was Liu Hsiu, a Confucian scholar, who later received the title Kuang Wu Ti, Glorious Martial Emperor. He again unified the empire, encouraged education, and fostered morals and a heroic spirit. Men of reputation and character were employed as officials. The reforms of Wang Mang were abolished. Kuang Wu Ti reëstablished control of the Chinese possessions in Annam. Relations with the archipelago which is now Japan began in A.D. 57, when some of the tribes sent embassies to China. In the northwest, and in Sinkiang also, the first emperor of Eastern Han began a process of reëstablishing Chinese prestige and rule.

After the reign of Kuang Wu Ti those of Ming (58–75) and Chang (78–88) are considered the most prosperous and enlightened periods of the Eastern, or Later, Han. The most important development was the official introduction of Buddhism into China, traditionally in the time of Ming Ti. (See chap. xviii, below). Both Ming and Chang were outstanding patrons of Confucianism and literature. Punishments were light; there was little forced labor and no interference with the lawful pursuits of the people.

Toward the close of Ming Ti's reign a great general, Pan Ch'ao (32–102), through personal diplomacy and strategy extended the power of his country over western (later Chinese) Turkestan, and opened the way for an extensive silk trade with the Roman Orient. One of his agents, Kan Ying, penetrated to the Persian Gulf in A.D. 97. Chinese garrisons were established on the Oxus and in Kashgar, Yarkand, Khotan, and Turfan.

The reign of Ho Ti (A.D. 89–105) was one of transition. For three centuries the empire had, on the whole, been unified and strong, but with Ho Ti it began definitely to decline. The court was dominated by empresses or concubines and their relatives, by eunuchs and powerful ministers, and by party intrigues. Bandits and insurrections disturbed the country, and barbarian pressure became increasingly serious.

Insecurity of life and property contributed to the rise, in the second century, of Taoism, a cult of mysticism and occultism which promised longevity or even immortality. After the central provinces had been swept for some years by an epidemic, a Taoist named Chang is reported to have discovered a magical cure—the drinking of pure water. Having gradually acquired many followers, Chang decided to revolt against the tyrannical administration of the eunuchs. Thus began, in the year 184, the Yellow Turban rebellion, so called from the headdress worn by the rebels. After this outbreak the empire dissolved into anarchy, though the dynasty endured until A.D. 220, when the last weak ruler was compelled to abdicate in favor of Ts'ao P'ei, son of Ts'ao Ts'ao.[8]

In the age of Ch'in and Han the significant political innovations were the examination system and the *yü shih,* or control system. These institutions, peculiar to China, are still in use—reëmbodied in two of the five yüan of the contemporary National government. In art the Ch'in dynasty handed down beautiful stone inscriptions in seal characters. The Han produced bronzes inferior to those of Shang and Chou, but its glazed potteries, painted clay figures, and painted vessels are very fine. In sculpture the tomb of Ho Ch'ü-ping (d. *ca.* 117 B.C.)[9] near modern Sian, and that of Wu Liang-tz'ŭ (A.D. 147) at Chia-hsiang, Shantung, are justly famous. Portrait painting, the carving of jade ritual objects, and lacquer work improved under the Han.

◇ ◇ ◇

The period from Shang to the end of Han was formative. Cultural development continued in spite of sporadic internal and external wars. After the Han came a period of cultural decline caused in part by political disunion and warfare. Invasions from north and west, with their concomitants of bloodshed and misery, emigration, and eventual racial assimilation, brought about marked deterioration in the standard of living. The administrative structure erected by Ch'in and Han could no longer be operated throughout the country and the cultural unity achieved by these dynasties was threatened.

Because of these circumstances the period of the Six Dynasties (220–589)—Wei, Chin, Sung, Chi, Liang, and Ch'ên—is often compared to the Dark Ages of Europe. In the Chinese Empire, as in the Roman, the cultured classes rapidly dwindled in numbers and importance. Barbarians streamed into the land and mingled with the population. Anarchy was not so marked as in Europe, however, nor were the changes so revolutionary. While the tribesmen who broke the power of Rome were still largely barbarians, those who settled south of the Great Wall were already deeply imbued with the principles of Chinese civilization. Accordingly, the break between the earlier and later periods of civilization was far less sharp than in Europe.

The Han empire was divided into three kingdoms: Wei (220–265), established by Ts'ao Ts'ao in central and northern China, with its capital at Lo-yang; Wu (222–280) in the lower Yangtze Valley, with its capital at Nanking; and Shu (221–263) in present-day Szechuan. These kingdoms, each with a large territory and great economic resources, fought each other for about half a century. The period of the Three Kingdoms (220–265), perhaps the most romantic in the history of China, may be compared to the age of chivalry in Europe.[10]

After the year 280 the country was loosely unified for a time by the Western Chin dynasty (265–317), with its capital at Lo-yang. The power of this dynasty was terminated by an invasion of a branch of the Hsiung-nu and China was again divided. In the south the Eastern Chin held feeble sway in Nanking from 317 until 420. Thereafter, until 589, the (Liu) Sung, Ch'i, Liang, and Ch'ên dynasties ruled.

Meanwhile (304–439) a series of barbarian houses established themselves in northern China by invasion and infiltration of various peoples who sought Chinese culture, followed Chinese precedents, and were rapidly absorbed. Along the northern marches were the Sixteen Kingdoms, established principally by leaders of the Turkish Hsiung-nu, the Hsien-pi (probably Mongol), the Ti,[11] and the Tibetan Ch'iang. After 439 most of northern China was unified for almost a century under the Northern Wei dynasty; later came the short-lived Eastern Wei and the Western Wei, the Northern Ch'i, and the Northern Chou.

The important feature of the period of the Northern dynasties (386–581) was the constant struggle between the Chinese in the south and the Chinese and non-Chinese in the north. Although in the course of this struggle the northerners frequently oppressed the southerners, the Yangtze Kiang was never crossed because the northern host was defeated at the Fei River, in northern Anhui, in A.D. 383. The battle at the Fei River is one of the decisive struggles in world history. Had the barbarians, or semibarbarians, succeeded in crossing the Yangtze at a time when Chinese vitality was at low ebb and the Chinese race and culture had not yet taken deep root in the relatively new territories of the south, probably all China would have been lost and it might have meant the end of Chinese

civilization. As it was, native elements and certain barbarian elements coalesced to form a new race, and Buddhism gradually gave
a new impetus and richness to Chinese culture.

The long period of political division after the fall of the Han
retarded cultural progress. There were, nevertheless, two important by-products: first, assimilation of foreign strains by the Chinese
race; and second, cultural expansion from northern into southern
China. Artistic products of the period include the calligraphy of
Wang Hsi-chih (A.D. 322–379); the paintings of Ku K'ai-chih (ca.
344–ca. 406); the famous rock sculptures at Yün-kang, Shansi, and
Lung-mên, Honan, dating from the latter half of the fifth century;
and other Buddhist statues of stone or bronze.

⟡ ⟡ ⟡

The age of the Six Dynasties (220–589), so marked by extremes in
culture and by decentralization and confusion, was followed by
that of the Sui and T'ang—perhaps the most brilliant in the history of China and one of the most brilliant in the world. The
country was unified, population increased, and commerce developed. Through long contact overland in the north and to a lesser
degree in the south, by way of the sea, with southern and western
Asia, there was much intermixture of blood, language and literature, art, fashions, and customs. The Sui (ca. 589–618) and the
T'ang (618–906) inherited these varied cultural elements (including Indian and Iranian) and modified and improved them. Considerable numbers of foreign merchants settled in the capital,
Ch'ang-an, in Canton, and in a few other cities. Thus the Sui-T'ang
age registered notable advances in civilization.

During this period Chinese civilization had great influence on
surrounding countries, including, especially, Japan. In the Pacific
region the Chinese are still called "the people of T'ang." A remarkably high level of creativeness was attained in art and poetry.
The development of Buddhism reached its climax under the T'ang,
and several foreign religions, such as Nestorian Christianity, Manichaeism, and Zoroastrianism, were introduced.

The T'ang rulers reëstablished and perfected the examination
system for appointment of officials which was followed until 1905.
(See chap. xxx, below.) Under their rule, military men held a pow-

erful position in society. Although civilian literary China has usually despised soldiers, many men of the T'ang age won respect and held advantageous positions in society.

The founder of the Sui dynasty, Yang Chien (jien), born in 541—known posthumously as Kao-tsu (gao-tsu), or Wên Ti (di)—at first ruled well. He suppressed rebellious factions and encouraged merit, honesty, and devotion to duty in his officials. He promoted frugality, sought out scattered works of literature, forbade and even burned the unorthodox *chan-wei* interpretation of the Confucian classics. In his later years, however, Yang Chien became corrupt and was killed by his second son, Kuang, who became the second Sui emperor and is known as Yang Ti.

Sui Yang Ti (605–618) was notorious in Chinese history, although modern scholars give him credit for being an energetic as well as an ambitious ruler. He was a capricious spendthrift, a pleasure-loving madman chiefly interested in the splendor of his palaces and the company of his women.

The two emperors of Sui, especially Yang Ti, were fond of public works construction. Chief among their feats were the building of a magnificent palace at Lo-yang, the repairing of the Great Wall, and the digging of a great canal. The last was formed by linking existing waterways from Lo-yang to the Yangtze. It was extended, in 608, to Cho-chow, Hopei, by a million laborers, and to Hang-chow, Chekiang, two years later. The Sui canal was not the same as the modern Grand Canal, which was constructed by Kublai Khan near the end of the thirteenth century. The term Grand Canal was not used in Sui dynastic history.

Under the Sui there were foreign wars against the T'u-chüeh, or Turks, in Kansu and in central Asia. An exhaustive war was carried on against Korea. Numerous levies of forced labor and of troops, forced contributions of goods and money, the flood of 611, and ever-increasing taxes collected in arbitrary and oppressive ways created disorder among both troops and civilians. In 614 more troops were enlisted and sent against the Koreans. "But now bandits and rebels arose like bees,"[12] and the Emperor Yang shut himself up in one of his pleasure palaces in Yangchow. In 618 some of the rebels forced their way in and murdered him. So ends the short history of the Sui dynasty.

In the course of the ensuing T'ang period (618–906) there were twenty-one rulers. The technical founder was Li Yüan, the Duke of T'ang (posthumously known as Kao-tsu), who was born in Ch'ang-an. His ancestors had held a title of nobility from the Western Wei (535–557). His father was a high military commander under the Northern Chou (557–581), a member of a non-Chinese tribe. His wife and his son's wife were also barbarians, Thus the early T'ang rulers, though in part Chinese, had a large admixture of foreign blood.[18]

From the beginning of the Sui period Li Yüan had held official positions. In 616 he was engaged in warring against the Turks and suppressing bandits and rebels who infested the northern provinces. With the help of his second son, Shih-min, Li Yüan gained prestige by his successes against his foes. Li Shih-min, the actual founder of the dynasty, urged his sire to take advantage of the geographical situation of the Shensi region, where it was relatively easy to attack but difficult for others to assail. At that time bandits and rebels had already started a revolution. After a short war Li Yüan ascended the throne at Ch'ang-an, on June 12, 618. He and Shih-min mainly concentrated on consolidating the empire and establishing political institutions. In 627 the first T'ang emperor abdicated in favor of his second son, who had killed two of his brothers to insure his own accession.

T'ang T'ai-tsung (Li Shih-min) was one of the ablest monarchs and had one of the most brilliant reigns (627–649) in China's long history. As emperor he was capable and energetic; in private life he was magnanimous. Since the people were war-weary, they particularly appreciated an enlightened government. T'ai-tsung completed the unification of the country, stimulated its culture, increased its prosperity, and placed it on a new pinnacle of power. All strategic points were carefully guarded by farmer-soldiers (fu-ping), who were drafted to serve between the ages of twenty and sixty. Most of the top-ranking local governers were military men who were relatives or personal friends of the imperial family. Three high official bureaus were instituted to control state affairs and to check on one another. Six government departments were established. All officials were appointed from the capital; great attention was paid to their selection through civil service examinations, which had been restored under the Sui. Local governors were given full power to develop their administrative abilities. The legal code was revised, and served as a model for China's subsequent dynasties and for other lands, as in Japan and Annam. Public granaries were re-instituted against times of scarcity.

The T'ang rulers entered also upon foreign conquest. They warred against the eastern Turks who had helped to found the dynasty but who subsequently raided Ch'ang-an. T'ai-tsung conquered his erstwhile friends, and later the western Turks, and expanded anew his country's frontiers into central Asia. Refusing to repair the Great Wall, he pursued the barbarians into Mongolia. Later, many states in and bordering the Tarim basin and along the old silk and other trade routes were made vassals. After T'ai-tsung's death the policy of conquest was continued. Finally, six military administrative protectorates were organized for the government of the frontier and newly conquered areas. One of these protectorates, organized in 679, with its capital in Tonkin, was called the Annam (i.e., pacifying the south) Protectorate.

At its height the T'ang exceeded the Han empire. What is known to Westerners as Manchuria, including the Amur territory, Korea, most of Inner and Outer Mongolia, Turkestan (Chinese and Russian), part of Tibet, Tashkent, Samarkand, Bokhara, Fergana, and Annam—all recognized the suzerainty of T'ang. The Han empire had never reached the Amur or the borders of India.

In the reign of T'ai-tsung's son Kao-tsung, political power fell into the hands of Wu Chao (woo jao), or Wu Tsê-t'ien, usually referred to as Wu Hou, or the Empress Wu, one of the three most powerful women rulers in Chinese history. Wu Chao was the daughter of a state minister in Shansi. T'ai-tsung had chosen her at the age of fourteen for her beauty and ability. On the death of that emperor she and other concubines entered a Buddhist nunnery, from which Kao-tsung took her into his harem. She was clever, witty, and versed in history and literature. In the year 655 she supplanted the empress and had her killed. After 656 Kao-tsung was frequently ill, and permitted Wu Chao to read all memorials and make decisions. Thus she wielded the actual powers of state throughout most of his reign.

The Empress Wu continued in power as dowager and deposed

in turn two puppet emperors, Chung-tsung (jung-tsung) and Jui-
tsung (jwei-tsung). In 684 she assumed actual control of the government, and in 690, as substantive empress, she changed the name of
the dynasty from T'ang to Chou.

Wu Hou promoted the literary civil service examination system.
The Li family were natives of Shensi and most of their relatives
and friends in high government positions were also Shensi people.
The empress changed this Shensi headquarters policy. Through
her emphasis on civil service examinations the common people of
Shantung and southern China began to enter both central and local
governmental posts. This breaking down of the Shensi headquarters policy was continued and completed in the reign of T'ang
Hsüan-tsung, or Ming-huang, the Bright Emperor (713–756).

It was in the middle of the eighth century that Chinese political organization and cultural achievement reached their climax.
T'ang Hsüan-tsung founded the famous Hanlin, or Academy of
Letters, through which men of extraordinary abilities might be
housed in comfort and luxury. Schools were established throughout the country. Buddhism and poetry reached the heyday of their
development. The achievement in historiography was also remarkable. Pottery making progressed, and printing had its beginning.
Such poets as Li Po, or Li Tai-po (705–762), Tu Fu (712–770), and
Wang Wei (698–759 or, more probably, 701–762), who was accomplished also in painting and music, lived in the reign of the Bright
Emperor.

The Japanese copied many of the T'ang political and social institutions, also the plan of construction of their first permanent
capitals, from Ch'ang-an and Lo-yang. Buddhist monasteries, pagodas, theaters, restaurants, foreign dance halls and bars, flower
shops, and fashion shows were all highly developed.

The life of T'ang Hsüan-tsung is in part unhappily reminiscent
of that of Han Wu Ti. In the early years of his reign he was guided
by able ministers and was frugal and dutiful; in later years he was
extravagant and spent much time and money at New Year's and
birthday celebrations. Worst of all, in 745, when he was sixty-one
years old, he added to his harem the twenty-six-year-old Yang Kuei-
fei, one of the most enchanting women of any age. Yang Kuei-fei
later fell in love with An Lu-shan, a general of mixed Chinese and

barbarian blood who frequently visited the palace. An Lu-shan was stationed in Hopei to guard against the Khitans in Manchuria. Traditional historians consider this appointment an intrigue of the chief minister, but since An Lu-shan had mastered six frontier languages, and the Hopei area was a special zone for barbarians, the appointment of an experienced warrior from that area to govern by a combination of diplomacy and force may not have been essentially a bad idea.[14]

Unfortunately, the abolition of the farmer-soldier system in 749, the overemphasis of the early T'ang rulers on protecting their Shensi headquarters, and a laissez-faire policy toward the tribes in Manchuria gave the peoples on the northeastern frontier a chance to attack China south of the Wall. This was a source of trouble not only under the T'ang but in later centuries as well.

An Lu-shan revolted in 755, and within a few months Lo-yang and Ch'ang-an were taken. The emperor and his court fled to Szechuan; on the way Hsüan-tsung was forced to have Yang Kuei-fei hanged. His "everlasting sorrow" has been described by many poets and story writers. The rebellion was finally suppressed in 763 by imperial forces with the help of foreign troops, especially the Turkish Uigurs, but the use of foreign troops to put down civil revolt caused the foreigners in China to become arrogant and led to frontier troubles. In the course of the revolt, eunuchs seized power, and eventually they menaced the emperor's authority. The generals in the protectorates became increasingly powerful as the integrity of administrative machinery was broken down and the power of the central government was weakened. Since a century and a half passed before the T'ang empire entered upon its final agony, the reign of T'ang Hsüan-tsung, especially the revolution of An Lu-shan, may be considered the demarcation line between the golden age and the fall of T'ang.

After 763 the central government lived on the old cultural prestige of Ch'ang-an and the financial support of grain from the lower Yangtze basin. In 766 Liu An, minister of financial affairs, introduced a new land tax and effective measures for state control of the salt business. He also improved communications on the Sui canal. Through these means the national revenues were considerably increased.

In the latter part of the T'ang era there were a few good emperors, but most of them were incapable, short-lived, and too much under the control of eunuchs. In the ninth century constant border skirmishes occurred with the T'u-chüeh, or Turks, the Uigurs, the Tibetans, and the Nan Chao, who had their capital at Tali, Yünnan. Many governors were insubordinate. The eunuchs, who were mostly barbarians or poorly educated Chinese from the borders of Szechuan, Kuangtung, and Fukien, became increasingly disobedient. Hsien-tsung (806–820) was the first emperor to meet a violent death at the hands of eunuchs. Their power was derived, in large part, from the fact that they controlled the imperial palace guards, the state papers, and the confidential documents.

The eunuchs were divided into two groups. Each allied itself with learned men outside the court. The classical and conservative scholars who belonged to aristocratic families in Shantung were organized under the leadership of Li Tê-yu.[15] The other faction, composed of scholars who were successful candidates in the civil service examinations, was led by Niu Sêng-ju.[16] The Li and the Niu factions opposed each other on such matters as succession to the throne and the necessity of military action against foreign invasion. The struggle lasted until near the end of the T'ang period.

Contemporary poetry revealed the political and social insecurity. The masses were helpless. Many were superstitious. Taoism grew stronger. Numbers of the people turned to Taoist charms against devils and misfortunes, and sought the elixir of immortality. The popularity of Taoism and of Buddhist and Taoist priests, who were exempted from military conscription and taxpaying, caused widespread religious persecution in 845, when Buddhists, Taoists, and followers of other religions, including Nestorian Christians, suffered greatly. (See chaps. xiii, xv, xvii, xviii, below.)

Unbearable social conditions and repeated famines, which ravaged a large part of northern China, made bandits and outlaws of many. In 874 a rebellion broke out in Shantung and spread throughout the country. One of the leaders, Huang Ch'ao,[17] who had earlier failed in the official examinations, occupied the lower basin of the Yangtze and cut off transportation to the north by way of the Sui canal. This was as fatal a blow to Ch'ang-an as was the British action at Chinkiang to the Peking government almost a thousand years later. Huang Ch'ao then progressed from Honan through Hupeh, Kiangsi, and Fukien to Canton, which he took in 879. According to an Arab account, many Chinese and foreigners in Canton were massacred.[18]

The distressed emperor, Hsi-tsung (874–888), looked to the tribes north of the Great Wall and in the Tarim basin for assistance, and Li K'o-yung,[19] a general of Turkish descent, helped to suppress the rebels. After the death of Huang Ch'ao in 884 his lieutenant, Chu Wên,[20] transferred his allegiance to the T'ang, and was rewarded with a principality in Honan.

Huang's rebellion was finally suppressed in 885, and many eunuchs were wiped out in 903 through the help of Chu Wên. Chu, however, murdered the last T'ang emperor in 907 and became the first emperor of the Later Liang dynasty. Although the imperial Li family history was sordid, the cultural and political achievements of the T'ang dynasty made it perhaps the most brilliant in the history of China and one of the most notable in world history.

CHAPTER VII

From the Fall of T'ang
to the Fall of Ch'ing (906-1912)

BY FRANZ H. MICHAEL

THE LAST NINE HUNDRED YEARS of Chinese imperial history have sometimes been called a period of stagnation. China had taken form within the limits of its territorial expansion and inner colonization. The political system and philosophy had been established. It has been said that the dynasties which ruled the empire during this time, whether alien or Chinese, did little more than carry on a tradition which had become stale and uncreative.

Yet it was a great tradition. The empires of the Sung, the Yüan, the Ming, and the early Ch'ing (tsing) not only were more populous but were vastly superior to any state in Europe or elsewhere in splendor and general advancement. Moreover, there are ample grounds for arguing that the period was not one of stagnation; rather was it a consummation of all the preceding developments in Chinese history. Reintegration of the old north and the newly colonized south, with its new economic center in the Yangtze region, constituted the basis for this consummation. Division of north and south had been overcome. New cultural influences, among them the once alien Buddhist, had been absorbed. After centuries of division China had been reunited by the military might of the Sui and the T'ang. As, twelve hundred years before, the military empire established by the First Emperor of the Ch'in dynasty had revived the Confucian ideology in the Han period, so the values of this same ideology were revived to serve as the foundation of a new cultural life in the great T'ang edifice.

The T'ang dynasty had fallen principally as a result of economic depression and inner military struggles. It was followed by a group of five short-lived dynasties: Later Liang (907–923), Later T'ang (923–936), Later Chin (936–947), Later Han (947–951), and Later Chou (951–960). Each of these was but a succession to temporary power of a victorious general and his family. None had been able to extend its sway over more than a part of northern China. In the southern and central western sections of the country seven autonomous states came into being. These developed the cultural values of the T'ang period and proved more stable than the military houses in the north, the rulers of which lost what is today northern Hopei and northern Shansi to the Khitan tribes from Jehol.

Into this mixture of political forms, loosely held together by the ancient idea of the empire, the Sung house (960–1279) brought order. The founder of this dynasty, Chao (jao) K'uang-yin (posthumously known as the Grand Founder, T'ai-tsu, 960–975), came from an official family whose ancestral home was near Peking, but he himself had been a military man. In 960 he was sent with an army against the Khitan in the north. The government of the Later Chou dynasty was in the hands of a regency ruling for a child emperor. On the march northward Chao's officers conspired one morning, entered the tent of their sleeping general, and hung around his shoulders the yellow imperial robe. Thus compromised, Chao K'uang-yin had to accept the lead and return to the capital, K'aifeng, as emperor of the Sung dynasty. It seemed at first merely another military change; but the new emperor introduced from the beginning the principle of peaceful victories and civil government. No blood was shed, and members of the former ruling house were permitted to live comfortably in the capital.

The new ruler faced a double task. He had to reëstablish a centralized system out of the many, more or less local, autonomous areas which the downfall of the T'ang had left; and he had to replace military officers of marked independence and doubtful loyalty by an efficient and obedient civil apparatus.

Governmental emphasis immediately began to shift from the military back to the civil offices which had been set up under the T'ang house but which in recent years had been subordinated to military rule. To create civil loyalty to the system of unified em-

SUN YAT-SEN
Founder of the Kuomintang Party and
Father of the Chinese Republic

pire the Confucian educational system was revived. In this task the emperor and his brother who succeeded him found an able helper and administrator in their first minister, Chao P'u.

Typical of many leading officials of his time, Chao P'u had not had much classical education. This now had to change. T'ai-tsu, it is said, advised his chief minister to study, and thereafter Chao P'u "was never seen without a book in his hands." Confucian education regained its former prestige.

Local civilian officials were raised to the rank which the military had held, and were selected by a governmental board of officials. Both military and civil administrations were centralized. The taxes were again sent to the capital. Local militia, or troops of local leaders, were reorganized into imperial bodyguards and were either kept at the capital or sent out to new garrisons under central control. A new provincial administration was created. Thus a new empire with political, financial, and military centralization emerged.

The military leaders who had mutinied and elevated the first Sung emperor were not left out of this cleansing process. But here the emperor had to act personally, and he did so with an originality indicative of the times. In the first year of his reign T'ai-tsu invited these men to a banquet. At the feast he complained to his former comrades that he could not sleep for worrying over which of his officers would dethrone him. They protested their loyalty, but the emperor reminded them of how he himself had been forced into his position by their rebellion, and added that there was nothing to preclude another similar rebellion. When they asked how his distrust could be removed, he suggested their resignation from military command. Each would then receive civil rank and an estate in the provinces, with an income that would let him enjoy a peaceful old age and the happiness of family life instead of the dangers and uncertainties of court rivalries. The emperor's proposal was accepted: all resigned, and the military camarilla gave place to civil government.

On the basis of these reforms the empire was reunited. Most of the states submitted to the strength of the new organization and the principle of a unified empire without fighting; the weak resistance of others was soon overcome. But the northernmost part of the country remained separate. The new appeal for unity did not affect the Khitan (or Ch'i-tan) state in the north, with its Liao (Iron) dynasty (907–1124). After much fighting, later Sung rulers gave up their claim to the lost territory, and, in 1005, even began paying the Liao house an annual subsidy for preserving what amounted to a stalemate peace. In the northwest another "barbarian" state, Hsi-hsia, consisting of parts of modern Kansu, Shensi, and the Ordos country, remained outside the Sung fold.

At home the Sung dynasty had to deal with the economic problems which always arise after a period of prosperity. Leaders of the gentry succeed in gaining ownership of large estates in times of peace. Increased wealth strengthens their local power and enables them to impose high rents while escaping their just share of taxes. Thus the tax burden of the small farmer increases. This, and unequal division of taxes, has characterized the decline and fall of all Chinese dynasties. Government income suffers, and the weakened central power is rendered unable to control profiteering groups of landowners and officials, who divert larger and larger parts of public wealth to private use. Order breaks down. Leaders of rebellious farmers arise and destroy some members of the exploiting group, force others into line, defeat the troops of the central government, and finally set up a new dynasty with—at the outset—strong central control. But members of the scholar-gentry class are always needed as officers of the civil government, and they soon rediscover and exploit the possibilities of graft. This leads to repetition of the cycle—and, to a degree, history repeats itself.

The Sung dynasty proved no exception. In the middle of the eleventh century signs of economic crisis became apparent. Whereas under former dynasties the military struggle within the country had tended to blur an economic background of increasing difficulties, now a government of civilian officials brought the old economic problems into focus. The military threat of the Khitan Liao dynasty (907–1124), originating in southeastern Mongolia, made the solution of these problems all the more urgent. Accordingly, in this period was made the greatest attempt in China's history to break the economic cycle by a different form of political and economic control of government. Violent discussion and rivalries arose between the reformers and the conservatives who held power alternately under the later Sung emperors.

Wang An-shih (1021–1086), one of China's greatest reformer-statesmen, was born into a poor official family. After passing his first examination he held a series of positions related to hydraulic engineering, juridical and financial matters, grain administration, and several other functions of government. In 1058 he memorialized the throne on the need for reorganization of the civil service. He proposed that, instead of training in the ethical concepts of Confucian ideology, officials should be educated in practical administration with concentration upon definite fields. Instead of literary scholar-officials he wanted experts who, being paid adequate salaries, should be rendered at least relatively immune to the temptations of graft. Military subjects were to be taught to army officers, who were to supplant the hired riffraff and untrained scholar-officers in defending the country.

This brilliant official at the age of forty-eight became vice grand councilor under the sixth Sung emperor, Shên-tsung (1068–1085), who throughout his reign remained Wang's protector. Wang An-shih put reform measures into practice despite the violent opposition of conservative scholar-officials, who gathered around the outstanding figure of the historian Ssŭ-ma Kuang (sz-ma guang) (1019–1086). Wang's reforms constituted an attempt at economic planning and state activities in opposition to the laissez-faire philosophy of conservative Confucianism.

He began by establishing a special financial counselor as a kind of "brain truster." Then he changed the current system of grain taxation. Instead of transporting the grain taken in taxes to the capital, where it was formerly sold at half its local value, he had it distributed locally for the adjustment of scarcity and surplus. This led to a form of price control, elimination of private speculation and hoarding, and eventually to what was practically a state trade monopoly. Connected with this measure was a system of agricultural loans. Exploitation of farmers by moneylenders of the scholar-gentry class had long been one of the worst of China's economic problems. From the government granaries, loans of grain were advanced to farmers at seedtime to be paid back after harvest. All these measures were meant to bring about regulation of market prices. Farmers had been required not only to pay taxes but also to labor on public works. The wealthy scholar-gentry had escaped this burden. In order to divide the load, Wang An-shih introduced the Public Services Act. Instead of being drafted, public labor was to be hired by the government. A tax was added which all shared on a prorated basis. An equitable land-tax measure, with periodic classification of land, was also introduced to shift more of the tax burden to the shoulders of the wealthy.

Together with these reforms, which aimed at fairer distribution of the tax burden and control of the economic system in general, Wang instituted a Militia Act to strengthen the state in its fight with the northern rivals. The Sung government had abolished the local troops of earlier times and had created in the capital what became a large and expensive army of mercenaries. With military virtues at a discount, these mercenaries lacked training, became lazy, and often were too old for active service. Wang attempted to dissolve the mercenaries by stages, reducing their number from 1,200,000 to 600,000; at the same time he built up local militia. These were composed of the best elements in the agricultural population, locally sustained, and trained under local leaders. At first the militia protected their own regions only; later they were organized into a conscript army for defense of the country. Horses were bred to equip these troops to fight the mounted enemy in the north.

In addition to these measures Wang An-shih introduced educational reforms. His officials were trained in schools which taught practical administration. In order to provide textbooks Wang himself reinterpreted and commented on some of the standard Confucian works—for with all his innovations the great minister did not mean to ignore the Confucian ideology of the past. He defended his measures by quoting from the classics. What he attacked was not Confucianism but what he considered a wrong interpretation of the Confucian theory.

In the seventeen years during which Wang's measures were applied they seem to have worked well. There is no record of farmer rebellions or serious disorders—only of the complaints of the scholars who opposed him. The weakness of Wang's system, according to these critics, was the lack of a trained group of loyal officials willing to carry out his ideas. There was much sabotage and disregard or misuse of orders, which may have led to corrupt practices counteracting his reforms. Wang's personality may have made

his task more difficult. Unmindful of himself to the point of physical neglect, he was criticized for lack of personal cleanliness.
Moreover, he alienated many people by his arrogant manner and
would not tolerate independent minds around him. The ambitious young men who tried to carry through his ideas did not increase the popularity of his reforms. The history of this episode,
however, comes from records written by the opposition—which
eventually triumphed.

Wang's laws were repealed after the death of the Emperor Shên-
tsung. The conservative party, under Ssŭ-ma Kuang, came back
to power and with it the laissez-faire policy of the past. Thus a
great attempt at economic reinterpretation of the Confucian form
of Chinese society failed. Thereafter, the orthodox ideas of the
Confucian system prevailed. With the uncontrolled play of economic forces in China, there continued that cycle of agrarian crises
which had led, after a period of prosperity, to the fall of dynasty
after dynasty.

If the Sung rulers did not rebuild the political structure of the
Chinese state they at least gave it a philosophical background and
added a period in which art and literature reached a development
not later surpassed. The new Confucianism of the time was greatly
influenced by the Taoist and Buddhist religions. Confucianism in
the past had been but a political system based on ethical grounds.
The thinkers of the Sung time added to it a metaphysical system
which they borrowed from these religions.

Chou Tun-yi (jou dun-yi) (1017–1073) was the first of the Neo-
Confucian philosophers. (See chap. xvi, below.) In the *I Ching*
(Book of Changes) he discovered a principle, the *t'ai-chi* (tai-ji), or
Supreme Ultimate, which he regarded as the creating force of the
universe. (See chap. xxi, below.) A philosophy based on a system
of natural law was developed by a number of other conservative
philosophers and was finally brought into a complete system by
Chu (ju) Hsi (1130–1200). Chu Hsi became the recognized com-
mentator and interpreter of Confucian classical texts for all later
ages. The Confucian social doctrine became a cosmic system;
the law of nature became the moral law which was to determine
human conduct. As the *t'ai-chi* operates through the positive and
negative forces, the *yin* and the *yang*, it creates the world of phe-

IN THE YANGTZE GORGES

Lucille Douglass

nomena with its moral law and the four main human virtues through which it works: benevolence, righteousness, reverence, and wisdom. The duty of man, who by nature is good, is to follow the middle way in the rules of this law.

The philosophy thus created was conservative. At the time of the struggle of the two parties Wang An-shih had tried to create his own interpretation and commentaries on the Confucian writings, but when the conservative school won, Neo-Confucian philosophy became the ideological background of the economic policy of laissez faire and was accepted by succeeding dynasties.

Nature's harmonies also formed the content of the greatest of Sung arts, landscape painting. (See chap. xxii, below.) An impressionistic style led to the omission of color except in the portrayal of flowers, birds, and the like. Shading in ink and the masterful technique of brush strokes became the means of expressing the atmosphere of philosophical speculation. Man and his emotions were not made the center of interest. Ideas and feelings of beauty and tranquillity were put into a portrayal of nature in which man and animals took a minor place. A brush wielded by a painter trained in the art of calligraphy could, with a few quick, daring strokes that permitted no correction, produce a spirit and life symbolic of the artist's emotions. The observer was not nailed to a definite point in the foreground; a perspective that put him in the position of a flying bird permitted him a placeless participation in that aspect of the painter's world in which essentials were emphasized while distances disappeared in clouds and mist.

Sung culture embraced many realms in addition to those of philosophy and painting. The revived emphasis on scholarship produced achievements in history, textual criticism, and archaeology. Block printing gave great impetus to literature. Sung porcelains, with their greenish grays and exquisite patterns, testify to the refined taste of the time. Some Chinese accomplishments affected the Western world through the intermediary of Arab, Jewish, and Persian traders at Canton.

Thus the Sung period was a time of renaissance. Enriched by Buddhism and by many new ideas and trends from the recent past, the Confucian system reasserted itself and established the political and cultural pattern which China followed to modern times.

Throughout their rule the Sung emperors were threatened by powerful neighbors both outside and within northern China. The initial attempts to drive out the Khitan Liao failed. But the Liao dynasts (907–1124), with their mixed Chinese-steppe society between the Chinese in the south and other tribal peoples pressing in from the north, were themselves not strong enough to defeat the Sungs and conquer their empire. They were vulnerable on both sides. When the Jurchen (ru-jen), a Tungusic forest tribe from the Amur River region, attacked the Liaos from the rear, the Sung emperor made common cause with this invader, and the Liao dynasty perished in 1124. The Sung rulers tried to use the occasion to regain northern territory, but they clashed with the new invaders. When the Jurchen, who in 1115 had established the Chin (dzin), or Gold, dynasty—"Iron rusts, but Gold does not"—threatened the capital, K'ai-feng, Sung Hui-tsung (1100–1125), the artist emperor, abdicated in favor of his son. A treaty was concluded in which the Chinese government promised to pay a huge tribute to the Chin rulers, but this treaty was not kept. The Sung forces were again defeated by the cavalry of the Jurchen. K'ai-feng was captured by the Chin army and Chin troops swept into the Yangtze Valley, looting and sacking Chinese cities.

But the Chin were not strong enough to hold central China. Under a heroic general, Yo Fei (1103–1141), the Sung dynasty regained the Yangtze region as far as the Huai River and established for another one hundred fifty years what became known as the Southern Sung dynasty (1127–1279), with its capital at Hangchow. Under the Southern Sung and the Chin of the north, China remained divided. Sung relations with the Chin, as formerly with the Liao dynasty, were a succession of wars and treaties, and both suffered from a deteriorating economic situation.

The weakness of the Liao (907–1124) and Chin (1115–1234) "barbarian" dynasties was caused by the difficulty of controlling both agrarian China and the outer tribal territories whence they had come. To rule the empire they needed a Chinese political and administrative organization. For their own people they kept their tribal or feudal systems. This duality led to inner difficulties, and yet it could not prevent their being vulnerable to the attacks of new groups from the tribal world. On losing their mobility in an agrarian world and adopting a new form of government all tribal invaders of China faced the same danger from beyond the border.

Tribal power depended on mobility and the organization of tribal territory by men who could assure predominance of their group. The decisive factor was control of pasture rights. Each group of nomadic tribal people moved in a region within which they rotated their pastures. Whoever was strong enough to dictate and guarantee the use of pastures to a number of groups in return for their support and the payment of tribute could form a powerful organization. Where such an organization grew along the borders of Chinese settled life its leader profited through trade and tribute. He also gained insight into Chinese organization—which was useful in planning penetration and conquest. Such a frontier organization, growing out of rivalry and disunity, would in general not be undertaken by men who had inherited secure positions and were thus disinclined to risk what they had for doubtful gains. But knowledge of political conditions and organizing ability were necessary for success. The leader of a rising frontier power was therefore likely to come from the lower border aristocracy—a man who knew the game but whose position was endangered and who in fighting for survival had the possibility of winning greater stakes. As in many inner Chinese rebellions, it was the hanger-on of the old order, one who was experienced but was threatened by existing conditions, who led discontented groups to establish new power. Such a one, on the steppe border of China, was Temuchin—known to history as Jenghiz Khan (1162?–1227). A small tribal leader fighting for survival and recognition, Temuchin, by 1206, had gained the position of Great Khan of the steppe tribes on China's north-western border. Under him these tribes received the name of Mongols.

The difference between Jenghiz Khan's Mongol empire and the Khitan and Jurchen states before him was the direction taken by their political development. All three started on the Chinese border. But whereas the Khitan and the Jurchen turned immediately into China and there set up dynasties which were open to further attack from the tribal world, Jenghiz Khan, after taking Yen-ching (modern Peking) in 1215, returned to the steppe and to the oasis world of Turkestan and the Tibetan Tangut Hsi-hsia state on the northwestern frontier of the Sung empire, with its capital at Ning-hsia. Defeating and then uniting the peoples of Mongolia and central Asia, Jenghiz created a base from which he could carry the Mongol attack in any direction: into Russia, Europe, the Near East, India, and China. He and his successors formed the greatest continental empire the world has seen. But they turned back from Europe and all but the northern part of India; so China became the most important part of their holdings.

Under Ogotai, Jenghiz Khan's successor, K'ai-feng, the capital of the Chin rulers, was captured in 1233, and in the following year the Chin empire disappeared under the combined attacks of the Chinese and Mongols. Mongol assaults upon Europe and disputes about the succession delayed their attack upon the Southern Sung empire. This was taken up under Kublai Khan in 1251 and was completed in 1276, when the capital, Hangchow, fell. The last Sung pretender soon thereafter died. Kublai made Peking his capital in 1263 and established there the Yüan dynasty (1260–1368).

When the Mongols made China their base in order to endure, they had to adopt and adapt Chinese forms of administration. The larger internal unity of the Mongol power gradually weakened. In 1295 the western Mongol khans were converted to Islam, and dissolved their loyalty to the empire of Kublai; so the outer forms of this unity also disappeared. Although the Mongols in China had nothing to fear from the steppe—except for family quarrels—they now became subject to the Chinese economic cycle.

The Mongol campaigns had caused enormous losses of life, particularly in northwestern China. The impoverishment of this region was such that its waterworks could not be maintained, and it never fully recovered economic importance. But the following decades of peace, the tolerant policy of the Mongols, and the opening of the ancient trade routes through central Asia gave China a flourishing period of which Marco Polo, in China *circa* 1275–1292, bore witness.

The Mongols first learned Chinese administration from the officials of the defeated northern Chinese dynasties. Yeh-lü Ch'u-ts'ai, eight feet tall, and of Khitan royal blood, who had been an important official under the Chin empire, is credited with echoing to Jenghiz Khan the saying of Lu Chia to the Emperor Kao of the Han dynasty: "You have conquered the empire on horseback, but you cannot rule it from horseback." Under Jenghiz and his successors Yeh-lü Ch'u-ts'ai became a trusted official and organizer. Many other officials of the defeated dynasties, including the Sung, entered the service of the Yüan. Having broken into agrarian societies other than that of China, the Mongols had an unusually large reservoir of trained men to draw from. Administering their empire were representatives of peoples from all parts of Asia and even Europe. All creeds, including those of Buddhism, Islam, and Christianity, found tolerant protection. Though the invaders attempted to remain apart from the Chinese by prohibiting intermarriage and by requiring the use of their own system of writing, the majority of their officials were Chinese.

The Mongols gave China more than half a century of peaceful prosperity. Nevertheless their end came for essentially the same economic reasons which had caused the fall of preceding dynasties. Their policy accentuated and accelerated the development of large landed estates with even less consideration for the fate of the farmers than had been shown under earlier dynasties. The cycle was shorter and the collapse correspondingly quicker. Seeking to avoid complete dependence on the Chinese Confucian educational system, the Mongols favored the Buddhist hierarchy in their administration. The support given to monks and monasteries increased the problem of landlordism: managers of large ecclesiastical estates were often harsher toward the farmers than were lay landlords.

Moreover, the extremely orthodox Confucianism in state theory upheld by the Mongols to the end of their rule—in order to retain the support of Chinese officials—excluded reform. Decrease in public income resulted in weakening of the government and neglect of its functions with respect to both public works and control over local administration. While the monasteries, the gentry, and many officials grew rich, the state and the masses suffered. China became ripe for a farmer rebellion which might restore the balance of land-ownership and of the tax burden.

Under Kublai Khan (1260–1294) the Mongols reached the height of their power. Commercial intercourse through Arabs, Persians, Italians, and other Westerners traveling to China and Mongols going to Europe gave the Western world hints of the wealth and glories of the greatest empire on earth. A short cultural revival, mainly in the fields of the novel and the drama, contributed lasting works to Chinese literature. But the hazards of the elements and the bravery of the Japanese broke the Mongols' attempted conquest of Japan, while climate, natural barriers, and other factors defeated their penetration into southeastern Asia and the islands of the Pacific.

Economic weaknesses were increased by monetary inflation caused by the printing of paper money in an attempt to save public finances. In the fourteenth century farmer rebellions broke out all over China. Misery was increased by the Yellow River floods resulting from neglect of the dikes. Floods, together with neglect, impaired the use of the Grand Canal, the most important link between Peking (bei-jing) and the richest agricultural region in the Yangtze delta. Unity and order disappeared.

The Yüan dynasty fell before an uprising of exploited tenant farmers against landlords, officials, and nobles of both Chinese and Mongol stock. The man who finally emerged as the leader, Chu Yüan-chang (b. 1328, reigned 1368–1399), came of a farming family, of slender means, in Anhui province. When his parents and elder brother died in a famine he entered a monastery. As monasteries had property and political influence, he gained an understanding of the mechanism of local power although he had no share in it. But when his monastery was destroyed in local uprisings he joined a force of peasant rebels and quickly rose to be their leader.

The critical moment in a Chinese farmer rebellion is that at which the bands turn from looting and fighting to organizing control over territory. The negative task of resistance changes to positive construction of a new administrative order. Such a task requires men with experience in administration, taxation, allocation of labor, and the carrying out of public works. The leader of the rebellion must compromise with members of the official and landowning upper group whose services are needed. This act transmutes the bandit leader or revolutionary into a new head of the state.

Chu Yüan-chang was not the only successful rebel leader of his time. All over southern and central China the old order had collapsed and brigand chiefs had arisen. But they did not turn north against the Mongols. They first fought among themselves for supremacy. In 1356 Chu gained Nanking, which became his capital;

from it he controlled the greatest economic key area—the Yangtze Valley. He now became a local ruler, supported by scholar-gentry officials, contesting with similar rulers in other parts of the country for the supreme position of emperor and founder of a dynasty. The enemy hereafter was no longer the rich official class, but the alien Mongol emperor, who had been guilty of tyranny and corruption. Only a Chinese should rule the Middle Empire—and Chu was the man to drive out the Mongol oppressors.

Chu's army moved against Peking in 1367 and in the following year the city fell. Without resistance the Mongol court fled into Mongolia, but Chu's armies followed the Mongols into the steppe. In 1372 Karakorum, the steppe capital of the Mongols, was burned. In later years the Chinese power was extended again into both Turkestan and Manchuria.

Chu called his dynasty the Ming (1368–1644). He himself is remembered as the Hung-wu emperor, the name chosen for the years of his reign. Henceforth the emperors of the Ming and Ch'ing dynasties who accepted his practice of having only one year-period for their entire rule are historically known by this style rather than by their names.

The main task of the Ta Ming, or Great Bright, dynasty was that of reintegrating the various groups in the Chinese state. The few Mongols and other foreigners who remained in the country were to be assimilated by preventing them from marrying any but Chinese. The Chinese administration itself was reorganized, and the system of civil government as it had existed before the Mongol conquest was formally reintroduced.

The Ming government divided the country into fifteen provinces—which, with later subdivisions and additions, constitute the present Chinese provinces. Although the administration remained bureaucratic, foreign invasions, the weakness of the Sung government, and the example of the Mongol garrisons in China had shown the need for a stronger military organization than that of the Sung mercenary armies. The old problem of local militia versus professional army came again to the fore. The disadvantage of a militia is the danger of local war-lordism and such rivalry between military men as had occurred in the latter part of the T'ang period. A professional army composed of riffraff led by scholars who were trained only in the ethics of Confucius had proved to be inadequate for the defense of the country.

The Ming rulers found a new solution in a dual military and civilian organization. The majority of the districts and higher administrative units were organized under civilian government with civilian scholar-officials chosen through the traditional, newly revived examination system. But within this civil administration certain districts of highly strategic importance were organized as guards (*wei*) under a military bureaucracy. These districts were freed from ordinary land tax and labor services, but had to organize themselves as military units. The men were simultaneously soldiers and farmers; the officers served also as civil authorities. The *wei* were islands of autonomous military organizations subdivided into posts and stations in border regions and at threatened points. Most of these districts were on the northwestern and northern borders, where they had the twofold function of constituting a defense belt against outside attacks and a springboard of political and military control for outer territories. Others were on the coast for defense against Japanese pirates and for the protection of the Grand Canal, which had been restored by the third Ming ruler, the Yung-lo emperor (1403–1424), after the capital was transferred from Nanking to Peking. ·

The Yung-lo emperor completed the work begun by the first Ming ruler. His empire was expanded far beyond the military bureaucratic zones at the frontier of China proper. He established outposts as far north as the Amur River and controlled the tribes in Mongolia. He also extended Chinese influence through southern and western Asia by naval expeditions—particularly the seven of the eunuch admiral, Chêng Ho, between 1405 and 1431—to Annam, Cambodia, Siam, Java, Sumatra, India, Ceylon, Arabia, and the Somali coast. Some of these politico-economic ventures resulted in short-lived Chinese political control. Although the land route to China had practically been closed after the collapse of the Mongol empire, the sea routes were thus kept open by the Chinese.

The majority of the Europeans who reached China in the sixteenth century created an unfavorable impression of the Western world. Numbers of the first Portuguese, Dutch, and English were not the best representatives of their homelands. Too many of them were adventurers who turned to looting and brigandage, assumed that the principles of Christianity did not apply to the "pagans" of the East, and appeared to the Chinese as uncivilized half-pirate people to be watched and warded off.

The missionaries, who arrived late in the century and thereafter, were of a different type. Of outstanding importance in this period were the Jesuits, who became highly respected because of their gentility, their character, and their specialized knowledge of astronomy, cannon casting, and other sciences. Their position was weakened, however, through quarrels largely forced upon them by the Franciscans and Dominicans. For a time, under the Yüan dynasty, the Franciscans had carried on a devoted work in both northern and southern China. Franciscans and Jesuits, more especially the latter under the Ming and Ch'ing dynasties, constituted the earliest channels through which knowledge of the peoples and civilizations in the eastern and western extremes of the Eurasiatic continent passed back and forth on a considerable scale.

The Ming period was one of comparatively little originality in thought and art.[1] Certain minor arts, however, flourished: jade and ivory carving, cloisonné, color ceramics, and weaving. In architecture the Ming constructed works of outstanding importance. The Forbidden City, the Ming tombs, certain city walls, pagodas, and temples, and the sinuous line of the Great Wall as seen today bear witness to the Roman temper of the Ming mind.

In literature the creative spirit turned to the less respectable—from the Confucianist scholar-official viewpoint—but highly popular forms of the novel and the drama. The great novels of the time offer a popular interpretation of Chinese history: they describe Chinese middle-class society in daily life and the proletarian adulation of rebel leaders fighting in behalf of the suppressed.

By the sixteenth century, exploitation of the farmer masses, corruption at court, the sale of offices, and the enrichment of a small number of profiteers had grown to scandalous proportions. This process led to decay and disorganization, large-scale rebellions, and the fall of the dynasty.

Disintegration south of the Great Wall gave a chance not only for a capable rebel leader to found a new dynasty but also for in-

---

[1] For notes to chapter vii see pages 525–526.

vasions from without. There might even be competition between
inner and outer Chinese forces for the establishment of a new
regime. Such was the state of affairs at the end of the Ming period.
The country was swept by farmer rebellions. One of the rebel
leaders, Li Tzŭ-ch'êng (dz-cheng),[2] succeeded in gaining a foothold
in the Han Valley whence he marched north through the mountains of western China to take Peking. The last Ming emperor
hanged himself, but Li, although proclaiming himself emperor, was
not able to retain the throne. The Manchus contested his power.

The Manchus were a small Tungusic tribal group descended
from the Jurchen Tatars, part of whom had ruled northern China
as the Chin (Gold) dynasty (1115–1234). They had lived on the
northeastern border of the Chinese pale in Manchuria, mainly in
what is now Kirin province. At a time of weakened Chinese border
control a minor chieftain, Nurhachu, or Nurhaci (1559–1626),[3] had
succeeded in fighting his way upward against the established frontier hierarchy. He thereby set up a strong border state which proceeded to conquer piecemeal the agricultural lands of the Chinese
in Manchuria.

The problem of all earlier invaders had been to reconcile their
feudal or tribal society with the civil bureaucratic system within
China. The political organization of newcomers never succeeded
in integrating the two types of society. The Manchus, however,
more nearly succeeded than any of their predecessors. They found
a model for their adjustment in the frontier organization of the
Ming government. The Ming frontier guards, with their military
bureaucracy, became the pattern for the eight Manchu banners
(units of military administration) in which the invaders had been
organized for peace and war. With the growth of Manchu power,
Mongols, Koreans, and a large proportion of the Chinese in Manchuria were welded into one state. Leadership remained in the
hands of the small group of Manchu nobles, although the military
bureaucracy could include any leading Chinese official who joined
the Manchu side. Above the eight banners the Manchus organized
a central government that was patterned on the Chinese system:
the political ideology of the new Manchu state, which conquered
and organized Manchuria up to the Great Wall, was orthodox
Confucianism.

It was this frontier state that became the competitor of Li Tzŭ-ch'êng for the Dragon Throne. In this contest Li had the advantage of having conquered Peking, whereas the Manchus were still outside the country. But success depended on his capacity to establish a new governmental organization and secure the support of the leading scholar-gentry and officials. Here the radical Li failed. This failure was dramatized in the decision of a former Ming official, Wu San-kuei (san-guei), who had been entrusted with the defense of the Manchurian border pass at Shanhaikuan. This man opened the way for the Manchus into China, helped in the defeat of Li Tzŭ-ch'êng, and later in obtaining the submission of southern China, after the Manchus had moved into Peking and established the Ta Ch'ing (da tsing), or Great Pure, dynasty in 1644.

The story of Wu San-kuei has been interpreted as the decision of an outraged lover. Wu's concubine had been caught by Li's men and was later regained by Wu in battle. But there were several reasons for Wu, and others who acted similarly, to turn to the Manchus instead of supporting Li. Wu San-kuei himself came from a Manchurian Chinese family and well knew that the Manchu political organization was Chinese enough to give him the same kind of position that he and other members of the official class had previously held. The easy victories of the Manchus over Li, who was chased back into obscurity and to an ignominious death, can be attributed to the fact that the Manchus were more orthodox Confucians than the native rebel leader and thus had the support of the men who mattered.

The Manchus brought their banners into China. But for China proper they had to accept the Chinese civil bureaucratic organization. The banners were used only to garrison the capital and strategic points in the country. Banner members remained segregated by the prohibitions of intermarriage with the Chinese and of taking up any profession except that of farmer-soldier. Banner soldiers in China lived at public expense, but since they lost military experience and practice in years of peace they soon became completely useless.

In their civil organization the Manchus divided authority between Manchu and Chinese officials. Whereas the Chinese were selected through the traditional examination system with its severe competition, the Manchus, with their much smaller numbers, had comparatively easy access to official careers. After the conquest the south was given at first to certain influential Chinese military leaders such as Wu San-kuei. These were made hereditary rulers of three largely autonomous states. Only under the second Manchu ruler, the K'ang-hsi emperor (1662–1722), did the Manchus succeed in destroying the independence of these rulers and in establishing firm control over the whole country.[4]

Under the K'ang-hsi emperor and his grandson the Ch'ien-lung emperor (1736–1796) the Manchus reached the apogee of their power.[5] They gained the greatest territorial expansion that China has ever achieved. Manchuria, Mongolia, Turkestan, and Tibet were dependencies; Korea, Annam, Burma, and lesser areas remained in the Chinese orbit as vassal states. But by the latter half of the eighteenth century signs of decay began to appear. Farmer unrest was organized by one of the secret societies, the so-called White Lotus sect. Soon after the death of the Ch'ien-lung emperor in February, 1799, the first outbreaks occurred. The emperor, fearing for Manchu authority, had persecuted certain groups of the scholar class for their anti-Manchu and antiorthodox attitude by burning their books and sentencing them to capital punishment or banishment.

The nineteenth century was marked by steady decay of the Ta Ch'ing dynasty, with the usual characteristics of weakening central control, corruption, and large-scale rebellion. China also felt the impact of the West. The Western world was drawing China into its orbit, and trade was taking the merchants of Europe to China in ever-growing numbers. But Chinese agrarian society, with its official control of economic activity, discouraged an independent trading class. The Manchu-Chinese imperial government was opposed to expansion of trade in Western manufactures which its society did not need. When, consequent upon the arbitrament of war (1839–1842, 1856–1860), the Westerners protected themselves in the Treaty Ports by force and the principle of extraterritoriality, their interference contributed to the further economic disintegration of the Ta Ch'ing empire.

What had been landlordism in the past became absentee landlordism in the late nineteenth century, when Western luxuries attracted wealthy Chinese to the ports and Chinese compradors invested their surplus funds in land. Chinese handicraft industries suffered from machine competition. The weakening of the central government through defeat at the hands of Europeans and through deflation of currency as money was drawn out of the country were new factors which contributed to the strain on Chinese economy. When a great farmer rebellion broke out in 1850, the reasons were fundamentally a mixture of old Chinese and new Western politico-religio-economic problems.

The T'ai-p'ing (Great Peace) rebellion (1850–1864) was begun under the leadership of Hung Hsiu-ch'üan (hsiu-tsüan),[6] who was greatly influenced by the tracts of Protestant missionaries. At the time of a nervous breakdown which followed his third failure to pass the government examinations, he experienced confused visions of God, Jesus Christ, and Confucius, who commanded him to establish a new order in China. The group of followers which he assembled included not only desperate farmers, but, in the beginning, Hakkas and Miaos, minorities in Kuangsi (guang-si) province, who had suffered even more than other peasants from local exploitation. Under the leadership of Hung and others, who vied in out-trancing each other, a swelling horde of rebels moved north from Kuangsi to the Yangtze region, took city after city, and for a time appeared likely to succeed in overthrowing the Ch'ing dynasty and establishing their Heavenly Kingdom.

But although the T'ai-p'ings magnificently succeeded in destruction, they failed in the reorganization of production and administration in the regions they controlled. The confused Western ideology which they harbored made it impossible for Chinese scholar-officials to join their side, and their fanatical destructiveness and perhaps their partly un-Chinese origin aroused bitter resistance by farmers in the regions through which they moved.

Although Manchu imperial forces were defeated and annihilated, local Chinese leaders organized farmer militia to defend their homes against attack. The central government appreciated the value of this sporadic resistance and entrusted the leaders—Tseng Kuo-fan (dzeng guo-fan),[7] Tso Tsung-t'ang (dzo dzung-tang),[8] and Li Hung-chang (hung-jang)[9]—with military commands and high government positions. Through their efforts, aided in the later years of the movement by American, British, and French military leaders, the T'ai-p'ings were defeated, and China developed a stronger national policy.

There also appeared a Chinese renaissance which for a time seemed to promise a modern national development. But fundamental changes were prevented by the reactionary orthodoxy of the Manchu-Chinese court at Peking and the official classes as a whole. Real reform demanded structural change which was not possible under the leadership produced by the classical system of education. The revival of the second half of the nineteenth century germinated a military reorganization and tradition which, through the imperial government's military reforms and its academy at Paotingfu (bao-ding-fu), culminated in Sun Yat-sen (sun yi-hsien), Yüan Shih-k'ai (shzh-kai), Chiang Kai-shek (jiang jie-shzh), and the relatively modern armies of the latter two.

The new leaders looked for outside support in their national policy and for a time hoped to find it in Japan by making common resistance against Western imperialism. In 1871 the two nations concluded a treaty which, following the advice of Tseng Kuo-fan and Li Hung-chang, carried a clause of alliance against aggression. But while China hoped for friendship and coöperation, Japan's leaders planned from the beginning for predominance in eastern Asia, as was revealed by their growing interest in Korea and Formosa. In 1894, when China and Japan clashed over control of Korea, Japan was so much further advanced in reforms and modernization that Manchu-Chinese resistance was quickly broken and the empire was utterly defeated.

The European Powers immediately took advantage of China's weakness by forcing the lease of certain ports and territories and the granting of spheres of influence. Dissolution of the Manchu-Chinese Empire was prevented mainly by the Anglo-American policy of the open door, by China's reactions, and by inability of the Europeans to agree upon a division of the spoils. Hasty reform attempts in 1898, advocated by K'ang Yu-wei, a modern-minded scholar-adviser of the young Kuang-hsü (guang-sü) emperor, failed in part because of the conflict between cliques at the court. Tz'ŭ-hsi, the grand empress dowager ex-regent, was the center of a group of conservative statesmen at court who saw with displeasure the ambitious plans of the Reform party. A coup d'état to eliminate this obstacle backfired, K'ang Yu-wei fled, the young emperor became the prisoner of Tz'ŭ-hsi, his imperious as well as imperial aunt, for the rest of his life, and the Conservative party returned to power. Reaction contributed to support an anti-Manchu, antiforeign, and, particularly, anti-Christian and antimissionary rebellion of farmers. The court turned this outbreak entirely against the foreigners to distract attention from its own shortcomings and with a naïve hope of freeing China from contact with the West. Defeat of the Boxers in 1900 by the Western Powers and Japan led the court to a belated policy of reform. But the Manchus and the Chinese mandarinate were unfitted to carry through the reconstruction of the country's economic, social, and political life which was necessary in order to create a modern Chinese nation out of the "universal" empire of the past two thousand years. The new leadership, in and after 1911–1912, came not from the Confucian classically trained scholar-officials, but from the modern, Western-trained Chinese students and merchants, who eventually joined forces with those who represented the Chinese heritage of great statesmen, thinkers, reformers, and military leaders in China's own history.

CHAPTER VIII

Chinese Society and
the Dynasties of Conquest

BY KARL AUGUST WITTFOGEL

THE LIAO–IRON–EMPIRE (907–1124) is generally classed with the dynasties of the Chin–Gold–(1115–1234), the Yüan (1260–1368), and the Ch'ing (1644–1912). These four share one fundamental feature: they were established by inner-Asiatic peoples who invaded Chinese territory and ruled over a population mainly Chinese. The recent history of the Far East has greatly increased interest in the four dynasties of conquest among both Chinese and foreign scholars.

A detailed analysis of Liao society and a preliminary survey of subsequent periods have given new insight into the dynamics of political and military institutions and of religious and secular thought and ceremonial under conditions of conquest.[1] These studies have shown the methodological inadequacy of what may conveniently be called the theory of absorption, advocates of which believe that nomadic Tatar invaders, such as the Ch'i-tan—or Khitan—founders of the Liao state, were "soon conquered" by Chinese civilization (Paul Pelliot), or that "the same curious process ... took place which seems always to have followed the intrusion of Tartar conquerors into China. . . . The intruders themselves adopted Chinese manners, ceremonies, literature, and civilization" (Sir Henry Yule).

Such statements note correctly the far-reaching influence which China's ancient and mighty civilization exerted upon its tribal conquerors; the situation, however, which established permanent con-

---

[1] For notes to chapter viii see page 526.

tact and, as a corollary, unusual opportunity for culture change simultaneously barred the way to any complete or one-sided cultural fusion (absorption).

History shows that in their determination to wield power the Tatar overlords were loath to accept the military and political institutions of newly acquired subjects in their traditional form. They preferred to maintain, with modifications, certain well-tested devices of dominance, particularly in the military field. Chinese administrative institutions were confined mainly to the Chinese among the population; whenever they were employed without restriction, the Tatars were careful to manipulate them so as to guarantee maximum protection against possible revolt.

Such arrangements in the fields of military and political organization were supplemented by similar measures in the social sphere. In general, intermarriage was forbidden, and patterns of privilege and prestige evolved that were not typically Chinese. Underlying considerations of power politics even retarded or limited the acceptance of language and literature or the refined habits of consumption of an advanced agrarian society which, although culturally desirable, might still be politically objectionable. The Manchu conquerors, who readily accepted the comforts of Chinese living and many patterns of behavior, forbade their women to wear Chinese dress and compelled Chinese men to adopt "barbarian" Manchu clothes and the queue.

The invaders' willingness to accept things Chinese varied according to their political significance and function. The saturation point of culture change was highest in the realm of consumption, material and artistic. In the primary institutions of power this point was much more quickly reached, and, once reached, was far more rigidly fixed. Sun Yat-sen (sun yi-hsien), who had great practical understanding of the nature of conquest society, held this fact responsible for the Manchu rulers' inability to reform their tottering government: "By reformation they would be absorbed by the Chinese people and would lose the special rights and privileges which they were enjoying."[2]

Culture change assumed different shapes at different times in a period of conquest. Initial eagerness to adopt Chinese customs in the seemingly neutral spheres of life might give way later to a vigorous anti-assimilationist (nativist)[8] policy if the adopted changes proved detrimental to the institutional and psychological foundations of power and privilege. In general, readiness to accept elements of Chinese civilization responded to the intensity of the culture contact. Acceptance was apparently greatest at court and among the nobles and commoners who dealt directly with the subject people. The aristocracy might simultaneously take special pride in preserving certain of their former national traditions. The large number of tribal commoners who lived in separate military settlements in China proper were less influenced, and those tribesmen who continued to dwell in the regions north of the Great Wall were little if at all affected by Chinese culture.

Particularly important in adaptation to Chinese civilization were the invaders' traditional economic and cultural standards. The attractiveness of an alien culture is determined not only by its immanent values but also by the recipient peoples' disposition to understand and appreciate them. The pastoral Ch'i-tan and the Mongols were not so well equipped to operate the basic institutions of Chinese agrarian society as were the founders of the Chin dynasty, the Ju-chên, or Jurchen (ru-jen), and Tungus, and those of the similarly descended Manchus of the Ch'ing dynasty—peoples who had been familiar with agricultural techniques generations before they set out to conquer China.

The tribal invaders were greatly influenced by Chinese civilization, but their reactions, on the whole, were much more complicated than the word "absorption" indicates. Because of the conquest situation, the adoption of certain institutions, ideas, and attitudes was retarded, frustrated, or not attempted. Even though in some instances assimilation went very far, in others tribal traditions were preserved unaltered or only slightly modified. At times the elements of a new third culture emerged. Complete cultural fusion became possible only after the power structure of the conquest society collapsed. Then, although some of the former ruling people were killed and some sought refuge in their inner-Asiatic homelands, others survived within the Chinese world with no political barriers to block further assimilation.

The unilinear theory of absorption obscures the complexities that exist within the conquest situation. A comprehensive examination of the many factors involved in the process of acculturation reveals multiple and intricate forms of culture change under conditions of continuous firsthand contact.[4]

    ⋄ ⋄ ⋄

The Liao empire (907–1124) is a particularly rewarding subject for a study of the phenomena of acculturation.[5] As an extreme case, it conspicuously discloses the conflicting forces at work in a Chinese conquest society. The Ch'i-tan did not occupy the heart of China proper; they were able, however, after conquering important districts in northeastern China, to impose their sovereignty on a predominantly Chinese population. The Liao court remained in the original Ch'i-tan territory in Jehol. Ch'i-tan cattle breeders continued to live outside the conquered Chinese regions, which included, among others, Yen-ching (yen-jing), near modern Peking or Peiping. But a rather large Chinese population was settled in the newly built fortified cities north of the Great Wall, and many peasants, Chinese and P'o-hai, made their homes in the woodlands and on the open prairies of eastern Mongolia and western Manchuria. A network of Chinese administrative units was spread over the Liao empire. Its five capitals, with their palaces and government offices, their workshops, bazaars, and temples, reflected the life and needs of a sedentary Chinese population.

Despite such definite and important Chinese influences, the basic character of Ch'i-tan society was preserved. The masses of tribal commoners were still herdsmen, hunters, and fighters. The *ordo* armies, composed primarily of trusted tribal warriors, constituted the backbone of the empire's military system. The two divisions of the Liao state were administered by separate political organizations. The officials of the northern region had jurisdiction over the tribesmen; those of the southern region controlled the affairs of the empire's sedentary populations. Tribal officials with Altaic titles played an important part in the new central government; and the highest positions, though bearing Chinese names, were held primarily by top-ranking Ch'i-tan nobles. Throughout the dynastic period the Ch'i-tan preserved their inner-Asiatic tradition of inherited prerogative to office. Their sons entered upon a government career, not by passing an examination, but to satisfy a hereditary family claim upon a particular office. In fact, a Ch'i-tan whose literary ambitions prompted him to take the Chinese tests might be severely punished.

The Ch'i-tan method of selection seems also to have affected the choice of Chinese officials in the Liao government. Examinations for Chinese candidates were introduced in the first half of the tenth century, but the Chinese *yin* system (the right of certain sons of former officials to enter government service without examination) was easily extended under Ch'i-tan influence. A prominent scholar of the next dynasty, the Chin, observes that forty per cent of all Liao officials obtained office by virtue of the *yin* privilege. The statement is confirmed by biographical data in the *Standard History of the Liao Dynasty*. Evidently the proportion of those who held office because of their *yin* status was higher than that reported for any typically Chinese dynasty.

Chinese scholars found the atmosphere of the Liao court none too congenial to their special training. The semitribal rulers, though aware of the need for learning, maintained a significant interest in their former activities—hunting and fishing, horseback riding, and military maneuvers. The Ch'i-tan court and the nobles close to it adopted many Chinese customs; but the Liao ritual calendar included, besides typically Chinese and Buddhist elements, a great wealth of tribal ceremonial. At no time, so far as is known, did a Liao emperor perform the great agricultural ceremonies which were considered essential to the welfare of Chinese agrarian society.

Familiarity with the Chinese language and script soon became desirable for the ruling group. But such conspicuous acculturation was accompanied by an equally conspicuous insistence on time-honored tribal institutions and customs. Except for the two ruling families the Ch'i-tan maintained their tribal kinship organization and a pattern of marriage that differed completely from that of their Chinese neighbors. Even the imperial house and the consort family, which officially set themselves up as Chinese clans, continued to marry à la Tatar, in complete disregard of Chinese generation taboos.

The Chinese in the main preserved their habitual ways of life, but those who resettled in the north or came into contact with Ch'i-tan officialdom inevitably made adjustments to the new en-

vironment. Several high Chinese dignitaries were permitted—or
ordered—to take honorific Ch'i-tan names; some led the empire's
armed forces; a few held definitely tribal offices such as that of
t'i-yin. Little is known of the Chinese who became *ordo* soldiers,
but if their situation was comparable to that of Chinese bannermen in the Manchu period, the earlier Chinese *ordo* men must have
been greatly influenced by the tribal setting in which they were
forced to live. A contemporary Sung traveler reported that, as a
rule, Liao Chinese who dwelt north of the Great Wall continued
to use their mother tongue but changed their style of dress.

◇ ◇ ◇

No comprehensive investigation of acculturation in the three post-
Liao dynasties of conquest is at present available. Nevertheless, on
the basis of a preliminary survey it is evident that the barriers to
culture fusion were essentially similar.

The Chin dynasty (1115–1234).[6]—The Tungus founders of the
Chin—Gold—dynasty, the Ju-chên, were interested in agriculture
generations before their supreme chieftain, A-ku-ta (a-gu-da),[7]
attacked and defeated the decaying Liao empire. When A-ku-ta
(1069–1123) ascended the throne in 1115, his uncle made him a
present of "the nine implements of husbandry"—reminding him
of the importance of agriculture. This incident occurred several
years before the Ju-chên entered China south of the Wall.

Once established in northern China, the conquerors carefully
safeguarded their dominant position. The majority of their tribal
followers were settled in military colonies where, until 1191, intermarriage with the Chinese was interdicted. Ju-chên control in
military affairs was ruthlessly asserted; Ch'i-tan and Chinese were
eventually eliminated from the empire's elite army. Like their
descendants the Manchus, the Ju-chên found it unnecessary to support a dual administrative machine; they systematically placed
their own nationals in key positions of power and rigorously restricted the number of Chinese officials. However, Chinese applicants for office had to pass the traditional literary examinations,
whereas the Ju-chên, if they were examined at all, were exposed
to simpler tests, which, as one might expect, inquired particularly
into the candidates' military achievements.

The Ju-chên attitude toward less fundamental aspects of Chin society was more flexible. Immediately after the conquest the government ordered all Chinese, on penalty of death, to adopt Ju-chên clothes and hair arrangement; but midway in the twelfth century these regulations, which centuries later were persistently enforced by the Manchus, were relaxed. The removal of the capital to northern China and, perhaps, the unrest that plagued the reign of the Emperor Hai-ling (1149–1161)[8] may well have accelerated Ju-chên acceptance of many Chinese culture traits in housing, food consumption, music, adoption of Chinese clan names, and religious and secular ideas.

The use of the Chinese language increased noticeably among the Ju-chên nobility, but the masses of the Ju-chên people, who were concentrated in military settlements, were probably less affected by its spread. In 1183 the Chin courts still translated Chinese complaints into Ju-chên. Official documents were composed in Ju-chên, Chinese, and (or) Ch'i-tan. Ch'i-tan was used in their communications until Chang Tsung's[9] reign (1190–1209).

The end of the twelfth century witnessed a formidable nativist movement: in 1187 all Ju-chên who retained their adopted Chinese family names or continued to dress in Chinese style were penalized, and an attempt to introduce at court the Chinese manner of bowing was summarily repressed. Whether the Ju-chên interest in Buddhism and shamanistic practices was strengthened by Shih Tsung's (1161–1190)[10] nativist program is not yet known. It may be said, however, that the belated permission to intermarry with the Chinese did not alter the habits of the court. The rulers continued to choose their legal wives from the tribal nobility. Even among commoners the consciousness of nationality still barred the way to complete fusion. Growing Mongol pressure made the Ju-chên settlers increasingly predatory, so much so, in fact, that in the last decades of the dynasty the embittered Chinese peasants revolted. At times, in their fury, they seized their oppressors and threw them down the wells.

The Yüan dynasty (1260–1368).—In the predynastic period the Mongols raised their stock in the heartland of the great inner-Asiatic steppes, a region appreciably more distant from China than were the early Ch'i-tan grazing grounds. Classical representatives of pure nomadism, these Mongol invaders had much less understanding of the benefits of agriculture than their Ch'i-tan predecessors. An early khan's naïve proposal to turn all Chinese fields into pastures contrasts strikingly with the first Liao ruler's friendly appreciation of his new subjects' agricultural techniques.

Duality in government institutions, so marked in the Liao empire, was equally conspicuous in the Yüan period. The Mongol armies and their tribal auxiliaries, the core of the empire's defense system, were strictly separated from the Chinese, who were used as local militia and, under later rulers of the dynasty, as guards along the southern frontiers. The civil administration, which was concerned with the affairs of an overwhelmingly Chinese population, was so organized that the Mongols and their non-Chinese aides controlled the key positions of power not only in the central government but also in the provinces.

The Mongol attitude toward the civil service examinations was largely negative. They did not require their nationals to pass the Chinese tests, and at first even their Chinese officials were nominated without recourse to the famous competitive system. Until 1267 they were freely chosen; from 1267 on, the *yin* system was recognized. Only in 1313 was the examination system restored. It restricted but did not replace the earlier *yin* policy.

Mongol and Chinese (and Uigur) were considered official languages, and not infrequently public announcements appeared in other Asiatic languages as well. It is therefore not surprising to learn from Chavannes' analysis that in this mixed linguistic environment the style of documentary Chinese perceptibly deteriorated.

Many scholars have been puzzled by Marco Polo's limited understanding of things Chinese and his detailed and accurate observations on Mongol life and culture. This apparent contradiction disappears when it is recognized that the Venetian, who was in China *circa* 1275–1292, was the friend and employee of the Mongol rulers of China. Residing for a time in inner Asia, he became familiar with Mongol customs and language, but as a Mongol *Gauleiter* he found it unnecessary to learn Chinese. He does not discuss the Chinese script, nor does he mention tea; he confuses inner-Asiatic and Chinese marriage practices. Not unlike the last Liao emperor, who did not know that his Chinese subjects disliked dairy products, Marco Polo ascribes definitely pastoral food habits to the Chinese.

Possibly, other Mongol officials were better informed on Chinese life and manners, but it is significant that under Kublai Khan (1260–1294)[11] a foreigner could become an official, and a successful one at that, with so limited a knowledge of the Chinese people.

The Mongols, while retaining many of their early preferences—among others their taste for mare's milk (Kublai Khan's palace possessed "ten thousand" white horses to assure his household's supply)—gradually adopted numerous Chinese ways of living and habits of consumption. Eventually, they even reintroduced such typically Chinese institutions as the examination system. But their concessions to cultural assimilation were too little and too late. The basic dichotomy in government organization was crassly maintained. This inability to establish a tolerable symbiosis with subject peoples accounts in no small degree for the limited duration of the Mongol empire.

The Ch'ing dynasty (1644–1912).—Owen Lattimore makes the challenging statement that "it has never been sufficiently emphasized how *Chinese* the Manchus were by the time they entered China."[12] Like their Ju-chên ancestors, the Manchus were breeders of cattle and primarily farmers. But, firmly established in villages and towns or on castled estates, they were more familiar with the problems of an advanced agrarian society such as China. The Manchus encouraged irrigation and flood control before they entered Peking in 1644. Eighteen years before that significant date their ruler had begun to perform the great Chinese agricultural ceremonies. Their first emperor, Shih Tsu Chang, or the Shun Chih emperor (1644–1661), showed particular favor to his Chinese officials. The Manchu noble, Singde,[13] who died forty years after the conquest, achieved such perfection in his treatment of literary Chinese that he became one of China's preëminent poets.

The willingness of those Manchus who settled within China proper to "turn Chinese" is so evident that their cultural resistance to complete assimilation is all the more remarkable. Again, considerations of power immanent in the conquest situation played a decisive part in shaping Manchu nativist policy. Despite the many conciliatory gestures of early rulers the Manchus were military conquerors. Military prowess continued to be a primary Manchu virtue, and their banners remained the pillars of the empire's defense system until the T'ai-p'ing rebellion (1850–1864). This great upheaval might well have succeeded had it not been for the energetic aid of certain members of the Chinese scholarly bureaucracy who rallied an army of Chinese volunteers to support the government. Political expediency caused the Manchus to form a kind of political bloc with their Chinese rescuers, but they neither disbanded their banners nor permitted them to be absorbed by the reorganized and enlarged Chinese armies.

In the field of political organization the Manchus followed the example of their near-relatives, the Ju-chên: they continued to use existing Chinese institutions. As under the Chin dynasty (1115–1234), control was safeguarded by a quota system. Chinese applicants for office had to pass the regular examination. But the Manchus, who were first tested in military performance, were not expected to excel even in the simplified literary examinations which they, like the Ju-chên, might be asked to take. Commenting on the situation before 1864, a competent student of Ch'ing history has recently written: "No bannerman should receive high honors in the civil service examinations, since he presumably had other opportunities to become an official and at any rate should traditionally devote himself to military affairs." In another passage dealing with "a typical Manchu nobleman" of the early nineteenth century, Fu-lung-an, the same scholar states that this gentleman's literary qualifications were "mediocre"—so mediocre, indeed, that in 1802 his appointment to the post of superintendent of the printing press had to be annulled because of "his inadequate command of written Chinese."[14]

Although literary achievements were not the road to political success, talented Manchus developed fair skill in composing *tz'ŭ*, a literary form derived from the songs of dancing girls and public entertainers. Others wrote popular novels. The first eighty chapters of the *Hung-lou Mêng* (Dream of the Red Chamber) were the most outstanding achievement in this field. But Manchu creative contribution to Chinese scholarship remained marginal. Both before and after the T'ai-p'ing rebellion it consisted in the main of translations and compilations. Dr. Hu Shih calls the Manchu nobles of the later period "ignorant." A statistical study undertaken by a Chinese investigator reveals that from 1646 to 1894 top honors were awarded to three hundred twenty-one Chinese and three bannermen. Of the latter, two were Chinese and the third, who significantly won fame in the year 1865, was a Mongol. On the evidence it would seem that Giles is well justified in observing that "the scholarship of a Manchu became . . . a bye-word and a joke."[15]

Because they resided in China south of the Wall and had adopted the Chinese language and numerous Chinese ways of life the Manchus found it all the more necessary to underline conspicuously their political dominance. They compelled all Chinese men to wear Manchu clothes and grow the queue as a symbol of submission; they forbade Manchu women to marry Chinese men. South of the Great Wall, where most of the population was Chinese, they published official documents and made formal announcements in Manchu as well as in Chinese—thus freshly exposing the national roots of the existing political dichotomy.

The Manchus upheld their national religion;[16] as late as the Ch'ien-lung period (1736–1796) their native priests were still called shamans (Manchu, *saman*). Pork, particularly favored by the sedentary Tungus tribes, continued to be the primary meat offering at Manchu ceremonials, even when the prayers sought to increase the horse herds. The joint participation of men and women contrasted strikingly with Chinese tradition. The Manchu shaman has vanished from the scene, but Manchu religion still finds adherents. It is obviously a remnant of the social institutions which, according to the late Professor S. M. Shirokogoroff,[17] were openly or covertly perpetuated even after the collapse of the empire in 1912.

✧   ✧   ✧

The data analyzed indicate the complex and contradictory nature of culture change under conditions of conquest. The four dynasties discussed rose to power in a period of cavalry superiority, which was probably inaugurated by the invention of the stirrup sometime before the middle of the first millennium, and which acquired full momentum in inner Asia when the mounted warriors of the steppes added a clocklike organization to their already terrifying mobile warfare. This crucial change seems to have occurred after the collapse of the Turkic and Uigur empires in the eighth and ninth centuries, but before the rise of Mongol power. It is more than possible

CHIANG KAI-SHEK
President of the National Government of China

MADAME CHIANG KAI-SHEK

that the Ch'i-tan were the first to develop the new tactics which a few centuries later were so magnificently coördinated by Jenghiz Khan.[13]

Barbarian control over Chinese soil and people was established by a combination of military attack, diplomatic maneuver, and "invitation" in the pre-Liao period, when tribal warfare demonstrated increasing effectiveness without, however, attaining its later formidable strength. Like other northern tribes, the T'o-pa (to-ba) were "invited" to settle within the Chinese borders in the hope that they would serve as armed auxiliaries or could be appeased by gifts of good grazing land. Like other tribal "guest" intruders, they soon fought for—and attained—supreme power, setting up, under the name of Wei (386–ca. 556), three dynasties, not of conquest but of infiltration.

During their early residence in China proper the T'o-pa adopted many Chinese customs. When establishing their imperial house they were, therefore, considerably better prepared to deal with the Chinese and their institutions than were the Hsiung-nu founders of the two short-lived Chao dynasties (304–352). Details of culture change during the Wei period have still to be written, but there is enough evidence to indicate a complex process of acculturation which anticipated the pattern of later dynasties of conquest.

Attention has been paid in recent years to the conquest situation in two of China's great early dynasties, the Chou (ca. 1027–255 B.C.) and the royal, and later imperial, Ch'in (tsin) (255[221]–207 B.C.). The Chou people, whose armies invaded and overthrew Shang, the center of Chinese civilization, originally lived among the Jung (rung) and Ti (di) tribes. Tradition has it that they renounced their barbarian customs in the fourteenth century when they abandoned their homes in Pin (bin). The philosopher Mêng Tzǔ (meng dz), or Mencius, speaking of the father of the founder of the Chou dynasty, King Wên, calls him "a man of the western barbarians." In the twelfth and eleventh centuries B.C. the culture of Chou was in some respects simpler than that of Shang, and differed in other ways also. For these reasons the contemporary historian Hsü Chung-shu (sü jung-shu), of the Academia Sinica, finds a structural similarity between the Chou and the four later dynasties, Liao, Chin, Yüan, and Ch'ing.

The comparison is suggestive—even if further study necessitates fundamental qualification. In the twelfth century B.C. the Chou way of life differed radically from that of the predynastic Ch'i-tan and Mongols, for among the Chou people stockbreeding was a secondary occupation and agriculture was the basic economy. Recent excavations of early neolithic sites in northwestern China give added credibility to historical records and songs which refer to early Chou agriculture and assert that walled cities were constructed before the days of King Wên. Thus, on the eve of their conquest of Shang, the Chou people may be said to have most closely resembled the furthest advanced among the later invading barbarians, the Manchus—if indeed the Chou can be looked upon as barbarians at all.

Many elements of Shang culture were present among the neighboring Chou people, probably adopted either before the conquest or shortly afterward: weapons, script, shell money, ornaments, the use of mats, and the style of binding the hair. Wang Kuo-wei (guo-wei) and other students of Shang and Chou inscriptions, however, point also to important differences between Shang and Chou institutions. In the Chou state, royal princes were enfeoffed as nobles; under the Shang they were not. Under Chou rule the kings succeeded each other according to the principle of primogeniture; Shang tradition favored the succession of brothers before sons. Ancestor worship and mourning practices indicate a different emphasis in kinship relations. The Chou month had four weeks; the Shang had three ten-day periods. Proper names with cyclical designations, popular with the Shang rulers, were rarely resorted to by the Chou, who, on the other hand, specifically indicated sex differences in their nomenclature. It is significant that in all these areas of culture the Chou rulers compelled their new subjects to accept Chou tradition. In so doing they influenced Chinese institutions more fundamentally than did any of the four last great dynasties of conquest.

Another phenomenon deserves mention. Neither Chou proper names nor Chou titles betray inner-Asiatic (proto-Altaic) features. The absence of such linguistic evidence is noteworthy, particularly since Wang Kuo-wei, Pelliot, and others have recognized the non-Chinese character of certain early tribal names. The question, therefore, may well be asked whether the Chou people at the close of the second millennium B.C. were not an important, if somewhat primitive, variant of the complex Chinese agrarian civilization of which Shang was then the core. Present knowledge of Shang and Chou culture suggests an affirmative answer.

At the close of the Chou period another western border state, Ch'in, rose to power, eventually conquering and, in 221 B.C., unifying the Chinese world. There is no need of discussing here the reasons which enabled Ch'in to create a united, nonfeudal empire; suffice it to say that basic institutional changes had prepared the way for this decisive event. It is necessary only to investigate the alleged barbarian background of the conquering state.

The Ch'in people lived in the northwestern border region of China in the old Chou homeland. Contrary to Chou legends, which emphasize the agricultural activities of the Chou forebears during the years spent in Pin and even earlier, Ch'in national tradition stresses early pastoral pursuits. Their historical records reveal close contacts with western tribes and indulgence toward the barbarian way of life. A pre-Confucian ode describes human sacrifice as part of a great Ch'in funeral ceremony. Deplored though it was, the rite continued to be practiced until the fourth century B.C. In the seventh century B.C. a Ch'in ruler, Duke Mu, was accused of violating the *li*, the rules of proper Chinese behavior. A few years later this same duke listened attentively when a delegate of the Jung barbarians argued the superiority of barbarian institutions. Even after the days of Confucius, Ch'in was occasionally classed with the barbarians. According to the *Shih Chi* (shzh ji) (Historical Record), until 361 B.C. the Ch'in people were treated like the I (yi) and Ti (di) barbarians; as late as 266 B.C. the minister of an enemy country reproached them for having "the same customs as the Jung and Ti."

Such statements reveal convincingly the barbarian milieu in which Ch'in civilization developed, but they are insufficient to prove that Ch'in society was essentially barbarian during and after the middle of the first millennium B.C. The criticism of 266 B.C. was made in an atmosphere of political hatred more favorable to propagandistic distortion than to objective judgment. Other data reveal that the Ch'in people had close contact with the surrounding barbarians but not an identical culture.

Pastoral beginnings were distinctly recalled in historical times, but the Ch'in people, it must be remembered, had engaged in agriculture hundreds of years before Confucius was born. In the seventh century B.C. this agriculture was so well advanced that in a period of severe famine their western neighbors, the old Chinese country of Chin (dzin), asked for a loan of grain and received it. Irrigation and flood control were as well known in Ch'in as in most other agrarian states along the shores of the Yellow River and its tributaries. A Ch'in bronze inscription made in the sixth century B.C. refers to Yü, the legendary Chinese pioneer of flood control, who, according to a protohistorical tale, was assisted by an early ancestor of the Ch'in ruling house. The digging of canals in Ch'in is recorded for the century following; and the construction of the Chêng Kuo (jeng guo) canal, even if instigated by political intrigue, reveals that before 221 B.C. the Ch'in government was able to create what was probably the greatest irrigation system in eastern Asia at that time.

The preimperial Ch'in army was organized in orthodox Chinese style. Within the Ch'in government, centralization began early, perhaps because of the need for frontier defense. Its officialdom conformed to the Chinese pattern; a powerful eunuch is mentioned in a pre-Confucian Ch'in ode. The poets and craftsmen of Ch'in produced poems and bronzes modeled after those of the inner Chinese states. The Ch'in language, like that of early Chou, was Chinese, not inner Asiatic.

Within historic times Ch'in society reflected in many ways the country's frontier situation. In fact, its tribal roots may well have been eliminated considerably later than those of the inner states of the Yellow River region. But there can be little doubt that when Ch'in became historically conspicuous in the eighth and seventh centuries B.C. it was already part of contemporary Chinese civilization. The final conquest of "all-under-heaven" was the triumph of Chinese power, not the result of a barbarian invasion in the style of Liao, Chin, Yüan, and Ch'ing.

CHAPTER IX

The Republic: Phase of War-Lordism (1911-1928)

BY HARLEY FARNSWORTH MACNAIR

FROM 1644 TO 1911 the Ta Ch'ing (da tsing), or Manchu, dynasty held the Mandate of Heaven to rule China with its dependencies old and new. From the accession to the Dragon Throne of the House of Nurhachu (or Nurhaci)[1] until well toward the end of the eighteenth century the grip of the Manchus upon the Mandate was strong and sure. From that period through the first decade of the twentieth century their hold became weaker and ever more hesitant until, in February, 1912, they relinquished it.

When, however, according to Confucian thought, the surrender of the Mandate took place, it was not into the hands of a new dynasty, as on occasion through almost three thousand years, but back to Heaven itself. Republicanism, parliamentarism, modernism, committees, and ballots have small need of heavenly mandates. The abdication of Pu'i ("Henry Pu-yi"), the Hsüan-t'ung emperor (1908–1912), the last of his line, betokened something unprecedented in the thirty-five hundred years of authentic Chinese history. Through the modes of civil or foreign wars, diplomacy, treachery, usurpation, sedition, privy conspiracy, murder, and rebellion, dynasties had fallen and others had risen, but monarchical government, royal or imperial, had been maintained.

In 1911 there came into being a channel and form of centralized governmental power hitherto not experienced by the inhabitants of the Middle Country. Truly a new kind of revolution was entered upon, in conjunction with aspects of mutation old in China's

---

[1] For notes to chapter ix see page 527.

story. Before considering the incidents leading immediately to, and flowing from, this fundamental change, not only in the relocation of sovereignty but also in the habitat and form of sovereignty's manifestation, it is desirable to consider briefly some of the deep-seated contributory causes. As with all great movements, these causes are chronologically far-reaching, in number considerable, and in nature complex. They fall into two divisions, domestic and foreign, of approximately equal importance.

Despite their Sinicization to a degree which made them at times appear almost more Celestial than the sons of Han and T'ang, the Manchus, from the day they irrupted south of the Wall to that on which they abdicated the throne, were looked upon and plotted against as aliens by innumerable members of Chinese secret societies. This fact goes far to explain the difficult solution of China's foreign as well as domestic problems under the Ta Ch'ing dynasty, especially during the nineteenth century. Consciously or unconsciously, almost every problem faced by the central government was considered primarily from the dynastic, and only secondarily from the national, angle.

As Western and Nipponese pressure increased upon the Manchu-Chinese Empire, as vassal dependencies were lopped off, and as the people of the Eighteen Provinces themselves suffered slights and exploitation at the hands of aliens, the tendency became more and more marked, preceding and following the Revolution of 1911–1912, to blame the Manchus for China's misfortunes. The attempt of the Boxers in 1900 to hold accountable the foreigners resident in the country and to punish them forthwith had conspicuously and disagreeably failed. In accord with the ancient Chinese doctrine that for everything evil occurring within the confines of the empire someone is liable, and in conformity with the human principle that it is pleasanter to hold others than oneself blameworthy for the imperfections of life, the Manchus were the logical scapegoats. To a degree they were responsible, but not more so than the Chinese who from the outset coöperated with them in the rule of the empire.

Overpopulation, maldistribution of population, and overweening pride on the part of the peoples and their rulers in China's patriarchal civilization; conflicts of interests between rural agricultural and urban industrial-commercial areas and groups; corruption, in a thousand ways, of officialdom and populace; venerable institutions—for example, the examination and the guild systems—of worth in essence, but not broadened in scope or modernized to keep up with the times; the impact upon China of Western peoples with conflicting interests and with strange ideas and institutions (social, religious, philosophical, educational, economic, political, military) subversive of those which had made China great for thousands of years: these and others combined to launch the country upon a revolution as many-sided as the ideas and institutions mentioned.

China's revolution really began, as a Chinese once remarked, with the arrival in Canton, in 1807, of Robert Morrison, the first Protestant missionary. More than two centuries earlier (1582), European Jesuits had begun work in the Middle Kingdom. Their work had resulted in partial enlightenment of China's intellectuals with respect to the culture of Europe, and of Europe's concerning the culture of China. The magnificent labors of the Jesuits, however, had no revolutionary political repercussions at either end of the Eurasian continent. But British and American Protestant evangelists and educators, primarily because of the nature of their religious, social, and political faiths, unintentionally constituted "fifth columnists." That these religious workers were, in the main, unconscious agents of political, and not merely religious and social, revolution rendered them none the less potent: new wine is innocent of ulterior motives as it enters old bottles.

Southeastern China, particularly the province of Kuangtung (guang-dung), where Western Protestants first established themselves in China proper, has for many centuries been more influenced by aliens and alien thought than any other section of the empire, not only because of the many foreigners who have penetrated thither and thence, but also because of vast numbers of traders and laborers who have gone abroad from this part of the country for temporary trade or for long, or even permanent, residence, and who have carried or sent back to the land of their ancestors funds and ideas from overseas. It was neither an accident nor a coincidence that Kuangtung served in the nineteenth century as the seedbed of revolution. In this province were born Hung

Hsiu-ch'üan (siu-tsüan),[2] prominent leader of the antidynastic
T'ai-p'ing rebellion (ca. 1850–1864); K'ang Yu-wei,[3] literary political evolutionist of the last years of the nineteenth century; Liang
Ch'i-ch'ao,[4] scholar-editor and constitutional monarchist; and the
indefatigably peripatetic, anti-Manchu, pro-Republican revolutionary, Sun Yat-sen.

If revolutionary thought and action flourished in the south,
weight of precedent and power rested mainly in the north. Cultural
and political struggle between north and south is never-ending in
China. Rarely, however, has this been manifested so dramatically
as in the decade preceding the outbreak of revolution in 1911, and
the first fifteen years of the Republican era. For a quarter of a
century the south proposed while the north disposed; but by 1928
the south had disposed of the north—for the time being.

Between 1898 and 1911 three major attempts were made to preserve the Ta Ch'ing dynasty and seek national salvation—the first
and the third by reforming China from the top downward, the
second by reforming from the bottom upward. The first attempt,
that of the Hundred Days, was made by the Kuang-hsü (guang-sü)
emperor (1875–1908) with the aid of southern reformers, notably
K'ang Yu-wei. This was ended by the Empress Dowager Tz'ŭ-hsi
(b. 1835–d. 1908).[5] It was followed by the Boxer rebellion, a move
at reform from the bottom upward.

The third attempt, that of Tz'ŭ-hsi herself, was undertaken in
1901, after the return of the court to Peking (bei-jing) from its
flight to Sian in Shensi. China was now to be transformed into a
constitutional monarchy under the Ta Ch'ing dynasty, which
Article I of the Draft Constitution of 1908 (verbally inspired by the
Nipponese Constitution of 1889) optimistically declared "shall rule
over the Ta Ch'ing Empire forever, and shall be honored through
all the ages." Instead of immortality and endless honor the descendants of Nurhachu were given short shrift in the autumn and winter
season of 1911–1912.

The suggestion that the Ta Ch'ing dynasty fell from power because the Mandate of Heaven was withdrawn might appeal to
Celestials of the pre-Republican period, but it means little or nothing to contemporary Chinese and Westerners. For a long generation
after the T'ai-p'ing rebellion the authority of the Manchus was

maintained on borrowed time—borrowed, and for the most part wasted, by that dominant lady the Empress Dowager Tz'ŭ-hsi. During some three-quarters of a century, beginning shortly before the First Anglo-Chinese War (1839–1842), the Western Powers and, after 1870, Japan worked concurrently with the native enemies of the dynasty to sap the foundations of the Manchu-Chinese state.

Defeat of China by Nippon in 1894–1895, followed by a series of attacks by aliens upon the dignity of the rulers and the empire's territorial and administrative integrity, contributed directly to the success of the plots of Sun Yat-sen and his co-conspirators. In 1911 two rebellious movements and an explosion heralded the revolution. In the city of Canton, in April, the general commanding the Manchu troops was assassinated and the official residence of the viceroy was attacked. A provincial autonomy movement, in opposition to plans of the imperial government for assuming control of the country's railroads and rail construction, culminated in Chengtu, Szechuan, in a student strike in August, followed by rioting in September. Finally, as an immediate consequence of a bomb explosion in Hankow, Hupeh (hu-bei), on October 9, the antidynastic and pro-Republican revolution was prematurely born on October 10.

Dr. Sun Yat-sen, the father of the revolution, was abroad, but he returned at the end of the year to accept what proved to be a stopgap election as president of the provisional government. "Shortly afterward in solemn state he appeared before the tomb of the Hung-wu emperor, the founder of the last native dynasty—the Ming—which had ruled China. To the spirit of the man who had ousted the Mongols, Sun announced the expulsion of the alien Manchus."[6]

If spirit, daring, and initiative in plot and action characterized Dr. Sun and his southern followers, the weight of official dignity—civil and military,—experience in administration, and control of the northern Chinese armies tipped the scales in favor of Yüan Shih-k'ai.[7] The Revolution of 1911–1912 was comparatively bloodless, primarily because of the balancing of power between north and south and the marked tendency of the Chinese to resort to reason and compromise instead of to the absolutism of doctrinaire dogmatism and bayonets. Sun was experienced in plotting but not in administration; Yüan was adept at both. In 1911–1912 the revolutionists of the southern and central provinces were unable by force of arms to conquer the north; the north was equally unable to extirpate the revolutionists and their movement in central and southern China. A compromise was reached: the Manchu dynasty abdicated in the person of the Hsüan-t'ung emperor,[8] who, however, retained his title, also his residence in the northern part of the Forbidden City; Sun Yat-sen resigned the provisional presidency after functioning in Nanking for six and a half weeks; and Yüan Shih-k'ai, who remained in Peking during the negotiations, was elected Sun's successor as provisional president.

But the compromise was more apparent than real; neither party relinquished its objectives:

Sun's followers disagreed with Yüan, and what he stood for, on almost every point. They desired a popular, democratic republic in reality, based on a wide franchise, and a powerful legislature which should dictate to the executive. They wanted change over night. They expected Yüan to be their willing tool, and to retire as soon as a permanent government should be formed.

Yüan needed southern revolutionary support, and intended to use the revolutionists in bringing the country under his control. He had no intention of hastily attempting to bring the people into a participation in the central government for which nothing in their background had prepared them. Moreover, he had no intention of accepting dictation from anyone—least of all from a popularly elected legislature controlled by southerners. As events proved, he had no intention of retiring from the executive position; on the contrary, there is reason to believe that he planned a return to monarchy from the beginning. Above all, he was not interested in socialism, state or otherwise, and this Sun and most of his followers were working for. Yüan was willing to bring in gradual reform in line with the experience of the Chinese people; he was unalterably opposed to deep-rooted revolution and a complete break with the past. Provincialism was much stronger than nationalism, and . . . Yüan was a northerner with little love for the southerners, or for the ideas of overseas Chinese who had been so lacking in a sense of propriety as to leave their homeland and ancestral tombs to reside, and to seek a living permanently, among "barbarians."[9]

A breach developed rapidly between the liberal-radical, Western-trained, Cantonese medical doctor, Sun, of peasant origin, and his National People's party, the Kuomintang (guo-min-dang), on the one side, and the typically conservative-reactionary, civilian-militarist, Honanese ex-viceroy, Yüan, of official family, and his northern military henchmen, on the other. Parliament was not convened until April, 1913. Before organizing for business it attempted to block negotiations for a foreign loan to the government. Nevertheless, the provisional president and the English, French, German, Russian, Belgian, and Japanese bankers carried through in May a "reorganization loan" for £25,000,000. The executive position was by so much strengthened at the cost of the legislative—and Yüan entered upon the consolidation of his power.

One means chosen by the president was the supplanting of revolutionist provincial governors by his own militarists. Dr. Sun resorted to a second revolution in July, 1913—this time to overthrow Yüan instead of the Manchus. On failing, he escaped to Japan. Yüan, in October, persuaded those parliamentarians who had not fled Peking to elect him substantive president of China. The means adopted were simple: Yüan's guards in the houses of parliament prevented exit of members until a majority had agreed upon the right candidate. When the parliamentary constitutional committee proposed an instrument of government providing for a president whose every act must be approved by a premier responsible to parliament, Yüan, in November, destroyed parliament's quorum by expelling all members of the Kuomintang. Parliament was suspended in December, 1913, and dissolved in January, 1914.

That constitutionalism should not disappear from the good Chinese earth, the president's followers prepared a new document, the Constitutional Compact, which concentrated power in the presidency, lengthened the term of that office from five to ten years, and established no limit to reëlection. With rebellion quelled, with the southerners again in the south—or in Japan—and with ample funds, his own constitution, unicameral legislature, and a council of state in his pocket, and in reality an unlimited term of office, Yüan was now in a position far more powerful than that attained by most emperors of China. He was a dictator. But for the problems connected with non-Chinese peoples, Asiatic and European, and their governments, he would probably have succeeded in establishing a dynasty in accord with his finally avowed objectives.

Unfortunately for the effectuation of the president's aims, the Middle Country was not at the moment functioning in a vacuum, as to all intents and purposes it had so often done in the past. The international problems faced by the China of Yüan Shih-k'ai had basically to do with demonstrations of imperialism: those of China with such outlying areas as Manchuria, Outer and Inner Mongolia, Sinkiang (sin-jiang), and Tibet, and those of the West and Japan with respect to China itself and these same outlying areas. Whether imperialism be considered reprehensible or praiseworthy, or merely a phenomenon of human nature and historical development, the fact that imperialism is peculiar to no time, place, or people, and that the Chinese people and their rulers have been through the ages and still are—when and where given the opportunity—as imperialistic as most other peoples, must ever be borne in mind. That the channels and methods of Chinese imperialism may differ from those of other nations merely illustrates the diversity of human inventiveness.

At various times in and after the second century B.C., China constituted a magnet which by the superiority of its culture and (or) its military and economic strength drew surrounding territories and peoples. In the nineteenth and twentieth centuries the situation was reversed, and the empires of Britain, France, Russia, and Japan became magnets which drew the remnants of the disintegrating Manchu-Chinese Empire. So it was in the days of Yüan Shih-k'ai—and later. At no time since 1898 had the governments and certain nationals of several of the Great Powers made clearer their expectation of, and on occasion their determination to bring about, a fatal termination to China's illness. Rarely in that country's history, moreover, have so many of its sons exhibited such willingness to play into the hands of aliens and to bring about the fall of their homeland as during the period under consideration.

Domestic and foreign disputes and diplomatic negotiations with Great Britain, Russia, and Japan served to encourage rather than hinder Yüan Shih-k'ai in his monarchical aspirations. In the autumn of 1915 a series of provincial "elections" of the president to the throne was carried out with extremely suspicious success. After observing the amenities by declining three times, the dictator announced the date of his enthronement, January 1, 1916.

Meantime Dr. Sun, from the vantage point of Nippon, continued his plots against the would-be emperor and monarchism. Sun's followers, and other enemies of Yüan who were not followers of the Cantonese leader, worked to thwart the emperor-elect. Nipponese representatives, having earlier joined those of Great Britain and Russia in advising Yüan to delay, at length warned him he must not continue with his plan.

In December, 1915, a rebellion broke out in Yünnan which was joined by other provinces. In March, 1916, the monarchical scheme was definitely abandoned. By April, five provinces south of the Yangtze River had declared their independence. In May a rival southern government was instituted under the presidency of General Li Yüan-hung, a leader in the Wuchang revolt of October, 1911, and subsequently vice-president in the government of Yüan Shih-k'ai. Heaven ended the 1916 impasse between north and south: President Yüan, the strong man who had willed to become the Hung-hsien (Glorious Constitutionalism) emperor, died in his palace in Peking on June 6.

The heyday of war-lordism had dawned. It proved a long and tiresome period in the course of which a succession of inconsequential executives, parliamentarians, and other politicians, militarists, and even a child emperor passed ghostlike across China's stage. An acting president declared war on Germany and Austria in mid-August, 1917. This step had followed: (1) two attempts (rebuffed in 1914 and 1915) of President Yüan's government to enter the war; (2) a request (November, 1915) by the Allies that Japan join them in persuading (as a substitute for discouraging) China to join the war; (3) an invitation by the United States (February, 1917) to Peking and other neutral governments to break relations with Germany; (4) a squabble between militarist President Li Yüan-hung and his rival militarist, Premier Tuan Ch'i-jui (duan chi-rui), over—*inter alia*—the wisdom of breaking relations with the Central Powers; (5) a declaration by Premier Tuan's friends, the military governors of Fengtien, Chihli (jzh-li), Shantung (shan-dung), Hupeh, Anhui, Chekiang (je-jiang), and Fukien (fu-jien), of the independence of their provinces from President Li's parliamentary government in Peking; (6) the dismissal of parliament (the members of which fled southward) by President Li at the instigation of queue-wearing General Chang Hsün, whom the president invited to save the country by mediating between himself and Premier Tuan; (7) the dispatch (June 6, 1917, the first anniversary of President Yüan's death) to Peking by the American government of a note suggesting that China's attitude toward Germany was less important than "the maintenance . . . of one central, united, and alone responsible government," and expressing the hope that China would "work for the reëstablishment of a coördinate government and the assumption of that place among the powers of the world to which China is so justly entitled"—a note which had no perceptible influence on the quarreling Celestial militarists, but which angered the young bloods of the Rising Sun because Washington had, from their viewpoint, interfered in Chinese affairs without consultation with Tokyo; (8) the restoration (at 4:00 A.M., July 1, 1917), for less than a fortnight, of the twelve-year-old Hsüan-t'ung emperor; (9) the resignation of President Li; (10) the consequent elevation of Vice-President General Fêng Kuo-chang, of the Chihli faction of the Northern Military party, to the acting presidency; and (11) the quarrel between Fêng and Tuan Ch'i-jui, of the rival Anhui clique of the Northern Military party.

Declaration of war upon the Central Powers assured China of representation in the Peace Conference, suspension of Boxer indemnity payments for five years, and cancellation of extraterritorial and other special prerogatives enjoyed by the governments and nationals of the Teutonic Powers, as well as temporary expulsion of their influence from the country. It did not, despite the labors of President Wilson, guarantee justice of treatment for China at the Peace Conference; it did not guarantee protection from either Nipponese or other foreign military and economic aggressions in the meantime; it did not guarantee general consent of the Powers to China's national aspirations.

Nor did technical participation by China in the First World War have a noticeably debilitating effect on military excursions and alarms at home. The bartering of national resources, mineral and industrial, to Japan in exchange for loans of millions of yen—250,000,000 yen in 1918 alone—contributed both to the boiling of the military pot and the indignation of patriotic students throughout the country. Generally credited with profiting most from Nippon's loans were members of Premier Tuan's Anfu Club (*An* of Anhui, also meaning "peace," *Fu* of Fukien, also meaning "joy"). They and Chang Tso-lin's Fengtien (Manchuria) clique and Ts'ao Kun's Chihli clique flourished during the administration of Hsü

Shih-ch'ang, foster brother to Yüan Shih-k'ai, who, in October, 1918, had been elected to the presidency at Premier Tuan's instigation by his specially packed parliament.

The three cliques felt crowded in Peking. Accordingly, in the summer of 1920 the Chihli and Fengtien militarists warred on the Anfuites and quickly overthrew them. Generals Wu P'ei-fu and Fêng Yü-hsiang of the Chihli faction played conspicuous roles at that time and for approximately two decades thereafter. Premier Tuan retired to Tientsin to study Buddhism while Chang Tso-lin, sometime swineherd and bandit but now war lord of Manchuria, largely dominated Peking. In the spring of 1922, however, Chang was driven back to the Manchurian frontier by generals Wu and Fêng, and at once declared himself independent of Peking. President Hsü Shih-ch'ang, unable to control either his enemies or his friends, resigned the presidency and, like Tuan, sought solace in the conning of Buddhist sutras in Tientsin. Whereupon, from that foreign-controlled and foreign-protected Treaty Port, former President Li Yüan-hung was with difficulty persuaded by Wu P'ei-fu to return to Peking in June. Parliament was reconvened on August 1. Wu hoped that restoration to their orbits of Li and the somewhat worn and travel-stained parliamentarians might serve again to bridge the chasm between north and south.

But Wu P'ei-fu's master, Ts'ao Kun, war lord of Chihli, desired to round out his unremarkable career by becoming president. Certain of Ts'ao's henchmen succeeded in straining relations between the restored President Li and his chief restorers, General Wu P'ei-fu and General Fêng Yü-hsiang, with the result that Li, after a military demonstration against him, fled again to Tientsin on June 13, 1923, having held office for a year and two days. By an expenditure estimated at fifteen million silver dollars, Ts'ao Kun obtained from parliament an election to the presidency on October 5. He assumed office five days later and at once promulgated a new "permanent" constitution.

The rivalries of Chang Tso-lin and Wu P'ei-fu again exploded into war in the summer of 1924 in both northern and eastern central China. On October 23 Fêng Yü-hsiang shocked his superiors, Ts'ao Kun and Wu P'ei-fu, by seizing Peking, imprisoning the president (who resigned his costly office on November 2, but was held prisoner until April, 1926), and ordering the arrest of the parlia-mentarians who had bartered the presidency.

On November 5 the Manchu emperor's palace in the Forbidden City was invaded by Fêng's military. The eighteen-year-old Hsüan-t'ung emperor was requested to resign his title and accede to a revision of the favorable-treatment agreement made in 1912 on the occasion of his abdication. This he declined to do, and on the same day withdrew from his palace to that of his father. Thence he escaped to seek refuge in the Japanese legation, as numbers of the Anfuites had done in 1920, and later resided in Tientsin until his voluntary or involuntary withdrawal to Manchuria early in 1932.

General Wu, taken by surprise, and with his communications cut, withdrew with a few thousand trustworthy troops by sea and river to Nanking and Hankow. Somewhat later he reached his former headquarters at Lo-yang, Honan.

Out of the imbroglio of 1924 the former premier, Marshal Tuan Ch'i-jui, emerged as the provisional chief executive, after a con-ference with Chang Tso-lin and Fêng Yü-hsiang. As titular head of the Peking government Tuan was no more influential than his predecessors since Yüan Shih-k'ai. Fêng and Chang did not long remain at peace: by the autumn of 1925 the former had allied him-self with two lesser militarists—one of them, Kuo Sung-ling (guo sung-ling), was a hitherto trusted general of Chang's in Man-churia—with whose aid Fêng hoped to eliminate Chang Tso-lin not only from China south of the Wall but from Manchuria as well. The Japanese, however, at the eleventh hour made it clear that they were not yet ready to dispense with Chang's services. Fêng's plan accordingly failed, and one year after Wu P'ei-fu and Chang Tso-lin had been at war with each other they became allies against Fêng. The latter now decided that a journey to Moscow would not only broaden his perspective but strengthen his relations with, and increase his supplies from, the Soviets. He therefore spent the spring of 1926 in Russia.

Contemporaneously, Provisional Chief Executive Tuan, who had suppressed student riots with harshness, was ousted from office. In accordance with custom he retired to Tientsin. Marshals Chang Tso-lin and Wu P'ei-fu now differed for a period over the type of government which should be instituted with the passing of the undistinguished but not humdrum administrations of President Ts'ao Kun and Marshal Tuan Ch'i-jui. Without a president, or the means of obtaining one, after the manifestation of Marshal Fêng's rude attitude toward parliamentarians, it was decided that a regency cabinet would serve to maintain the theory that Peking was the seat of China's legitimate government in the face of the southerners' pretensions to rule the country from Canton. By June, 1927, Chang Tso-lin had sufficiently organized his military position on both sides of the Wall to warrant establishing himself in Peking as T'ai-yüan-shuai, or dictator, a position he maintained for about a year. On the night of June 2, 1928, when the southern Nationalists were approaching the capital from which Kublai Khan, but not himself, had ruled a great part of the world, he felt it expedient to visit Manchuria. The Japanese military by this time had decided that Chang was no longer indispensable to their welfare in either the Eastern Three Provinces or in China south of the Wall. His car was bombed and he was killed as his train entered Mukden.

The outline of developments in China north of the Yangtze during the regime of Yüan Shih-k'ai and his successors has indicated that the retirement of Dr. Sun Yat-sen from the provisional presidency in February, 1912, and from China to Japan in the summer of 1913 did not betoken his withdrawal from public life or from a position of personal and ideological influence even when physical power was lacking. If amid civil wars, banditry, and treachery an attempt was made to maintain a semiconstitutional, conservative government in the north, equally vigorous attempts against similar and no less numerous difficulties were made to initiate and maintain a constitutional, liberal-progressive government in the south—which eventually should rule all China. Between 1917, when the parliamentarians dismissed by President Li Yüan-hung had journeyed to Canton, and 1925, when Dr. Sun Yat-sen died in Peking within sight of the imperial yellow-tiled roofs of the Ming and Ch'ing palaces, the indomitable revolutionary leader alternated between holding office in the province of his birth and plotting to return to office from his Shanghai home in the French Concession. At all times he engaged in the dissemination of his doctrines and made plans for the unification and modernization of his country.

In the years 1919–1920 a powerful student movement had been organized on a national scale as a threefold result of China's bitter disappointment at certain decisions of the Paris Peace Conference, the unbridled corruption of the Peking government, and the success of the Russian Revolution. Contemporaneously, offers of assistance to China, north and south, were made by Bolshevist agents. In mid-January, 1923, those of Abram Adolf Joffe were accepted in Shanghai by Dr. Sun. The two agreed, however, that "the Communistic order or even the Soviet system cannot actually be introduced into China, because there do not exist here the conditions for the successful establishment of either Communism or Sovietism."[10] For his acceptance of Red aid while rejecting Red thought the founder of the Kuomintang has been described as "the first of many world statesmen to fall victim to the fallacy of the 'popular front.'"

Dr. Sun became for the fourth time a leading figure in Canton in a south-China aggregation of power. This government, unfortunately for his reputation during the last two years of his life, was malodorous and tyrannical in the extreme. Without the coöperation of socialist-revolutionary Russia and the Chinese student masses the posthumous reputation of Dr. Sun and the development of China after his death would have been conspicuously different. With the arrival in August, 1923, of Comrade Michael Borodin and Russian funds, Dr. Sun's Kuomintang was reorganized, with the Communist party serving as a model. Its membership was soon opened to Chinese Communists, whose numbers had been noticeably increasing in recent years. This merging temporarily strengthened the Kuomintang. It strengthened also the Communists, led to antagonisms between members of the new and the old Kuomintang, and contributed both to the increasingly autocratic attitude of Dr. Sun and to the struggle, avowed and unavowed, between his party and the Communists from 1927 to the present day.

After suppressing a rebellion in Canton against his government, Dr. Sun accepted an invitation from Fêng Yü-hsiang, Tuan Ch'i-jui, and Chang Tso-lin to go north to confer regarding reorganization and reunification of a national government. The distinguished revolutionist set forth, by way of Shanghai and Japan, for the city of his enemies—Manchus and northern Chinese militarists—of

thirty long years. On the way thither, as opportunity offered in
Japan and in China, he denounced imperialism and preached Pan-
Asianism. In so doing he further contributed to the Russian orientation which he and Joffe had initiated some two years earlier, and
unconsciously strengthened Nipponese ideology and plans for the
"Greater East Asia Co-Prosperity Sphere" which were to plague his
countrymen—and others—for decades thereafter.

Sun's death in Peking on March 12, 1925, was followed by an
apotheosis of the hero at the hands of certain of his Russian advisers and Chinese followers of the more radical type. What Lenin,
dead, had become for revolutionized Russia, Sun, dead, should
become for a revolutionized China. And so to a considerable degree
it has been. Dead, the leader could make no more mistakes, and
those made, plus the imperfections attributed to him by critics,
were officially soon forgotten. But the colleagues in the south,
whom death had not yet rendered heroic, were left to struggle
among themselves and with Dr. Sun's enemies and their own. This
they did with gusto.

In part through his own ability, in part by the maneuverings
of Comrade Borodin and General Blücher (contemporary alias,
Galens), Chiang Kai-shek rose to control of the southern Nationalist movement. Born in 1889, a native of Chekiang, Chiang was a
student in the Tokyo Military College at the age of nineteen.

While there he became a follower of Dr. Sun.... On the outbreak of the 1911
revolution at Wu-ch'ang he returned to China to participate in the struggle....
For a time he was one of Dr. Sun's secretaries. The failure of the "second revolution" in 1913 ... interrupted his military career, and for a time he was in
business in Shanghai. Later he became chief-of-staff to Ch'en Ch'iung-ming [a
militarist rival in Kuangtung to Dr. Sun]. During the struggles of Ch'en with Sun,
Chiang found difficulty in serving two masters; his earlier loyalty overcame his
later and, while officially serving Ch'en, he advised Sun to attack the latter. After
this Chiang again entered into discreet obscurity; then, in August, 1923, after
Sun's and Joffe's *rapprochement,* he was sent by the former as confidential representative to Moscow to meet Lenin, Trotsky, and Chicherin, to study Bolshevist
strategy, ideology, and revolutionary technique, and to seek aid of a material
nature from Moscow. Returning to China, he was appointed principal of the
Russian-inspired, recently established Whampoa [Military] Academy. The pro-
tégé first of Sun Yat-sen and later of Borodin, a man of decision and iron nerve,
Chiang, who was now reckoned a Communist, seized the opportunity so carefully

prepared by Borodin. So successfully did the two men coöperate for the nonce that during the remaining months of the year 1925 all opposition to the Communist-Kuomintang forces in the Kwangtung area was overcome.[11]

One of the ever-recurring dreams of Dr. Sun Yat-sen's last years was the dispatch northward of the southern armies which, eliminating his opponents, should unify the country and make possible the effectuation of his political doctrines. The summer and autumn of the year following that of Sun's passing witnessed the irruption into the Yangtze Valley and the provinces of Fukien and Chekiang of Kuomintang forces under the guidance of Chiang Kai-shek and his Russian helpers, notably Borodin and Blücher. Meticulously prepared and disseminated propaganda, printed and vocal, the use of silver, lead, and steel, and the hopeful idealism as well as the war-weariness of the people explain in large measure the relative ease of the southerners' advance. The same facts appeared to demonstrate also that progeny not altogether worthless may issue from a marriage of convenience. But participants in, and progeny of, such a marriage may quarrel, and so it happened this time: successes of Kuomintang-Communist leaders, advisers, and forces were followed in the spring of 1927 by a split between Chiang and Borodin and their respective followers and forces.[12]

An important incident connected with the break within the Kuomintang and between that party and the Communists was the premeditated attack on foreign nationals and interests (with the killing of six Westerners and wounding of others) in Nanking, on March 24 and several days following, by the Communist-controlled Hunanese troops of one of Chiang's rivals.

More important politically were: the turning of Chiang to the middle-class merchant-banker leaders of Shanghai and to those older—and also more recent—members of the Kuomintang who were opposed to Russian and Communist influences, Chinese or non-Chinese; the establishment in Nanking by Chiang of his own Kuomintang government as rival to that established in Wuhan by the Russian-inspired radical Left Kuomintangists; the expulsion, in the summer of 1927, of Borodin, Blücher, and other agents of the Third International; the withdrawal to Moscow of Dr. Sun's second wife (Soong Ch'ing-ling) following charges that the agrarian and social revolution in which her husband had been most deeply interested from his early youth was being betrayed by Chiang Kai-shek and his adherents; the announcement, in June, by Fêng Yü-hsiang (who had returned from Moscow in October, 1926, where he had been since early May) of his support of Chiang; the intervention of Japanese troops in Tsinan, Shantung, in July, to prevent Chiang's and Fêng's advance to seize Peking, where Chang Tso-lin had just established himself as T'ai-yüan-shuai (Generalissimo); and finally the sudden resignation of office by General Chiang Kai-shek on August 12, 1927, as a means of restoring unity within the party following the expulsion of Chinese Communists therefrom and that of the Russian advisers from the country.

Chiang's position was strengthened personally and politically by his marriage (an earlier wife having been divorced) in the following December to Miss Soong Mei-ling, a younger sister of the second wife of Dr. Sun and of the outstanding government financier of the Kuomintang, T. V. Soong. Intricate permutations and combinations having contemporaneously taken place within the party, Chiang was invited on December 10 to resume his position as commander in chief. In January, 1928, he returned to dominate the situation in Nanking.

Reorganization of the government was entered upon, and plans were renewed by Chiang and Fêng Yü-hsiang for the conquest of the country's theoretical capital, Peking. In May the Japanese military again intervened at Tsinan; blood was shed on both sides, and Generalissimo Chiang was hindered from reaching his objective. To prevent Fêng Yü-hsiang from accomplishing what he himself was blocked from doing, and to insure that that wily, if patriotic, opportunist should not obtain control of the metropolitan area, Chiang appointed Yen Hsi-shan, governor of Shansi, as commander of the Peking and Tientsin gendarmerie. On the night of June 2, 1928, Chang Tso-lin withdrew from his position as T'ai-yüan-shuai of Peking and went to Mukden, where, as earlier mentioned, he passed from China's troubled scene. A few days later, Governor Yen and General Pai Ch'ung-hsi, the Kuangsi leader, entered the capital city.

In theory and claim the unification of China proper was now complete. On July 6 the Nationalist leaders repaired to the magnificent Pi Yün Ssŭ (bi yün sz) Buddhist monastery[13] in the Western

Hills outside the former capital—now renamed Pei-p'ing, or "northern peace,"—to announce in the presence of their late leader, Sun Yat-sen, the official consummation of part of his plans, even as he, in 1912 outside Nanking, had announced to the spirit of the first Ming emperor the expulsion of the Manchus and the beginning of a new dispensation in China's history.

CHAPTER X

The Republic: Phase of Resurgence (1928-1946)

BY PAUL MYRON ANTHONY LINEBARGER
AND ROBERT E. HOSACK

THE PERIOD OF THE CHINESE REPUBLIC after 1928 differs so much from the preceding one that it is hard to believe that the same general social, political, and military pressures were responsible for both. In the earlier phase, enormous energy was squandered in what appeared to be a rigmarole of transient power politics. China progressed—but into the unknown. "Where there is no vision the people perish,"—and the Chinese, as a political entity, were for a time without a grand illusion to illuminate and justify their collective existence. They could not ascribe a purpose or role to their own being, since the splendid Heaven-Man-and-Earth synthesis of the Confucians had lapsed from public faith and no longer commanded general assent. For lack of such a public fiction the people turned to those modes of existence, always present in China, which are basically antistatist and escapist.[1]

Part of the strength of the Chinese social system through the ages has been the unusual ability of the people to get along without political government and to employ, instead, less formal and more intimate modes of social and economic control. In the early phase of the Republic the institutional facilities of the family, the guilds, other *hui* (consociations), and the ideological justifications offered by Taoism, or a generally pragmatic and materialistic spirit, had made it possible for the Chinese to live maturely and relatively well without access to those profound gratifications—moral, intel-

---

[1] For notes to chapter x see page 527.

lectual, and personal—which are made possible only by the presence of an active, vigorous polity. Nevertheless, they sensed their
loss, since in all societies public activity is a part of individual life.

The year XVII (1928) marked the settling of revolution into the
form of government; this was the first full year of the National
government under the five-power constitution, and it was the year
in which the Kuomintang-Communist war broke forth with full
virulence. Chinese domestic politics became thenceforth increasingly involved in the struggle to control an existing government or
to expound and modify a way of thinking which was both official
and widely sanctioned. The struggle toward government was over.
The struggle for government had begun.

The mere existence of a state form and a national ideology was
enough to qualify all phases of China's domestic and international
relationships. Under the fantastically impotent Republic at Peking, China's domestic affairs had been almost completely divorced
from its foreign relations. Until the establishment of the National
government China's foreign relations had channeled through a few
more or less able diplomats who exploited all the aid they could get
from the power configuration of world empires. No representative
was in a position to speak for all China; nor was there a leader able
to command enough military or economic force to do more than
amuse, or irritate, the rulers of other countries and exploit his
country's resources to his own advantage. Increasing unification,
in and after 1927, meant that each step forward in the domestic
field had its concomitants in the realm of international politics.
Weakness in the interior led to bluff or appeasement on the coast;
national unity enhanced China's influence on the world.

In this light, the developments in China after 1928 formed part
of a single general process: the reconsolidation of society in terms
acceptable to the people and to the rest of the world. The fall of
the Szechuan war lords was one extreme in a series of events in
which Japanese invasion constituted another. The connecting link
was the appearance of true government for the country as a whole.

Domestically, the Chinese were still struggling in 1946 for unity
and power. Phases included elimination of the *tuchün* (dujün),
prolonged Red insurrection, development of the National government, and counterdevelopment of puppet governments.

Internationally, the Chinese struggled to obtain control of their homeland. This involved an attack on imperialism and the vested legal rights which imperialist states had acquired in China in the past hundred years. But the international phase, which might have been one of the Middle Country against the world—if the government had been forced to deal with a world at peace,—became vitally connected with the slow and piecemeal extension of the so-called Second World War,[2] eventually to China's great benefit.

The prescience of wisely wishful thinking, as much as any one factor, sustained the real leaders of China in the long resistance to Japan, and provided their countrymen with indomitable belief in their eventual triumph over that country. Historically minded Chinese sensed that another great war was coming, not because they were innately more astute than Westerners, but because they had had long experience in trying to conciliate an insatiable aggressor and because they had faith that the conscience and material interest of mankind, in conjunction with the madness of the aggressors, would in due time bring allies to their side. Since the Chinese knew that their war was bound to be long, and realized that they could not win by their own efforts, they saw that coalition was the inescapable price of victory. The leaders, therefore, made their country politically and morally one of the United Nations long before that organization came formally into being.

Two major problems remain even beyond victory—problems which overshadow the events of the period from 1928 to 1946. The first is that of China's relationship to other major Powers; the second is that of the country's internal unity. To attempt to brush aside or minimize them is utter folly. The Chinese are not likely to find the problem of their relations with the Soviet Union, the British Empire, and the United States easy to solve. Questions of regional rights, peripheral and marginal zones, world commerce, relative rights of industry, finance, and world production quotas, world-wide migration, military security, and monetary control are inescapable. It is not to be expected that the Chinese will accept mere national independence unaccompanied by those powers which are necessary to their right to progress. Indeed, the Chinese may on occasion again prove touchy, proud, and even arrogant; their always keen sensitivities may be sharpened by vic-

tory; and the peace of eastern Asia and of the world will depend
upon the justice, breeding, tact, and good humor which the victorious Americans, British, Chinese, and Russians show in their
relationships with one another.

The problem of internal unity is one which the Chinese follow
with avidity. Britons and Americans at times read contemporary
Chinese history as though it dealt with their own nations. They
overlook the facts that Outer Mongolia, a sometime dependency of
China, was completely closed to Chinese officials for years before
the outbreak of hostilities in 1937, and was neutral toward Japan
throughout China's life-and-death struggle; that Chinese central
Asia has often been but uncertainly under central governmental
control; that in the war with Japan certain large armies obeyed
Generalissimo Chiang's commands because he never ordered them
to do anything distasteful to themselves; that throughout the
war a radical, fanatical minority party had its own armed countryside, its own defensive system, its own army *within* Kuomintang-
controlled China; that other military groups were united with the
center only (or at least mainly) for the purpose of fighting the invader; and that at the end of the war the Chinese had ample reason
to suspect that global reformation—especially the thoughts and
actions of certain Americans, British, and Russians—was not yet
so far advanced that China could feel itself immune to private or
covert, if not public, foreign meddling until unity could be implemented, if need be, by force. Under these circumstances the desire
for unity—among large groups of the military and the Kuomintang,
most educated men, and the majority of farmers, shopkeepers, and
workers—takes precedence over social reform or political harmony
purchased at the price of *de facto* division.

In the background of Chinese unification and *étatisation,* it is
possible to note divers patterns which give fairly precise indicia
of the significance of recent events. The elemental materials of politics may be regarded as land, people, doctrine, force, and law. The
first two need not be discussed here, but the developments taking
place in doctrine, military and economic force, and law, including
systematized government, indicate patterns which Westerners as
well as Chinese may find meaningful.

At the time of the founding of the National government, in 1928, all major political factions had shared in the experience of transition from the Great Revolution to nationalism. Within the Kuomintang the deepest fissure lay then, as now, between those who chose to follow ideas and policies leading to rapid and remorseless national unification and those who felt that social and economic reform should be given priority, or who believed that reform alone could achieve the foundation of unity which their antagonists professed to desire.

The Communists, also, were in a state of ferment and disagreement in China and throughout the world. The intellectuals were in opposition, and there were powerful political groups which had not yet outlined a clear doctrinal position.

Kuomintang and government alike were dominated in 1928 by the informal triumvirate of Hu Han-min, Chiang Kai-shek, and Wang Ching-wei, each of whom typified an inner ideological division. On the Right, with Hu, were those whose predilection for a sound and stable, disciplined and powerful national government which should be representative and republican made them suspicious of sudden change which might again permit opportunist agitation from the Left. In the center was Chiang, outstanding in prestige and technical military prowess; but it was momentarily impossible to discover what ideology he and his adherents supported, beyond a forceful pragmatism. At the other pole, with Wang, gathered those party members who sincerely desired immediate democratization and land reform, or who feared a break with the Communists more than the risk of Communist boring from within, together with those erstwhile Communists who placed national unity before Leninism.

So far to the Left as to be officially out of sight were the disciplined Communists who followed the party line, insisting upon radical reforms led by the infinitesimal Chinese proletariat. Other influential personalities held a wide range of opinions, but were not backed by the definite political pressure which supported the triumvirate and the Communist party.

The power of the center, led by Chiang Kai-shek, was increased in 1931, when, as a result of conflict over financial and constitutional questions, Hu Han-min retired and Wang Ching-wei returned from exile to a governmental position. In the same year

Japanese aggression in Manchuria was added to the civil war against the Reds by which the Kuomintang was seeking internal unity. Both crises demanded that zealous, disciplined, and energetic action which was Chiang's forte. To this end the generalissimo urged moral and social reform, epitomized by the New Life Movement, which was formally inaugurated in 1934. A blend of the cardinal Confucian virtues and Protestant Christianity, this was at first a potent ideological weapon.

Japanese aggression increased China's patriotic fervor, but the government, under Chiang and Wang, championed appeasement. The tension created by this divergence between public opinion and official policy exploded in the Sian incident of December, 1936. Under Japanese pressure the friction generated by the direct clash between Chiang's demand for disciplined unity, the demand for popular representation and for resistance to Japan, and the Communist demand for recognition and for political and economic reforms created a political temperature high enough to fuse all three in an unofficial united front. Those who clung to appeasement were isolated, and the door was opened for the exit of Wang Ching-wei. This left Chiang Kai-shek to dominate an apparently united China.

Active in achieving this fusion were unrecognized minor parties, particularly the National Salvationists, whose role was peculiarly ideological since they did not seek power. Putting unity of country first, they acted as an ideological catalyst. The Third party, an organization of former Kuomintang and Communist members, avowedly worked to the same end. Other splinter parties existed, but ideologically they can be classed with the Third party.

Outbreak of the full United Nations war in 1941 affected the Chinese in two contrary ways. On the one hand, civilian and reformist groups were strengthened, since they were not slow to exploit the close Chungking-Washington contact in the hope that, as an ally of the democracies, the National government would develop more liberal policies. On the other hand, the fact that Chungking could turn directly to the West for fiscal and managerial aid and related services made the military more independent than ever of the intellectuals and capitalist-experts to whom formally democratic objectives were of the highest concern. Prospect of large-scale military modernization made the generals less inclined to purchase civilian support at the price of loosening their control over opinion and political action in wartime.

The excessive joy with which the Chinese greeted Japan's final blunder—the psychological mistake of Pearl Harbor—was followed by a period of intense disillusionment as the Chinese observed their outer defenses, particularly Malaya and Burma, falling to the enemy for what many felt to be political reasons. This depression and the suspicion of Anglo-American motives were gradually superseded by a more serene outlook. The ending of extraterritoriality in the treaties signed with China by the United States and Great Britain, in January, 1943, helped confirm the Chinese in their hope that the United Nations system promised an honorably prosperous role for them and their government.

Throughout 1943 Chinese morale was fairly well sustained, but thereafter it went into a slow decline. The domestic armistice between the Kuomintang and the Chinese Communists continued. The small parties had a minor but unterrorized position. Inasmuch as mere survival was the first criterion, there was widespread satisfaction with the immediate situation and a tendency to hold out for victory before risking anything on the hazards of domestic conflict. Even Japan's "too-little-and-too-late," soft policy of giving its puppet, Wang Ching-wei, unprecedented honors and allowing him weapons, including planes—unusual for puppets—did not succeed in shaking the leadership of Chiang and the Kuomintang over the Chinese people. Critics could not suggest any other feasible way of running the government, nor could they adumbrate doctrines better adapted to China's ideological needs. The Kuomintang, like any In group, was subject to merciless diatribes from the Outs, but the latter had no hope of taking over control. Criticism, domestic and foreign, indicated mainly impatience with conditions which might be remedied by victory and unification.

The rising tide of Soviet Union victories in the West and the increasing prospect of Soviet participation in the war against Japan, together with the most serious Chinese losses since 1938, gave new force to this criticism in 1944, as the major group of Outs caught the glimmer of a prospect that in future they might take a large measure of control. This change brought an offer of immediate share in the government to the Communists, who rejected it as inadequate. Even yet, however, in the realm of ideas the contest was between democracy and unity as the primary political value for Unoccupied China.

The prevailing official doctrine consisted of the teachings of Sun Yat-sen—as supplemented by comments of Generalissimo Chiang Kai-shek. The latter sought to combine ideal justice with political horse sense in his emphasis upon the personal and social phases of reform and his avoidance of any widening of the breach between military men and civilian liberals. Chiang's political influence continued to be paramount in National government doctrine. The publication of his *China's Destiny,* touchily patriotic in tone, highlighted his personal appreciation of the unity of China's political and military efforts, which he reiterated in his speeches to the nation.

The generalissimo's patience and sagacity were reflected in his extensive coöperation with the United Nations war effort. Despite numerous peace offers from Japan and personal disagreements with high-ranking American advisers there was no observable shift in China's basic position vis-à-vis its Western allies.

The stability of the country's international course was epitomized in Chiang's solemn assurance to the Thaï people, and thereby to the rest of the world, that China would respect its small neighbors. Inflation, the torture of delay, the agony of false hope, and other adverse factors at times made Chinese leaders sound chauvinistic; but the underlying moderation of Chinese character, the indisputably democratic type of official ideology, and the bitterness of the people against Japan and all it stands for were sufficient guaranties that China, ideologically at least, would keep aligned with the democracies of the world.

⋄ ⋄ ⋄

The Republic of 1928 represented a China just emerging from almost undiluted militarism. Likewise, the succeeding dozen years marked a progress from internecine banditry to honored participation in a world war, and from anarchic manifestations of monarchial greed to the status of a republican nation-state. Throughout there was close correlation between military and political aspects.

Rival military camps developed from the divorce of the Kuomintang and the Communists. (See chap. ix, above.) The latter employed the military devices most readily available for spontaneous mass action, whereas the Kuomintang created a professional army. Each group reflected a political ideal: revolution on the part of the Communists, as opposed to the Kuomintang aim of stabilizing a regime by the imposition of order by experts. Pitted against each other, the two armies constantly perfected their respective methods. Without its rival neither could possibly have grown so rapidly in military stature.

Though diametrically opposed, the two armies were sharply differentiated from the armed hordes of the *tuchün* and other war lords. This was especially true of the Red Army, which did not attempt to copy the organization or tactics of European national armies. The Nationalists compromised with the existing military system; but after a period of testing by fire, under the influence of Chiang Kai-shek's moral, political, and technical ideals, the National Army began to attain a professional morale notably absent in the armies of the *tuchün*. The victory in 1930–1931 over the northern *tuchün* conclusively proved the superiority of the National Army.

This superiority was based on four factors. First, the army was led by a nucleus of professional officers trained in Kuomintang military academies. Second, the army as a whole had a better status in literacy, pay, subsistence, and regularity of control, which gave it greater prestige and self-respect. Third, mechanization and road building gave the army greater mobility than its rivals enjoyed. Last, but perhaps most important, the National Army had a practical monopoly of air power. Aviators and other military technicians were generally recognized as types of scholars worthy of first place in the Chinese social scale.

These advantages were made possible by a relatively large and stable income—which, in turn, required the services of a modern, highly integrated state. The peripheral *tuchün*, therefore, in return for the crumbs which fell from the Nationalists' table, accepted the organizational details and the long-range plans that were proposed by the central government.

The inheritance of these semiautonomous armies, inflated by

the necessity of giving employment to the economically distressed and providing for the exigencies of endemic civil war, reduced the efficiency of the National Army. Nevertheless, it vigorously pursued its policy of creating a nuclear core, especially recruited and equipped, and with intensive political and military training. Formally undistinguished from other units, "Chiang's own" formed a crack unit and was a mass demonstration of China's modernization. Thus the whole military system—the Red Army aside—began to resemble that of modern armies, which exist for defense or aggrandizement of national states.

The Japanese attacked in 1937, at the moment that the National and Red armies had come together in common opposition to external dangers. Japan faced, therefore, both a veteran professional army, taught by German specialists, and a guerrilla force possessed of more practical experience in that art than any other organization. It was a formidable combination.

The first effect of invasion was to enhance the relative power and prestige of the Communists. As the less-prepared party in the struggle, the Chinese had to consider the guerrilla tactics of which the Red troops were masters. The Red Army, then the Eighth Route Army, and later the Eighteenth Army Corps became famous for their heroism. An even greater boon to the Communists was the fact that their tactics and organization were ideally fitted for action in Occupied China. As a result, the Communists, free from all but nominal governmental control, organized the people and directed resistance against Nippon in a large section of the most populous areas of the country—all in the interests of national China, to be sure, but the immediate credit and popular influence were theirs.

A guerrilla leader must utilize popular support. For this reason foreign observers have hailed the Chinese guerrilla as the great democratic force in modern China, often without appreciating the fact that the guerrilla's democracy is a military necessity, irrespective of his political beliefs. The guerrilla areas are training grounds for Chinese democratic action of a populist, or *völkisch*, variety—a fact which is bound to influence postwar Chinese politics.

Japanese aggression also increased the prestige of the National Army, of which the Eighteenth Army Corps is a part only in name.

T. V. SOONG

President of the Executive Yüan

SUN FO
President of the Legislative Yüan

The courageous formal defense of Shanghai, Soochow, and Hankow burnt up the core of the German-trained divisions; the front
about Ichang was finally stabilized; and the successive reverses suffered by Japanese expeditions against Changsha contributed to
popular appreciation of the value of the new-style army, which was
not humiliated until the great Japanese railway campaigns of 1944.
The ability of the National Army to contain the Japanese after
seven months' successive reverses in the first important positional
warfare since 1938, and later to return to the policy of limited
offensive, gave it the chance to redeem its reputation and to restore
to Generalissimo Chiang the prestige sorely needed for domestic
military hegemony. Meanwhile, Chinese successes, with American
training and partial American equipment, in northern Burma,
western Yünnan, and Hunan, served to restore the self-confidence
of National government troops. Transfer of troops to critical fronts
in the interest of national resistance helped to dissolve provincial
loyalties. Friction, ignorance, and inefficiency were not eliminated,
but the central troops became more truly a national Chinese army
than any other in modern times.

The realization, in late 1941, that China was justified in hoping
for help against invasion had the immediate effect of increasing
the prospect of national victory. Though limited by military exigencies and the isolation of the country, the resources of the United
Nations were potentially at the disposal of Chiang Kai-shek. His
troops obtained modern arms to repel the Japanese—a factor which
laid the foundation for preponderance in domestic power during
the postwar era. In consequence, the autonomous Communist army
became increasingly loath to place itself under Chiang's command,
and in 1945–1946 China's military mastery appeared less certainly
assured to the National government than at any time since December 7, 1941. Nevertheless, in prestige and prowess it appeared to
be paramount in the domestic field.

◇ ◇ ◇

China is still passing through the crises of several simultaneous
revolutions—notably the industrial and social revolutions—with a
concomitant shift from quasi-colonial status to that of a well-
rounded national economy. In and after 1842, Western traders

secured a privileged position epitomized by extraterritoriality and the treaty tariffs. Thus screened from Chinese competition and regulation, Westerners introduced the machine to China in order to take advantage of cheap Chinese labor rather than to develop the country's resources. The machine largely ruined Chinese handicrafts without being fully utilized in China's economy. From this fact came, in part, the nationalistic aspirations of the Kuomintang to end the privileged position of foreign economic interests in China—which coincided with the international anti-imperialism of the Comintern.

Communist demands for socialization, however, met with little sympathy in Kuomintang ranks, which were drawn from the merchant class and some gentry. Moreover, the establishment of native capitalism was markedly disapproved by Chinese Communists. As occurred in the military organizations following the violent break of 1927, each party selected that portion of its former joint economic program which was best adapted to its own ideology. True to their mass appeal, Chinese Communists pushed first for agrarian reforms, including redistribution of land. The Kuomintang, with its ideal of nationhood for China, concentrated upon industrialization[3] and better communications.

In and after 1928 the National government secured several noteworthy reforms. One of the most outstanding was the attainment of tariff autonomy, which reflected attempts to create a sound national fiscal system. To achieve such a system the government relied upon the normal economic controls of the modern state, but these, especially the issuance of a national, managed currency, were veritable miracles in China.

Fiscal reforms were paralleled by improved communications. Wire and wireless communications, railways, highways, and airways were created, improved, and extended. Industrialization proceeded less rapidly. A contributing factor was foreign competition. Both Chinese and foreign capitalists were lured by immediate profits into the same coastal industries, and both neglected the development of Chinese internal resources. Difficulties led the government to sponsor directly those industrial installations for which it had immediate need, exactly as it had done with respect to communications. There was a distinct trend toward state capitalism.

Kuomintang economic policies thus displayed a mixture of Hamiltonian and state socialist principles. These pragmatically successful policies contained three sources of danger for the government. First, a clash with the vested interests of foreigners was implicit in the effort to establish Chinese industry. Second, exploitation of the small but strategically placed Chinese proletariat by native capitalists created resentment. Third, the Kuomintang program ignored in large part the chronic peasant distress.

The reforms by which the transition might be made from agricultural to industrial economy infuriated many farmers and laborers. Pressure was increased by the fact that the Chinese Communists were organized and willing to direct this fury in an effective anti-government action. Fortunately, Kuomintang leaders were wise enough to yield when opposition became too bitter. By articulating demands for reforms to which Nationalist officials, for the most part recruited among the landlords, were normally apathetic, Communist agitation sometimes secured redress of the worst grievances and involuntarily acted as a safety valve for the body politic.

The threat to foreign economic privilege finally elicited a direct counterchallenge from Japan. Of all the foreign Powers with interests in China, Japan was the most deeply committed. Moreover, as China's nearest powerful neighbor, it was the most directly threatened by competition with a modernized nation. Efforts to prevent this eventuality caused spontaneous retaliatory boycotts among the Chinese and thereby transformed a future threat into an immediate irritation. When economic and political pressure proved inadequate, Japan resorted to military aggression.

Invasion in 1937 and later years destroyed the political base of the coastal capitalists, both native and alien, and made the inland development of China vitally important. Thus occurred in China, through war, what the Soviet Union accomplished through planned economic strategy, both before and after the outbreak of war: industry was moved from accessible, world-communicating ports and areas to the hinterland. This partially rounded out the national economy. Simultaneously, loss of power by independent private enterprises facilitated state socialist tendencies, which were controlled by the Kuomintang or the National Army. Thus the economy became more and more like that of contemporary Germany or England: which of these it would eventually resemble would be decided not by technical and economic but by ideological pressures. If the existing power group found itself constantly challenged and in danger of subversion from the Left—whether from within China, from the Western democracies, or from Soviet power,—the tendency might be to keep the economy strictly under wartime control and to resist a democratization which might open up new economic forces against the prevailing authority. Thus the direction of China's modernization is likely to depend on the internal ideological stresses of power, on the character of inter–United Nations financing, and on the opportunities for profit and power which may be open to postwar free capital and postwar coöperative labor, as against government-owned or -managed syndicates.

The much-publicized Chinese industrial coöperatives may indicate the direction of certain future developments; but the prosperity of China depends not so much on the forms of control of industry, or even upon industry itself, as upon solution of the Chinese agrarian problem and attainment of the politico-economic climate of peace. The surrender of Japan in 1945 potentially opened the way to Chinese prosperity. It also placed the world's most tragic economic problems in the laps of Chungking, Washington, and London.   ◇   ◇   ◇

After the demise of its Hankow rival in the summer of 1927, the most formidable problem which faced the Nanking regime was the formalization of its rule. Following the period of operating under the Organic Law, Nanking, in 1931, adopted a Provisional Constitution, which was intended to cover a preliminary five-year period of political tutelage. But the Organic Law and the Provisional Constitution continued to function throughout the war as the basis of government in Unoccupied Kuomintang China.

Theoretically less admirable than earlier, ineffective constitutions, these fundamental laws possess the merit of attempting to make their provisions correspond to actual practice. This governmental structure is characterized by (1) explicit subordination of the government to the party, (2) concentration of power in the supreme agencies, (3) fivefold division of power and function, and (4) lack of provision for a representative assembly.

Under the tutelage of Soviet advisers (1923–1927) the government was a mere tool of the party; but, even so, it had definite power. Following Dr. Sun's teaching, and expecting the Kuomintang to guide the country's first steps in popular government, the Kuomintang-controlled National People's Convention wrote into the constitution a unique provision making the Kuomintang superior to the National government.

The party organs to which the determination of national policy was thus formally entrusted were the Party Congress and its Central Executive Committee. Inasmuch as the Party Congress meets irregularly at long intervals (six sessions in two decades), whereas the plenary sessions of the Central Executive Committee are held regularly every six months or oftener—and are by far the best-established political process in the Chinese state—the latter constitute the real nexus of political power. To provide continuous exercise of the party's sovereign power over the government, the Central Executive Committee elected a Central Political Council. Though not concerned with administrative details, this council for a time had power to decide basic principles of legislation, execute governmental policies, and appoint and dismiss government officials. In 1938, however, another party agency, the Supreme National Defense Council, replaced the Central Political Council.

Prior to 1931 the Council of State, the supreme governmental body, served as chief control agency. Under the Provisional Constitution, however, its function became primarily that of transmitting instructions of the Central Political Council as orders to the appropriate governmental agency. The chairman of the Council of State is the titular head of the Chinese state. This post Chiang Kai-shek assumed in August, 1943, upon the death of the former incumbent, Lin Sen. The president of the National government and the Council of State are important only for ceremonial functions.

In the five-power constitution two essentially Chinese powers, examination and control, are added to the familiar three of the West: legislative, executive, and judicial. The National government includes a yüan (board) for each of the five. The two first-mentioned powers, according to Sun Yat-sen's theory, are to enable the bureaucracy to keep itself clean, efficient, and high-minded by means of an all-inclusive civil service (examination) and an institutionalized impeaching, auditing, and inspecting power (control). Of the five, the Executive Yüan is the real governing agent. It includes thirteen ministries and, as consultative and unifying agency for the entire executive, resembles a cabinet. Its president, Chiang Kai-shek, is the highest executive officer of the government.

The constellation of powers about the Executive Yüan has eclipsed the other boards. The issuance of ordinances by the Executive Yüan has relegated the Legislative Yüan to the drafting of a permanent constitution and the codification of administrative law. Through its power to appoint and dismiss higher officials the Executive Yüan also by-passes the Examination and Control Yüan. These continue to function in civil service reform, inspection, and auditing, but only as secondary agencies. The Judicial Yüan serves as the administrative staff agency for the actual prosecuting and judicial bodies, though it does make some effort to unify judicial procedure and interpretation of laws and orders.

The fact that this highly departmentalized bureaucracy has survived the impact of total war without major change testifies to its fundamental soundness. At the apex of the National government only two changes have been made in the arcanum of power. Neither implies radical change from prewar practice. Two changes immediately below the apex of government have been more significant shifts in the tenure of power. All sprang from the Emergency Party Congress of 1938.

By the first, Chiang Kai-shek was elected to the newly created post of Tsung-ts'ai (Chief) with all the powers originally held by the Tsung-li (Leader), a title held in perpetuity by Sun Yat-sen. As Tsung-ts'ai, Chiang is chairman of the Party Congress and of its Central Executive Committee, with a veto over the acts of both bodies. Actually, this was a recognition and regularization of Chiang's position rather than a substantive addition to his power.

By the second change the Supreme National Defense Council, till then the National Defense Council, replaced the Central Political Council. More significant was a further modification permitting this body to issue direct commands to any party, government, or military organ. So far as it exercises this right the Supreme National Defense Council is not merely the guiding authority over government—it *is* the government. Some facts are still hidden by military secrecy, but it is known that Chiang Kai-shek is chairman and that heads of all ranking party, government, and military organs are members ex officio. This constituency makes the highest political agency of Kuomintang China representative of more than the party, for some of these figures (despite nominal Kuomintang membership) are independent. Furthermore, it is believed that Chiang does not act on basic issues without consulting it.

At the next lower level of government the Military Affairs Commission was inflated almost beyond recognition when it was charged with the military prosecution of the war. Such a commission has existed in some form ever since the Great Revolution, but it was to have been absorbed in the Ministry of War. Now that ministry is but an adjunct of the commission which is headed by Generalissimo Chiang; it consists of seven or nine other key military officers designated by the Supreme National Defense Council. In addition to supervision of the armies, the commission deals with war work of all kinds, including social work, relief, education, propaganda, espionage, many economic activities, and the promotion of social reform. It has become almost a third government parallel to party and government structures.

At the same level of government the Emergency Party Congress of 1938 also created a representative assembly, the People's Political Council. It was provided that government and party bodies for the respective areas should nominate the representatives for geographic regions, whereas the Supreme National Defense Council should nominate the representatives for cultural, professional, and economic bodies. The final election was reserved to the Kuomintang Central Executive Committee. The People's Political Council is a deliberative advisory body to which the government is bound, except in emergencies, to submit all important measures before they are put into effect. Moreover, the council has the right to demand and hear reports from the yüan and ministries, and to interpellate officers of state. Because Kuomintang leaders were wise enough to select truly representative figures from other factions, this council is the nearest to representative government that China has ever known. It has obtained important concrete improvements in government and party through its criticism and airing of issues.

The organization of the National government clearly sets forth certain general tendencies in Chinese politics. The most important of these, the basic viability of the five-power system, was evidenced by the ability of that system to conduct modern warfare. The most sincere testimony to the fundamental position which that system occupies in modern China is the fact that the Japanese installed a duplicate at Nanking, under Wang Ching-wei and his successors.

Nevertheless, one may discern a tendency toward trifurcation of power in Chungking. Technically, the government receives all its power from the Kuomintang, but years of successful peacetime administration lodged a degree of power in the hands of the bureaucracy and the exigencies of war increased the weight of the army in the councils of state. But though party, government (bureaucracy), and army may at times appear to be rivals, they are not mutually hostile. Their respective personnel overlap to a high degree. According to their common ideology, both party and army play temporary roles, after which they will surrender power to the civil government.

Nevertheless, delay in the democratization of China is strengthened by rivalry between the three power groups. This delay is continually highlighted because all groups agree that democracy is their eventual objective and the Leftist liberal opposition keeps demanding more rapid progress in this direction. The People's Political Council is steadily becoming more prominent, but the opposition's criticism emphasizes the gap between political realities and the political ideal. The disparity is further emphasized by the continual postponement of the ratification of the Draft Permanent Constitution. This document was first published in 1936; its ratification was definitely arranged for in 1937 and again in 1940, only to be postponed to the war's end because of the military situation. Such vacillation led many to question the sincerity of the Kuomintang and its government in pledging to introduce democracy. However, at the Party Congress in May, 1945, Generalissimo Chiang promised that a national assembly would meet in November to adopt and promulgate a constitution under which all political parties would have legal status and enjoy equality. A proposal was made, also, for the immediate creation of a wartime political council within the Executive Yüan on which other parties, including the Communists, would have representation. (See chap. xi.)

Those who fear an illiberal trend in the Chinese government are further disturbed by the drift toward centralization which has been noted in both economic and military spheres. It is prominent in purely intragovernmental affairs, also, and in the increasing number of posts held by Chiang Kai-shek. As Tsung-ts'ai, Chiang is head of the Kuomintang; as president of the National government he is head of the state; as president of the Executive Yüan he is the chief bureaucrat; as chairman of the Military Affairs Commission he is generalissimo. Nor does this exhaust his titles.

Because of the military background and preoccupation of so many Chinese officials, the government is predisposed to apply the military "chain of command" to civil government. Chiang himself is zealously devoted to the virtues of loyalty and discipline. Meanwhile, as the war dragged on, tensions increased, and official tolerance of divergent behavior or opinion correspondingly decreased. In spite of their formal ideal of complete popular control, the Chinese are faced with the practical problem of the minimum limits of democratic toleration. Nevertheless, it is beyond question that a democratic ideology reigns supreme in the field of doctrine. No one proposes monarchy, separatism, or permanent dictatorship. Differences of opinion are solely with respect to how and when. This situation, in conjunction with the fact that China's future depends upon that of the great democracies, makes democracy an inescapable attribute of Chinese government—unless democracy should become as discredited in the future as monarchy is today.

Nationalization, centralization, bureaucratization, a slow but basic democratization, and the emergence of a half-Western nation-state: these characterize the progress of Chinese polity since 1928. The growth in stature of the National government is witnessed by the place taken by China among the United Nations. As a member of the Pacific War Council (the Allied Far East Military Council, formed in Chungking, was their first formal international military agency), as the signator of a master lend-lease agreement, as co-sponsor of the United Nations Conference on International Organization, as one of the major belligerents, and accepted as one of the future's "Big Five," the Chinese National government is today one of the principal characters on the international stage.

The present phase of Chinese affairs shows every indication of indefinite continuation of much the same problems and issues. With victory over Japan the strains of the war years became increasingly evident. The forces which were in abeyance owing to the pressure of war from the outside again made themselves felt. The leadership of Communist Yenan possessed popularity and skill which could be opposed only if they were matched. Reoccupation of formerly Japanese-controlled areas by Nationalists and by Communists, with the resulting attempted settlement of questions brought up by dissolution of the Japanese puppet regime, involved political issues and events of the highest magnitude. There is no time limit on the settlement of China's destiny. The crisis, already decades long, may remain and seem perpetual.

Broadly considered, nonetheless, the history of China will be, for a time at least, that of the United Nations world to a far more definite degree than the history of America, Russia, or Britain. China will be the prime beneficiary of the United Nations system— if the system works. International Soviet-American understanding has become the *sine qua non* of China's domestic tranquillity. The Chinese may be willing to pay the price of democracy everywhere; Nationalists and Communists may accept current compromises and relinquish ideal ends and violent means where these endanger the preservation of benefits already attained. But this will occur only if the United Nations system is global in effect and creates a settlement which satisfies all the major Powers. Then, perhaps, the constitutional and political anomalies of the Chinese will help them to serve as a bridge between the Western democracies, on the one hand, and the postwar political world of an increasingly liberated Asia and of the Soviet Union, on the other.

This statement presupposes that the United Nations can and will set up an international system strong enough to support the requirements of good faith, of the living together of peoples, and of military security. If the United Nations fail, they will have destroyed the Axis system only to find that *three* worlds are potentially, if not actually, in conflict. The *ecumene* (the world of the political and ideological "we-group") of the Axis has been destroyed. The *ecumenes* of the Western democracies and of the Soviet Union, not always in harmony, have triumphed without consolidating. China is a potential third *ecumene* to be reckoned with among the survivors. If the United Nations system becomes an *ecumene,* and all mankind is encompassed by the single system of reciprocal understanding which is necessary to maintain both military security and economic prosperity, China may be the central pivot—again the Middle State, the neutral ground of most understanding—of such a system, equally respected by all, equally friendly to all partners, an ally, a supplier, and a market to its co-working and truly co-prospering nations.

But if a shortsighted "realistic" view of immediate gains should lead the world again to disaster, if Russia and the Western democracies remain separate and hostile in spirit, if both Russia and the Western democracies connive at the hindrance, or attempted subjection, of China, the recent political and military history of that country suggests that the Chinese may have the courage and skill to create a world for themselves, and to resist incorporation into any narrowly Soviet or narrowly Anglo-American system. This long-range choice confronts the nations of today: world unity or world schism. The Chinese have demonstrated their preference for world unity, but in that choice, which can be made only partly by themselves, they will choose for the new world: central pivot or third *ecumene.*

CHAPTER XI

The Social Revolution

BY AGNES SMEDLEY

The masses of men are not born with saddles on their backs, and a chosen few booted and spurred to ride them legitimately, by the grace of God. THOMAS JEFFERSON

THE TRANSFORMATIONS taking place within China are an integral part of global, social-revolutionary change. They are as significant as those which caused the fall of Rome, or the American and the French revolutions, which constituted the final chapter in the rise of the middle class to power.

Like their prototypes in capitalist democracies, conservative elements in China condemn social-revolutionary changes as due to evil men, and resent the invocation of the name or writings of Sun Yat-sen on behalf of basic changes in property relationships. Dr. Sun and his followers, nevertheless, constituted definite, if at times confused, expression of one aspect of the social revolution. Since Sun's death in 1925 some of his more conservative followers have tried to interpret his writings to suit their personal interests and thereby to hold back tides uncontrollable as those of the sea. The only result has been to unleash class hatred, the end of which is not yet in sight.

For half a century the weak middle class of China has been struggling against the Manchu dynasty and its aftermath, and against foreign attempts to dismember and (or) control China. The T'ai-p'ing rebellion (*ca.* 1850–1864), the Boxer rebellion (1900), the Revolution of 1911–1912, and many smaller uprisings foreshadowed the present social revolution. The T'ai-p'ing rebellion greatly influenced Dr. Sun's generation. Folk songs and tales are still current in praise of T'ai-p'ing attempts to burn title deeds and mortgages and to divide the land among the peasants.

In his formative years Sun was affected also by the conflicting principles of British and American capitalist democracy, the latter in particular. In his later years the founder of the Republic came under the sway of Marxian ideas emanating from Soviet Russia. He was branded first as a traitor by the Manchus, and later as a visionary and troublemaker by many foreigners in China. Like all revolutionaries, he was, indeed, a troublemaker for the forces of reaction and oppression. The Revolution of 1911–1912 which he instigated, and the Republic which he and his followers helped to found, had to struggle for years against internal reaction and decay and external interference.

The unilateral treaties imposed on China, in and after 1842, were part of an attempt, conscious and unconscious, to harness China to the cart of imperialism. Many of China's natural resources and its customs service gradually fell under foreign control and were used to a considerable extent for the benefit of aliens. Foreign Powers gained special privileges, including extraterritorial rights, by a "gunboat policy." Heavy indemnities imposed upon the country in the nineteenth century and following the Boxer uprising, many forced loans thereafter, and the support of war lords by various foreign Powers, in conjunction with innumerable domestic factors, drove China deeper into poverty and impotence. Mainly on account of the unequal treaties, Chinese industry and trade developed slowly and had difficulty in competing with foreign trade even within China itself. Recent Chinese surveys have shown that 75 per cent of manufactured goods in even the most remote villages were of foreign origin. Under these circumstances social-revolutionary ideas naturally developed.

Americans do not like to think that their government and countrymen had anything to do with such conditions; they believe that the United States has consistently been "China's friend." They like to think that the open-door policy prevented China from dismemberment and subjection, that the Washington government helped China by returning part of its share of the Boxer indemnity to found a college in China and to send Chinese students to this country to be educated in "American ideas and ideals." It is true that American policies exercised a slightly alleviating effect upon foreign aggression. Basically, however, the open-door policy was an instrument by which American business interests claimed the right to an equal share in the wealth of China along with other foreign nationals. Educating the Chinese at home and abroad was a good thing, indeed, in the days when Americans themselves did not shrink from new ideas. But some Chinese declare that American philanthropy has been aimed at producing imitation Americans to serve American interests instead of educating Chinese as patriots who will first of all serve their own country.

Christian missionaries, it is claimed, have accomplished great good in China by advocating social reforms and introducing modern science. This they have done—but they have, in a variety of ways and for the most part unintentionally, exacted their price. Preceding and in the course of the Boxer year many missionaries were attacked and injured or killed, partly because of their modern or revolutionary ideas, but particularly because they and their converts were linked, in the minds of considerable numbers of Chinese, with foreign aggression, and, living in the interior, were vulnerable, as residents of the Treaty Ports were not.

In the past some foreigners considered China's poverty and backwardness a proof of the inferiority of all classes of Chinese. Foreigners talked of the sanctity of foreign lives and property, but rarely of the sanctity of Chinese lives and property. Not only were the Chinese labor, peasant, and student movements regarded as a menace, but ordinary nationalism was regarded in the same light. Students, as exponents of the spirit of revolt, were especially suspect; certain Japanese expressed the general nonmissionary foreign attitude by declaring that the outlook of students was characterized by "ignorance and arrogance." The words "mob" and "riot" were often used to describe meetings of the people. Also, English-speaking Chinese—and there are millions of them—at times used these words without realizing their connotations.

The Russian Revolution opened a new era in history and began to work incalculable change on the Chinese mind. It proclaimed the rights of subject nations and peoples to independence, sovereignty, and racial equality. It heralded the dispossessed classes as the source of a power destined to give birth to a new social order. Some Occidental writers branded the Soviet Union as "the enemy within the gates of the white world." They raised the old cry of the "yellow peril," but meanwhile ignored the "white disaster" which for centuries had helped to keep a billion Asians in inferior positions, poverty, and servitude.

Dr. Sun sent many of his followers to the Soviet Union to study. Thousands of youths, mostly poor intellectuals, streamed to Moscow to study Marxism and the technique of revolutionary struggle. A number of these men and women returned to found the Kung-chantang, the Chinese Communist party, in 1919, to organize labor unions and peasant leagues, and to form study classes for workers and peasants. The first unions and study groups were formed among railway men, textile workers, and seamen. Student unions, uniting in common action with labor unions, became powerful.

It is at this point that the development of the mass movement in China differs from the labor movement in Western countries. From its inception the Chinese mass movement was political and was led by Chinese Communists. It has followed two major lines of thought and action: struggle against foreign control, and struggle for an agrarian revolution to eliminate feudal or semifeudal agrarian conditions and introduce democratic practices. Reactionaries, native and foreign, were horrified at the demands of labor unions for shorter hours and higher wages, for freedom of speech, press, and assembly, and for the right to strike. Even at present there are Americans as well as Europeans who ask if anyone is foolish enough to believe that Chinese coolies should have the right to vote. Similar questions were hurled at Thomas Jefferson.

In 1924 Dr. Sun, with the aid of military and political advisers from the Soviet Union, reorganized the Kuomintang (guo-min-dang), the Nationalist party. Thereafter, Communists were admitted to membership. This reorganization constituted a social-revolutionary action: the Kuomintang, hitherto led by the middle and upper classes, now represented the masses as well. More than 85 per cent of China's population is made up of workers and peasants; their entrance into the party transformed it into a mass revolutionary organization of limitless potentiality. The Kuomintang, however, did not "go Communist," although some foreigners so branded it and until 1927 often referred to the national revolutionary movement as a "Red" movement.

Dr. Sun died in March, 1925, soon after the reorganization of his party. Thereupon many of his old followers began to organize cliques to meet the new mass menace to their former privileges and power. Although serious breaches took place within revolutionary ranks, they were patched up long enough to enable the new southern army to begin its northern expedition in 1926. This swept all before it in the march from Canton to the Yangtze. Labor unions and the new peasant leagues welcomed the advancing Nationalist forces with general strikes. Certain foreign groups, particularly British and Japanese, countered with violence in which numbers of Chinese were killed, and again it looked as though there might be large-scale foreign intervention against revolutionary upheaval.

The Communist-organized peasant leagues were inspired by Dr. Sun's advocacy of land reform. He had urged that rent be reduced by 25 per cent. Peasants had been paying 50 per cent of their crop in rent, much as do American white and Negro sharecroppers in the South. Chinese peasants also were burdened by heavy debts to landlords who were simultaneously landowners, officials, usurers, judge, and jury. But many officers in the Chinese revolutionary army—the sons of landlords or factory owners—thought the mass movement should be directed only against foreign imperialism.

These issues resulted, in 1927, in a twofold split in national revolutionary ranks: in the interior, the poorer fought the more prosperous peasants; in Shanghai, stronghold of imperialism and citadel of Chinese industry, trade, and banking, part of the laborers struck against their employers, defeated the local mercenaries of the war lords, and opened the city to the revolutionary army.

Certain Chinese businessmen, bankers, factory owners, and army commanders demanded that the Shanghai workers disarm and return to their factories. Various foreign business interests threatened armed intervention. But the workers refused to lay down their arms. General Chiang Kai-shek, commander of the revolutionary army, cast the die on April 12, 1927, by beginning a "purge of Communists." Many Shanghai workers and some students were killed. The gates of the foreign concessions were opened and hordes of armed gangsters were allowed to attack the strikers.

A group of conservatives and semiconservatives now formed a government in Nanking to rival that previously established in Hankow by the Communists and Left-wing Kuomintang. Chiang's government was soon recognized by the Powers—except for the Soviet Union—as the legal government of China. The Nanking government broke off relations with the Soviets and drove their advisers from the country. Several Soviet consular officials were killed. This was applauded by some foreigners, who then used such events to prove that the Powers could not afford to abolish extraterritorial rights. Foreign and native police in Shanghai hunted down Chinese revolutionaries and surrendered them to the Chinese authorities to be killed or imprisoned.

At the time of this purge Mrs. Sun Yat-sen, with a large number of middle-class Chinese revolutionaries who still held to the national united front, fled to Europe. Mrs. Sun refuses to allow her name to be used by the Kuomintang because, as she has publicly stated, it wages war on the poor.

The National government at Nanking undertook to industrialize and modernize the country on a capitalist basis. It campaigned against the unilateral treaties and extraterritoriality—and got nowhere. Foreigners tried to use the new government for their own interests—and they got somewhere. American financial advisers and German military advisers became attached to the National government. A British subject, Sir Frederick Whyte, acted as adviser to the Ministry of Foreign Affairs. Soon thereafter, when Generalissimo Chiang was baptized, various foreign missionaries swung into line to excuse and support almost everything the government did.

When, in 1927, the terror against the masses swept like wildfire through the country, units of the revolutionary army, some of whose leaders were Communists, revolted in Nanchang and Hankow. The rebel Kuomintang troops tried to fight their way back to Canton, which they hoped to transform into a new mass revolutionary base, but they were defeated and almost decimated in a running fight across southern China. General Chu Teh (ju de), one of their leaders who had become a Communist, gathered the survivors and led them into the mountains of Kiangsi (jiang-si), where they were joined by Mao Tze-tung (dze-dung), a leader of thousands of peasant troops. Other Kuomintang troops joined by battalions and regiments, and a peasant revolution began on a gigantic scale. Some two years later this revolutionary army was called the Chinese Workers and Peasants Red Army, with General Chu Teh as supreme military commander and Mao Tze-tung as supreme political director.

The political system of the Chinese Red Army had been introduced into the southern revolutionary army at the suggestion of Soviet political and military advisers, who had observed its effectiveness in the Soviet Red Army in educating troops called upon to fight not merely for military objectives but for a new social system. The precursors of these political leaders were Cromwell's Agitators, who made of the Ironsides that unconquerable instrument, a thinking army. After the "purge of Communists" began, the Kuomintang abolished the political system in its army since its troops thereafter were called upon to fight not for a new social system but for the old.

In the years following 1927 the soil of China was soaked in the blood of the people—blood which was shed by those who advocated and by those who opposed the Communist cause. Few Chinese families remained unaffected by the revolutionary movement. Landlords, scholars, and high government officials were always trying to save some son or daughter accused of communism and condemned to die.

Five great military campaigns were waged by the Kuomintang Nanking government against the new Red Army of Workers and Peasants. Yet this badly armed remnant eventually grew into a powerful force. Its strength was based upon political training and the system of guerrilla warfare which of necessity it developed into a military science. Red Army troops were imbued with the conviction that they were the people's army of liberation. When harvest uprisings were defeated by armed landlords, militia, and "peace preservation" corps, the peasants poured in countless small streams to the Red Army. Some Kuomintang units sent to suppress the "thinking army" mutinied and joined it.

In the fifth and last campaign—prior to the "Long March"—of the Kuomintang against the Chinese Red Army the latter suffered tremendous losses when it was encircled by a million troops. The strategy of this campaign was formulated not by the Chinese but by a German *Reichswehr* officer, General von Seeckt, head of the German military mission to the Chinese government at that time, and later one of Hitler's henchmen.

In the course of this struggle much missionary and other foreign as well as Chinese property was destroyed. When eleven missionaries were killed, tremendous propaganda on their behalf was put forth in the Treaty Ports and in Western countries. The Red Army charged that missionaries and native Christians were connected with imperialism and acted as spies for foreign Powers. Some doubtless did, and a few engaged in propaganda activities in conjunction with the Kuomintang armies. While it protested against the killing of foreign missionaries and their converts, the foreign press manifested less indignation over the killing of hundreds of thousands of Chinese in both camps.

The Red Army, though defeated, could not be broken. The system it had introduced in great areas under its control took root. The Communists built schools, hospitals, small arsenals, and agrarian institutions. They published newspapers and textbooks and founded theaters and clubs. They introduced suffrage for workers and peasants over eighteen years of age. After extensive educational campaigns, elections were held to soviets, or councils. Traffic in opium was made a crime punishable by death.

It is notable that the Communists did not nationalize the land in the areas they controlled. Instead, they confiscated it and divided it among the peasants, much as their predecessors had done in earlier revolutionary periods. (See chap. vii, above.) But, unlike them, Chinese Communists, after dividing the land, did not merely wait for history to run the vicious circle of past ages—which would eventuate in violent revolutions against another landed gentry. Their goal was a coöperative, or socialist, form of society in which the means of life would be owned and managed for the welfare of all. To this end, consumers' and farmers' coöperatives were organized, and pools of agricultural implements and draft animals, on which all peasants could draw, were provided. Peasants and troops in large areas banded together to help till the soil and harvest the crops. Never as individualistic as Western farmers, the Chinese take naturally to such methods.

Yet, to the owning classes of China and to non-Russian foreign nationals and governments, these concepts and methods served as danger signals. Private property—which most Westerners are taught to regard as sacred—was involved, and this terrified the owning classes. But it was mass coöperation which gave the Chinese Red Army the stamina to survive the five campaigns directed against it by Generalissimo Chiang between 1928 and 1934 and the years of Japanese invasion which followed.

Defeated but not annihilated in Kiangsi in 1934, the Communist forces broke through a powerful blockade to begin that "Long March" which became an epic not alone of Chinese but of world military history. Their objects were to save a nucleus for the spreading of Red doctrines to regions yet untouched and to come into direct conflict with the Japanese invaders then occupying vast areas of the country. The Communists fought their way across the face of western China. They crossed rivers and mountain ranges and pressed into Tibet; enemy troops converged against them from every direction. Nearly two years later they emerged in the far northwest, where Red Army forces from other regions joined them.

Civil war continued in new territory. The Nanking (nan-jing) Kuomintang National government, practically ignoring the Japanese occupation of one province after another, continued to hope that the Red forces could be annihilated. In late 1936 Generalissimo Chiang journeyed to Sian in Shensi for an anti-Red military conference. There, on December 12, he was captured by generals under his own command, who refused to continue civil war while the Japanese pressed ever deeper into the country. Leaders of the Red Army were flown to Sian. The world was told that Chiang had been killed and that red flags flew over the walls of the ancient city. Meanwhile, plans were being laid for the termination of civil war and the formation of a united front against Japan. Then Generalissimo Chiang was released and flown back to his capital.

The cessation of civil war and the formation of a united front were great blows to the Japanese, who, throughout the Republican era, had utilized internal conflict to transform Manchuria and northern China into bases for the conquest of all China and the Far East. To consolidate the national front the Communists agreed to desist from confiscation and division of land and formation of class soviets; to change the name of the Red Army to Eighth Route

Army, and place it under the general command of the National Military Council of the government. They refused, however, to surrender command of their army or give up control over its political system. They called this system their "life line" because it prevented the development of militarism and maintained the army as an educated, social-revolutionary force.

In return for making such concessions the Communists demanded that the Kuomintang government make immediate preparations for armed resistance to Japanese aggression, release all political prisoners except Japanese agents, liberate antifascist organizations, which until then had been officially banned, and introduce democracy so that the people might have a voice in the government that ruled them.

The demand for democracy caused a deadlock which was maintained throughout the war period. Some demands were granted, including the release of most political prisoners. Among them were seven leaders of the democratic National Salvation Association who had been imprisoned for advocating conclusion of civil war and commencement of armed resistance to the Japanese.

Negotiations for incorporating the Red Army into the National Army dragged on for months. Not until September 10, 1937, was this achieved and the name of the Red Army officially changed to Eighth Route Army. A few months later it was renamed Eighteenth Group Army. Branches of the old Red Army, which had been left south of the Yangtze to continue the revolutionary struggle, were permitted, in April, 1938, to reorganize as the guerrilla New Fourth Army. Their theater of operation was along the Japanese-occupied territory in the lower Yangtze Valley.

When the Japanese saw that civil war had terminated and that the nation was united, they struck on July 7, 1937, and actual, if not technical, war began. The northern Nationalist Twenty-ninth Army began fighting around Peiping, but it was ten days before the Chinese government at Nanking made up its mind to fight.

In the course of these events the writer was with the Chinese Red Army, having gone to observe its techniques in January, 1937. Some of its units had but recently emerged from the Long March, during which tens of thousands of marchers and their opponents had been killed or had died of hunger, cold, and exhaustion. The survivors were inadequately clothed and fed, and there was a good deal of sickness. The Red Army lacked qualified doctors and medical supplies. Despite such difficulties the veterans of a thousand battles were physically tough and, what was of greater importance, were imbued with boundless enthusiasm. They were filled with a conviction that China was entering upon a new era of liberation and that they themselves were the advance guard in a revolution of the common people.

The Red Army is the most literate and best informed of all Chinese military forces in regard to national and international developments. The political directors in its ranks, many of them men and women of high educational attainment, had the duty of educating the troops. The directors, but not all the troops, were Communists, since party affiliation was not compulsory. The soldiers were informed of the rise of Hitler, the Italian conquest of Abyssinia, and the meaning of the German-Italian fascist war on the Spanish Republic. To these soldiers fascism appeared the last desperate effort of the owning classes to destroy parliamentary democratic institutions in an attempt to prevent the final victory of the common people of all countries. Such convictions had given them what John Brown in his day had called "an armor against affliction."

From the moment in December, 1936, that civil war was ended by the capture of Generalissimo Chiang in Sian, and while negotiations were secretly proceeding for the formation of the national united front, the army began intensive ideological retraining and military reorganization for the national war of liberation against the Japanese. Thousands of workers, students, and other intellectuals made their way to the Red Army from every part of China, either to join as fighters or to study in Kangda (Resistance University), the nonparty school, Shanpei, or the newly organized Lü Hsün Art Academy, at Yenan in northern Shensi. Peasant volunteers for the fighting units were so numerous that the army could not provide uniforms for all.

After incorporating the Red Army as the Eighth Route Army on September 10, 1937, the National government provided it with money and ammunition—but not with new uniforms or new guns. Wearing their Red Army caps with the red star gleaming, the troops immediately crossed the Yellow River and began forced marches to reach the rear of the advancing Japanese columns, which were now scattering the poorly equipped but ferociously fighting regular armies like chaff from a threshing floor.

The 115th Division of the Eighth Route Army reached the Wutai Mountains of northeastern Shansi in late September; it split up and deployed its units over a great area in the rear and on the flanks of the Japanese and began a battle which culminated, on September 25, in the victory of P'inghsingkuan, a pass near the Great Wall. In this battle the Eighth Route Army shattered the powerful Itagaki division, wiping out an entire brigade of three thousand men and capturing invaluable documents, maps, battle orders, arms, ammunition, food, medical supplies, and even the divisional banner presented by Premier Konoye.

This first Chinese victory was obtained when the people and armies of the north had all but lost confidence in their ability to defeat the Japanese. It was of tremendous significance in setting an example of the kind of military-political tactics necessary for success against a powerfully equipped enemy.

The Eighth Route Army followed up the victory of P'inghsing-kuan with a long succession of lesser ones. It began the recovery of a large area in the rear of the main Japanese lines. On January 10, 1938, seven northern cities were recaptured and hundreds of miles of railway were destroyed. Replenishing its losses from the volunteers who poured in, the army established its first guerrilla base in the Wutai Mountains. Here was formed the first regional government—known as the Shansi-Hopei-Chahar border government—which the National government recognized as the equivalent of a provincial government.

The army sent political workers throughout the north to organize and train the civilian population in anti-Japanese associations of peasants, workers, youth, women, and children. These activities aroused anew the darkest fears of the ruling classes, who had hoped that the Eighth Route Army would be transformed into a mere military instrument for killing Japanese—after which the landlords and other gentry could return to their old haunts.

The Eighth Route Army, however, accepted—and practiced—the Three People's Principles of Sun Yat-sen, which aim not only at national independence but at democracy and improvement of living conditions. The civilian organizations in the north constituted one of the chief means by which, for the first time, Sun's principles were effectively implemented. In fact, the army was convinced that only as the whole people were drawn into the war could China win final victory.

But to draw in the masses necessitated giving them a cause and a goal worth fighting and dying for. Accordingly, special schools were set up to train local leaders for the people's organizations. In the guerrilla base in the Wutai Mountains, and later in five other guerrilla bases in recovered areas, military-political training schools were established for extensive training of military and political cadres.

Local self-defense corps of older men were organized in every village, and a volunteer people's militia of able-bodied men from sixteen to fifty was built up. These organizations did not ordinarily engage in military operations beyond their village or hsien (county). They guarded their own regions and in times of battle acted as auxiliaries of the Eighth Route Army.

According to a report published in July, 1942, there were more than ten million members in civilian organizations and about eight million in local militia. Membership in local self-defense corps was virtually compulsory. These corps were responsible for observation of Japanese movements and for passport control designed to prevent the infiltration of Japanese agents. Women and children in the people's organizations served as passport inspectors in the more thickly settled regions. Females, in particular, were drawn into the network of industrial coöperatives which spread throughout the liberated areas. They manufactured all the cloth used by the army and the civilian population, and made cloth shoes for the soldiers.

Miners, railway workers, and engineers established small foundries in each hsien to teach the people's militia iron founding and the manufacture of ammunition. The militia were armed with old guns or spears and large swords, but their main weapons were hand grenades and land mines. Special training schools taught guerrilla tactics and methods of demolition, destruction of enemy communication lines, current events, and political science.

A primary school system was fairly well established in the liberated areas, as were high and normal schools wherever possible. There was one university. In the Shansi-Hopei-Chahar border region a school for the training of mass-movement local leaders enrolled eight hundred students in 1942. Great emphasis was laid on the eradication of adult illiteracy; schools for this purpose functioned in winter, when there was little farm work to do. In the areas west of the Peiping-Hankow railway 300,000 adults learned to read and write, with 1,200 characters as the standard of literacy.

A few qualified Chinese and foreign doctors found their way to the Eighth Route Army to direct the care of the wounded, who were housed in villages that served as hospitals. The New Fourth Army in northern Kiangsu and southern Shantung had its own excellent medical training school. The main medical school, however, offering a three-year course, was in Yenan, in northern Shensi. The foreign doctors who gave aid during these years included an American, Dr. Norman Bethune, known as Dr. Ma Hai-teh, a Canadian, one anti-Nazi German refugee, one Russian, and five surgeons sent by the Indian National Congress. Dr. Bethune died at his post, as did Dr. Dwarkanath Kotnis, an Indian.

After the disaster at Pearl Harbor a number of Westerners escaped from Peiping and joined the Eighth Route Army. Among these were the American banker, G. Martell Hall, who spent eight months in the guerrilla regions, and Professor Michael Lindsay,[1] an Englishman from Yenching University. Dr. William Band, professor of physics in Yenching University, and his wife taught for a year and a half in the army's radio school.

Up to 1944 the Eighth Route and New Fourth armies together had wholly liberated 277 hsien and partially liberated 178 others. In the occupied areas the Japanese held strategic walled cities, but the countryside for the most part remained in Chinese hands. According to reports from the region in 1943, the population totaled some fifty millions.

When, in late 1937, the Eighth Route Army first fought its way into this territory, the Nationalist armies had already been driven out. Government officials and rich landlords had piled their families and valuables into government trucks and fled with the armies. Some simply moved into Peiping and Tientsin under Japanese

[1] For notes to chapter xi see pages 527–528.

"protection." As the Japanese established puppet governments and armies, the Eighth Route Army rendered their positions untenable.

According to the Kuomintang, at this point the Eighth Route Army became "rebels" against the National Chungking government. The army should have regarded itself as only a military tool of the Kuomintang: that is, it should have cleaned out the Japanese, called back the old appointed officials and the old armies, and protected them from Japanese invaders. Instead, according to Chungking, the Eighth Route Army began to "stir up the people and disturb the social system." Anti-Japanese people's organizations were founded, trained, and armed. Instead of calling back the old officials, the army undertook educational campaigns in democracy (Sun Yat-sen's Second Principle) and granted suffrage to men and women over eighteen, except for criminals, the insane, and Japanese agents. Elections were held in liberated villages and the higher administrative units, the chün and the hsien. The Shansi-Hopei-Chahar border government, first of six regional governments established before 1944, was formed. It consisted of three hundred members, elected every two years, except for ten per cent "coöpted" members to represent special groups such as the army, the new university, Mohammedans, Mongols, and Manchus.

Candidates for election in village, chün, and hsien were usually put up by the various people's organizations, though individuals, also, might run. The Kuomintang contested the 1940 elections for the border government. There were Kuomintang members in the various regional governments, but none in the villages. The chairman and the vice-chairman of the Shansi-Hopei-Chahar government were Kuomintang members. The Communist party, the largest in northern China, limited its representation in any elected body to one-third. Its aim was to have another third made up of progressive nonparty people and the rest of "upper-class elements": landlords, merchants, and gentry. "Upper-class elements," however, did not constitute a third of China's population. In fact, in some northern regions not one such person could be found to run for election. In others the Communists failed to muster even their allotted third.

The laws passed in the northern liberated regions guaranteed freedom of speech, press, assembly, religion, residence, and movement, and the right to own property. Marriage by choice, instead of by family arrangement, and the right to divorce were guaranteed. Concubinage, child marriage, and traffic in opium were forbidden. The Kuomintang charged that efforts to effectuate Sun Yat-sen's Third Principle—improvement in the people's livelihood—"disturbed the social system." Although private industry was permitted, industrial, consumer, and marketing coöperatives were promoted on a vast scale.

As for agrarian policy, a single progressive land tax, with a fixed minimum, was introduced. Burdens now began to fall on those best able to bear them. Landlords who returned from Peiping or other cities were paid rent by tenants, but never more than 37.5 per cent of the produce. Money interest was radically lowered and the newly established regional banks granted loans to farmers at low rates. Extensive breeding of livestock, especially sheep, helped provide much-needed food, also wool for clothing. Experimental farms were established, 15,000 acres of new land were brought under irrigation, and other measures were taken to improve living conditions.

The Shansi-Hopei-Chahar border government declared that its expenses were being kept within the taxation yield—which was quite possible in view of the coöperative basis of economy and the absence of war profiteering, hoarding, and official corruption. Soldiers, officers, and officials were paid a bare maintenance allowance, and no person was permitted to profit from the sufferings of soldiers and people.

Since Kuomintang leaders had declared that the revolution was not finished and that everyone must struggle on until the goal was reached, they might have been expected to welcome the improved conditions in the northern provinces and to compare them favorably with the war profiteering, food hoarding, inflation, nepotism, and widespread official corruption in the Chungking-controlled areas. For the most part, however, they did the opposite. In 1937, when the war began, Wang Ching-wei branded guerrilla warfare and the mobilization of the people as "banditry." Nor was he the only leader of his party who so argued, and who urged the government to accept Japanese peace proposals to prevent a social revolution. When Chiang's government failed to heed such advice, Wang

deserted to the Japanese in late 1938 and with his followers established the Nanking puppet regime. He and his invading masters
raised the Chinese national flag over Nanking, inscribed with the
characters for "Chinese People's Anti-Communist Government."

This flag, with its new inscription, was not without effect upon
members of the Kuomintang. On January 21, 1944, the Roman
Catholic newspaper, *Yi Shih Pao,* of Chungking, published an editorial which had first received official sanction. It read, in part:
"The Chinese people have always been noted for their political
broadmindedness. Instances are by no means lacking in Chinese
history where traitors who reformed themselves were pardoned
and given a chance for self-redemption." The editorial went on to
say that if Wang Ching-wei and Henry Pu-yi, the puppet "Emperor
of Manchukuo," repented and reformed, "they will be given a
chance to become Chinese anew, and may be granted freedom of
assembly, association, speech, and publication"—rights which are
not universal in Unoccupied China. In reply to questions asked by
Westerners about this editorial, Dr. K. C. Wu, of the Foreign Ministry, declared that Wang Ching-wei "cannot be called a traitor
because you can do that only after he is judged guilty."

Chungking, however, dealt otherwise with the Eighth Route and
New Fourth armies and with various other democratic elements.
The two Communist armies were repeatedly called traitors, and
attacks were made upon them. Their anti-Japanese people's organizations were called Communist cells and the elected northern
administrative organs were branded as soviets. In 1941 the government ordered one of its most powerful armies, 500,000 strong, commanded by General Hu Tsung-nan, to throw a cordon around the
rear and southern flank of the Communist headquarters at Yenan.
No money, ammunition, and medical or other supplies were thereafter permitted to reach the Eighth Route Army. To prevent medical supplies from reaching the wounded, even of the enemy, is a
violation of international law.

Simultaneously, the Chungking government began widespread
operation of its secret military and political police, of which there
were, in 1944, three divisions: that headed by General Tai Li, a
Blue Shirt fascist unit which emulated the Gestapo; another headed
by the C.C. clique (with Chen Li-fu, then minister of education,

as leader) directly under the Kuomintang, which was engaged in hounding intellectuals for "dangerous thoughts"; and a third, Generalissimo Chiang's personal outfit, which investigated anyone suspected of opposing his supreme power. Among the innumerable "achievements" of the secret police systems was the establishment of concentration camps for those who disagreed with Kuomintang orthodoxy.

None of these or similar developments could be divorced from the rise of international fascism. For more than a decade before 1939, Kuomintang leaders and publications openly praised Hitler and Mussolini and declared that fascism was the new social system best suited for China. Generalissimo Chiang had Mussolini's biography translated into Chinese and sent a copy to each of his officers. The Kuomintang National government imported Italians to train Chinese fliers. German military advisers were officially attached to the government from the early years of the civil war. In July, 1938, the Germans were recalled by Hitler, who acted on Japanese demands. Their chief was General Alexander von Falkenhausen, subsequently military governor of Belgium.

In attempted justification of its frequent assaults upon the Eighth Route and New Fourth armies, Generalissimo Chiang's government at divers times declared that these armies had attacked the Nationalist armies but had never fought the Japanese. Government censors permitted such statements to be circulated abroad and attempted to suppress all evidence to the contrary. Violent fighting between Japanese and Communist armies was not reported by Chungking. These armies, however, issued annual reports of battles fought, of casualties, of trophies captured, and of war prisoners taken. According to such reports, from June, 1940, to June, 1941, the Eighth Route Army alone suffered 48,383 casualties, and 63,847 in the following year. The increase in number of dead and wounded, they declared, was due to the government blockade which had shut off ammunition and medical supplies. From 1940 to 1943, according to other reports, the two Communist armies almost continuously engaged thirteen Japanese divisions, or 44 per cent of the total Japanese troops in China. The only ammunition consisted of what the Communists could capture or manufacture in their own small arsenals. Many battles were fought hand to hand, and often the guerrillas had no weapons except hand grenades. The writer was, on occasion, with Chinese guerrillas who possessed only ten rounds of ammunition each. When this supply was used up the guerrillas had to vanish.

Early in 1944, American military men in China requested permission to send observers to the Eighth Route Army to study guerrilla tactics and Japanese positions and installations. Generalissimo Chiang refused, on the grounds that the Communists were "rebels" guilty of countless crimes. The Communists invited foreign correspondents and military observers to visit their armies and seemed to have no fear of the results. In 1938 they welcomed Colonel Evans F. Carlson, of the United States Marine Corps, who later successfully used the military and political tactics of the Eighth Route Army against the Japanese in the South Pacific. Westerners, however, were asked to accept Chungking official charges against the Eighth Route and New Fourth armies instead of being permitted to obtain firsthand evidence. Finally, in the summer of 1944, a group of foreign correspondents was permitted to visit sections of the Communist-controlled areas in northwestern China.[2]

No account of the phenomenal social transformation taking place in both Occupied and Unoccupied China would be complete without mention of democratic individuals and organizations in the western provinces. The Chinese Industrial Coöperatives are of such basic significance in the transformation of Chinese society that they are nothing less than revolutionary. Organized in 1938 by Rewi Alley, a New Zealander, they are said, in official reports of the Chinese Industrial Coöperatives, to number 1,400 to 1,500 units. It is asserted that in 1944 they supported some thirteen million civilians. Owned by the men and women who work in them, the Chinese Industrial Coöperatives produce vast quantities of supplies for the armies and the people. Regionally federated, the individual coöperatives are small, self-governing republics which maintain primary schools, night schools for adults, hospitals, theaters, and newspapers. They, too, have been harassed by officials and by secret police and on occasion are reported to have been forced to disband. Many of their leaders have been thrown into prison, released, and then arrested again. American and British supporters have thus far enabled them to continue to exist.

Modern Chinese medical workers have made deep inroads on scientific ignorance and the ancient indifference to the suffering of soldiers in wartime. In the early years of the war the Chinese Red Cross Medical Corps and the Emergency Wartime Medical Training Schools (the latter under the Army Medical Administration), organized and directed by Lieutenant General Dr. Robert K. S. Lim, performed historic service in the care of the wounded. Dr. Lim and former Surgeon General Loo Chih-teh standardized military medical supplies. They and their followers, working with the National Health Administration, laid the foundation for socialized medicine in China, with free clinics in all unoccupied territory. However, not even this work was free from the blight of political intrigue and ambition. Some of China's finest medical men were driven from their positions and reduced to futility, or coerced, and even threatened with death.[3]

Official censorship of foreign press dispatches has, in large measure, prevented the Western world from hearing about the great number of democratic-minded Chinese of the educated classes. To the present day, few outside China know of the Federation of Democratic Parties—an organization similar to the Canadian Coöperative Commonwealth Federation—which was founded in March, 1941. It is composed of the Young China party, the Third party, the National Socialist party (Social Democrats), the Rural Reconstruction Association, the Vocational Guidance Association, the National Salvation Association, and unaffiliated individuals. On October 10, 1941, this federation issued a ten-point program for democracy.

Among the points of the program are: (1) termination of one-party rule; (2) cessation of government financing of the Kuomintang; (3) discontinuance of governmental use of political power to force membership in the Kuomintang; educational officials (specifically, Mr. Chen Li-fu, minister of education) to cease forcing teachers, students, and others to join the party; (4) abolition of Kuomintang organizations within the armies; (5) abolition of concentration camps; (6) introduction of free speech, free press, and free newspaper circulation; (7) abolition of inequality of war economics "by which profiteers are becoming fantastically rich and the poor poorer."

Members of the Federation of Democratic Parties hold a few seats in the People's Political Council which the government, under popular pressure, inaugurated in 1938 as an approach to democracy. Three days before the Council convened, on November 20, 1941, a government spokesman informed foreign correspondents that the Council provided "an auspicious opportunity for introducing democratic institutions into China in wartime" and that the government was willing to hear criticism. The Federation of Democratic Parties thereupon presented its ten-point program to the secretary of the People's Political Council. The secretary gave it to Generalissimo Chiang, who, according to reports, forbade it to be presented. The bill was suppressed. Moreover, the Chinese press was forbidden even to mention it or the fact of its suppression.

On September 18, 1943, the twelfth anniversary of the Japanese invasion of Manchuria, Dr. Chang Piao-fang (Chang Lan), president of the Federation of Democratic Parties and former president of Chengtu University, issued a manifesto entitled "China Needs True Democracy."[4] Following an analysis of the dangerous internal situation and a defense of international democracy as "the political form most suitable for mankind and the times," his document challenged the Kuomintang dictatorship as a violation of Sun Yat-sen's Three People's Principles, upon which the Kuomintang maintains it is based. The war was in its seventh year, the manifesto declared, yet "Neither the party nor the government can reach the people with their propaganda, to encourage and arouse them [in continued resistance]." It added:

For the past several years the officers of the government have been openly corrupt. Juniors have imitated their seniors. Laws and decrees have both become scraps of paper...the government is hated on every side, the people are harassed...people who have no grain are still made to pay grain...homes that have no men must still provide men....

Ever since the single-party dictatorship has been established, able men outside of the party are wasted and all political parties and groups have been severely repressed. No open activities are permitted. Many able men feel this to be a great injustice. A particular case is the Communist Party with several hundred thousand troops in seven or eight provinces, under the continual threat of another civil war....

Our British and American friends feel that China, the so-called democratic country, has not really been carrying out democracy...they will eventually and naturally not wish to support and help a government which is democratic in

MAO TZE-TUNG
Secretary-General of the Chinese Communist Party

CHU TEH

Commander-in-Chief of the Chinese Communist Armies

name, but carries out in practice anti-democratic single-party rule. China today is fighting shoulder to shoulder with the other United Nations. But unless true democracy is carried out soon, it will be difficult for us to gain freedom, equality, and independence either during or after the war.

On February 23, 1944, Sun Fo, son of Dr. Sun Yat-sen, who is president of the Legislative Yüan—an exalted position without power—delivered a frank speech in defense of democracy before the Central Training Institute in Chungking. He said, in part:

If we had strictly observed the principle of democracy during the past twenty years, the democratic spirit of the Kuomintang would today shine brilliantly. Unfortunately, we have not strictly observed this principle for various reasons. As a result, the organization of the Kuomintang now moves, on the contrary, from the top down to the bottom. The members of the committees of the provincial and municipal party headquarters, for instance, are appointed by the central party headquarters. The organization of the Kuomintang has thus become a governmental or even bureaucratic organization contrary to the spirit of democracy.... We must frankly admit the fact that in these twenty years the machinery and practice of the Kuomintang have turned in a wrong direction, inconsistent with the Party Constitution drafted by Dr. Sun Yat-sen in 1923 and contrary to the spirit of democracy. The practice of the revolutionary party has consequently become the same as that of a bureaucratic regime.... I feel strongly that to realize democracy in this state, we must first democratize the Kuomintang. The democratization of the Kuomintang is the condition precedent to the democratization of the state and to the establishment of the democratic government as aimed at in the *Min-Chu'an-Chu-I* [democracy].... we cannot think that the Kuomintang should permanently be the party in power and permanently be the ruling caste of China. We must fully realize that a political party is the vanguard of its people. The making of sacrifices for the country and people is its inescapable duty. It should by no means become the ruler of its people, neither a ruling class nor a noble caste in the state....

Unfortunately, we have in the past assumed unwillingly the attitude and habit of a ruling caste. The suppression of outside criticism against our party, and even criticism by our party comrades, bespeaks this fact. The number of our party members is less than one per cent of the Chinese population. The Kuomintang is simply a minority in terms of population. But we have come to regard ourselves as if we were the sovereign power entitled to the enjoyment of a special position and to the suppression of all criticism whatsoever against us.[5]

Sun Fo further declared, "We have already spent sixteen years in political tutelage. Yet there is not a single councillor of the hsien People's Political Council or a hsien administrator elected by the people." Criticism from America and Great Britain, he declared, is not due to "Communist influence," as officials state, but to the fear that "China is taking the road to fascism." And he observed:

There is a great deal of harmful talk by Chinese so narrow in vision as to hide behind the Communist bogy, and worse, to accuse critics of being over-friendly toward the Chinese Communists and influenced by them.... China must find her own democratic path, but it ought to run in the same general direction as in the democratic countries, rather than along the courses of Japan, Germany, and Italy, as—let it be candidly stated—has been the recent tendency.

One of the many pronounced instances of fascist development in China was the publication, in October, 1943, of a government decree affecting Chinese students who wish to study abroad. After complying with countless provisions, the candidate for study abroad must attend an official training school in Chungking to be indoctrinated with orthodox Kuomintang ideas. Then he must pass an oral examination "in deportment and thinking." Clause 14 of the decree reads:

Self-supporting students abroad must absolutely receive directions and control from the Superintendent's Office [the superintendent of Chinese students abroad] and the Embassy in connection with all their thinking and deeds. If one's statements are contrary to the Three People's Principles and his deeds are irregular, after they have been verified and reported to the Ministry, his qualifications to study abroad will be promptly canceled, and he will be compulsorily required to return to China.

When questioned, Chinese official spokesmen defended the decree on the grounds that a similar decree had been passed in 1873, when the Manchu dynasty (the London legation of which kidnaped Sun Yat-sen) sought to prevent Chinese students abroad from becoming contaminated with democratic thought. No Chinese of intellectual integrity could comply with the provisions of such a decree. Even if he did so, he would still be subjected to political espionage from the Chinese superintendent of studies and the Chinese Embassy in the United States, the country to which most of the students, for a time at least, will be coming.

This "educational" decree is but one example of the reaction which has been developing during the past few years. Censorship of the Chinese press, for instance, transcends all military necessity and is primarily designed to control thought. All newspapers, magazines, plays, poems, and historical essays are rigidly censored.

Even translated poems of Robert Burns and the novels of Sinclair Lewis have been censored, and fascism may no longer be mentioned in publications. Censored manuscripts are filed as evidence against authors and publishers. University professors and administrators for the most part must either join the Kuomintang or lose their positions and receive no rice allowances to keep their institutions alive. Students are spied upon by the official Kuomintang Youth Corps, the only youth organization allowed to exist, and university authorities are required to present names of students who should join the Youth Corps, regardless of the students' desires. Mature scholars and newspapermen going abroad must pass official indoctrination courses; many are "invited" to become party members. Journalists or other Chinese seen with foreigners are watched and frequently called up for questioning. Intellectuals of integrity who refuse to knuckle under can get no work.

Censorship and coercion do not affect the Communists, who are mainly in the northwest. However, every intellectual is affected. Representatives of General Tai Li's Blue Shirts and of the C.C. clique of the secret political police are active in the United States. Few Chinese students in America dare express other than official views or appear in public with persons disapproved of by the Kuomintang. The writer knows of one secret Blue Shirt meeting in New York at which half-a-dozen South American students and one from India were special guests. The writer also knows of American-born Chinese students who were offered lucrative positions by Chinese government officials if they would join the Kuomintang Youth Corps. When these American citizens refused to do so, they were abused.

Coercive measures prevented full development of China's material and spiritual strength in the war of resistance against Japan. Yet they brought forth tributes to the strength and tenacity of the revolutionary movement within and without the country. Dictatorship has led to the formation of an adroit and determined underground movement through the channels of which uncensored information pours. China's democratic intellectuals are among the best informed politically of any in the world.

Neither the intelligentsia nor the common people as a whole can be regimented in the twentieth century, any more than could their ancestors in preceding centuries. By merely mentioning democracy the government unwittingly arouses hopes that cannot be stifled. In the halcyon days of the national united front, from 1937 to 1939, democracy was studied and discussed in some of the Nationalist armies. Under pressure of the people's movement the government had reintroduced political training in the armies, and progressive youths joined army political staffs to teach the soldiers everything from reading and writing to the history of their country and its relations with other countries; they reported news from every Chinese front, including the Communist. A few armies retain such political educators today, though most have been replaced by spies whose duty is to ferret out "dangerous thoughts."

Soldiers in the Nationalist armies had to listen to propaganda lectures against their guerrilla countrymen, but they went away to talk among themselves. The writer heard soldiers say, "Eighth Route Army soldiers have the same food, clothing, and pay as the officers; and no officer can beat or curse a soldier as ours do. They don't pay enough—yet they have clubs and theaters, and a man can study."

The military-political training system of the Communist armies had great influence on other armies in the early months of the Sino-Japanese War of 1937–1945. However, no Nationalist army developed training to so high a degree. Instead of a few weeks or months, as in the Nationalist armies, the military-political training schools of the Eighth Route and New Fourth armies gave from nine- to twelve-month courses in military and political science and in general knowledge.[6]

After presenting such courses, the political educators, who are attached to all units of guerrilla armies, are held responsible for keeping the soldiers informed of events and conditions. A glimpse into this system of training may be gained from an article written by General Chen I, commander of the New Fourth Army, in its monthly magazine, *Kangdi* (Resistance). The article deals with the state of learning among the troops:

A man who has spent years in this army will have listened to thousands of reports, attended thousands of conferences, read hundreds of books, and taken part in tens of hundreds of battles. If, after this, he has not yet learned to drive forward to help create a new world, there is something wrong with him and not with the system of training.

General Chen concluded his article by calling upon the troops to preserve and emulate China's ancient respect for learning, and quoted maxims which indicate how poor men in the past studied under the most difficult conditions:

Tie your head to a pillar by your belt to keep from falling asleep while you study.
Put a pin in the back of your jacket while you study.
Cut a hole in your wall and steal light from a neighbor.
Study by the reflected light of snow.

Slogans on walls and buildings throughout China express the hopes and aspirations of soldiers and people. In western China, where protofascist armies are under direct control of the Kuomintang, one of the chief slogans is reminiscent of Nazi ideology: "One party, one principle, one leader." But the slogans of the Eighth Route and New Fourth armies are quite different in their emphasis:

Where there is no struggle, there is death.
Only by knowledge can youth be strengthened to reconstruct the new world.
Men should be proud of all things constructed by labor and intelligence.
Carry out all the Three People's Principles.
A more equitable distribution of war burdens.
China fights for world democracy.

The writer made a practice of asking soldiers in the war zones of China what they were fighting for. A group of New Fourth Army guerrillas once explained what they meant by "a new progressive China." "After the Japanese are driven from Chinese soil," they said, "there will be no rich or poor, but all will be equal. Men who grow rice will have rice to eat and not go hungry; men who grow cotton and weave cloth will have clothing to wear. There will be work for everyone, and all men can get an education and be cured when sick without cost."

No men on earth are more hungry for knowledge than Chinese soldiers of all factions. When they lack paper and pencil, squads may be found tracing characters and figures in the dust with sticks. Many young officers teach their troops reading and writing in their free time. The speech of many officers in the best Nationalist armies is permeated with democratic and socialist thought.

In 1940 a divisional commander in a Kuangsi army asked the writer these questions: "Do you believe that America, Britain, and

France really wish us Chinese to win the war and emerge strong
and independent? Aren't the British afraid that our victory would
inspire the people of India to emulate us? The French fear for the
people of Indo-China, and the Dutch for the people of the Dutch
East Indies. Do not Western nations rather hope that both China
and Japan will become so exhausted by this war that we shall be
more easily exploited in the future than in the past? How else can
we Chinese explain the sale of war materials to Japan by America
and Britain?"

The Chinese officer and his staff members also asked if the writer
thought China should adopt the capitalist system, which, they said,
had failed to feed and clothe people in the Western world and had
led to wars of conquest. They even believed that members of the
American Congress, because of their refusal to fortify Guam, had
been bribed by the Japanese to follow Japanese policies.

Before December 7, 1941, most Chinese had tremendous respect
for America's presumed unconquerable armed might. When Japan
struck—as they were sure it would when the opportunity came—
they expected its defeat within a few months. After the disaster at
Pearl Harbor and the collapse of southeastern Asia they were disillusioned and became increasingly so for a time, as they were cut
off from outside supplies.

Certain powerful Kuomintang officials and military men might
have accepted Japanese peace terms at that time had they not
feared that some of the regular armies would form a bloc with the
Communist armies to continue the war. Many Chinese officials
were pleased at the defeat of white imperialist Powers at the hands
of an Asiatic Power and tried to emulate Japanese practices, as in
the decree concerning Chinese students.

Chinese Communists, viewing world history from a different
angle, that of historical materialism, believed that capitalist societies had all but run their course and were on the brink of a more
advanced and humane form of social organization. During the war
with Japan they held that a Nipponese victory would harness capitalist imperialism on the necks of Asian peoples for decades. They
maintained that they were waging a holy war and that they were
destined to help bring to birth a more nearly just form of human
society. This conviction, founded on at least a modicum of knowl-

edge of historical development, explains the birth of the Red Army, its endurance throughout the civil wars and the Long March, its growth since 1937 into a body of 470,000 regulars with 2,700,000 militia, and Communist control over territory with an estimated population of 86,000,000. This knowledge and faith formed their "armor against affliction," and explained why their armies had so few neuropsychiatric or other mental casualties, even though they fought under conditions so bitter that it is doubtful if many Americans could endure them. American soldiers at least have good food, proper clothing, and medical care.

When, prior to the summer of 1945, far-visioned Americans insisted that differences in point of view meant civil war, perhaps for decades, certain Kuomintang officials directly or indirectly threatened to make peace with the Japanese. They were advised by their countrymen, even by some of their own democratic-minded party members, that civil war could be prevented, the people inspired to fight the Japanese to the death, and the country strengthened in every way by the introduction of a democratic form of government—but they feared that change and reform would rob them of their power.

Such were the conditions when, on August 14, 1945, hostilities ended in Allied victory. The stage was set for a continuation of the "anti-Communist" civil war which Japanese aggression had brought to a temporary halt in 1937. On the day following the Japanese surrender offer, the twenty-year-old conflict flared up in northern and central China, thereby increasing international confusion and trepidation.

Throughout 1944 and in 1945 informed Westerners and Chinese had become increasingly alarmed by the deterioration of economic, military, and financial conditions in Kuomintang-controlled territory, as well as by the growing danger of civil war. Kuomintang troops had continued to swell the ranks of puppet armies until, by the end of 1944, a large majority of the 800,000 troops operating for the Japanese were former Kuomintang soldiers. Among these were some eighty generals and other high-ranking officers against whom the Chungking government had taken no action—not even depriving them of their commissions.

In October, 1944, the shroud of official censorship over Kuo-

mintang China was temporarily ripped asunder by the sudden recall—at the demand of Generalissimo Chiang Kai-shek—of General
Joseph W. Stilwell, commander of United Nations forces in the
China-Burma-India theater of war. Stilwell had repeatedly clashed
with Chiang over many decisive military issues: Chungking's reputed policy of "sitting out the war" after Pearl Harbor; the utilization of Kuomintang armies as political tools; paralysis of the war
effort by the anti-Communist blockade; poorly concealed collaboration with the quisling Nanking government, which included the
use of puppet troops against Communist-commanded armies; General Stilwell's refusal to deliver American lend-lease supplies to
the control of the generalissimo, using them instead for the American air force in China and for the supply of Allied armies fighting
to open the Ledo Road from India into China; General Stilwell's
delivery to the generalissimo of a suggestion from the American
government that an American officer (Stilwell) be given a command in China similar to that held by General Eisenhower in
Europe. This last was a move designed to create national unity. It
is interesting to note that General Chu Teh, the commander in
chief of the Communist-commanded armies, officially informed
General Stilwell of his willingness to place his armies under the
American general's command.

Following the recall of General Stilwell and the subsequent resignation of the United States ambassador, Clarence Edward Gauss,
Washington's policy toward China changed. The generalissimo
was apparently allowed to do as he wished with American lend-
lease, and to continue the policies which increasing numbers of
observers felt had all but wrecked the country.

In late 1944, after months of struggle with the Chungking censorship and press officials, a group of foreign correspondents and
one of American military observers were permitted to pass through
the anti-Communist blockade to visit Yenan and the Eighth Route
Army. Their reports were so favorable to the Communists that the
temporary rift in censorship was filled: the Kuomintang government not only suppressed facts but passed new "thought-control"
decrees against foreign correspondents.

The findings of the foreign press party in the northwest were as
follows: military and territorial losses suffered by the Communist-

commanded armies through Japanese offensives in 1941–1942 had been repaired from 1943 on. These armies reconquered lost territory and extended their gains until, by the end of 1944, they claimed to have liberated 331,000 square miles and 94,000,000 persons. Their bases behind Japanese lines had increased to a total of nineteen. Communist-commanded regulars, it was asserted, had grown in numbers to 865,000 by the end of the year and to 910,000 by May, 1945. Education, people's organizations, and industrial and agricultural coöperatives had been extended, and democratic rights had been granted to additional millions of people.

For these gains, the two guerrilla armies asserted that they had paid with 446,000 dead by the end of 1944, but had taken a toll of 1,360,877 Japanese and puppet troops. Foreign correspondents reported that agricultural and industrial coöperative production, literacy, morale, and general well-being were highest in the Communist regions. It was precisely these achievements of the people and their northern armies that led the Kuomintang to intensify reaction in its own territory and to hasten preparations for civil war against the Communists.

When, on August 10, 1945, Japan offered to surrender, Generalissimo Chiang issued a command by radio that all Chinese and puppet troops were to keep their weapons and remain in their assigned areas to maintain "peace and order." Japanese generals were not to surrender their arms to the guerrillas—an order obeyed with such willingness that the Japanese commanding general in Peiping issued a warning to Chinese Communist-commanded armies that he would fight if necessary to preserve "peace and order," because, as he piously added, "China has had enough of civil war."

For years the Communists had known of Kuomintang plans to use puppet troops, and perhaps Japanese, against them in civil war. Therefore, when Generalissimo Chiang issued his radio address to puppet troops to keep their assigned areas and maintain "peace and order," General Chu Teh ordered all Communist-commanded troops to attack Japanese and puppet troops. Fighting began.

In the following week the Chungking government revealed the extent of its collaboration with traitors by appointing three of them to official positions in northern China. Meng Chih-chung, former chief of the Japanese "Pacification Office" in Peiping, was appointed Chungking's "peace preservation" commander in that city. Wu Hua-wen, former commander of the puppet Third Front Army under the Japanese in Shantung province, was appointed Kuomintang "peace preservation" commander in Tientsin. Li Hsien-liang, former commander of the Imperial Japanese Collaboration Army in the Tsingtao Special Area, was appointed mayor of Tsingtao.

In Shanghai the Kuomintang "underground" emerged and was revealed as the notorious Green Gang, corresponding to the Black Dragon Society of Japan. Tu Yueh-seng, leader of the Green Gang, who had been known for decades as the "opium king," "white-slave" trafficker, and leading racketeer of China, flew by American plane to Shanghai to resume control of this gang.

As crises developed, the Kuomintang government was so weak that it had to depend on foreign—including Japanese—support. American planes began to transport Kuomintang troops into walled cities. These troops could not have passed through Chinese territory without foreign assistance. Thousands of General Hu Tsung-nan's troops were transported from Sian to Peiping; others penetrated Communist-controlled areas north of the Yellow River.

On September 7, after American planes had flown Kuomintang troops into Nanking, a New York *Times* correspondent reported watching a fully armed Japanese military expedition moving into the countryside against the Communist-commanded New Fourth Army. Chinese quislings of the Nanking puppet regime were at least temporarily left in power, and felt secure enough to call a press conference, at which they proclaimed their "love for China." They had served as Japanese puppets, they said, only to earn a living. Meanwhile, Chinese Communists, who had never deserted to the Japanese, but had fought to the death through poverty and disease, were being hunted down in Nanking, the former Kuomintang capital, and in the surrounding countryside.

On August 14, 1945, a Sino-Soviet treaty of alliance was signed in Moscow in an effort to prevent another world war. Conservative sections of the American press proclaimed that the treaty had "knocked the props out from under the Chinese Communists." One might ask, what props? For years Moscow had recognized and dealt with only the Kuomintang National government. The only "props" on which Chinese Communists could depend were the

Chinese people, whose interests they represented. Since the needs of the people had not changed, the Communist and guerrilla armies did not evaporate when the Sino-Soviet treaty was signed.

The day after the signing of the Sino-Soviet pact, Generalissimo Chiang invited Mao Tze-tung, secretary-general of the Chinese Communist party, to proceed to Chungking to negotiate for peace and unity. Mao rejected the invitation, but offered to send a representative. Two more invitations were sent. The third, issued on August 22, Mao accepted. The new American ambassador, General Patrick J. Hurley, flew to Yenan and returned to Chungking with Mao Tze-tung, General Chou En-lai, and Wang Jo-fei.

The Communist delegation, however, took nothing new to the Chungking negotiations. They repeated the demands for democratization of the country which they and the Chinese Democratic League had been making for years but which the generalissimo and the Kuomintang had rejected. The Communist delegation again offered to surrender the Eighth Route and New Fourth armies to a freely elected National government and a joint High Command purged of grafters and traitors. The Yenan delegates added that the Kuomintang must also surrender its armies to these bodies. The Chinese Democratic League issued a similar proclamation, insisting that grafters and traitors should be arrested as war criminals and that all Chinese parties should participate in the Japanese surrender and in war reparations.

In October the Kuomintang armies, supplied with every type of American weapon, were transported by American planes into the heart of the Communist-commanded regions of northern and central China. Some 53,000 American Marines landed at key coastal cities in northern China to clear the way for additional Kuomintang troops, which were carried northward, with all their American equipment, on American naval vessels.

Civil war began. United States officials stated that American aid in landings was for the purpose of disarming and repatriating Japanese troops. Yet General Yu Fei-eng, communications minister for the Chungking government, officially stated on November 6 that his government was "employing 30,000 Japanese engineering troops" to repair the two main railway lines of northern China over which the Kuomintang troops were pouring into the north

against the Communist-commanded armies. The Eighth Route
Army reported that Japanese divisions and Chinese puppet troops
were fighting side by side with Kuomintang armies against guerrillas; on November 6 the Chinese Communists listed eight instances of direct American action against the Eighth Route Army.

Washington's policy after General Stilwell's recall was summarized in the New York *Herald-Tribune* of October 30 as follows:

> Ambassador Hurley's all-out support of the Kuomintang Government has
> created a situation in which Americans are giving military aid to one Chinese
> faction in its quarrel with another. American planes are being used to transport
> Chungking Government troops to strategic cities in North China—cities which
> are islands in a Communist sea—and some coastal cities are controlled directly
> by American Marines pending the arrival of Generalissimo Chiang Kai-shek's
> soldiers. . . . In China's internal war America is a virtual ally of the Kuomintang
> regime, which is extremely conservative to say the least, and often is denounced
> as reactionary.

With civil war raging, negotiations for peace and democratic
unification broke down. On November 6 the Kuomintang minister
of information, Dr. K. C. Wu, stated that Chinese Communists
were trying to force public opinion in the United States to exert
pressure for withdrawal of American troops from China. "They
will never succeed," he declared.

In the meantime, according to Washington reports, Chinese officials in the American capital began to recruit discharged American
fliers to go to China. On October 30, while en route to China,
General Albert Wedemeyer asked Americans "not to make up their
minds" about American armed intervention in China, adding,
"There is no doubt that the turn of events in an area embracing
half the world's population must inevitably affect our country—
economically, psychologically, and perhaps militarily." These and
other events seemed to point to American military and financial
support of a Kuomintang regime which would transform China
into a military base for another world war.

On November 27 General Hurley resigned as American ambassador to China, charging that intrigue within the foreign service
made it impossible for him to carry out American policy. He stated
that he was opposed both to colonial imperialism and to Communist imperialism. President Truman then appointed General

George C. Marshall, retiring chief of staff, as special envoy to China. Secretary of State Byrnes stated, on December 4, that the United States "favors the creation of a strong, united, and democratic China and feels that collaboration among China, the United States, Britain, and Russia is essential to Far Eastern peace." When General Marshall left for his post by air on December 15, President Truman issued a statement of policy requiring cessation of hostilities and civil war, and a national conference of major political elements to bring about the unification of China, promising American financial, economic, and military assistance should China broaden its one-party government to give effective representation to other parties.

Chungking and the Communists accepted General Marshall as a mediator on January 3, 1946, and a week later a formal truce was announced at the opening of the Political Consultation Conference of thirty-eight members—of whom eight represented the Kuomintang, seven the Communists, five the Youth party, nine the Democratic League, and nine were not party members. This conference concluded its labors successfully on February 1, agreeing to the calling of a National Assembly of 2,050 members, made up of 900 delegates chosen before the war, an additional 450 to be elected (of which 150 were to come from Manchuria and Formosa), and another 700 to be appointed: 220 by the Kuomintang, 190 by the Communists, 120 by the Democratic League, 100 by the Youth party, 70 by nonparty groups. It was agreed that the new constitution to be worked out by an all-party committee of thirty-five must be adopted by a three-fourths majority.[7] All this is an indication of progress. Whether it will result in a peaceful all-party government and constitution for China remains to be seen.

Upon the ending of Kuomintang-Kungchantang hostilities and the establishment of peace between them, with consequent uniting of all factions of the Chinese people, depends the future of China and, in large measure, the future of Japan, Korea, and all subject peoples of Asia—not to mention the prosperity of the Western world. A freely elected democratic government in China may result in peace and progress and certainly will strengthen the liberation movements of subject Asian peoples and the democratic movement in Japan.

CHAPTER XII

International Relations: The Twentieth Century

BY ESSON M. GALE

THE OPENING YEARS of the twentieth century disclosed China weak, militarily discredited, and internationally humiliated. One of the reactions of the nation to the measures taken by European Powers to acquire spheres of interest or influence and to grab concessions had been the Boxer uprising.

Russia's role in the Far East had been played, for the most part, as a lone-hand affair. Attempts to secure a foothold in Chinese Turkestan had been unsuccessful. Muraviev, however, by the Treaty of Aigun in 1858, had obtained co-possession with China of what became, in and after 1860, the Maritime Province, with its valuable harbor at Vladivostok. The Russo-Chinese boundary now reverted to the Amur; navigation of this river and of the Sungari and the Ussuri was reserved for Russians and Chinese—unlike the great waterways in China proper, which were open to all commerce. Transfrontier trade remained unregulated.

By intervening with Germany and France on behalf of China, after the Sino-Japanese War, Russia helped evict Japan from its newly won position in Manchuria and, not long afterward, secured the right to build the Chinese Eastern Railway across northern Manchuria, with a branch extending southward from Harbin. Thus the Trans-Siberian line was linked with Vladivostok and the Kuantung-Liaotung Peninsula, with the latter's naval harbor of Port Arthur and commercial port of Dalny—later Dairen. From 1898 to 1904, Russia was dominant in China's Eastern Three Provinces, known to the West as Manchuria.

[200]

The position of France in China was of little significance. Territorially, it was represented by the so-called French Concession at Shanghai (administered by a consul and an elective council, but chiefly by the former); part of the island of Shameen at Canton; and the commercially unimportant but strategically situated port of Kwangchouwan (guang-jou-wan), which faces Hainan Island and Indo-China, and which had been obtained in 1898 to balance contemporarily acquired British, Russian, and German positions. The special interest of Paris continued to be protection of Catholic missionaries, established in China by the Treaty of Whampoa (1844). Trade was a relatively minor consideration. The ruthless, if gradual, acquisition of the Indo-Chinese peninsula had absorbed French attention and had terminated China's shadowy overlordship in that region.

The role of the United States in the international complex in China had been unique. Denying imperialistic ambitions, the Washington government and American citizens, both merchants and missionaries, had logically and legally—by virtue of the most-favored-nation clause in the Sino-American treaties—enjoyed rights and privileges secured in successive treaties exacted by Great Britain and France by means of diplomacy—and armed action. American-Chinese relations had in general been friendly. In the nineteenth-century wars against China the United States government had almost invariably observed the principle of abstaining from coercive measures.

In spite of the fact that the brunt of the Boxer attack had fallen upon American missionaries, residing in the interior without government protection, American Commissioner William Woodville Rockhill pursued a conciliatory role in 1901 with respect to indemnities and other punishments. Some two years earlier, Rockhill and Alfred E. Hippisley, an Englishman, had been mainly responsible for the formulation of the commonly designated Hay open-door policy in an effort to check European aggression and to preserve equality of opportunity for Americans and others in China.

By the end of the nineteenth century Great Britain's pioneering mission had virtually been fulfilled. It was England that had taken a strong stand with Manchu-Chinese treaty commissioners. The latter had usually stood between the devil of foreign importunity and the deep sea of imperial court reactionaries, who attempted to hold the commissioners strictly accountable for any yielding to the unmanageable foreigners, who were backed by gunboats.

The British had acquired the largest trading stake in China. Except for the Russians in Manchuria, they also had the largest holdings in the form of leaseholds and residential concessions. The crown colony of Hongkong, emerging from the barren island ceded in 1842, at the close of the First Anglo-Chinese War, had become a flourishing emporium with territorial expansions on the mainland totaling 405 square miles. Shameen (Canton), Shanghai (International Settlement), Hankow, and Tientsin (British concessions) were to a large extent under British control. Almost every other open port had its orderly British Concession; these constituted havens from the misgovernment and squalor of surrounding areas.

In addition, British influence, through a highly trained official personnel experienced in the language and customs of the Chinese, or through powerful banks and trading companies and their agents, maintained leadership in the international communities of China and in relations with Manchu-Chinese officialdom. In the staffing of certain imperial government services, such as customs, posts, railways, and harbor and river conservancy works, British talent predominated. Thus satisfied, Great Britain was prepared to maintain a *status quo* in which it was first among relative equals.

Certain other nations were not so content. German plans for obtaining a foothold on the coast of China had long been under consideration when, happily for the kaiser, the murder of two German Catholic missionaries occurred on November 1, 1897, in the interior of Shantung. Demands upon Peking (bei-jing) were immediately made, and in the following March a provisional lease for ninety-nine years was granted to territory about the Bay of Kiaochow (jiao-jou), including the port of Tsingtao. Except for undeveloped and costly residential concessions at Tientsin (tien-dzin) and Hankow, Germany possessed no other leaseholds in China. As an act of grace on the part of the British and the Americans, one German was permitted to be nominated to the Shanghai Municipal Council, to represent his rapidly expanding national community. German trade developed and soon two regular steamship lines connected German ports with the Far East. The flamboyant gesture of the kaiser in dispatching an overstaffed punitive expedition to China in 1900, which, under the swashbuckling Count von Waldersee, had practiced unnecessary brutalities, had not endeared official Germany to the Chinese people. But the tact of German merchants eventually overcame earlier prejudices.

A generation before 1900, Japan had determined to revive its traditional policy of seizing territory on the continent. Yet the Japanese government acquiesced with outward grace in the "advice" proffered by Russia, Germany, and France at the close of the Fourth Sino-Japanese War,[1] that of 1894–1895, to forego territorial acquisitions in Manchuria in return for increased indemnity. But Japan did obtain Formosa and the Liu-ch'iu (Riukiu) Islands. It participated with distinction in the international expedition against the Boxers, but, following Western examples of looting, seized large quantities of silver bullion from the government treasuries at Tientsin and Peking and, like the European Powers, exacted indemnity out of all proportion to its losses.

Portugal and Belgium maintained footholds on Chinese territory. The former retained the somnolent gamblers' paradise of Macao near Hongkong. Belgium and Austria held minute and for the most part undeveloped concessions at Tientsin.

The "awakening" of China was yet to take place. The first four decades of the twentieth century witnessed a struggle of cumulative intensity against the Powers. As far back as 1894, Dr. Sun Yat-sen had submitted memorials to the throne advocating reform. Similar representations were made by K'ang Yu-wei, Liang Ch'i-ch'ao, and others. Although the Empress Dowager Tz'ǔ-hsi and her partisans were bitterly opposed to the reformers, her nephew, the Kuang-hsü (guang-sü) emperor, had come under their influence. Sweeping edicts were issued in the course of the Hundred Days of Reform, June–September, 1898. In a palace coup d'état the dowager secured the person of the emperor, and the reform movement was driven underground. Sun Yat-sen nevertheless maintained an antidynastic movement which eventuated in abdication of the Manchus in February, 1912. Revision of treaties with Western Powers and Japan was thereafter stressed as one of the cardinal principles of the revolution.

---

[1] For notes to chapter xii see page 528.

The leading actors in the drama now emerge as the eastern Asiatic antagonists, Japan and China, with the Western Powers, for the most part, enacting the roles of passive onlookers. Internally, China was engrossed by revolution; externally, in the main, with attempts at curbing the onslaughts of Japan upon Chinese territories and resources. Included in the play of rivalries were proposals for the neutralization of railways in Manchuria, advanced in 1909 by American Secretary of State Knox. One result of this grandiose but awkward gesture was to make more ardent Japan's and Russia's embraces begun in 1907, less than two years after the conclusion of their war. A series of open and of secret agreements (1907, 1910, 1912, 1916) envisaged, *inter alia,* the division of Manchuria into northern (Russian) and southern (Japanese) mutually exclusive spheres of economic and political activity and the development of Russian and Japanese interests in Outer and Inner Mongolia, respectively.

Beginning in 1910, various loans to Peking—for the Currency Reorganization, the Hukuang Railways, the 5 per cent Gold Reorganization (1913)—were proposed or consummated. From four to six Powers negotiated upon these transactions through a consortium composed of banking representatives from each nation involved. The object was to prevent monopoly by any one Power in the financial control of China. Because of President Wilson's dissatisfaction with the terms of the loans, the American members of the original consortium withdrew before the completion of the reorganization loan, which was left to a five-nation (quintuple) group. Before the end of the First World War, however, the Wilson administration came to advocate American participation in the international financing of China. The achievements of the new consortium were negative only: no loans were made by the second consortium, but irresponsible and ephemeral Chinese administrations were prevented from hypothecating (as in the Nishihara loans) the country's national credit or resources and subsequently wasting or embezzling the proceeds of the loans.

After Japan's seizure of Manchuria, in 1931–1932, the United States government collaborated with the League of Nations in the dispatch of the Lytton Commission to examine into the dispute. The Stimson doctrine of nonrecognition of governments established by *force majeure,* contrary to the will of native populations, eventuated.

No "short-of-war" measures served to stop Japan's advances into China. The Roosevelt-Hull appeasement of Japan by granting tacit consent to the shipment of strategic and essential war materials while giving lip service to China's plight—an amoral policy of "running with the hare and hunting with the hounds"—resulted, in part, in Japan's attack upon Pearl Harbor and open warfare. Attempts at justification of this policy were made by its exponents on the ground that it gave the United States time to "prepare."

In the third and fourth decades of the century France confined its attention increasingly to the economic exploitation of Indo-China, alternately stimulated and retarded by a fluid political situation in Paris tending to impose direct control on France overseas.

Under the terms of the Anglo-Japanese Alliance, prior to 1922 Great Britain left to Japan the policing of the eastern seas. The empire-commonwealth's immensely rich holdings in southeastern Asia encouraged a relatively static colonialism, which finally resulted in their temporary forfeiture to Japan.

The United States became more and more engrossed in philanthropic and educational enterprises as instrumentalities of a policy designed to develop a strong China. Educational institutions, largely American in type, grew up in eastern and central cities and even in Szechuan province in the far west. (See chap. xxix, below.) Many of the intellectual elite obtained their education in these and in American universities.

Between 1912 and 1919 a triangular struggle went on in Tibet between the British, the Chinese, and the lamas ruling the Roof of the World. In the last years of their occupation of the Dragon Throne, determined and not always tactful moves had been made by the Manchus to rule Tibet with firmness, to attach it ever more strongly to their empire, and to strengthen to a dictatorial position that of the imperial representative in Lhasa, at the expense of the Dalai Lama. President Yüan Shih-k'ai and his successors continued this assimilation policy in various attempts at uniting Tibetan and Inner Mongolian territory with that of China to form new provinces. An attempt in the summer of 1912 to enter upon military conquest in Tibet was checked by Great Britain.

The independence of Tibet was declared early in 1913 by the Dalai Lama, who negotiated a treaty with the Hutukhtu of Urga— third in rank in the hierarchy of Lama Buddhism after the Tibetan Dalai and Panshen, or Teshu, lamas—in Outer Mongolia. Each was to recognize the independence of the other's theocratic state. At a triangular conference at Simla, held intermittently between October, 1913, and July, 1914, Tibet demanded independence, China defended its claims to continued suzerainty, and Great Britain advocated subdivision of the country into Inner and Outer Tibet—with itself acting as intermediary between vassal and sovereign. When Peking proved obdurate, Britain and Tibet signed a trade agreement (July 3, 1914) in which the former recognized the autonomy of the latter; and Britain's interests and influence in Tibet continued to expand at the expense of China's.

The abdication of the Ch'ing dynasty in 1912 had important repercussions also upon the relations of China proper with Sinkiang (sin-jiang), Mongolia, and Manchuria. In these vast areas Russia's influence expanded coincidentally with that of Japan in Inner Mongolia and southern Manchuria. In Mongolia and Manchuria, Russia and Japan were helped by the aggressive policies and actions of both Manchus and Chinese, as Britain was helped in Tibet for somewhat similar reasons.

Outer Mongolia had been drawn into the Chinese state system, on the most recent occasion, by the Manchus in 1691. President Yüan Shih-k'ai's hopes for its union with the Republic of China were disappointed in November, 1912, by Russia's treaty recognizing Mongolia's autonomy. This was followed in January, 1913, by the Tibetan-Mongolian treaty. In November, 1913, by agreement with China, Russia recognized Chinese suzerainty over Outer Mongolia, whereas Peking recognized Outer Mongolian autonomy.

The outbreak of the First World War in Europe in 1914 startled the comfortably established Treaty Port communities of China. Social solidarity of the white man in the Orient was split asunder and subjects of the Central Powers withdrew from international social clubs. The European populations suffered immediate diminution as men owing allegiance to the Allied Powers embarked for Europe to join home forces. Those of Germany and Austria-Hungary were hastily mobilized at Tsingtao. Promptly beleaguered by a Japanese military and naval expedition, in which a small British token contingent participated, the survivors of the garrison were carried as prisoners of war to Japan. Subsequently they and their compatriots in China were repatriated by the Allies. The Far East was swept clear of German and Austro-Hungarian subjects. This was at a time when the Germans, through trading sagacity, tactfulness in dealing with the Chinese, and technological superiority, were equaling if not surpassing British and Americans in competitive Chinese markets.

The exigencies of war markedly reduced the volume of Anglo-Chinese trade. Both Japan and the United States took advantage of this situation. The former was relatively unhampered because of its limited participation in the war; the latter was free to expand its Far Eastern market until its entry into the war in 1917. The number of nationals of both countries in China greatly increased in the interval. The extension of American influence in the great trading centers of Shanghai, Tientsin, Hankow, and even the crown colony of Hongkong, beginning with the war years, was noticeable.

Japan, however, was not content with mere commercial gains. The opportunity to effectuate the messianic mission foretold by Lord Hotta (1858) and Lord Tani (1887) had apparently arrived.[2] The United States suggested a limitation of the area of hostilities in the Far East; China proposed neutrality. Japan promptly acted, ostensibly under the terms of the Anglo-Japanese Alliance,[3] to declare war on Germany on August 23, 1914. Attacked by land and by sea, Tsingtao fell on the following November 7. When Peking requested that Japanese and British troops be withdrawn upon termination of hostilities, the Japanese minister personally presented Twenty-one Demands to President Yüan Shih-k'ai.

These demands called for guaranties and (or) expansion of Japan's interests in Shantung, Manchuria, and eastern Mongolia, and in China's foremost iron and coal company. Assurance was demanded that no further cessions of territory would be made to other Powers. Control over China was sought through a system of advisers in all departments of government and through monopolistic concessions and unique rights and privileges. For the first time in the modern era Japan threw off the mask to give effect to the program of conquest of China which Toyotomi Hideyoshi had exemplified in the last decade of the sixteenth century and which had again been intimated in memorials of statesmen of the post-Restoration era. Theatened by an ultimatum, China, through two treaties and supplementary notes, agreed in truncated form to most of the demands.

The treaties dealt, respectively, with Shantung, southern Manchuria, and eastern Inner Mongolia. In all three areas Nippon's position was strengthened and expanded, as also by the exchange of notes on the Yangtze Valley and the province of Fukien (fu-jien). In addition to its advances in China at this time, both within and without the Wall, Japan's final objective—control of the Eighteen Provinces and as much more as possible in the dependencies of the former Ta Ch'ing empire—was clearly foreshadowed.

Nippon's policies and deeds with respect to its continental neighbor in the next twenty-five years were, in the main, but the effectuation of its earlier intimations of immorality. Vast sums, including the so-called Nishihara loans, were advanced to more or less subservient and ephemeral governments at Peking, especially after the death of President Yüan in 1916. (See chap. ix, above.) In addition, a series of secret agreements with the Allied Powers assured Japan of its gains after the war. A carefully worded exchange of notes took place, on November 2, 1917, between Secretary of State Lansing and Viscount Ishii. The text was publicized to the world by Japan as America's recognition of Nippon's special position in China. Thus the island empire availed itself of the opportunities presented by the suicidal gestures of Occidental nations to achieve extensive military, political, and economic influence over China and other Far Eastern areas.

While the Anglo-Japanese attack on Kiaochow was under way, Russia—as a natural sequence of its treaties of 1907, 1910, and 1912 with Nippon—signed two agreements with the Outer Mongolian government on September 30, 1914. By one of these, St. Petersburg "obtained a concession for a telegraph line . . . by the second, Mongolia was pledged to seek Russian advice in the determination of railway routes, to adopt the Russian gauge, and to consult Russia before granting railway concessions to non-Russian foreign nationals."[4] Following the negotiation of these agreements, Chinese, Russian, and Outer Mongolian representatives entered upon eight months of discussion of a tripartite agreement. These discussions were not without influence upon Tokyo, which forced Peking to agree to its Twenty-one Demands less than a fortnight before the Sino-Russian-Mongolian agreement was signed on June 7, 1915. By the latter, China and Russia again recognized the autonomy of Outer Mongolia; and Russia became co-suzerain with China in that area, as Great Britain had become, in practice, with Tibet.

Peking's hopes for obtaining redress against Japan's aggressions now centered on the Paris Peace Conference. Such expectations were disappointed, however, for the Treaty of Versailles sanctioned the reversion of Germany's interests in Shantung to Japan, and Chinese representatives refused to sign. Nevertheless, China had made substantial gains at the expense of the Central Powers in the renewed struggle for revision of the treaty status of foreigners in China. German residential concessions at Hankow and Tientsin, as well as Austrian at the latter port, reverted to Chinese jurisdiction with all government properties. These areas were immediately converted into "special administrative districts" and were provided with efficient municipal governments under Chinese auspices. The grossly inflated German share of the Boxer indemnity was canceled, together with several private and semiofficial German and Austrian loans.[5] Similarly, extraterritoriality lapsed for citizens of the Central Powers—the first breach in the solid front of the Treaty Powers' rights and privileges in China. Considering the passive role played by China as a belligerent, because of Japan's opposition and its own political chaos, Chinese outright gains were by no means inconsiderable.

The younger statesmen of China, notably the American-educated V. K. Wellington Koo (gu), Cheng-t'ing (jing-ting) Thomas Wang, Alfred Sze (shzh), Wang Ch'ung-hui, and C. C. Wu, with the sympathetic support of American official quarters, persisted in the battle of diplomacy against Japan. An extraordinary spectacle was thus presented. While China was being exploited at home by a reactionary military mandarinate, bribed and corrupted by Japanese money, a Young China contingent was battling abroad—primarily to oppose Japan's pretensions, but also to reduce the foreigners' special status in China. This procedure was the reverse of that carried out by Japanese statesmen in the post-Restoration era.

Then, every effort had been made to reform and modernize Japan before arguing for the withdrawal of limitations on Japan's sovereignty. Another curious contradiction has been pointed out by a Western scholar: China's foreign policy from 1919 to 1937 was primarily attuned to "revisionism," whereas China's weakness demanded adherence to the *status quo* system of collective security.[6]

The Washington Conference of 1921–1922 was ostensibly convoked to deliberate primarily on limitation of armaments. It necessarily related to the Far Eastern situation, unsettled as that was by virtue of the unsatisfactory Treaty of Versailles. Japan was reluctant to attend: the "tripartite intervention" of 1895 had not been forgotten, nor was American policy with respect to China misunderstood. Japan feared loss, in part, of recent acquisitions in China, and nonrenewal of the Anglo-Japanese Alliance, which, twice renewed since 1902, was now due for renewal or abrogation. Both these contingencies occurred. The Alliance was replaced by the innocuous Four-Power Pact, which guaranteed the *status quo*. Of prime importance was the arrangement, by means of direct conversations in the presence of British and American observers, for eventual restoration to China of Germany's former holdings in Shantung.

It would not have been meet to hold Japan exclusively accountable for its recent aggressions upon Chinese sovereignty while ignoring those of the judges on the bench, the Allied and Associated Powers. Thus the status of Weihaiwei and Kowloon (British) and Kwangchouwan (French) came under consideration. Only the first was eventually returned to China. It was agreed to withdraw post offices maintained without treaty right by alien governments in China. Certain of these post offices were often instruments of smuggling, especially of narcotics. The Chinese postal service, under the administration of foreign officers employed by the Chinese government, had earned an enviable record. Inadequate ad valorem tariffs based upon obsolete schedules were forthwith to be revised upward. More thoroughgoing revision would be effected in future by a tariff commission. Extraterritorial jurisdiction exercised by alien courts established on Chinese soil was similarly to be discussed by a commission *ad hoc* as to whether the time was ripe for its relinquishment.

Once more the Powers—not including the defeated Central states and ostracized Soviet Russia—collectively appointed representatives to deliberate on the unfinished business of the Washington Conference. The Tariff Conference convened at Peking in October, 1925. Chinese grievances stemmed fundamentally from the treaties imposed almost a century before. These, although terminating the arbitrary rates collected prior to 1842, had erred in the other direction by subjecting the tariff schedule to the will of the foreign Powers and by fixing rates so low as to strangle China fiscally. With mounting costs of indemnities and loan services, relief was imperative. The Commission on Extraterritoriality passed a resolution approving tariff autonomy in principle and presumably consenting to tariff autonomy as from January 1, 1929. China undertook the abolition of *likin* (li-jin), the troublesome levy on goods in transit. The resolution came into full effect in 1928, Japan's tardy signature being affixed in 1929.

Thirteen nations were represented at the convening of the Commission on Extraterritoriality in Peking on January 12, 1926. The juridical anomaly of extraterritoriality had grown out of conditions attending the administration of justice in China prior to 1842. However suitable to the peculiar conditions existing in China, extraterritoriality was an infringement on China's sovereignty which led to confusion of jurisdictions and laws. For persons of foreign nationality who were charged with crimes and who had escaped the country, there was no system of extradition. Asylum was given to China's political refugees in foreign-administered enclaves on Chinese soil. New and modern codes had been drafted by the Chinese Law Codification Commission. Admirable as these were on paper, however, Chinese courts were still subject to military and other pressures, and a trained judiciary was only in the making.

Taking these factors into consideration, in a time of widespread political chaos and disintegration, the Commission contented itself with various recommendations: Chinese administration of justice must be "effectively protected against any unwarranted interference by the executive or other branches of the government"; improvement of codes, laws, procedure, and prisons was needed; extraterritorial and consular courts should continue to administer

Chinese law as far as possible, and correct their own current abuses, "pending the abolition of extraterritoriality." The latter consummation was postponed to January, 1943, when the United States and Great Britain negotiated treaties with China ending the juridical device which had been instituted a century before. Whether the cautious stipulations of the Commission on Extraterritoriality will be met by the government in postwar China remains to be seen. It may be remarked in conclusion, however, that complaints of unredressed oppressive action by military and other authorities against business and church properties of foreigners in Nationalist China are already on record in the files of the embassies concerned.

Standing apart from the Allied and Associated Powers and the defeated Central European states as well, the Union of Soviet Socialist Republics pursued an independent and *sui generis* policy toward China after the twofold Revolution of 1917. Though absorbed in consolidating the new regime over the Eurasian continent, the Soviet Union, as early as July 25, 1919, renounced, in theory, all "imperialist" concessions exacted from China by the tsarist government, including extraterritorial status for Russian citizens. This was apparently done by Moscow with tongue in cheek, since all Russians in China at this time were adherents of the old regime. As such, they remained subject to the jurisdiction of tsarist officials there resident until recognition of the latter was suspended by Peking in September, 1920. Moreover, the Soviets made reservations and displayed inconsistencies in their self-denying ordinances. For example, a treaty between the Soviet Union and Mongolia, signed on November 5, 1921, ignored the traditional pretensions of China's sovereignty in that area. Full share was also claimed in the Chinese Eastern Railway crossing northern Manchuria.

Soviet missions, one after another, were dispatched to China between 1920 and 1923. The envoys alternately negotiated with *de facto* Peking and *de facto* Canton authorities. (See chap. ix, above.) In September, 1923, Ambassador Karakhan established relations with Peking, contemporaneously with the arrival of Comrade Borodin to aid Dr. Sun in Canton. On May 31, 1924, the Koo-Karakhan Agreement on General Principles was signed in Peking. This formally annulled the tsarist treaties and granted nominal recognition of Outer Mongolia as "an integral part" of China. The Chinese Eastern Railway still remained a joint enterprise. In 1929, however, the virtually independent Chinese authorities in Manchuria seized the railway and ejected Russian officials—an action the significance of which was well understood by the Nipponese. The railway was purchased from the Soviet Union by the Japanese-made government in Manchuria, with a Japanese guaranty of payment and transfer of title on March 23, 1935. Diplomatic relations between China and the Soviet government, severed in 1929, partly as a result of controversy over the railway, were resumed in 1933, after discussion in the League of Nations of the Manchurian dispute between China and Japan.

An occasional cause of friction between Moscow and Chungking was the ebb and flow of Russian influence in and near Sinkiang (for example, the completion, in 1930, of the Turk-Sib railway), scene of Russo-Chinese controversies in the 1870's. The year 1943 witnessed the withdrawal of the Soviet troops which had been sent a decade earlier to aid the Chinese government of Sinkiang against Moslem enemies.[7] Moscow furnished limited supplies to China via Sinkiang during the Fifth Sino-Japanese War (1937–1945). For a time following the Japanese blockade and the partial destruction of the Burma Road, the only foreign goods—except those obtained through trading with the invader—came from Russia.

China's relations with other nations after the outbreak of hostilities in July, 1937, were somewhat fluid. The seizure of Manchuria in 1931, followed by a short but bitter armed clash at Shanghai between Chinese troops and a Japanese "landing party," signalized the end of the truce obtained by the Washington Conference and resumption of the age-old Nipponese policy of expansion at China's expense. The abortive Brussels Conference was a ghostly apparition evoked from the Four-Power Pact and the Nine-Power Agreement. Japan contemptuously ignored a second time, as it had in 1932, its conviction as an international brigand. Until Japan's capacity to wage offensive war, or China's will to survive, is permanently destroyed there will probably never be more than an armistice between the two great eastern Asiatic antagonists.

The awakening of powerful nationalism in China was based on exploitation of the innate xenophobia of the Chinese masses and upon the repetition of grievances and injustices, both actual and fancied, sustained by China through the nineteenth-century treaties. Nonmilitary campaigns were conducted with such vigor as to equal or exceed the effectiveness of the military front against Japan. Moreover, the diplomatic victories of Nanking and Chungking over the Treaty Powers, in and after 1928, but especially in the course of the war with Japan and the Axis, were at least as brilliant as those against the traditional island enemy. The Powers found it expedient to fall back, yielding one line of defense after another—tariff, residential concessions, leaseholds, and, at last, extraterritoriality.

The impositions of the 1840's had been liquidated by the mid-1940's. As at the end of the sixteenth century, Japan had been forced to retire from the continent. With foreign aid the Nationalist Chinese armies appeared from the heartland of western China to reoccupy the riverine and maritime provinces containing the rich former Treaty Ports. Hongkong in time must revert to China—its position having been demonstrated to be as vulnerable to Chinese economic warfare as to Japanese land and naval attack. Chinese and British diplomacy will solve the problem by peaceful means. With the abrogation of the century-old extraterritorial practice, alien river and coastal shipping, banking and insurance franchises, and a host of lesser rights and privileges now fall under the sovereign control of China. A Chinese government staffed in key positions with a personnel skilled in many of the Western arts of public administration and diplomacy will contrive such conditions of intercourse as exist between nations equal and free.[8]

Nevertheless, the war's end leaves unsolved many problems of the continuing relationships of a still amorphous Chinese political, economic, social, and judicial system, with citizens of Western Powers still resident on Chinese territory. The structure painfully erected to meet the special circumstances of an exotic civilization cannot be demolished without substantial replacement. For this reason official and unofficial explorations* are already under way

---

* For example, the American State Department has deputed the Hon. Milton J. Helmick, former judge of the United States Court for China, to examine the judicial adjustments necessary for the continuance of trade and residence by American citizens in China; the American Chinese Trade Council, an aggregation of American business interests, has been constituted to explore methods of trade with China under the new conditions presented.

to reconstruct a suitable procedure which will recover for Chinese enjoyment and profit the unusual privileges and opportunities hitherto accruing to foreigners in China and, at the same time, offer such inducements and safeguards as will continue to attract foreign capital and enterprise to China. China in its present undeveloped and impoverished condition, needing all manner of technical skills and mechanical tooling, cannot afford to estrange the Western world.

Typical of forthcoming readjustments is the new series of agreements represented by the Treaty of Alliance and Friendship signed in Moscow on August 14, 1945, by plenipotentiaries of the Union of Soviet Socialist Republics and the National government of the Chinese Republic.[9] This alliance supplemented the American-Anglo-Chinese agreement entered into at Cairo on December 17, 1943. At the moment of the military collapse of Japan the two great contiguous Asian states pledged themselves, as they had done in the secret Li-Lobanov Treaty of May, 1896, specifically against their common insular enemy.

The Li-Lobanov Treaty was followed by the contract of September 8, 1896, establishing the position of the two governments in China's Eastern Three Provinces, known generally to Westerners as Manchuria. It provided for construction of a jointly controlled railway in Heilungkiang, the northern province of Manchuria, linking the newly built Trans-Siberian Railway with Russia's Maritime Territory (Primorskii Krai)—gained from China in 1860—and the fortress port of Vladivostok on the Sea of Japan. Two years later, provision for an extension of the Chinese Eastern Railway line from Harbin to the ice-free port of Dalny—later Dairen—and the naval base of Port Arthur was obtained by Russia. The agreements detailed the respective parts which the two governments or their representatives were to play in the C.E.R.'s administration. In the ensuing years, control of the lines oscillated between Russia and China and for a time reverted to Japan. Out of this grew the network of railways traversing Manchuria from the Amur to the Gulf of Chihli and from the Liao to the Yalu rivers.

The main trunk lines built by Russia in Manchuria at the close of the last century formed an enormous letter T. The transverse part, measuring some 950 miles, crossed northern Manchuria from

Manchouli in Siberia on the west to Pogranichnaya in the Maritime Territory in the east—on the way to Vladivostok facing the Sea of Japan. The upright section dropped southward from Harbin to Dalny and Port Arthur, another 646 miles. A line built by Japan during the Russo-Japanese War of 1904–1905 runs from Mukden to Antung on the Yalu River border of Korea, with a short cut from the southern Manchurian section to the Peking-Mukden line on the way to Shanhaikuan, a traditional corridor into northern China.

The early part of the twentieth century was a period of international competition for railway concessions in Manchuria. These proposed to penetrate the rich agricultural area west and north of the existing trunk lines. A road was built from Ssupingkai as far as Taonan, almost due west of Harbin; eventually, under the Japanese puppet regime, it was extended to Heiho opposite the Siberian city of Blagoveshchensk. Where Korea, Manchuria, and the Russian Maritime Territory (Primorskii Krai) meet on the Sea of Japan, a network of railways came to center. With the surrender to them of the southern section of the Chinese Eastern Railway from Changchun to Dairen, as a fruit of the Russo-Japanese War, the Nipponese finally assumed control of all lines in Manchuria by forcing the Russians to sell the remainder of the Chinese Eastern Railway to them in 1935. After this date, having evicted Chang Hsueh-liang, the Chinese war lord of Manchuria, in 1932, and substituted as puppet ruler the last Manchu emperor of China, the Japanese virtually blacked out this most important region of eastern Asia to the outside world. The capitulation of the Japanese Kuantung army in Manchuria to Russian forces occurred in the late summer of 1945, following the collapse of resistance in the home islands and the formal signing of the surrender instrument on September 2.

By the Russo-Chinese Treaty and annexed Supplementary Agreements of August 14, 1945, the historic cycle was completed, with Soviet Russia, successor to the tsarist policies of the nineteenth century and earlier, once more a full participant in control of the original trunk lines and the terminal commercial and naval harbors of Dairen and Port Arthur. Aside from the alliance against Japan, in eight articles, there is a minutely drawn railroad agreement. This provides that the entire former Chinese Eastern Railway and the South Manchuria Railway "leading from the station in Manchuria (Manchouli [Lupin]) to the station of Pogranichnaya and from Harbin to Dalny [Dairen] and Port Arthur shall be joined into one railway system under the name of the Chinese Changchun Railway. This railway system will become the joint property of the Soviet Union and the Chinese Republic and will be jointly exploited by them" (Art. I). There follow detailed arrangements for such control. Similarly, the agreements on Port Arthur and Dairen divide control between Chinese and Soviet authority. Two other agreements deal with the relations which are to exist between the two governments in respect to military and civil administration of the Eastern Three Provinces and their government, while confirming China's full sovereignty therein and acknowledging the National government as the central government of China. A final agreement offered a solution to the rivalry of Russia and China in Outer Mongolia by leaving the determination of the form of government to its people by means of a plebiscite. A vote for independence (under the aegis of the U.S.S.R.) was a foregone conclusion. The fate of Manchuria, China's richest possession, is dependent upon the sincere implementation of the terms of the treaty and agreements mentioned above.

The autumn of 1945 disclosed a China well on the way to recovery of all the outlying possessions of which it had been shorn in the century of humiliation beginning with the unilateral treaties of 1842–1844. The historic Moscow Conference communiqué issued by the American, Russian, and British foreign ministers on December 27, 1945, reaffirming adherence to the policy of noninterference in the internal affairs of China, apparently left henceforth to China the shaping of its destiny in the community of nations.

Part Three

PHILOSOPHY
AND RELIGION

CHAPTER XIII

Chinese Thought

BY HU SHIH

THE HISTORY OF CHINESE THOUGHT can be divided into three periods of about one thousand years each. The ancient period covers the major part of the first millennium B.C. The medieval period covers the first millennium of the Christian era, during which Taoism and Buddhism flourished in China. The modern period of intellectual and philosophical renaissance begins in the tenth century, with extensive printing of books, and continues with the rise of secular Chinese philosophy in the eleventh and twelfth centuries.

The ancient period includes the classical age—the indigenous, original, and creative age of intellectual and philosophical activity. It is the period of Confucius (551–479 B.C.), Lao Tzŭ, and Mo Ti, or Mo Tzŭ; of Mencius, Chuang Tzŭ, and Han Fei (d. *ca.* 233 B.C.). (See chaps. xv, xvii, below.) Philosophers of the classical age are better known to the Western world than those of later periods. The classical age not only set the pattern of Chinese thought of all subsequent ages, but also furnished the inspiration and intellectual tools with which Chinese thinkers of the medieval and modern periods labored for their philosophical and cultural renaissance.

The intellectual heritage of the classical period is threefold. First is its humanism, with special emphasis on man, his life, duties, and relations in this world. Second is its rationalism, or intellectualism. (Since rationalism has something of a theological connotation in the Western world, the term "intellectualism" may be preferable to indicate its special emphasis on knowledge and education.) Third is its spirit of freedom and democracy which champions the supreme importance of the people and advocates the social and political responsibility of the intelligentsia.

The classical age was humanistic in that it consistently and distinctly concerned itself with human life, human conduct, and human society. It scrupulously avoided supernatural and otherworldly problems. When Confucius was asked how to serve the gods and the spirits, he replied, "We have not yet learned to serve men. How can we serve the gods and the spirits?" Asked "What is death?" he answered, "We have not yet learned to know life. How can we know death?" Preoccupation with man and his life in this world is a characteristic which differentiates Chinese thought, at least ancient thought, from that of India, Persia, and Israel.

A useful sourcebook on Indian and Chinese thought has been compiled by Dr. Lin Yutang, bearing the title *The Wisdom of India and China*. It is instructive to compare the section on India with that on China. The former discusses the gods, future life, and the religious life; the latter discusses, in the main, human nature and human problems, man's relation to the family, the state, and the world—education, government, and law. This fundamental difference runs through the history of the intellectual life of the peoples of India and China. Ancient China, which produced a great civilization with highly developed theories of human nature, moral conduct, and political organization, seems to have taken little interest in problems of religion. It was almost primitive in its religious and theological thinking, and spent little time in speculation about life after death. It is the predominant interest in man and his problems that constitutes the first heritage bequeathed by the classical age to China.

The classical age is noted for its strictly intellectualistic approach to the problems of thought. The Chinese are the least mystic of peoples, but among them were thinkers who tended toward mysticism. Lao Tzŭ, for example, declares that without going outdoors one can know the world and that without peeping out the window one can know the ways of Heaven. He goes on to say that the farther one goes the less one knows—which would appear to constitute a mystical approach! But, on the whole, the classical tradition of China places most emphasis on knowledge—on empirical and exact knowledge, on learning and thinking.

Confucius laid down the dictum, "Learning without thinking is confusing, but thinking without learning is perilous." This observation is representative of the intellectual tradition of the classical period. One of the later Confucianists expressed the intellectualistic attitude in a fivefold formula: "Study widely, inquire minutely, think carefully, analyze clearly, and then practice earnestly."

It was the intellectualistic approach that led most Chinese scholars to stress the importance of education, of learning, and of thinking. The most influential leader in China's national life during the last twenty-five centuries, the idol of countless millions of Chinese youth, was not a military hero or a messiah, but a schoolmaster—Confucius.[1] He described himself merely as one "who never grew tired of learning, and never grew weary of instructing others." Never to grow tired of learning or of instructing others—that is indeed the ideal of a schoolmaster! Confucius sums up the intellectualistic attitude—the most valuable and characteristic gift inherited by China from the ancient period.

The classical age was one of mental freedom and independence, an age of democratic ideas. It bequeathed to later ages a spirit of freedom of thought and speech, of independence of character, and of the worth and dignity of personality. It was primarily an age of independent and warring nations. Because of the juxtaposition and coexistence of so many states, a thinker persecuted in one state could usually find political asylum and welcome in another. It was also an age in which the scholarly class was making its influence felt on the internal and external policies of the states. Because of these two factors, thought and speech were relatively free and the thinkers of the age were fully conscious of their moral responsibilities. One of the great disciples of Confucius said, "The scholar must needs be stout-hearted and courageous, for his burden is heavy and his journey is long. Humanity is the burden he imposes upon his own shoulders: is that not a heavy burden? And only death ends his toils: is that not a long journey?"[2]

This sense of the grave responsibility of the individual, especially of the educated individual, was shared by most of the social and political thinkers of the classical age. Mencius, whose moral and intellectual influence was second only to that of Confucius, often

---

[1] For notes to chapter xiii see page 529.

spoke of "the individual shouldering the heavy burden of the world." The sense of social responsibility of the intelligentsia is a peculiarly Chinese tradition. Every Chinese schoolboy remembers the saying of Ku Yen-wu, a seventeenth-century patriot, "The humble individual, however humble, has a share in the responsibility for the prosperity or the downfall of the empire." He may not realize, however, that this remark goes back to Mencius and to the school of Confucius.

The feeling of responsibility gives to the educated individual a sense of dignity and a spirit of independence. Mencius said: "Who is the great man? The great man is he who cannot be tempted by wealth and honor, who cannot be budged by poverty and lowliness, and who cannot be bent by authority and power. That is the great man."

From the sense of moral responsibility for the well-being or the misfortune of the nation has emerged the classical tradition of the individual's duty to be outspoken and to fight unrighteousness, misrule, and corruption. It has become a tradition for scholars to fight against tyrannical monarchs and corrupt officials in the interests of the state and the people. From this stems China's fight for freedom and democracy through the ages. The democratic tradition has developed primarily from Confucianism, one of the most orthodox schools of thought of the classical age.

In the *Hsiao Ching* (Book of Filial Piety), a tiny classic of doubtful authorship, which for more than two thousand years was read by every schoolboy as his primer, Confucius is made to say: "In the face of unrighteousness it is the duty of the son to fight it out before his father and it is the duty of a minister to fight it out before his sovereign. Therefore, I say, in the face of unrighteousness, fight it out." And in the *Meng Tzŭ* (Works of Mencius), which was used as a second reader, Mencius taught: "When a ruler treats his subjects like grass and dirt, then it is the right of his subjects to treat him as a bandit and an enemy." (See chap. i, above.) Any ruler violating the principles of benevolence and righteousness is no longer a ruler, but a robber and a murderer whom the people have a duty to overthrow and kill.

These dangerous and revolutionary doctrines are contained in the classical works which have been the required reading of every

Chinese student through more than two thousand years, and which have been used throughout the last ten centuries in the competitive civil service examinations for selection of government officials. Such is the heritage of freedom and independence, social responsibility, and democratic control which has come down through the ages.

◇　◇　◇

The threefold heritage of the classical age has been the bedrock of China's intellectual life. It has given the Chinese the criteria with which to evaluate imported ideas and institutions—and the antitoxin to neutralize the poisonous effects of certain of these. It has served also as the soil to which many kinds of foreign thoughts and institutions have been transplanted and have grown to flowering and fruition.

The classical age ended about 200 B.C., when the country became a united empire. In such an empire it was no longer possible for a thinker persecuted in one part of the country to find asylum in another; nor was it possible for a book banned in one province to be published in another. There was, in consequence, less intellectual freedom and independence. But it is the glory of the Chinese that, in spite of the unified empire and in spite of several thousand years of monarchical rule, there has been maintained a tradition of comparative freedom of thought and scholarship—thought and scholarship that often came into conflict with the established ideas and practices of the great religions of the Middle Ages.

The medieval period lasted approximately from 200 B.C. to A.D. 1000. Chinese thought, in this period, had to cope with two gigantic problems. The first was to build up not a military but a civilian government of continuity and stability which should soften the harshness of absolute rule in a unified empire; the second was to rescue China from the fanaticism brought about by mass conversion to the Indian religion of Buddhism and by the rise of its native, imitative counterpart in Taoism. (See chaps. xvii, xviii, below.) Secular life and civil institutions had to be carried on in the midst of wholesale conversion to otherworldly religions, and the torch of intellectualism had to be kept alight in the midst of a population going mad under the strange attraction of such religions.

It was no easy task to maintain the tradition and authority of civilian government in empires and dynasties often founded or controlled by warriors or by men and women who arose from the lowest strata of society. The intelligentsia, however, steadily accomplished the task by following the classical tradition.

Four instrumentalities were responsible for the continuity and stability of civilian government in the medieval period. First was the founding of a civil service examination system for the selection of government officials. Begun in the year 125 B.C., the examination system became, through the centuries, one of the most important weapons in the struggle of the people for equality of political rights. Confucius had laid down a democratic educational philosophy in four words: "With education, [there is] no class." This germinal idea was worked out in the civil service examination system, which was competitive, objective, and open to practically everyone of ability. It broke down class distinctions, feudalism, and artificial barriers of race, tribe, religion, and color. Prior to its abolition in 1905 it was China's most effective tool in the fight for political equality.

Second was the founding of a national university in 125 B.C. Opening with only fifty students, it had ten thousand by A.D. 4, and in the second century as many as thirty thousand students. With the rise of a national university, numerous private schools were established, some of which had thousands of students. The spread of learning was necessary to supply educated personnel for the civil service.

Third was the development of a codified law which came to be one of the greatest systems in the world. There exist today five completely preserved codes of the last five great dynasties between A.D. 600 and 1900; there are, also, fragments of nine codes antedating the year 600. This body of codified law is one of the most important tools in the development and maintenance of civilian government.

Fourth was the establishment of a canon of Confucianism, not only of standard texts for use in the schools but, more particularly, of sacred scriptures. The Confucian canon gradually acquired authority equivalent to that of basic law in limiting monarchical power and protecting the people against the encroachments of rulers and administrators. An important illustration is the *Mêng Tzŭ*, which contained many democratic and even revolutionary doctrines. This was one of the works used in the examinations for selection of public officials. In 1372, Chu Yüan-chang, founder of the Ming dynasty, who apparently had not read Mencius' book in his boyhood, discovered that it contained dangerous ideas. So he ousted Mencius from the temple of Confucius and later (1394) ordered a third of the book expurgated. But the desired results were not achieved. The *Mêng Tzŭ* continued to be read in its entirety and to be cherished by the nation. The authority of Mencius was greater than that of the Hung-wu emperor (1368–1399).

❖   ❖   ❖

The second great problem of the medieval period was how to rescue China from religious fanaticism. Buddhism was introduced perhaps in the first century B.C.—or earlier. By the third century of the Christian era it had become popular and powerful. China had become Buddhized and Indianized to a considerable degree. Mass conversions took place, for the native religion was too simple to satisfy the yearnings of many. No heaven, no hell, no future life: Chinese classical thought was too simple! Indian Buddhism offered China not one heaven but thirty-two heavens, not one hell but sixteen or eighteen hells! In place of the old idea of retribution of good and evil, India gave China the doctrine of karma, the iron law of causation, which teaches that moral retribution runs through all existences, past, present, and future. It was a situation which a Chinese proverb describes as "A little witch conquered by a great witch": a simple religion was conquered by a great religion.

For a time it seemed that Chinese rationality and humanism might be submerged by Indian thought and belief. Hundreds of thousands of men and women withdrew from their families to enter the monastic life. Fanaticism swept the country. A zealous monk would burn a finger, an arm, or even his whole body as a supreme sacrifice to a Buddhist deity. Thousands of the pious, sometimes including members of the imperial court, flocked on occasion to a mountainside to witness and wail at the self-destruction of a great monk by slow burning.

Otherworldliness and inhuman fanaticism finally shocked the people back to their senses, to reason and humanity. Behind governmental persecutions of Buddhism was always the protest of

Chinese civilization against the "barbarization" of the country. The imperial edict of the great persecution of 845, for example, said: "The government cannot abandon the human beings of the Middle Kingdom to the following of the life-denying (*wu-sheng*) religion of a foreign country." Humanism revolted against the Indianization of Chinese thought and civilization.

The greatest representative and most articulate leader of the revolt against Buddhism was Han Yü (768–824),[3] who pointed out that the ideal of Chinese thought was that moral and intellectual cultivation of the individual must have a social objective and that this objective was the ordering of the family, society, the state, and the world. Individual cultivation which aims at personal salvation by denying life and fleeing the world is antisocial and un-Chinese. Han Yü's famous battle cry for this revolt was "Man their men!"— that is, restore the monks and nuns to their humane life.

Han Yü's severe criticism of Buddhism, especially his attack on the imperial court's patronage of the Buddhist religion, brought about his exile in 819. However, twenty years after his death his ideas were carried out by the great persecution of Buddhism (845).

But persecution has never succeeded in uprooting a religion which has taken a strong hold on the intelligentsia as well as on the vast majority of the people. It was the thousand years of preservation and slow spread of classical education which finally achieved the task, a few centuries after Han Yü's death.

Paper had been invented *circa* A.D. 105. A living secular literature of prose and poetry arose in the medieval period. Printing with wood blocks came into vogue about A.D. 800. Book printing on a large scale took place in the tenth century. Confucian classics, with standard commentaries, were printed under government patronage. Schools were established in increasing number in the tenth and eleventh centuries. Printing from movable types was invented in the middle of the eleventh century.

A Chinese renaissance was taking place. The middle age was passing away.   ◇   ◇   ◇

In the eleventh century there were two outstanding movements toward political, economic, and educational reform. The first, in the middle of the century, was led by a great Confucian scholar,

Fan Chung-yen (989–1052),[4] who is remembered for his saying, "A scholar ought to worry [over the problems of the time] before anyone else begins to worry [about them], and ought to enjoy life only after everybody else has enjoyed life." In this dictum is seen arising a new spirit which harks back to the classical tradition of the Chinese scholar taking upon himself the burden of humanity. How totally different from the otherworldliness of the medieval period!

The second reform movement was led by another great statesman, Wang An-shih (1021–1086),[5] who brought about numerous economic, educational, and political reforms. The cry of the age was: Revive the social, political, and educational ideas and institutions of the classical age, and make them sufficiently attractive to the youth and the best minds of the nation. Then, but not until then, the otherworldly, antisocial, and un-Chinese religions of the middle age will surely die a natural death!

Revival of a secular and indigenous philosophical movement opened the third, or modern, period of Chinese thought. It was the age of Chinese philosophical renaissance. In the course of the nine hundred years of modern Chinese philosophical development there has been a new flowering of the humanism, intellectualism, and spirit of freedom of the classical age.

In the earlier stages of Neo-Confucian, or rational, philosophy (see chap. xvi, below) monastic and moral austerity and much sterile scholastic speculation still survived from the age of medieval religion. On the whole, however, the spirit of intellectual freedom encouraged the development of rival schools of thought, some of which succeeded in breaking away almost completely from medieval influence. Speculation became more methodical and scientific; moral teaching became more humane and reasonable.

In the twelfth century the school of Chu Hsi (1130–1200)[6] laid special emphasis on the intellectualistic approach to knowledge. The slogans of this school were: "Go to the things and investigate into the reasons thereof." "From your own body to the reason-of-being of Heaven and Earth, everything is an object of investigation." "Every grass and every shrub must be studied." "Investigate one thing at a time. Understand one thing today, another tomorrow. When you accumulate sufficient knowledge, you will some day understand the whole."

This strictly intellectualistic spirit and methodology gradually brought about a new rationalism in Chinese thought. Lacking, however, the tradition and technique of experimenting with objects of nature, this scientific ideal did not produce a natural science. (See chap. ii, note 7, above.) But its spirit came gradually to be felt in historical and philological studies. It has, in the last three hundred years, produced a scientific methodology in the study of classical and historical literature. It has developed textual criticism, higher criticism, and a philological approach to ancient texts. Scholars who were seeking to overthrow traditional commentaries now perfected a tool in the form of a methodology by which they were in a position to sweep aside subjective interpretation and traditional authority, with the strength of philological evidence and inductive reasoning. The old rationalism became scientific and the spirit of intellectual freedom found a powerful weapon.

This brief summary of the foundations of Chinese thought may be concluded with two anecdotes. Wu Ching-heng, China's oldest living philosopher, was presented in his teens to the master of the famous Nan Tsing Academy at Kiangyin. When he entered, he saw a wall scroll with eight characters written in the large, bold writing of the master himself. The inscription read, "Seek the truth and do not compromise."

In looking over my father's unpublished writings some years ago, I found volumes of notes made when he was a student at the Lung Men Academy in Shanghai, about 1875. These were written on notebooks printed by the Academy for the use of its students. On the top of every page was printed in red a motto reading, in part: "The student must first learn to approach the subject in a spirit of doubt. . . . The philosopher Chang Tsai [A.D. 1020–1077] used to say: 'If you can doubt at points where other people feel no impulse to doubt, then you are making progress.'"

Approach every subject in the spirit of doubt; seek the truth; do not compromise. That has been the spirit of those Chinese thinkers who have kept the torch of intellectual freedom burning throughout the ages. That is the spirit which has made Chinese thinkers feel at home in this new world of science, technology, and democracy.

CHAPTER XIV

Folk Religion

BY LEWIS HODOUS

T HE CHINESE often speak of the Three Religions: Confucianism, Taoism (daoism), and Buddhism. But these religions are not to be regarded as fixed entities, each with a certain number of adherents. Influences have passed from one to another. Confucianism has taken elements from Taoism and Buddhism. Taoism has been influenced by the other two. Buddhism has been reconstructed in the Chinese environment. The people express the situation thus: "The Three Religions are one religion," that is, all three are concerned with the fundamental order of the universe.

Folk religion is behind and within the Three Religions. Since it has evolved from the cultures of eastern Asia and from the islands southeast of Asia, its origins go back into the twilight of history. It is a source of later religions and has conditioned the philosophies of subsequent generations. To it the western nomadic, the northern proto-Tungus, the Yüeh, the Sino-T'ai, the Li, and the southwestern cultures all made contributions. The western nomadic culture centered in Shensi and Kansu (gan-su), and was probably the bearer of the astral cult which began to penetrate China in the fourth and third centuries B.C. The northern proto-Tungus culture centered in northern Shansi and Hopei, and introduced northern shamanism. The Yüeh culture centered in southern Shantung (shan-dung), Kiangsu (jiang-su), Anhui, Chekiang (je-jiang), and Fukien (fu-jien), and was strongly influenced by the Austroasiatic culture of the islands southeast of Asia. The Sino-T'ai culture of southern Honan, Hupeh (hu-bei), Hunan, and the great southern regions introduced southern shamanism. Its bearers were the groups who used the Chinese and the Siamese languages. The Li culture (Austroasiatic?) was in the territory south of the Yellow River, but was dislodged early. The proto-Tibetan southwestern culture centered in Szechuan, and was assimilated by the Chinese under the Chou dynasty.

Knowledge of folk religion is based upon artifacts found at neolithic sites in northwestern China and Manchuria, and upon the Oracle Bones of the Shang dynasty found in Honan. The *Shih Ching* (Book of Poetry), when divested of Confucian moralism, contains interesting insights into the folk religion of the early part of the Chou period, in the twelfth and eleventh centuries B.C. Although the *Chou Li,* the *I Li,* and the *Li Chi* are late books, they contain material about folk religion. For the modern period the chief sources are legends, stories, proverbs, inscriptions upon tombs and contents of tombs, provincial and local histories, decrees of national and local government officials, and direct observation of religious practices.

◇ ◇ ◇

*The Shang dynasty (tradl. 1766–1122 B.C.).—*The religion of the Shang (see chap. iv, above) was that of ruling families who did not govern a kingdom but held sway over groups paying tribute to priest-kings. Religion was not an individual matter; it was the concern of the whole group. Although the people of the soil carried on religious practices which differed from those of the ruling groups, their objectives coincided to an appreciable degree.

Throughout this period religion was a fertility cult. The people were tillers of the soil whose religious ceremonies were connected with the tensions of agricultural life: seedtime, harvest, rain, drought, pests. Most of the gods were earth gods and sky gods. The chief god was Shang-ti (shang-di), the Ruler on High. He was not supreme in all matters, nor were the other gods subordinated to him in every respect. The God of the Wind was regarded as a messenger of Shang-ti. There were also gods of rivers, the God of Earth, and Rulers of the Four Quarters. Many deities were female, as was common in eastern Asia in this period. The Eastern Mother, the Western Mother, and the Dragon Woman were goddesses. One word which is still meaningful is *ling,* or magic power. The character is composed of the symbols for rain, three mouths, and a shaman who is passing over fire to prepare himself to pray for rain.

To the gods were offered cattle, horses, sheep, dogs, and, at times, human beings. Ordinarily, offerings were burned or buried in the ground, but on certain occasions the worshipers partook of them. Liquors were poured on the ground. There were at least forty kinds of offerings.

A second aspect of Shang religion was connected with tensions in clan and family life: marriage, birth, sickness, and death. This, too, was a fertility cult. Kuo Mo-jo (guo mo-ro) has discovered, in the Oracle Bone records, mother right with ancestor worship. This cult centered about the ancestral temple, the funeral, and the grave, which was dug in the loess soil. At the bottom of the pit was built a small shrine in which were placed vessels and utensils, often of exquisite workmanship. Chariots and horses were also put into the pit. Offerings were made because the people believed that the dead would be unhappy if not properly nourished and would bring calamity upon the living. The dead were regarded as a part of the living social group. The shaman was the mediator between the two groups.

A third tension was connected with interclan and intergroup life. This was related to the continuity of rule of the priest-king.

A fourth aspect of Shang religion was connected with tensions of agricultural, intergroup, and social life. Rulers and people needed advance information on such matters as weather, agricultural prospects, hunting and fishing, battles, and other questions connected with the social and political life of the day.

There is evidence that religion was not merely a means to immediate material advantage. Creel mentions one symbol on the Oracle Bones representing a devoted son bowing before his ancestor. But apart from this the object of religion was to integrate the groups of that day with the total psychic imaginary world. This included the satisfaction, to some extent, of man's deeper nature.

Religious life was not confined to times of tension, which were simply the high spots of religion. The daily routine of cultivation of the soil, social intercourse, intergroup relations, and political life was regarded as religious and was performed with deep insight and fervor.

The Chou dynasty (ca. 1027–255 B.C.).—The Chou people (see chap. v, above) conquered the Shang state and, according to tradition, began to rule in 1122 B.C. The actual date was about 1027 B.C. The Chou rulers worshiped T'ien, Heaven. Both Shang-ti of the Shang people and T'ien of the Chou people were sky gods. In the Chou period the two concepts coalesced and the term used was Hao-t'ien Shang-ti, Lord on High of Exalted Heaven. This god was worshiped by the emperor until A.D. 1912. Under the Chou dynasty Ti (di), Earth, was regarded as the consort of Heaven. The classics speak of T'ien-ti (Heaven and Earth) as the father and mother of all living things.

Under Chou rule folk religion continued as a fertility cult. That of the peasants centered about a small mound outside the village, near trees and water. Festivals were celebrated at these mounds, in spring and autumn, to guarantee the fruitfulness of the soil. Here, also, marriages were sanctified, and a court of justice was established under the eyes of the Earth God. Individuals and groups which at other times were rivals were united by the festivities. Contests in poetry and games and a kind of initiation took place. The object of the cult was to promote social unity and the fruitfulness of Mother Earth.

In this circle of society and intimately connected with it is the family. Granet believed that woman occupied an important place in peasant life. He held the theory that two clans or great families formed a marriage group in which sons married their cousins, that is, daughters of the brother of their mother—a marriage system which passed from cross-cousin marriage to sororate and to free exogamy.

The ancestral cult is the fertility cult in another form. The substance of death is believed to penetrate the family soil. It disincarnates itself near the dark corner of the dwelling where the seeds are stored which, put into the earth, germinate. In the same corner was set up the conjugal couch.[1]

By the latter part of the Chou period (*ca.* 479–255 B.C.) the feudal system was disintegrating. The larger states swallowed the smaller. The old religion was losing its hold on the upper classes, but confusion and uncertainty brought about a revival of folk religion

---

[1] For notes to chapter xiv see page 529.

among the people. As the old order passed, a new view of the heavens, called the astral theory, emerged. It came to China from the West, and was developed by the *yin-yang* school of diviners. The ancient Chinese regarded the earth as a solid square block surrounded by water. The heavens, stars, and sun revolved about the earth. This revolution—called the *Tao* (dao), or *T'ien-tao,* the way or movement of the heavens about the earth—was produced by two interacting forces, *yin,* the negative, and *yang,* the positive. Earth, responding to this Order of Heaven, produced the seasons, seedtime, and harvest. Man likewise must respond to the order and adjust himself to it and thus do his part in promoting its harmonious operation.

With *Tao* was associated the term *Tê* (de). This means the *Tao, Universal Order, in action. Tê* operates in nature and in man. In both it is the harmonious operation of *yin* and *yang.* Harmony in social life is attained by right relations between classes in society, that is, the five relations of ruler-subject, father-son, husband-wife, elder brother–younger brother, friend-friend. Right relations in society are also the object of the operation of *yin* and *yang.* But in human society right relations depend on moral conduct. The ethical includes all requirements arising in social life from which rights and duties are built up. *Yin* and *yang* are directed to the operations of nature and to moral conduct. Together they make an integrated whole. Right behavior is an integrating power in the world process.

Moral influence is clearly seen in the relation between a good ruler and social welfare. According to Confucius (see chap. xv, below), a good ruler makes for good subjects and a bad ruler brings out the evil in his subjects. This effect does not come about by his example only: goodness is a force which coöperates with cosmic forces and makes for goodness.

These concepts and this theory developed in the Chan Kuo, or period of the Contending States, *circa* 480–222 B.C. The literati and various groups detached from the feudal system came to doubt the reality of the gods. In the fifth century B.C., Mo Ti—commonly call Mo Tzŭ,—bewailing the skepticism of his day, tried to prove the reality of the gods by quoting the sages of antiquity and giving concrete instances of the power of the spirits and the gods. His efforts had little influence.

The *yin-yang* school of diviners (see chap. xvii, below) explained the phenomena of the world by the interaction of the forces *yin* and *yang* without the intervention of the gods. In comparison with these cosmic forces, the intervention of the gods in personal matters cut a sad figure. Shang-ti came to be regarded as Heaven, a mere materialization of *yang*. Sovereign Earth and, in general, all the minor gods of Earth were materializations of *yin*. Thus the gods, great and little, were reduced to natural forces.

The literature of the period contains examples of this attitude. When the King of Ch'i (tsi) wanted to offer his prayer to Shang-ti, his minister, Yen Tzŭ (yen dz), dissuaded him: "If the Lord on High is powerful, your prayer will not deceive him; if he is not powerful, your prayer will not serve any useful purpose" (*Yen Tzŭ Ch'un Ch'iu*). A similar doubt appears with respect to the souls of the dead. Toward the end of the Chou period the phrase frequently occurs, "If the souls are conscious." Confucius said, "Worship the gods as though they were present." The Confucian school interpreted this to mean, "In sacrificing [to the spirits of ancestors] one should act as though the ancestors [in their own person] were present; in sacrificing to the gods one should act as though the gods were present."

Thus two religious attitudes developed among the literati and their supporters. On the one hand, the religious ceremony must be performed at the right time and in the proper place. The worshiper must purify his mind and rectify his intentions. He must cultivate his spirit. Religious festivals were intended to bring about harmony between the *Tao* of Heaven (i.e., between the operation of *yin* and *yang*) and the *Tao* of man in the moral world.

The second attitude discarded the gods and explained the ceremony rationally. For example, at an eclipse of the sun it was the custom for armed men to proceed to the altar of the God of the Soil to arouse him to defend the sun against the attacks of a monster. For this mythology the philosophers substituted the theory that the sun was light, *yang*, and was being obscured by *yin*. But the earth is *yin* and the God of the Soil is *yin;* so the armed men attack the God of the Soil, who represents *yin*. This new interpretation changed the superficial meaning of the ceremony, but the object and method of the ceremony remained the same.

A similar process took place in ceremonies for the dead. Man is a compound of the animal soul (*p'o*) which comes into being at conception and the higher intelligent soul (*hun*) which is added at birth. The *p'o* goes with the body to the grave and unites with the *yin*. The *hun* goes above and unites with the *yang*. The offering consisted of a libation which was poured upon the ground for the *p'o*. The odor of incense and the burnt offering went above to the *hun*.

These theories were formulated at the end of the Chou age, and became the orthodox belief of the official class under the Han dynasty (206 B.C.–A.D. 220). They have continued to modern times. A rural cycle was carefully followed. Special offerings were made at critical times of the year. At the winter solstice an offering was made to Heaven by the emperor, at the altar south of the capital. North of the capital, at the summer solstice, an offering was made to Sovereign Earth. Peasants took part in special ceremonies in spring and autumn. This was the fertility cult. These festivals were not for individual advantage but for the benefit of the country, the district, and the village.

An ancestral cycle was observed by the nobility at the beginning of spring, summer, autumn, and winter, and at the equinoxes. On these occasions, offerings were made to ancestors. Besides the regular offerings, special ceremonies were held at eclipses of sun and moon and in times of flood, drought, and pestilence. Through ceremonials and festivals, officials and peasants assisted nature in its operations, and harmonized relations between individuals and classes. Ceremonial regulations were embodied in the calendar which was issued by the emperor. These patterns of behavior were intended to bring about harmony between nature and man, and between man and man.

In connection with this world view there developed an aspect of religion which has had large influence. This is known as *fêng-shui*, literally, wind and water. The idea behind the system is that man is the product of the forces of the universe. Accordingly, his institutions, his dwelling, and his burial place must be so arranged as to harmonize with these forces. The earth is regarded as a square block set in the midst of the sky, surrounded by water and by the twenty-eight mansions of the moon. The year cycle is dominated

by the breathings of nature: birth in the spring, growth in the
summer, drying in the autumn, death in the winter. Likewise the
day has its breathings. To avoid evil and bring blessing, man and
his works must be carefully adjusted to the forces of the universe.

◇ ◇ ◇

Influence of Buddhism on folk religion (A.D. *25–1900*).—Prior to,
or early in, the first century of the Christian era Buddhism entered
China. (See chap. xviii, below.) Taoism, which had started as a
philosophy, was emerging as a religion. Confucianism was split
into sects. The Taoists acted as hosts to the Buddhists. This enabled
Buddhism to become acclimated more rapidly than would otherwise have been possible. In A.D. 335, under the Eastern Chin dynasty (317–420), the first edict of toleration for Buddhism was
issued and the Indian religion gradually grew strong. By the beginning of the fifth century nine families out of every ten were
Buddhist. By the sixth century most Confucian schools were closed.
(See chap. xii, above.)

Why did Buddhism prosper? Primarily because disorders in the
country loosened many people from their traditional homes and
ways of life. On the borders of the empire were numerous groups
already under the influence of Buddhism. Through its monasteries
the harassed peasants were given a degree of moral and physical
security. It brought vital, glowing hope to every person, with respect both to this world and to the world to come.

Buddhism did not oppose Chinese folk religion. Native beliefs
were regarded as ways of salvation. Incomplete and partial, they
were nevertheless sincere attempts to find salvation.

In the course of centuries, Indian influences interpenetrated
folk religion and confirmed, developed, and fulfilled it. The alien
religion introduced a large number of gods into the Chinese pantheon. This addition is especially noticeable at the beginning of
the T'ang age (A.D. 618–906). Before the seventh century, gods were
few and public worship was rare. Under the Sung dynasty (960–
1279) many new gods were added by the Taoists. In the ancient
festivals few gods had been worshiped, and the symbols were those
of natural forces. But, after the introduction of Buddhism, T'ai
Shan, a majestic mountain in Shantung, came to be worshiped as

a god presiding over a section of Hades. Temples to this god and to his consort and assistants were erected in the eastern suburbs of walled cities. The magic power associated with the God of the Kitchen materialized in a messenger mediating between the family and Yü-huang Shang-ti. The Chinese began to worship the City Guardian and many other gods.[2]

Buddhism is usually charged with introducing images into the religion of China. This is incorrect if symbols are included. In ancient China there were images.[3] For example, the Rain God was represented by a frog. The Dragon was represented by various symbols. Heaven was represented by a disk or a circle: the altar of Heaven and that of the Sun were round. Earth was symbolized by a square: the altar of Earth was square with ditches on the sides. The Count of the Yellow River had a human face and the body of a fish. But Buddhism introduced gods in human form.

Again, Buddhism, with its personalized gods, introduced a new phase in ritual. Hitherto, ritual had been regarded as a mechanical process to influence nature. This characteristic did not disappear at once, but a personal god required a different approach. Prayer was introduced along with magic formulas and incantations. Even these were responsive to the new atmosphere. The formula found in many parts of China at dangerous places along the roads, *Namo O-mi-t'o-f'o* (in Sanskrit, *Nama Amitābha*), means "I put my trust in Amitabha Buddha." The stones found occasionally at the end of dead-end streets bear the inscription "T'ai Shan will consume any spirit which dares to approach."

Buddhism introduced another insight which has not always been understood or employed. Taoist and Buddhist gods were worshiped for material benefits. Offerings were made in return for anticipated favors. In the third and fourth centuries people were considered to be afflicted by all sorts of spirits. Demon possession was a psychic disturbance to which the wars and confusion of the times contributed. Both Taoist and Buddhist gods were employed to exorcise demons. But Buddhist leaders, although condoning the practice, taught that gods had spiritual blessings, also, which were available to the believer. This attitude transformed some of the folk festivals into joyful occasions for recreation, and people acquired a new awareness of their psychic imaginary environment.

APPROACH TO T'AI SHAN

Lucille Douglass

Lucille Douglass

TEMPLE ON T'AI SHAN

Even the demons were transformed. They were partly sublimated by the Buddhist atmosphere which gradually permeated folk religion. It is not easy to evaluate this aspect of the subject. Some hold that the Chinese live in fear of demons, and numerous stories seem to confirm this idea. But, although the Chinese believe in demons and talk about them, the question arises whether demons are not symbols of undesirable things, of experiences to be avoided. Well-written and widely read stories about demons form a considerable part of their literature.[4] This leads to the suggestion that they constitute a genre of literature comparable to Western mystery stories. Dante consigned some of his contemporaries to reserved places in the Hades of his conception. Chinese writers have given similar honored places to officials who plucked them in the state examinations.

Another contribution of Buddhism was the conferring of personal immortality upon ancestors. In ancient China, ancestor worship was a fertility cult; it was directed to the family soul rather than to the souls of individual ancestors. Graves and funerals constituted the foci of ancestor worship. This concentration has continued to modern times.

Buddhism did not diminish the importance of the family soul and of elaborate funerals and graves, but it gave a new status to individual ancestors. The individual was immortal. His immortality did not depend upon offerings or position in this world, but was dependent rather upon his character and conduct. There was a moral relation between this life and the condition of the soul in the next life.

Buddhism introduced the theory of karma, the equivalence of deed and award. Karma and transmigration have proved great boons in easing the tensions of life. Poverty and wealth, sickness and health, happiness and misfortune can be explained by these formulas. The Western Paradise presided over by Amitabha (in Chinese, O-mi-t'o-f'o), which is open to all who have faith in Amitabha, improved the status of ancestors and brought comfort to the survivors. But the great contribution of Buddhism was Hades! (See chaps. xiii, xviii.) The Taoists also seized upon the idea of Hades and adapted it to local conditions. It is a vital force in the imaginary environment of the Chinese.

Folk religion from 1900.—Participants in the Boxer uprising attempted, in 1900, to employ mass magic by the state to drive out the foreigner and all his works. It was a throwback, the last gasp of a disintegrating system. Abolition of the old examination system in 1905 marked the end of traditional Confucianism based on the philosophy of Chu Hsi (A.D. 1130–1200). In the early years of the Republic religious images were smashed, certain public religious ceremonies were forbidden, and pilgrimages were discouraged. Temples were converted into schools, or were occupied by soldiers; some were demolished. Folk religion was regarded as a superstition unworthy of a modern and democratic nation.

The impact of the West, the loosening of social ties, the dislocation of many family groups, the realization that the village, the clan, and the family can no longer provide adequate security, the growing conviction that the nation alone can give security—all these influences are changing the center and the pattern of village religion. They are sweeping away superficialities and bringing out fundamentals.

In recent years the cultural unity of the Chinese has gripped the masses. They have a profound conviction that the family is rooted in universal cosmic forces. Man is the product of these universal forces, is subject to them, and is connected with his ancestors by means of them.

The New Life Movement fostered by Generalissimo Chiang Kai-shek is an attempt to formulate deep collective instincts and to provide techniques for their implementation in a modernized state. Its objectives may be summarized as follows:

1. *Li* contains the basic—and regulated—attitude toward nature, society, and national affairs. With reference to nature, this means acceptance of the findings of science. As to society, it means obedience to rules of social etiquette. In national affairs it means discipline.

2. *Yi,* or right behavior, embraces conduct in accordance with natural law, social rule, and national discipline.

3. *Lien* means discrimination. Whatever agrees with *li* and *yi* is right; whatever lacks agreement with them is wrong.

4. *Ch'ih* is conscientiousness. When a person realizes that his action is not in accordance with *li* and *yi,* he is ashamed. When he

sees that the action of others is not in accord with these fundamentals, he is disgusted.

Folk religion in China is again reviving fundamentals. Some traditional ways will be discarded. Others will be modified, but the great racial and cultural realities will find expression in new patterns suited to the times.

CHAPTER XV

Confucianism

BY JOHN K. SHRYOCK

ONFUCIANISM is usually assumed to be a religion, but the assumption may be questioned. It is, more accurately, a complex system of thought—an attitude toward the universe. It includes elements which are generally considered to be religious, and it can be used as a basis for religion. But it is possible for an agnostic, a materialist, or an atheist to be an orthodox Confucian; nothing in the Confucian system of thought compels religious belief, as the person of average education understands the term. Heaven has been interpreted as an impersonal force, without raising the question of the interpreter's right to be considered a Confucian. It is better to leave unanswered the question whether Confucianism is a religion, because of the difficulty of defining religion and because it is impossible to give a conclusive answer. In any case, there is a Confucian system which contains religious elements, and its origins and development may be briefly described.

The Confucian classics contain material which dates from the second millennium B.C., including a few sacrificial odes. The odes show that sacrifices were made to ancestors, nature spirits, and a divinity called the Emperor on High, or Heaven.

The classics also contain legends dealing with men and events of the third millennium. The characters may have existed, but on the basis of existing materials they must be regarded as culture heroes and the stories largely myths, although there are a few historical references to local rulers of the second millennium.

About 1027 B.C. the Chou (jou) dynasty came into power. (See chap. v, above.) Its founders were regarded with great respect by

Confucius, who maintained that he was merely carrying on their traditions. How far this statement is true and how far he made original contributions to tradition, it is impossible to say. He called himself only a transmitter, but *he selected what he transmitted*— and, therefore, must have used a standard of selection which in itself was largely original. Scholars have tended to underestimate Confucius' own contribution to the system that goes by his name.

The Chou dynasty was feudalistic; after the first few rulers its kings became little more than figureheads. The division in society corresponded roughly to the distinction between noble and serf in the feudal period in Europe. Members of the noble caste were called "superior men" and commoners were called "small men." "Superior men" were supposed to live according to a code somewhat like that of chivalry, called *li,* which is usually translated "propriety," though it is often used to cover the whole of morality.

With dissolution of the central authority, intensification of warfare, growth of cities, and increase in wealth, a corresponding looseness in morality developed in the ruling class. This decay was shown not only in terrible scandals which broke from time to time, but in such minor symptoms as licentious songs and dances.

As confusion throughout the country increased, groups of mercenary soldiers and scholarly advisers in the art of government traveled from one state to another offering their services for hire. The leaders of all the schools of thought in the later feudal period, including Confucius, arose from this body of wandering politicians.

The word Confucius is a Latinized form of the Chinese phrase for "the Master K'ung," and was introduced by early Jesuits. There are many accounts of Confucius' life, but all are based on that given in the first Chinese dynastic history by the great historian Ssŭ-ma Ch'ien (sz-ma tsien). This work was written in the first century B.C.

Confucius was born in 551 B.C., in a family of the petty nobility descended from an ancient king. While yet a young man he became well known as a scholar and took up politics as a profession. At first his career promised to be successful, and he is said to have become the minister of justice in his native state of Lu (modern Shantung). Learning that it would be necessary either to give up his career or to compromise his principles, he quit politics and never again held public office. Gathering a small group of disciples, he devoted himself to teaching and literary work. By tradition he is considered to be the author of the *Ch'un Ch'iu,* or Spring and Autumn Annals, and the editor of other classics, particularly the *Shu Ching* (Classic of History) and the *Shih Ching* (Book of Odes—or Poetry, or Songs). The exact amount of Confucius' personal contribution to the system which goes by his name will never be known. Although he did not do all that tradition has assigned to him, he certainly made a contribution sufficiently important to justify the use of his name.

Confucius was a conservative and supported the feudal system associated with the Chou dynasty. He also stood for a strong central government, such as he believed to have existed at the beginning of the dynasty. He upheld the most characteristic feature of Chinese culture: loyalty to the family complex. This included the absolute authority of parents over their children, the preëminence of family loyalty, and the concept of family and clan as including both living and dead members.

The religious aspect of Confucianism involved a cult the chief feature of which was a communal meal, which was supposed to be shared by both living and dead. This cult is known to Westerners as ancestor worship. It necessitated a great number of observances and rituals, particularly emphasis upon funerals, the cult of the dead, and the keeping of clan records. All these, as well as the other forms of behavior required of a gentleman, were included in the primary virtue of *li.*

Confucius taught a philosophic doctrine which has been interpreted as similar to Plato's theory of ideas. The single principle underlying the universe he called Heaven. The reality of an object depended upon the degree to which it realized what Heaven had intended it to be. A prince or a father had reality only so far as he embodied what Heaven had decreed a prince or a father should be.

The moral standards of Confucius were high and included admirable conceptions of benevolence and justice. A sincere Confucian would be recognized as a good man in any civilization. Confucius described knowledge as the realization of one's achievements and limitations: knowledge of what one knows and what one does not know. His methods of teaching, habits, and sayings were collected by his disciples in a small volume, the *Lun Yü,* or Analects.

Confucius was in no sense a religious leader or the founder of a religion. He made no such claims for himself. He was a political reformer who was forced by his politics into stating philosophical, religious, and moral positions. It has been debated whether he was even a religious man. It seems wise to interpret him as accepting Heaven as a personal and purposive principle. He never attacked religion, though he seems to have ignored the current nature worship. He "sacrificed to the [ancestral] spirits as if they were present." He regarded himself as the instrument of Heaven, which was using him as a bell.

Confucius' teachings contain no developed system of thought. The records, with their random accounts and sayings of the Master, are more like the Gospels than like the works of Aristotle. Confucius was a wise and good man who endeavored to reform the corruption of his time. He never dreamed of the weight which future generations would place upon his lightest utterance. He was, however, a man who firmly believed that he had been called to a definite mission, and to this he unswervingly devoted his life.

In what he deliberately attempted, Confucius failed. The feudal lords neither appointed him to office nor adopted his principles. His life was not outwardly tragic, however. He lived into old age, dying in 479 B.C., and always he commanded respect.

Before, during, and after Confucius' lifetime, warfare and the dissolution of morality went on unchecked. A few large states absorbed the lesser. Finally, after a desperate struggle, the northwestern border state of Ch'in (tsin) alone remained, and the empire was founded as a result of its triumph in 221 B.C.

In this period the followers of Confucius constituted one of several schools of thought which molded the intellectual life of China. The Sage left a considerable number of disciples who, in turn, had their own disciples; so the tradition endured.

Yet it was an unpopular and unsuccessful tradition. Wandering scholars were appointed as advisers by the feudal lords, but the Confucians were too much interested in righteousness and ritual to be administrators in time of disorder. Their attitude was especially disliked in Ch'in, whose rulers despised and opposed them. They did, however, produce a number of important men, of whom the greatest were Mencius (a Latinized form of Mêng Tzǔ) and

Hsün Tzǔ (sün dz) (*ca.* 298–238 or 340–245 B.C.). Mencius (fl. 324–314 B.C.) was particularly disliked because of his teaching that a ruler who did not realize the obligations of his position could properly—and should—be deposed.

The chief Confucian discussion of the period centered about human nature. On this subject there are four possible positions: human nature is either good, or bad, or both good and bad, or neither good nor bad. It is probable that the subject was discussed more thoroughly than ever before or since. The chief protagonists were Mencius, who held that human nature is fundamentally good, being the image of Heaven within us, and Hsün Tzǔ, who held that it is essentially evil. For several centuries the view of Hsün Tzǔ predominated. This contributed to the unique development of Chinese education and the scholar class, since, if human nature is evil, the only remedy lies in education. The final decision of orthodox Confucianism—made many centuries later—was that Mencius was right. But in the closing centuries of the feudal period, Confucians for the most part engaged in academic discussions.

The empire was unified by Ch'in Shih Huang Ti, or First Emperor of the Ch'in dynasty, in 221 B.C. (see chap. vi, above), and Confucianism seemed to be at its lowest point. The Ch'in dynasty lasted but a few years, however, and was succeeded by the Han. The position of the Confucians was bettered, but it was not until 136 B.C., in the reign of the Emperor Wu (140–87 B.C.), that they noticeably enjoyed the imperial patronage.

Han governmental policy was based on a mixture of earlier theories. Certain elements of Ch'in government were continued, but a modified and innocuous feudal system was restored. The Confucians never became the sole party in the government under the Former, or Western, Han (*ca.* 206 B.C.–A.D. 9), but in certain directions they acquired great influence, particularly in education, literature, and ceremonial.

Confucius had laid especial emphasis upon correct ritual and, by the time of the Han dynasty, was generally recognized as the final authority on such matters. When the Han emperors began to develop their court, Confucians were called into power since they were regarded as experts in the rules of cultured behavior.

In 136 B.C. the Emperor Wu was persuaded by certain Confucian scholars to found an imperial university. Its graduates, appointed to official positions directly from the common people, aided the Emperor Wu and later rulers in curbing the nobility. This was the beginning of the most remarkable and long-lived system of education ever developed in any land.

Succeeding emperors enlarged and perfected the system until, toward the close of the Han period, about A.D. 200, the students in the capital alone were numbered in tens of thousands. A series of examinations was devised and those who passed them were given official careers. The system endured, with ups and downs, until 1905. On the whole it worked well and gave the country a long line of capable officials. In theory, almost any man might aspire to the highest position; in practice, a relatively small number of scholarly families possessing wealth and leisure supplied most of the officials.

From the beginning, the examination system was controlled by Confucians; indeed, the terms scholar and Confucian became almost synonymous. The civil service of the state, and to an appreciable degree the military also, was Confucian throughout the larger part of Chinese imperial history.

Confucians also contributed greatly to the development and fixation of the language, particularly through the preparation of the first dictionary, near the end of the first century of the Christian era. The written language is ideographic, like Western mathematical and musical notations; the symbols stand for ideas, not sounds. Not being subject to a fluctuating pronunciation, Chinese writing has a permanence not found in phonetic script. This, in turn, has contributed to the stability of culture.

There is little or nothing to indicate that Confucianism was a religious movement in the pre-Christian era. A few traditions, however, came to be generally accepted by Confucians. It has been said that not long after Confucius died he became an object of worship to a religious cult. This is thoroughly unreliable. There is also a reference in the first dynastic history, which was copied into the second as well, that Liu Pang, i.e., Han Kao-tsu (206–195 B.C.), the founder of the Han dynasty, sacrificed to Confucius. This is at best improbable. By about the middle of the first century of the Christian era, however, more than five centuries after his death, sacrifices were offered to him. The cult developed until, in the

HU SHIH
Poet, Philosopher, and Statesman

CONFUCIUS

The Sage of China

seventh and eighth centuries, it became the religion of the state
civil service and the scholar class. Great temples were built, which
were filled with images and various works of art, and fixed times
and rituals of sacrifice were decreed by the government.

Worship was not limited to the Sage himself. It became the custom for his disciples, ancient and modern, to share in the cult.
Beginning with his personal followers, and including the great
Confucians of later ages, many names were honored in the state
Confucian temples, which thus became halls of fame of all that
was best in Chinese culture. Inclusion in the Confucian temples
became the greatest honor—always a posthumous one—that could
come to a public servant. The custom continued into the period
of the Republic.

How far the development of this cult, as the expression in religious terms of the civil service of the state, may have been due to
such external influences as Buddhism, it is impossible to say. Such
influences certainly existed. The cult of Confucius was paralleled
by a similar military cult, which has not been adequately investigated by scholars. There were also many other cults of semideified
men, such as the patrons of guilds and trades.

A Confucian reaction to Buddhist and Taoist influences began in
the Sung period (960–1279). Eventually this resulted in a Confucian reformation, and in 1530 the emperor destroyed all temple
images, which must have included numerous works of art. Thereafter, the only objects of reverence or worship were wooden tablets
inscribed with names and titles. The central tablet bears the legend,
"Confucius, Perfectly Holy Teacher of Antiquity."

From the sixth century, civil officials were required to perform
rites in the Confucian temples. How far this was genuinely religious
may be questioned. It could be performed as a religious act, or
merely as a patriotic act, resembling the ceremonies held at the
tombs of unknown soldiers. In later times most Christian missionaries decided that their converts could not take part. It is noteworthy that a similar situation developed in the twentieth century
with respect to Shintoism, which has been influenced by Confucianism. In Japan and Korea some missionaries have permitted
Christians to participate in the state rites; others have not.

Leaving the question of the cult of Confucius, which has never

been essential to his influence, the history of the Confucian movement may now be further considered. In the later, or Eastern, Han
period (A.D. 25–220) Confucianism was all-powerful. The time was
eclectic and late compilations were accepted as genuine. Enormous
commentaries were produced, also the first of the two standard
interpretations of classic literature.

Following the collapse of the Eastern Han dynasty came a reaction against everything Confucian, even morality. Into this intellectual and religious vacuum flowed Buddhism and Taoism. Chinese
thought in the period of the Six Dynasties, from the fall of Han to
the rise of Sui (220–589) (see chap. vi, above), was characterized by
toleration: Confucianism, Taoism, and Buddhism were regarded
as three ways of reaching one goal. This situation continued, to
some extent, under the T'ang dynasty (618–906). Most of the
T'ang rulers patronized Taoism and maintained that they were
descended from its founder. But Buddhism, also, flourished for a
time; and Confucianism progressed as the religious aspect of the
state civil service.

Under the Sung dynasty (960–1279) a Confucian reaction all
but submerged Buddhism and Taoism as respectable systems of
thought. (See chap xvi, below.) Several distinguished thinkers,
in formulating the second of the two great Confucian schools of
interpretation, used the Confucian canon to attack Buddhist
idealism. In this reaction against the once alien religion, Chu Hsi
(1130–1200) and other Confucians emphasized certain parts of the
Confucian canon, including two sections of the *Li Chi,* or Book of
Rites: the *Ta Hsüeh,* or Great Learning, and the *Chung Yung,*
or Doctrine of the Mean; also the *Lun Yü,* or Analects, and the
Mêng Tzŭ, or Works of Mencius. The question of the nature of
man was now finally settled for orthodox Confucians in favor of
Mencius, who was given greater honor than ever.

After the Sung age, Confucianism hardened into the mold prepared by Chu Hsi. In the Ming and Manchu periods it was influential but sterile so far as philosophy was concerned, although it
included some brilliant critics and historiographers. The most important figure of the late period was Wang Yang-ming, or Wang
Shou-jên (1472–1529), who differed with Chu Hsi on "the investigation of things." Although Wang has had much influence, par-

ticularly in Japan, Chu Hsi remains the standard interpreter of the philosophy of Confucius.

The Sung Confucians were influential also in Japan, where they affected a number of important writers who, in turn, contributed to the nationalistic revival in the middle of the nineteenth century. The Japanese, however, in both earlier and later times, selected those features of Confucianism which appealed to them, such as loyalty to the throne, and ignored those they did not like, such as Mencius' sanction of revolution against a degenerate ruler.

Under the Republic, Confucian sacrifices were at first continued, but later they seemed to lose their significance and fell into disuse. The old connection with the civil government is gone and the state temples are dilapidated. Japanese imperialists tried to revive the cult after 1931, but their attempts helped neither them nor Confucianism. It appears unlikely that the cult of the Sage will be revived. Nonetheless, Confucius is a unique figure, and Confucianism will continue to represent the characteristic Chinese attitude toward the universe. How great is its importance can be perceived from the position of the family in Chinese life. Taoism and Buddhism ignore or deprecate family relations. Yet the family remains at the heart of Chinese culture. It is indeed a handicap sometimes, as when an official puts family loyalty above loyalty to the public good. But the predominance of the family in Chinese society is due mainly to the influence of Confucianism.

Confucian literature remains important, although it will never again be the sole basis of education. Its moral teachings, particularly those of Confucius himself, will always endure. But perhaps the most lasting effect of Confucianism is found in the position of the scholar class and the general reverence for education. There is no other land where culture and education, particularly literary ability, receive such honor and so directly lead to power. Although the subject matter of scholarship now includes science and other modern or Western subjects, reverence for the scholar remains an outstanding Chinese characteristic. Accordingly, the influence of Confucius and Confucianism is decidedly a factor in the life of a great nation, the most populous in the world. And Confucianism is well worth the study and consideration of those who, as Confucius said of himself, "desire to know men."

CHAPTER XVI

Neo-Confucianism

BY CHAN WING-TSIT

IT IS IMPOSSIBLE to understand the Chinese outlook on life and the thought underlying much of modern China's transformation without some knowledge of the intellectual movement from the twelfth to the twentieth century. The story of this movement, which is called Neo-Confucianism[1] in the West, is virtually the story of modern Chinese thought.

Neo-Confucianism arose in the eleventh century partly as a development of the humanism of Confucius and Mencius and partly as a protest against Buddhism and Taoism. Taoism advocated the "preservation of the pure nature" of the individual, to the neglect of society, and Buddhism rejected society altogether. Against these antisocial philosophies the Neo-Confucianists launched vigorous attacks. They denounced the two heterodox systems as entirely "unsubstantial."[2] To them the Buddhist belief in existence as illusory was but a confession of inability to understand reason, nature, and destiny. Buddhist pessimism was a failure to understand man.[3] Neo-Confucianists criticized Buddhists for looking upon all things, including clothing and food, as void—and yet using these things every day.[4]

They condemned the Buddhist desertion of the family as dangerous in practice because such renunciation would eventually annihilate mankind, and as untenable in logic because, although a man might desert his family, he could not escape society as long as he set his feet on earth. Even Buddhists formed a society of masters and pupils. The Buddhist attempt to transcend, and the Taoist

---

[1] For notes to chapter xvi see pages 529–531.

attempt to ignore, birth and death were based, it was argued, not only on fear, but on selfishness. Both were branded as unjust and cowardly in that they encouraged working solely for one's own interests, thereby avoiding social responsibility, and as socially destructive in that they resulted in the rejection of empirical knowledge in favor of transcendental wisdom. Buddhists were conceded special ability in self-discipline; but their asserted total lack of ability to deal with others was deplored.[5] In short, both Buddhists and Taoists, in the eyes of Neo-Confucianists, were "incompetent to promote and bring human affairs to successful conclusion."[6]

But the Neo-Confucianists went much further: they attacked Buddhists and Taoists (see chaps. xviii, xvii, below) in their intellectual foundation, their doctrine of the Void. Under the influence of Buddhism, Taoists had transformed Lao Tzŭ's (lao dz) teaching of "spiritual tranquillity" and emotional "vacuity" (humility) into a metaphysical vacuity, and had carried Chuang Tzŭ's (juang dz) doctrine of "equality of things and opinions" to the point of making no distinction between the One and the Many. In Buddhism the idea of the Void was developed to an extreme. As interpreted by Nagarjuna of India, the Void means essentially "being devoid of all specific characters," or the negation of names, characters, self-nature, and independent reality for things, which are accepted as phenomenally and temporarily, but not ultimately, real. This amounts to outright denial of the phenomenal world in favor of an absolute.[7]

In the T'ien-t'ai and Hua-yen schools of Buddhism, both essentially Chinese, an effort was made to save the world of appearance. According to T'ien-t'ai, all things are void since they depend on causes and therefore have no independent reality; but because they are produced they enjoy temporary existence. Being both void and temporary is the nature of dharmas (elements of existence); and by this is meant the Mean. Thus the Void, Temporariness, and the Mean involve one another—they are both three and one. "Material existence is not different from Void and Void is not different from material existence."

The Hua-yen school advocated the doctrine of universal causation, or mutual causation of all dharmas. Because all dharmas have the six characteristics of universality, speciality, similarity, diversity, integration, and differentiation, they are interoriginated, interrelated, interdependent, interpenetrated, and interidentified. They are thus both One and Many, and result in a world of "perfect harmony without obstacle."

In these schools the humanistically minded Chinese tempered Indian Buddhism and brought it closer to earth. Chinese Buddhism, however, reached its climax not in the T'ien-t'ai and Hua-yen schools but in the meditation school, the Ch'an (Japanese, Zen). Ch'an Buddhism teaches "directly pointing to the human mind, and to become a Buddha by seeing one's nature." By nature is meant the Buddha-mind in its highest attributes and true essence. The Buddha-mind "knows no distinction of manifestation and silence, mind and its objects, or enlightenment and ignorance." It is the Void, which is "neither holy nor unholy, neither cause nor effect, neither good nor evil, neither form nor characteristics, neither the root nor the attachment of feelings, and neither the Buddha nor sentient beings." The world of multiplicity, with its specific characters and distinctions, is the result of man's ignorance and attachment, and so is but a dream. Thus, although Ch'an, or Zen, was based on T'ien-t'ai and Hua-yen, it practically denied what these two schools had tried to affirm. Nowhere else in Chinese Buddhism has its negativistic philosophy gone to such an extreme.

Neo-Confucianism protested furiously against this otherworldly, mystical, and negativistic philosophy. To the Buddhist Void was opposed Reason, which is identical with the Great Ultimate. "The Great Ultimate moves and generates the active principle, *yang*. When its activity reaches its limit, it becomes tranquil, engendering the passive principle, *yin*. When the Great Ultimate becomes completely tranquil, it begins to move again. Thus movement and tranquillity alternate and become the occasion of each other. . . . By the transformation of *yang* and its union with *yin*, the Five Agents—water, fire, wood, metal, and earth—arise. When these five forces [*ch'i*] are distributed in harmonious order, the four seasons run their course."[8] As a result, "The One and the Many have each their own proper state of being. The great and the small have each their determinate nature."[9] Thus reality is a progressively evolved and well-coördinated system.

This is true because of a universal principle called Reason. In the words of the brothers Ch'êng (Ming-tao, 1032–1086; I-ch'uan, 1033–1107), "We say that all things are one reality because all things have the same Reason in them," and they all have Reason simply because things "must have their principles of being." As Reason is the universal principle, "The Reason of a thing is one with the Reason of all things."[10]

Reason needs an agency through which to operate, and also needs to be embodied. It must, therefore, be supplemented by a substantiating and particularizing principle. This is *ch'i*, or vital force, which, working through the Five Agents and the two modes, *yin* and *yang*, differentiates the One into the Many. But it is not to be sharply contrasted with Reason. Basically, there is no distinction between them, for, as the greatest Neo-Confucianist, Chu Hsi (1130–1200), said: "The Great Ultimate is Reason, whereas activity and tranquillity are the vital force. As the vital force operates, Reason operates. The two are mutually dependent and are never separate."[11]

Because of this coöperative functioning of Reason and the vital force, the universe, with all its myriad things, is a harmonious system. "Centrality is the order of the universe, and harmony is its unalterable law."[12] Thus the cosmos is a moral order and therefore a social order. Consequently, nothing can stand by itself; everything has its opposite; no two things are exactly alike; nothing is purely *yin* or purely *yang*; nothing is permanently in the state of activity or of tranquillity; everything is in process of growth and decay; and every production is a new creation.

All these characteristics of the universe are but its Reason. It is the duty of man to comprehend Reason in order to appreciate fully the meaning of his existence. We must "investigate things to the utmost." "A thing is an event. A perfect understanding of an event can be obtained by investigating to the utmost the Reason underlying it." When perfect understanding takes place, our nature will be realized and our destiny will be fulfilled since "the complete realization of the Reason of things, the full development of one's nature, and the fulfillment of destiny are simultaneous."[13]

To achieve full understanding of Reason, the human mind must undergo severe discipline. The mind must be sincere (*ch'êng*) and serious (*ching*). By seriousness, according to Chu Hsi, is meant "apprehension, as if there were something feared. Sincerity is truth and the utter absence of anything false."[14]

In this rationalism appears an influence of Buddhism. Many Neo-Confucianists had studied Buddhism in their youth, and remained fascinated by it even when they attacked it. The Neo-Confucian idea of the mutual dependence of the One and the Many can be traced to Hua-yen. The doctrine of sincerity and seriousness has a definite connection with the meditation and insight of both T'ien-t'ai and Ch'an.

But the spirit of Neo-Confucian rationalism is diametrically opposed to that of Buddhist mysticism. Whereas Buddhism insisted on the unreality of things, Neo-Confucianism stressed their reality. Buddhism and Taoism asserted that existence came out of, and returned to, nonexistence; Neo-Confucianism regarded reality as a gradual realization of the Great Ultimate.[15] Buddhism denied the particular; Neo-Confucianism affirmed it. Buddhism and Taoism cherished the state of absolute tranquillity; Neo-Confucianism preferred the harmony of activity and tranquillity. Buddhism taught the cycle of formation, duration, deterioration, extinction. Neo-Confucianism held that things are always in process of transformation.[16] To the Buddhists, existence was an aimless cycle; to the Neo-Confucianists, the universe was perpetually new. Buddhists attempted to transcend birth and death; Taoists sought immortal life; and Neo-Confucianists accepted life and death as processes in the operation of *yin* and *yang,* and taught "complete realization of one's nature" as the best way to deal with them.[17] Buddhists and Taoists identified birth and death, and right and wrong; Neo-Confucianists regarded the sense of right and wrong as the foundation of moral life. Buddhists—and, to some degree, Taoists as well—relied on meditation and insight to achieve supreme wisdom; Neo-Confucianists chose to follow Reason.

In ethics, Confucius advocated a life of *jên* (ren)—true manhood, benevolence, love, or goodness—as a matter of good sense. The Neo-Confucianists, however, placed this doctrine on a solid metaphysical foundation. Since all things have the same Reason in them, they argued, "All people are our brothers and sisters and all things are our companions." We should not entertain attitudes of discrimination or inequality, but must love all universally.[18]

Religion, too, was put on a rationalistic basis, and Heaven was equated with Reason. *Kuei* (guei) and *shên,* instead of being heavenly and earthly spirits who bestowed blessings and sent punishments, were interpreted as "the natural functions of the two modes of the vital force,"[19] or "the manifestation of the creative power."[20] As Chu Hsi put it, *"Shên* is the extension and *kuei* the intension of the vital force." Spiritual beings, the unfolding of a flower, lightning, and all conceivable phenomena are manifestations of the vital force.[21] The attitude toward such manifestations should be not fear but sincerity and seriousness. Sacrificing is essentially an expression of this attitude. The rationalistic approach to religion has been characteristic of the Chinese intellectual movement to the present.

In government and education Neo-Confucianists followed Confucius and Mencius faithfully. Like their masters, they advocated "benevolent government." They insisted on benevolence and righteousness instead of profit and force as the foundations of government. They declared that only the virtuous and competent were fit to rule. They urged fair and light taxation, reduction in conscription, impartial selection of military leaders, willingness on the part of rulers to accept criticism and advice. These were regarded not merely as sane measures but as necessary applications of Reason. A good ruler adopts these measures as a carpenter uses the compass.

In education Neo-Confucianists, following in the footsteps of Confucius and Mencius, recommended the study of books and sages to the end of "manifesting the clear character of man, giving new life to the people, and dwelling in the ultimate good." These are necessary not only because they are sound but also because they are dictated by Reason. In short, the Neo-Confucian movement of the Sung dynasty (960–1279) represented an effort to make objective and self-evident Reason the foundation of life.

In the Ming period (1368–1644), however, objective and self-evident Reason gradually became subjective. To the great Neo-Confucianist scholar-general-statesman, Wang Yang-ming, or Wang Shou-jên (1472–1529), the Confucian ideal remained the central objective. The *Ta Hsüeh,* or Great Learning, sums up the ideal thus:

When things are investigated, then true knowledge is achieved. When true knowledge is achieved, then the will becomes sincere. When the will is sincere, then the heart is set right. When the heart is set right, then the personal life is cultivated. When the personal life is cultivated, then the family life is regulated. When the family life is regulated, then the national life is orderly. And when the national life is orderly, then there is peace in this world.

Wang's whole system is built around this passage. But he regarded the mind as the embodiment of Reason or identical with it. Instead of investigating *things,* said Wang Yang-ming, one should investigate the *mind.* The original nature of the mind is good. Consequently, one possesses the native ability to know good and with it the native ability to do good, for, in his novel theory, knowledge and conduct are identical. The starting point of a good life, therefore, is to "exercise one's mind fully." This can be done only by "tranquil repose," in which alone can the highest good be attained.[22]

In this idealistic tendency the influence of Ch'an (Zen) may be perceived. Many Neo-Confucianists of the time were so overwhelmed by Zen that they were called "insane Zen Buddhists." Neo-Confucianism resembled "Confucianism externally, but Buddhism internally," for it had become subjective and speculative. The time was ripe for revolt.

In the beginning of the Ch'ing period (1644–1912) the revolt broke out. Scholars demanded a return from contemplation to experience, from the abstract to the concrete, from the transcendent to the immanent, from the universal to the particular, from the remote Great Ultimate to everyday human events, and from the speculative philosophy of Sung and Ming to the sociopolitical teachings of Confucius and Mencius. "The study of the sages," said the leader Ku (gu) Yen-wu (1613–1682), "was limited to ordinary speech and ordinary conduct. It did not consist of speculative books and diagrams."[23] Learning from everyday experience and practical application of knowledge were insisted upon. "Sung and Ming scholars," cried Ku, "ignored the distress and want of the world, and talked about subtlety, essence, and unity. I am at a loss to understand."[24] Sincerity and seriousness should not lead to a mental vacuum, the Ch'ing scholars insisted, but must be related to practical affairs—and they emphasized human desires. "Reason is embodied in human desires," said Wang Ch'uan-shan (1619–1693). "Without human desires there can be no expression of Reason."[25]

This empirical philosophy was not formulated by accident, but was a result of the early Ch'ing scholars' new interest in science, their new attitude of doubt, and their new method of verification. Their researches and writings dealt with astronomy, mathematics, geography, and mineralogy. Exceedingly strong in creative spirit, they doubted the authenticity and traditional interpretations of the Confucian classics and insisted on historical and objective evidence. Ku, for example, assembled 160 examples to prove the ancient pronunciation of a single word! Emancipating themselves from the dogma of Sung and Ming Neo-Confucianism, the philosophers returned to the ancient classics, declaring that "investigation of things" meant nothing other than investigating the Three Things: the Six Classics, Six Meritorious Deeds, and Six (Liberal) Arts. They even asserted that "without the classics there can be no system of Reason."

On the surface, the movement was a return to the past—but its object was primarily to understand the present. Ku made this clear: "I have nothing to do with any literature that does not deal with that part of the Six Classics which has a direct bearing on the affairs of our present-day society."[26] Current affairs were studied in the light of past experience. The intellectual rebirth of seventeenth-century China resembled the earlier renascence of western Europe. Like their counterparts in Europe, the Ch'ing scholars reëxamined classical philosophies, emancipated themselves from speculation, were independent in thinking and critical in judgment, employed methods of induction and verification, and rediscovered the particular, the present, the individual, and society.

The movement reached high tide in the eighteenth century, especially in the person of Tai Chên, or Tai Tung-yüan (1724–1777), who may be taken as representative of the new philosophy. In him the emphases on practical application and human desires reached the highest degree. At the age of ten Tai asked, "How did Master Chu Hsi know that it was so?" Tai's guiding principles were: "Rely on facts and seek what is practical," and "Never accept anything unsupported by evidence." He rejected in its entirety the philosophy of early Neo-Confucianists, especially those of Sung, who had considered Reason to be above events.

In spite of their conscious effort not sharply to contrast Reason and the vital force, early Neo-Confucianists had considered Reason to be above corporeality—pure, refined, and universal—and the vital force to be corporeal—mixed, crude, and particular. Tai Tung-yüan vigorously criticized this bifurcation of reality: "The distinction of what is corporeal and what is above corporeality refers to operation of the vital force. . . . What is corporeal is that which has taken a definite shape, and what is above corporeality is that which has not taken a definite shape. . . . Thus corporeality means the transfiguration of things and not the vital force."[27] The vital force—with its Five Agents and two universal principles, one active and the other passive—was not inferior to Reason. To Chu Hsi and his circle, Reason was the moral law which was above the vital force. To Tai Tung-yüan, on the other hand, the moral law meant nothing but the operation of the vital force. There was no distinction, then, between Reason and the moral law, on the one hand, and the vital force, on the other. Reason and the vital force together constituted the moral law.

> The moral law refers to the incessant transformation, whereas Reason refers to the complete fullness of the moral law. . . . That which produces life is the source of transformation, and that which produces life in a systematic order is the flow of transformation. . . . As there is growth, there is repose, and as there is repose, there is growth. This is how the universe keeps on forming and transforming. That which produces life is called *jên*, and that which is responsible for the orderliness of life is called propriety and righteousness.[28]

Thus the moral law finds expression in constant and orderly transformation, the realization of which is Reason. In other words, Reason is discoverable only in the operation of the vital force in everyday events. As Tai said, "Human relations and everyday affairs . . . are Reason."[29]

From the eleventh to the sixteenth century the general opinion in the discussion of Reason was that good action proceeds from Reason, whereas evil action proceeds from desires. Thus Reason and desire are sharply contrasted. To Tai Tung-yüan this opinion was erroneous because "men and creatures all have desires, and desires are the functions of their nature. Men and creatures all have feelings, and feelings are the operations of their nature."[30] Since feelings are inborn, they "should not be violated."[31] If their functionings "do not err, they are in harmony with Heaven and Earth."[32]

Tai defended desires and feelings not only because they are in-born but also because desire and Reason are inseparable. "Desire refers to a thing, whereas Reason refers to its principle. . . . A thing is an event. In speaking of an event, we cannot go beyond daily matters such as drinking and eating. If we cast aside all daily matters and say that herein lies Reason, that is not what the ancient sages recognized Reason to be."[33] Furthermore, feeling, which engenders desires, does not violate Reason. On the contrary, "Reason never obtains where feeling does not. . . . When feeling is expressed neither too much nor too little, it is called Reason."[34] When we harmonize feeling and desires with Reason, we shall then come into harmony with the universe. When all men and things are in harmony with the universe, there will be complete fulfillment of the moral law.

The spirit of Tai's philosophy was the central emphasis of all Ch'ing scholars, namely, practical application. However, the interest of Tai and his immediate followers was, for the most part, literary and intellectual. Like their predecessors, they built their system around the Confucian classics as interpreted in the Han period (206 B.C.–A.D. 220), and considered that almost anything from Han was good. Han tradition gradually became a dogma—and another revolt was in order.

This revolt was started by K'ang Yu-wei (1858–1927), who threw overboard all Han and later classics as unauthentic. He boldly declared that Confucius was not a conformer, but a reformer who attempted to "transform social and political systems on the pretext of ancient examples." He held that the ancient sages had invented the ideal emperors and had made these their authority. Confucius, according to K'ang, conceived history as an evolution through the Three Periods: those of Disorder, of the Well-to-Do State, and of the Great Commonwealth.[35] "When *jên* prevails, the period becomes that of the Great Commonwealth. When righteousness prevails, the period becomes that of the Well-to-Do State."[36] The Period of Disorder is characterized by nationalism, capitalism, and individualism. In the Period of the Well-to-Do State these still exist, but they are subordinated to internationalism and socialism. When the Great Commonwealth is established, unity and harmony will reign in society and government.

When the great Way prevailed, the world became a common state. Rulers were elected according to their virtue and ability, and good faith and peace were restored.... The old people were able to enjoy their old age, the adults to employ their talent, the young people to respect their elders, and the widows, orphans, and cripples to have support. The men had their respective occupations and the women had their homes.... This was the Period of the Great Commonwealth.[37]

K'ang was a rebel. He felt that the ideal of practical application must be translated into actuality in society and government. He therefore became a vigorous reformer, even to the point of risking his life by interrupting an imperial procession to present his petition for reform. Eventually he engineered the Reform of 1898, which, if successful, would have changed the course of Chinese history. It failed, and K'ang was sent into exile. He later became an ultraconservative; nevertheless, his philosophy and earlier political activities brought into bold relief the empirical sociopolitical philosophy which had been evolving for some nine hundred years.

What effect did this long period of intellectual evolution have on the Chinese outlook on life—and on the spirit of modern Chinese transformation? With respect to the former, it strengthened the rationalistic, this-worldly, humanistic, and practical tendency of the Chinese, which gained momentum with the overcoming of Buddhism and Taoism in the Sung period and reasserted itself in the Ch'ing. It is not surprising that in the late Ming and early Ch'ing periods Christianity was well received, chiefly, perhaps, because it offered astronomy, mathematics, and medicine. Nor is it any wonder that, when serious dissemination of Western thought was undertaken in 1897 by Yen Fu (1853–1921), books by Mill, Adams, Darwin, and Huxley were the first to be translated. The Chinese were and still are, on the whole, rationalistic, this-worldly, humanistic, and practical in their outlook on life.

Modern Chinese transformations—social, political, and intellectual—are expressions of this temperament. These transformations resulted, in part, from the impact of the West. But why has China accepted Western culture more spontaneously, wholeheartedly, and thoroughly than India or Japan? The answer is that in China there was a long evolution toward a rationalistic, practical, and humanistic sociopolitical philosophy. To be sure, the ruling class of the decadent Manchu dynasty and the conservative Confucianists, in their resistance to science and to social and political reform, were neither rational nor practical. But when search is made beyond the immediate past, which was saturated with dogmatism, traditionalism, and conservatism, it is discovered that modern transformations come into line with a series of renascence movements in Chinese history. Dr. Hu Shih called the Sung movement China's second renascence and the Ch'ing movement China's fourth.[38] The twentieth century was ripe for another rebirth.

Furthermore, even beneath the official and Confucian conservatism ran strong currents of transformation.[39] T'an Ssŭ-t'ung (1865–1898),[40] one of K'ang's pupils who was executed for his part in the abortive reform, attempted to synthesize Confucianism with Western science by propounding the theory that *jên* was all-pervasive and all-penetrating, identical with ether and electricity. Liang Ch'i-ch'ao (1873–1928), another of K'ang's pupils, advocated wholesale introduction of Western culture and contributed more to the modernization of Chinese thought than any other Chinese except Hu Shih. Chang T'ai-yen (1868–1936), a noted Confucianist who was influenced by the democratic philosophy of Neo-Confucianist Huang Tsung-hsi (1610–1695),[41] started a political revolution. In a real sense, these men paved the way for the renascence of 1919. This renascence, under the leadership of Hu Shih, has put Chinese reforms on the basis of Western science and rationalism. Only a beginning has been made in China's transformation. But because of the intellectual background and the impact of the West, there is no doubt that, as time goes on, the spirit of rationalism and humanism—and with them science, democracy, and social welfare—will become stronger.

CHAPTER XVII

Taoism

BY HOMER H. DUBS

TAOISM HAS BEEN A PROTEAN MOVEMENT. Beginning as a philosophy that ranks among the world's greatest presystematic bodies of thought, Taoism (daoism) became the outstanding opponent of Confucianism. In that capacity it adopted many alien features, such as magic, alchemy, and even a pantheon. In the twentieth century, Taoism manifests itself chiefly in two forms: as a mystical philosophy that continues to exert great influence on Chinese thought, and as a popular, superstitious religion. The temples, images, and priests of the latter are still found throughout China. Although Taoism as a religion is dying, philosophical Taoism maintains an important position.

The founder of philosophical Taoism was called the Lao Tzŭ (lao dz), a recluse who lived at the end of the fourth century B.C. His clan name was Li, his given name, Erh, and his courtesy name, Tan (dan). Surnames were often changed in those days, and the Lao Tzŭ's son Tsung (dzung), following the common practice, took for his surname the name of his fief. In 273 B.C., as a general in the state of Wei, he arranged peace between Wei and Ch'in (tsin) and in reward was made Viscount of Tuan-kan (duan-gan). The name Lao Tzŭ probably means "venerable viscount."

The Lao Tzŭ's birthplace was within a hundred miles southwest of that of Confucius. There is a tradition that the Lao Tzŭ became keeper of the royal archives at Lo-yang, the Chou (jou) capital, and was visited by Confucius. This account, however, almost certainly originated in Han times in an attempt to bolster Taoism, which was being discriminated against.

In those days government office was largely hereditary, and the Lao Tzǔ probably belonged to a clan of hereditary generals. In despair at the suicidal militarist policy of the Wei court, he seems to have retired to private life to cultivate a philosophy that denied war and many other values prized at court. He left a brief but extremely brilliant book, later entitled *Tao Tê Ching* (dao de jing), or the Classic concerning the Way and Values.

Chuang Chou (juang jou), second founder of Taoism, was a younger contemporary of the Lao Tzǔ. He is usually called Chuang Tzǔ, literally "the master surnamed Chuang." (Tzǔ has various meanings: viscount, sir, gentleman, master.) Chuang Tzǔ came from the same region as the Lao Tzǔ. Chuang Tzǔ, likewise, retired from the world. He illuminated the teachings of the Lao Tzǔ by his brilliant writings and added his own philosophy: absolute skepticism, mystical practices, and contentment with fate, including death itself. The last of these additions was opposed by certain later Taoists, who called the Lao Tzǔ's philosophy Huang-Lao, that is, the teaching of the Yellow Lord and of the Lao Tzǔ.[1] Chuang Tzǔ's teaching was called Lao-Chuang—a synthesis of the Lao Tzǔ and Chuang Tzǔ. In reality there is no disagreement between the two Taoist founders.

The Lao Tzǔ and Chuang Tzǔ were not the first important Chinese recluses. Two noble brothers, Po-i (bo-yi) and Shu-ch'i (shu-tsi), are said to have gone into retirement when, about 1100 B.C., King Wu rebelled against his overlord, the King of Shang, and founded the Chou (jou) dynasty. Half a millennium later Confucius in his travels met various recluses who derided him for attempting to reform a declining age. But the honorable company of protestants against iniquitous government to which Confucius belongs has remained so continual a feature of Chinese life that its members have sometimes been given a separate chapter in standard Chinese histories. The Lao Tzǔ and Chuang Tzǔ were men who would normally have attained high official position, but they deliberately refused it. Their thought was in opposition to their times. In this respect they were characteristic of the Taoist philosophy which has benefited China by its criticism of the dominant Confucian ethic and other doctrinaire policies.

---

[1] For notes to chapter xvii see page 531.

In the fourth century B.C., China was in turmoil. Wars between its petty states had for centuries been increasing in intensity; large areas had become depopulated, and the country's wealth was exhausted. Any plausible doctrine could find a home in one state or another, and a variety of philosophic systems developed. The Confucians upheld a high ideal of moral life and righteous government and asserted that Heaven, highest of the gods, destroys a wicked ruler. Mo Tzŭ[2] and his followers were even more idealistic in their attacks on war and their preaching of love for all people. Both Confucians and Mohists declared that Heaven governs the world righteously, rewarding virtue and punishing wickedness. But Chinese politicians were realists and were skeptical of moral idealism.

The Lao Tzŭ and Chuang Tzŭ despaired of moral idealism and of political realism. With keen insight they attacked the underlying assumptions of both: "Heaven and Earth [the greatest gods of China] are not humane. They treat people and things like herbs or beasts" (*Tao Tê Ching*, chap. 5). According to the Lao Tzŭ, then, the universe is neither kindly nor righteous. It goes its way regardless of human desires and human standards of conduct. The person who tries to reform morals or to right wrongs is wasting his efforts, for he is fighting the way of the universe. With greater insight than his predecessors, the Lao Tzŭ comprehended the weakness in Confucian moral idealism, attacked its metaphysical presuppositions, and challenged Confucian optimistic attempts at reform.

In that age of blood and terror, when the brute force of Ch'in (see chap. v, above) was rapidly engulfing the land, the Lao Tzŭ could discover no moral government in the universe. He belongs with Spinoza and Schopenhauer, who emphasize the difference between human ideals and the way the universe acts: "The perfection of things is to be judged by their nature and power alone; nor are they more or less perfect because . . . they are beneficial or prejudicial to human nature" (Spinoza, *Ethics*).

The Lao Tzŭ was the *enfant terrible* of ancient China who destroyed the metaphysical foundations of Confucianism, Mohism, and popular religion. He pointed to the abundant evil that is continually present in the universe: unless the universe is moral, why should man cultivate virtue? The true ruler, says the Lao Tzŭ, should be like Heaven and earth, nonmoral, in that he, too, "should not be humane and should treat the people as herbs or beasts" (*Tao Tê Ching,* chap. 5).

What, then, are moral ideals? They are mere human creations, existing only in human thought. They are relative to one another; when good arises, evil too must occur:

It is only when people generally consider beauty to be beautiful that the idea
   of ugliness occurs and only when they recognize goodness to be good that
   the idea of wickedness comes about.
For existence and nonexistence give birth to one another,
   The difficult and the easy come into existence because of one another,
The long and the short are determined by one another,
   The high and the low depend upon one another,
A note and its sound correspond to one another,
   Before and after follow one another. (Chap. 2)

Thus, if anyone is to recognize the good, he must also know its correlative, evil. By admitting the notion of goodness one simultaneously creates a notion of evil. Nothing can be good except in relation to something that is evil, as nothing can be in front except in relation to something that is behind. Evil is not escaped by stressing goodness, for, whenever goodness is emphasized, evil also is emphasized. The way to avoid evil is to go behind both good and evil to the primeval unspoiled universe, which is beyond merely human moral concepts.

Confucian morality is, then, a mistake, not because it should be displaced by the concept of mutual struggle, as Nietzsche somewhat later urged, but because morality represents a decline from the primitive, unitary, and undifferentiated state.

Not until the great highroad [*Tao*] of acting naturally was done away with
   Did there come about [Confucian] virtues of benevolence [*jên**] and justice
   [*i,* or *yi*],
Not until knowledge [*chih*†] and astuteness appeared
   Did there come about people's great hypocrisy.
Not until family relationships were no longer harmonious
   Was there emphasis upon filial piety [*hsiao*] and paternal kindness.
Not until states fell into confusion and rebellion
   Was there any emphasis upon loyalty [*chung*‡] and trustworthiness [*hsin*§].
   (Chap. 18)

---

* Pronounced ren.   † jzh.   ‡ jung.   § sin.

Hence, when the great Way [the *Tao* of acting naturally] is lost, virtue [*tê*] is esteemed;
    When virtue is lost, benevolence is esteemed;
When benevolence is lost, justice is esteemed;
    And when justice is lost, proper conduct [*li*, one of the greatest Confucian virtues] is esteemed.
Verily, the principles of proper conduct are the thinning out of loyalty and trustworthiness
    And the beginning of disorder. (Chap. 38)

The Confucian teaching of benevolence or humaneness (*jên*) and of the principles of proper conduct (*li*) was, according to the Lao Tzŭ, a decadent phenomenon, an ineffective substitute for the method of clinging to the aboriginal Way (*Tao*) of the universe.

The fundamental mistake of moralists is their failure to see that what benefits one person injures another. When a ruler lives in luxury, his people live in poverty.

Whose government is unostentatious, quite unostentatious,
    His people will be prosperous, quite prosperous.
Whose government is prying, quite prying,
    His people will be needy, quite needy.
Calamity is that whereupon happiness depends,
    Happiness is that wherein calamity lurks.
        Who knows their turning point?
        There is nothing fixed about it. (Chap. 58)

Chuang Tzŭ illustrates the relativity of good and evil in his brilliant story of the cripple. This man's chin was hidden in his navel, and his shoulders were higher than the crown of his head. His spine pointed to the sky. His thighbones were like ribs. But his bent condition enabled him to make a good living by sharpening needles, washing clothes, and cleaning rice. When the government impressed citizens for labor, he was not taken. When the government levied soldiers, he had no need to hide himself. When the government gave alms to the poor and suffering, he received more than anyone else (chap. 4). Thus the cripple's apparent calamity was really his greatest blessing. Man's judgments of value are worthless and should be discarded as mistakes, for the universe (*Tao*) knows nothing of them.

Knowledge of *Tao*, the Way of the universe, should replace the mistaken moral ideals of Confucianism.

There is a Being formless yet complete.
  Before Heaven and Earth it came to be.
    How solitary it is! How alone!
It depends on nothing and does not change.
  It pervades everything and fails not.
    So that it is worthy to be mother of the universe.
I do not know its true name.
  As a courtesy name, I call it the Way [*Tao*]...

Man has for his model Earth,
  Earth has for its model Heaven,
    Heaven has for its model the Way,
But the Way has for its model its own spontaneity. (Chap. 25)

Tao gave birth to One [*Tao* is self-created].
One gave birth to Two [*yin* and *yang*],
Two gave birth to Three [Heaven, Earth, and Man, the Confucian trinity],
And Three gave birth to all things [Heaven and Earth gave birth to all things,
    and man is lord over them]. (Chap. 42)

It is not surprising that the following passage appears at the beginning of the Lao Tzŭ's book:

The Way that can correctly be considered as the Way is not a uniform Way
  And names that can be correct names are not unchanging names.
Our name, nonexistence, denotes that from which Heaven and Earth began,
  Yet our name, existence, denotes the mother of all things.
Hence,
Concerning any supposed uniform nonexistence, we need to watch its hidden
    subtleties
  And, concerning any supposed uniform existence, we need to watch its paths.
These two [nonexistence and existence]
  Arise from the same source [the Way], but have different names.
That they have the same source, we can but call a mystery,
  A mystery upon a mystery,
    Which is the door to all hidden subtleties. (Chap. 1)

The Lao Tzŭ thus developed a complete metaphysical and cosmological theory—something that Chinese philosophers had not previously attempted. Thereafter, Confucians were forced to engage in similar speculations. This attempt continued with varying success until Sung Neo-Confucianism (see chap. xvi, above) produced a cosmology by incorporating many Taoistic elements.

Taoism contains a conception new to Occidental thought. According to the Lao Tzŭ, the real name of the absolute source of all cannot be known, but it may be called *Tao,* or the Way. Before there was anything, there must have been nothing. Hence out of nonexistence arose existence, and out of existence arose all things. But nonexistence has definite characteristics of its own. Here is a solution to the problem of creation which is new to Western philosophy: the universe can arise out of nothing because nonexistence itself is not characterless or negative. The Lao Tzŭ dwells upon the virtues of nonexistence:

When thirty spokes unite into one hub,
  By taking advantage of their nonexistence [the hole in the hub]
    The wheel has its utility.
When clay is molded and becomes a vessel,
  By taking advantage of its nonexistence [its hollowness],
    The vessel has its utility.
When one cuts out doors and windows [as in a loess cliff] so that there comes to
      be a house,
  By taking advantage of its nonexistence [the empty space within],
    The house has its utility.
      Thus, as from a thing's existence comes its beneficial character,
      So from its nonexistence comes its utility. (Chap. 11)

Nonexistence is as important as existence—omit the emptiness within a house or a bucket and it becomes useless.

Here is a metaphysical system which starts, not with matter or with ideas, but with law (*Tao*), nonexistence, and existence as the three fundamental categories of reality. Nothing similar is found in Occidental philosophy. After Parmenides declared that nonexistence cannot exist, Western philosophers never attempted to challenge his dogma. The nonbeing of Plato and Plotinus, like the empty space of the Greek atomists, was given no positive character. Only Einsteinian space-time—which is nothing, yet directs the motion of particles—comes at all close to the Lao Tzŭ's concept of nonexistence. The Lao Tzŭ perceived no contradiction in speaking of the existence of nonexistence. He boldly recognized the need to assert the reality of nonexistence as well as of existence and to give to nonexistence determinate and observable characteristics. His teaching often seems paradoxical because the West has a different philosophical heritage.

For the Lao Tzŭ the chief characteristic of *Tao,* or the Way, is effortlessness, or nonaction (*wu-wei*), a term which he probably took from the Confucian *Chung Yung,* or Doctrine of the Mean (chap. xxvi, 6). The Lao Tzŭ declares, "*Tao* never acts, yet there is nothing but is done through it" (*Tao Tê Ching,* chap. 37). To take a modern example, the law of gravitation does not change or move, yet all material entities are controlled by it. The Lao Tzŭ would say that this law partakes of nonexistence in that it is not a concrete object. It makes no effort, yet everything is ruled by it. Similarly, *Tao* does not seek to impose itself upon anyone. It is humble and passive. Like a valley which, because of its emptiness, lowness, and passiveness, draws to itself waters from the surrounding mountains (chap. 66), *Tao* is the most powerful of all entities because it does nothing. Regardless of whether man recognizes and honors *Tao,* it continues its humble and effortless nonexistence, seeking no recognition, even shrouding itself in mystery upon mystery—yet all things obey it.

Tao should be the model for the philosopher's life. Instead of wearing himself out in fruitless efforts to reform the world, as did Confucius and Mo Tzŭ, the wise man should set himself in harmony with *Tao,* which orders and molds the world without striving. Part of this harmoniousness consists in returning good for evil (chaps. 63, 49), a precept which was rejected by Confucius (Analects, XIV, xxxvi). War is likewise condemned (*Tao Tê Ching,* chaps. 30, 31). If only man does not interfere with the order of nature, *Tao* will give their due place to all things and will produce complete harmony. What man has been doing ever since he invented civilization is to alter the natural course of affairs, with disastrous results. As an illustration of this, Chuang Tzŭ tells the story of three gods:

> The divinity of the Southern Sea was Sudden Change, the divinity of the Northern Sea was Destruction, and the divinity of the Center was Chaos. Sudden Change and Destruction often met in the territory of Chaos. Chaos treated them well, so that Sudden Change and Destruction planned to repay Chaos for his kindness. They said: "All men have seven orifices for seeing, hearing, eating, and breathing. Chaos alone has none. Let us try to bore some for him." So each day they bored one orifice. On the seventh day, Chaos died. (Chap. 7)

Thus human interference, instead of improving conditions, has really carried mankind farther and farther from the ideal situation in which *Tao* alone controls. Herein lies the mistake of morality.

Any attempt at positive morality brings corruption and trouble because it interferes with the natural harmony and order of the universe.

The wise man should imitate the passivity and humility of *Tao* and purposively do nothing: "The sage relies upon actionless activity and carries on wordless teaching. Whatever anything does, he does not refuse to accept it." (Chap. 2)

> The sage knows without running about,
> Understands without seeing,
> Accomplishes without acting. (Chap. 47)

The Lao Tzŭ continually preaches the lesson of effortlessness. If only man will recognize the nature of the universe and imitate it, he will achieve the great harmony—in which he welcomes whatever happens because it comes from the One and All.

The foregoing is fundamentally a mystical doctrine, although it is not known positively that the Lao Tzŭ was a mystic. Chuang Tzŭ, however, did experience mystical ecstasy. In this ineffable condition man feels that he is united with the One and All, so that the ultimate secret of the universe is revealed to him—the unity of all being. In India this mystical experience was the source of the Upanishads; in Europe it produced Christian mysticism; in China it has been an integral part of Taoism. When Buddhism came to China, three centuries after the time of the Lao and Chuang, the Taoists had already prepared the way by their mysticism and renunciation of worldly goods.

From the experience of unity with the All arises complete contentment with whatever happens. Chuang Tzŭ carried this doctrine to its logical conclusion—contentment even with death. He describes how Tzu-lai's wife wept over him as he lay gasping at the point of death. A friend came to visit Tzu-lai, and admonished the wife, "Hush! Go away or he will not accomplish his due metamorphosis." Then, leaning against the door, his friend said to the dying man, "Great is metamorphosing power! What will it make of you? Will it make you into the liver of a rat? Will it make you into the leg of an insect?"

Tzu-lai replied, "Wherever a parent tells a son to go, east, west, south, or north, he obeys. The creative *yin* and *yang* forces of

Nature are more than my parents. [See chap. xiv, above.] If they bring me to the point of death and I demur, then am I rebellious. How could they do wrong? Nature gives birth to me in giving me a body, she recompenses me in giving me life, she gives me repose in giving me old age, and she rests me in giving me death. What makes my life good makes my death good also. . . . Calmly shall I rest and contentedly shall I go to sleep" (chap. 6). As Chuang Tzŭ says elsewhere, "Death and life, existence and nonexistence, are one and the same."

Resignation, then, is not a duty; it is the ultimate wisdom. Contentment with whatever happens is not unnatural; it is man's proper response to the universe. Life, death, enjoyment, pain—all are welcome to the true mystic; they come equally from the universe and are equally and equably to be received.

He who understands this doctrine can pass unscathed through the bitterest suffering; he can live serenely in a country where everything seems to be decaying and apparently nothing worth while remains, for he can find peace and harmony within himself. Chuang Tzŭ says:

Death and life, preservation and destruction, ill and good fortune, poverty and wealth, worth and degeneracy, criticism and fame, hunger and thirst, cold and heat—these are chance events and the operation of destiny. Day and night they succeed one another, but knowledge cannot espy their origination. Hence they are not worthy of being allowed to disturb one's harmony and one should not allow them to enter one's mind. One should make his mind harmonious, contented, and comprehending, so that it will not lose its cheerfulness. One should make it free from faults day and night, so that it can be at home with all things. The person who clings to the foregoing practice, so that he creates his own environment from within his mind, may be said to have a perfect character. (Chap. 5)

Chuang Tzŭ went further than the Lao Tzŭ in denying not merely the foundation of morals but also the foundation of knowledge: "Speech is not merely an emission of the breath. It is intending to say something. But it cannot be absolutely determined whether what one says is true or not" (chap. 2). Winning the argument in a debate does not prove that the winner is right, for judges have their preconceptions. How can one know that what one now considers true may not be false an instant later? This absolute skepticism doubts even the permanence of truth.

Perhaps Chuang Tzǔ's most famous passage is that concerning the butterfly:

> Once upon a time, I, [who am called] Chuang Chou, dreamed that I was a butterfly, a butterfly flitting about, enjoying myself just as I liked. I did not know that I was Chuang Chou. Unexpectedly I awoke and accordingly was Chuang Chou again. I do not know whether I am Chuang Chou who dreamed that I became a butterfly or a butterfly who dreamed that I became Chuang Chou. Yet between Chuang Chou and a butterfly there is certainly a difference, so that such a change is merely an example of the metamorphosis of things [as in death].

If knowledge of one's own identity is doubtful, what, indeed, can be known? Nothing. "Sages harmonize systems of right and wrong, and rest in the evolution of Nature"—that is, they allow things to follow their own spontaneity. Knowledge is vain; one can but retreat into mysticism.

This philosophy is more than stoicism; it is mystical union with the universe and contentment with all that happens—because all is one. It is the ideal philosophy for a recluse. Confucianism has often been the philosophy of those in power; the same persons, when events have driven them into obscurity, have not infrequently taken refuge in Taoist mysticism. They find contentment in their misfortune by believing that it, too, comes from the universe and so must be good. For example, the Emperor Ming (713–756) of the T'ang dynasty (better known by his temple name, Hsüan-tsung, the Subtle Exemplar) sought refuge in Taoism after the death of his favorite, Yang Kuei-fei. Confucianism has been the philosophy of those who have succeeded or hoped to succeed. Taoism has been the philosophy of those who have failed—or who have tasted the bitterness of success.

In the Occident a philosophy is considered complete when it provides a refuge from trouble and turmoil. Not so in China, where problems of society and government have been uppermost. Hence even mystical, individualistic, and quietistic Taoism from its inception developed political aspects. The Lao Tzǔ came from the official class and drew political implications in his teaching:

> If we stop looking for persons of superior morality to put into power [a Confucian ideal],
> People will not be jealous of one another.

If we cease prizing goods difficult to obtain,
  There will be no more thieves.
If we do not look at what kindles desire,
  Our hearts will remain unconfused.
Therefore the sage rules
  By emptying their hearts
    And filling their bellies,
  By weakening their ambitions
    And toughening their sinews,
Always striving to make the people knowledgeless and desireless,
  And seeing that those who have knowledge dare not interfere.
By thus acting through inaction,
  All things are controlled. (Chap. 3)

The ideal of the Lao Tzǔ was to allow *Tao* to work its way without interference. Government should merely restrain the attempts of interested persons to control natural laws. "Govern a great state as you would cook a small fish" (chap. 60)—the less one disturbs it the better. Thereby great harmony is attained wherein all things find their natural goal.

The Lao Tzǔ's program was that of extreme laissez faire: In his age the Chinese states interfered with economic life in many ways. The manufacture and sale of salt constituted a government monopoly whereby certain rulers made great profits. Iron manufacture was also a government monopoly. In Han times, a hundred thousand convicts were employed in the iron industry alone. There were severe sumptuary restrictions upon the common people. At times, fermented liquors were under government monopoly. The Han dynasty engaged in speculation, buying goods when they were cheap and selling when they were dear. Large granaries were maintained not only as a preparation for famines but also as a source of profit. Merchants were penalized in various ways because they made large profits and were thought to be parasites upon the body politic. Rulers, in order to protect their people from these parasites and to enlarge their own revenues, tended to take over especially profitable enterprises. (See chap. vi, above.)

Confucianism originally supported state monopolies. Chinese state socialism reached its ancient apogee under Wang Mang (9 B.C.–A.D. 23), who attempted to create a completely Confucian state. His spectacular fall, and the failure of his many state enterprises and those of later rulers, however, brought a reversal in Confucian attitude. As a consequence, Taoist advocacy of laissez faire entered more and more into Confucian teaching, especially in the Sung period (960–1279). The last and most Confucian dynasty, the Ch'ing (1644–1912), upheld an almost completely laissez-faire policy. (See chap. vii, above.) Even government coinage was finally restricted to the lowest denomination of money, so that bullion had to be used for large payments. At least the economic teaching of the Lao Tzŭ attained realization through the medium of Confucianism.

But the Lao Tzŭ did not stop with mere laissez faire. He went on to exalt primitive times, when, before civilization had arisen to disturb men's lives, *Tao* operated unchecked. In a final chapter he describes the ideal country:

> In a small state with few people,
> Let there be military organizations,
>   But do not make use of them.
> Induce people to be willing to die doubly [in defense of their homes],
>   But not to migrate to a distance.
> So that, although they had ships and carriages,
>   No one would ride in them,
> And, although they had armor and weapons,
>   There would be no reason to array troops for battle.
> Induce people again to knot cords
>   And use them [in place of writing],
>   To delight in their food,
>   To beautify their clothing,
>   To be satisfied with their homes,
>   And to rejoice in their own customs.
> Then a neighboring state might be within sight,
>   And the sounds of its cocks and dogs might be within hearing,
> Yet the people might grow old and die
>   Without ever having gone there. (Chap. 80)

The Lao Tzŭ rejected civilization, writing, and all mechanical devices for the sake of bringing contentment and peace to the country. His anarchism and opposition to civilization were intended to allow *Tao* to work its effects without interference. As Chuang Tzŭ said, the sage "wanders on the road of freedom and ease, of aimless and unregulated enjoyment, and of ever-changing evolution" (chap. 6). Thereby is complete harmony attained.

Under the Han the importance of Taoism varied inversely with that of Confucianism. From about a generation after 141 B.C., when an imperial edict ordered the dismissal of non-Confucians from office, to almost the end of the first century B.C. there were few Taoists. When Wang Mang's attempt (A.D. 9–23) to set up a Confucian ideal government resulted only in another and worse tyranny, Taoism again secured adherents, some of whom came from Wang Mang's own clan. The Eastern, or later, Han dynasty (A.D. 25–220) was at first even more Confucian than had been the Western, or Former, Han (206 B.C.–A.D. 9). After the time of Wang Mang, however, Taoists were never uncommon, and, in the year 103, Fan Chün (jün) persuaded the Empress Dowager née Teng (deng) to reverse the prohibition of 141 B.C. and appoint Taoists to the bureaucracy. Perhaps in protest against Confucian criticism of his rule, the Emperor Huan sent a court official, in 165, to sacrifice at the ancestral shrine of the Lao Tzŭ in his native hamlet. On September 20, 167, sacrifices to the Yellow Lord and to the Lao Tzŭ were offered in the Cho-lung Palace, in a park at the capital.

As the later Han dynasty decayed and its emperors came under the influence of palace eunuchs, the rulers became less and less Confucian. The Confucians had an irritating habit of memorializing the throne upon the occurrence of such heavenly portents as eclipses, droughts, and floods, reproving the emperor for some fault supposed to have occasioned the portent. Confucians blamed, especially, the eunuchs and endeavored to remove their corrupting influence. But after 168, when the eunuchs succeeded in massacring the Confucians in the capital, Confucianism lost its hold upon many intelligent people. The fall of the dynasty caused the majority of Chinese intellectuals to turn to Taoistic ideas.

Taoists reacted against Confucianism; some even went so far as deliberately to shock Confucian sensibilities by violating the Confucian code of conduct, which had become increasingly puritanical, rigid, and detailed. Toward the end of the third century, opposition was headed by a group of Taoist poets and litterateurs, called the Seven Sages of the Bamboo Grove,[8] who were officials or came from families prominent in the bureaucracy.

Confucians considered filial piety a most important virtue. When an official reported a case of matricide to the throne, Yüan Chi (dzi), one of the Seven Sages, remarked, "Alas! If he had killed his father, it might have been all right. Has he come to killing his mother?" The courtiers were shocked, and the emperor said, "Killing one's father is the worst deed there is. How do you say it might have been all right?" Yüan Chi replied, "Animals know their mothers but not their fathers. Killing one's father is brutish, but killing one's mother is something not even a brute would do." For this he was applauded by the court.

Liu Ling, another of the Seven Sages, wrote a poem praising the virtues of wine. He was homely, and rode about the capital in a mean cart, holding a pitcher of wine and followed by a man with a spade. To him Liu had given an order worthy of Chuang Tzŭ, "If I should die, bury me immediately, just as I am."

The followers of Chuang Tzŭ were not, however, mere roisterers. They were seriously intent upon breaking the overelaborate Confucian code of conduct, which had become inflexible, an obstacle to sincere treatment of problems, and the source of much hypocrisy. In its place they offered the Taoist ideals of simplicity, naturalness, and harmony with the rhythm of life. This skeptical attitude in regard to all codes of conduct has become a permanent feature of Taoist tradition, and has prevented the Chinese from accepting uncritically any totalitarian program.

Despite its philosophic greatness and splendid literary form, ancient Taoism could never become universally popular. It could serve as a powerful critique against abuses, but it could not organize a governmental program. There is too little positive teaching in an essentially skeptical system. Consequently, before it could become widespread, Taoism was forced to alter its ethical ideal and adopt certain ideas and practices from Chinese occultism, as well as from early Chinese popular religion, Mazdaism, and Buddhism.

The change in the political status of Taoists from that of recluses who criticized the government to that of officials who governed the country necessitated a change in Taoist ethics. The ancient conception of effortlessness, or nonaction (wu-wei), now became unsuitable. This fundamental Taoist virtue had been manifested in the refusal of Taoists to take part in the government. Nonaction had been mere quietism. The necessary reinterpretation was not difficult. The Lao Tzŭ and Chuang Tzŭ had taught that Tao is the total spontaneity of all things, that it "does everything by doing nothing." Whereas the Taoist founders had stressed "doing nothing," later Taoists emphasized that *Tao* "does everything." Hence effortlessness came to mean, not refusal to enter political life, but emphasis upon spontaneity, naturalness, simplicity, refusal to impose one's ideas upon others, and laissez faire. Commentators upon the early Taoist writers, such as Wang Pi (bi) (226–249) and Kuo Hsiang (guo siang) (d. *ca.* 312),[4] read this new concept of nonaction into the writings of the Taoist founders. Kuo Hsiang wrote: "Nonaction [*wu-wei*] does not mean doing nothing and keeping silent. Let everything be allowed to do what it naturally does, so that its nature will be satisfied."[5] Or, as he puts it elsewhere:

A workman practices nonaction [*wu-wei*] in cutting into wood, since he acts directly only in using his axe. Likewise a prince practices nonaction in managing affairs of government when he acts directly only in appointing his ministers. A minister's special ability lies in attending to government business and a prince's ability lies in appointing his ministers, just as an axe's special ability consists in cutting wood and a workman's ability consists in employing an axe. When everything works in accordance with its special ability, Nature controls, since things are spontaneous and not by being acted upon. . . . This is perfection of nonaction.[6]

These Taoists also transformed the Lao Tzǔ's and Chuang Tzǔ's repudiation of civilization. They reinterpreted primitivity as harmony with the nature of things. Kuo Hsiang wrote:

Some people have heard [of the return to primitivity] that one should adapt himself to the nature of a horse, and have interpreted it to mean that one should set horses free and not hitch them up. They have heard of effortlessness, and have consequently said that walking is not as good as lying down. How could they live without contradicting such an interpretation?[7] Hence civilization and culture are not mistaken if they are natural developments. Only a perverted civilization, or a forced cultivation, is objectionable.

Along with emphasis upon naturalness went rejection of the Confucian ideal of imitation of the ancient sages. Kuo Hsiang argued that times change and that what suited ancient times may not be adapted to the present. Great personalities cannot be imitated; as great artists become artists spontaneously, so only spontaneously can sages become sages. Imitation is harmful because it forces human nature to become different from what it would naturally be.[8] Instead of imitation there should be spontaneity, nonaction, "living according to one's self."

In this doctrine, however, Taoists denied to themselves the feature which, more than any other, has been the source of Confucianism's power: its emphasis upon education. All the great Confucians were teachers and acquired their influence through their pupils. But spontaneity cannot be taught; it can only be caught. Taoists could not stress teaching without contradicting their own philosophy. Hence medieval Taoism was seriously handicapped in its competition with Confucianism.

Occultism, which also entered and changed Taoism, was originally distinct from that movement. Under occultism may be included such practices as the cultivation of supernatural powers by man, mediumship and traffic with supernatural beings or immortals, foretelling the future, astrology, the prolongation of life, magic and the performance of miracles, and alchemy and other pseudosciences, especially the cure of disease. These partly religious and partly prescientific practices and beliefs arose out of the early popular religion (see chap. xiv, above). Occultism was absent from the teachings of the historic Lao Tzŭ and Chuang Tzŭ, as it was also from the genuine sayings of Confucius and Mencius. Hsün Tzŭ (sün dz),[9] the great Confucian philosopher of the third century B.C., attacked occultism and even denied the existence of spirits.

Occultism was given a philosophic foundation by Tsou Yen (dzou yen), who lived in the first half of the third century B.C. He elaborated a cyclical theory of history based upon a doctrine of transmutation among the five powers, or elements: earth, wood, metal, fire, and water. Each was equated with one of the five colors, the five virtues, the five ancient rulers, the five planets, and so on. As each element, in turn, came to rule, it brought to power a new dynasty; as the power of that element weakened, the dynasty fell. The months and seasons were also supposed to be under the control of certain elements. Such ideas accorded with the superstition of the age. Tsou Yen's doctrine quickly became popular and received much elaboration. Correlations were set up between the ruler's conduct and natural phenomena. If the ruler did not accord, in the colors of his clothing and in his ordinances, with the element dominating that month, it was believed that natural calamities would occur. Speculations about taboos to be observed in each month and season were accordingly developed at great length.

PAGODA, REVOLUTIONISTS' MEMORIAL, NANKING

MAUSOLEUM OF SUN YAT-SEN, NANKING

In an age when virtually everyone believed in spirits and miracles, only unusually bold and intelligent minds could remain free from superstition. Confucianism and Taoism were not merely speculative philosophies which attempted to explain the universe; they also attempted to guide their devotees to the best life. The latter endeavor led both to become religious, as had Stoicism. Confucianism and Taoism had to make terms with the popular religion of the day.

Confucianism also admitted large amounts of occultism. The *I Ching*, or Book of Changes, which had originally been a book of divination, was made, in Han times, the first of the Confucian Five Classics. The *Shu Ching*, or Book of History, the second of the classics, which was recovered in Han times, contains a chapter, "The Great Plan," which is in harmony with Tsou Yen's ideas. To the *Li Chi*, or Book of Rites, a Han compilation of writings on proper conduct which later became one of the Five Classics, was added a chapter, "Ordinances for the Months" (*Yüeh-ling*), containing taboos and superstitious requirements for governmental activities of each month. In conformity with these ideas the Han rulers had executions performed only in the winter months. Occultism pervaded Confucianism until the Sung Confucians, in the spirit of Hsün Tzŭ, reinterpreted and moralized occult practices by means of symbolism.

Taoism produced no thinker who attacked superstition as Hsün Tzŭ had done. Hence Taoism was much more open to occult influences than its competitor, and was more easily misinterpreted, as in the following passage from the Lao Tzŭ's book:

> He who contains within himself richness of [*Tao's*] virtue
>> Is like a babe.
>>> Poisonous insects do not sting him,
>>> Fierce beasts do not seize him,
>>> Birds of prey do not strike him.
>> Although his bones be weak and his sinews tender,
>>> Yet his grip is strong. (Chap. 55)

This literary hyperbole was easily misunderstood to assert miraculous powers for the Taoist adept, and it was used by later Taoist miraclemongers to justify their claims.

Many medieval Taoists attempted to transmute base metals into gold and to compound the elixir of immortality. This movement is exemplified in Ko Hung (254–334), who wrote under the pseudonym of Pao-p'u Tzŭ (Master Who Maintains the Pristine Simplicity of His Nature).[10] Alchemy was an ancient Chinese art which probably originated with Tsou Yen and was already well known in the second century B.C. As early as 144 B.C. it had been prohibited under penalty of capital punishment, but it was secretly cultivated in spite of this law.

Liu An,[11] King of Huai-ñan, who was executed for rebellion in 122 B.C., possessed secret alchemical books. Liu Hsiang[12] inherited these books from his father, who had secured them from the king. About 50 B.C., Liu Hsiang persuaded the Emperor Hsüan to employ the imperial resources in an attempt to make alchemical gold. When Liu Hsiang had wasted much money without success, he was sentenced to death, and was saved only through the esteem of the emperor—and the payment of a large ransom by his elder brother. Liu Hsiang's outstanding failure seems to have put a quietus upon the alchemistic movement for a time, but the collapse of Confucianism, in the second century of the Christian era, revived alchemy and the search for the elixir.

The attempts to make gold and to prolong life were far from being pessimistic symptoms of the Taoist attitude toward this world. On the contrary, they were decidedly optimistic: this life is not bad but good; what one needs is prolonged life and wealth with which to enjoy it. Ko Hung and the alchemists repudiated Chuang Tzŭ's teaching that death is unimportant: death was now regarded as an event to be put off as long as possible. The alchemists were Taoists—but they attached themselves to the Lao Tzŭ, not to Chuang Tzŭ. Optimism became a permanent feature of Taoism and served to distinguish the Taoist attitude from that of pessimistic Buddhism.

The alchemistic doctrine later current in Europe had its origin in Chinese philosophy.[13] Both Chinese and European alchemists believed that gold could be made by combining the two prime principles (*yang* and *yin*) in the form of sulfur and mercury (from cinnabar). Chinese alchemy was distinguished from European in that its main purpose was not the creation of material wealth but the preparation of a grand elixir which would prolong life and confer immortality. Unending life was not usually insisted upon—several centuries or half a millennium was considered sufficiently long. The theory of the elixir was that, since gold is indestructible, being unaffected by reagents, the eating of gold would incorporate indestructibility into the body. Real gold was beyond the means of most Taoists. Alchemical gold, because of its mysterious properties, was considered more efficacious for compounding the grand elixir.

Alchemy was accompanied by certain semimagical and mystical processes, such as prolonged meditation and control of the breath—usually an attempt to take in more breath than was expelled. This often led to mystical ecstasy. Alchemy also involved the picking of magical plants, especially spiritual fungi, on mountains and wastelands; the avoidance of grain and other dietary regimes to promote health; and, sometimes, communication with immortals and other supernatural beings. Failure in alchemical attempts was blamed upon the absence of the proper spiritual ingredients.

Mercury was an important ingredient in formulas for the elixir. This element, however, is extremely poisonous. The story is told of an alchemist who, retiring to a remote place, succeeded in compounding the elixir. He drank of it and died immediately. One of his pupils went for help, but the other, loyal to his master, drank some also. The first pupil returned to find both dead. Many Taoist masters and at least one emperor were poisoned by the elixir. But alchemists learned that death could be avoided by taking the potion in minute doses over a long period of time.

In the second millennium, when alchemy had long been unsuccessful, the attempt to produce material gold was sublimated into an attempt to produce spiritual gold, that is, mental and spiritual powers. Mystical and bodily—instead of chemical—practices now came to be cultivated. The same terms were used as before: sulfur, mercury, gold, the Tiger, the Dragon, but now they denoted spiritual qualities. Thus new wine was put into old bottles. In part, this spiritualized alchemy returned Taoism to its ancient mysticism, often with addition of magical notions, and in part it became a pseudoscientific medical doctrine for cultivating health and curing disease. Taoists became physicians and Taoism became a health cult.

A quite different development took place in the second century of the modern era. Buddhist missionaries were then coming to China via Persia. Chang Ling, later known as Chang Tao-ling (jang dao-ling), began at this time, in what is now Szechuan (sz-chuan), to preach a strange doctrine. Only a few brief descriptions of his cult remain. From them it can be determined that his religion was actually the Persian Zoroastrianism of that day, which is perhaps better called Mazdaism, since in it Zoroaster had become unimportant. Chang Ling cured diseases by having his patients confess their sins and pray to the three high, divine officials, Heaven, Earth, and Water (the last of whom is almost certainly the Persian Anahita). The monotheistic God of Mazdaism, Ahura Mazda, was in Persia commonly called "the Creator," the Avestic word for which is Dadhvah. Chang Ling turned this name into the Chinese word Tao (dao). He established a fire temple on top of a hill north of Chengtu (cheng-du). He also made much of angels, who abound in Mazdaism, and stressed the Mazdean doctrine of purity. He taught his converts to tell the truth and to be generous, both of which were Persian virtues. Because his priests, in accordance with this virtue of generosity, made the modest charge of five *tou* (dou, *ca*. nine quarts) of grain a year, this cult came to be called the Religion of Five *Tou* of Grain (*Wu-tou-mi Tao*).

Chang Ling's grandson Chang Lu spread this religion in southwestern Shensi and, after he surrendered to Ts'ao Ts'ao, took it to Lo-yang, Honan. When Hun invasions drove the Chinese court to the present Nanking, this religion moved too, and became one of the chief cults in the Eastern Chin (dzin) court. Among its adherents were the great minister Wang Tao (dao), who has been honored in China ever since as the outstanding example of loyalty, together with his cousin, the commander in chief Wang Tun (dun), who overshadowed even the emperors, the famous calligrapher Wang Hsi-chih (hsi-jzh), and various ministers and governors. It became the dominant religion of the Yangtze (yang-dz) delta, and spread to present Hupeh (hu-bei), Kuangtung (guang-dung), Kuangsi (guang-si), and farther south. The great rebellion led by a priest of this cult, Sun En, in 399, almost succeeded in overturning the Eastern Chin dynasty, but the cult was finally crushed by Liu Yü, founder of the Liu Sung dynasty of the fifth century.

Although ancient Chinese Taoism and the Religion of Five *Tou* of Grain had little in common, they both used the word Tao for the supreme power in the universe. In 415, in Lo-yang, the Taoist practitioner K'ou Ch'ien-chih (chien-jzh) amalgamated the Religion of Five *Tou* of Grain with Taoism and gave himself the title previously held by Chang Ling and his successors—Heaven's Apostle, T'ien-shih (tien-shzh).

Thereafter the amalgamation of the two religions proceeded rapidly. By the beginning of T'ang times the two had become one, and the derivation of many Taoist ideas from Mazdaism was forgotten. It is not mentioned in any extant Chinese source. But the present head of Taoism, who still calls himself the T'ien-shih, claims descent from Chang Ling. Taoism took over the ritual and many practices of Chang Ling's religion. Thus it became a positive religion with a developed pantheon, at whose head was the Jade Emperor. (Jade is a symbol of purity.) This god, who is first mentioned by that name in the ninth century, when he was already a fully developed and well-known figure, was almost certainly Chang Ling's supreme god, Tao, who was Ahura Mazda.

At the same time Taoism took over many Buddhist practices and established monasteries and temples. Taoism was cultivated by Chinese rulers as a "home product" to compete with alien Buddhism. The T'ang emperors were persuaded that they were descendants of the Lao Tzŭ, and in 1012 the True Exemplar, Chentsung (jen-dzung), of the Sung dynasty (960–1279), adopted the Jade Emperor in the state pantheon. This period represents the apogee of Taoism. But even then Buddhism was perhaps more popular than Taoism among the common people.

An important Taoist—religious, not philosophical—doctrine is that good and evil deeds are duly repaid. The *Kan-ying P'ien,* or Book on Responses Evoked [by good and evil deeds], often called the Book of Rewards and Punishments, a late medieval work which incorporates many ancient ideas, is today perhaps the most popular of Taoist tracts. Familiar divinities (see chap. xiv, above), such as the Kitchen God and guardian spirits, watch the deeds of individuals and report them to the Jade Emperor and other gods in heaven. The God of the Northern Bushel (the Dipper), who from his place overhead can see all, keeps a record of each person's deeds and lengthens or shortens his life accordingly. Calamities are sent upon the wicked; good luck comes to the virtuous. If a person's full reward or punishment is not attained on earth, it is visited either upon his descendants or upon himself after death, in heaven or in hell. Accordingly, human life becomes a balancing of good against evil deeds. Chinese beggars do not ask for alms. They cry, "Do a good deed!" The fear of hell is inculcated by life-sized, brilliantly painted wooden figures in the courtyard of a temple, usually that of the City God, depicting sinners being tortured in each of the ten hells. Thus, ironically enough, popular Taoism came to accept the moral government of the world which the Lao Tzŭ had so vigorously denied.

Religious Taoism developed a pantheon, as had Mahayana Buddhism. Ancient hermits and mystics became minor gods, worshiped for the favors which they were supposed to grant. Myths and fabricated history supported the cult of these "immortals." Taoist divinities were made of planets, stars, ancient heroes, presiding spirits of various occupations, metals, human activities—for example, robbery, fornication, drunkenness—and insects and animals such as grasshoppers, snakes, dragons, tigers. Monasteries, temples, and rites were patterned after popular Buddhist practices. A canon of Taoist writings was formed analogous to the Buddhist Tripitaka.

A supreme trinity was conceived, paralleling the Buddhist trinities. To it belong the Lao Tzŭ—who has retired from active government, in harmony with his exaltation of nonaction—the Jade Emperor, and the future Savior. With his ministers and assistants, subordinate gods, immortals, miracle-working beings, and spirits, the Jade Emperor controls the spiritual world. His control, however, is far from complete and is frequently as lax and inefficient as that of many emperors of China.

The ordinary Taoist priest makes his living chiefly by calling upon members of the divine hierarchy to defeat the machinations of devils. Evils of all sorts—blindness, pain, disease, plague, wind, thunder, fire, flood, and drought—are blamed on the actions of spirits. To deal with these evils it is necessary to know what spirit caused them and which divinity can oppose that spirit. Taoist priests are ready, for a consideration, to drive away malignant spirits with the necessary charms, religious ceremonies, divinatory selection of drugs, and rearrangements in the geographical orientation of buildings. If the first attempt is unsuccessful, they propose a more powerful—and more expensive—performance. Inasmuch as a certain proportion of their attempts are successful (since many sick recover without medical attention), their reputation is maintained.

Among these Taoist priests, the head of the clan, descended from Chang Ling,[14] who is entitled the T'ien-shih, heads the Taoist organization. This position was confirmed by large imperial grants of land in the hills of Kiangsi (jiangsi). Although Occidentals call him the Taoist "pope," the head of the clan does not control a unified hierarchy. Rather is he the most famous magician among many; Taoist priests and devotees come to him to be invested with spiritual powers. Nominally and legally, this Mr. Chang is the superior of the Taoist organization; in practice, he does little.

Contemporary religious Taoism is a thoroughly superstitious and loosely organized system which uses only the name and fame of the philosophic founders of Taoism. Its priests make a living chiefly by selling charms, and spend a good part of their time stirring up unrest among the people—thereby creating trade for themselves. Such a religion is unable to withstand the criticism of modern science. Each patient who is cured by modern medicine discredits Taoism. Educated Chinese since the time of Hsün Tzǔ have tended to be skeptical. Religious Taoism has been dying for centuries, and modern science is speeding up the process. Philosophical Taoism, however, with its exaltation of mysticism, naturalness, and simplicity, securing solace in misfortune by cultivating inward calm, laissez faire, skepticism of doctrinaire programs, and optimism, cultivating bodily as well as spiritual health, is likely to remain an important part of China's heritage.

CHAPTER XVIII

Buddhism

BY CLARENCE HERBERT HAMILTON

AFTER CONFUCIANISM the most pervasive cultural influence in China is Buddhism. As India's gift to the Celestial Empire, this religion through the centuries has assumed forms congenial to its new environment. So rich and varied are its expressions in literature, philosophy, art, architecture, and folklore that it is an inalienable part of Chinese cultural heritage. Through two thousand years it has served as a link in the spiritual relations between India and China; it serves the same purpose in the present, when the peoples of these subcontinents are being brought into closer relationship than at any time since the seventh century. Important studies by modern Chinese scholars bear witness to the interest in reappraisal of Buddhism.[1] (See also chap. xx, below.)

It is not known when Buddhism entered China. Tradition says A.D. 67 or 68, when two Indian monks were welcomed at the court of the Emperor Ming (58–75) of the Eastern, or later, Han dynasty. This may mark the earliest official cognizance of the religion, but it has no direct relation to the first contacts, which undoubtedly were unofficial in character. Dr. Hu Shih is inclined to believe that advances had been made among the common people long before Buddhism was officially adopted.[2] (See chap. xiii, above.) In any case, the Sutra of Forty-two Sections belongs to the latter half of the first century and forms incontestable evidence of Buddhist activity at that time on Chinese soil.[3]

How the Chinese responded to this "first ray of the law" is not known. It taught the sanctity of animal life, transmigration, the law

[1] For notes to chapter xviii see pages 531–533.

of moral retribution (karma), the value of asceticism and meditation. Among a people accustomed to revere the ethical and political
wisdom of Confucius and to exalt filial piety, such ideals must
initially have appeared incongruous and alien. Yet interest in the
new teaching could not have been lacking since, before the close of
the Eastern Han, A.D. 220, more than three hundred fifty other
works had been translated into Chinese by twelve Indian monks,
half of whom came from India and half from central Asia.[4]

Transference of Indian ideas into China continued apace. In the
troubled period of the Three Kingdoms (220–265) the translation
of monastic rules indicated that many Chinese had turned to Buddhism. By the year 381, nine-tenths of the inhabitants of northwestern China were said to be Buddhists. Divisions and foreign
invasions, moreover, down to the beginning of the Sui dynasty, in
the years from 581 to 589, deepened the sense of religious need,
which Confucian and Taoist traditions failed increasingly to satisfy. Thus Kumarajiva, a gifted Indian teacher and translator who
had undergone stressful experiences in the turmoil of central Asia,
could, in the early years of the fifth century, receive patronage from
an emperor and attract great numbers of disciples.[5] The teachings
emphasized by Kumarajiva were those of Mahayana Buddhism, the
type, since characteristic in China, which exalts pity and mercy for
all suffering beings, together with the ideal of becoming, after many
transmigrations, an enlightened savior of such beings in a heavenly
realm.[6]

As Chinese monks became adepts under their Indian teachers,
the more learned among them aided in the multiplication of translated scriptures. Devotees such as Fa-hsien (fl. 399–414), Hsüan-
chuang (juang) (602–664), and I-ch'ing (yi-dzing) (635–713) made
the perilous journey over deserts and mountains to visit sanctuaries
in India, to study, and to bring back sacred books in Sanskrit which
they and other monks, Indian and Chinese, translated into their
native tongues. Others studied Sanskrit at home, aided the great
teachers, and assisted in establishing various sects. The number of
Buddhist books which thus came into being was enormous.[7]

Meanwhile, the monastic institutions set up in China prospered
or suffered persecution according to the attitude of rulers in different dynasties.[8] Restrictive legislation first appeared in the fifth

century. Struggles with Confucians and Taoists marked the T'ang dynasty (618–906). In 845, for example, Buddhism and other religions suffered persecution at the instigation of court Taoists: more than forty thousand temples were ordered demolished, temple lands were confiscated, and more than a quarter of a million monks and nuns were commanded to return to secular life.[9] Motives for persecution appear mainly to have been political, since Buddhists rivaled Confucianists and Taoists in influence at court. Yet Confucian scholars were not lacking who attacked the faith on grounds other than political: Han Yü (768–824) opposed Buddhism on principle as a foreign faith incompatible with basic Chinese traditions.[10] Nevertheless, in spite of opposition, Buddhist institutions continued to transmit the characteristic rituals and teachings through succeeding generations.

Under the Sung dynasty (960–1279) Chinese art, especially painting, drew much of its inspiration from Buddhism. Artists caught the meditative charm of landscapes seen from monastic retreats. On the other hand, a resurgence of Confucian reflection on the part of a galaxy of scholars led by the Neo-Confucianist philosopher, Chu Hsi (ju hsi) (1130–1200), although owing something to Buddhist example, tended to offset the attractions of high Buddhistic metaphysics for the intellectuals.

Under the Mongol rulers of China, in the thirteenth and fourteenth centuries, Buddhism, since it had grown up on Chinese soil, was consistently favored by Kublai Khan and his successors. The personal preference of these conquerors, however, was for the Lamaism of Tibet and Mongolia, one temple of which has been maintained in Peking since their epoch. In the Ming period, 1368–1644, Confucianism returned to a position of dominance in the nation's life. Yet Buddhism, though subjected to occasional restrictive decrees, was, on the whole, respected, and early Roman Catholic missionaries found it their chief rival.[11]

◇ ◇ ◇

Since the founding of the Manchu dynasty in 1644 there has been little change in the structure of Chinese Buddhism. Its past is a function of its present. Accordingly, the general character of Mahayana Buddhism may now be considered

Although Chinese Buddhists are aware of the story of the Indian prince, Gotama, his teachings, and the religious community which he founded, and recognize that these are venerated in southern Asia, they regard the early developments of the religion as but preliminary to another phase of doctrine and practice which developed in India in the first and second centuries of the Christian era. In this advanced phase, called the Mahayana, or Great Vehicle (i.e., the Great Way of Salvation), as contrasted with the earlier Hinayana, or Little Vehicle (Little Way), the historic Gotama is seen as but one of countless enlightened beings who are manifestations of a cosmic "Buddha-source." Dr. Karl Reichelt,[12] a noted Norwegian Christian missionary with unusually intimate understanding of Buddhist meanings, has called this cosmic source "the eternally latent divine power."

Individuals awakening to the divine power are known as enlightened ones, or Buddhas. Such attainment is rare, but it may be pursued in the same way as any goal of perfection. They who strive after it are known as bodhisattvas (in Chinese, *p'u-sa*). It is held that some of these beings on the path to enlightenment are worthy—because of good deeds done throughout many previous lives—to enter the transcendent state of nirvana, but through pity they forego that good and are reborn many times into this suffering world so that they may save others from the sea of ignorance and misery. Some of the bodhisattvas are Kuan-yin (guan-yin), so-called Goddess of Mercy; Wên-shu, Lord of Wisdom; and Ti-ts'ang (di-tsang), savior of suffering spirits from hell. These personages, although superhuman, are not yet completely enlightened. Those who have attained supreme enlightenment are Buddhas and reign in celestial glory. Such is Amitabha, or O-mi-t'o, Lord of the Western Paradise. Chinese Buddhists are thus conscious of a pantheon of superhuman beings (theoretically innumerable) leading up to an impersonal metaphysical origin, which is the quality or status of Buddhahood.

The consequence of such conceptions for religious living is interesting. One may regard these pitying, self-sacrificing beings as saviors having superabundance of merit from their multiplied good works, and may call upon them for help. In popular religion this has a wide appeal. Or one may aspire to be eventually of their number by taking vows and practicing the world-renouncing, unselfish life through many reincarnations until one gains supreme enlightenment—thereby becoming a Buddha presiding over some heavenly realm for the benefit of others. The piety issuing from the first attitude is observed in the faithful chanting of the words *Nan-mo O-mi-t'o Fu* (Adoration to Amitabha Buddha). This signifies the turning in reverence and trust to the great Buddha whose vast merit has prepared a "Pure Land," or Western Paradise, in which to save all who invoke his name. This piety has given rise to the Pure Land sect of Buddhism and has found many forms of expression: in art, supplying motifs for paintings of Amitabha and his paradise; in literature, offering impressive devotional poetry,[13] as in the following hymn addressed to O-mi-t'o:

> Thou perfect master,
> Who shinest upon all things and all men,
> As gleaming moonlight plays upon a thousand
>   waters at the same time!
> Thy great compassion does not pass by
>   a single creature.
> Steadily and quietly sails the great ship
>   of compassion across the sea of sorrow.
> Thou art the great physician for a sick
>   and impure world,
> In pity giving the invitation to the Paradise of the West.

For the monastic life a much more disciplined piety is required. From whatever motives monks enter monasteries—whether they are given as children by families in straitened circumstances, or enter because of sorrow, frustration, old age, or genuine desire for religious guidance—all follow the time-honored program designed to set the devotee on the path to Buddhahood. First, they must learn the commandments of Buddhist ethics: not to kill, steal, commit adultery, lie, or take intoxicating liquors; to abstain from perfumes and flowers, singing and dancing, and overcomfortable beds; to abstain from food at certain times; and to forego valuable possessions. These are the great commandments; others, in detail, number more than three hundred. After an ordination ceremony lasting many days, the candidate takes his vows and receives the title of bodhisattva, that is, one committed to the journey toward enlightenment, cherishing love and sympathy for all beings. The ceremony culminates with the burning of marks on the scalp of each candidate—three to eighteen according to his zeal—which betoken the avowed priest.[14]

Monks are entitled to make pilgrimages among temples and monasteries and are assured of the fellowship of the monastic community and of a welcome throughout China. Members of monasteries attend worship, practice meditation, listen to religious lectures, and perform rituals, including masses for the dead. A few monks become hermits; others become learned in the scriptures or in a particular school of thought. Since ten different schools or systems have developed, there is ample scope for study. Several schools have coalesced, however, and at present there are four chief sects: the Ch'an Tsung (Zen in Japan), or contemplative, school; the Lü Tsung, or legalistic, school; the T'ien-t'ai school, founded by Chih I (d. 597);[15] and the Ch'ing T'u, or Pure Land—which emphasize, respectively, meditation; learning; meditation, learning, and ritual; and devotion to Amitabha.

◇ ◇ ◇

Twentieth-century Chinese Buddhists have been buffeted by the winds of political and social change. Events culminating in the fall of the Manchu dynasty in 1912 brought clergy and laity alike to a realization that monasticism and otherworldliness were not sufficient for survival in a new age. Buddhist associations of lay members and ordained monks began to be formed. Most important at first was the National Buddhist Federation, organized in 1910 to purify the monastic order of ignorance and abuses and to assure a better representation in public affairs. In the early days of the Republic this society participated in the struggle for religious liberty when there was a tendency to exalt Confucianism as the state religion.[16] Although the principle of religious liberty was finally recognized, the National Buddhist Federation incurred hostility from the government and was closed when it objected to official supervision of temples and monasteries.

Activities of other Buddhist associations continued. In many places lay devotees supplied funds for rehabilitation of monasteries and temples which had fallen into disrepair. Religious liberty made possible the increase of accessions to various orders. Publications and popular lectures became instruments of wider appeal. By 1915 the general movement toward revival found its spokesman in a young monk (later abbot) by the name of T'ai-hsü. (See chap. xx, below.) He became chief among popular lecturers, inspirer of new associations, and editor of the leading Buddhist monthly, *Hai-ch'ao-yin* (Sound of the Tide).

Although he was acquainted with the seclusion of monastic life on the sacred island of P'u-t'o, T'ai-hsü belonged to the generation of youth who felt the impulses of the renaissance of 1917. This movement, started by Hu Shih and his confreres in Peking National University, became widespread among the younger intellectuals. It promoted the use of the vernacular in writing, questioned everything traditional, and sought new learning and reforms. T'ai-hsü, sensing the temper of the times, unhesitatingly pointed out the shortcomings of monks: lack of social service, ignorance of scientific knowledge and current thought, and failure to attain their professed goals. He deplored also the inability of monastics to interpret their doctrines acceptably to the modern mind. At the same time he appreciated the earnestness of their ascetic devotion, their tolerant spirit, and their feeling for universal humanity which, he felt, made them true internationalists.[17] By way of reform T'ai-hsü advocated a national system of Buddhist institutions with a central monastery and a university at the capital, and stricter discipline and more manual labor for the monks. Also, he projected propaganda work through periodicals, the formation of Buddhist associations, the conduct of orphanages, and the visitation of jails.

T'ai-hsü's efforts did not appeal to conservatives, but young liberals among both monks and laity gathered about him. In time, vigorous reformists such as Ta-hsing, Chih-feng, Fa-fang, Yi-huan, and others led the movement called New Buddhism. Radical at first, and ready to break with all tradition, the leaders of this group became more moderate as they themselves assumed important offices or became administrative heads of monasteries. After twenty years most of T'ai-hsü's institutional plans remained a dream; by 1937, nevertheless, he could count to his credit the founding of Buddhist seminaries in Wuchang and Fukien and a Chinese-Tibetan Buddhist college in Szechuan, as well as the stimulation of numerous local Buddhist associations.[18] Meanwhile, through his preaching, teaching, and writing, he has acquainted the literate public with his purpose of propagating the essence of Mahayana Buddhism in a form pertinent to the times.

In his teaching the Abbot T'ai-hsü has emphasized the inter-relatedness of humanity and the universality of Buddhist doctrine. "Buddhist doctrine," he holds, "is fully capable of uniting all the existing forms of civilization, and should spread throughout the world so that it may become a compass, as it were, for the human mind."[19] His central message, however, maintains continuity with tradition. There is inherent in human nature, he declares, the pos-sibility of a higher state called enlightenment, a perception or insight into the ultimate nature of the universe and life which is perfect, universal, infinite, and supreme.[20] Only once in history has such perception been attained—that was by the Indian prince, Gotama. Nevertheless, for others it may become a goal toward which progress is made "by devoting ourselves to the promotion of good and to the diminishing of evil." Scholars can readily recog-nize here the ancient doctrines of Buddhahood and karma, but, as a contemporary Christian bishop, Andrew Y. Y. Tsu (ju yu-yü), has pointed out, there is a modern correlative in the conception that the present human condition is the accumulated result of the inter-action of countless lives. Because mankind lives so interdepend-ently, only coöperative effort will enable man to realize a better world order.[21] "Humanity is a whole," says the Abbot T'ai-hsü. "To help others is to help oneself, and to hurt others is to do oneself double injury, and yet, we find all nations today [1928] living in mutual distrust and preparing war under cover of apparent peace. ... The Buddhist doctrine alone can make us abandon the false conception that life is necessarily based on struggle and competi-tion, and bring us to adopt a policy of mutual aid by which we can attain to lasting peace."[22]

❖ ❖ ❖

Apart from the reforming, propagandizing movement of the Abbot T'ai-hsü and his co-workers, another trend of contemporary Bud-dhism is to be noted in renewed scholarly research in the ancient classical texts and history of the religion. In part, such work springs from religious motivation and, in part, from purely scientific interest in the history of culture. The most notable center for such study has been the Nanking Buddhist Institute (located in western China throughout the recent war years), headed by Mr. Ou-yang Ching-wu. Younger scholars of this group utilize the Sanskrit, Pali, and Tibetan languages to aid their investigations into Chinese sources.

More especially has the Institute busied itself with critical re-editing of texts of the Wei-shih (wei-shzh) philosophy, a complex and subtle system of metaphysical idealism imported from India in the T'ang age as a result of the labors of the famous pilgrim-scholar, Hsüan-chuang (602–664),[23] and his notable disciple, K'uei-chi (kuei-ji). Since the arguments of the Wei-shih philosophy are dialectically keen, well organized, and well articulated, it has always been regarded as a mountain peak in the development of Buddhistic rationalism. In times of reflective ferment, as under the present impact of Western systems of thought, the Wei-shih literature tends to attract the more strongly speculative minds.[24]

Studies in the history of Buddhism have been written by non-Buddhists and Buddhists alike: Liang Ch'i-ch'ao, Liang Sou-ming, Hu Shih, T'ang Yung-t'ang, Lü Ch'eng, Chiang Wei-ch'iao, Huang Ch'an-hua. Among recent essays have appeared Wu-Ting-ti's "Buddhist Influence on Chinese Culture,"[25] Hu Shih's lecture before the Harvard Tercentenary Conference on "Chinese Culture before and after Indianization,"[26] and T'ang Yung-t'ang's "Notes on the History of Chinese Buddhism."[27] In the field of philosophy a courageous effort to utilize both Buddhist and Western thought is exemplified in an essay entitled "A New Interpretation of Wei Shih," by Chu Pao-ch'ang (ju bao-chang), who attempts to relate certain ideas in the Wei-shih system with concepts of Alfred North Whitehead.[28] Cultural studies of this character are an authentic phase of China's intellectual renaissance.

The long-range importance of contemporary researches in China's Buddhistic culture cannot be assessed. To the minds of some it may appear as the beginning of a critical process that will eventually dissolve the Indian elements in Chinese civilization in favor of closer affiliation with Western scientific elements. To others it will appear as a purifying factor, eliminating the worthless and setting in clearer light the spiritual values held in common by India and China.

With the increasing tension in Sino-Japanese relations in the fourth decade of the century, Chinese Buddhists had to face extraordinary conditions. In 1936 the government ordered that monks should be given military training, but granted their petition to substitute relief work, on the basis that Buddhist commandments prohibit the taking of life. Upon the outbreak of hostilities in July, 1937, the Chinese Buddhist Association published an open letter to Japanese Buddhists, urging them to awaken their militarists from their continental dream. In the same month the Abbot T'ai-hsü cabled the Japanese Buddhist Association, calling upon its members to urge their government to use diplomatic instead of military methods in handling Sino-Japanese difficulties.

Soon thereafter the Chinese Buddhist Association, under the leadership of the Abbot Yüan-yin, began war-relief activities in the Shanghai area. Some hundred and twenty monks were summoned from fourteen neighboring cities to carry on first aid and relief work at the front. By October the Abbot Yüan-yin was touring the Straits Settlements and South Sea Islands to raise funds from overseas Chinese for war relief. As the tide of invasion deepened about Hankow, Wuchang, and Hanyang, a rescue corps of sixty monks from sanctuaries of that region, under the leadership of the Abbot Hai-ching (hai-jing) of the large Hsiang-shan Monastery, acted as stretcher bearers dispensing first aid and meeting wounded soldiers at railway stations and wharves. Relief activities in Shanghai and the three central cities were small compared with the need, but they indicate the changed spirit within monastic orders. Meanwhile, some temples were occupied by soldiers, some were destroyed, and others were turned into havens of refuge for the homeless and destitute. In a temple at Hangchow, Buddhists and Christians worked side by side.[29]

In step with the military occupation of China, Buddhists from Japan attempted to cultivate relations with Chinese Buddhists on the basis of common religious sentiment for furthering pacification. It is not clear how far such attempts succeeded, since Chinese monks are inclined to regard the specifically Japanese forms of Buddhism as departures from the norm. The outstanding religious leaders, furthermore, fled to Unoccupied China. T'ai-hsü moved his Wuchang Buddhist seminary to a place near Chungking, where he continued his propaganda activities and gave full support to the National government in its resistance to invasion. How far popular Buddhism may be subject to political exploitation remains to be seen.[30]

It is impossible to envision Buddhism's future in China. That it has had a long and distinguished past and is integral to the cultural heritage of the Chinese people is evident. That it exhibits stirrings of new life under the impact of modern conditions is clear.[31] Whether it can fully adjust itself in the world of tomorrow without departing radically from its past is open to question. Possibly there is something prophetic in the fact that, in China's far west, Buddhists participate readily in an All-China Interreligious Association that includes, as members of its board, a Roman Catholic bishop, Paul Yü-pin (yü-bin); a Methodist bishop, W. Y. Ch'en; a Moslem general, Pai Ch'ung-hsi (bai chung-hsi); and a Buddhist abbot, T'ai-hsü.[32]

CHAPTER XIX

Christianity

BY KENNETH SCOTT LATOURETTE

C HRISTIANITY IS PROMINENT in China, but that prominence is of comparatively recent date. It is chiefly of the present century and is growing. Christianity is felt much more deeply and extensively than the numerical strength of its adherents would lead one to expect. Any attempt to understand contemporary China and to look into its future or to forecast the possible contribution of the country to the world must, therefore, take into account the Christian faith.

Three times Christianity has been introduced into the Middle Empire. Twice it was present for several generations and then died out, leaving, as far as is known, little impression upon the national culture. The third time it won a continuing foothold, but not until late in the nineteenth century and early in the present one did it have a striking effect upon the life of the people as a whole.

Christianity seems to have made its first appearance in China in the seventh century, in the reign of T'ang T'ai-tsung (tai-dzung) (627–649). Hints have not been lacking that it came earlier, but no evidence establishes a date before the seventh century. Under the T'ang several other non-Chinese religions were present, including Islam, Manichaeism, Mazdaism, and Judaism. The Christians in central Asia were chiefly Nestorians. It was from central Asia, by way of the caravan routes across Sinkiang (sin-jang), or Chinese Turkestan, that Christianity seems first to have come to China. The fullest record is an inscription on a monument erected near the T'ang capital, Ch'ang-an, in A.D. 781. This reviews the history of what it calls the Luminous (or Illustrious) Religion of Ta Ch'in (da tsin). Presumably, it was Christianity in its Nestorian form. The date given for its arrival in Ch'ang-an is A.D. 635.

In the ensuing two centuries the religion became rather widely disseminated in China, but it was represented only by minorities composed largely of aliens. In the declining years of the T'ang the Christian communities gradually disappeared, partly because of government-directed persecution (not against Christianity only, but against other non-Chinese cults also, notably Buddhism), partly because of the disorders attending the decay of the dynasty. So completely did Christianity vanish that the date of its demise is not known, though there have been conjectures of continuing influences of the faith in religious customs and semisecret societies.

Although Nestorianism disappeared from China proper near the close of the ninth or the early part of the tenth century, it survived for some three hundred years among the peoples of central Asia and on the northern marches of the empire, in parts of what are now Sinkiang, Mongolia, and Manchuria. Some of these Christians moved inside the Great Wall and conformed, in part, to Chinese culture. The border folk and the Chinese themselves were conquered by the Mongols in the thirteenth century. Through intermarriage with the ruling line of one of the central Asian peoples, some of the Mongol princes, descendants of Jenghiz Khan, had Christian mothers and were baptized as children.

It was therefore during the Mongol rule of China, in the thirteenth century, that Christianity again became fairly widely extended in China proper. At its height the Mongol empire embraced not only that country but also most of central Asia and considerable parts of western Asia and Europe—areas in which Christians were then numerous. Many of these (mainly Nestorian) Christians settled in China, some as officials under the Mongols, some as contingents in the Mongol armies, others as civilians.

The Roman Catholic form of the faith also was carried to China from western Europe in the Mongol era. A few western Europeans were in Mongol employ; numbers of others, mostly from Italy, went as merchants. In addition, there were missionaries, notably Archbishop John of Montecorvino, of the Order of Friars Minor, which was then in its heyday. Franciscan houses were established in several Chinese cities.

With the decline of the Yüan, or Mongol, dynasty (1260–1368), change in the political environment was again accompanied by the disappearance of Christianity—so utterly that it is not known when the last Christian groups died out. Land travel across Asia now became less secure and contacts of the Chinese with central Asiatic peoples were less frequent. Most of the Nestorian communities in central Asia also died out, either perishing amidst the disorders of the times or becoming converts to Islam or to Lamaistic Buddhism. Commercial intercourse with Europe lapsed.

The third entrance of Christianity into the Middle Kingdom was through the channel of the Roman Catholic Church, in the latter half of the sixteenth century, as a phase of European expansion. This time, Christianity, reinforced by the Russian Orthodox Church and by various forms of Protestantism, came to stay. It has now existed in China longer than at either of its other two appearances and seems to have become an integral part of Chinese culture.

For the first century and a half of its renewed course in China, Catholicism made relatively rapid strides. Its leading missionaries were Jesuits, the first of whom was Francis Xavier, a companion of the founder of the Society of Jesus. He died in 1552, off the coast of China, in a vain endeavor to gain access to the mainland. The Society did not allow his dream to fade; before the end of the century, footholds had been established centering in Macao, a Portuguese enclave.

Chiefly responsible for carrying the faith into the interior was Matteo Ricci, an extraordinarily able and devoted Italian who, by his skill in mathematics and astronomy and his knowledge of the Chinese classics, won the respect of several members of the ruling scholar class. Through them he obtained a residence for the Society in Peking. Later, the Jesuits in the capital were given subsidies from the imperial purse and for decades were in charge of the official bureau of astronomy. From time to time they were also entrusted by the emperor with other assignments involving the use of Western techniques, in which they were adepts.

Ricci, moreover, adopted a tolerant attitude toward ancestral and Confucian cults. This made it possible for converts to be loyal both to their traditional background and to their Christian faith. Among early Jesuit converts was a scholar-statesman, Hsü Kuang-ch'i (sü guang-chi), whose family village, Zikawei (sü-jia-huei), on the outskirts of Shanghai, became the chief Jesuit center in China in the nineteenth and twentieth centuries. Among Hsü's descendants are Mesdames Chiang Kai-shek and Sun Yat-sen.

Through the favor shown to Jesuits in Peking, much practical toleration was secured for Christian missionaries in the provinces. Several orders and societies were soon represented. By the dawn of the eighteenth century, Roman Catholic Christians were to be found in most of the provinces, and probably exceeded two hundred thousand.

Late in the seventeenth century, Russian Orthodox Christianity was introduced by Russian captives who had been given quarters in Peking. They were followed, in the first half of the next century, by a small but continuing Russian ecclesiastical-commercial-diplomatic mission in Peking.

In the eighteenth century, Roman Catholic Christianity in China fell upon evil days. Prolonged controversy among missionaries over the propriety of the tolerant attitude taken by Ricci and his successors toward traditional Chinese rites divided Western representatives of the faith and led to the expulsion of some of them from the empire. Recurring persecutions were part of a general state policy to discourage all societies, religious or otherwise, which might conceivably become a political threat to the Manchu dynasty. In 1773 the Society of Jesus itself was suspended by the pope and could therefore send no reinforcements to China. The wars and revolutions from which Europe suffered in the latter part of the eighteenth and the first few years of the nineteenth century handicapped assistance from the West to other Roman Catholic organizations. Christianity by no means died out. Indeed, it may not have declined seriously in numbers, yet the Christian communities suffered in morale and found it impossible to make many gains.

It was in these difficult years that Christian missions to China had important repercussions in Europe. Through Jesuit missionaries, Europeans began to be made acquainted with Chinese philosophy, government, and art. As a result, the Celestial Empire was idealized and things Chinese became a fad. China had more effect upon the Occident through missionaries than the Occident as yet had upon China.

In the nineteenth century the Christian enterprise was greatly strengthened throughout Asia. By the dawn of the twentieth century, Europeans dominated most of the world. Sixty years earlier they had forced their way into China and constrained the government to permit them to reside therein and trade. The revival of Roman Catholicism in China and the introduction of Protestantism constituted manifestations of the pulsing life of Europe and North America. Missionary enterprises were undertaken which in extent have not been equaled in the history of any other religion.

The spread of Christianity was facilitated by the treaties which the Western Powers exacted of China. Particularly by those of 1842–1844 and 1858–1860, several ports were opened to the residence of foreigners, including missionaries; travel of Westerners—and later of Japanese—throughout China was legalized; extraterritorial status was given to citizens of the Powers; Christian missionaries were expressly permitted to teach their faith and Chinese were allowed to accept it. In their claims to the protection of the treaties, Western governments supported missionaries along with others of their citizens. After 1919, however, the rights thus acquired were seldom appealed to by missionaries, and later American and British agreements have removed most of them. (See chap. xii, above.) But for more than half a century they were important instruments in the penetration of the country by the Christian church.

Roman Catholics of many orders and societies went to China in the nineteenth and twentieth centuries. Prior to the First World War most of them had gone from the continent of Europe; following the conclusion of that war an increasing number went from the United States. By 1937 they totaled more than 4,000 priests, lay brothers, and nuns.

The first of the Protestant missionaries landed in 1807. The majority of their staffs have been drawn from the British Isles and the United States, especially the latter in recent years. They have also gone from the continent of Europe and from some of the British Dominions and have represented all the major, and some of the minor, ecclesiastical branches of Protestantism. In 1937 the Protestant missionary staff totaled about 5,700, approximately two-fifths more than the Roman Catholic foreign staff.

All Christian forces from the West suffered a reduction in, and after, 1937. A few reinforcements succeeded in making their way into the country, but many more missionaries were forced out as new territories were occupied by the Japanese.

Russian Orthodox missionaries and converts were never prominent. The small mission established in Peking in the eighteenth century continued to function, but not until the twentieth century was there much expansion—and this did not begin to approach the dimensions of Roman Catholic and Protestant activities. The overthrow of the tsarist regime in Russia and the rise of communism cut off help from the mother church and the mission suffered greatly.

Effects of Christianity upon China in the twentieth century have been pronounced. Nevertheless, although it has shown rapid gains, the numerical strength of Christian communities is not impressive. At present Roman Catholics probably number about three million, whereas Protestants are about two-thirds of a million. The Russian Orthodox are only a few thousand, possibly now only a few hundred. That is to say, those who call themselves Christians are less than one per cent of the population. These figures, however, represent great increases for Roman Catholics and Protestants: for the former a two-and-a-half-fold growth since 1911, and for the latter a threefold growth since that year.

More significant is the way in which both great divisions of Christianity have begun to establish themselves. Roman Catholics have been adding to the body of Chinese clergy. Within the past twenty-five years they have created a national organization supervised by an apostolic delegate. Moreover, a Chinese episcopate is being rapidly developed. Before the 1920's only one Chinese had been raised to the episcopate, and that was in the seventeenth century. In 1926, in a striking ceremony in St. Peter's, with Pope Pius XI officiating, six Chinese were consecrated bishops. Since then the number has been greatly augmented. In 1946, Bishop Tien, of Tsingtao, was elevated to the cardinalate. He is the first of his race to be so honored.

Protestants have been no less active in putting Chinese to the fore in their enterprises. Only a minority of Protestants are in episcopally organized bodies, but these have had several Chinese bishops. Most educational, medical, and social institutions now have Chinese as heads. A large proportion of executive posts in

Protestant bodies have latterly been filled by Chinese. Like the Roman Catholics, Protestants have developed a nation-wide organization under what is termed the National Christian Council. The Protestant Chinese leadership is both able and young, a happy augury for an enduring place in Chinese life.

Outside the realm of the ecclesiastical, Christianity has been making a deep impression upon various phases of the life of China. In this development the Protestants have had a larger share than the Roman Catholics, primarily because of a difference in programs. The latter have been chiefly concerned with building the Church as the means through which the salvation of souls for eternity is to be achieved. Protestants have had the objective of bringing into being and nourishing permanent churches, but, in addition, they have been interested in touching helpfully as many phases of this life as possible—even if these efforts do not directly result in conversions. The distinction between the policies of the two wings of the Christian enterprise is not always so sharp, however, as this simple statement would indicate. Some Roman Catholic undertakings, particularly of late years, have only indirectly contributed to the numerical growth of the Church, while many Protestants, too, have devoted themselves almost exclusively to preparing souls for the future life. Yet in its broad outlines the generalization is valid.

Christianity, especially in its Protestant phases, has had a striking effect upon Chinese life, partly because it was for long the chief agency in the introduction of Occidental culture—a culture which proved of advantage to the Chinese as they entered fully into relations with the modern world. Under the Manchus (1644–1912) China attempted to keep the West at arm's length by maintaining some degree of isolation and so preserving the old culture. This policy was understandable, especially in view of the generally high character of that culture and the violence and predominantly commercial motives with which the Occident forced itself upon the empire. It was, nonetheless, foredoomed to failure. Many missionaries and some Chinese—most of whom the missionaries had trained—foresaw that this would be so and, in the face of indifference or active opposition, introduced various phases of Western culture which had values for the country. Whenever the Chinese undertook to make adjustments, Christians, foreign and Chinese, and Christian institutions were at hand to be of help. Moreover, there are qualities in the Christian faith which have reinforced in many Chinese the disinterestedness, courage, and persistence that have made for creative leadership in the dark and difficult years the nation has recently undergone.

The influence of Christianity has been felt especially in the field of education. (See chap. xxviii, below.) Yung Wing (rung hung) is one of many who owed his introduction to Western learning to an early Protestant mission school. He was chiefly responsible for the educational mission of the Chinese government which sent several scores of youths to schools in the United States in the 1870's and 1880's. An American missionary, W. A. P. Martin, was president and teacher in the T'ung-wên-kuan maintained by the Tsung-li (dzung-li) Yamen (Foreign Office) to acquaint future officials with the ways of the West. Martin was also the first head of the Imperial University in Peking. Timothy Richard, a British missionary, had much to do with encouraging modern education. He produced literature which circulated by hundreds of thousands of copies in the 1890's and early 1900's, when Chinese were groping for guidance in the adjustments made urgent by the Sino-Japanese War of 1894–1895 and the Boxer outbreak. For more than a generation, secondary schools, colleges, and universities founded and maintained by Christian agencies have been among the outstanding educational institutions of China. A distinguished Christian, Chang Po-ling (jang bo-ling), was the chief creator of Nankai, formerly at Tientsin, which was later moved to a temporary site near Chungking (chung-ching) because of the Japanese occupation. James Y. C. Yen, serving under the Young Men's Christian Association in connection with the Chinese Labor Corps in France in the First World War, developed the methods of the mass-education movement for which he has become famous.

In several specialized types of education Christian forces have also been prominent as pathbreakers. They have devised systems for teaching the blind to read and have trained them for useful livelihood. They have embraced experimentation and training in agriculture and forestry: an outstanding pioneer school in this field was developed in connection with the University of Nanking (nan-jing), a Christian foundation. Christian institutions have given great initial impetus and have had a continuing share in higher education for women through coeducational and women's colleges.

It is not only in the field of education that China is indebted to Christianity. All the earliest medical schools of consequence for training physicians and surgeons in modern techniques were begun by Christians. Preëminent has been the Peking Union Medical College, created through Rockefeller beneficence and the united enterprise of several Protestant missionary societies. In the practice of medicine and surgery and in the founding and maintenance of hospitals, Christian missions have been the outstanding pioneers. The hospital, along with the school and the church, has constituted a normal feature of the Protestant mission station and has frequently accompanied Roman Catholic efforts. More than a century ago Dr. Peter Parker, the first Protestant medical missionary to China, opened at Canton a hospital which has had a notable career in that southern metropolis. One of the later physicians in charge of the institution led the way for scientific treatment of the mentally ill in asylums.

The modern nursing profession was introduced by Christian missionaries, who gave most of the first training in nursing. Indeed, a large proportion of it is still in the hands of Christians. The initial effort at country-wide public health education came through the Young Men's Christian Association. Physical education owes much to the Christian forces.

In its political effects Christianity has been notable. Shortly after the middle of the nineteenth century the T'ai-p'ing rebellion took place. It was an abortive movement, partly agrarian, for political reform, originating primarily through contact with Protestant Christianity. The unhappy record of destruction which it left should not be allowed to obscure the fact that it was, in part, an attempt to expel the Manchus, who were foreign in origin, and to give to the empire a better life.

More striking and more lasting has been the Christian contribution to the Republic. Sun Yat-sen, chief founder and patron saint of the Republic, had his formal education almost entirely through Christians—at first in Honolulu, in a school maintained by an English bishop, later in Hongkong, and in Dr. Parker's hospital in

Canton. Through these contacts Sun became a Christian and remained one. Much of his idealism and, through him, much of the program of the Republic came through Christian channels. The Soong family owes its leadership, in part, to the education given to the elder Soong by American Christians and to the faith which he acquired through them. The Christian faith of Generalissimo and Madame Chiang Kai-shek is well known. Both have repeatedly given public expression of their debt to Christianity. These names are but the most distinguished of the Christians who have occupied prominent positions in the political scene under the Republic. Through them, something of Christian idealism has entered into the complex of Chinese politics.

Other fruits of Christianity, less tangible but at least equally important, have appeared in the transformation and development of character of vast numbers of persons. Some have found hope after despair. Some have been freed from crippling vices. Others have been emancipated from fears, hates, and superstitions. Many have been nurtured in attitudes of unselfishness and faith.

In the sympathetic interpretation of China to the peoples of the West, Christian missionaries have played a conspicuous and influential part. The Jesuits were chiefly responsible for creating, in the Europe of the Enlightenment, the idealized picture of China which was cherished by the intellectuals of that day. The greatest of British sinologists, James Legge, who was the first professor of Chinese at Oxford, and the translator of many Chinese classics, served as a missionary throughout most of his adult life. In the United States a majority of early scholars in things Chinese were missionaries. Through books on China prepared for the education of their constituencies, missionary societies have given to hundreds of thousands of Americans almost all the very little information on China they possess. Usually they have presented the more favorable aspects of Chinese life

It is interesting to speculate on the contributions which Chinese Christians will eventually make to world-wide Christianity. There can be no possible doubt that such contributions will be made. Christianity has become so well rooted and has evoked so much of native ability and leadership that China has already added, and must add much hereafter, to the heritage of the Church Universal.

Numbers of Chinese have traveled widely among the churches of the West, speaking for Christianity, and have taken their places in ecumenical councils.

The Chinese heritage is largely one of personal and social ethics. From the standpoint of China's most influential philosophy, Confucianism, a religion is to be judged by its power to produce worthy character and a just social order. Presumably, it is this note which Chinese Christians will stress in their contributions to the Christianity of the twentieth century. Because of it the entire world will be the richer.

CHAPTER XX

Trends in Contemporary Philosophy

BY CHAN WING-TSIT

LIVING PHILOSOPHIES in China are varied and conflicting, consisting of the new as well as the old, of the Western as well as the indigenous, and of the extreme as well as the moderate—each fighting for supremacy. Basically, the struggle is between Confucianism and Western philosophy. As the rise of Neo-Confucianism (see chap. xvi, above) in the eleventh century terminated the traditional rivalries between Confucianism, Buddhism, and Taoism, so the introduction of Western philosophy ended the domination of Neo-Confucianism, which had been unchallenged for about eight hundred years.

As a result of the impact of the West, the foundations of Confucianism were shaken in the nineteenth century. In the latter part of that period a few enlightened Confucianists earnestly advocated the adoption of Western science and industry. They still clung, however, to their old heritage and insisted on "Chinese learning as the basis and Western learning as utility." Toward the end of the century a serious attempt was made to reconstruct this basis. K'ang Yu-wei (1858–1927) revolted against the Neo-Confucianism of Chu Hsi (1130–1200) and Wang Yang-ming (1472–1529), rejected the Confucianism of Han and T'ang, and interpreted Confucius (551–479 B.C.) in his own way. He advocated the Confucian ideal of a "Great Commonwealth," where the "nine distinctions . . . of nations . . . classes . . . races . . . sexes . . . human relationships . . . the rich and the poor . . . injustice and selfishness . . . natural species . . . and any condition that results in suffering"[1] are eliminated. "The Way of

---

[1] For notes to chapter xx see pages 533–535.

the Great Commonwealth," declared K'ang, "is perfect equality, perfect justice, and perfect love [jên]." In the world of suffering, jên expresses itself in what Mencius called the "unbearing mind," that is, the mind that cannot bear to see the suffering of the world. It is not a subjective state; rather is it objectively real, comparable to ether, the basis of all existence.

K'ang's young follower and comrade, T'an Ssŭ-t'ung (1865–1898), elaborated this doctrine. To him the first principle of jên is universal application, in the sense that it is all-pervasive and all-penetrating, like ether, electricity, and spirit. When jên is realized, there will be fourfold unity: the unity of all states, classes, sexes, and the ego and its alter ego. Furthermore, jên is the origin of Heaven and Earth and the myriad things, the source of spirit and intelligence. It is eternal and one, by virtue of which all distinctions and inequalities are unreal and should be eliminated.[2]

This interpretation of jên is nearer to those of Chu Hsi and Wang Yang-ming than to that of Confucius. But, in general, K'ang and T'an were true to the spirit of the Confucian renaissance. They reaffirmed the central sociopolitical position of Confucianism and actually attempted to put its philosophy into practice. They reëstablished the authority of Confucius himself. They brought the philosophy of the secular, the particular, and the concrete into closer contact with life.

In trying to create the state of jên in China, K'ang realized that his country must follow certain steps of the West. He was convinced that the Western nations were prosperous and powerful because they had a constitution and a religion. Consequently, he advocated political reform and the promotion of Confucian teaching as the "Confucian religion." In opposition to those in power, he secretly planned with the Kuang-hsü emperor (1875–1908) for a comprehensive and radical reform of the government. Their attempt in 1898 failed utterly and resulted in the emperor's virtual imprisonment by the Empress Dowager Tz'ŭ-hsi and K'ang's flight abroad.

During his years of exile K'ang's devotion to Confucius and the emperor grew deeper and deeper; he became the staunch promoter of constitutional monarchism and the "Confucian religion." Later, in 1917, he participated in the abortive restoration of the Hsüant'ung emperor (1908–1912). He was no longer K'ang the radical,

but K'ang the reactionary. In the face of growing belief in republicanism and science, his movement was exceedingly unpopular.
His failure came to be interpreted as the inability of Confucianism
to cope with modern situations; his conservatism was taken to mean
the inability of Confucianism to advance with the world. For the
solution of its problems the Middle Country turned to the West.

◇ ◇ ◇

The introduction of modern Western philosophy into China began
in 1897, with the translation of Huxley's *Evolution and Ethics*,[3]
which was soon followed by the translation of the works of Mill,
Spencer, Darwin, and Montesquieu. At the turn of the century
the ideologies of Schopenhauer, Kant, Nietzsche, Rousseau, La-
marck, Tolstoi, and Kropotkin made their appearance in China.
The movement soon gained momentum. As a result of the renaissance of 1917, many books were translated. Dewey was invited
to lecture in 1919 and 1920, Russell in the latter year, and Driesch
two years later. Special numbers of learned journals were devoted
to Nietzsche and Bergson. In the next decade important works
of Bacon, Descartes, Spinoza, Berkeley, Hume, James, Bergson,
Eucken, Russell, and Dewey became available in Chinese. Almost
every trend of Western thought had its exponents in China; a few
of these developed into schools.

Pragmatism.—Pragmatism was the first Western philosophy to
become a concerted movement in China. It was the guiding philosophy of the renaissance set in motion by Dewey's pupil, Hu Shih.
Its philosophy of ideas as instruments to cope with actual situations and its emphasis on results had special appeal to reformers.
Hu Shih's article, "Pragmatism," exerted great influence in 1919.[4]
When books and lectures by Dewey became available, the following of pragmatism grew considerably. The movement reached its
zenith around 1924. Since then, however, there have been few
writers on the subject. Pragmatists, including Hu Shih, have been
devoting themselves to education, social reconstruction, and political reform. Nevertheless, the influence of Dewey and Hu Shih remains appreciable, particularly among educators and writers on
social problems. Only a few years ago a second version of Dewey's
Reconstruction in Philosophy appeared. Although certain of the

works of James and Dewey still await translation, the educated class in China have a clearer idea of pragmatism than of any other Western philosophy.[5]

Since Hu Shih is the central figure of this movement, a survey of his philosophy will reflect the spirit of the school. Hu declared that he learned from Huxley how to doubt and from Dewey how to think. The result is a naturalistic conception of life and the universe, and belief in social immortality in place of the Chinese traditional "three immortalities of virtue, of service, and of wise speech." Hu Shih faithfully follows Dewey in the conviction that truth is an instrument changing with circumstances and that natural laws are hypotheses tenable only until more satisfactory hypotheses are formulated. He advocates "more investigation of problems and less talk about theories." The literary revolution in which Hu Shih and his co-workers freed Chinese thought from the classical style and created a new literature of the spoken language is, he holds, the "practical application of evolutionism and pragmatism." He rejects the idea that Oriental civilization is more spiritual than Western civilization. On the contrary, the opposite is the case, since the invention of the automobile, for example, is very much an activity of the spirit.[6]

Hu Shih's writings have been extensive and varied. He is at once an authority on philosophy, literature, Buddhism, and history. His chief contribution in philosophy is his *Chung-kuo Chieh-hsüeh Shih Ta-keng* (Outline of the History of Chinese Philosophy), published in 1918, which covers the ancient period. It is the Chinese version of his *The Development of the Logical Method in Ancient China,* written the year before. As a pioneering work, it contains many bold theories, some of which—such as the logical system of Confucius and the evolution of Chuang Tzǔ—are untenable. Others, like the discovery of Mohist scientific method and Neo-Mohist logic (which no one before him could understand), are permanent contributions. Publication of the *Outline of the History of Chinese Philosophy* practically revolutionized the approach to Chinese philosophy. Hu Shih accomplished this, first, by "investigating the evolution of Chinese philosophy," second, by "discovering the causes of this evolution," and third, by "critical study." He saw more pragmatism in ancient Chinese philosophy than actually exists: the book was written for a particular purpose. As a general history it is being replaced by later studies which have benefited by its methods and discoveries; nevertheless, as a monument of creative and revolutionary thought its importance will increase with the years.

Pragmatism, the philosophy of China's social and intellectual revolution, has been critical of all indigenous Chinese philosophies, especially that of Confucius, which it singled out for attack, although it could have found certain sympathetic notes in that ancient system of thought. Both systems are humanistic and practical. Both emphasize social values. Both regard knowledge primarily as power. Both are interested in specific problems instead of *a priori* principles. Confucius said, "Obtain wide and extensive knowledge; critically inquire into it; carefully ponder over it; clearly sift it; and earnestly carry it out."[7] These words might have come from Dewey. But pragmatists found Confucianism decadent and generally regarded it as the symbol of China's poverty and weakness. In their eyes it was incompatible with the modern world. They therefore demanded its total rejection, an attitude they have not altered to this day. In the early 'twenties pragmatism dealt Confucianism an almost fatal blow. This work of active hostility, however, has passed on to the materialists.

Materialism.—As pragmatism was the driving force of intellectual and literary reform, materialism has become, to some extent, the moving power of economic reconstruction. However, like pragmatism, materialism is working for a completely new society involving revolution in every phase of life. There are two trends, critical naturalism and dialectic materialism: the first reached its peak around 1920, and the second a decade later. When the materialistic tendency was under way, a series of articles on Haeckel's monism of substance gave it added impetus.[8] It was reinforced by the translation of his *Riddle of the Universe, The Wonders of Life,* and *History of Creation,* and later by Mach's *Analysis of Sensations* and Poincaré's *Science and Hypothesis.* Ch'ên Tu-hsiu (1879–1942), cofounder of the renaissance of 1917, was one of the principal advocates of this philosophy. Later, Ch'ên joined the Communist party and promoted dialectic materialism.

Drawing from both German and Russian sources, the dialectic

materialists have propounded most vigorously a materialist metaphysics, a dialectic epistemology, and a materialistic interpretation of history. Mainly, they follow Karl Marx, whose general
introduction to China dates from 1919, when an article on his
philosophy was published.[9] With few exceptions, members of this
group are now Communists. They base their doctrine on Marx
and Engels, and closely follow Lenin, Bukharin, and Plekhanov,
many of whose works have been translated into Chinese. In numerous periodicals the materialists interpreted the dialectic method
of Hegel, Fichte, Kant, and Lenin in the same light. In the late
'twenties the materialistic interpretation of history became a fashion and even opponents of communism rode with the tide. So many
books were printed to promote these two lines of thought—materialism and the materialistic interpretation of history—that special
sections were devoted to them in book catalogues as late as 1935.

Materialism has been, and still is, an influential movement, particularly among China's youth. It is a mass movement, represented
not by a few outstanding scholars but by a great number of writers.
However, the number of its publications, mostly propaganda, is not
proportional to the number of its intellectual converts. Needless
to say, this school aims at the overthrow of all traditional philosophies, especially Confucianism, which last it holds to be the foundation of Chinese feudalism. To the materialists, Confucianism,
feudalism, and backwardness are synonymous. In 1940 Chinese
Communists proclaimed the "new democracy," in which restricted
capitalism is accepted as a transitional stage to socialism. This
change in ideology is purely political opportunism. The materialistic philosophy of the Communists remains unchanged.

Neorealism.—At the same time that Marxism was introduced, a
group of young intellectuals systematically advocated neorealism.[10]
After Russell's lectures in 1920 the movement reached new heights.
In the following two decades a large number of professors preached
its doctrine. Articles on the subject have been numerous and are
increasing. But it is represented by younger men whose beliefs and
convictions are still in process of evolution and who lack the cru-
sading spirit of the intellectual and economic reformers. They
show even more diversity of opinion than do Western realists.
Furthermore, although such works as Russell's *Introduction to*

Mathematical Philosophy and *The Problems of Philosophy* and Montague's *The Ways of Knowing* are available in Chinese, other important works await translation. The neorealist movement, therefore, needs outstanding writers and standard works on which to focus.

Chinese neorealists follow closely those of England and America, although most of them attended American and not English universities. Fung Yu-lan, one of the earlier leaders of the school, has become a Neo-Confucian rationalist. His shift suggests no rejection of the philosophy but is a natural growth. The belief that nature has objective reality is a basic tenet of Neo-Confucian thought.

Vitalism.—The three foregoing schools have little in common, although they agree in upholding the efficacy of science. Science is considered to be the solution, not only of China's immediate social and economic problems, but of all problems of life. Belief in science gradually became a dogma which reduces existence to physico-chemical phenomena and condemns metaphysics as futile speculation. Naturally, reaction should arise from many directions—from idealists and from followers of Eucken, Bergson, and Driesch.[11] Disciples of Bergson and Driesch vigorously and systematically defended metaphysics against science, and life against mechanical laws, thereby precipitating, in 1923, a long controversy which involved most of the leading scholars, including Hu Shih, Ch'ên Tu-hsiu (1879–1942), Liang Ch'i-ch'ao (1873–1928), and Chang Tung-sun.

The leader of vitalism is Professor Chang Chün-mai, a faithful follower of Driesch and the central figure in the controversy. From articles dealing with the episode, now collected in three volumes, it is clear that the basic difference between vitalists and scientists did not concern the usefulness of science but the extent of its validity. Vitalists insisted that life has five qualities: subjectivity, intuitiveness, synthesizing power, free will, and personal unity—none of which is characteristic of science.[12] They placed Bergson's *élan vital* and Driesch's entelechy above science, which, based on the theory of necessary laws, presented only a closed universe. They defended free will, creative intelligence, purpose, and personality. They concluded that the scientific laws of cause and effect are applicable only to matter and not to spirit, that the various branches of science need to be synthesized by metaphysics, and that solution of the problem of free will can be found only in transcendental science.[13]

The controversy did a great deal to restore the balance of Chinese thought and accelerated the growth of idealism. As a movement, vitalism today is not widespread. Driesch is not so prominent as he was. Bergson, however, is still influential. His works have been known to China longer than those of any other Western philosopher and are the best-represented in translation: *Creative Evolution, Matter and Memory, Mind-Energy, Time and Free Will, Introduction to Metaphysics,* and *Laughter.*

New idealism.—The center of this school is Professor Chang Tung-sun. His purely professional interest in philosophy, serious and independent thinking, persistent effort, ability to attract followers, and voluminous writing, in the second quarter of the twentieth century, have made him one of the few creative philosophers of contemporary China.[14] Professor Chang calls his system "revised Kantianism." In 1937 he systematized and summed up his previously expressed views in an article entitled "The Pluralistic Theory of Knowledge Re-stated." Although in general accepting Kant, he rejects Kant's bifurcation of reality into the manifold and unity, and the division of the nature of knowledge into the given and the innate. He starts with cognition as a basic fact comprising intuitive synthesis, conceptual synthesis, and idea, not as three stages but as component parts. He believes that in cognition there is no need of a self which is transcendent and has no reality. There is only subjectivity, which in the language of Stace is "later construction."

In place of Kant's categories, Chang proposes postulates which he holds are identical with Schiller's "methodological assumptions." Following C. I. Lewis, he asserts that these are products of society and culture. They are not entirely *a priori* since they are within the realm of experience. There are, however, three *a priori* postulates. The first is the basic law of logic, that is, the laws of thought. The second includes space and time as forms, which are *a priori* in intuition. In cognition there is always the "this" and the "what." The "this" is the particular; the "what" is the universal—and the universal is impossible without duplication in space or time. The third is the subject-object relation in cognition, which is a given fact.

Sensation is neither mental nor physical but "the nonexistent," an illusion, an appearance. Analysis of sense content shows that the external thing is but what realists call a construction, which bears certain formal similarities to sensation. Even other minds can be explained in this way. This construction is not an entity but "the correlated." The nature of this structure is the natural order, which is not entirely independent of the mind but is a factor of cognition having three intrinsic qualities: atomicity, continuity, and change. Because of the common nature of mind, the universal conditions of space and time, and social intercourse, there is the common mind and, therefore, the common world. Thus, in cognition, there are four worlds: the world of substructure, the world of sense or shadow, the world of constructions, and the world of interpretations. The last includes science, philosophy, aesthetics, ethics, and religion. These worlds are overlapping and constitute multiple factors of knowledge.[15]

Professor Chang admits that his epistemology is a synthesis of various Western theories, "following Kant in his main tendencies." He claims, however, that his position is a new one, whether in China or in the West. Not all his followers accept his theory in totality, nor can he be said to represent all idealists. But he is the only one in this school to have formulated a well-thought-out system. In doing so, he has raised new idealism to a position of dignity.

In addition to these five systems, such philosophers as Eucken, Whitehead, Schiller, Morgan, Hocking, Perry, and G. E. Moore have their own following.[16] Although Chinese thinkers are varied in their tendencies and are often confused and obscure, they agree that Western philosophy is that of the future, in contradistinction to Confucianism, which most of them regard as the philosophy of the past. The spread of Western philosophy in China was achieved mainly at the expense of Confucianism, which is now on the defensive.

◇ ◇ ◇

While the struggle between Western philosophy and Confucianism continues, Buddhism (see chap. xviii, above) attempts to retain a place for itself by reviving medieval scholastic philosophy. This revival is significant in that Buddhism is the only school in China that looks to the past. In the last two decades there has been great interest in Taoism. (See chap. xvii, above.) This interest, however, has been almost exclusively centered around the date of Lao Tzŭ and the authenticity of the *Tao Tê Ching*. Because of its practical sociopolitical doctrines, democracy, and scientific method, Mohism has been popular. But this popularity has not crystallized into a movement. The only conscious and persistent effort to revive the past is the effort of Buddhism.

The first attempt in recent times to revive Buddhist philosophy was made in 1880, when lost texts were brought back from Japan by a profound scholar, Yang Wên-hui (1837–1911). Although this Buddhist layman aimed at a revival of Buddhist philosophy and eventually circulated more than a million stitched volumes (*chüan*) of Buddhist literature, his chief effort was directed to the regeneration of the Hua-yen philosophy.[17] This school flourished in China in the sixth century and was essentially a Chinese product, although certain sources can be traced to India. It started with the theory of "causation by mere ideation"; it developed the theory of "universal causation of Dharma-dhātu," or "universal causation of the realm of the law"; it culminated in the totalistic philosophy of One-in-All and All-in-One. It originated the "ten profound propositions," to the effect that all elements of existence (dharmas) are perfect and real, that they reflect one another, and that all are at once simple and complex, one and many, exoteric and esoteric, pure and varied, so that the universe is a "grand harmony without any obstacle." For four decades Yang maintained a center in Nanking. After his death, his followers scattered. Small institutes have been organized and dissolved and occasional treatises have been published, but, for the most part, the movement has subsided.

About 1918, however, an effort was made to bring Buddhist mysticism back from Japan. Buddhism exists in China primarily as a mystical religion.[18] In philosophy it treats the universe as the spiritual body, or the "body of law," of the Buddha, which manifests itself as the "realm of diamond elements," that is, the world of principle, and the "realm of matrix repository," that is, the world of entities. These two phases are, however, but different manifestations of the same Buddha. Accompanying this philosophy is an elaborate system of magic and esoteric practice. Mysticism in its pure form has little attraction nowadays for Chinese intellectuals, let alone a system of mysteries with charms and magic verses. No wonder, then, that nothing resulted from the visits of Japanese priests to China or the mission of Chinese students to Japan.

One hears today a great deal about Ch'an (Zen, meditation school). Ch'an is essentially a method of "direct intuition into the heart to find Buddha-nature," and thus is not a philosophy. Interest in it is purely historical in China, the most important contributions coming from critics like Liang Ch'i-ch'ao and Hu Shih.

The chief effort to revive Buddhism does not lie in these schools. It lies rather in the mere-ideation school,[19] the basic tenet of which is that consciousness alone is real. Consciousness is divided into eight categories, namely, the five senses, the sense-center consciousness, which forms conceptions, the thought-center or self-conscious mind, which wills and reasons on a self-centered basis, and the *Ālaya,* or ideation-store consciousness, where energy to produce manifestations, called "seeds," is stored. This last consciousness is ever in a state of instantaneous change, perpetually "perfumed" (influenced) by incoming perceptions and cognitions from external manifestations. At the same time it endows perceptions and cognitions with the energy of the "seeds," which in turn produce manifestations.

These three elements—"seeds," manifestations, and "perfuming"— keep on evolving and influencing one another, acting at the same time as cause and effect. Thus all dharmas are but manifestations of consciousness, which alone is real. The world, the self, and all dharmas are instantaneously issued from the *Ālaya* consciousness and restored to it at once, thereby constituting man's life of ignorance and illusion. Because of ignorance, man accepts the reality of "things of false existence," or things of purely imaginary nature, such as mistaking a rope for a snake, and also the reality of "things of merely temporary existence," or things of dependent nature, that is, depending on others, as the rope depends on many causes and factors. Only with perfect wisdom can man comprehend the reality of "true existence," the reality of ultimate nature, which is "thusness," the true noumenon, and the true nature of dharma transcending all specific characters and conditions.

It is unnecessary to go into the details of this system. Its psychological analysis is thoroughgoing and its arguments for idealism are strong.[20] But it enjoyed only a short life in China because its extreme idealism was too one-sided for the moderate temper of the Chinese. Why, then, is it revived today? The answer lies, first, in the fact that great enthusiasm was aroused by the reappearance of important mere-ideation texts which had been lost since the ninth century and which Yang Wên-hui brought back from Japan; second, its subtle psychology has a certain fascination for Buddhists; third, the spread of idealism in the West raised the hopes of Buddhist idealists in China; and finally, prominent Confucianists in the last three hundred years have exhibited interest in the mere-ideation theory.[21]

The revival of this philosophy is chiefly the result of the work of two distinguished scholars: Ou-yang Ching-wu, a layman, the founder and director of the Institute of the Inner Learning, formerly in Nanking; and the Abbot T'ai-hsü (see chap. xviii, above), until recently the director of the Buddhist Institute in Wuchang.[22] Ou-yang, a more profound scholar, concerned himself mainly with the investigation and elucidation of the doctrine through teaching, whereas T'ai-hsü has been active in writing, lecturing, and religious reform. The two differ not so much in their interpretation of the basic texts as in their attitude toward the question of "thusness." Ou-yang and his followers attacked *The Awakening of Faith in the Mahāyāna Doctrine*,[23] which teaches that "thusness," the ultimate nature of all dharmas, manifests itself according to causes, either pure or tainted. They refused to admit that "thusness" is affected by the process of "perfuming" and that this ultimate nature has distinct characteristics. They insisted that "thusness" is the noumenon, the nature, whereas the world as manifestation is the realm of characteristics.

T'ai-hsü, on the other hand, accepts no parallel between the nature and the characteristics of dharmas. He refers to a basic doctrine of the mere-ideation school, the theory of the "three object-domains." The first of these is the "object-domain of nature," or immediate perception, that is, the object which has its original substance and presents itself as it is. The five sense-consciousnesses and the eighth consciousness perceive an object in this way. The second is the "object-domain of mere shadow," or illusion, having no real existence and appearing only from the imagination of the sixth consciousness. The third is the "object-domain with the original substance." The object has original substance and yet is not perceived as it is, because in the seventh consciousness it is seen from the subjective point of view. It is due to this "perfuming" in consciousness that nature is discriminated, thereby giving rise to specific characters. But the original substance itself is also manifested out of ideation, not entirely free from "perfuming," and, because of this, it is a characteristic in a certain sense. Accordingly, T'ai-hsü maintains that there should be no opposition between the nature of dharmas and their characteristics.[24]

Ou-yang and T'ai-hsü revived two traditions of the mere-ideation philosophy, but added nothing new. Although T'ai-hsü calls his doctrine the "new" mere-ideation theory, there is no indication in his works that he has departed from the past except in regrouping the component parts of consciousness and giving them new names.[25] Ou-yang's pupil, Hsiung Shih-li, who is regarded as the most promising, has attempted, however, to reconstruct the mere-ideation philosophy. He conceives the universe as a process of constant transformation in which there is no distinction of consciousness-domain and object-domain, matter and mind, the Many and the One. This process is incessant change, involving intension and extension. Intension is the characteristic movement of material elements, whereas extension is that of mental elements. But neither material elements nor mental elements have self-nature. Only constant transformation is real. As such, it is the self-existent and self-sufficient function, vital energy, life, or simply the "great current of production and reproduction in this universe," and can only be intuited by the mind.[26] Obviously, this "new" mere-ideation philosophy is Buddhist scholasticism in terms of Bergson, Hua-yen (Kegon) totalism, and the Confucian philosophy of change.

The movement is weak and limited, attracting only a small group of Buddhists. The main difficulty is that the mere-ideation philosophy is today, as it was over a thousand years ago, fundamentally an Indian scholastic philosophy transplanted to Chinese soil. There is no indication that the China of today provides better soil for it than did the China of old. Modern China is definitely not in the mood for a second Indianization of its thought. China's choice is not between Confucianism and Buddhism. The option lies between Confucianism and Western philosophy—with a possible synthesis of the two.

◇   ◇   ◇

Because of the onslaught of Western philosophy, Confucianism has lost practically all its influence in education and a great deal of its power in society. As an ethical dogma and a social force, its rapid decline has been spectacular. But this does not mean total rejection of its philosophy. Sun Yat-sen (1866–1925), in no sense a Confucianist, was influenced by Wang Yang-ming (1472–1529) in his theory that it is "easy to act, but difficult to know." The Kuomintang, or Nationalist, party has no special sympathy for Confucianism; nevertheless, it has for its motto the eight Confucian moral ideals: loyalty, filial piety, benevolence, love, fidelity, righteousness, harmony, and peace. The New Life Movement, sponsored by the party and the National government, chooses for its ethical objectives the Confucian "four binding principles for the country," that is, *li,* propriety, or regulated attitude; *yi,* righteousness, or right conduct; *lien,* honesty, or clear discrimination; and *ch'ih,* integrity, or self-consciousness. Even the new Buddhism contains the Confucian element of change.

Generalissimo Chiang, in his *China's Destiny,* shows a strongly Confucianist tendency. His political and economic doctrines are essentially Confucian. He points out that in modern Chinese thought there has never been a real cleavage between the Confucian emphasis on government by morals, which represents the harmony of human sentiment and human reason, and the legalists' emphasis on government by objective and impersonal law, since Confucianists also accept law as indispensable. But, like all Confucianists, Chiang insists that law must be based on natural reason and human sentiment. These facts are living testimonies that, although Confucianism, since the impact of Western philosophy upon it, has been reëxamined, readjusted, and reconstructed, it has definitely not succumbed to Western philosophy.

Significantly, the modern changes in Confucianism have been wrought, not by the Confucianists themselves, but by others. Only the two most outstanding of these will be mentioned: a mere-ideationist and a neorealist who have turned Confucian.

The first is Liang Sou-ming, whose lectures, in 1921, stirred the Chinese as violently as did Hu Shih's publications. Liang's lectures were published in the same year under the title *The Civilization and Philosophy of the East and the West,* a celebrated book.[27] In his lectures Liang rejected Buddhism in favor of Confucianism at a time when everyone else regarded the latter as decadent, outmoded, and doomed. After carefully examining both Indian and Western philosophies, Liang boldly declared that Confucianism was "the only way China should follow." He did not oppose the adoption of Western civilization; in fact, he urged it. But he insisted that Confucianism, in its philosophy of change as "production and reproduction," in its doctrine of Reason as a universal principle of existence, and in its theory of incessant transformation resulting from the constant operation of the universal active and passive forces, offered the most suitable philosophy for China in a modern dynamic world.

The intuition of the fact of universal production and unceasing creation, he said, is *jên,* which is "the way by which a man is to be a man," as Mencius put it. To comprehend the dynamic universe and the principle of *jên,* Liang said that man can rely neither on sensation nor on intellect but on intuitive knowledge. In this he followed closely the Neo-Confucianism of Lu-Wang. Instead of accepting Wang Yang-ming's "tranquil repose," however, Liang advocated *jên* as a dynamic philosophy of life. Recalling that Confucius said, "The firm and strong and resolute . . . are near *jên,*" he demanded a philosophy of action.[28] Eventually, he resigned from teaching and devoted himself to rural reconstruction. He is now actively engaged in the work of national salvation. In the meantime his few followers scattered and the new Lu-Wang school faded out of the academic world.

The second reviser of modern Confucianism is Professor Fung Yu-lan, author of the standard *History of Chinese Philosophy,*[29] whose views were systematically presented, in 1939, in a volume called *The New Rational Philosophy.*[30] Fung says that he continues, but does not follow, the rational philosophy of the Ch'êng-Chu school, and reconstructs it from the viewpoint of objectivism. To him as to the Sung Neo-Confucianists, especially the brothers Ch'êng and Chu Hsi, Reason (*li*) is that by which a thing is what it

is. As such, it is self-existent, eternal, and not affected by its objec-
tification in the world of actual entities. It belongs to the realm
of truth and not to the realm of actuality. It is neither in nor above
the world since it does not enter into spatial or temporal relationship. Consequently, the question whether Reason is prior to actuality is meaningless. Although Reason is not *in* the world, every event,
condition, or relation in the world must follow Reason. The sum
total of the Reason of all entities is the Great Ultimate.

Contrary to the opinion of Chou Tun-yi (1017–1073) and other
Sung Neo-Confucianists, Fung holds that Reason and the Great
Ultimate do not create. The realm of actuality is self-existent, although individual entities in this realm must have a beginning and
an end. According to the Neo-Confucianists, entities come into
being by virtue of a material principle called *ch'i,* or vital principle.
Analyzing this concept in greater detail, Fung explains that, in
coming into being, an entity is not only modeled after Reason but
is also based on the vital principle. The latter is the "material" on
the basis of which an entity becomes actual in accordance with
Reason. In a relative sense, *ch'i* is the "what" of an entity, like the
bricks of a house, but, in an absolute sense, it is matter, a logical
concept, which Fung proposes to call "the vital principle of the
true prime unit," using Ch'êng I-ch'uan's term in a new sense. Although this vital principle, being the principle of actualization, has
the characteristic of existence, it is neither in Reason nor in the
actual world. In this, Professor Fung departs from Neo-Confucianists like Chang Hêng-ch'ü (1021–1077) and Ch'êng I-ch'uan (1033–
1107), who considered *ch'i* to be *in* the actual world.

In actualizing, the vital principle necessarily follows the Reason
of activity and, by implication, that of passivity. These two primary
modes, called *yin* and *yang,* are neither subtle matters, as some Neo-
Confucianists believed them to be, nor an energy that can influence
the world, as their predecessors believed, but merely logical concepts. They have meaning only with reference to particular entities
and cannot be regarded as self-existent universals. Furthermore,
activity and passivity are relative, as activity to one entity is at the
same time passivity to another. Both are indispensable to existence
since every entity has constructive elements which constitute its
activity, and destructive elements which constitute its passivity.

As every entity consists of many elements and follows many principles of Reason, and as these are shared by other entities, the activity and passivity of an entity are, therefore, at the same time, those other entities. By virtue of this, there is internal relation between entities.

This means that every entity is internally related to many other entities but not to all other entities, as no entity follows all principles of Reason. When Chu Hsi (1130–1200) said, "Every person and every thing has each a Great Ultimate," he merely meant that each entity has the "sum total of all the principles of Reason." Even here Chu Hsi went too far in assuming that "the human mind embodies all the principles of Reason," which is not the case. It is impossible for an entity to follow all principles of Reason because its destructive elements and passivity are always present to prevent it. There is, therefore, nothing perfect. By the same token, there is nothing permanent.

On account of the two modes of activity and passivity, an entity is forever in a state of flux; the world is therefore a stream of transformation. As the Neo-Confucianists put it, the universe is "daily renewed." In somewhat Buddhist fashion, Fung calls this process "formation, development, decay, and destruction," and describes it in terms of "daily renewal by cyclical process . . . by progression toward and retrogression from Reason . . . by the increase and decrease in the actualization of entities . . . and by the appearance of new classes." The last process is dialectic, resulting in new and higher qualities.

This movement of perpetual transformation involves the vital principle, all the principles of Reason, activity and passivity, and actualization. In its dynamic state, it is the *Tao* of the Taoists, or creation; in its static state, it is the universe, or the Whole. In this continuous flow of *Tao,* Reason is gradually actualized. Since Reason involves an infinite number of principles, its complete realization requires infinite time. The world as man knows it is therefore only a part of that process in which individual entities are becoming actual.

When an entity becomes actual in accordance with Reason, its nature can then be said to be realized and its destiny fulfilled. From the viewpoint of the realm of truth the nature of an entity as such is neither good nor evil, but from the viewpoint of the realm of actuality it is good, since it always follows Reason to some degree. Evil is merely the privation of good. From the practical standpoint, however, when an entity fails to follow a higher principle of Reason it becomes evil. The origin of moral evil, then, is to be explained in terms of "the failure to develop one's capacity," as in the Neo-Confucianists and Mencius. When an entity follows Reason completely, both its reason and its nature are fully realized. In this respect Fung completely agrees with the brothers Ch'êng and Chu Hsi that "the complete realization of Reason, the development of one's nature to the utmost, and the establishment of one's destiny are simultaneous."

To accomplish these, one needs to "investigate things" and to "extend knowledge." To the brothers Ch'êng and Chu Hsi this meant speculation. Chu Hsi believed that the mind was the embodiment of all the principles of Reason and therefore could know the whole of Reason by knowing a part of it. To Fung, on the other hand, the contents of Reason can be known only by objective and systematic study. He therefore insists on the inductive method and experimental logic. By analyzing actual entities, one may know the realm of actuality, and from this one may know the realm of truth. When one understands Reason perfectly, he "views things from the standpoint of Heaven," considers "the myriad things as one unity," lives according to jên—love, or the highest good—and moves in a transcendental world.

This outline is too brief to do justice to Professor Fung Yu-lan, but it is sufficient to show that, although he employs the same terminologies as the Sung Neo-Confucianists and arrives at similar conclusions, he has supplied new arguments, cleared up certain confusions, and removed some difficulties. More significantly, he has avoided the Buddhistic mysticism of the brothers Ch'êng and Chu Hsi. Furthermore, he has provided a logical foundation for the system, which Sung Neo-Confucianism sadly lacked, and has supplemented it with a modern epistemology. In addition, Fung has reaffirmed the objective character of existence from the standpoint of Western objectivism. Above all, his philosophy is a synthesis not only of the Sung philosophers but also of Neo-Confucianism, neorealism, and, to a small degree, experimentalism.

Certain points, such as how transcendental Reason and experimental logic can be reconciled, need clarification. Professor Fung is justified in criticizing the Ch'ing philosophers as illogical in contending that Reason was *in* things, and in asserting that there could be no Reason without them. He has undermined their philosophy of immanence and with it their practical and this-worldly spirit. Nevertheless, the system is a solid proof that Confucianism is not being entirely rejected, but is rather being reconstructed in the light of Western philosophy. The reconstruction will result in a synthesis of East and West.

Part Four

THE ARTS,
LITERATURE,
AND EDUCATION

CHAPTER XXI

Calligraphy, Poetry, and Painting

BY FLORENCE AYSCOUGH

I F ART BE THE FINE FLOWER of man's spirit, it is important to recognize the root from which it springs. Therefore this study is divided into two parts. The first discusses origins; the second describes the six manners in which calligraphy, poetry, and painting in China have woven themselves into a brocade of beauty.

To make clear the commonly held belief in the unity of all created things, attention may first be directed to the *t'ai-chi t'u*, or Plan of Ultimate Principle. This paradigm of Neo-Confucian philosophy is engraved on the tombstone of Chu Hsi (1130–1200), the great Sung-dynasty exponent of this system of thought. The diagram (see overleaf) was drawn by Jean-Joseph-Marie Amiot (1718–1793), a learned Jesuit missionary, and is more easily comprehensible to European eyes than the original.[1]

From the Ultimate Principle which is brought forth by *ch'i*, breath of the Creator, spring the two essences, *yang* and *yin*. *Yang*, positive essence, corresponds to all masculine elements—to strength, light, height. *Yin*, negative essence, corresponds to all feminine elements—to weakness, darkness, depth. By their interaction and perfect balance *yin* and *yang* bring forth *wan-wu*, the ten thousand "creatures." These, including men, animals, insects, plants—all created things—are bound in close brotherhood. Man, although one of the Three Powers, of which Heaven and Earth are the other two, is closely akin to the innumerable manifestations of nature with which he is surrounded.

---

[1] For notes to chapter xxi see pages 535–536.

Realization of this philosophy is essential to comprehension of the arts of China. Nor does realization of this philosophy only suffice. One must take into consideration also the preoccupation of many Chinese with the region they call the Western Paradise. Here dwell forever, under perfect conditions, those fortunate beings who, by a life of abstraction, have attained *hsien*-ship. This world of fantasy, where dwell the *hsien* (sien), often seems more real to the artist than the world of actuality.

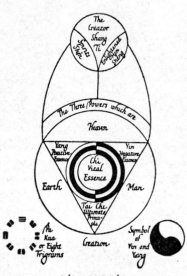

T'AI-CHI T'U

The Chinese, essentially logical, delight in seeking origins, but they have never been hampered by that passion for proof which so complicates the lives of Occidentals. Nor do they consider it necessary to attribute all origins to human agency. Believing that all things are bound in close brotherhood, that Heaven, Earth, and Man form an indissoluble trinity, and that mortals, by transmutation, can become immortal, it is easy for them to ascribe a supernatural origin when the human origin is unknown. Hence many legends, as delightful as they are unscientific, have grown up. In the attempts of the Chinese to deal with origins, legends play an important part.

Calligraphy.—Let us, in imagination, go to the banks of the river Lo, where, in the dim mists which veil the dawn of history, stood Fu Hsi, first of primeval lords. Sunlight glinted from the scales which covered his body, dazzled the three eyes in his head, and was reflected from the surface of the waters. Suddenly the waters parted and a dragon-horse arose. Upon its back the creature bore a diagram, the *pa-kua* (ba-gua), or Eight Trigrams. Fu Hsi copied it and deduced therefrom a method which superseded that of keeping records by means of knotted cords.

The Eight Trigrams were introduced to Chinese thought at an early date; later they formed the basis of the *I Ching,* or *Yi Ching* (Classic, or Book, of Changes). Recognition and application of this design may be called the first great invention in Chinese art. This was but the precursor of greater ones. It remained for Ts'ang Chieh (tsang jie), minister to the Yellow Lord, to carry it further. Chinese accounts state, "He observed the shapes of things in Heaven, the forms of things on Earth, and the footprints of birds upon sands." He must have observed with deep concentration, thanks to the four eyes which he is said to have possessed. A great idea flashed across his mind—and the art of writing was born.

Histories say that when the five hundred forty primitive characters were formed, nature was moved: Heaven rained millet; demons wailed in the night; dragons hid themselves in the depths. The characters, which formed the second great invention (and now one comes to the region of fact), for the most part represented natural objects: sun, moon, trees, streams, a mouth, a hand, an eye. Little pictures they were, drawn with life and vigor.

With pictures alone, however, one does not go far. It remained for an unknown genius to combine them so that ideas could be represented. This may be counted the third great invention. This genius wrote sun and moon together to suggest brilliance, floods and flames to mean disaster, two trees to signify a forest, three trees for deep shade. This and further developments have made the Chinese language a marvelous and beautiful vehicle for expressing thought, especially poetic thought. For example, the character *chai* (jai), which means a retired room or a scholar's study, expresses the place where "the heart is regulated to receive the instructions of Heaven." Is that not a poem—a poem full of depth and sensibility? It is interesting, too, to note how the Chinese use manifestations from the natural world to express human emotion. The character *ch'ou,* meaning sorrow, is made up of heart and autumn; the character for autumn shows grain combined with fire. Could sorrow be more vividly expressed?

As similes, too, the Chinese use manifestations of nature in a manner foreign to the West. No other people would describe a lovely lady in the terms used by a poet who writes about the concubine, née Chiang (jiang), of Marquis Chuang (juang) of Wei, who ruled from 811 to 757 B.C. The poem, from the second stanza of the *Shih Ching* (shzh jing) (Book of Songs), reads:

> Fingers like tender shoots of white grass;
> Forearm like viscid sap of fir trees;
> Neck like long white larvae of tree grubs;
> Teeth like row of melon seeds;
> Square-headed-cicada forehead, and moth-antennae eyebrows.*

The earliest examples of Chinese writing extant are the characters on the Oracle Bones found at An-yang, Honan. (See chaps. iii and iv, above.) Writing appears on bronze vessels of the Shang and Chou dynasties. Bronze and stone are especially valued since by inscriptions thereon they can be transformed into literary as well as historical documents. Early Chinese books were strips of bamboo or wood, from one to two centimeters wide, perforated at one end so that they could be strung together on a leathern thong. These strips bore single columns of characters written with a bamboo pen dipped in lacquer made from the sap of trees. Peripatetic scholars at times took with them veritable cartloads of books.[2]

Poetry.—No legends deal with the origin of poetry in China. The art was well developed in the earliest days of which there is knowledge. There are, indeed, folk songs among the Odes of Shang in the *Shih Ching,* which are traditionally ascribed to the period 1766–1122 B.C.

Apart from folk songs, the *fu,* or free verse, may be said to have had its rise in southwestern China, in the region known as the Land of Ch'u, or Land of Thorns. It dates from about 300 B.C. There lived the famous Ch'ü Yüan (332–295 B.C.), author of *Li Sao* (Falling into Trouble).[3] (See chap. xxvii, below.)

Painting.—It is not known how the earliest painting was done. The first examples of the art are traditionally ascribed to Lei, a younger sister of the legendary ruler Shun.[4] She is called "Painter Lei." An exasperated critic of later days exclaimed, "To think that this divine art was invented by a woman!" Chinese tradition refers, also, to representations of people and things at the dawn of time. Certainly, design was far developed in the days of Shang. By that time, and quite possibly by the late neolithic period, the fourth

---

* This translation and the translations of other poems quoted in this chapter were done by Florence Ayscough.

great invention, that of the writing brush, had taken place. Moreover, in the Shang and Chou periods, wall paintings existed, fragments of which have been found at An-yang. In a long poem, *T'ien-wên* (Heavenly Questionings),[5] Ch'ü Yüan describes those he saw in the ancestral temples of the kings of Ch'u. The description alone remains. It is not so, however, with the murals in the Ling-kuang (ling-guang) Palace, which was built in the second century B.C. Besides the account written *circa* A.D. 129 by the poet Wang Yen-shou, reproductions of these paintings were cut on stone.[6]

The fourth great invention, that of the hair-tipped writing brush, was followed by the fifth, that of paper, in A.D. 105. In the Han dynastic history it is stated:

In ancient times writing was generally on bamboo or on pieces of silk, which were then called *chih*. But silk being expensive and bamboo heavy, these two materials were not convenient. Then Ts'ai Lun [chief eunuch at the imperial court] thought of using tree bark, hemp, rags and fish nets. In the first year of the Yüan-hsing period [A.D. 105] he made a report to the emperor [Ho] on the process of paper making and received high praise for his ability. From this time paper has been in use everywhere and is called "the paper of Marquis Ts'ai."[7]

Although the equipment of Chinese scholars—a term which includes artists—had grown, it was not yet complete. An essential element was lacking, namely, ink. The invention of ink from lamp-black, the sixth great invention, is attributed by the Chinese to Wei Tan (wei dan), who lived in the fourth century of the Christian era. At last the black-haired people, as the Chinese love to style themselves, were provided with materials for writing pictures and painting poems. They use the term *hsieh* for both processes and call both writings and paintings "ink remains."

The chief requirements for the development of the scholar's art are firmness, lissomeness, and decision. Pressure on the brush must be nicely graduated and this graduation must be evenly maintained. The hand and the arm must be strong and lissome as silk. Absolute decision is inherent in a great artist. He must know precisely what he intends to do. Where the brush drops, thence it must depart; no erasure, no change, is possible. The fluid ink makes an indelible mark upon the absorbent paper or carefully prepared silk, and the author is committed to what he has done. Long mental preparation is essential. I once asked a Chinese art connoisseur whether a painter worked quickly or slowly. His reply was, "*Thinkee*, long time; *do*, chop-chop." The keynote of writing and painting in China is this absolute mastery of the brush, so that every gradation of tone can be faultlessly rendered. Gradation of tone is all-important, for therein lies the power of depicting distance.

Change comes gradually. The cursive style of brushwork was not fully developed until the third and fourth centuries of the modern era. Traces of it are found in the fourth-century work of Ku K'ai-chih (gu kai-jzh).[8] It is supposed to have been introduced to painting by Lu T'an-wei, who lived in the second half of the fifth century. No work of Lu's remains, but the scroll in the British Museum attributed to Ku K'ai-chih must be, if not an original, at least a very early work in the style of that master.

There grew up, too, a school of great calligraphists. The greatest of these, the master for all time, was Wang Hsi-chih (322–379).[9] He it was who invented the running brush stroke by which one character melts into the next. Of the two hundred forty-three scripts from his hand which are reported to have been in the collection of the Emperor Hui-tsung (1100–1125) of the Sung dynasty, only seven were in square script.

By the sixth century the cursive style had become firmly established, as is proved by mural paintings in a tomb at Gukenri, Korea, which bears a date equivalent to A.D. 550. The glorious dragon depicted on its eastern wall seems about to soar away upon a whirling wind.[10] Writing also had changed: the running hand and the grass characters, the despair of Western students, had developed. From the fourth century, then, when this cursive style was developed, the union of calligraphy, painting, and poetry was complete.

❖   ❖   ❖

There are six methods which exemplify the union of calligraphy, painting, and poetry.

First method.—Calligraphy and design are used as essential yet independent elements in one composition.

An exquisite remnant of silk from the grave mounds of Noin-Ula, near Urga, in Outer Mongolia, supplies a beautiful example of this method. The find of a dated lacquer cup places the group in the year 2 B.C. The silk is woven in a design of green and pale yellow on a red-brown ground. Birds, trees, and other natural objects appear, marvelous in their freshness. Lines of characters, regularly repeated, form the sentence, "May sons and grandsons prosper for ten thousand years." The pictures and the phrases, although independent, are integral to the design.[11]

Another beautiful example is a seventh-century mirror which is cast in light bronze and has a lovely green patina. The design provides a steppingstone to the freer style of the T'ang dynasty and is attributed to the Sui.[12] In the inner circle appear the animals of the four quarters: the blue-green dragon of the east, the vermilion bird of the south, the snow-white tiger of the west, the dark warriors (tortoise and serpent) of the north. On the smaller of the outer circles is cut a rhyming inscription of forty characters:

[The mirror] in O-fang—Palace of the Beautiful Region—reflects the gall. [The mirror] Jên Shou [ren shou]—Benevolence and Longevity—hangs in the palace. The water chestnut is hidden within the illuminated surface. The moon swings past the Pitcher. All forms which look in its center must be recorded; its luster, as of gems and flames, is like the wide bright sky. Hill demons dare not come forth; water sprites are humbled by the work. Then I wrote these jewel-like square characters and engraved them, for eternity, upon the pale green bronze.

The inscription offers difficulties and the allusions contained in the forty characters must be elucidated. According to legend, a mirror hung in O-fang Palace, built in 212 B.C. by Ch'in Shih Huang Ti (221–210 B.C.),[13] which reflected the "galls" of the palace ladies and revealed whether or not they were faithful. The Jên Shou Mirror took its name from the palace where it was hung, in the Ch'in (dzin) period, in the third century before the Christian era. It was concealed and so arranged that it reflected the faces of those who passed—although they were unconscious of the fact.

In the outer circle, on spaces separated by flower motives, appear the animals which govern the twelve branches: rat, tiger, hare, dragon, snake, horse, sheep, monkey, hen, dog, boar, bull.

Second method.—Writings, such as grave pieces or dedicatory inscriptions, are used on monuments, together with representations of natural objects and of the human form.

An excellent example of decoration in this much-used method

is shown in the Pin-yang (bin-yang) Cave at Lung-mên, Honan.[14] Processions of donors in flowing robes, some carrying lotus—sacred flower of the Buddhist faith—are among the best-known documents of Chinese art. The Pin-yang Cave is dated A.D. 525. The decoration provided by the inscription on the pillar was added in the year 641. This inscription is written in his best manner by the famous calligraphist, Ch'u Sui-liang (596–658).[15] The writing states that the Pin-yang Cave had been decorated in honor of the mother of T'ai-tsung (tai-dzung), second emperor (627–649), and founder of the T'ang dynasty. (See chap. vi, above.) The writing is principally concerned with cataloguing the virtues of the lady who closed her eyes in death at the age of thirty-six, but philosophical reflections are included also.

Third method.—Writings and paintings are used as essential and closely allied elements of the same design.

One of the most exquisite of paintings is that of the wild goose, "dropping to earth as a dead leaf drops," to borrow the words chanted by Tu (du) Fu (712–770).[16] It is attributed to Lo Ch'uang, an artist of the Southern Sung dynasty, who was a priest in the Liu-tung Temple on the West Lake, near Hangchow. The painting is now owned in Japan.[17]

The poem is placed so as to balance the dropping bird and thereby to complete the rhythm of the painting.

LONG ROAD

Wild goose at edge of Heaven drops!
  Turns its head!
On road south of river, where wind blows rain,
Flying aslant in dreary autumn it crosses
  pool by dyke.
Dead lotus blossoms; faded leaves;
  plumed rushes all yellow.

Fourth method.—Writings and calligraphic paintings may reveal precisely the same brush stroke.

Perhaps no more striking examples exist than the portrait of the Buddhist patriarch Ta-mo (da-mo), or Bodhidharma,[18] by the Japanese artist Sesshu, and the marvelous characters from the same hand.[19] Sesshu (1420–1506) spent years studying in China and is ranked by the Japanese among their greatest artists.

The character of the brush stroke is all-important: how impossible, for instance, to depict a tender Kuan-yin, like the well-known goddess by Mu Hsi,[20] with the dashing strokes used for Ta-mo!

Another example of the fourth method is the famous painting by Ying Yü-chien, of the Southern Sung period.[21] Like Lo Ch'uang, he was a priest and lived upon the shores of the West Lake in the Tz'u-ching (tz-dzing) Temple. His pictures are the oldest in what Japanese critics term the "broken stroke." To those who have not traveled in moisture-laden subtropical parts of China, the painting may seem exaggerated, but in just such an illusive manner do little villages peep from the mists. The poem, written in characteristic strokes, reads:

CLEAR AFTER RAIN AT MOUNTAIN MART AMONG SUMMITS

Rain drags at base of clouds
  which enshroud Ch'ang-sha,
Dim, dim remains of rainbow
  borne on evening afterglow.
Supremely beautiful, Mart shines clear
  rising from beyond willows.
Wine-shop flag flutters, flutters;
  It makes me think of home.

Brush strokes and characters! How deeply the Chinese feel about them! The wielding of the implement may fairly be described as a cult. Tu Fu[22] wrote, of the eighth-century calligraphist Chang Hsü:

SEEING, GAZING AT, THE GRASS-CHARACTER PICTURE BY CHANG HSÜ
[THE PROPERTY OF] YANG, SUPERVISOR OF IMPERIAL
GARMENTS AND UTENSILS

They say this man is dead!
Inspired writings by Enlightened One of Grass
  Characters are difficult to obtain.

Now, seeing, gazing at them, fire of grief burns
  in my head;
Overwhelmed by sadness, melancholy, my eyes
  fill to overflowing.

From small silk strip mournful autumn wind
  seems to rise;
Ancient characters appear amazing, unprecedented.

Clear! clear! as harmony of swinging jade;
High! high! as groves of towering pines.

Mountain ranges coil through their midst;
Virility of writing brush, irresistible as surging
water.

   . . . .

Wu hu! alas! dryad of Eastern Wu;
I recognize his leaping inspiration which rouses
pure emotion.

Sir Yang wipes clean, square bamboo book box,
Unrolls the scroll. We forget to eat, to sleep.

Remember strokes which formerly fell from tip
of his long, soft brush!
Not only for winedrinking did he manifest
genius!

Subdivision of the fourth method.—Writings and paintings may
be brought forth by the selfsame flash of inspiration, the thought
being expressed in part by words, in part by images executed con-
secutively, and providing equally important elements of the same
design.

One of the best examples of the intimate means by which the arts
of calligraphy, poetry, and painting are interwoven is provided by
an album from the brush of the Japanese painter Koetsu (1557–
1637). No reproductions can suggest the charm of these little
"poetry paintings," or "painted poems." Silver or gold and light
colors combine to form a perfect background for the strong black
strokes in which the poems are written.[23] One realizes that the
master, impelled by inspiration, availed himself simultaneously
of all modes to express his emotion.

Fifth method.—Writings are used instead of paintings.

This method, so characteristic of Far Eastern thought, is developed in a hundred ways. Under this division may be placed the
"written pictures" peculiar to Oriental art. These *tzŭ-hua* (dz-hua),
or "hanging-on-the-wall poems," which the Chinese consider the
perfect manner for self-expression, are less known and understood
in the West than any other form of Asiatic art. A lovely thought
perpetuated in beautiful handwriting and hung upon the wall to

suggest a mental picture—that is what they amount to. The Chinese artist considers the *tzŭ-hua* a far better means of suggestion than images.[24]

> A cold rain blurs the edges of the river;
> Night enters Wu.
> In the level brightness of dawn
> I saw my friend start alone for Ch'u Mountain.
> He gave me this message for his friends and relations
>   at Lo Yang,
> My heart is a piece of ice in a jade cup.

So runs the wording of a written picture in my possession.[25] It makes visual to the mental eye the drama of a man who leaves behind him the world and all he loves. One sees the torrential subtropical rain which so often deluges Wu, the region where the Great River debouches into the sea. This is succeeded by the brilliant dawn which follows such a downpour. In the brightness of this dawn, the man who is retiring from the world, whose heart is become as "a piece of ice in a jade cup," starts alone for the steep mountains of Szechuan, those first treads of the stairway leading to the Roof of the World. Nor is the one departing insensible of what he must leave behind. Friends and relatives are to a Chinese the beginning and the end of life.

A highly popular form of these written pictures are the *tui-tzŭ* (duei-dz) which form part of the decoration in even the most humble homes of China. The cultivated choose these antithetical phrases with the greatest care so that they will be appropriate to the place they are to adorn. The uncultivated depend upon others for their choice—but *tui-tzŭ* they must have!

Sixth method.—Paintings are used instead of writings.

There are three ways in which paintings take the place of writings. First, they are used to express a wish or a proverb, or to suggest a well-known tale. No pictures are more popular than those of flowers, trees, and birds, which are used as birthday greetings. The white-headed bulbul appears as a symbol of longevity, and various trees and flowers play symbolic roles.

A well-known picture by Mao Yi, of the Sung dynasty, shows a mother dog with four puppies.[26] This suggests that each shall take his turn on guard during one of the "five watches" of the night—

also the hope that five generations may live in peace under the same roof. Three egrets (because *ssu,* egret, and *ssŭ,* to reflect, have the same sound) express the proverb, "Think thrice, then act." Nine egrets mean "The scholar reflects nine times."

A favorite theme of painters is that of the Trees of Love. Perhaps it was first carved on the monument in Kansu (gan-su) raised, in A.D. 171, in honor of the prefect Li Hsi.[27] It is placed in the cliff wall facing a mountain road built by the prefect. Other motifs carved on the monument are the nine-eared head of grain and the tree of sweet dew, emblems of prosperity. The other trees, with branches entwined—what do they suggest? The answer is given by a charming if tragic story, which runs as follows:

Han P'êng, minister to the ruler of Sung, a feudal state under the Chou dynasty, had a beautiful wife whom he adored and who adored him. Tales of the lady's loveliness reached the ears of the the ruler, and desire awakened in his breast. He caused Han P'êng to be cast into prison, where he died. The widow was then transferred to the royal harem.

A day or two later the ruler invited her to walk with him upon a high terrace. Before accepting the invitation, the lady, realizing the ruler's intentions, dressed herself in a silk gauze robe. Together they ascended the terrace. The lady looked up to the bright blue sky and down to the fair green earth, taking from each a silent farewell. Then, to the horror of her companion, she sprang upon the parapet and cast herself into space. He seized the edge of her robe, but the frail gauze parted. He looked down and saw her lying dead upon the paving stones.

In her girdle was a letter which begged that her body might lie with that of her husband in a single grave. This petition the infuriated tyrant would not grant, and the graves of Han P'êng and his wife were dug side by side, but separate. There sprang, then, from each grave a tree, and the trees, bending toward each other, closely interwove their branches. Exquisite paintings of these twin trees have been made through the ages. To every Chinese they suggest undying conjugal love.

Second, paintings are used as illustrations. Under this head may be placed Buddhist and Taoist pictures which tell a definite story, as do Western religious pictures. Very beautiful is the *yü-lan* or fish-basket Kuan-yin in the style of Li Lung-mien. According to legend, the Bodhisattva appeared in one of her thirty-three manifestations, that of a beautiful girl offering fish for sale. Many suitors appeared, and she promised to accept him who could learn the P'u-p'in Sutra in one night. At dawn the next day twenty successful candidates presented themselves. The Diamond Sutra was proposed, and ten succeeded in learning it. The Lotus Sutra was then adopted. Only a youth named Ma passed the test. The lovely fish-vendor entered his house, but before becoming his bride she died and her body disintegrated. Later, the tomb was opened in the presence of a monk, who said, "It was Kuan-yin, come to convert you." Hence this manifestation of the Bodhisattva is also known as the Ma-lang-fu, or Kuan-yin, wife of young Ma. The somewhat cryptic inscription on the painting is signed by Ch'ing-yü, a mendicant priest:

> Hairpins awry, head-dress disheveled,
> Her lips affirm, her heart denies.
> There where eyes do not reach
> Is a basket in which are no fish.

Painters delight also in depicting historical events. A favorite theme is the story of Ts'ai Yen, courtesy name Wên-chi, a lady who lived in the second and third centuries of the Christian era. The daughter of a noted historian and statesman, she was possessed of distinct literary and musical talents. In the course of an invasion, in A.D. 195, she, a childless widow, was carried captive to the Tatar camp and there was forced to become the chieftain's bride. Her misery and disgust at this fate were expressed in eighteen songs called *Hu-chia Shih-pa P'o,* that is, Eighteen "Sweeping-of-the-Cords" (on hearing the Mongol flageolet). The third song reads:

> I go out from country of Han, hsi-i-i; I enter
>   precincts of Hu,
> My home has vanished, my person is violated, hsi-i-i;
>   it were better I had not been born.
>
> Felts and furs make my garments, hsi-i-i! My bones
>   and flesh shake as does thunder, tremble as does
>   a startled horse;
>
> Rank odor of wethers pervades food I must taste, hsi-i-i;
>   I sternly repress my disgust.

Drums of Ho resound, hsi-i-i; proceeding from night they
    enter bright dawn;
Winds of Hu blow a gale, blow a gale, hsi-i-i, at dark
    frontier camp.

Present anguish, former woe, hsi-i-i, third "sweeping-
    of-the-cords" is complete;
I control my grief, store my resentment, hsi-i-i; at
    what time will come peace?

In spite of initial despair, the lady became at least relatively
happy and bore two children to her barbarian lord. After twelve
years she was ransomed with gold and jade by Ts'ao Ts'ao (155–
220), who felt pity for her old father deprived of his only child.
A well-known painting shows the sad parting between Wên-chi and
her Tatar family.

Third, paintings are used to suggest some mood evoked by a
poem. There are innumerable examples of this manner. One can
find a poem to balance most of the masterpieces from the Chinese
painter's brush. The famous work of Ma Yüan, of the Southern
Sung, showing a tiny fishing boat in the midst of limitless space,[28]
is expressed in the following words of an anonymous writer:

Fishermen draw their nets
From great pool of T'an river.
They have hired a boat
And come here to fish by reflected light
Of sunken sun.

✧   ✧   ✧

One period of the T'ang age is especially noted for its poets, painters, and calligraphists, namely, the quarter of a century which
closed with the An Lu-shan rebellion in the year 755. There met at
that time in the capital, Ch'ang-an (near modern Sian, Shensi), a
group of men whose names glow in the annals of Chinese art. Then
lived Wang Wei (698–759, or, more probably, 701–762),[29] who expressed himself in both poetry and painting, and whose rolling
"Waterfall" is a world masterpiece. Then lived Li T'ai-po (li tai-bo)
(ca. 705–762),[30] who dubbed himself an Immortal of the Wine Cup,
and who chose the lyric as his principal means of interpretation.
Another giant, perhaps greatest of all, was Tu Fu (712–770),[31] in
whose poems, as the Chinese say, the history of the times can be

T'IEN HÊNG AND HIS FIVE HUNDRED FOLLOWERS

An oil painting, of mural dimensions, by Ju Péon

CITY GOVERNMENT BUILDING, SHANGHAI

read. And Chêng Ch'ien,[32] the eccentric Chêng Ch'ien, to whom the Emperor Hsüan-tsung (713–756), popularly remembered as Ming-huang, the Bright Emperor, gave a post at the Kuang-wên (gwang-wen) lodge entailing no duties—because Chêng Ch'ien would perform none. He lived in the Tz'u-en Temple—Temple of Compassionate Grace,—from the courtyard of which he collected persimmon leaves and decorated them with pictures or poems. One of his famous offerings to the ruler was a landscape with a poem in impeccable script, placed so that the balance of the composition was perfect. The emperor, with his quick aesthetic response, appreciated it keenly and exclaimed, "Chêng Ch'ien! The Three Perfections!" The term has been used ever since to describe such a composition.

In those days, poets, painters, and calligraphists banqueted together to listen to one another's poems and admire one another's paintings and writings. They made expeditions together and lived, indeed, a life full of aesthetic emotion. They visited the hills, where they listened to what Tu Fu describes as "the music of silence," and watched the Dragon float by in the clouds he governs, or heard the Tiger growl in the wind he controls. Then they were inspired to write—poetic frenzy seized them.

It is not to be doubted that in the writing brush—their fourth great invention—the Chinese, the Japanese, and the Koreans possess a medium for the expression of emotion which is denied to Westerners. With the brush, eastern Asians improvise much as musicians do. Intoxicated by the joy of execution, they are veritable virtuosi of the brush. Artists pour out their souls from the soft hair tip of the slender bamboo tube, and whether that which drops from the tip be a writing or an image, it is:

> That which is undefinable;
> That which is untranslatable;
> That which is universal;
> That which is—Poetry!

CHAPTER XXII

Art

BY CHIANG YEE

CHINESE ART has a history of at least four thousand years' duration and an infinite variety of media, of which jade, bone and ivory, stone, bronze, wood, enamel, lacquer, silk, pottery, porcelain, calligraphy, and painting are most important.

Thanks to the work of scholars such as Laufer, Bushell, Hobson, Binyon, and Sirén, Chinese art is no longer considered mysterious and exotic by Westerners. These men devoted much of their lives to revealing the beauty of Asian art, and Chinese as well as Westerners recognize their debt to them. It is a pity, however, that many younger students have paid so much attention to the symbolic aspects of Chinese art and its myths and legends rather than to its intrinsic beauty and interest. This misdirected zeal tends to foster the notion that Chinese art is difficult for Westerners to understand.

It is the essential beauty of the works that is of the first importance. Chinese admire ancient Egyptian and Greek works of art and the masterpieces of Michelangelo, Raphael, and Leonardo da Vinci without feeling handicapped by lack of knowledge of their symbolic meaning or their historical or mythical associations. Art speaks to the human heart, and any good work of art reveals itself to the person meditating upon it. Its appeal is for all time and for all places. Explanation of its meaning, though helpful, is not essential. Therefore it is proposed here, not to explain Chinese art, but simply to examine its origins and development and to suggest ideas concerning its future.

To state precisely how Chinese art originated some four thousand or more years ago is impossible, but it is safe to suggest that it arose out of the ordinary, everyday needs of men. Recent excavations at the tombs of the Shang (*ca.* 1766–1028 B.C.) and other rulers brought to light sacrificial bronze vessels and some tools, as well as early Chou bronzes (*ca.* 1027–500 B.C.). Examples of the latter have long been well known. The most important discovery was a large number of animal bones, generally known as the Oracle Bones, engraved with ancient Chinese characters. (See chaps. iii and iv, above.) Scholars describe these as containing portrayals of objects observed in the daily life of the times. The characters on bones and the inscriptions on early bronzes form tiny, well-constructed pictures. The perfection of the characters suggests that they must have been in use for a very long time.

In the most ancient days the forefathers of the Chinese doubtless made marks on trees and stones as a means of remembering events or transactions. According to traditions in the oldest books, a genius of the twenty-eighth century B.C., Ts'ang Chieh (see chap. xxi, above), after observing footprints and shadows of birds and animals, invented a script. The cutting of signs on bone was probably the next stage of development. The ancient scripts, especially the characters on bone, constitute the foundation of Chinese art. Each picture was constructed with only those lines or strokes essential to make the objects immediately recognizable.[1] Simplicity and lack of fussiness, in conjunction with the balanced use of space, have remained the chief guiding principles of Chinese art. Artists have *never* aimed at photographic reproduction of objects, nor have they desired to decorate all available space on the medium used for self-expression. If these points are clearly understood and remembered, it will be easy to follow the development of Chinese art.

One can but wonder at the hardness of the tools used for early bone inscriptions, and even more at the instruments invented for the molding and chiseling of Shang and Chou bronzes. Knowledge of chemistry and metallurgy was clearly at the disposal of the craftsmen. There must have been many stages of evolution before the creation, more than three thousand years ago, of the beautifully formed *yü* (a jar with a lid and a swing handle), the tall and slender vase-shaped *ku*, the three-legged *ting*, and the *chüeh* (a libation cup

---

[1] For notes to chapter xxii see pages 536–537.

with three sharply pointed, slightly flaring legs) characteristic of the Shang age. Their shapes have eternal artistic value because they are simple and not fanciful, solid and not weak in structure, dignified and pleasing to the eye. The Shang designs were the best in the days of their creation, and have remained the best throughout succeeding ages.

Some of the bronzes are round, some square, some triangular, and some rectangular. Some have legs like those of birds, beasts, or human figures; others have cylindrical legs. It may seem that these shapes have nothing in common with the ancient scripts, yet the guiding principles—simplicity and suitability to their purpose—are the same. Furthermore, the decorative designs on the bronzes are patterns of birds, animals, dragons, ogre masks, and cicadas and other insects which are based, not on photographic resemblance, but on the ancient scripts representing these objects. The cloud-and-thunder pattern, for example, is a repetition of the scripts for cloud and thunder. The minds of the artists were so well stored with the beautiful lines of the script that they could not but make use of them in their own designs.

It is not known whether artists chose a certain bird, beast, or insect because of a meaning attached to it or because of its beauty and suitability. Consider, for example, the bronze owl wine vessel of the Chou dynasty (*ca.* 1027–255 B.C.) in the Eumorfopoulos Collection of the British Museum. The owl may not be realistic, but the solid dignity of form, demanding little material for neck, wings, and legs, is suitable for a wine vessel. Probably only princes and dukes could afford to possess cooking utensils and sacrificial vessels of such beautifully fashioned bronze. It was natural that they should wish to put the artists' skill to the highest use. Hence it was that bronzes came to be associated with state ceremonial and ritual.

The ancient Chinese expressed their awe of the powers of nature (see chap. i, above) by establishing rules and ceremonies for the worship of Heaven, Earth, and other natural phenomena. Anthropomorphic images, however, formed no part of the worship. In this the Chinese differed from the Egyptians, Greeks, Indians, and Mexicans. This lack may be ascribed to various causes. The ancient scripts evolved through the forces of imagination, reasoning power, and logical combination in constructing characters. Perhaps this led early artists to pursue metaphysical ideas, such as the theory derived from Fu Hsi's Eight Trigrams in the *I Ching*, or Book of Changes (see chap. xxi, above), rather than to indulge in the construction of anthropomorphic images. The geniuses of Chou—Lao Tzŭ, Chuang Tzŭ, Confucius, and Mencius—stressed always that man is but one type of creature among thousands of others. That is one reason why no complex and highly integrated system of religion was developed in ancient China. The early bronzes, though they came to be closely associated with the idea of worship, seldom depict human figures. Lack of emphasis on man has remained characteristic of Chinese art to the present, in strong contrast to the art of the West.

This contrast is most marked in archaic jades: ceremonial disks, knives, and daggers, and decorated ornaments. Jade was usually carved in the shape of oxheads, buffaloes, tigers, bears, pigs, hares, birds, fish, cicadas, and other insects; rarely is it cut in human form.[2] Animals may have had symbolic meaning in the days when the early jades were made, but probably they were considered merely as common objects of nature. Dragons, *fêng-huang*, and other fabulous creatures seldom appear in archaic art. Patterns and contours of archaic carved jade show the direct influence of ancient scripts. Perhaps it was because jade was too hard to carve in realistic natural shapes. More likely, however, artists preferred to follow the principles of the ancient scripts by presenting simplified forms. The results attained are eminently satisfying in their simplicity and harmony, which are the keynotes of every branch of classical Chinese art.

By degrees, jade came to be used more than bronze, possibly because artists were trying to find a lasting material not subject to the difficulties of casting which attended bronze, or because jade was better suited for objects demanded by a more complicated way of life. Jade did not take the place of bronze, but supplemented it. Most archaic jades are small; indeed, it is difficult to find a piece of any considerable size which is good in quality. A Han jade horse's head in the Eumorfopoulos Collection is the largest known jade carving of that period. Accordingly, though jade has long been the favorite medium of Chinese artists, its scope is limited. The craftsmanship and decorative designs of jades and bronzes of the Shang period show that Chinese civilization had reached an advanced state of development by the fifteenth century B.C. Skillful use of the color and texture of natural stone calls for as much admiration as the casting and shaping of the ancient bronzes.

When careful examination is made of the potteries and porcelains of the post-Han period, as well as the wood and ivory carvings, glass, lacquer, and enamels, it is found that shapes and decorative patterns have remained more or less the same—so numerous and of such perfection were the beautiful designs accumulated in early days. All exemplified the values of simplicity and harmony and were characterized by a graphic approach, in contrast to the plastic emphasis of Western art. It may, then, be asserted that the evolution of Chinese art has been confined to changes in materials and subject matter, inasmuch as its root principles were established early and followed thereafter without deviation.

The rise of the fictile art, comprising all kinds of earthenware, stoneware, and porcelain, was probably due to the necessity of employing a more abundant and easily found material than bronze and jade. Stones other than jade were apparently little used in early days, although a few Shang marble sculptures in the round, as well as in relief, have been found. But jades have survived in the greatest numbers. Artists turned, however, to an easier medium in which to make small objects for daily use and discovered how to fire earth or clay in kilns. In the course of excavating the Shang tombs, specimens of black pottery, small molds made of stone, and pottery used for casting bronze have been discovered. The large bricks of the Great Wall, built in the Ch'in (tsin) period (255–207 B.C.), prove that the process of firing clay was by that time well established.

Of China's ancient architecture (see chap. xxiii, below) comparatively little is known. Only a few foundations of Shang buildings have been uncovered. The use of wood and brick apparently diverted the minds of builders from the possibility of using marble and other stone to any considerable extent. There are references, however, to Ch'in Shih Huang Ti's grand O-fang Palace and the beautiful Wei-yang Palace of the Han period, which were constructed, for the most part, of wood. With the exception of China's walls, no ancient ruins or relics of carved stone survive, comparable to those of Egypt, Chaldea, and Susa.

By the time of the Han (206 B.C.–A.D. 220), pottery was being widely used in everyday life. This is the first great development in Chinese art after that of bronzes and jades. With the introduction of glaze, a hard, compact, fine-grained pottery was produced; on percussion it gives a clear, musical note, and it is impervious to scratching with a knife. An excellent example of this pottery is a Han vase with iridescent green glaze, in the Bushell Collection of the Victoria and Albert Museum.

From pottery was developed porcelain, with its added qualities of translucence and vitrification owing to the use of a special kind of clay. Various clays found in divers places produce many types of porcelain. The best-known factories were at Ching-tê-chên (jing-de-jen) in present-day Kiangsi province, where the best quality of white clay was abundant. T'ao Yü, a native of this district, is said to have presented to the throne, in A.D. 619, the first white porcelains. They were called "false jade" vessels—which indicates the sequence of development in this branch of art.

The invention of porcelain opened a wide sphere to artists. The potters of the T'ang dynasty (618–906) not only achieved gorgeous effects in size of molding, but created a three-colored glaze, which was applied with the brush. This method was developed from the application of cinnabar to the unglazed part of the ware. The Sung dynasty (960–1279) potters excelled not only in the tranquil color schemes of their works, but also in the beauty of the markings and crackles they produced. Such markings and crackles—owing, in the first instance, to defects in the glaze—came to be looked upon with favor. Artists, realizing their possibilities, produced them by artificial means. Some markings show faintly through the glaze the shapes of fish roe, air bubbles, crab claws, and earthworm tracks; others, appearing on the surface of the glaze, resemble orange peel or dodder. There are "cold" crackles and "silk" crackles. The Ming-dynasty (1368–1644) potters followed closely the examples of their predecessors. But they added types of their own: a pure moon-white porcelain, a "blue of the sky after rain," and designs in underglaze blue. Under the Ch'ing dynasty (1644–1912) the potters elaborated both design and color.

With all the changes in molding, however, ceramic art continued to follow the shapes of ancient bronzes and jades. Realizing that these could not be surpassed, artists strove with redoubled energy to achieve distinction in technique and subject matter. Under the Han dynasty, for example, much colored glass—and glass vessels also—was imported from the Roman Empire. As long as ceramic art flourished, however, Chinese artists were not greatly interested in the manufacture of glass[8] for the creation of objects of art. But in the eighteenth century, when the porcelain art seemed to have reached its limit, they returned to the use of glass. In the Ch'ien-lung period (1736–1796) many beautifully colored glass vases and snuff bottles were produced. When, in the Yüan period (1260–1368), Kublai Khan extended his power over the Middle East, the Chinese must have become familiar, also, with the art of enameling as practiced in Arabia and Persia. But artists did not take up enameling until the Ching-t'ai (jing-tai) reign (1450–1456), in the Ming period. Many fine specimens were then produced, and this branch of art continued to flourish in the eighteenth and nineteenth centuries. Although glass and enamel manufacture were of foreign origin, the Chinese assimilated and adapted them so that they, too, show the influence of the early bronzes and jades, except for a few glass vases of the Ch'ien-lung period which are decorated with Arabic scripts.

To indicate the part played by change of subject matter, attention may be directed to the evolution of pictorial art. Painting is the chief flower of the nation's civilization. It has the closest relationship to the ancient scripts, which later developed into the art of calligraphy. (See chap. xxi, above.) Painting and calligraphy are sister arts and have developed along parallel lines. In painting and in writing the same brush and ink are used. As the shapes of bronzes and jades were influenced by the ancient scripts, so too, and even more strongly, does linear influence appear in painting.

Although wall paintings have been found in Shang-dynasty tombs, and figure paintings in lacquer were common at least as early as the first years of the Christian era, the earliest known Chinese silk-roll painting—now in the British Museum—is the "Illustrations of the Admonitions of the Lady Historian," also called "Admonitions of the Instructress in the Palace," by Ku K'ai-chih (ca. 344–ca. 406). The decorative designs on bronzes and jades of the Shang and Chou periods were probably first sketched, but it is necessary to examine the lines of the horses, carriages, and human figures, with their cohesive and harmonious movements, in the bas-reliefs on Han bricks and stones or on the rubbings of first-century stone carvings on Hsiao-t'ang-shan to realize that Chinese pictorial art was, by Han times, highly developed.

In the days of Ku K'ai-chih, Chinese painting reached its first peak of perfection in the display of refined, flowing lines and the achievement of a harmonious, simplified form for the human figure. In spite of the tendency, from earliest times, to prefer metaphysical ideas to anthropomorphic images, Han bas-reliefs show that early pictorial artists did on occasion occupy themselves with human scenes depicting historical events. They were done at imperial command and used for the moral instruction of the people. This type of painting limited artistic genius; so, after the inimitable achievement of Ku K'ai-chih in depicting the human figure, artists were glad to find new subject matter and inspiration in Buddhist art.

Indian Buddhism was introduced into China at least as early as the first century of the Christian era and flourished from the third century onward. (See chap. xviii, above.) From time to time, Chinese intellectuals went to India and Indian monks arrived in China. It is remarkable how quickly the influence of Buddhist art, with its anthropomorphic images, spread in China. In the period from the rule of the Northern Wei through that of the T'ang dynasties (*ca.* 386–906), Buddhist bas-relief carvings, sculptures, and paintings multiplied. The most famous Buddhist sculptures are in the caves of Lung-mên and Yün-kang (yün-gang). Among the finest Buddhist paintings are the silk banners from Tun-huang, many of which are in the British Museum and in India.

Such was the enthusiasm for Buddhist thought that rulers, high officials, and intellectuals patronized artists who devoted their talents to producing works inspired by the Indian religion. The artists, thus freed from worldly cares, were able to do more than merely imitate a foreign art: they assimilated it, were inspired by it, and in time created one which was essentially Chinese in treatment of subject matter. Notable is the fact that the graceful lines of the draperies of Buddhist sculptures reflect the graphic linear expression of calligraphy rather than the plastic muscular strength of Hellenic and Hellenistic sculpture.

The T'ang-dynasty (618–906) sculptures of horses are noted for their realism and fine proportions. The pottery figures of persons, horses, and camels in the Eumorfopoulos Collection offer additional examples of these qualities.

Chinese love of nature, the influence of which is so strongly marked in the shapes of ancient bronzes and jades, was not lessened, however, by the flowering of Buddhist art. From the moment that T'ang T'ai-tsung (627–649) claimed Lao Tzŭ as his ancestor, Taoism[4] (see chaps. xvii and i, above), with its stress on withdrawal from the world and meditation on nature, again sprang into prominence and flourished side by side with Buddhism as an influence upon the national art. Taoism and the new school of Ch'an Buddhism both reminded man that he is only one of the millions of kinds of creatures. Therefore, artists continued to turn for their subjects to birds, animals, insects, flowers, trees, and, above all, to landscape painting.

Landscape art is the most characteristic type of Chinese painting. Confucius once said, "The wise take pleasure in lakes and rivers; the virtuous, in mountains." *Shan-shui,* the term for landscape, means mountains and water. Only in landscape can the artist express depth and distance. In the fourth century, Ku K'ai-chih attempted landscape painting as a background for his figures. Artists of the Sui dynasty (*ca.* 589–618) evidently occupied themselves with landscape painting; there are many records of their discussions on this subject, though no examples of their efforts have as yet been found. It is in the mid-T'ang period that landscape painting—with such masters as Li Ssŭ-hsün,[5] a great-grandson of the first T'ang emperor, and his son Li Chao-tao (jao-dao), Wu Tao-tzŭ (dao-dz), and Wang Wei—becomes all-important.

Perhaps it was the unlimited variety of composition offered by landscape painting which made artists so rapidly, if apparently belatedly, prefer it to all other subjects. There could be no dogmatic rules for executing a landscape painting; the artist's genius had free play. Wu Tao-tzŭ and Li Ssŭ-hsün were commanded by the Emperor Hsüan-tsung (hsüan-dzung) (713–756) to paint a stretch of the Chia-ling River scenery in the upper Yangtze region. Li began immediately, and finished his work in three months. His painting revealed the utmost care and thought and showed refined treatment of brush strokes and rich coloring. Wu awaited the moment of inspiration. When the scenery appeared more beautiful than ever before, he seized his brush and, in the full light of vision, recorded his impression in a single day. When the two works were brought before the emperor, the artists received equal praise.

This story not only illustrates the freedom of the artist, but also draws attention to the change in the brush stroke which took place in the eighth century. Li Ssŭ-hsün's was the method traditional since the days of Ku K'ai-chih: fine, careful, exact. Li became the founder of the Northern school. Wu, with unhesitating genius, enfranchised the brush stroke and set the example for broad, bold treatment. Wang Wei introduced a still freer, swifter, impressionistic movement of the brush. He is considered the founder of the Southern school. The terms Northern and Southern have no geographical significance; they refer solely to the treatment of brush strokes. The most essential element of landscape painting—indeed, of all types of Chinese painting—is the brushwork. Under the Sung dynasty (960–1279) this was the chariot in which many great masters won the race to fame.

Good figure paintings were produced in the Sung period, but most of the Sung artists distinguished themselves in the painting of landscapes, birds and flowers, and animals. This may have been because of the period of chaos following the collapse of the T'ang dynasty. When China was at peace and reunited, people turned more than ever to nature to forget their sufferings. Few subjects in nature had been neglected by T'ang artists, but, except for the innovations of Wu Tao-tzŭ and Wang Wei, strict conventions had governed brushwork. Brushwork, then, was the field open to Sung artists for the expression of original ideas. As a result, more great masters appeared in this period than in any other—not because artists were more numerous, but because each could achieve something distinctive in brushwork and composition. Painters had reached the stage of seeking what was essential, spontaneous, and alive, and of rejecting what was unessential. The value of empty space as a factor in design was now discovered.

From this time there is a marked preference for monochrome, that is, pure ink-painting. The artist had decided not to be distracted by the rendering of surface appearance and texture. He was ready to dispense with the help of colors, pigments, and other media such as light and shade. Ma Yüan, Hsia Kuei (guei), Kuo Hsi (guo hsi), Fan Chung-cheng (jung-jeng), also called Fan K'uan, and Mi Fu, or Mi Fei (1051–1107) were among the most noted masters of the time.

After the great creative Sung period, artists did not have an easy task. Their scope was narrowed by the reduction of media. One might have expected them to find fresh inspiration in the Mongols, with their exotic types of faces, costumes, and habits. This people poured into China in the thirteenth century. But the invaders despised the Chinese and the latter were not interested—aesthetically—in the invaders. So artists continued on the same path, and little either new or remarkable was produced under the Yüan dynasty (1260–1368). There were, however, four noted landscapists: Wang Meng; Huang Kung-wang, also called Tzŭ-chiu; Wu Chên, also called Chung-kuei; and Ni Yün-lin. Each managed to develop a distinctive style of brushwork not tried by the Sung masters. Ni Yün-lin declared that his idea of a painting was a few swiftly made strokes, not with the intention of copying reality, but merely to give pleasure to himself. At this point Chinese painting attained a high ideal: unconcerned with any medium, it reveled simply in the rhythmic vitality of the brush stroke.

In the Ming period (1368–1644) there was no change in the themes pursued by Chinese painters. Masters such as Tung Ch'i-ch'ang (1555–1636),⁶ T'ang Yin, Shên Chou, Mu Ch'i, and Lin Liang produced masterpieces, but only the last two achieved innovations. They developed an extremely free hand in depicting birds and flowers and added some personal brush strokes to the conventional manner of painting.

Drastic change in a well-established art can be brought about only by unusual circumstances. The effect of the introduction of Buddhism has been noted. In the Ch'ing age (1644–1912) China came increasingly into contact with the West and was again under foreign rulers—the Manchus. This in itself might have brought new inspiration, but the Manchus had neither the wish nor the ability to upset Chinese ways of thinking. Not only did they encourage artists to continue to work along traditional lines, but they themselves imitated Chinese methods.

In the sixteenth century and thereafter, Christian missionaries went to China in small numbers. Possibly they had an opportunity to interest the intellectuals, as early Indian Buddhist monks had done; possibly they did not. In any event, with the exception of a few Jesuits, they failed to do so. In the main, they did not realize what influence the knowledge of the great achievements of Western art might have on the Chinese mind; consequently, Christianity, unlike Buddhism, has as yet produced no notably new phase in Chinese art. Two Jesuit fathers, Jean-Denis Attiret (1702–1768) and Joseph Castiglione (1688–1766), who were attached as painters to the imperial court in the early eighteenth century, attempted to introduce European art. They indicated how it used the science of anatomy; they showed its plastic value and its effects of light and shade; but, in the end, they took up the Chinese brush and painted in the Chinese manner.

In the last fifty years, however, primarily as a result of increasing contact with the West, certain new developments have taken place in Chinese art. For years, intellectuals have been writing on the need for changes in artistic expression. Young artists were sent abroad, mostly to Paris, to study the art of other countries. This acted as a spur to those who stayed at home and continued to work in the traditional style. The latter have created many variations on old themes. Jên Po-nien (ren bo-nien)[7] achieved distinction in new variations on themes of birds and flowers, and Wu Ch'ang-shih (1844–1927), a famous calligrapher, with bamboo, wistaria, and other flower subjects. Their influence on modern artists is very great. Ch'i Pai-shih (tsi bai-shzh) is noted for painting shrimps, crabs, and chicks. His arrangement of these creatures is without parallel, and his brush strokes display a strange, transparent quality. Huang Pin-hung (bin-hung) and Chang Ta-ch'ien (jang da-tsien) have presented new versions of landscape themes, as they have traveled more widely than most of the old masters.

The effect of China's contact with Western culture is not yet so evident in art as it is in literature. Translations of art cannot be read, and no reproduction can convey the feeling aroused by the original. There is constant dispute—both Westerners and Chinese participate in it—whether Western art should be allowed to influence Chinese art at all. Many non-Chinese who have studied and who love Chinese art are—perhaps sentimentally—horrified when they find a Chinese using Western technique or painting in Western style. Other Westerners declare that Chinese artists have shown no creative power for several centuries. The artist may thus find himself in a dilemma. Change is inevitable, however, and the artist's genius must assimilate and blend it with tradition. China is no longer in the position in which it was at the end of the eighteenth century. It rarely has been, and certainly is not now, isolated; it plays its part in the world community. Ways of life based on native traditional thought are being readjusted. Art cannot stand aside; it is bound to be involved.

There will be many difficulties and false beginnings before a new art is developed. A number of Chinese who have studied in Europe describe themselves as followers of Rembrandt, Rubens, Corot, Manet. Other returned art students are cubists, Fauvists, impressionists, expressionists, or surrealists. Their work may have merit, but they can hardly be said to represent modern Chinese art. Fortunately, China maintains its power of assimilating what it has taken from other sources; so this stage of hurried copying has already yielded to a stage of readjustment. Professor Ju Péon (sü pei-huang), who studied in Paris for eight years and became skilled in the use of oils and chalks, now paints animals and figures with Chinese brush and ink and produces good results. Professor Liu Hai-su, an admirer of Cézanne and Van Gogh, has adapted a new type of brush stroke to landscape themes.

The war which Japan directly and indirectly waged upon China for many years left artists little opportunity for peaceful contemplation. They turned their attention from landscape painting to the sufferings of the poor. Chiang Chao-ho (dziang jao-ho) shows great talent in depicting their life. Chao Wang-yün paints ruined farms. Fêng Tzǔ-k'ai portrays peacetime and wartime life, frequently with children predominating, and with humorous touches. Yeh Ch'ien-yü (tsien-yü) and Chang Kuang-yü (jang guang-yü) excel in caricature and cartoon. In addition, art has been used to teach farmers and illiterates how best they could help defend the country. This propaganda technique, a new development in the history of Chinese art, brought remarkable results artistically and practically. (See chap. xxvii, below.)

Tung Ch'i-ch'ang (1555–1636), a great calligrapher and painter, once remarked that a good artist must read ten thousand books and travel ten thousand *li*. The mass movement of the Chinese from Occupied China, a few of whom took refuge in Europe and America, gave artists an opportunity to see many new subjects. The artist has much to assimilate—his own new way of life and all the storehouse of Western art. He must choose, and discard, with discrimination. The use of oil alone may lead to a great phase in Chinese art. One wonders what certain of the T'ang and Sung masters of flower painting—Chao Ch'ang (jao chang), for example,—might have achieved with oils. As Chinese travel more in this modern world, they will delight in new subjects for their brushes: the architecture, mountains, trees, animals, birds, and flowers of other countries. Again, interest in the modern interpretation of man's relation to man and his place in the universe may arouse enthusiasm for human beings as subjects for art; so figure painting, which has played little part in Chinese art, may spring into prominence.

In sculpture, what an opportunity is presented to the Chinese to develop their genius with new freedom! They know how to carve stone, as they have demonstrated from the days of the Shang, but they have much to learn from Western sculpture in order to express with new life their own aesthetic points of view. Several well-known modern sculptors, such as Li Chin-fa and Wang Yü-chiu, have occupied themselves with molding living models according to the Occidental method. It is to be hoped that eventually they may create something essentially Chinese in genius which will live for all time and for all people, as the great works of Western sculptors have done.

Tolstoi said that the task of art is enormous. "Through the influence of real art, aided by science, guided by religion, that peaceful coöperation of man which is now maintained by external means—by our courts, police, charitable institutions, factory inspections, and so forth—should be obtained by man's free and joyous activity. Art should cause violence to be set aside." Apparently, he was referring to the task of art within one country. But, although art represents the mind and life of the people which creates it, it has, at the same time, a universal appeal to man's passion for beauty. No one can deny the great part played by the exhibition of Chinese art in London, in 1935–1936, in stimulating interest in China.

Now that the war has ended, the governments of various countries should consider it one of their responsibilities to arrange for frequent interchange of art exhibitions so that all peoples may benefit. China would profit tremendously from such a plan, for it has perhaps fewer examples of foreign art than any other country. The Chinese government should, in turn, help artists and craftsmen to travel widely to see the wonders of Western art in their own setting. China has no lack of artists and craftsmen. They have not ceased the struggle to exercise their talent, even in the chaos of the last few decades. They will work eagerly when order is restored. But they will need refreshment for their eyes and minds. They will then go forward in freedom to contribute their share to the new art of the world.

CHAPTER XXIII

Architecture

BY HENRY KILLAM MURPHY

I
N CHINA is found one of the great architectural orders of the world—one generally considered to be not only superior to those evolved in other Asian countries, but comparable to the great orders developed in the West. Like the latter, Chinese architecture has met the test of adaptability to modern requirements of planning and construction.

"Culture," says Lin Yutang, "is a product of leisure—and we Chinese [*which* Chinese not being specified] have had four thousand years of leisure!" On this basis of reasoning, and because architecture is a product of culture, Chinese architecture may be said to have a history of four thousand years.[1] Instead of attempting an analysis based on a history of such longevity, however, it seems wiser to try to discover, through artistic analysis, how Chinese builders of earlier times achieved the beauty, dignity, and splendor which have moved certain architectural critics to call Peking's Forbidden City the finest group in the world; to determine the essential elements of that architecture; and to show how the renaissance is translating the salient characteristics of old China's style into modern scientific construction to meet new China's needs.

The most striking characteristic of this order of architecture—so striking, indeed, as to lead many of those attempting its adaptation into the error of thinking it the only feature essential to preserve—is the curving roof, upturned at mitered corners, with its great sweeps unbroken by windows. Nowhere else have builders realized its splendid possibilities. When to the curving grace of

---

[1] For notes to chapter xxiii see page 537.

form is added the glory of color—the Chinese roof tiles ranging from sober gray through midnight blue, jade green, and turquoise to the magnificent golden tints of imperial yellow—the architectural result is unmatched.

Second in importance in ancient Chinese architecture is the orderliness of arrangement which is seen in its formal grouping of principal buildings around vast rectangular courts, and in its marked attention to axis throughout. The principle of axial planning, which is found in nearly all styles of architecture, has been developed to its ultimate in the Middle Country. The greatest axis in the world today—as it was, in part, when Marco Polo saw it and marveled—runs due south from the central pavilion of Coal Hill in Peking, through the centers of the principal buildings of the Forbidden City, through Ch'ien Mên (the towering Wall Gate near the railway station), and ends five miles away, at Yung-ting Mên, between the Altar of Agriculture and the glorious Altar of Heaven. This formal grouping of buildings is marked, not by rigid symmetry, but by that nice feeling for balance which is characteristic of all the art of the Chinese, especially of their poetry. By avoiding exact duplication on opposite sides of an axis, Chinese architects introduce just enough variation to avoid monotony.

The third essential feature of Chinese architecture is its frankness of construction—"keeping the bones of the building on the outside"—with the great columns, whether free-standing or partly engaged in walls, actually doing, as they appear to do, the work of supporting the structure. The massive roof timbering, in its exposure from below, gives a feeling of tremendous strength and dignity. In using structural members as elements of beauty Chinese builders have observed most successfully the sound maxim that architects should decorate their construction—not construct their decoration.

The fourth essential feature of Chinese architecture is the lavish use of gorgeous color, not only in roof tiles, but glowing from columns, lintels, and beams, from richly bracketed cornices, and from broad expanses of stuccoed walls. The great column shafts, though sometimes a quiet brown or dull black, are usually of rich, deep red, which changes at the bottom of the lowest horizontal member to a band of sharply contrasting color. The beams, lintels, and brackets are profusely decorated with panels and bands of pure earth-pigment greens, yellows, and blues, often outlined in white and accompanied by dull gold. In the architecture of the ancient Greeks there may have been a parallel to this feature of Chinese architecture, but in nothing now extant can Western architecture approach the richness of old Chinese buildings in their use of color.

In addition to the four features listed as essential in adaptations of Chinese architecture, there is a fifth fundamental to success: the method of approach. One reason for the artistic failure of many modern adaptations is that their designers started with foreign architectural conceptions into which they merely introduced features of Chinese architecture. The inevitable result has been that the completed designs remain essentially foreign. For successful adaptation of Chinese architecture, Chinese conception must be maintained. Foreign architectural elements should be introduced only when clearly needed for practical purposes.

The most magnificent architectural group in China—one which elsewhere is scarcely equaled and assuredly is not surpassed—is the Forbidden City in Peking. The innermost of three concentric walled rectangles (of which the Manchu City is the second and the great fifteen-mile northern Peking city wall is the outermost), the Forbidden City is about three-quarters of a mile square and is laid out in a series of rectangular, marble-paved courts varying from one or two hundred to nearly a thousand feet in extent. Through one of the largest of these courts winds a white marble balustraded waterway which is fed from the lovely Jade Fountain several miles northwest of the city. The principal buildings are raised on terraces, with balustrades of richly sculptured white marble. The more important structures have simple hip roofs; the less important combine a small gable with the hips at each side of the ridge. The roofs are covered with glazed tile, glowing in imperial golden yellow.

At the middle of the southern wall of the Forbidden City is the finest architectural unit in the country—the great Wu Mên, a central building some two hundred feet long, on a balustraded terrace, flanked by a pair of square, sixty-foot pavilions. The four-hundred-foot composition is raised on a wall base fifty feet high, stuccoed in dark red, and pierced by five arched tunnel entrances.

Projecting three hundred feet south are two flanking wings of the wall base; at the outer ends of these, a second pair of pavilions repeat those of the main group. The effect is one of overpowering majesty and breath-taking beauty. Fortunate are those visitors to Peking whose hosts insist that they make their first entrance to the old capital up the axis from the railway station and through the Wu Gate into the Forbidden City. Perhaps equally fortunate are those who obtain their first impression of the great city wall with its massive gateways in the quiet middle hours of a starry night.

In its millennia-old architecture China's love of symbolism[2] finds its most intricate and thought-compelling expression. In stiff rows down the curving hips of the typical roof sit, like watchdogs, the protective beasts of legend; these guard against the escape of the lonely Wang, who, for his sins, is condemned to sit forever at the very tip, astride the ignoble hen. Along the main ridges, friendly dragons—symbols of the imperial attributes of courage, strength, and wisdom—meet at the center to support the "priceless pearl" whose perfect sphere symbolizes the fusing of the complementary principles, *yang* and *yin*. (See chap. xiv, above.) On the even balance of *yang* and *yin* depends the well-being of the universe. Chinese builders throughout the ages have fashioned the decorative finials at the ends of their roof ridges into huge sea monsters, created to drink the rain water falling on the roof, so that it might not drown the people within.

Up the center of the approach to the terraced main building, in many of the old and in some new groups, is the Spirit Way, a sumptuously carved slope of white marble extending from the ground to the top of the terrace, with a flight of stairs on either side. This inclined path is for the use of spirits, who need no steps for their ascent. In their honor the pious sculptors of olden times fashioned in low relief, over the entire surface of the Spirit Way, exquisitely delicate clouds, waves, birds, and dragons.

The most purely symbolic of Chinese buildings and the most distinctive man-made feature of the Chinese landscape is the pagoda. Not indigenous to China, having come from India with Buddhism, probably soon after the beginning of the Christian era, the pagoda became an element of the elusive *fêng-shui* (wind and water auspices—harmony with the elements) to bring prosperity to a neighborhood by helping to ward off evil spirits. There are hundreds of pagodas throughout the land.[3] As odd numbers are favored in Buddhism, these buildings always have an odd number of stories, usually five, seven, or nine. An occasional thirteen-story structure appears, such as that at Tung-chou; this was reproduced for the water tower of the imposing American-financed Yenching University group, built in adapted Chinese architecture, in the 1920's, near Peking.

In the Revolutionists' Memorial, likewise built in adapted Chinese architecture, in the 1930's, just outside Nanking, Chiang Kai-shek, at the suggestion of its American architect,[*] authorized the inclusion of a 175-foot nine-story pagoda. In this, as in the rest of the group, purely Chinese architectural features were carried out in reinforced concrete construction, with curtain walls of light granite and buff stucco. The roofs are of glazed, jade-green Canton tile and the ridges and starting tiles are deep blue. On the interior of this memorial pagoda and on both exterior and interior of the other buildings in the group the full Chinese color scheme, red columns with polychrome entablatures, was used. All are in permanent cement colors built in without the use of paint. The tower of the Revolutionists' Memorial has been called the most beautiful pagoda in China.

The architecture of the Chinese garden[4] symbolizes, generally in miniature, the kind of world in which its successive owners would have liked best to live: tiny artificial lakes, carefully placed with a view to the most pleasing reflections, cunningly curved to simulate distance, and gracefully spanned by "tiger-back," or "camel-back," bridges; steep little hills, built when the lakes were dug, around the far sides of the garden to shut off the outer world; dwarfed trees of widely varied shapes among which wind alluring paths; and, best loved of all, the little pavilion that lends perpetual charm to Chinese poetry. A dozen centuries ago the poet Li T'ai-po sang:

> Out in the artificial lake
> there is a pavilion of green and white porcelain;
> it is reached by a bridge of jade,
> arched like the back of a tiger.[5]

---

* Henry Killam Murphy, author of this chapter, who is anonymously referred to several times hereafter.—EDITOR'S NOTE.

Loveliest of all garden features is the "moon" doorway, a circle large enough for one to pass through without stooping and artfully placed to frame the most entrancing bit of landscape. Sometimes its form is varied to an octagon or to the still more typically Chinese hexagon; always it is dramatic. Occasionally, upon its frame is carved a bit of philosophy, like that adorning a monastery gateway in Canton:

> Standing by my stone doorway,
> I can look between the clouds
> And behold the stars.

Although little has yet been attempted along these lines, Chinese architectural forms and colors are readily adaptable for use in other lands. The garden pavilion—sometimes square, sometimes round, sometimes polygonal, always graceful and inviting—could well be transplanted intact. The alluring "moon" doorway would add immeasurably to the picturesqueness of any European or American garden and of many Western homes. Balustrades and furniture would lend themselves to the endless fascination of the Chinese grille (e.g., in Chinese Chippendale).[6] The Chinese rooms in which, all too rarely, Western homes, clubs, and hotels indulge are universally popular. But the most promising field is in modernistic architecture: its great exterior planes cry out for Chinese use of color. Pilasters, cornices, moldings, and surface breaks of all kinds are being eliminated. On the resulting smooth expanses of wall, why should not Occidentals, taking a leaf out of the Chinese book of architecture, "let themselves go" with a symphony of colors which would warm Western souls as they are warmed by the first sight of the peerless Forbidden City?

The renaissance of Chinese architecture, now thoroughly established, dates from the early years of this century, when several missionary educational institutions—notably St. John's University in Shanghai,[7] Nanking University, Shantung Christian University in Tsinan, and Yale-in-China in Changsha—tried out the possibilities of introducing Chinese architectural features (at first usually limited, unfortunately, to roof treatment) into the otherwise foreign-style buildings then being erected. A great step forward was taken when the Rockefeller Foundation built the great Union Medical College group in Peking; in this the Chinese character was carried much further than in earlier groups. But not until the completion, in the early 1920's, of the first buildings of Ginling (Women's) College at Nanking, and Yenching University at Peking (built at a third the cost of the Rockefeller buildings), were the possibilities of adapting Chinese architecture to modern structures fully realized. It was the universally recognized success—aesthetically, functionally, and economically—of the Ginling and Yenching buildings that finally established the renaissance. When, in 1928, a Chinese commission made a world tour to select five foreign advisers to guide the development of the new China, the use of this adapted Chinese architecture had become so thoroughly a part of the National government's program that the members of the commission chose as their architectural adviser the New York architect who had come to be recognized as its leading exponent.

An architectural competition open to any style was held in 1926 for the great Sun Yat-sen mausoleum at Nanking. A striking proof of the strength of the architectural renaissance was the choice of a design, in adapted Chinese architecture, by Lu Yen-chih (Y. C. Lu). After being graduated from the Cornell School of Architecture, this young Chinese studied the principles of Chinese architecture in New York under an American later chosen by the government as architectural adviser. The untimely death of Mr. Lu robbed the renaissance of its most promising Chinese exponent. Just prior to his death, however, Mr. Lu completed the designs, later carried out by Poy G. Lee, of the magnificent Sun Yat-sen memorial auditorium in Canton. This is a much finer piece of work, architecturally, than the mausoleum and is more purely Chinese in basic concept as well as in details.

In addition to the memorial pagoda at Nanking and the auditorium at Canton, the most impressive buildings of the architectural renaissance are the administration building of Yenching University and the enlarged adaptation of it erected, in the early 1930's, as the main building of the Greater Shanghai Municipal Center. This splendid city hall (severely damaged by Japanese bombs in 1937) is the work of another brilliant Chinese architect, Dayu Doon. The consulting architect was the American architectural adviser in whose New York office Messrs. Doon and Lu had studied the principles of their country's architecture. In this great building the three-part, in-line composition of a two-story central body, with lower, two-story wings—first successfully used in the main building of the Ginling College group at Nanking and improved in the Yenching administration building—reaches its finest form. It is superposed on a massive granite basement story, which is projected to form an elevated, encircling terrace. This new composition is an accepted addition to the basic traditional forms of Chinese architecture.

The 1929 report of the Nanking city planning bureau, a Chinese group with two Americans as architectural and engineering advisers, called for construction of a National government center, in adapted Chinese architecture, on the southern foothills of Purple Mountain, close to the Sun Yat-sen mausoleum outside the east gate of the capital. The architectural adviser drafted plans for some two hundred buildings, thirty of which were to house the government as then constituted. But the instability felt increasingly by the Nanking government led to the abandonment of this extramural project for the greater security of an intramural site in the old Ming Ku-kung, and on a much more modest scale. Revised plans in 1930 included a railway station inspired by the Wu Gate in the Forbidden City. Even this modified project was not carried out. The various ministries continued to erect separate buildings about the city in varying styles of architecture.

The renaissance thus suffered a tragic aesthetic loss in the abandonment of the plan to build a vast unified government group, in adapted Chinese architecture. This would have rivaled the Forbidden City in beauty and would eventually have exceeded it in extent. However, some of the buildings erected, notably the Ministry of Railways (1930), by Robert Fan and Shen Chao; the auditorium (1931) for Generalissimo Chiang's officers' club, by Shen Chao; and the Ministry of Communications (1934), by a Russian architect (one of the most attractive buildings in Nanking), are excellent examples of the possibilities of the renaissance.

When Japan started full-scale war on China in 1937, the development of that country's architecture came, perforce, to a standstill. Judging by its attitude of critical analysis in the 1920's, China may find it wise to take time to scrutinize all its institutions to insure that only the best will survive. As one of the beneficial results of the crushing of Japan and Germany—the two nations which in recent time have gone to the most radical extremes of ugliness in architecture—it may be that China will experience a revulsion from the tendency of a few years ago to follow similar tendencies, and will demand beauty in architecture. If so, the intense nationalism of postwar China will strengthen the hands of those who are working to prove, through the renaissance, that in its own ancient architecture China has a priceless heritage of beauty.

CHAPTER XXIV

Drama

BY HSIUNG SHIH-I

CHINESE DRAMA did not reach maturity until the thirteenth century. The Chin, or Golden, dynasty (1115–1234) of the Jurchen Tatars, in northern China, fell to the Mongol armies of Ogotai Khan in 1234, and the Southern Sung dynasty was overthrown by Kublai Khan's forces in 1279. Between these two dates, drama blossomed into perfection.

In the fifth century of the Christian era and thereafter, Chinese Buddhist monks related stories and legends of Gotama for the entertainment of persons attending their services. In the light of holy candles and the mist of burning incense, Buddhist Gathas were chanted. With the passage of centuries, public storytellers imitated the art and method of the monks in secular material. A form of literature known as *pien wên* (revised literature) was developed for the narration of Buddhist stories. This was a combination of prose and poetry. When the poetical part predominated, it constituted the primitive form of verse drama. When the prose part was developed, it constituted the primitive form of the novel. The original form of the novel contained verses. In contrast to classical works, both drama and novels were colloquial in style.

But this is only one phase of the story. Description of the development is incomplete without mention of dancing and music, comical incidents and human stories, and the imaginary and actual characters which contributed to the perfection of thirteenth-century drama.

In ancient times men sang ballads and proclaimed their first battle orders. There was a time when the priestess or sorceress *wu* danced in worship of the native gods. The pictograph *wu* shows the long-sleeved *kung* dancing. In the *Li Chi* (Book of Rites) the officials of the sage-king Yao were called "a hundred *kung*." In addition, *kung* means workers; the archaic character for surgeon is *yi*, which contains the character *wu*. Thus in early times the priestess *wu* danced on religious occasions, was an official of the court, controlled the general working of society, and cured diseases. Communicating with the divinities, she swayed the fortunes of men.

According to the history *Ch'u Yü* (in *Kuo Yü*), communication with divinity, once the function of a special class of men and women, became common practice. "Upon the decay of the reign of Shao Hao [tradl. date 2597–2513 B.C.] . . . ," it says, "everyone could offer sacrifices to the gods and in every family there lived a priestess or recorder." From this it appears that the ancient monopoly of religious affairs by the state or by professionals had disappeared. In the Ch'un Ch'iu age (722–481 B.C.), in the course of the long period of decline of the Chou dynasty, the state of Ch'ên, in the middle of the Yellow River Valley, became a center of spirit worship. The poems of Ch'ên in the Confucian anthology *Shih Ching* (Book of Odes, or Songs) describe these dances. There are two references to Wan Hill, where people wearing heron feathers danced under the oaks. The marketplace was another center of dancing; girls, throwing aside their hemp weaving, went there to dance. Dancing was no longer an art for professionals alone, but a popular amusement.

To the south, in and around present-day Hupeh, was the state of Ch'u. Not long civilized and still highly superstitious, the people of Ch'u, near the end of the fourth century B.C., considered religious dances to be of the greatest importance. Their priestess was called *ling* (the spirit). Dressed in a brilliant costume, she diffused fragrance as she danced in the ceremonial hall and sang in a loud voice accompanied by music. According to one of the poems of Ch'u, "Five notes made an enriched combination."

The later *ch'ang* might occasionally tell a story. In the Han period, when "the rich prayed to the famous mountains and streams, offering to the spirits the sacrifice of a whole cow, and beating drums," the *ch'ang* danced. He might appear, also, when the emperor offered sacrifices to Heaven and Earth. On occasion, the *ch'ang* wore masks while dancing. According to an annotator of the *Han Shu* (History of Han), his masks represented fish, lobster, and lion. The *Shuo Wên* (*ca.* A.D. 100) of Hsü Shên,[1] the earliest surviving Chinese dictionary, says that the *ch'ang* was a kind of *yu*, or court comedian. Thus, when the professional *wu* had disappeared from the ceremonial scene, *yu*, whose function was primarily the entertainment of men, was borrowed for the entertainment of the gods.

A long tradition of *yu* exists in Chinese history. In 500 B.C. Confucius attended the Duke of Lu at a meeting with the Duke of Ch'i. The latter entertained his ducal guest with a comedian who mocked the Sage. Confucius ordered that this comedian should be put to death.

Volume LXVI of the *Shih Chi* (Historical Record), by Ssǔ-ma Ch'ien (*ca.* 145–*ca.* 87 B.C.),[2] under "Lives of Comical Characters," includes several references to famous court comedians. It is regrettable that little attention was paid to the careers and art of these comedians. A passage in the introduction to this volume, however, indicates clearly that the historian's interest was limited to the effects of their actions on state affairs:

The comedian Chan was a jester and a dwarf in the court of Ch'in. He was very good at making jokes, which always contained great truth.... Once the First Emperor [Shih Huang Ti, 221–210 B.C.] proposed to have a grand hunting park extending as far east as the Pass of Han Ku and as far west as the districts of Yung and Ch'ên-ts'ang. The comedian Chan said, "Good! Put as many animals within it as possible. If invaders come from the east, you order the stags and deer to butt them; that would be quite sufficient!" The First Emperor accordingly abandoned his scheme.

When the Second Emperor [Erh Shih Huang Ti, 209–207 B.C.] ascended the throne, he wished to paint the Great Wall. The comedian Chan said, "Good! Even if Your Imperial Majesty had not spoken, I should have requested Your Majesty to do it. Though painting the Great Wall will distress the people and involve them in much expenditure, yet how fine it would be! Standing grand and majestic is the painted wall; the invaders would not be able to climb over it when they arrived! Even if they wished to come near it they would soon be covered with paint. But it would hardly be a blessing for your descendants!" The Second Emperor laughed at this and abandoned the idea. Not long afterward he was assassinated. The comedian Chan went to the court of Han, where he died a few years later.

---

[1] For notes to chapter xxiv see page 537.

The comedian Mêng was described as a musician (*yüeh jên*). It seems that he acted to the rhythm of music and was clad in a costume designed for his performance.

A description of a play of the Han period is preserved in the *Hsi Ching Tsa Chi:*

> Chü Tao-lung, whom I knew, was skillful in magic arts. He related some ancient stories, and told me about one Huang Kung of the Eastern Sea district, who practiced magic in his youth. Huang Kung, he said, could control snakes and tigers. He wore a sword of red gold, and bundled his hair with a piece of red silk. He stood up, and clouds and mist were released. He sat down, and the landscape was transformed. When he got old his strength faded. Moreover, he drank too much and was unable to exercise his art. About the end of Ch'in a white tiger appeared in the Eastern Sea district. Huang Kung tried to control it with his red-gold sword. His magic power was no longer effective and he was killed by the tiger. The people of the suburban towns of the capital played this story. The emperor of Han adopted it in his acrobatic sports.

How the story of Huang Kung was played is not known, but that it was a popular entertainment is certain.

In the fourth century, when the capital of the Eastern Chin was moved to Nanking, northern China fell into chaos. Many tribes who marauded their way south of the Wall established short-lived kingdoms. Among the petty princes was one Shih Lo,[3] who appointed a *ts'an chün* (state counselor) to govern the district of Kuant'ao. This man embezzled "tens of thousands of silk pieces from the official treasuries," and was condemned to death. Shih Lo spared his life, but subjected him to mental tortures. When the prince entertained guests, the sometime state counselor was put among his jesters, wearing a silk garment. Then his humiliation followed. When the jesters asked him, "What post do you hold among our cast?" the *ts'an chün* was compelled to answer, "Once I was a state counselor, but alas! [shaking his silken garment] it was because of this stuff that I am thrown among you, the jesters." This amused the audience and his former lord and colleagues.

But it was not only such relations between players and audience which made these performances popular. Every court included some embezzlers, and it was a pleasure to see them punished, even in a play. Thus the *ts'an chün* became a symbol and an inseparable part of early comical performances. There was no playbook in those days; comedians worked out the details of their parts on the stage.

It is recorded that the *ts'an chün* theme was much used in the reign of the Bright Emperor, Hsüan-tsung (713–756), of the T'ang dynasty, and in that of his son, Su-tsung (756–762). Several actors are mentioned as able performers of this play; a certain Li Hsien-ho (the Immortal Crane) was nominated a counselor of Shao Chou for his merit. Women players are on record; one of them was said to have worn a green garment and held a bamboo *chien,* which symbolized the authority of an official. A woman player sang and her voice "hovered high in the clouds." From these statements it is inferred that in a *ts'an chün* play theatrical costumes were used and the player sang, probably accompanied by music. There might be dances in the interim, since singing and dancing were inseparable in ancient entertainments.

The *ts'an chün* character became permanent in ancient plays, to represent any official. The name was later shortened to *tsing,* an important term in the modern theater, represented by the "painted face." The *ts'an chün* was a dignified character, but was invariably placed in an awkward position. He was always the butt of a witty clown, who was, perhaps, in the beginning his servant. The latter was known as the *ts'ang t'ou,* or "blue head." This was the ancient name for a servant, who wore a blue turban to signify his humble social position. As time passed, the *ts'an chün,* or official character, became such a fool on the stage and the *ts'ang t'ou,* or clown, became so witty that he could give commands to his ridiculed master. To cause laughter among the audience, the clown usually hit the official. He was to him as the falcon is to the little birds; the clown, therefore, came to be known also as the *ts'ang hu,* "blue falcon." The *ts'an chün* and the *ts'ang hu* were popularly accepted characters in the T'ang period (618–906). The poet Li Shang-yin wrote, of his spoiled son:

> Don't imitate the official again,
> Shouting for his Blue Falcon.

Several other plays, probably combining singing and dancing to narrate stories, are recorded as popular before the T'ang period. All were foreign in origin or influence. The play *Tai Mien* (The Substitute of Face) tells the story of Prince Lan-ling of northern Ch'i. He was a brave warrior but of an effeminate appearance;

so, to frighten his enemy, he wore a mask in battle. The play presents his daring exploits by means of songs and spear dances performed by men in masks.

Another play was based upon the popular story of a scholar, Su, of the Northern Chou dynasty (557–581). Su had a broad nose, a beautiful wife, and a brutal character. When he was drunk he would beat his wife, who lamented loudly in the street, wriggling her body. The neighbors saw the funny side of it and the complaining wife became a comical figure in a play. Her appeals were made into a song and her movements into a dance. This play was taken to Japan, where it was called *Hu Yin Chiu* (A Barbarian Drinking Wine). The name Su had been "translated" into *hu*, a barbarian.

One play tells of a *hu* from Pa T'ou who was killed by a tiger. His son went to the mountain and killed the tiger. Because the mountain path had nine turnings, the play, according to history, contained nine *ch'e*. In later drama this word meant an act. As the play of the Pa T'ou family was a dancing story, the dancers presumably danced nine times in the course of the performance as representing the adventures of the young man avenging his father's death.

These dancing plays survived in the T'ang period; others of a similar type must have been lost. The rise of dancing plays was connected with the introduction of foreign music into China, in the warring centuries before the unification of the country by the T'ang house of Li. The historian Tu Yu,[4] in his great work, *T'ung Tien,* wrote:

In the beginning of the Wu-têh period [the reign of Li Yüan,[5] the first T'ang emperor, 618–626], the popular banquet music [*yen yao*] followed the system of the [preceding] Sui dynasty. It included (1) the banquet music, (2) the pure Shang, (3) the music of western Liang, (4) the music of Fu-nan [Cochin China and southern Cambodia], (5) the music of Korea, (6) the music of Kucha, (7) the music of An-kuo [Parthia], (8) the music of Su-lê, and (9) the music of K'ang-kuo. In the reign of T'ai-tsung (627–649), Kao-ch'ang [the Turfan capital] was conquered, and the music from Kao-ch'ang was added to the system to make up ten sections.

The banquet music, which formed the first section, was the music of northern China, an amalgamation of native and foreign influences. It had an appreciable influence on the dancing plays. Only the second section, that of the pure Shang of southern China, comprised native music. The music of the remaining sections came from foreign countries. Classical music, known as "elegant" music, was used only when sacrificial offerings were made to Heaven and Earth and the imperial ancestors. It had no relation to popular entertainment.

In the T'ang period (618–906) more foreign music was introduced into China—for example, the famous tune called "The Rainbow Petticoat and Feather Garment," which the Lady Yang, concubine of the Emperor Hsüan-tsung (713–756),[6] loved so much. According to Po Chü-i,[7] this tune was presented to the court by Yang Ching-shu, governor of western Liang Chou, a state which had been conquered by the arms of T'ang. The tune was native to this border area, and contained twelve sections (*pien*).

In 714, the second year of his long reign, the Emperor Hsüan-tsung, a great lover of music, founded the musical school known as Chiao Fang (Teaching Shop), near P'êng Lai Kung (Palace of the Fairy Island). Its purpose was to train star musicians in the foreign-influenced, fashionable music of the day. The classical, or "elegant," music was controlled by a board of music, the T'ai Ch'ang (Great Constancy). By order of the emperor, students were examined by officials of the Ministry of Music. The best were classed as the Sitting Department and were allowed to sit inside the hall during performances. The second group belonged to the Standing Department; its members stood during performances. The least-talented candidates were sent to the Ministry of Music to learn only the stereotyped, traditional music in order to amuse spirits, not men. The Chiao Fang schools were divided, also, into Left and Right groups: the members of the Left were dancers; those of the Right were singers.

From the Sitting Department, the elite of young musicians, the emperor made a further selection of three hundred of the best. These were housed in the imperial Pear Garden and were trained by the emperor personally. Several hundred young girls from the palace, or singsong girls selected from professional entertainers, lived in the Agreeable Spring Court of the Pear Garden to receive training. These boys and girls were known as the Emperor's Students of the Pear Garden. They learned to sing, dance, and play;

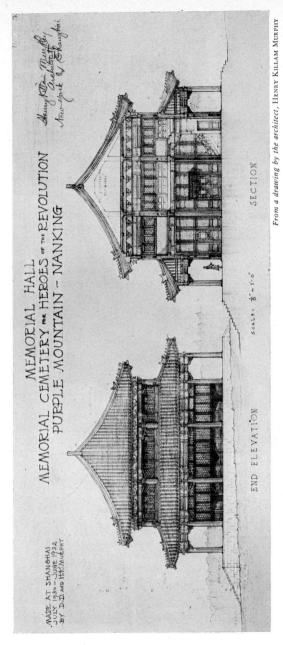

From a drawing by the architect, HENRY KILLAM MURPHY

DESIGN FOR MEMORIAL HALL, PURPLE MOUNTAIN, NANKING

From a drawing by the architect, HENRY KILLAM MURPHY

DETAIL OF RIDGE-FINIAL
SCALE 1" = 1'-6"

DESIGN FOR MEMORIAL HALL, PURPLE MOUNTAIN, NANKING: DETAILS

accordingly, the term Pear Garden has come down as a symbolic name for the Chinese theater. Hsüan-tsung is honored as the patron saint of the theatrical profession.

In his reign, many wrote a form of poetry known as *yao fu* (musical house poetry). Such poems were composed in the spirit of the ballad, but usually they were in the traditional form of seven syllables to the line. Musicians rewrote them in irregular forms and adapted them to tunes composed on the same theme. Toward the middle of the eighth century a type of poetry called *tz'ŭ* was developed. First a tune was composed, then words were written for it. These poems all bore the title of the tune. As the poems were written in irregular musical forms, they were also called *ch'ang tuan chü* (long and short lines). In the Sung period (960–1279) it was the practice of poets to narrate a story by a number of *tz'ŭ* written to the same tune. Thus, when the poems were sung, the tune was repeated by instruments. In this way long stories were related, such as the eleven poems set to the tune of *Tieh Luan Hua* (Butterfly Loves Flower), which tells the romance of the damsel Ts'ui Ying-ying and the scholar Chang Chün-jui. The poet was Chao Ling-ch'ih, who lived in the twelfth century.

A group of *tz'ŭ* was usually introduced by a poem in the traditional form of seven syllables which was not sung. In some, narrative poems which were not designed for singing were intermingled with *tz'ŭ* which were sung. Further changes took place with time. At first there was interlacing of *tz'ŭ* with "regular" poems. Then came mingling of *tz'ŭ* of two different tunes—a form of narration called *ch'uan ta,* or *ch'an ta.*

This was an important step in the development of the Chinese drama and was apparently the original form of an act of a thirteenth-century play. The tunes used in the second act of Chêng T'ing-yü's *K'an Ch'ien Nü Mai Yuan Chia Chai Chu* (Miser's Tragedy) and an anonymous author's *Chang Ch'ien T'i Sha Ch'i Tsa Chü* (Dream of Chang Who Killed His Wife) shows this evolution in a remarkably clear manner. The tunes used by the former are: *Chêng Kung Tuan Chêng Hao, Kung I Hsiu Ch'iu; T'ang Hsiu Ts'ai, Kung I Hsiu Ch'iu; T'ang Hsiu Ts'ai, Kung I Hsiu Ch'iu; T'ang Hsiu Ts'ai, Kung I Hsiu Ch'iu; T'ang Hsiu Ts'ai, Sai Hung Ch'iu;* Conclusion. Those used by the latter are: *Tuan*

Chêng Hao, Kung I Hsiu Ch'iu; T'ang Hsiu Ts'ai, Kung I Hsiu Ch'iu; T'ang Hsiu Ts'ai, Kung I Hsiu Ch'iu; T'ang Hsiu Ts'ai, Kung I Hsiu Ch'iu, Tao Tao Ling; Epilogue.

It is to be noted, however, that dramatists of the thirteenth century were not limited by this regulation. The examples quoted have retained the fossil impressions of ancient growth.

In the reign of the Sung Emperor Jên-tsung (1022–1063) many forms of folk literature came into being, among them the narrative poetry known as *chu kung tiao* (modulations). Usually, several poems narrating a long story were composed to the same tune, which the minstrels played over and over. This had a wearying effect; so a famous bard, K'ung San-ch'uan, who sold his songs in the Northern Sung capital, Pien Ching (K'ai-feng), invented a new method. He used a number of tunes, and changed the keynotes (*tiao,* or *kung tiao*) frequently. This was the writing of a narrative song or groups of songs on a grand scale. A complete example of this form of poetry is seen in the immortal work of Tung, *Hsien So Hsi Hsiang* (The Western Chamber in Spring). This presents the romance of Ts'ui Ying-ying and the scholar Chang Chün-jui, which Wang Shih-fu dramatized. The details of Tung's life and his personal names are not known. He lived about the end of the twelfth century or the beginning of the thirteenth.

There are two fragmentary versions of *chu kung tiao,* in addition to the complete poem by Tung. One of these, which was probably an earlier work than that of Tung, describes the story of Liu Chih-yüan, who became king in the Later Han (947–951). Some seventy-six sets of songs are preserved in five of the original twelve sections. Another *chu kung tiao* was by Wang Po-ch'êng, who lived in the first part of the fourteenth century. Wang's poetical narration tells the story of the Emperor Hsüan-tsung and Yang Kuei-fei. Fifty-five sets of songs are preserved in early quotations.

The form of drama which prospered throughout the period of the Yüan, or Mongol, dynasty (1260–1368) was known as *pei ch'ü* (Northern drama). It had only four acts, but sometimes it consisted of several four-act plays, which increased the number of acts in multiples of fours. Only one keynote was used in an act. Not more than one of the leading players, the hero or heroine, could sing in each act. He or she was the "host" of the act and the rest of the cast were "guests." Every member of the cast could speak on the stage. The monologue was called *pai* (explanation) and the dialogue *pin* (with guests). This reflects the tradition that the *tz'ŭ* used in the drama were once subjective and lyrical. Then the poet himself was the "host" and the readers were "guests." In the drama this atmosphere was still retained in the Yüan period.

All these restrictions disappeared in the Southern drama (*nan ch'ü*), which originated near the end of the Mongol period. A variety of keynotes might be used, and in any act of the play. Every character, whether important or not, could sing, and in the same act. There was no definite number of acts in a play, which usually contained from forty to fifty. The first masterpiece of the Southern drama, *P'i P'a Chi* (The Balloon Guitar), written by Kao Ming at the end of the Yüan period, contains forty-two acts.

Apparently, the Southern school of drama can be traced to an origin earlier than that of the Northern plays. Freedom to adopt various keynotes to the tune of one act was a tradition of the *chu kung tiao*. When the Chin, or Golden, Tatars occupied Pien Ching, capital of Northern Sung, in 1126, the Sungs moved southward across the Yangtze and finally established their capital in the beautiful lake town of Hangchow. Below Hangchow, to the southeast, is the rich coastal town of Wenchow. Both Hangchow and Wenchow had an eventful history in the Southern Sung period. Many entertainments are recorded, among which is the Southern play.

Playbooks were known as *hsi wên* (dramatic literature). While the *chu kung tiao,* in which the bard played a stringed instrument and sang a story, was still a Northern entertainment, the *hsi wên* play was prosperous in the south. It had assumed the form of drama, with singing, talking, and performing. No masterpieces have survived, inasmuch as the *hsi wên* were seldom written by men of letters. They were intended for the guidance of actors, not for reading as literature. When the great Northern dramatists such as Kuan Han-ch'ing and Wang Shih-fu began to write, the *hsi wên* play gradually disappeared. Throughout the period of the Mongol conquest it was declining and in the second part of the fourteenth century, when Mongol influence was decaying and the Northern drama had spent itself, it gave way to the Southern drama. The achievements of Northern dramatists, however, facilitated the growth of the Southern drama, and Kao Ming and his contemporaries developed the popular Southern play of Sung into the distinguished literary form of the Southern drama of Ming.

The prethirteenth-century drama was either a dancing play or a farce, and comedians were the most important participants. As previously mentioned, the *ching* (i.e., *ts'an chün,* state counselor) and the clown, *ts'ang hu* (blue falcon), were established characters in the cast of every play. In the dancing plays the *ts'an chün* became a leader who recited the explanatory poetry of the dances. He held a bamboo pole to direct the performances and was therefore called the *chu-kan tzŭ* (bamboo-pole man). The chief dancer was called *wu t'ou* (first dancer), or *wu mo* (dance ender). The latter name was soon shortened to the single word *mo*. This character became very important in thirteenth-century drama.

As the duty of the *ts'an chün* changed, his old function was taken over by a character called *fu ching* (assistant painted face). Meantime, the old blue falcon was renamed *fu mo* (assistant ender), and he was the clown. There was sometimes a woman in the play, or a nobleman who was not a comic character. There would then be a character in the cast called *chuang tan* (pretended girl) or *chuang ku* (pretended noble). *Tan* was the singsong girl of ancient times.

Thus, according to records written toward the end of the Sung period, at least four, and possibly five, permanent characters existed in the drama. These were the ender (*mo* or *mo ni*), the painted face or introducer (*ching* or *ying hsi*), the assistant painted face (*fu ching*), the assistant ender (*fu mo*), and the pretended noble or the pretended girl (*chuang ku* or *chuang tan*).

The thirteenth century was a period of dramatic revolution. Not only did the form undergo transformation, but the dramatic spirit took a new direction. Plays were written not merely to provoke laughter or to give a sly dig on a topical subject: their aim was to appeal to the sympathy of the audience. Suddenly emerging from the ranks of popular entertainment, the drama became serious literature in the time of Kuan Han-ch'ing, Wang Shih-fu, Pai P'u, and Ma Chih-yüan. Most of these prominent dramatists flourished before the year 1234.

Kuan Han-ch'ing, who was a native of Ta Tu (Peking), was an official physician in the court of the Chin dynasty (1115–1234).

After its fall he refused to enter the service of the Mongols. He wrote *The Orphan of the Chao Family* and several other great plays. Wang Shih-fu, whose immortal play, *Hsien So Hsi Hsiang* (The Western Chamber in Spring), is hailed as the masterpiece of Chinese drama, was also a native of Ta Tu and a contemporary of Kuan Han-ch'ing. They wrote on the same theme, the romance of the girl in the Moon-Worshiping Pavilion, with the background of the Mongol invasion of the Chin, or Golden, empire. Pai P'u, also, refused to take up a post in Kublai Khan's court, preferring to roam about until the end of his days writing nostalgic poetry about the vanished Chin dynasty.

This period is known as that of the Northern drama since most of the dramatists were northerners. In this school the technical terms for dramatic parts underwent changes. The part of the hero was played by the chief ender (*ch'êng mo*), that of the heroine by the chief girl (*ch'êng tan*), and that of the odd figure by the painted face (*ching*). Their roles are divided into three classes. The ender group included the noncomic male members, with the chief ender in the leading part. The girl group included the noncomic woman members, with the chief girl in the lead. The remainder, including the painted face (*ching*), the clown (*chu*), and the extra (*wei*), comprised villains, clowns, rustics, and all the odds and ends of comic elements in the play. For the insignificant roles of soldiers or executioners no technical names were given.

Since the thirteenth century the material for dramatic stories has come mostly from history and fiction. Romantic stories of the T'ang and Sung periods, known as *ch'uan-ch'i* (melodrama), were particularly favored by dramatists, especially those of the Southern school in the fourteenth century and later. The examination system which promoted young scholars to official rank was a favorite subject for early story writers and late dramatists. The success or failure of scholars and their love, marriage, and separation from their sweethearts were common subjects in the Southern drama. A character called the scholar (*shêng*) appears in the average Southern drama playing opposite the girl (*tan*).

Throughout the Yüan period the Northern drama flourished. In the Ming (1368–1644) and early Ch'ing periods to the Ch'ienlung reign (1736–1796) the Southern drama was in the ascendancy.

A branch of the Southern drama called the *k'un* tune school arose in the sixteenth century. This was the most influential of the many local schools of the Southern drama. These schools made new versions of the traditional music of plays and revised the text, using local accents and pronunciation. When the *k'un* tune school became powerful, it monopolized the Southern drama, crushed its rivals, and eventually became a classic. One of the *k'un* tune's merits was the introduction of the flute into its orchestra.

K'un tune held sway until the eighteenth century, and was favored by the court and the noble houses in Peking. A less influential local school from the northwest, probably a branch of the *k'un* tune, called Shensi tune (*ch'en ch'iang*), by this time had also found favor with the nobles of Peking. A characteristic instrument used by its members was the *pang tzǔ;* hence the school was known as *pang tzǔ* tune. A branch of this school used a skin fiddle (*p'i ku*) instead of the *pang tzǔ* and came to be known as *hsi p'i* (western skin), as the tunes came from west of the capital. Toward the end of the eighteenth century, in the last years of the Ch'ien-lung reign, famous local troupes were summoned to Peking to aid in the celebration of the emperor's eightieth birthday anniversary. *K'un* tune, which retained most of the traditions of the verse drama of the Southern school, had now become classic. Its plays were officially called *ya pu* (the "elegant" section). Other local schools of drama, including the Shensi tune (*ch'en ch'iang*) and a school originating in the central area of the Yangtze Valley, known as Anhui tune (*hui tiao*), were grouped under the general name of *luan t'an* (mixed music). As was historically the tendency, the popular schools were always more favored by the audience than were the classical, and the *k'un* tune was soon neglected.

Four great institutes of the Anhui school were organized in Peking. Two of them, San Ching (the three celebrations) and Ssǔ Hsi (the four happinesses), became the most powerful in the theatrical world until the end of the nineteenth century. In spite of the fact that they were known as the Anhui school, they originated in the districts of Huang P'i and Huang Kang, in the Han Valley. Their tune was called the Han tune or *erh* Huang (the two Huangs). When this influence was amalgamated with the *hsi p'i* branch of Shensi tune, it was called *p'i* Huang. The chief instrument of the *p'i*

Huang school is a *hu ching* (foreign fiddle). This is now the "opera" in the Chinese theater.

The stories were still taken from history and fiction, as in the old Northern and Southern dramas, but poetical interest in the language began to be neglected. Verse writing was neglected by poets after the nineteenth century; fewer songs and more dialogue came into the text. The text writers were more often unknown professional hands than poets. Accordingly, drama became more commercial than poetic.

Scenery and properties for Chinese plays are extremely simple. Two flags with wheels represent a carriage. A rider makes a gesture of mounting an imaginary horse. A small painted screen indicates a citadel. Four soldiers represent an army. This was necessary for several reasons. The Chinese theater has a tradition going back prior to the thirteenth century. It was the custom for princes, noblemen, and rich writers to keep private troupes for themselves and their guests. No grand public theater was permanently established until the nineteenth century.

Furthermore, the drama was composed of essentially narrative poems; the language and music were more highly regarded than were acting and background. The Chinese still say "listening" to drama instead of "seeing" it, and critics incline to criticize only the voice. Dramatists preferred that freedom should be given to their poetry, without technical restrictions. When the poet-playwright described, with poetic imagination, the background of hundreds of miles of rivers and mountains, or a war fought by a thousand men, or when ten years passed in the story, there was no consideration of a principle analogous to that of the Greek trinity. Theatrical managers had to give way to the poet; the imagination of the audience was the quality essential for appreciating the beauty of the play. To the two reasons mentioned must be added the fact that the Chinese always prefer spiritual effects to material details.

Conditions have changed and traditional influence is gradually giving way in the new plays. Drama, like other cultural institutions of modern China, has been influenced by Western culture, and writers and producers now work, to a great extent, in imitation of Westerners. (See chap. xxvii, below.) Whether or not one approves of this, it is an important phase in the history of Chinese drama.

CHAPTER XXV

Traditional Literature: Nature and Limitations

BY WANG CHI-CHEN

THERE MAY BE no universally accepted definition of literature, but concerning Western literature there is little room for disagreement concerning its content and ideals. In the West, literature includes epic and saga, fiction and drama—in other words, poetry and prose in all forms and varieties. It begins with narrative accounts of racial myths and legends and culminates in such great works of the creative imagination as *War and Peace* and *The Brothers Karamazov*. It is conceived of as something which embodies an abstract ideal, something which has its own reason for being, which enriches and illumines life but is not subservient to it. It is thought of as Art with a capital "A."

This conception of literature is typical of the idealistic civilization of the West, which because of its interest in abstract truth has developed the most elaborate philosophical systems and political institutions for the emancipation or for the enslavement of man. Because of its interest in pure science it has developed the most advanced technology both for the benefit and for the destruction of humanity. Finally, it has glorified genius and originality instead of mediocrity and tradition, as the Chinese have done in the past. This attitude toward literature is as typical of the idealism of the West as the lack of it is typical of the rational and utilitarian civilization of the Chinese, whose "cleverness" and "wisdom" have cost them their early leadership in the race for progress.

The Chinese have had no conception of literature in the modern sense of the term. There is no Chinese word for literature in its broadest sense (that is, anything written)—only such concrete images as scriptures, books, records. Similarly, for literature in the narrower sense the Chinese can speak only of particular literary forms—poetry and prose and their subdivisions. Literature as an abstract ideal does not exist. The term *wên-chang* comes close to it, but refers to form or ornamentation, as opposed to substance, rather than to literature. The term *wên-hsüeh,* now used to translate the Western word literature, is historically a contraction of the phrase *wên-chang po-hsüeh* (ornamentation and learning), and until recently has generally been used to describe an individual quality, an accomplishment, rather than something achieved or created.

More significant, perhaps, in this connection is the fact that, though theirs is one of the oldest of literatures, the idea of making a systematic study of it never occurred to the Chinese until after the literary revolution heralded by Hu Shih and Ch'ên Tu-hsiu in 1917. The first history of the subject was written not by a Chinese but by an Englishman, Herbert A. Giles, and this—*A History of Chinese Literature*—did not appear until 1901. Such a fact can mean only that the Chinese had no general conception of literature. Otherwise they would have produced a history of their own literature long ago.

Although Chinese epics commemorate ancestral deeds, fiction and drama, according to the old Chinese literati, have no place in literature. Moreover, prose and poetry in their broadest sense have served functions quite different from those in the West. These statements may appear somewhat academic; actually, they are of fundamental significance. The divergent conceptions and functions of Chinese and Western literatures bespeak markedly different historical developments. Literature, Occidental and Oriental, can be understood only in its historical setting. Failure to approach Chinese literature historically has resulted in failure to understand the true character of the writings of traditional literati and of popular literature and to explain their shortcomings and weaknesses. It has resulted, also, in many false alarms about this or that "masterpiece" of classical Chinese literature—and hence bitter disappointment, and subsequent indifference, on the part of the more cultured readers of the West.

Though it is customary to think of literature in terms of the written word, man devised the art of writing for much more practical ends. Writing was originally a difficult and costly process, and was used only to mark or commemorate important places and events, to identify ownership of valuable objects, and to record such documents as deeds, contracts, and codes of laws, and the word patterns and formulas used in ancient ritual. As far as early literature was concerned, that is, epic and saga—narratives to which people enjoyed listening, but which were of no immediate practical value—it was thought sufficient to memorize it and communicate it by word of mouth when occasion arose.

In the Western world, however, as writing became generally practiced and less costly, all sorts of things came to be written down, regardless of their practical value. First the legends of the race were preserved in writing, then the current oral literature of the people, as well as philosophical speculations, histories, and other original compositions. Thus the groundwork was laid for the convergence of classical and popular traditions and for eventual emergence of a single national literature existing primarily in the written medium. It was practiced by a class of people with high regard for their calling who devoted a large part of their time and energies to it although they did not necessarily derive their livelihood from it.

The earliest specimens of Chinese script are found on the Oracle Bones, crude records of consultations held with the gods by the people of the Shang period (*ca.* 1523 [tradl. 1766]–1028 B.C.). Next are the bronze inscriptions. They identified the ownership of the vessels on which they were cast, or solemnized important deeds and occasions. The Chinese of this period must have used writing for important documents also—mantic poetry, form hymns, and ritual songs—as evidenced by the *Shu Ching* (Classic of History, or Book of Documents), the *Shih Ching* (Book of Songs, or Odes), and the *I Ching* (Book of Changes), which have come from Shang-Chou times. Then there were books on ritual and annals of the royal court and of various feudal states, which were considered important adjuncts to the practical art of government and social intercourse.

This seems to have been the extent to which writing was used to the time of Confucius (551–479 B.C.), more than a millennium after the invention of writing in China, whereas in Greece oral literature, in the form of the Homeric legends, was committed to writing within a comparatively short time after the invention of this all-important art. The reduction to writing of popular literature in China apparently was little practiced until about the ninth century, well over two millennia after the invention of writing!

What accounts for this time lag between the invention of writing and its use for the preservation of literature, in contrast to the preservation of word patterns serving useful ends? Three reasons may be advanced. The first is the nature of Chinese script, which—whatever its merits—is more difficult to learn and more laborious to execute than the alphabetical variety. The second is the unfortunate type of writing materials used by the early Chinese. Their slips of wood and bamboo were distinctly less manageable than the papyrus of the Egyptians and Greeks. Incidentally, such records were less portable because of their weight and bulk, which rendered them particularly liable to destruction in times of disturbance. This suggests the possibility that the Chinese may have preserved, earlier than has been indicated, their epics and sagas in writing; but if so, it was not done on a scale large enough for them to survive permanently the ravages of time and human destruction. The third reason lies in the practical nature of the Chinese genius. It may sound like begging the question to say that the Chinese wrote only of things they considered of practical value because they were a practical people, but it is true—unless it be denied that a people has a genius and a character which distinguish it from other peoples.

The practical nature of Chinese literature before the time of Confucius has been mentioned. Confucius and his contemporaries had high regard for records which moderns might consider unworthy of preservation on bamboo and silk. At this time, annals, hardly more than lists of dates, were being compiled in various feudal states. Confucius was reputed to have had a hand in the *Ch'un Ch'iu* (Spring and Autumn Annals) of the state of Lu. Soon thereafter, more detailed chronicles began to be compiled, such as the *Tso Chuan* (Tso Chronicle), a commentary on the *Ch'un Ch'iu*. This use of writing was in accordance with earlier tradition, since the Chinese have always regarded history as a mirror which serves at once as guide and warning to those who would rule.

The only book representing a new departure—an extension of the use of writing—was the *Lun Yü* (Analects, or Conversations and Sayings, of Confucius) as recorded by his disciples. But even here the intent was practical, for the burden of the Analects is the art of ruling and social intercourse, though it served no immediate practical ends. The same may be said of all the books of the period: of the colloquies of Mencius, Mo Tzŭ, and Hsün Tzŭ, to say nothing of the *Shang Chün Shu* and the *Han Fei Tzŭ,* works associated with the realist or legalist school of philosophy. The *Chan Kuo Ts'ê* (Strategies of the Warring States) is almost entirely taken up with intrigues of itinerant politicians, who were (to use Mr. Waley's apt analogy) interested either in the collective security of the various independent states or in the world domination of the state of Ch'in. Even the leading Taoist philosophers, Lao Tzŭ and Chuang Tzŭ, pondered the same problems—only they pondered in reverse fashion, insisting that the true art of ruling lies in not attempting to rule at all!

What appears to have taken place in the early stages of the invention of writing in China was that, as soon as a man acquired the difficult art, he became a member of the ruling class or qualified as a candidate for membership therein. Gradually there evolved that peculiar product of Chinese civilization, the literocrat, a man who was privileged to govern by virtue of his ability to read and write. Confucius was a literocrat, as were the philosophers of the "hundred schools" of his time and the centuries immediately following. He was a literocrat without portfolio, hence his peregrinations from one feudal court to another in search of a patron. One has only to read the *Chan Kuo Ts'ê* to realize how, by the fourth century B.C., the desire to serve in some governmental function had overshadowed all other ambitions. And small wonder, for the rewards of a successful literocrat were large and often spectacular, as was shown, for example, by the careers of Chang Yi, Su Ch'in,[1] and other office seekers of the Warring States period (*ca.* 480–*ca.* 222 B.C.). By that time China had already become a literocracy, although official recognition of literocrats as a privileged class did not come until later, through the system of literary or civil service examinations.

[1] For notes to chapter xxv see page 538.

Since the literocrat was primarily a government official and a man of affairs, it was but natural that, like all good bureaucrats, he should be a stickler for precedents, conventions, and correct form. So he is found writing, not in the living speech of his time, but in a highly artificial language as different from the vernacular as Anglo-Saxon is from modern English. It is natural, also, that the literocrat should have been interested chiefly in writing things which had to do with the art of government or social intercourse. For him, literature was not an art which had its own reason for being, but "a great factor in the government of the state, a glorious thing that never dies," as Ts'ao P'ei,[2] an emperor-literocrat of the third century, put it. This may seem a lofty conception of literature, but what Ts'ao P'ei actually had in mind were edicts and memorials, reports and proclamations, and the similar functional stereotypes expected of a successful literocrat.

These stereotypes became, so far as prose was concerned, the staple of post-Han literature, supplemented by such functional compositions as obituaries sent by the bereaved to relatives and friends; biographies, with or without eulogies in verse, for tomb monuments; addresses to the dead; prefaces to celebrate the compilation of a book, or such communal or social occasions as the building of a temple or the gathering of friends. Of a more personal nature were letters, essays, and descriptions of places, but these formed only a fraction of the whole, and they are generally more stereotyped than expressive of genuine feeling. In this sterile and artificial literature are found amazing feats of verbal virtuosity and acrobatics.

If it is suggested that this criticism of literocratic prose does not apply to Chinese poetry, the answer must be that, on the whole, it does. A third or more of the works of the principal poets is made up of poems of an occasional nature addressed to friends or presented at parting, impromptu rhymes exchanged at feasts and picnics, doggerel of the type encountered in guest books of American homes. Many others are either imitations of earlier poems or variations on ancient themes (most of the so-called music-school verse [see chap. xxiv, above] belongs to the latter category), humorless parodies which no truly literate adult of the West would dream of composing. Most Chinese poetry, then, is also practical in purpose; it differs from prose only in that it usually served social rather than political functions.

There are, of course, exceptions to the general rule. There have always been independent spirits—witness T'ao Yüan-ming, or T'ao Ch'ien (A.D. 365–427),[3] who did not regard an official career as the only objective in life. Others of great talent, finding the doors to an official career closed to them, turned to writing and meditation as their chief occupations. For instance, Ssŭ-ma Ch'ien (ca. 145–ca. 87 B.C.)[4] originated the topical history, and is accounted one of the greatest prose masters. Hsi K'ang (A.D. 223–262)[5] wrote eloquent and cogent essays instead of new arrangements of clichés. In poetry, such men as Tu Fu (712–770)[6] and Po Chü-i (772–846)[7] wrote out of their own experience and reflected their own times. The genius and power of Li Po (ca. 705–762)[8] enabled him to rise above the limitations of his vision and his themes. Even in the strictly occasional pieces there is no lack of material, both in prose and in verse, which has great beauty and manifests sensitivity and genuine emotion. On the whole, however, the collected works of the proud literocrats present a rather dreary picture, and are no more truly literature than are the collected speeches, letters, and resolutions of the average politician, Occidental and Oriental.

In the field of popular Chinese literature are found the virtues and limitations common to all literature that stems from an oral tradition. It is simple and direct and is written in the language and idiom of the people, but it suffers from the fact that it reflects, and appeals to, the lowest common denominator of popular taste. Greatness and vision ordinarily do not go hand in hand with popularity, although since the literary revolution the tendency in China has been to glorify traditional popular literature because it was written in the language of the people. On the whole, less should be expected of popular literature in China, since its creators appear always to have occupied a lower economic and social position than their brethren in the West.

Little or nothing is known of ballad singers and storytellers before T'ang times (618–906), nor is much of their work extant. The only surviving oral literature of pre-T'ang times consists of a few score lyrics and festival songs preserved in the *Shih Ching* (Book of Songs, or Odes)[9] and a somewhat larger number of lyrics (usually

of four lines) and ballads dating from the Han (202 B.C.–A.D. 220).
The earliest tales and story cycles, both in prose and in verse, constituted the main body of popular literature to beguile the peasants and city dwellers of antiquity, as later stories have beguiled
their descendants since late T'ang days.[10] Not only, however, were
these not preserved, but there are few references to them by pre-
T'ang writers. The average storyteller was illiterate and learned his
stock in trade by word of mouth. Some late T'ang oral literature
of the *chantefable* type has come to light through the Tun-huang
finds. Among these are several pieces which show great skill and
beauty of imagery, but they were exceptional and were probably
preserved in writing for that reason. The same may be said of certain storytellers' tales of Sung-Yüan times (960–1368). Most of the
written versions of this literature were, in the early stages, mere
skeleton outlines, prepared by half-literate scribes, which served
as promptbooks for storytellers who were able to read a little.

Crude as it was, however, popular literature served as a stimulus
to the general stream of Chinese literature and kept it from becoming completely sterile. In fact, all the creative elements of traditional Chinese literature were of popular origin, as Hu Shih has
pointed out in his history of *pai hua* (plain speech) literature. The
reason why Chinese poetry achieved a higher degree of excellence
than any other branch of classical literature was that the literocrats
did not hesitate to learn from popular poetry. From late Han times
of the early third century the language of classical poetry has been
essentially the same as that of popular poetry, instead of being radically different from the living speech, as in classical prose. The
poetry of some of the literocrats—notably Po Chü-i—was written
in such simple language that it was, in effect, indistinguishable
from popular poetry and was therefore widely circulated among
the populace.

Then again, from late T'ang times, the literocrat-poets began
writing lyrics in the pattern of the popular airs of the time, thus
preparing the way for fraternization between the lyricists of the
popular theater and the literocrats themselves on a more or less
equal footing in Yüan times. In the Ming age (1368–1644) many
of the less orthodox literocrats actually wrote plays—lyrics, dialogues, and stage directions—and were not ashamed to sign their

names to these compositions. Here is to be observed, in some degree, that type of convergence of literary and popular traditions which in western Europe made possible the emergence of great modern literature and, consequently, a body of theatrical literature of comparative merit.

The literocracy was somewhat slow in making use of the popular story form. The *ch'uan-ch'i* tales which came into vogue among T'ang scholars were similar to popular literature in theme and intent, but they were written in the literary style. In the sixteenth century, however, scribes with some pretension to classical attainment began editing and publishing popular tales and story cycles in more elaborate forms than had previously been available. By the end of the century or a little later the great story cycles and novels based on traditional material had been published in the fully elaborated versions in which they exist today.

Most of the writers were only editors and transcribers, as, for instance, the still unknown authors of the *San Kuo Chih Yen I* (Romance of the Three Kingdoms)[11] and the *Shui Hu Chuan* (Story of the Liangshan Bandits),[12] generally ascribed to Lo Kuan-chung and Shih Nai-an, respectively. Others, like the unknown author of the *Chin P'ing Mei* (The Golden Lotus)[13] and Wu Ch'êng-ên, literocrat-author of *Hsi Yu Chi,* translated into English under the title *Monkey,*[14] used traditional material only for the framework of their narratives and actually wrote original novels.

By this time the existence of a considerable body of what may be called lay readers—that is, those who read for pleasure and not to gain knowledge or prepare for examinations—had brought about the author-reader setup without which it is impossible for literature, in the modern conception of the word, to flourish.

Some of the readers were literocrats. Although most of them were too proud or too timid to be caught reading such "vulgar trash" as fiction, at least one literocrat, Chin Jên-jui (or Shêng-t'an),[15] an eccentric of the seventeenth century, proclaimed that the best of the novels and plays were no less great as literature than the chronicles of Tso or the history of Ssŭ-ma Ch'ien.

Several works appeared soon thereafter to justify his claim. P'u Sung-ling (1640–1715),[16] who had a great reputation among literocrats for his collection of anecdotes and tales—*Liao-chai Chih-i*—in the literary tradition, produced *Hsing-shih Yin-yüan Chuan,* a satire, in one hundred chapters, on henpecked husbands. This work is realistic in spite of having a supernatural apparatus imposed on the framework of the narrative. About the middle of the eighteenth century, Wu Ching-tzŭ (1701–1754)[17] wrote *Ju-lin Wai-shih* (Unofficial History of the Literati), a satire on the literocrats themselves. Ts'ao Ch'an's (*ca.* 1715–1763) autobiographical novel of the same century, *Hung-lou Mêng*[18] (Dream of the Red Chamber), is without parallel in its scope and power of synthesis in traditional Chinese literature. These novels, however, are only exceptions that prove the fundamental soundness of the characterization of traditional Chinese literature—for the tendency of the two traditions to merge was never fully realized.

Such, then, is the development of Chinese literature to the beginning of the twentieth century, when the influence of Western literature made itself felt, as the achievements of Western science and technology had done some decades earlier. The absurdity of a situation in which literary men spoke one language and wrote another began at length to dawn upon the more progressive minds. Tradition, however, was too deeply entrenched for early reformers to attack it by frontal assault. They admitted the supremacy of the classical written language, but they argued that the vernacular might profitably be used to enlighten the masses. Among apologists for the vernacular were Christian missionaries and their converts, who were interested in carrying the Gospel to the people in language they could understand—as the Buddhist missionaries and their converts had done in earlier times.

The dual standard in language served its purpose to a certain extent, but it did not contribute to the advancement of literature as such. Radical advocates of the *pai hua* style, recognizing the untenable position of the double standard, began, in 1917, a concerted movement for adoption of the *pai hua* as the one medium for writing. They vigorously attacked the traditional literature of the literocrats as sterile and dead—which it certainly was—and extolled the virtues of the literature of the common people, which they somewhat overevaluated in their enthusiasm for the living tongue. Although the leaders of this literary revolution were interested primarily in advancing the cause of democracy and science, they succeeded in bringing about general acceptance of the *pai hua* medium and in introducing Western notions of what the ideals of literature should be. Thus they prepared the way for the emergence of a new literature in China in the 1920's and thereafter.[19]

Writers of the new school now dominate the scene, although the classical tradition is by no means dead; for example, the national anthem sponsored by the Kuomintang is composed in the archaic meter and idiom of the *Shih Ching*. Through the efforts and achievements of the new leaders, Chinese literature has at last been channeled into the main stream of world literature. Oral tradition, nevertheless, will continue to play an important part among the illiterate masses as it does in other countries.

China's literary revolution of the twentieth century constitutes no mean achievement, especially in view of the weight of tradition against which new writers have had to struggle. Compared with traditional Chinese literature, the new literature is as the automobile to the wheelbarrow. Whatever sophists may say about the eventual advantages and disadvantages of wheelbarrow and of motor-car civilizations, humanity—including the sophists themselves—will always rush for the motor car, as well as for other advantages of modern civilization. This, incidentally, is not to say that China itself may not some day evolve the best automobile, or astound the world with a sudden efflorescence in literature as the Russians did in the nineteenth century. It must be remembered, however, that before these things can happen China must acquire the spirit and methods that made possible the achievements of the West. China seems to have fulfilled the preliminary requirements for a new period of progress. May it not be retarded by encouragement from any source to look backward!

CHAPTER XXVI

Chinese Literature in Today's World

BY PEARL S. BUCK

THE INTEGRATION of the Eastern and Western worlds in the twentieth century has rendered indispensable for Westerners, particularly North Americans, a knowledge of what the Chinese people have that will be useful in the postwar era. Are the Chinese ready to take part in solving the complex problems which are looming? Or will they be merely an added burden to the accumulated medievalisms which remain to be cleared before the modern world can begin to function?

These are important questions. It is of the utmost value if Americans can count on a nation across the Pacific whose people are ready to think in constructive world terms. The Japanese cannot at present do so. It is doubted by some whether the Russians can. From India, Westerners have arbitrarily cut themselves off, or been cut off, with a determination which can scarcely be comprehended—or quickly changed. It is pertinent, therefore, in studying the Chinese, to ask: Will the Chinese be alien in the modern world?

Short of living among them, there is no better way to become acquainted with a people than to study their literature. Literature is the accumulation of a nation's thought and feeling, the essence of its ways of life. Even where that literature is distilled chiefly through a few individuals, those individuals are themselves the distillations of their people and their times.

Chinese literature is peculiarly the mirror of the Chinese mind because it is not confined to a handful of great names. Many men and women who were totally illiterate, and others with no genius beyond a modicum of scholarship, have contributed to Chinese literature. There is a large amount of anonymous literature which reveals the thought and life of the people. The anonymous literature of China would constitute an engrossing study. But there is space only to mention it as significant in its revelations and to suggest why there has been more anonymity in China than in any other country. The reasons reveal much about the Chinese nature.

The people of the Middle State have always distrusted the spectacular individual. The common man, the golden mean of a man, has been and still is to them the reliable man. The people of China—and perhaps all peoples more than they realize—have suffered from the man who is unusual. In China he has too often been a tyrant. He has broken laws and conventions which during countless centuries the people had so developed that in them the best men and women found freedom and security combined. The individual who destroys, even once, these walls of security and the areas of freedom within them, arouses the disapproval of his fellows; there is united effort to put him down and prevent his rise to power. The *great* man, in Chinese estimation, has always been the *controlled* man, not the willful man. Personal ethics as well as social approval affirm this.

When in the past, therefore, an individual felt the surge of self-expression, he veiled it in anonymity* unless he was indeed an uncontrollable and rare genius. If a scholar longed for complete freedom, but lacked courage in the face of disapproving family and friends, he remained hidden behind an assumed name. Because so much of Chinese literature has been anonymous (see chap. xxv, above), the name of a man was less important than what he wrote.

Emphasis on material rather than on authorship has persisted into modern times. This is revealing, for although the Chinese have regarded the individual as of supreme importance, so that the greatest consideration is paid to saving the feelings of individuals, high and low, the Chinese have no humility before great names. Prudence moves the common man in China to bow low before the temporarily great, but behind his sober face he often hides laughter that is hearty or even ribald. The highest in China, the richest, the most seemingly secure, knows that his foundations are shaky be-

---

* Confucius, be it remembered, *claimed* to be, *not* an originator or innovator, but a transmitter and restorer.—EDITOR's NOTE.

cause the deepest instinct of the people is their belief in the essential equality of all humans in the eyes of Heaven and therefore in their own eyes—for the average Chinese has no undue reverence for Heaven, either.

The sooner the West obtains access to Chinese literature, the closer Westerners will feel to the Chinese people and the surer of brotherhood with them. But inasmuch as that access depends on two different steps, that of many Westerners learning Chinese and of the translation of many books, it is helpful for those who have been fortunate enough to live in the atmosphere of Chinese literature to pass on what they can

Viewing a literature which flows from millions of people over thousands of years, one feels lost in its immensity. One must, therefore, choose two strands for guidance: folk literature and classical literature. These two strands, often so unlike in their expression, run parallel and yet intertwined. Both existed long, long before the time of Confucius, but in the sixth and fifth centuries B.C. the Sage defined the classical—and by defining one defined the other. Thereafter the two strands continued separately until modern times. Folk literature developed out of the people, in songs and fiction; classical literature developed through scholars, in poetry, essays, history, and philosophy. In spite of this separation, commingling persisted through anonymous writings of scholars and through a certain robust folk quality which showed itself in individuals such as Li Po (705–762) and even in Tu Fu (712–770), Li's contemporary and complementary classical rival. Wherever a genius appeared in the classical school, his power flowed from the folk quality in his own character and thinking. Folk quality came from physical heredity or from experience. Where it was lacking, a desiccated, though occasionally exquisite, literature was the result.

Since folk spirit so permeates all that is vital in the literature of China, it is necessary to examine its qualities and test its universality. It is an essential quality of the Chinese people or it would not be so pervasive. It is the secret, too, of their vitality, or there would not be vitality where it appears—and no vitality where it is lacking.

Much classical writing can be dismissed because, although it has the form of literature, it is without substance. (See chap. xxv, above.) Thousands of volumes of Chinese classical writing cannot be called literature since they are nothing but commentaries upon real literature. Wherever the precious quality of vitality existed, scholars recognized great literature. When they were unable to produce with vitality, they satisfied themselves by explaining and commenting upon it—and, in the fashion of some scholars in other countries, sometimes by killing it. Or they copied it in diluted versions, plagiarizing the form without being able to re-create the meaning. Classical literature in China was at times almost stultified by slavish copying of what had once been an original creation.

But there were individuals in China who knew this and who, whenever they appeared, revivified classical literature. It is doubtful, however, if these few could have kept classical literature alive had it not been for the folk literature which flowed, an unimpeded torrent of story, song, and poetry, from the heart of the people. (See chap. xxvii, below.) Folk literature was not touched by scholastic formalisms, for they were unknown to the people. Of the classical writings, only those of a few great men are significant and revelatory, but all folk literature is significant and revelatory.

Since Confucius, through the medium of ethics, defined the laws of classical literature so clearly, it is simplest, in briefly viewing classical literature, to consider Confucius in the light of his relationship to the world. Confucius' was the first permanently recorded world mind produced in China. That there were others before him is obvious: his work is a synthesis of Chinese civilization to his time. From many sources he gathered what seemed to him the most admirable thoughts and records of his people. For almost twenty-five centuries his idealistic, universally thinking mind has been permeating the minds and spirits of the Chinese people. This surpasses in length of time and concentration even the influence of Jesus, who, in an entirely different fashion, accomplished the same synthesis of the best in his people and the same infusion of his own quality of personal idealism.

There have been brief periods when Confucius was put aside, as in the generation following the Revolution of 1911–1912. But these periods were short, and the latest is passing, for the people of China have been unable to find in any other figure the comprehensive satisfaction they have found in Confucius. To them his direction has always seemed the most practical and the most lofty. This is because Confucius, although he expressed the essence of Chinese idealism, was also universal in his thinking. The Chinese demand both qualities in those whom they admire and trust.

The influence of Confucius upon his people has been twofold: first, through his selection, from a large number of writings, of those facts, forms, and ideas which seemed to him finest and most worth preserving; second, through his own personality as evidenced by his selections. In the Five Classics, Confucius preserved the very best—according to his judgment—of his countrymen's historical writings, poetry, philosophy, ethics, and records. He compiled a thesaurus. Had he not done this, much of China's past would have been lost and the people would not have become the spiritual and cultural unit they are today. It would be interesting to speculate on what the Chinese might have become if another than Confucius had made the selection. It was probably fortunate that Confucius was the one to put his hand to the task since he was able to think of his people in terms of mankind and not, as a lesser man might have done, in terms of a nation. From antiquity the Chinese, guided by the universal mind of Confucius, have been accustomed to think of themselves as part of the whole human race.

Opposition to Confucius appeared in the teachings of Lao Tzŭ (lao dz) and Chuang Tzŭ (juang dz), who could not endure his formalism, especially as it was reflected and repeated in smaller men. These two rebelled against it and sought the fresh springs of the individual human heart. But Lao Tzŭ and Chuang Tzŭ themselves were influenced by the world mind of Confucius and expressed their opposing thoughts in terms of all mankind. The sayings of Lao Tzŭ, such as "Follow diligently the Way in your own heart, but make no display of it to the world," "Do nothing and all things will be done," have now become the possession of the people. Yet these were actually a balance to the definitions set by Confucius and have remained so through the centuries. This means not only that the Chinese have had world minds, as had their leaders and the founders of their thought and civilization, but that the very differences between their leaders were expressed in terms of the universal or world mind. For the conservative, Confucius was a guide; for the liberal, there was Lao Tzŭ. (See chaps. xv, xvii, above.)

The two are not mutually exclusive. It is to be expected that the young should tend to follow the spirit of Lao Tzŭ. During the sober, hard-working middle years of a man's responsibility he leans upon the ethics of Confucius for the solidity of his family and social relations. But when willful and whimsical old age comes, when a man is no longer responsible for anybody and his sons lift the burden from his shoulders, he returns to Lao Tzŭ.

As the Chinese see it, the two great schools of literature and thought are not mutually exclusive. The ofttimes harsh restrictions of the Western code, which, for example, forbids a Protestant to be at the same time a Catholic, is, in general, foreign to the modern Chinese. To him such differences are not so fundamental as to require that he remain all his life in one region of the mind or spirit. His is a free mind, a free spirit, and he wanders where he finds most satisfaction for his changing needs. This breadth of view is a direct result of the world-mindedness of the men who were founders of Chinese thought and literature. And this is not because these founders were solitary and lonely geniuses, but because they were able to put into words, through their synthesizing gifts, that which was, and is, the nature of the sons of Han and T'ang, the two great natural trends of all people, the conservative and the liberal. Because these men were great enough to be universal and thought of all mankind when they spoke of and to their own people, they taught the Chinese universality.

The result of this teaching throughout the centuries is that today the people of China are more ready for world organization and world coöperation than any other. They realize intuitively and traditionally—and one need only talk to an ordinary Chinese to discover this—that all people are dependent on one another. Even Chinese nationalism tends to become a part of internationalism and not to constitute an end in itself. For this the world is indebted to the founders of classical Chinese literature, who in the beginning, although they emphasized uniquely Chinese qualities, pointed out that these were manifestations of the universal and not qualities which marked them as chosen of God or in any wise supernatural or divine. Emphasis upon the human as well as the universal is what the world most needs today.

And all the while, in a separate stream, folk literature was increasing—the literature of those who, unable to read and write, were dependent upon songs sung and stories told and plays enacted before their eyes. The earliest folk literature was probably made up of ballads and songs. There has been little group singing in China until recently, except for songs sung in unison by laborers to lighten the tedium of their work or the chants of priests in temples. But the individual singer has always been important in his relation to the people: the wandering singer, the minstrel, the blind fiddler who walks the streets and the countryside, singing and sometimes begging. Somewhere, sometime, the singer became also the story-teller. And the storyteller found his material in the daily lives of the people and their memories. That he might find more stories, he also learned to read—and thus met Confucius and Lao Tzŭ. Folk literature, springing up through thousands of simple persons, brought the classics back to the people with whom they had begun and the people accepted them. Today the balancing forces of Confucianism and Taoism unify Chinese thought; the world-mindedness of two great sages has become instinctive with the Chinese people.

But folk literature, which thus adopted the ethics and philosophy of classical literature, found new forms. The Chinese wanted stories and novels and plays about persons like themselves. The founders of Chinese Buddhism discovered that they could never make their religion, imported from India, take hold until it had reached the imagination of the people. The theater developed in China, as it did in the West, through religious plays at temples. Other drama (see chap. xxiv, above) did not appear until relatively late in the Yüan period (1260–1368). The novel, too, did not appear until late. Its first definite, though still rudimentary, form may be traced to the age of the Sung (960–1279). Neither drama nor novel was accepted as part of literature by the rigid classical school, the very poetry of which had to be written by set standards.

It was but natural, however, in the democratic, or semidemocratic, society of imperial China, where sons comparatively rarely inherited their father's honors, that original minds, even among classicists, should sometimes find release through folk forms. Many popular novels and plays are signed by pseudonyms, but their excellent technique is proof that they must have been written by scholars. Yet so strong was the classical prejudice against these popular forms that scholars dared not set their names to them. The situation was something like that obtaining among scientists, who seem to fear they will ruin their scholarly reputations if the ordinary man can understand what they have written.

Vigorous, trained minds nevertheless followed the classical tradition to the extent that they did not feel it necessary always to be entirely original, even in nontraditional forms of folk literature. The vast and extremely vital novel *Shui Hu Chuan* (Story of the Liangshan Bandits), for example, is a compilation of many popular legends which sprang from history, imagination, local tall tales, and Robin Hood stories, but which are so interwoven that only a great novelist could have made the final compilation into a single work of intricate art. Confucius himself set no store on originality; under his influence the delicacies of plagiarism have never troubled the Chinese mind.

The folk literature of China, which includes the forms forbidden to scholar-acknowledged literature until Western influence arrived, is so vast and so rich, so varied in humor and tragedy and all that goes to make up the life of a people—especially the Chinese people, with their emphasis upon the value of the human—that it is impossible to mention here individual names or works without giving them undue emphasis. It is more significant to say that no names are superlatively important and that the greatest works are compilations, infused, in the Confucian and Taoist sense, with the personalities of one or more writers of genius who modeled them anew. It is indicative of a certain difference that American school children are, in the main, taught literature by learning first the names of great authors and then—sometimes—what they wrote. Last of all, and sometimes not at all, do they read the masterpieces themselves. In Chinese schools, literature is taught by great works, and authors' names are often either ambiguous or unknown.

And yet it would be wrong to give the impression that to the Chinese the individual does not matter. He matters, and matters intensely. Chinese literature, especially folk literature, is centered on individuals, and the utmost effort is expended in describing their actions and feelings, their tragedies and joys. Still, one always senses that these individuals are important not because they have names and live in a certain town but because they carry in themselves the world of human beings everywhere. And the important ones behave and think and feel as they do because they partake of that larger humanity. They are important because they are human beings named Wang or Smith and not because they are Wang or Smith.

The sort of writing, superb as it is, in Steinbeck's *The Grapes of Wrath,* for example, is essentially Western in its regionalism, both geographic and social. Many a Chinese novel or story begins with a meticulous setting of place and character: "There lived once, in the city of ——— in the province of ———, in the year of ———, a man named ——— and surnamed ———." All this may be set down with a precision which no Western novel, originating in the brain of one individual, could match. Yet somehow that beginning, precise as it is, puts the man named ——— into his place in time and space among humankind.

This is the ancient habit of the Chinese mind, which, through literally thousands of years, has realized the infinite value of a human being, and yet knows that he is but one of all mankind. This, it seems to some, is the spirit which the present age needs above all others. In the West there are two opposing beliefs: the belief, expressed through modern democracy, that the individual has the right to be free and to maintain his own being; and the belief, now labeled as fascist, that the individual is of no value and is merely part of the mass. But the Chinese have achieved a balance between these notions: they have lived with both so long that they have synthesized the two. It is not a new synthesis. Chinese life, mirrored in both classical and folk literature, shows the synthesis as it has developed in the daily life and thought of the people. This synthesis of individualism and universalism is China's peculiar gift to modern times.

Are the Chinese alien in the modern world? No; less alien than many Westerners. For while many in the West have been busily perfecting machines of communication, the Chinese for centuries have been perfecting the one belief that is essential for a shrinking world—the belief that all men belong to one race, the human race, and that therefore All Men Are Brothers.

CHAPTER XXVII

Letters and Arts in the War Years

BY DRYDEN LINSLEY PHELPS

A HEADY TORRENT has been gushing from attic studios, fly-by-night back-room presses, and guerrilla encampments in the land of Cathay. From Kunming, Kueiyang, Chungking, Chengtu, and Yenan stream literary miscellanies faster than any librarian can index them. Bamboo-fiber rag sheets carry odd-sized type which wobbles down the page with haste and fervor, graphic woodcuts by peasant artisans, vernacular ballads and racy tales that hop, skip, and jump among the ponderous ranks of essays, novels, and dramas.

Eagerness to write is matched by eagerness to read. A wealth of reprints and new translations has appeared to meet the voracious demand. "Free Reading—Welcome!" shout the bookstore placards of Chungking, and along Culture Street are several shops where a poor man may drop in and snatch a chapter or two of his favorite novel, washed down with numerous cups of free tea.

Several decades ago the agile brain of James Yen was fired with the idea: what if millions of Chinese farmers could read in the long winter months! Then came the uprooting convulsion, and suffering was followed by the possibility of freedom—literally new life. When Chang Tao-fan, sometime minister of information and later chairman of the Central Cultural Movement Committee of the Kuomintang, observed, in an article, "Wo Mên So Hsü Yao Ti Wên I Chêng Tseh" (The Literary Policy We Need), that literature should no longer be for the leisure class only but should now portray for the people the Chinese ideals of life gleaned from the struggle of war, he was merely stating what the people had already discovered.

Now it is the people who are talking and the people who are listening—for it is not too early to proclaim the discovery that a high literary or artistic I.Q. is no monopoly of the well educated. Farmers make up ballads to new tunes. They perform in impromptu peripatetic scenarios called "living newspapers," and their fellows write them down. Countrymen and soldiers relate tall tales which someone turns into stories and novels. Peasants dash off satirical cartoons on rice paper or carve woodcuts. Each artist uses the medium of spontaneous utterance with which he is most familiar.

This literary and artistic expression, unlike former Chinese renaissance movements, is not primarily a self-conscious intellectual process, but a tremendous upsurge from below. *Wên i fu hsing* (renaissance) is too stereotyped a term for what has been happening in modern China. Recent events, indeed, stand in sharp relief when contrasted with earlier periods of new birth in Chinese literature and arts.

Hu Shih discovers four great relatively early periods of renaissance in Chinese history. The first was the rise of the great poets under the T'ang dynasty, with a simultaneous movement for new prose literature modeled after the style of the classical period and the development of Ch'an Buddhism as a Chinese reformation of its Indian heritage. Reform movements of the Sung dynasty in the eleventh century, with subsequent development of a powerful secular Neo-Confucian philosophy which gradually replaced the medieval religions, constituted the second awakening. The rise of the thirteenth-century dramas, with the great novels, a little later, glorifying the joys of life, constituted the third. And the fourth was the revolt, in the seventeenth century, against the rationalistic philosophy of the Sung and the Ming dynasties and the development, in the last three hundred years, of new philological and historical techniques based on documentary evidence. But all these, according to Hu Shih, lacked a sense of their historical mission; so they never achieved the work of revolution, but were swept away by the conservative force of tradition. Although they brought in new patterns, they never obliterated the old.

In and after 1917 a coterie of intellectuals led chiefly by Hu Shih, and followed by students and younger writers imbued with their passion, gave birth to the now famous vernacular renaissance. Its similarity to three features of the European renaissance was recognized: a conscious movement to promote a new literature in the language of the people to replace the classical literature; a conscious protest against ideas and institutions in the traditional culture and a conscious attempt at emancipation of individuals from tradition; a new movement led by scholars who knew their cultural heritage and proposed to study it with the methodology of modern historical criticism.

These leaders set out to destroy that in the past which obstructed new modes of expression. They wanted a new scholarship; a new language for popular education; a new literature capable of expressing the feelings and thoughts of the people; and a new outlook on life and society to break the shackles of tradition, make the people feel at home in the new world, and prepare them for active participation in modern sciences.

Magazines like *Hsin Ssŭ Ch'ao* (New Thought) and *Hsin Ch'ao* (New Tide) gave expression to this new birth intellectually of an old people and an old civilization. Government students at Peking University established a monthly magazine in 1918 and called it *Renaissance*.

The new literary movement spread among the colleges like a prairie fire. Its highly self-conscious intellectual enthusiasm was realistic in depending on the language of the people to give expression to the thoughts and feelings of the people.

Lü Hsün, pen name of Chou Hsü-jên (1881–1936), gave voice to the revolutionary ferment which for decades had been gathering in China, but he spoke in a way profoundly different from that of 1917: not as a self-conscious intellectual with an intellectual purpose, however democratic, but as one of the people. His passion was to portray men and women hurled from a traditional past into the modern cataclysm. His writings profoundly stirred the scholars, but even more the people, since his stories expressed the "common" man's intense sufferings and blazing hopes. Thus Lü Hsün unknowingly ushered in the war literature of China.

Another great writer, Kuo Mo-jo, in a radio address in May, 1942, under the auspices of the Chungking Sino-American Institute of Cultural Relations, affirmed the determination of the Chinese to carry on the creative activities of the renaissance, not in spite of the war with Japan, but *because* of the war:

When the war broke out, we feared that its wanton destruction would cripple literature and the arts, that pens, chisels, and batons would be laid aside for more patriotic weapons. But war against aggression stirs man's creative activities, literary and artistic. The fight against falsehood, brutality, disorder, and unreasonableness brings about the ascendancy of a nation's literature and art. A nation engaged in a war of aggression, however, compels its writers to whitewash brutality and turn the muses into monsters. But an antiaggressive nation defends itself, as well as the people and civilization of the aggressor. So I have coined a new term: our artistic war. Our Chinese artists have been led into a new awakening. Art for war's sake and war for art's sake are indivisible. The fecundity of literature and the arts manifests the common feeling. . . .

Before the war, China's old literature and arts were confined to imitation of lifeless ancient masterpieces, while the new literature imitated foreign works and was no more than a childlike make-believe. Writers of both schools, alienated from reality, gathered in a few modern cities like Shanghai and Peiping, or shut themselves in their studio ivory towers. Whether of the new or of the old school, whether leftists or rightists, they were all bombastic and untruthful. But the bugle has awakened them all and summoned them to the street, the front, the countryside. Only then did the new arts take root and the old arts revive. The distinction between the old and the new has gradually disappeared, for only that which has life is art. Art with life is new even for ten thousand generations; art without life is old in a single day.

Before the open conflict with Japan, plays and stories directed against Japanese fascism were sharply censored. During the war, growlings against native fascism and outcries for Chinese democracy increased to a thunderous roar. This was more than sound and fury; it was the highly intelligent, articulate voice of writers and poets, playwrights, musicians and dancers, scholars and historians, professors and lawyers, speaking for the people of China.

On February 20, 1945, three hundred such men and women, including the topmost creative writers, artists, and thinkers, signed the "Wên Hua Tso Chia Hsüan Yen" (Declaration of the Cultural Workers):

"When there is no way out, a change is necessary." This is the universal appeal at present. The political situation of China is such that there is no need for us to "frighten the people with alarmist views," nor does it allow us to "paint it with flashy words."

In internal politics we have not achieved unity; in the government, corruption and bribery . . . cultural and educational fields suffer restrictions and oppression.... We have not the necessary strength to check the advance of the enemy nor to coördinate the counteroffensive of our Allies. At a time when the World War is approaching victory, we are laggards in the new era ... A thousand critical eyes stare.

The way is right at hand, a simple way, to realize democracy at once. Day and night the people appeal. Even the government has publicly declared its purpose to end the party rule and return power to the people.

"When the sun is up, it is time to work; when the knife is at hand, it is time to cut." In the present critical situation, the mere talking of democracy resembles the attempt "to stop hunger with picture cakes," and the empty promise of democracy is like "quenching thirst by gazing at sour plums." Obstructions to democracy we must abolish....

Then follow definitive demands on the Chungking government, signed by Kuo Mo-jo (1891 [?], or possibly 1887, or 1893–), Mao Tun, pen name of Shên Yen-ping (1896–), Pa Chin, pen name of Li Pei-kan (1905–), Lao Sheh, pen name of Shu Shê-yü (1898–), Ts'ao Yü, pen name of Wan Chia-pao (1909–), Ku Chieh-kang (1893–), and colleagues of similar caliber in all the arts.

China's resistance movement against fascist imperialism enlisted all its intelligence and discovered skills and imaginative powers now become articulate. These many forms of expression are being woven in novel patterns by the quick shuttle of events. Visions of a new life in an old land, bitter experiences of broken homes, surging emotions of pity and of love, galvanic ideas like the plans for a TVA of the upper Yangtze are mingled in the new literature with the conviction that in grass-roots democracy lie at hand all the possibilities for genuine political, economic, and spiritual freedom.

Writers, women as well as men, served as volunteers in medical and dramatic corps or as soldiers and guerrillas at the front. Startling peasant resourcefulness, the quick thrust of danger, and sudden death punctuated their war reporting. Although much of the war writing did not go beyond reports, such personal experiences were grist for stories and plays which caught and held the popular imagination. Lao Sheh's long story, *Huo Tsang* (Cremation) (printed by the *Literary Vanguard*), depicted the guerrillas incinerated in their own village when they refused to surrender. "These men are *Chinese,* our own brothers. Today they conquer the Japanese imperialists. Tomorrow they build China!"

Many intellectuals, writers, and artists, fleeing across their own land before the oncoming storm, saw for the first time the towns and countryside, the rivers and hills which they had long known only from ancient stories and poems. They have written of these journeys in the new national tongue, well salted with provincial variations. Lao Sheh uses the Peking dialect; Sha Ting—pen name of a young novelist—the pithy vernacular of western China; Pi Yeh—pen name of a young northern writer—the idiom of the north-west. Border tribes enter the current literature in the quaint, racy flavor of a Chinese Zane Grey style. Tuan-mu Hung-liang, a young writer from the northwest, in *Steppe of the Khorchin Banner,* depicts Mongolian life in northern Jehol in 1931, when the Japanese invaded the northeastern provinces. This novel was published in 1937. *Beyond the Willow Palisades,* another novel by the same author, describes the agricultural Mongols of the northeast under the Japanese. Pi Yeh's short story, "Wu Lau Pu Lang Ti Yeh Chi" (The Night Sacrifice at Ulanblan), pictures Suiyuan Mongols fighting the enemy. Lao Sheh's ten-thousand-line autobiographical poem, *Chien Pei Pien* (North of Chienmenkuan), describes his journey into the limitless northwest.

Not only geographical and ethnological but religious and class barriers have been broken down. Lao Sheh, distinguished author of poems and dramas, stories and novels, in his play *Kuo Chia Chih Shang* (The State Comes First), written in collaboration with the playwright Sung Chih-ti (1914–), portrays a stubborn Moslem who is finally convinced that to win the war he must discard racial and religious prejudices and coöperate with his fellow Chinese of other faiths. Now the Mohammedans are urging him to write more plays about the great Moslem leaders of the past.

China has been making a fresh discovery of its own past. Throughout these death-grappling years the country has called on its reserves—the heroes of the war days of long ago. And so, amid the welter of new books, are throngs of the old favorites: *Shui Hu Chuan* (All Men Are Brothers), *San Kuo Chih Yen I* (Romance of the Three Kingdoms), *Hung-lou Mêng* (Romance, or Dream, of the Red Chamber). Their renewed popularity reveals how China has returned to the rock from which it was hewn.

In the early years of the struggle with Japan, the people's day-to-day literature was characterized by romantic glorification of

heroism and a tremendous sense of release. The nation's future
rose before all eyes. In later years military setbacks, political chican-
ery, social evils, and human suffering, attended by weariness and
loss of faith, drove writers to more objective, penetrating insights.

The Chinese are born raconteurs. Mellow with unnumbered
centuries of living, they are the most human of earth's peoples.
Their war stories and novels, filled with wit and satire, make excellent reading aloud. All sorts of people flock through the pages
of Lao Sheh: big-drum players, acrobats who peddle medicine,
ricksha coolies, actors, peasant soldiers, and fat officials.

Many stories and novels were penned with direct propagandist
purpose. Ch'ên Shou-chu's novel *Ch'un Lei* (Spring Thunder) tells
how the villages of silk-producing Wusih organized to fight the
enemy. Its racy satire and humor are heightened by the tang of
the Wusih dialect. Yao Hsüeh-ying's *Liu Ch'üan-te Yü Hung Lo
P'u* (Liu Ch'üan-te and the Red Turnip) contrasts Liu, a tough,
professional soldier, with the Red Turnip, a timid, ignorant peasant soldier. Liu, the camp "slicker," sacrifices himself in the end
to save the Red Turnip, formerly his personal enemy. Yao Hsüeh-
ying spent years in the Tapieh Mountains of the Honan-Hupeh
border region, and wrote novels about the life of the political workers at the front. *Ch'un Luan Hua K'ai Ti Shih Hou* (Spring Brings
Blossoms) describes the activities of these workers, who brought
about and kept such close coöperation among people, guerrillas,
and militia. Perhaps Pearl Buck got the clue for one of her novels
from Mao Tun's *Tsou Shang K'ang Wei* (Assume Your Post), which
tells of the removal of a factory from the lower Yangtze to the interior. Pa Chin's *Huo* (Fire) is one of the favorite novels of student
life. Fêng Wên-shu, a middle-class girl of Shanghai, nurses the
Chinese defenders of that city, with the foreign settlement as background. The second volume depicts her as a member of a propaganda corps at the front. The third volume is in the writing. This
novel and Pa Chin's prewar *Chia* (Home), *Ch'un* (Spring), and
Ch'iu (Autumn) continue to be best sellers.

To meet the insatiable demand for the printed page some Chinese novelists have been turning out love stories not unlike those
of the American cinema in their portrayal of luxurious, erotic life
in the cities. "Not a bad omen," remarks the veteran critic, Sun

Fu-yüan, of this love-story craze. Writers popular before the war—Lao Sheh, Pa Chin, Kuo Mo-jo, Mao Tun, Ping Hsin (Ice Heart, pen name of Hsieh Wan-ying, 1905–), Ts'ao Yü—continue to respond to the tremendous demand. Their romances and volumes of amusing plays find constant buyers.

The propaganda play, however, like the novel with a purpose, is more characteristic of wartime China. The undercutting of foreign imperialism and of native fascism, whether through open battle or underground resistance, is material for the stage. A struggle that uses eight-year-old gamins to lead Japanese into guerrilla ambush, and venerable Taoist priests and Mohammedan mullahs to arouse the people, provides dramatic material for improvised stages on the streets or country roads and for elaborate five-hour plays in the great city theaters.

When Japan invaded China in open assault, the reverberating cry of resistance sounded in stirring plays throughout the land. Novels, short stories, incidents of heroism at the front, and dark plots of sabotage were dramatized. Troupes of children were organized to go on the road to awaken the farmers by means of song and play and recitative.

A reactionary censorship, more fearful of the people's demand for democratic freedom than of Japanese invasion, clamped down on this dramatic outburst. More than fifty plays were banned between 1937 and 1943. The censorate was suspicious not only of plots but also of techniques. These performances were too stirring, too vivid. They portrayed too sharply the new versus the old, the rich above the poor, the feudal landlord against the peasant, the conniving merchants of Shanghai and Hongkong who were disloyal to their own country. The censorate feared that both playwrights and actors were pro-Communist.

Hsia Yen's *Fa-hsi-ssǔ Hsi Ch'ün* (The Fascist Bacillus; or, The Typhoon) was banned; then, under stiff pressure, it was released. So elaborate was the presentation of this drama that the producer lost $200,000 on the Chengtu performances. But he made up the loss on his next play, *K'ung Ch'iao Tan* (The Peacock's Gall), by Kuo Mo-jo. Incidentally, the Chinese version of *Mourning Becomes Electra,* "though it had nothing to do with the present war," as a Chinese producer commented, was banned.

In order to present their message to the nation, therefore, play-wrights chose heroic themes of ancient history. How could a censor ban a tale of the T'ang or Sung dynasty and preserve face? Wu Tsu-kuang's *Chêng Ch'i Ko* (Song of Righteousness) played to packed houses night after night in Unoccupied China.

It was estimated that during the war more than a thousand dramatic troupes, professional and amateur, operated in Unoccupied China. This number does not include the many impromptu performances of one-act plays and "living newspapers" in guerrilla areas behind the Japanese lines. Theatrical art made remarkable progress. Chungking and Chengtu were full of experienced directors, actresses, and other theatrical workers. If they had been in Soviet Russia during the war, as Kuo Mo-jo remarked, many of them would have been awarded medals and called heroes.

The government and the theater owners reaped profits: from a third to a half of all box-office receipts went to Chungking and a third to the theater owner, leaving only a third or less for the producer, actors, and production costs.

Brief biographical sketches of two dramatists will represent the many in this field. Hsia Yen was born in 1900, in a small-landlord family of Hangchow. There he was graduated in 1919 from a technical school in time to join Hu Shih's literary renaissance movement. In 1925 he was graduated from the Kyushu Engineering School in Japan. But, as in the case of Lü Hsün, political events interfered with his scientific career. He joined the Northern Expedition of 1926–1927, and thenceforth gave himself solely to writing for the sake of modern China. He translated several works of Gorki and Chekhov, and soon after the Japanese invasion he edited one of the literary miscellanies which aroused students and the masses generally. But playwriting was his central interest. Of his plays, *Within One Year* deals with the first year of war. *Shanghai Yeh* (Under Shanghai Roofs) describes the poverty and misery of the common people in Shanghai even before the outbreak of war. *Fa-hsi-ssŭ Hsi Ch'ün* (The Fascist Bacillus) is the story of a Japanese-trained Chinese physician who brings his Japanese wife back to China and has to bear the insults which his countrymen fling against his wife and child, and the violence of the invaders, who destroy his life's work in bacteriological research. *City of Sorrow* portrays the dangerous life of progressive writers in Japanese-occupied Shanghai. *The City's Little People* is a collection of one-act plays dealing with various social strata of Shanghai under Japanese and puppet regimes. Hsia Yen collaborated with Sung Chih-ti and Hsü Lin in writing *Birth Struggles of the Modern Play*.

Sung Chih-ti, born in 1914, in Hopei, is the son of a farmer. His family wanted him to become a railway engineer—an unusual ambition in agricultural China—so the boy went to work with an uncle on the Peiping-Suiyuan railway. The pace of political events in 1927 turned him toward books of social implication. He was influenced by such writers as Tolstoi, Dostoevski, Balzac, and Lü Hsün, "the Chinese Gorki." In 1928, after the railway explosion that killed Chang Tso-lin, the Manchurian war lord, Sung Chih-ti took part in an anti-imperialist, anti-Japanese school play. The Mukden "Incident" of September 18, 1931, terminated his college career midway. With many other students, he joined the National Salvation Movement. Their patriotic propagandist plays frequently involved him with the police in the days when China was appeasing Japan. No publisher dared accept his writings. The outbreak of the Fifth Sino-Japanese War in July, 1937, started Sung Chih-ti on his playwriting career, and he later toured western China with a troupe staging his own and other modern plays.

Sung's first play, *Tzŭ Wei Tui* (Self-Defense Corps), depicts the guerrillas. *Fa* (Punishment) concerns a young magistrate who takes the place of a corrupt old official. *Wu Chung Ch'ing* (Foggy Chungking) describes the backwash of the war's initial wave of patriotism. Enthusiasm flags and greed mounts; youth is cynical, disillusioned; corruption rots the structure even of the new China. The hero of *Tsu Kuo Ti Hu Shêng* (Fatherland Calling) is a physician who remains behind in Occupied China to give medical aid to his fellow countrymen until finally he is forced to admit that the Japanese yoke makes an objective stand impossible, and he slips through the lines to Unoccupied China.

To witness such plays as *Chia* (Family), staged by Mr. Chang, a graduate of the Yale School of Drama, in which his wife, the beautiful and talented Pei Yang, played with distinction, is a thrilling experience even to a sophisticated Western theater-goer. Rage, jealousy, passion, exaltation, craftiness—surging and sly emotions expressed through every device of repartee, complex situation, modern make-up, and stage setting: this is the new theater in China. (See chap. xxiv.) Yet the Chinese stage, so rapidly becoming modernized, must still retain the old five- and six-hour performances to satisfy the insatiable demand of packed houses. The Chinese have a passion for the theatrical, either as actors or as spectators. They have turned their history into an endless procession of plays, and the Chinese *Comédie humaine* is familiar in scenes and acts to millions who can neither read nor write.

Before the war, to call a man poet was to brand him an effeminate dilettante. But in the war years "the extreme sensitivity of the lyric poets became in itself a war bugle." Poetry magazines sprang up like mushrooms, many published by the Association of Poets.

The main sources of poetic inspiration were incidents at the front, the emotions of the country recruit, the breakup of ancestral homes under the fury of bombing, the separation from family and beloved friends—a perennial theme in Chinese poetry,—the intense suffering of long journeys to western China, the exultation of refugees at beholding the rivers and mountains of their own land.

T'ien Chien's collection of individualistic poems, *Dedication to the Sentries in the Snowstorm,* recalls the mood of Hsü Ssŭ-ch'i's great painting of tigers buried in snow, with flocks of birds wheeling high above—a symbol of China's elite soldiers killed at Nanking and the rising of the people's militias to replace them.

Tsang K'ê-chia's *Shu Shang Ti Hua Pao* (Blossoms of an Old Tree) tells the story of the Shantung guerrilla leader in five thousand lines. His short poems describe the rural scenes he came to know in his life with farmers and soldiers at the front.

The poet Pien Chih-lin spent a year among the guerrillas with his poet friend Ho Ch'i-fang and then went to that greatest center of literary activity, the National Southwest Associated Universities in Kunming, to teach and to work on a novel.

Ko Chung-ping's "Great Wrecking Work of the Pinghan [i.e., Peiping-Hankow] Railway Workers" and Yüan Sui-p'o's "Hou Chieh" (Back Street) in the latter's collection, *The People,* are widely contrasted types of poetry, the first a heroic hymn awakening the masses to action, the second a melancholy meditation on the life in city slums.

Kao Lan's two volumes contain *Lang Sung Shih* (Recitation Poems) such as the 340-line "Wo Ti Chia Tsai Hei Lung Chiang Shang" (My Home Is on the Amur River), which recounts the happy life in northwestern Manchuria before the miseries of the Japanese invasion.

The *Shih Ssŭ Hang Shih* (Fourteen-line Verse, or Sonnets) of Fêng Chih, called by Yang Kang, of Radcliffe College, "the first book of philosophy in poetry in our Chinese modern literature," was influenced by Rilke. Auden, Eliot, Yeats, and Burns, too, have their young followers.

As in other fields, the heavy hand of the censor influenced poetic titles and themes. Members of the resistance movement—antifascist within China, as well as anti-Japanese—chose Christian titles and stories such as "The Death of John the Baptist" and "The Casting Away of Adam and Eve" to describe the massacre of the New Fourth Army by order of the Chungking government (see chap. xi, above) or the emancipation of the northwest by the Yenan border government.

The metrical structure of the new poetry varies in length of line from sharp, stabbing, one- and two-character lines to the long, regular lines of orthodox verse. All kinds of stanzas are used, and every form of verse from the many-thousand-line narratives of Lao Sheh and Wang Ya-p'ing to the clipped lyrics of T'ien Chien.

Much of China's war poetry, like that of the West, is evanescent. But there is much that will remain. Of all the war writers, the poets and dramatists have been perhaps the most skilled and conscientious workmen. But he would be a hardy critic who would venture to place any one type of literature in the forefront of war activity. Who shall say whether the war stories and novels of Lao Sheh, Kuo Mo-jo, and Pa Chin, like an army with banners, or the plays of Ts'ao Yü, like a signal corps, or the poems of Pien Chih-lin, like lonely patrols, have played the most stirring part?

Of all countries, China has had the longest-sustained taste for serious literature. The great popularity of essays throughout the war years offers striking confirmation of this fact. Kuo Mo-jo's story about Ch'ü Yüan (see chap. xxi, above), the scholar-hero of centuries ago, who drowned himself in protest against the evils of his day, sold ten thousand copies in the first few weeks after publication.

The essay-lectures of the philosopher Fung Yu-lan (see chap. xx, above) on historical and political themes attract great numbers of students and teachers, and are constantly being reprinted. Dr. Sun Fêng-wên's *Modern Chinese Social Problems,* Dr. Ma Yin-ch'u's *Outline of Economics,* and Dr. Lo Chia-lun's *A New Outlook on Life* have continuous sales; the last-mentioned has had seven printings.

The monthly magazine *K'ang Chan Wên I* (Wartime Literature) is published by the Ch'uan Kuo Wên I Chieh K'ang Ti Hsieh Hui, or National Writers Antiaggression Association, now reorganized as the National Writers Association. The Central Cultural Movement Committee publishes *Wên I Hsien Fêng* (Literary Vanguard). The Time and Tide Institute prints *Shih Yü Ch'ao Wên I* (Time and Tide Literature), which is devoted to translations of Western literature. *Shih Chieh Wên Hsüeh* (World Literature), in the same field, is edited by three university professors. The dramatist Hsiung Fu-hsi (1900–) edits *Tang Tai Wên Hsüeh* (Contemporary Literature) and *Wên Hsüeh Ch'uang Tso* (Creative Literature) in Kueilin. *Hsin Wên Hsüeh* (New Literature), in the same city, had to reprint its first issue to satisfy the demand.

Many wartime translations of foreign works have been made, for example, Wendell L. Willkie's *One World,* Joseph Davies' *Mission to Moscow,* John Gunther's *Inside Europe* and *Inside Latin America,* and biographies of Franklin Delano Roosevelt and Winston Churchill. Works by Tolstoi, Gorki, and Turgenev have appeared in several translations. A bookstore in Kueiyang systematically republishes the complete works of Shakespeare and Dickens in new and revised editions. Kuo Mo-jo's translation of Goethe's *The Sorrows of Young Werther* enjoys a steady popularity. The Writers Bookstore in Chungking profits by the Chinese flair for French literature in new translations of Victor Hugo, Flaubert, Maupassant, and Balzac.

Recent fiction from America and England in translation includes Eric Knight's *This Above All,* John Steinbeck's *The Moon Is Down* (in half-a-dozen translations appearing about the same time) and *The Grapes of Wrath,* two versions of Margaret Mitchell's *Gone with the Wind,* Daphne du Maurier's *Rebecca,* Ernest Hemingway's *For Whom the Bell Tolls.*

The arts, especially painting and woodcutting, have been making great strides. Ju Péon, in Chungking, has equal mastery in Western techniques of oil painting and in Chinese brush painting of bamboos and misty landscapes. His versatility is amazing: huge Veronese-like murals of canvas depicting ancient revolutionary scenes, wild horses on the run, portraiture in oil and crayon. (See chap. xxii, above.) Ju Péon is but one of many artists who have freed themselves from the past and from the West. Their exhibitions in Chungking and Chengtu draw vast crowds, and many war loans have been launched by their splendid paintings.

In the northwest the Lü Hsün Hsüeh Yüan Art School of Yenan University, named for Lü Hsün, has produced peasant wood engravers of realism and power. Their illustrations, now printed in many a Western book (e.g., Gunther Stein's *The Challenge of Red China*) and magazine, bring home the humor and stark experiences of *The People* vs. *Fascism.*

The theme of all the wartime music—concertos, operas, soldiers' road songs, students' college songs, chanted recitatives—is the death struggle against fascism. Orchestral concerts, and operas like *Akiko,* in which musicians and poets collaborate, have been presented in Chungking. Collections of Yangtze River boat songs have been printed.

Are the arts and literature of wartime China an enduring part of the country's eternal culture? It is too early to say. No one involved in the conflict has had time, as yet, to make intellectual or artistic appraisal. In the words of a Chinese student, "I still maintain that the Chinese people are mere caterpillars painfully wriggling in the dust of the Earth, and that ultimately they will be butterflies flitting in the sunshine, their wings dusty with the gold of Heaven. They will be no longer the victims of Japan, but spirits emancipated for wide adventure."

CHAPTER XXVIII

China: A Frontier in American Literature

BY ALICE TISDALE HOBART

LITERATURE SEEKS FRONTIERS in either the intangible outposts of mind and spirit or the more tangible outposts of new lands and industries. This is because literature is born of the imagination—an imagination made pregnant by events which stimulate individuals or nations to daring adventure, romantic living, struggle, suffering, growth.

American literature was early informed with the rich and gorgeous frontiers of the East. Old Europe, in avid pursuit of the riches of the Indies, discovered America and bequeathed to the continent's earliest white settlers the heritage of its adventurous craving for that extreme eastern frontier. Scarcely had the young United States finished cutting itself off from England and begun looking around for external sources of wealth than it settled upon trade with Canton. Long before its citizens had reached out to the virgin lands of the Middle West and the gold of California, their ships had rounded the Horn and the Cape of Good Hope to enter the harbors of China. America's first great fortunes came from Cathay.

This outpost was at first exclusively one of trade, a frontier different from all other frontiers the young nation was to know. Men found it not raw, unsettled territory like that of the West, but settled and old in tradition, steeped in the refinements and finesse of ancient cultures. Its products—teas, porcelains, carvings, and silks—lent beauty and graciousness to the material life of the new republic, heretofore bred chiefly to the stern simplicities of an undeveloped country. The mental qualities of ancient China, its age-old philosophies, its smooth shrewdness in bargaining, and its suave and at times slightly mocking politeness, which character- ized business as well as social relationships, on occasion developed sophistication in the rough and ready pioneer sea captains.

Stories told by returning sailors stimulated the imagination of their listeners. The adventures of long voyages, the customs and dress of the strange and faraway Chinese, came to form part of the lore of the new United States. Today in New England one finds numerous relics of the clipper ship era and of eighteenth- and early nineteenth-century China. In small white cottages as well as in ship captains' foursquare mansions with lookouts to the sea one is apt to note a fragile bit of porcelain or a carved wooden chest handed down from more romantic times.

It is impossible to estimate either the direct and conscious or the indirect and unconscious influence of China on American litera- ture. From the days of the pioneers, who told and read stories in the flickering light of pine knots and homemade candles, to the days of luxurious homes and world-famous museums, men and women have repeated to their children the tales which their fathers told them, and which family traditions have preserved, of the Salem trade, of pirates and opium, of shipwreck and danger, of tea clip- pers racing each other from Canton to London.

Generations of boys and girls dreaming in the firelight have had their imaginations stirred and have gazed beyond the horizons of their own land to that more ancient one peopled by such figures as those of Yang Kuei-fei, Kublai Khan, and the Hong merchant, Houqua. In the mind's eye they have watched the tragic parting of the T'ang Emperor Hsüan-tsung and the Lady Yang, or witnessed the farewells of Kublai Khan and Messer Marco Polo, and of Marco Polo and the lovely princess whom he escorted to a royal husband in Persia, they have looked with fascination upon Houqua—in his day "the richest man in the world"—and meditated upon his glow- ing eyes, his hollowed cheeks, his calm and remote bearing. In imag- ination, with their grandfathers or great-grandfathers, they have walked with Houqua in his gardens at Canton, down paths the tiny stones of which were embedded in the packed earth to form patterns of birds and flowers, and have stood with him on small

arched bridges looking into the waters of artificial lakes abloom
with lotus and flashing with gold and silver and copper-hued fish.

Some of them pondered over the restricted lives of American and
English merchants, members of the little foreign colony outside the
walls of Canton—virtual prisoners since they were not allowed by
the mandarins to leave the small area allocated to them for ware-
houses and temporary residences.

In the early days, what writing was done in the new American
nation drew consciously for its forms and often for its substance
upon Europe, of which it was an offshoot. Nevertheless, the influence of Asia was at work in the new nation.

The first Americans in Macao and Canton were men of action
and business. Their chronicles were limited in the main, but not
exclusively, to business reports, ships' logs, family letters, and an
occasional diary kept to satisfy the personal need for expression.[1]
Most of these writings lie untouched and forgotten in attics here
and there in New England, New York, and Pennsylvania, and in
far Canton—rich treasure to be sought out some day by historians
and novelists. Such records are the raw material of literature.

But China was not always to be simply a frontier of trade. It
proved to be a frontier of the mind, discovered and rediscovered
by succeeding waves of explorers. It was not long before American
Protestant missionaries began going to China, as European Roman
Catholic and Greek Orthodox workers had been doing for centuries. In time these American religious, social, and scientific intellectuals, or semi-intellectuals, penetrated beyond the seaports of
traders into the hinterland of China. They were an expressive
group, these missionaries, pouring forth letters and reports in vast
quantities. In some cases their genius was sufficiently sustained to
produce books. They wrote, as had their forerunners, about the
geography of the country, about the people and their customs,
about the country's religions and philosophies. Some of these works
were descriptive and not without beauty; others were passionate
polemics in which beauty was not a predominating characteristic.

For many an American village in the nineteenth century these
books were among the few that drifted in from the coast cities.
And through them China once more became a frontier of the imag-

[1] For notes to chapter xxviii see page 539.

ination. Much of the writing was marred by narrow-mindedness or even intolerance, but here and there an author saw beyond the limitations of his own civilization and religious sect and wrote without condescension or disapproval of the Chinese, their ways of living, their outlook on life. Occasionally, one of these accounts came close to being a classic. Some man or woman far from his own shores, seeking to give expression to the beauties as well as the terrors of a great experience, succeeded in making China live in all its color and mystery. In half-forgotten mission and other libraries one comes across such books. They are a part of America's heritage.

Thus men and women bent on trade or on "saving the souls" of Chinese performed for their own countrymen this other function. Through such works another generation of Americans living in prairie towns and mountain settlements was introduced to the ancient Middle Kingdom. They came to know the great northern plains of Asia, an unrelieved land of yellow-red-brown soil and yellow-red-brown, mud-walled villages. They learned about the rich valley of the Yangtze with its thousand-hued banks. They learned of another order of architecture, as classically magnificent as any elsewhere evolved—ornate and beautiful, and therefore strangely disturbing to certain puritanical Americans drilled to simplicity and repression.

Gradually a minority of these Americans, bent on spreading their interpretation of life and religion, became acquainted with a few Chinese philosophers such as Confucius and Lao Tzŭ. Most missionaries, hypercritical of non-Christian ways of thought, impressed upon home audiences how inadequate or even wrong were such ways of thinking and living. But the "new" Chinese ideas took root in certain minds and again imagination was stirred and made to reach out to alien frontiers of thought. These can be traced in the writings, *inter alia,* of Ralph Waldo Emerson and Emily Dickinson. Emerson consciously and unconsciously drew on the Confucian philosophy of human relations. And who of the students of Lao Tzŭ, in reading Emily Dickinson, is not aware that she knew something of his mystic thought? Her terse couplets with their vivid imagery make one suspect, too, that she may have been influenced by the strict discipline of form of Chinese poetry as well as by its imagery.

But only within the last few decades has China broken through and become a consciously exploited frontier of American literature. American writers have at last discovered China for themselves, have realized the rich gifts it has given and yet has to give, and frankly made use of them for their own country's and for China's good. At first, unhappily, Western writers—for example, Bret Harte—tended to portray the "Celestial" as sinister and gave the world the picture of a wicked, long-nailed villain—the stock figure of mystery thrillers. Then suddenly, or so it seemed, writers began to explore that far-off frontier of culture and to look at it through the eyes of realism, of truth.

In the past few decades a few—a very few—travelers, social workers, scholars, and poets have traveled to China with the object of trying to understand the country and its inhabitants. In addition to these and the missionaries in China who for more than a hundred years have been attempting the same thing, a minority of Occidental residents within the Middle Country—diplomats, businessmen, nonmissionary educators, and, on occasion, the wives of these individuals—have set themselves the same objective. A wave, or at least a ripple, of intelligent appreciation and a wealth of books—travel, biography, and fiction—have been the results. Nevertheless, only the surface of China and its civilization has been scratched; the complacent ignorance of America's population as a whole, including most of its intelligentsia, has not as yet been dented.

Still, Joseph Hergesheimer has produced his exquisite *Java Head*, which combines in one short novel the adventurous New England of the sailing ships and the languid sophistication of self-satisfied China. The Chinese wife thrown against the background of the New World *is* China with all its disturbing sophistication and exotic beauty.

No student of literature of this generation will ever forget the impact of Pearl Buck's *The Good Earth*. For the first time the peasant of China was drawn with the clear lines of realism. This faraway frontier was seen to be made up of people bound into the brotherhood of humanity by the common suffering and struggle.

In the following year Alice Tisdale Hobart's *Oil for the Lamps of China* was published, thereby strengthening the sense of mutuality and universality of experience in the contrasting cultures of

East and West. Through the defeats and triumphs of two men in business, a Chinese and an American, China came to life as the latest frontier of the industrial era. *River Supreme,* by the same author, describes with stark realism the ruthless forcing of China into the machine age. Here China is seen as an unwilling frontier of the Industrial Revolution. In *Yang and Yin* is depicted the entrance of modern medical science and public health into China through missionary channels, and some of the effects therefrom.

The author of *The Good Earth* followed her second masterpiece (the first having been *East Wind: West Wind,* the unfortunately little known but not the less valuable study of the social and intellectual conflict between old and new China and between China and the West) with equally true portrayals of Chinese bandits, war lords, and patriots, presenting contemporaneously, in *The Patriot, Dragon Seed,* and *The Promise,* pictures of China and the Chinese despoiled by Japanese aggression.

In this period also was published Dorothy Graham's *The China Venture,* a three-generation story of Western impact upon China; James W. Bennett's *Son of the Typhoon,* a stirring tale of student action culminating in the affair of May 30, 1925; and Nora Waln's *The House of Exile,* a romantic tale which sets forth with considerable idealism, in the form of an autobiography, the life of certain of China's materially fortunate groups.

As in the days of America's beginnings, through these novels Westerners were brought close to the life of that ancient race living on the other rim of the Pacific. Year by year the rich tapestry of China's culture—its philosophy, its history, its poetry—has been increasingly revealed to Occidental eyes, disclosing frontiers of thought never dreamed of before.

Florence Ayscough gave to the Western world charmingly colorful and scholarly essays on the foundations of Chinese culture, and translations of the lovely imagery which lies in Chinese poetry. At first, with Amy Lowell, she put many of those images into the forms best understood by Westerners. Then, with the spirit of the true explorer, she began translating literally the works of Tu Fu, greatest of Chinese poets. Through these translations she has led students of poetry and comparative literature into a new land, a wholly Eastern land. (See chap. xxi, above.)

Many others, such as Eunice Tietjens and Witter Bynner, have put into verse and drama the beauty and the ugliness, the joy and the tragedy of China—the grandeur of its rivers and mountains, the slow march of camels along a city wall, the whine of its beggars, the sound of its temple bells at evening, the echoes of battles, the moans of the starving, a Gobi dust storm half concealing, half revealing the yellow-tiled roofs and rose-tinted walls of the Forbidden City.

And in yet another way China is being developed as a frontier of American literature. There is a group of men and women scholars who are seeing to it that the vast store of books centered around Chinese ideals of human relationships shall become part of the West's cultural heritage. In the Library of Congress, and in less formidable collections over the country, Chinese books are being studied, translated, digested, and stored for future generations. Arthur Hummel, curator of the growing treasure of Orientalia at the Library of Congress, profoundly influenced by the Confucian conception, has spent many years gathering these works—ancient, medieval, and modern—and seeing that the best are translated.[2] What such a contribution may mean to Western thought and to world literature can but be guessed. Perhaps only those closely attuned to Chinese conceptions of art, religion, and philosophy will be conscious that these infiltrations *are* infiltrations. It is possible that the rank and file will think them indigenous. If so, the East will indeed have penetrated the West, for only as the written word absorbs and re-presents ideas and makes them its own does it become literature.

CHAPTER XXIX

Modern Education

BY FRANCIS LISTER HAWKS POTT

CHINA OWES THE BEGINNINGS of modern education to the efforts of Christian missionaries, especially to those sent from the United States and England. The establishment of elementary schools became part of the policy of both Protestant and Roman Catholic missions. There were, however, striking differences between the methods of these two bodies. The Roman Catholics aimed chiefly at providing, for children of their converts, both religious and elementary secular education. The Protestants opened their doors to non-Christian as well as Christian students as a means of broad evangelization and modernization of the state. For some time, Roman Catholics neglected the development of higher education on a wide scale. They had institutions for educating candidates for the priesthood, but none for the youth of the country in general. In later years they changed their policy, as was demonstrated by the founding of Aurora University in Shanghai and Fu Jên University in Peking.

The interest taken by Protestants in education may be ascribed to many causes, among which was the difficulty experienced in making an impression on the adult portion of an extremely conservative people. Wherever the Protestant missionary gained a footing, he opened primary schools, especially for children of the poorer classes. These schools taught classical Chinese literature, but also gave instruction in the Christian Scriptures, arithmetic, geography, and natural science. At first the teaching was done in day schools. Later it became possible to open boarding schools for boys and for girls. The schools for girls constituted a novelty.

The first boarding school was founded in 1807 by Robert Morrison, the first Protestant missionary to China, who had earlier established the Anglo-Chinese College at Malacca. Chinese, English, and modern science were taught in this school. After Morrison died, a boarding school to perpetuate his memory was established, first in Macao and later in Hongkong (1849).

As evidence that these elementary schools founded by Protestant missions had an influence far beyond that envisaged by their founders, reference may be made to the career of Yung Wing (rung hung),[1] a student in the Morrison School. When the Rev. Samuel Robbins Brown, in charge of the school, was forced by ill health to return to the United States in 1847, he took with him Yung Wing and two other Chinese students. After studying in a New England preparatory school, Yung was admitted to Yale University, from which he was graduated in 1854—the first Chinese to obtain a degree from an American institution. After his return to China, Yung Wing set to work to persuade the government to send a selected number of youths to study in the United States. In spite of opposition he succeeded, in 1872, in organizing the first Chinese educational mission to America. For four successive years, groups of thirty Chinese lads were sent, with Yung himself heading the mission.

At first the experiment worked well, but charges were later made that the students were being denationalized and that on returning home they would become a disturbing factor. In 1881 a hundred students were recalled before they had finished the college course. Although Yung Wing's project was abandoned, seed had been sown which came to fruition. Some of the students educated in this way—for example, T'ang Shao-yi and Liang Ju-hao (ru-hao) (courtesy given name, Mêng-t'ing)—occupied prominent positions at the time of the Revolution of 1911–1912.

Christian mission schools had a clear field for many years and met with no competition from government schools and colleges. Eventually, several preparatory and high schools developed into colleges and universities. Thirteen such institutions were founded, two of which—Ginling and Hwa Nan—are colleges for women.

In the spread of higher Protestant mission education two things

[1] For notes to chapter xxix see pages 539–540.

were extremely important. One was the use of English as the medium of instruction in "Western" studies—mathematics, modern science, history, political science, sociology, economics, and philosophy—partly because of the scarcity of Chinese texts for these subjects. Moreover, knowledge of English opened the door to the great storehouses of knowledge of the Western world. Many students in missionary colleges were eager to continue their education in the United States or England and therefore needed thorough grounding in English. A study of *Who's Who in China* reveals that a rather large number of prominent men received their first education in Christian institutions and later studied in American universities.

The other was that, as many missionary institutions in China had been founded by Americans, a relatively close relationship developed between these institutions and the American system of education. That the work of their colleges in China might be recognized and obtain for the graduates privileges similar to those enjoyed by college graduates in the United States, mission boards took steps to incorporate their Chinese higher educational institutions in the United States. In this way they obtained the right to confer degrees. This was an important, if unforeseen, extension of the privilege of extraterritoriality conferred by treaties between the United States and China. Some Christian institutions of higher learning obtained charters from the Board of Regents of New York State or from other states; one was incorporated in the District of Columbia.

It is impossible to trace the far-reaching influences, direct and indirect, of Protestant and Catholic missionary educational institutions in China. It may be said without exaggeration, however, that Christian education has been one of the chief causes of that country's awakening, with subsequent resurrection to a position of world importance, and that influence in this direction was exerted long before government and private colleges came into existence. Christian education has supplied to China many of its most distinguished leaders, men who have taken prominent positions in government and who have been leaders in Christian and other philanthropic movements.

When the central government somewhat belatedly decided to

establish a new system of education, its members found missionary institutions well established and providing models for the proposed government institutions.

◇ ◇ ◇

The Fourth Sino-Japanese War, that of 1894–1895, revealed that one of the causes of China's defeat was its antiquated system of education. In the course of the brief attempt at reform made in 1898 by the liberal Kuang-hsü emperor,[2] one of the proposals put forward was for a complete change in education.

By a coup d'état the Empress Dowager Tz'ŭ-hsi[3] resumed the regency and a desperate attempt was made by conservatives to stem the tide of liberal-radical reform. As a consequence, in part, the reactionary Boxer movement assumed serious dimensions when the Boxers attempted to "drive the Westerners into the sea." Their failure forced the empress dowager to change her policy, at least outwardly: in 1902, while still a fugitive in Sian, Shensi, she issued an edict enjoining officials to acquaint themselves with international law and political science.

After her return to Peking, Tz'ŭ-hsi appointed a commission to draft a public school system. The two commissioners were Viceroy Chang Chih-tung (jang jzh-dung),[4] who issued a famous work entitled *Ch'üan-hsüeh P'ien* (Learn, or Exhortation to Study), published in 1898, and Chang Po-hsi,[5] minister of education. The report of the commission, issued in 1904, recommended a system of education largely copied from that of Japan. It provided for the training of boys only, although some attention was elsewhere given to the founding of private schools for girls. Yet, aside from what missionaries were doing, the education of girls was generally neglected until after the Revolution of 1911–1912.

Previous to 1904 certain provincial authorities had established private schools offering modern education, but as long as the government maintained the ancient examination system and as long as that system served as the ladder to official employment the new schools were not popular. (See chap. i, above.)

On September 1, 1905, an imperial edict abolished the almost two-thousand-year-old imperial examination system. In consequence, great enthusiasm was manifested for the establishment of modern schools. Old temples were turned into schoolhouses and money was raised from taxes and private sources to carry out the projects. One of the chief difficulties was the lack of well-trained teachers; for a time those who had been employed and (or) educated in mission schools were in great demand. The first years of the experiment were characterized by confusion and inefficiency, but determined efforts were made to surmount difficulties.

Interest in the modernization of learning was stimulated by the action of the United States government in remitting a large portion of the Boxer indemnity fund. In the administration of President Theodore Roosevelt, more than $12,000,000 was remitted. The imperial government decided to use this money for educational purposes. A large amount was used for the founding of Tsing Hua College (later University) near Peking. In its early years the chief aim of this institution was the training of young men so that they might complete their education abroad. Many of its graduates have rendered valuable service in the modernizing of their homeland. The privilege of studying in the United States was extended subsequently to students selected by competitive examination from other schools. It is interesting to note that Dr. Hu Shih, ambassador to the United States from 1938 to 1942, was one of the earlier successful candidates in these examinations.

When it was found that the sum retained by the United States government was still in excess of the damage wrought by the Boxers, there was a further remission of the indemnity fund, amounting to $10,400,000. The actions of the Washington government were, on the whole, deeply appreciated by the government of China, and helped to promote international good will. Other nations followed in the footsteps of the United States, although their governments did not give to China so high a degree of control over the funds remitted as did that of the United States. There are ten Chinese and five Americans on the board of control of the American indemnity fund.

⋄   ⋄   ⋄

With the establishment of the Republic in 1911–1912 great hopes were entertained for the progress of modern education. Political conditions, however, seriously hampered the movement. The attempt of President Yüan Shih-k'ai to make himself emperor plunged the country into civil strife. (See chap. ix, above.) War lords controlling various sections contended with one another for supreme mastery and costly confusion ensued.

If the abolition in 1905 of the imperial examinations be taken as the starting point of official adoption of the new education in China, its history extends over less than forty years. The thirty years preceding the Japanese invasion of 1937 may be divided into three periods.

The first period, from 1905 to 1918, was one of experimentation. In addition to the previously noted lack of qualified teachers there was a scarcity of textbooks in the Chinese language. This need was met in part by rapid growth of educational publishing firms, such as the Commercial Press in Shanghai.

The period was also marked by a utilitarian spirit. The ancient educational system had been regarded primarily as the pathway to official employment; the new system was looked upon in the same way. The conception of the vast content of modern thought and education was inadequate; consequently, the idea prevailed that the road to their acquirement was short and easy. During these years great numbers of students went to Japan: at one time as many as 30,000 Chinese were attending Japanese schools and colleges. The majority of these students hoped that, through the medium of the Japanese language, they might find a short cut to Western or modern learning.

The second period extended from 1918 to 1928. This decade was revolutionary. The First World War and the Russian Revolution of 1917 resulted, in part, in the development and dissemination of many ideas regarding democracy and freedom. Communism exerted strong influence. Many students turned away from what was avowedly old and accepted with avidity all that was accredited with being new. They resented school discipline and agitated for control over teachers, educational authorities, and curricula. Numbers of them became extremely censorious of the government and vociferously criticized its weaknesses in policy and action.

This period was marked also by student strikes. On occasion, members of the student body, female as well as male, in order to arouse public opinion on national affairs, refused to continue academic work and expended their efforts in political propaganda. Clashes between youths and politico-military authorities became frequent; these disturbances resulted at times in lamentable consequences. Even in the early postwar years, however, student political efforts met with considerable success, and the student movement is now recognized as having constituted a factor of the utmost importance in the National Salvation revolution. One of the most notable student activities was the prevention of the Peking government from agreeing to the terms of the Treaty of Versailles because it gave to Japan the rights formerly possessed by Germany in Kiaochow (jiao-jou) and elsewhere in Shantung province. Interfering on many other occasions in business as well as political matters, student groups sometimes went to excess and, to many adults at least, seemed to act very unreasonably. As a result, students were at times regarded as a turbulent element by many of the commercial, military, and official classes, native and foreign.

The third period, that of centralization, extended from 1928 to 1937. Gradually the government became conscious that if the new education was to prove of the utmost value it must be brought under control. To effect this purpose, full powers of administration were given to the Ministry of Education, which began to determine qualifications of teachers, scholastic standards, discipline, school revenue, and appointment of administrators. Registration of all institutions—governmental, missionary, and private—was required by the Ministry of Education. Only those conforming to this regulation received recognition of their diplomas and degrees and were privileged to receive government subsidies. Centralization of authority helped to bring order out of chaos and led to a period of remarkable growth in numbers of institutions and students in attendance. The students were no less politically minded than formerly, but they came again to recognize the value of thorough education for those who wished effectively to serve their country.

❖ ❖ ❖

In 1921–1922 a group of educational experts from the United States visited China under the leadership of Professor (later President) Ernest DeWitt Burton, of the University of Chicago. Chinese educators coöperated with the visitors, whose purpose was to make "a thorough study of Protestant education in China, and to formulate recommendations for future development." The report issued by the group members, Chinese and foreign, was of great value. Unfortunately, however, it aroused suspicion in non-Christian Chinese educational circles. Some were jealous of the work and discipline of Christian schools and colleges; others feared that Westerners would develop a separate and independent system of education in the country. A wave of intense nationalism spreading through vast areas in and after 1919 led to a determined effort to bring all educational institutions under government control.

Passage of time was necessary to allay suspicion with reference to the purposes of the Burton group. Gradually, however, it became evident that its members, as well as other Western and Chinese Christian educators in China, aimed at coöperation with the central government in the enormous task of extending modern education, and that most missionary and other nongovernmental educators were ready to accept governmental regulation of private institutions.

Missionary institutions, although rendering valuable service and continuing to exert an appreciable influence, have been overshadowed in recent years by government institutions. This is evidenced by the fact that of the 108 colleges and universities in China only 13 are supported by Protestant missions. The percentage of students in missionary schools and universities is small when compared to the total number.

At the request of the central government in Nanking a mission of educational experts, appointed by the League of Nations, visited China in 1932. Its object was to make a thorough study of the national system of education and to offer recommendations for improvement. The ensuing report charged that the Chinese system was based to too great a degree upon that of the United States.

Education in contemporary China owes much to the nineteenth- and twentieth-century efforts of American educators. After the central government and several provinces had begun to foster modern education in contrast to the ancient classical system, Dr. Paul Monroe, of Columbia University, acted as adviser to the Chinese Ministry of Education in organizing the new system. It is therefore not surprising that American influence has been strong, educationally speaking, in present-day China. The criticism by the League of Nations experts may be somewhat discounted in view of the fact that it was made exclusively by men educated in Europe. Nevertheless, their report contained valuable recommendations, especially for secondary education: the need for better laboratory education in middle (i.e., high) schools was emphasized.

In recent years the Chinese Ministry of Education has been influenced by European educational theory and practice to a somewhat greater degree than was formerly the case. Chinese who have studied in France and Germany have been appointed to important posts in the field of education. How far this was due to the report of the committee appointed by the League of Nations it is not possible to say.

◇ ◇ ◇

Reports issued by the Ministry of Education in recent years indicate a remarkable growth of modernism in ideals, methods, and results under the Republic. The following comparison of the figures reported in 1912, the first year of the Republic, with those reported for the year 1937, at the time of the Nipponese invasion of northern China, reveals phenomenal progress. In 1912 there were only four government institutions of university status, with an enrollment of 481 students. The amount appropriated for their support was $735,780. In 1937 there were 108 colleges and universities, including the 13 founded by Protestant Christian missions, with an enrollment of 42,920 students. Expenditures amounted to $33,574,000.

In secondary education the increase is even more remarkable. In 1912 there were 373 middle schools with an enrollment of 52,000 students and expenditures of $3,034,703.[6] In 1937 the total number of middle schools, including normal and vocational schools, was 3,047; these reported an enrollment of 546,212 students and expenditures of $55,299,839. This showed a tenfold increase in number of schools and pupils.

The figures for elementary education are astonishing. In 1912 there were 83,319 schools with 2,795,475 pupils, with an expenditure of $19,334,480. In 1937 there were 259,000 schools with a total of 11,684,300 pupils; expenditures amounted to $93,625,513.

The Ministry of Education is aware of the innumerable problems still to be solved. Compulsory elementary education has not received sufficient attention. In a country with so low a standard of living as that prevailing in China—where child labor greatly helps in the support of the family—it was impossible to carry out immediately this drastic reform. Attempt is being made to reach the goal by progressive steps extending over a number of years. In 1932 a one-year compulsory course was introduced for all children of school age. It was thought at first that eight years might be needed to effectuate the program of three years' education for all children of school age, but this period had to be extended. Lack of funds, also, made the introduction of free education a strain on government resources. In 1931 it was estimated that children of school age in the entire country numbered 50,140,000, of whom less than 30 per cent were under instruction.

Another great problem to be faced is the high percentage of illiteracy among the adult population. Two men have played leading parts in attempting to bring education to illiterates. A generation ago Dr. Hu Shih realized that one of the chief stumbling blocks to the spread of knowledge was the continued use of the classical literary style. He advocated introduction of *pai hua,* or the spoken language, in its place. In this way a vernacular literature was developed which is comprehensible to those of limited education.

The other leader in the adult education movement is Dr. Y. C. James Yen. In order to reach illiterate adults he compiled a list of the thousand—later thirteen hundred—characters most frequently used in *pai hua* literature. By experimentation in teaching adult classes he demonstrated that these characters could be mastered by soldiers and laborers in a comparatively short time. Knowledge of these characters makes it possible to read simple, specially prepared literature.[7] It has been found, moreover, that a knowledge of a thousand characters serves as a spur to the acquisition of a larger number. The Ministry of Education has encouraged the mass education movement by supporting night schools and special classes.

Attempts have been made to introduce a system of phonetic writing into elementary schools so that reading may more quickly be acquired. Primary school textbooks, with phonetics by the side of the characters, have been published. The phonetic system is intended to serve the purpose that *kana* does in Japan. It has not

met with general favor, however, partly because it calls for the production of a new literature printed in phonetics, and partly because
the Chinese, conservatives and liberals alike, are devoted to their
age-old and aesthetically satisfying system of writing with ideo-
grams. (See chap. xxi, above.)

The Ministry of Education, keenly aware of its responsibility, is
endeavoring to improve methods of learning. Indeed, new regulations are so constantly introduced that at times institutions find
it difficult to act in accord with the changing requirements.[8] The
tendency toward experimentation is strong—which is not to be
wondered at, in view of the vastness of the task involved in educating China's four or five hundred million.

◇ ◇ ◇

The war in and after 1937 caused a serious setback in carrying out
the program of the Ministry of Education. As soon as it was realized
that educational institutions were marked by the Nipponese for
destruction, it was decided to remove them to Unoccupied China.
Faculties and students in great numbers, carrying what equipment
they could, undertook a trek of fifteen hundred miles or more to
the west, northwest, and southwest. The number of those who went
to Yenan, Shensi, in Communist-controlled China is not known.

Seventy-seven institutions (universities, colleges, and technical
schools) left their homes. Of these, seventeen moved to Szechuan
and Hunan, fifteen to Yünnan, Kueichow (guei-jou), and Kuangsi
(guang-si), two to Shensi and Kansu, and eighteen to other districts
in the interior. Chengtu in Szechuan and Kunming in Yünnan became the leading educational centers; their institutions rendered
marked assistance to newcomers. Twenty-one higher educational
institutions in the neighborhood of Shanghai sought refuge in the
International Settlement and the French Concession. Four of these,
St. John's University, Soochow (su-jou) University, the University of Shanghai, and Hangchow (hang-jou) Christian College, entered into temporary coöperation in the International Settlement,
occupying one large building and sharing library and scientific
equipment.

Before its fall, Hongkong gave shelter to the colleges of Canton and of Kuangtung (guang-dung) province. Seventeen colleges

were obliged to close temporarily. Buildings of several well-known universities were damaged, and Nankai University in Tientsin was obliterated by systematic Japanese bombing and burning.

The value of buildings and equipment destroyed amounted to several hundred million dollars in Chinese currency. Of the five and a half million books which before the war had been accumulated in college libraries, more than half are reported to have disappeared. Losses in scientific equipment, also, were extremely heavy. In occupied areas more than a third of the middle, or high, schools were rendered inoperative and large numbers of students were deprived of educational facilities. In elementary education some six million students were affected.

Another result of the gigantic struggle between China and Nippon[9] was a decrease in numbers of students traveling to the United States for advanced study. In 1929 there were 1,034; in 1937 the number had declined to 366; in 1938 it had dropped to 59. This interruption in the flow of Chinese students abroad will be felt for years to come.

Students in Chinese universities were not generally encouraged to enlist in the armed forces. The government, realizing how few students there were, did not wish to interrupt their education. Since there is only one college student to every ten thousand persons in China, and no lack of man power, the reasons for this policy are easily appreciated.

In the war period the Ministry of Education adapted the curriculum to emergency conditions. Special emphasis was laid on technical studies and on military science. Although there may have been a decrease in the total number of students, all schools and colleges were overcrowded. Standards in college work were lowered from lack of preparatory training in the lower schools and from loss of library and scientific equipment. But the splendid morale of faculties and students and their determination to carry on under the most adverse circumstances are forever to be admired.

✧   ✧   ✧

With the conclusion of Sino-Japanese hostilities, divers educational movements in China will advance with increased momentum. The policy of governmental control of education will become stronger and all educational institutions, government and private, will be obliged to conform to standardized regulations. A stereotyped system of education may hinder freedom in experimentation; missionary and other private colleges will probably lose some of their former privileges. Schools and colleges founded by private enterprise or by philanthropic organizations will have the same status as those supported by government funds.

Another trend is toward making education less humanistic and increasingly utilitarian. The Chinese are a practical people and take naturally to the philosophy of pragmatism. The value of education in the liberal arts may for a time be overshadowed. The Ministry of Education now attempts to determine the proportion of students to be admitted into arts and science courses and seeks to increase the number of the latter. It also exercises authority by determining, or attempting to determine, which students shall go abroad after indoctrination in Kuomintang principles, what studies shall be pursued by those who go abroad, how such students shall think while they are abroad, and how students returned from abroad shall be indoctrinated before entering upon careers in their homeland.

Research institutions will probably receive increasing attention. The Ministry of Education has long been conscious of this need. The Academia Sinica was founded for the purpose of stimulating research. With excellent laboratories and splendid equipment, it was carrying on valuable work when its labors were interrupted by the outbreak of war in 1937. Work in special research institutions will be supplemented by graduate study in the larger government universities under supervision of the Ministry of Education.

The old educational system in China produced scholars who devoted their lives to absorbing and dispersing humanistic learning. That class is rapidly disappearing. The government is anxious to replace it by men who will devote themselves to scientific study and research. ◇ ◇ ◇

In this review an attempt has been made to show the stages through which modern education in China has passed and how such education has introduced a new ideology which is leavening the old civilization politically, socially, and industrially.

Dr. Tsur Ye-tsung (jou yi-chun), one of China's leading educators, under whose administration Tsing Hua College became one of the foremost institutions in the country, gives the following estimate of the influence of modern education and of modern-trained students:

It does not seem possible to give an adequate estimate of what the students as a whole have done for their country. But probably it is within the bounds of safety, as well as propriety, to say that it has been due entirely to their efforts and influence that the country is being modernized. To be specific, the early returned students from America and a few from Great Britain toiled hard to clear the soil and sow the seed. Those coming after them, though in larger numbers, had naturally a much easier task to perform. To them as a class must be credited, in spite of the very decided and far-reaching contributions by other parties, the introduction of Western ideals and ideas, the institution of fundamental reforms, and the gradual transformation of the social and political order of the country along modern lines. More than anything else that will stand out as a monument to their achievement and influence is the change of the country from a monarchy to a republic, from an absolute despotism to a popular democracy, from an antiquated conservatism to a modern liberalism.

Judging from what modern education[10] has already accomplished there is good reason to be optimistic concerning its achievements in the postwar period.

CHAPTER XXX

China's Examination System
and the West

BY TÊNG SSǓ-YÜ

THE IMPORTANCE of school and civil service examinations is widely recognized. Few people, however, realize that the ancient Egyptian, western Asiatic, Greek, and Roman empires made no use of civil service examinations, and that China was the first country to develop open competitive examinations for school and governmental purposes. In the adoption of civil service examinations by England and other countries in the nineteenth century, the influence of the precedent established by the Han, Sui, T'ang, and Sung rulers of the Middle Kingdom was by no means small.

A system of recommendations and examinations stressing moral excellence was instituted in China under the Western, or Former, Han dynasty in 165 B.C. Thereafter, examinations were used at intervals. In A.D. 622, however, a solid foundation was laid for essentially open, competitive literary examinations which took place periodically both locally and at the capital. Beginning in 1066, examinations at the capital were held triennially.

From 1370 on, the system was so adjusted that the student who passed a district examination was known as a *hsiu-ts'ai,* or budding genius; one who passed at a provincial capital became a *chü-jên* (jü-ren), or promoted man; and one who was successful at the national capital became a *chin-shih* (dzin-shzh), or achieved scholar. The three honors corresponded roughly to the Western bachelor's, master's, and doctor of philosophy degrees. The examinations stressed classical literary knowledge rather than technical learning. A probationary period was imposed for civil servants who had passed the official examination. The system was generally conducted with regularity and rigidity until its abolition in 1905.

Though the earliest Western university oral examination is traceable to "a period subsequent to 1219," yet, according to *The New English Dictionary*, "examination" is a word not used in the sense of "test" until 1612. Most combinations of the term, such as "examination paper" and "examination questions and answers," first appeared as late as the nineteenth century. The year 1702 is considered by most writers to mark the beginning of written examinations in Europe. In 1747 the mathematical tripos was instituted; in 1802 appeared the first real examination for the bachelor's degree.

France adopted a civil service examination system in the course of the Revolution of 1791; Germany, around 1800; India, in 1855. England applied the Indian system to all home services in 1870. Thus scholastic examinations were held not much earlier than civil service examinations.

◇   ◇   ◇

Although there were contacts between the ends of the Eurasian continent before the Christian era and in the Middle Ages, no direct bearing of these relations upon the examination system can be traced. In the sixteenth century, European adventurers, traders, and Jesuit missionaries traveled to China. The most famous of the Jesuits was Matteo Ricci, who reached Macao in 1582, Canton in 1594, and Peking in 1601. Ricci was appointed to a high official position in the imperial government and associated with many Chinese scholars. He and other missionaries—also merchants, travelers, and diplomats—made reports to Europe on many subjects, including the Chinese examination system.

The earliest source mentioning selection of officials by "trial made of their learning," and the degrees of licentiates and doctors, is an account by Gaspar da Cruz, who sailed to China in 1556 and published a narrative of his travels[1] in 1569. A more detailed account is contained in the work of Juan Gonzales de Mendoça, entitled *The Historie of the Great and Mightie Kingdom of China, and the Situation Thereof*, published in London in 1588. Mendoça was a member of the abortive Spanish embassy to China in

---

[1] For notes to chapter xxx see pages 540–541.

1584. The fourteenth chapter of his first volume deals with competitive examinations, degrees and ceremonies, and methods of appointing officials.

In Samuel Purchas' *Hakluytus Posthumus*[2] there is "an excellent treatise of the Kingdome of China, and of the estate and government thereof," in which the Chinese examination system is described and praised. In the same collection (XII, 414–472) there appeared "A Discourse of the Kingdom of China taken out of Riccius and Trigantius." This contains a detailed description of examinations for degrees, both "philosophical and militarie," and outlines the governmental structure of China. The statement seems to have been based upon personal observation. Other detailed descriptions of examinations are to be found in Nicolas Trigault's *Du Voyage de la Chine*[3] and in Robert Burton's *The Anatomy of Melancholy*.[4]

In 1655, to satisfy "the curious and advance the Trade of Great Britain," an English translation of *The History of That Great and Renowned Monarchy of China* was published in London. This work had lately been written in Italian by Alvarez Semedo, a Portuguese, after a residence of twenty-two years at court and in the famous cities of China. It contained, *inter alia,* three chapters systematically explaining the procedure of the Chinese examination system.

One of the most influential works of the eighteenth century was Du Halde's *Description de la Chine,* published in Paris in 1735. It was soon translated into a number of languages and was widely read and reviewed.   ◇   ◇   ◇

Partly owing to the works mentioned above and partly to the political, social, and religious dissatisfaction of certain thinkers in Europe, there developed in France and England much admiration for Chinese civilization. Perhaps the most zealous of these thinkers was Voltaire, who considered China not as a country in which despotism flourished but as an absolute monarchy established on paternalism. He admired the dutiful Chinese officials who observed Confucian doctrine and were devoid of fanaticism: "The human mind certainly cannot imagine a government better than this one where everything is to be decided by the large tribunals, subordinated to each other, of which the members are received only after several severe examinations."[5]

Montesquieu, in *De l'Esprit des lois,* and Diderot, in his *Encyclopédie,* praised Chinese public administration and civilization. Rousseau regarded China as a country where scholarship led to the highest dignity of the state.

François Quesnay, in his *Discours sur l'économie politique,* eulogized the administration and justice of China, and wished to introduce the Chinese competitive examination system into Europe. Since he was the leader of the physiocrats and the most notable theorist of the neomonarchist school, Quesnay's ideas were influential. For this reason Ferdinand Brunetière, in the *Revue des Deux Mondes,* wrote that the physiocrats were united in the attempt to introduce "l'esprit chinois" into France. Brunetière believed that French education was really based on the Chinese principle of competitive literary examinations, and that the idea of a civil service recruited by competitive examinations owed its origin to the Chinese system which was popularized in France by the philosophers, especially by Voltaire.[6] This definite conclusion that the French system had its origin in China was adopted by several others.[7]

In England, Temple, Johnson, Addison, and Goldsmith expressed their appreciation of Chinese ideas. Several magazines advocated adoption of the civil service examination system. As early as 1733 an article on China in the *Gentleman's Magazine* pointed out that "the Chinese excell all other Nations in the Art of Government" and that "their Honour and Titles are not Hereditary" but are conferred once a year at the metropolis of China with writing as the only test.[8]

In *A Letter to Cleomenes, King of Sparta,* Eustace Budgell asserted that China was the best-governed of all empires, and discussed in detail the system of competitive examinations and of public censors:

> If any modern Politician should take it into his Head that this Maxim, however excellent in itself, cannot possibly be observed in so large and populous a Kingdom as Great Britain; I beg to inform such a Politician, that at this very time, this glorious Maxim is most strictly follow'd and observ'd in the *Largest,* the most *populous,* and the *best Govern'd* Empire in all the World; I mean in China.[9]

The merits of the competitive examination system were summarized in 1775 by John Nichols[10] in the following five points:

[First] The youths, whom idleness and sloth never fail to corrupt, are by constant employment diverted from ill courses. Secondly, study forms and polishes their wits. . . . Thirdly, all offices are filled by able men, and if they cannot prevent that injustice which proceeds from the covetousness and corrupt affections of officers, at least they will take care to hinder that which arises from ignorance and immorality. Fourthly, since the places are given, the emperor may with great justice turn out those officers whom he shall not find deserving. . . . Lastly, no fees are paid for the administration of justice.

These excerpts indicate that English intellectuals, as early as the seventeenth and eighteenth centuries, had a favorable impression of the Chinese examination system

Before going as first British ambassador to China in 1793, Lord Macartney had been governor general of Madras and Bengal, where he had fought against "enormous abuses in administration." In an abridged journal of the life of Macartney it is related that on his way to Peking the ambassador and his retinue stayed overnight at the examination hall of the provincial capital of Kiangsi. Sir George L. Staunton, secretary to Lord Macartney's embassy, praised the examination system and the government of China.[11]

His son, George T. Staunton, who followed him to China, wrote *Miscellaneous Notices Relating to China,* in which he says: "The short residence in China of Lord Macartney's Embassy, was amply sufficient to discover that their superiority over other nations is in point of knowledge and of virtue. . . . These literary degrees . . . are in fact the sole regular channel of introduction of official employment, and consequently to rank and honours, in the empire."[12] The younger Staunton's idea of Chinese government was widely quoted in contemporary works. He became so interested in Chinese governmental and legal systems that in 1812 he translated one of the most important codes, entitled *Ta-ch'ing Lü-li.* Two years later a French translation was produced incorporating regulations for the examinations.

⬦ ⬦ ⬦

In the nineteenth century many descriptions of the Chinese examination system appeared. The most important is in *A Dictionary of the Chinese Language,* by Robert Morrison. Other excellent accounts may be found in the writings of Charles Gutzlaff, W. H. Medhurst, and Thomas Taylor Meadows. In the first part of the Morrison *Dictionary* appears a long section on the examination system, its historical development, regulations, and practices.[13] It is based on primary sources and to this day constitutes one of the best accounts in the English language.

In 1834 Charles Gutzlaff wrote *A Sketch of Chinese History*,[14] containing an accurate and compact statement on the examination system. In another work published in 1838, *China Opened,* he declared: "In China, only talent, without the least respect to persons, is promoted. The principle is noble, and well worth the adoption of other countries."[15]

W. H. Medhurst's *China: Its State and Prospects* also contains a succinct chapter describing literary examinations. After listing advantages and disadvantages, this author concludes, "The system itself is truly admirable and worthy of imitation."[16]

In 1836 Hugh Murray, in *An Historical and Descriptive Account of China* (p. 169), and, in 1838, C. T. Downing, in *The Fan-qui in China* (II, 255), expressed their esteem for the principles of the Chinese examinations. Edouard Biot's *Essai sur l'histoire et l'instruction publique en Chine,* published in Paris in 1841, contains nearly all the information extant on the subject, digested in an extremely lucid manner.

The most persistent, indeed almost fanatical, advocate of the adoption of the Chinese system, however, was Thomas Taylor Meadows,[17] who reached China early in 1843 and returned to England on furlough in 1854. In two works, *Desultory Notes on the Government and People of China* (1847) and *The Chinese and Their Rebellions* (1856), he strongly recommended that England adopt a system of civil service examinations. In the preface and in several sections of the latter work (pp. 246–249), he summarized what he had written previously, and continued his promotion of "some well-digested system of local and metropolitan general examinations, for all British subjects, like that which has existed with little variation in China for the last thousand years, but in more useful matters, and followed by special metropolitan examinations, to be passed before admission to the various subdivisions of the executive."

It is to be noted that Meadows stressed the principle, not the details, of Chinese methods, so that a "well-digested system" might be worked out. Before he died, in 1869, he believed that he had accomplished something in this direction. However, an anonymous article in *Macmillan's Magazine* condemned his "eccentric work, both in its views and in the manner of expressing them" and adversely criticized the Chinese examination system as being of a country where "offices are notoriously sold to the highest bidder" (Vol. 135, 1871, pp. 216–223). This article was too late to influence the adoption of the British system, since the principle of civil service had already been passed in 1855 and had been put into effect in all offices in 1870. Proof of Meadows' influence is found in a comment regarding his work on China in the *Eclectic Review* (Vol. 104, 1856, pp. 550–560), in which the writer called on the reader to accept his opinion.

These are but a few examples of nineteenth-century accounts of the Chinese system.   ◇ ◇ ◇

The civil servants of the East India Company, originally called "factors" and "writers," were trained by an apprenticeship of several years. In 1789 the idea of a preliminary course for "writers" is said to have emanated from the Company's factory at Canton, and in the 'nineties resulted in a year's training in London in the tea trade for youths destined for service in China. In May, 1806, a college was established at Haileybury, near London, in which, until its abolition in 1858, Indian civil service probationers took a two-year course in general and Oriental education.

Haileybury College had no tests or examinations in its first seven or eight years. According to *Parliamentary Papers* (1831–32, 9 Indian Company 2 Public, 234), a law was enacted in 1814 for a test in "Orientals," and in 1819 for a similar test in European languages. The term "examination" was adopted in 1821. Results of the examinations of the East India College at Haileybury were announced in the *Asiatic Journal*.

Civil service examinations for India were apparently initiated in 1829 for those who had not passed through the East India College. In 1832 the Act of 7 Geo. 4, c. 56 operated to supply civil servants by examination without college residence. In 1833 an act prescribed that in future four candidates should be nominated for each vacancy at Haileybury; the nominees were then to compete in "an examination by such examiners as the Board of Control of the Company shall direct." Although this early attempt to introduce limited competition was soon suspended, Professor Herman Finer, in *The British Civil Service,* expresses belief that the germ of the idea of open competitive examinations "was generated in the reform of the English administration in India and was carried out in the Charter Act of 1833."[18]

In July, 1835, Robert Inglis, a British resident in China, wrote: "The British East India Company . . . have adopted the principle as far as election to the civil service . . . The full development in India of this Chinese invention is destined one day, perhaps, like those of gunpowder and printing, to work another great change in the states-system even of Europe."[19] In 1836 Mr. (later Sir) John Francis Davis, His Britannic Majesty's chief superintendent of trade in China, described Chinese civil service as "a plan not unlike that which has lately been adopted in the civil Government of British India."[20] No great change took place in the Indian civil service until 1853, when the queen's letter nominated and approved a commission to inquire into the organization of a permanent civil service. In 1855 the civil service examination for India was adopted.

Before 1855, England itself had no civil service examinations. But proposals had earlier been made for the improvement of the corrupt administration. One of the earliest was offered in 1776 by Adam Smith, in *The Wealth of Nations* (II, 270), that every man "undergo an examination or probation before he can obtain the freedom in any corporation to be allowed to set up any trade." According to M. F. Sadler's interpretation (*Essays on Examinations,* p. 55), Smith was influenced by the French Encyclopedists, who in turn were influenced by Chinese philosophy and government.

The first effective challenge to the system of patronage in domestic government appointments was given in 1853 when Gladstone commissioned Sir Charles Trevelyan and Sir Stafford Northcote to inquire into the organization of the "permanent civil service" and to report upon the best method of recruiting it. These gentlemen had had long connection with the East India Company. The Trevelyan-Northcote report of 1853, entitled "The Organization of the Permanent Civil Service," laid the foundation of the civil service examination system in England.

In June, 1853, Sir Charles Wood introduced the Act of 1853 to the House of Commons and made a speech strongly urging the House to pass the bill, "and pass without delay." In July, 1854, he asked Macaulay to head a committee of well-known men to report upon the recruitment of the Indian civil service. The "Report on the Indian Civil Service," signed by Macaulay and others, was immediately submitted to Parliament.

There is clearly a similarity between the ideas of the Macaulay report and the principles of the Chinese literary examinations. The report recommended that a central board of examiners should be constituted—as in China; that the examination should be a "competing literary examination in all cases"—as in China; that the competition should be not for specific appointments but for general knowledge—as in China; that the examination should be periodic and open to all—as was approximately the case in China; that the examination for the lower class of appointments should be local—as in China; that promotion should be made by merit instead of by favoritism—as was ordinarily the case in China. Emphasis on the moral character of candidates, a period of probation, and similar recommendations in the report are principles which had in general been practiced for more than a thousand years in China. How strange a coincidence, if there was no Chinese influence at all!

The *Edinburgh Review* (Vol. 139, p. 339) observed in 1874, "In fact the procedure resembles nothing in life so much as the system obtaining in China." *Fraser's Magazine* declared, "A great deal of clap-trap argument in favor of this system has been advanced, on no better foundation than its alleged success in China" (N.S., Vol. 7, November, 1873, p. 343).

The parliamentary debates of this period contained many references to Chinese influence on English civil service examinations. In 1853, in the House of Lords, Earl Granville declared that one of the principal reasons why a small Tatar dynasty had governed the immense empire of China for upward of two hundred years was that its rulers had secured the talent of the whole Chinese population by opening every official situation to competition (*Hansard's Parliamentary Debates*, CXXVIII, June 13, 1853, p. 38).

When the Trevelyan-Northcote report was brought up in Parliament, Lord Monteagle attacked it with asperity. His argument was that "the only precedent which exactly applies is that of the Empire of China." China was not an enlightened country, and the open competitive system was therefore poor (*ibid.*, CXXXI, March 13, 1854, p. 651). Lord Monteagle continued with a series of comparisons between the Chinese system and that recommended in the Trevelyan-Northcote report. He made liberal use of W. H. Medhurst's account of Chinese examinations. At the second reading, on June 23, 1853, Lord Stanley, also, said, "The right hon. Gentleman . . . had introduced a principle unknown in this country, but which was said to prevail in China, and therefore it might be called the Chinese principle" (*ibid.*, CXXVIII, July, 1853, p. 619). In *Papers Relating to the Civil Service* (Vol. 20, 1854–1855, p. 159), Edwin Chadwick wrote, on August 1, 1854: "One nobleman, himself an eminent public officer, objects to the measures proposed, because . . . the plan is Chinese—the Chinese having examinations for their civil service . . . I should fully concur with the noble friend and other objectors on the same grounds." Dean Carlisle also remarked, "Many point ominously to China as the best examined country in the world." All these contemporary witnesses acknowledge, willingly or unwillingly, Chinese influence on their civil service examinations.

More than two decades later, various periodicals continued to attack the competitive examinations as "an adopted Chinese culture." In 1875, for example, the London *Fortnightly Review* (N.S., Vol. 17, pp. 843, 844, 846) published an article by A. H. Sayce, who wrote: "At present the Chinese theory is in full possession of the public. . . . The present Chinese current of popular belief has degenerated into a mere examining machine." Therefore, he urged, "try to stem the invasion of this new Chinese culture. . . . Successful or unsuccessful alike, all . . . are ready to propagate the new doctrine of an adopted Chinese culture."

⋄ ⋄ ⋄

Investigation of more than seventy items[21] written between 1558 and 1870 by scholars, missionaries, diplomatic officials, and merchants warrants the following conclusions: (1) The time was early enough for the Chinese examination system to influence the Western system; (2) East and West were well connected by the above-mentioned writers; (3) there are similarities between the examination principles of the two countries; and (4) before the adoption of the civil service examination system in England (1855) the Chinese system was well known to the intelligentsia of Great Britain.

Thomas Taylor Meadows wrote in 1847: "The existence of a system of examinations, based on this principle [that good government consists in advancing only men of talent and merit to official posts] is well known to every educated European; and it is literally impossible to conceive that the various writers on China, from the Jesuit missionaries who lived upwards of 150 years ago, to the sinologues of the present day, can have failed to perceive the effects of this institution" (*Desultory Notes*, p. 124). It is therefore clear that the Chinese had a very considerable influence upon the beginnings of the English civil service examination system.

Part Five

ECONOMICS AND RECONSTRUCTION

CHAPTER XXXI

Economic Development

BY WU CHING-CH'AO

FROM TIME IMMEMORIAL agriculture has been the chief occupation of the Chinese. Today the proportion engaged in farming is estimated at 75 to 80 per cent. It is because of the continuity in pattern of their livelihood that modern Chinese find the history of their country so interesting and instructive. The history of the Western Han dynasty (206 B.C.–A.D. 9), for example, can be read with especial profit since most of the economic problems which confronted the people at that time are problems demanding solution at present. Except in matters concerning contacts with the Occident, a Chinese seeking today to improve social and economic conditions naturally consults the national records for information. In these is found the practical wisdom accumulated through thousands of years.

Though rural life is not exactly the same as that of two thousand years ago, there is a Chinese way of making a living which holds as true for the present as for the past. The Chinese are predominantly small farmers working on tracts of a few acres. Most of them are owners or part owners, but a rather large proportion are tenants. Farmers consume most of what they raise; only a small margin of their products may be used in exchange for things that they cannot produce.

Because of the small size of their fields the majority of workers cannot produce a surplus in crops that will suffice to tide them over periods of scarcity. This has always been the central problem in Chinese economy.

For an understanding of the small farm as a prevailing institution in the past, one may consult the first family-budget study in China—that made about 400 B.C. by Li K'uei, a minister of the state of Wei:

> A farmer having a family of five usually cultivates a farm of 100 *mou*. [A *mou* of the Chou (jou) dynasty was smaller than the modern *mou*, which is approximately one-sixth of an acre.] From every *mou* he can get one and a half piculs of millet, making a total of 150 piculs of millet. From this total, one-tenth is taken as tax. So what remains amounts to 135 piculs. A person usually consumes one and a half piculs per month. A family of five will consume 90 piculs for the whole year. Subtracting this amount, the remainder will be only 45 piculs. At the price of 30 cash per picul, 45 piculs can be sold for a sum of 1,350 cash. On religious services 300 cash must be spent, leaving only 1,050 cash. For clothing one must spend 300 cash on every person, making 1,500 cash per family of five. Therefore the deficit at the end of a year is 450 cash. Nothing is put aside for such emergencies as sickness, funeral expenses, and extra taxes. Consequently the farmers are always in a state of poverty.[1]

It is interesting to note that the farmer in the Chou period spent 66 per cent of his net income on food alone—definite indication of a low standard of living. Modern studies of Chinese family budgets reveal similar conditions.

⬦ ⬦ ⬦

How to keep farmers well fed, well clothed, and contented has been the chief concern of Chinese statesmen. As rainfall in northern China is irregular and usually inadequate, irrigation works were developed as early as the Chou period (*ca.* 1027–255 B.C.) to insure reliable crops. Irrigation works were first developed on the plains of northern China in the states of Han and Wei. In the third century B.C. irrigation was begun in the state of Ch'in (modern Shensi). Since this laid the economic foundations for unification of China under Ch'in (tsin) Shih Huang Ti (221–210 B.C.), the story should be told in full:

> In order to prevent the eastward expansion of Ch'in by tiring it out with other activities, Han sent the hydraulic engineer Chêng Kuo [jeng guo] to Ch'in to persuade [the King of] Ch'in to tap the Ching [jing] River and construct a canal. . . . The proposed canal would be 300 *li* long and was to be used for irrigation. Before the construction work was finished, however, the Ch'in authorities became aware of the trick and intended to kill Chêng Kuo, who then said to them, "Although the project was intended as a trick, yet the finished canal will

---

be of great benefit to Ch'in." The work was then ordered to be continued. After completion it irrigated over 40,000 *ch'ing* [i.e., 4,000,000 *mou*] of alkali land with water laden with rich silt. The productivity [of these fields] rose to one *chung* [i.e., 64 *tou*] for each *mou*. Thus Kuanchung [guan-jung] [i.e., Shensi] became a fertile country without bad years. Ch'in, then, grew rich and strong and finally conquered all other feudal states. The canal was [named after the engineer and] called the Chêng Kuo canal.[2]

From Shensi, irrigation was introduced into Szechuan by Li Ping, a Ch'in official. He had a pass cut in a mountain and, directing the Min River through it, distributed its waters in a network of canals. As a consequence the Chengtu basin has never known a year of famine. Under the Han dynasty the knowledge of irrigation became common throughout the country, eventually as far as southern Sinkiang (sin-jiang). Technically, the Chinese had solved the problem of drought before the time of Christ. Whether they always put this knowledge into practice is, of course, another question.

Floods have been as devastating as droughts. The typical method used to guard against them was the building of river dikes. The relation between deforestation and floods has not been widely comprehended by the Chinese. Many hillsides have been stripped of trees, and many places of grass. The runoff of rain water is so rapid that masses of silt are carried into the rivers. The river beds gradually rise to levels higher than those of surrounding districts and the water is forced to run within the channel formed by the dikes. The breakage of dikes from the heavy rainfall is one of the chief causes of recurrent floods, especially in northern China.

F. W. Williams once remarked, "It is notable that in the history of China no great upheaval has occurred without its concomitant of famine."[3] Many dynasties have been overthrown by hungry mobs, notably those of Wang Mang (9 B.C.–A.D. 23), the Sui (A.D. 589–618), the T'ang (A.D. 618–906), and the Ming (A.D. 1368–1644). (See chap. viii, above.) Although many factors have contributed to famines, drought and flood have been the most important. Statesmen and able rulers have long recognized this fact; they know that the preservation of peace and order depends upon the prevention of famine. This problem has occupied the mind of the Chinese as, in modern times, the problem of unemployment has commanded that of Westerners.

Besides irrigation works and flood control the Chinese have used granaries to combat the scourge of famine. Li K'uei, earlier quoted, suggested the equalization of prices and supply of agricultural products by state purchase in times of plenty and sale in times of scarcity. According to his computation, an average farm of 100 *mou* may, in ordinary years, raise 150 piculs of millet. But in an extraordinarily good year the harvest may be four times the average yield, or 600 piculs. In a very good year the harvest may be three times, and in a good year twice, the average yield. Assuming that a family of five needs 200 piculs for consumption, the surplus for an extraordinarily good year is 400 piculs; for a very good year, 250 piculs; and for a good year, 100 piculs. In an extraordinarily bad year the harvest from the same farm may amount to only 30 piculs; in a very bad year, 70 piculs; and in a bad year, 100 piculs. It is a function of the central government to buy the surplus from farmers in good years and to sell it to the people in bad years. Thus farmers will not suffer in good years from decline in prices, and in bad years they will not endure hardships because of food shortage.

Whether Li K'uei put his theory into practice is hard to determine. But it is definitely known that in the reign of the Han emperor, Hsüan (süan) (73–49 B.C.), upon the recommendation of Kêng Shou-ch'ang, granaries were built on the frontiers for the purpose of equalizing prices of agricultural products. Under later dynasties, imperial edicts were often issued instructing local officials to build granaries so that in time of famine the population might be spared starvation. Besides local granaries the government usually built large ones in the capital, as well as along main lines of transportation such as the Grand Canal. This was necessary in a country where transportation was little developed and movement of foodstuffs to a great distance was well-nigh impossible. But no system was developed to guarantee that granaries would always be kept stocked and that officials would not sell grain for their own benefit.

When the granaries proved inadequate, the hungry people formed robber bands or migrated to other parts of the country. When Mencius (372–289 or 390–305 B.C.) went to the state of Liang, the king told him that to mitigate the misery of his people he had sent grain to the famine district and had removed part of its population. Although many migrations were directed by the government, others were made by the people themselves. In periods of famine, "wanderers" from the smitten district are met in adjacent territories. They return when the famine is over, or settle permanently in new places.

Chinese migrations connected with famine are discussed by Ellsworth Huntington in *The Character of Races* (chaps. x–xiii).[4] According to him, in the third century B.C., in the fourth and fifth centuries of the present era, and again in the twelfth and thirteenth centuries, prolonged periods of increasing aridity prevailed in central Asia. Non-Chinese have often invaded China, especially when chaos prevailed south of the Great Wall. As a result, millions have migrated southward or southeastward. Migration, mainly because of famine, has gone on for thousands of years. In this way old China expanded and the Chinese became accustomed to various types of climate. Unfortunately, the history of Chinese migrations has never been systematically studied. It is, however, well known that the Chinese, after centuries of acclimatization, have acquired a constitution that permits them to do hard work in any climate from cold Siberia to the hot East Indies.

◇ ◇ ◇

Another important aspect of the life of many Chinese is that of tenancy. It has been pointed out that the average size of farms is exceedingly small, and that even owners of these can with difficulty make a decent livelihood. If the farmer be a tenant, he and his family must live on only a part of the products of his field since the remainder must go to the landlord as rent. How wretched is the life he is condemned to live, can be imagined.

The problem of landlordism and tenancy has long occupied the attention of Chinese thinkers. Innumerable works have urged the advantages of the *ching-t'ien* (dzing-tien), or "well-field," system— the division of a piece of land into nine farms, resembling the Chinese character for a well. According to this system, each of the eight outer farms was to be assigned to a family, and the farm in the center was to be worked collectively by the eight families to raise income for the state. Whether such a system has ever been practiced is a moot question. There is, however, no doubt that at times the ideal has exerted an influence.

In the beginning of the Western Chin (dzin) (A.D. 265–317), the Northern Wei (A.D. 386–534), and the T'ang (A.D. 618–906) epochs, attempts were made to assign to each family a piece of land. T'ang practice may be considered as an example. In the year 624, Li Yüan, or Kao-tsu (gao-dzu), first emperor of the T'ang line, ordered that each male of a family be given a piece of land of 100 *mou*. Those who suffered from chronic diseases were given 40 *mou*. Widows were allowed 30 *mou*. Of this land, 20 per cent became private property, inheritable by the owner's sons; 80 per cent was public property, to be returned to the government on the death of the owner. Such a system could be put into practice at the beginning of a dynastic age, when population was scarce and land abundant, but it broke down when population outgrew the available supply of land. In consequence, the problem of tenancy arose under every dynasty.

One way to arrest the spread of tenancy was to limit the amount of land which an individual might hold. Tung Chung-shu (dung jung-shu), of the second century B.C., the foremost philosopher of the Western Han dynasty, first proposed the limitation of holdings. He has had many followers; but as his idea worked against the interests of landlords, who were always politically powerful, it was never seriously put into effect.

Probably the lack of primogeniture has been mainly responsible for the fact that landlords have never become a hereditary class in China. No family can remain in that class for many generations: when a landlord dies, his holdings are divided more or less equally among his sons. Consequently, sons are not ordinarily, at the outset, as large landowners as their father; when their holdings are in turn subdivided, each holding becomes so small that the owner cannot live on the rent from it alone. At this point the landlord is degraded. Since it takes a few generations for a landlord to fall in the social scale, it takes as long or even longer for a tenant to become owner of his land. Climbing on the agricultural ladder in China has always been slow because it is difficult to accumulate a surplus on a small farm.[5]

In the year 1937, according to the National Agricultural Research Bureau, distribution of farm tenancy was as follows: owners, 46 per cent; part owners, 24 per cent; tenants, 30 per cent. The

National government has tried to ameliorate the lot of tenants: first, by putting a ceiling on rent (37.5 per cent or less of total products); and second, by providing easy credit to farmers so that they will not fall prey to landlords in time of distress. Although these measures may contribute to the welfare of tenants, there is reason to believe that the problem of farmers in general and of tenants in particular must be solved in connection with economic reconstruction in other fields of Chinese economy.

◇ ◇ ◇

At this point the questions may be raised: Why has China remained an agricultural country for the last two thousand years? Why did industrialization not develop at a particular moment in China as it did in western Europe? These questions have puzzled historians and economists, and no satisfactory answers have yet been found. It may, however, be worth while to offer here some speculations.

The literary examination system contributed to the static nature of Chinese economic development. It was only through successful competition in literary examinations that an intellectual might raise his social and political status. For this reason the ambitious and the talented were induced to study the classics and to neglect the study of science.[6] They were encouraged to seek knowledge from the old instead of learning through personal observation and experimentation. Under such a system it was comparatively easy to produce volume after volume of commentaries on the classics, but it was difficult to produce a scientific invention. Thus the mind of the scholar was divorced from the daily problems of the masses. In a word, the intellectual foundation for industrialization in China was lacking.

From the days of barbarian invasions in the Chou period the non-Chinese who came into contact with the Chinese were, in the main, culturally inferior. They had much to learn from the Chinese, but the latter felt they had little or nothing to learn from aliens. Many who conquered China, such as the Mongols of the thirteenth century (see chap. viii, above) and the Manchus of the seventeenth century, assimilated much of the Chinese manner of living and thinking and lost much of their identity in the Chinese melting pot. For this reason, to the end of the nineteenth century the majority of Chinese believed that theirs was the most cultured nation in the world. This ignorance retarded diffusion of Western culture in China and prevented the spread of industrialization for at least a hundred years.

Some historians think that shortage of capital chiefly accounts for the lack of industrialization in China. There may be truth in this suggestion, but it should not be overemphasized. Throughout Chinese history countless individuals and families have accumulated vast wealth. The manner in which this wealth has been consumed deserves careful study. It has been spent mainly on luxuries or invested in land. It has helped to redistribute the national income, but it has not contributed to the production of new capital. It has brought about redistribution of national wealth without adding new wealth to the nation. There have been no channels for investment which would create capital goods. An agricultural economy may include millionaires, but their wealth will not of itself bring about industrialization if other conditions are not favorable.

◇ ◇ ◇

The present is the second of the two most important epochs in China's history. The first came in the middle years of the third century B.C., when Ch'in Shih Huang Ti unified the country. That was a period of political transformation from warring feudal states to an empire. Because of this transformation China was able to accomplish something which was not achieved by the Roman Empire. When the Chinese consider the bloody wars which have been fought among European nations in the past fifteen hundred years, they congratulate themselves upon their own good fortune.

In addition to political transformation in the present age, the Chinese are now passing through a momentous economic transformation which has been brought about principally through contact with the West. It may be said categorically that if China had not been brought into contact with the West it would have remained an agricultural country to an even greater degree than it is at present. Although for many hundreds of years a limited trade was carried on between the Middle Kingdom and the West, it was not until the end of the nineteenth century, particularly after the Fourth Sino-Japanese War (1894–1895), that the Chinese began to appreciate the culture of the West to any considerable degree, and then mainly in its material phases. This appreciation has grown with increase in the numbers of students trained in Western countries. But not until the outbreak of hostilities between China and Japan, in and after 1931, was the importance of Western industrialization made apparent to the general Chinese public. It is now held by China's leaders that without industrialization the country can never become prosperous and strong enough to defend its independence against aggression. Moreover, without industrialization the living standards of the common people cannot be raised.

This conclusion determines the nature of the task which the government aims to accomplish now that victory has been won by the United Nations. China will follow the road traveled by Great Britain, the United States, and Soviet Russia: it will be industrialized. The present occupational distribution of population, with 75 to 80 per cent engaged in farming, must be changed. With improvements in agriculture, the approximately 300,000,000 acres of farm land can be cultivated by less than 50 per cent of the population. The rest of the man power must be emancipated from rural districts and put to work at mining, manufacturing, communication, transportation, commerce, and other productive work. As more people migrate to the city to find better-paid jobs, the farmers who remain in country districts will have larger farms to operate and a wider market for their products. Thus they will receive more income and will be able to give their children better opportunities in life.

Industrialization will result, also, in opening up the country's natural resources, which thus far have been little touched. China's coal reserve has been estimated as being one of the largest in the world. Its iron ores, although not so abundant for large-scale exploitation, are sufficient for domestic use for the next fifty or even one hundred years. In the northwestern region, oil fields have recently been discovered and a preliminary estimate indicates that Chinese oil reserves may be one-third as large as those of the United States. With regard to metals used to make ferroalloys, there is a sufficient quantity of manganese, an abundance of tungsten, also a little nickel and cobalt. Although copper, lead, and zinc are insufficient, compensation is found in the existence of more antimony

and tin than are needed. All these and many other natural resources must be exploited for the benefit of China as well as for
the world.

There is yet another meaning to be attached to China's industrialization. The maintenance hereafter of peace in the Far East
requires a strong China. But the country cannot be strong if it is
not industrialized. Therefore, if China, with other nations, is to
shoulder the responsibility of maintaining peace throughout the
world, particularly in eastern Asia, it must be industrialized. The
Chinese must be prepared, economically and militarily, to put
their weight on the side of peace so that hereafter no nation will
dare to commit sustained acts of aggression. As the Chinese are a
peace-loving people, a strong China will be an asset, not a menace,
to other peace-loving nations.

The task of industrialization must be approached from many
angles. Prerequisite to other plans of development, China needs a
modern system of transportation. Instead of relying upon sailboats,
wheelbarrows, draft animals, and human carriers, increasing use
should be made of steamships, railways, motor trucks, and air liners.
Before 1937 there were little more than 100,000 kilometers of motor
highways, 10,000 kilometers of railways, less than a million registered tons of steamships, and only two airlines. Within a decade
after the conclusion of war China should build at least 20,000
kilometers of railway to link its most important centers of production and commerce. As water transportation is the cheapest means
for movement of goods and as there are several excellent waterways
running from west to east and a coastline stretching thousands of
miles, more steamships should be built to carry domestic trade and,
as soon as may be, to participate in international trade.

When the country is united by modern means of transportation
its economy will be transformed. Large-scale industries will flourish: the whole population will serve as customers. The interior,
with its vast natural resources, will be developed. There are many
reasons why, prior to 1937, industries were concentrated along the
coast, but the main one was that the coastal provinces had better
transportation facilities.

The development of modern transportation throughout the interior will lead to the establishment of modern industries. Seven

industrial regions can be visualized: (1) the northeastern region, with Mukden, Changchun, and Harbin as centers; (2) the northern region, with Peiping, or Peking, Tientsin, Shihchiachuang (shzh-jia-juang), Tsinan, and Tsingtao as centers; (3) the northwestern region, with Sian, Tienshui, and Lanchow as centers; (4) the eastern region, with Shanghai, Nanking (nan-jing), Hangchow (hang-jou), and Wuhu as centers; (5) the central region, with Hankow, Siangtan, and Hengyang as centers; (6) the southern region, with Canton, Luichow, and Kueilin (guei-lin) as centers; and (7) the southwestern region, with Chungking, Weining, and Kunming as centers. In all these areas raw materials and labor are abundant. Conditions for industrial development are ripe and await the transformation of potentialities into realities.

In every one of these regions there should be established all the important industries, so that each may stimulate and sustain the others: power, metals, machine tools and machinery, chemicals, armaments, foods, clothing, building construction, transportation and communication equipment, and printing. The first four are indispensable both for defense and for human welfare. Whether China should pay more attention to defense or to human-welfare industries in the postwar period depends, in the main, upon the international situation. If a system of collective security can be made to work, the government can devote a larger share of time and energy to human-welfare industries.[7] Otherwise China will not again rely mainly upon the good will of other nations for the necessary means of self-defense.

CHAPTER XXXII

Agriculture

BY A. KAIMING CHIU

No country can be industrially sound or strong unless both its agricultural technique and the agricultural part of its society are progressive and prosperous.

HENRY WALLACE

CHINA IS PREDOMINANTLY an agricultural country. Authoritative estimates indicate that from 75 to 80 per cent of the people are engaged in agricultural pursuits.[1] In normal years agriculture (including farming, livestock raising, and horticulture) contributes about 80 per cent of the national income and is responsible for nearly 80 per cent of the export trade. Agriculture is, then, the pivot around which the economic life of the country revolves. Before 1937 China led the world in the production of rice, soybeans, millet, barley, sweet potatoes, kaoliang, peanuts, tea, and silk. In 1932–1936 it ranked ahead of the United States and next to the Soviet Union in the production of wheat; in tobacco production it occupied, with the United States and India, first place, and in cotton production was surpassed only by those countries. Nevertheless, for a long time Chinese agriculture has been in an unhealthy condition; proof of this statement is found in the extremely low standard of living of the farming population as compared with that of rural groups in other countries.

Rural problems may be divided into two groups: natural and man-made. Under natural problems may be considered: (1) land limitations and population pressure, (2) insufficient, uneven, and uncertain distribution of rainfall, which brings about periodic

[1] For notes to chapter xxxii see pages 541–545.

droughts and floods, (3) poor varieties of plants and breeds of animals, (4) ravages of plant and animal pests and diseases, (5) partial exhaustion of soil fertility because of long tillage, and (6) lack of transportation facilities.

Under man-made problems, outstanding are: (1) bad political administration, (2) inequitable taxes, (3) unequal distribution of landownership and oppressive systems of tenancy, (4) poor credit facilities and high interest rates, (5) an uneconomical system of farm layout, (6) inadequate educational facilities, and (7) lack of coöperation among farmers.

The problems in the first group are mainly to be solved by scientific and technological improvements. Those in the second group must be attacked through political and economic measures.

An unusually small proportion of China's land area is suitable for agriculture. Thus, although the density of population for the country as a whole (taking the total area to be 11,173,558 square kilometers, or 4,314,097 square miles, and the population to be 450,00,000) is 40.27 per square kilometer, or 104.4 per square mile (which compares favorably with other important countries: Japan proper, 453; Germany, 365; France, 197; continental United States, 41.3; and Soviet Russia, 19.82 per square mile), that for populated and agricultural China is about 500 per square mile.[2]

According to Dr. W. H. Wong, the nation's foremost geologist, this portion of the country is populated in five regions: the northern plain, with a population density of 650 per square mile; the Yangtze Valley, 850 per square mile; the uplands which border these two plains, 350 per square mile; the southeastern coastal fringe, 350 per square mile; and the interior plain of Szechuan, 600 per square mile. In isolated places the density of population exceeds 1,000 per square mile. The five regions total only some 700,000 square miles (or a little less than 17 per cent of the total area of 4,314,097 square miles), but they support about 360,000,000 people, or a little more than 83 per cent of the total population; the remaining 17 per cent is spread over 83 per cent of the area.

Uneven distribution of population is caused by climate and topography. It is estimated that more than half the country has a mean annual rainfall of less than 20 inches. Dr. Wong further divides the land into classes according to altitude.[3]

According to this estimate, land suitable for agriculture amounts to less than 20 per cent of China's total area. Dr. Wong concludes that, except for Manchuria, the possibility of redistribution of China's population into new agricultural areas is limited; the northwest can at most absorb 10,000,000 new settlers to eke out a meager living. Hence the prospect for bringing about lessening pressure on congested areas is not bright.[4]

Relation to human habitation	Altitude (meters)	Percentage of total area
Most suitable.	Below 500	14
Fairly suitable.	500–1,000	18
Not quite suitable.	1,000–2,000	8
Unsuitable.	2,000–4,000	40
Most unsuitable.	Above 4,000	20

Professor J. Lossing Buck, in his monumental study, *Land Utilization in China*,[5] concludes, from a survey of 16,786 farms in 168 localities of eight agricultural regions, that for agricultural China there can be no great increase in amount of farm land. He estimates that an additional 10 per cent of the present area in farms—at most 23,000,000 acres for the eight agricultural regions, consisting of 232,000,000 acres of cultivated land—could be made available for profitable cultivation by the following means: removal of graves from farm land, elimination of land in boundaries after consolidation of fragmented holdings, and putting under the plow arable lands not now cultivated. The arable uncultivated area, Dr. Buck estimates, amounts to about 35,000,000 acres, or 11 per cent of all uncultivated land in the part of China (171 hsien, or counties) surveyed by his investigators.[6]

A result of land limitation and increasing population is that acreage of cultivated land per capita is extremely small as compared with figures for other important countries: China, 0.45; Japan, 0.44; United States, 8.04; Great Britain, 0.67; Soviet Russia, 2.01; Germany, 1.11; France, 1.29; Italy, 0.65. The figure for China is from the Government Directorate of Statistics for 1929–1931, a nation-wide estimate giving per-capita acreage as 2.97 *mou* and taking 1 *mou* as 0.152 acre. This is equivalent to a population density of 1,413 to each square mile of cultivated land. The figures for other countries are from *Annuaire International de Statistique Agricole,* published in Rome in 1932–1933.

The amount of cultivated land available to each Chinese citizen has been decreasing in the last three hundred years, as is shown by the accompanying table.

CULTIVATED LAND AND POPULATION IN CHINA, 1661–1931[*]

Year	Cultivated land (*mou*)	Population	Per-capita acreage (*mou*)
1661	549,357,640	104,707,086	5.24
1685	607,834,001	111,879,559	5.43
1724	683,791,427	141,541,697	4.83
1753	708,114,238	159,984,053	4.43
1766	740,449,550	182,076,774	4.07
1812	772,121,278	271,145,671	2.85
1872	819,453,194	329,563,216	2.49
1887	911,976,606	337,590,400	2.70
1900	919,504,897	366,810,000	2.51
1916	1,384,937,701	409,500,000	3.38
1931	1,248,781,000	419,957,000	2.97

* The figure for 1931 is from C. C. Chang, *An Estimate of China's Farms and Crops* (Nanking, 1932), pp. 11–14. Data refer to 25 out of 28 provinces; Sikang, Chinghai (tsing-hai), and Kuangsi (guang-si) are not included. Figures for other years are from Chen Chang-heng, "Some Phases of China's Population Problem," in *Bulletin de l'Institut International de Statistique* (Tokyo, 1931), Tome XXV, 4° Livraison, pp. 18–54.

In large parts of northern China the average precipitation is only 20 inches; a slight decrease or irregularity results in famine. One of the worst famines in the history of Shensi, Shansi, Hopei (ho-bei), Honan, and Shantung (shan-dung) was that of 1876–1879. For three years almost no rain fell; it was estimated that from nine to thirteen million people perished. In 1920–1921 the people in those provinces suffered a similar fate. No rain fell for nearly a year prior to the time for harvesting the autumn crop of 1920. Because of better means of transportation at the later date, however, the number of deaths is estimated to have been less than half a million.[7]

Occasional heavy rainfalls occur in all parts of China. Cyclones and typhoons cause frequent floods, especially in the southeastern provinces. In the period 1911–1932, according to a study made by K. Y. Cheng (jeng), of the National Research Institute of Meteorology, 56 floods occurred in the Yangtze Valley: 5 were due to thunderstorms, 42 to cyclonic storms, and 9 to typhoons.[8] In most parts of the country, from 70 to 80 per cent of the annual rainfall comes in the months of June, July, and August. A large amount may fall in a few days' time. Sudden swelling of rivers and slow drainage of the plains give rise to floods. That of 1931 caused property loss of two billion Chinese dollars; about a quarter of a million lives were lost. Some 25,200,000 Chinese farmers were affected—a figure almost equal to the total farm population of the United States in that year.[9]

◇ ◇ ◇

Poor varieties of plants and breeds of animals, ravages of plant and animal pests and diseases, and insufficient soil fertility combine to reduce crop yields and farmers' incomes. The accompanying table (on the page opposite) compares China with other countries in average yields of six important crops.

Although China has been practicing intensive farming for centuries, yields of most crops are not high as compared with those of other countries. Better than those of India and Russia, China's yields are not equal to those of Japan, Germany, Great Britain, and Italy. According to the Crop Reporting Service of the National Agricultural Research Bureau,[10] losses caused by insect pests and diseases ravaging five winter crops in 1935–1936, in terms of percentage reduction of normal yield, are as follows: wheat, 27 per cent; barley, 27 per cent; field peas, 30 per cent; broad beans, 28 per cent; and oats, 29 per cent.

Lack of economical and dependable transportation facilities has handicapped Chinese economic development for centuries. This has been a contributing cause in aggravating famines, and has prevented proper distribution and marketing of agricultural products.

The prohibitive cost of transporting rice from Hunan, Kiangsi, and Anhui to Shanghai and Canton has necessitated the ever-increasing importation of this cereal from Burma, Siam, and Indo-China. According to a study made by the National Tariff Commission in 1932, when rice imported from these countries was selling in Shanghai at Chinese $8.25 per picul (133.3 lb.), native rice of the same quality transported from Changsha, Kiukiang (jiujiang), and Wuhu had to sell at Chinese $10.89, $9.12, and $8.77, respectively, because the cost of transportation and other miscellaneous fees from these three centers to Shanghai were Chinese $4.07, $2.94, and $2.65 per picul each. Actual transport costs for rice per picul from various places to Shanghai were as follows, in Chinese dollars: from Rangoon, $0.525; from Bangkok, $0.516;

AVERAGE CROP YIELDS FOR EIGHT COUNTRIES, 1929–1933, IN BUSHELS PER ACRE
(EXCEPT FOR COTTON)

Country	Rice	Wheat	Barley	Corn	Irish potatoes	Cotton (kilograms)
China (a)	59	18	24	25	108	102
(b)	67	16	19	21	87	168
Japan	68	25	36	22	139	199
India	29	11	..	15	..	80
U.S.S.R.	..	10	16	15	128	188
Germany	..	31	38	..	233	...
Italy	93	21	21	28	85	188
Great Britain	..	32	37	..	244	...
United States	47	14	22	25	108	177

Data for China: (a) from the Government Directorate of Statistics as given in C. C. Chang, *An Estimate of China's Farms and Crops* (Nanking, 1932), in 25 provinces (1,781 hsien); (b) from a survey of 16,334 farms, 162 localities, 150 hsien, 22 provinces, by the Department of Agricultural Economics, University of Nanking, as given in J. Lossing Buck, *Land Utilization in China* (Chicago, 1937), chap. vii. Data for other countries from the *International Yearbook of Agricultural Statistics*, 1930–1931 and 1932–1933, as given by Buck, p. 226.
A bushel is figured as 60 lb. of wheat, soybeans, and Irish potatoes, 56 lb. of corn, 54 lb. of sweet potatoes, 48 lb. of barley, and 45 lb. of rough rice.

from Saïgon, $0.452; from Changsha, $0.952; from Kiukiang, $0.644; and from Wuhu, $0.433. Thus the high cost of transportation and the miscellaneous exactions on the way from the interior to the coast have barred native rice from the Shanghai market.

It is likewise with wheat. Flour mills in Shanghai and Hankow prefer to use Canadian and American wheat rather than native wheat; foreign wheat is cheaper on account of lower ocean freight rates. Transportation costs for wheat shipped to Shanghai from Canada and from Hsüchow (sü-jou), in Kiangsu, were, respectively, Chinese $0.60 and $1.00 per picul. Again, while American wheat was selling in Hankow at Chinese $30 per ton, Shensi wheat transported there must sell at Chinese $130–$140 per ton. Thus high transportation costs and tax levies on agricultural produce in transit make it difficult for China to compete with foreign countries exporting thither agricultural commodities.[11]

◇ ◇ ◇

Land taxes in China are of two kinds: the main tax and various surcharges. In the first few years of the Republic, the law of 1912 prevented surcharges from exceeding 30 per cent of the main tax, but incessant civil war led to the breakdown of this law. Before 1928 the main tax was collected by the central government and surcharges were collected by the local governments. In 1928 the main land tax was turned over to the local governments.

Since the breakdown of the 30 per cent surcharge law, the basis of assessment and the rates of surcharges have varied from province to province, from county to county, and from one surcharge to another. In recent years the number of surcharges has greatly increased: there are more than sixty kinds in Kiangsi, seventy in Chekiang (je-jiang), and a hundred in Kiangsu (jiang-su). The surcharges often total about twenty to thirty times more than the main tax.[12] Furthermore, surcharges on land are usually levied with the county as a unit; the result is that they are unequal in incidence and fall more heavily on the poorer localities.

The rates of land tax (main tax and surcharges combined) vary from 1.33 per cent to 6.6 per cent. In general, the land tax is about 3 per cent of the land value. The tendency is to charge a higher rate on less productive land.[13] On medium-grade land the average tax burden, as calculated by Professor Buck, is United States $1.79 per acre as compared with $0.90 per acre for the New England states and $1.15 per acre for the middle Atlantic and eastern north-central states in 1932 (when the average exchange rate for 1929–1933 of United States $1.00 = Chinese $3.54 is used).[14]

Another feature of the land tax and its surcharges is the fact that under the Republic, in many provinces, military governors have collected them years in advance—once, in Szechuan, according to report, a century in advance!—and often several times a year.[15] In addition, farmers have had to pay numerous taxes on farm implements, night soil, pigs, and so on.

Private ownership of farm land has prevailed since abolition of the feudal system under the Ch'in dynasty (221–207 B.C.). In 1865, cultivated land under private ownership amounted to 92.7 per cent and state land to 7.3 per cent.[16] In recent sample studies covering wide areas, the amount of privately owned land shows a slight increase, namely, 93.3 per cent of all cultivated land.[17] Most public lands are in mountainous and forested areas.

As for distribution of landownership, the nation-wide tenancy survey conducted in 1934 by the National Agricultural Research Bureau showed that in nine northern provinces more than 50 per cent of farmers were owners and less than 20 per cent were tenants; in a majority of southern provinces no less than 40 per cent of farmers were tenants and only 20–30 per cent were owners. For the country as a whole (891 hsien in 22 provinces) owners constituted 46 per cent, part owners 25 per cent, and tenants 29 per cent of all farmers.[18]

There are no accurate statistics on inequalities in landownership. According to an investigation[19] in 1926–1927 by the revolutionary Wuhan government, controlled by Communists and by the Radical wing of the Kuomintang, distribution of landownership was as follows:

Class of owners	Size of holdings (*mou*)	Percentage of population	Percentage of cultivated land
Poor farmers	1–10	45	7
Middle-class farmers	10–30	24	13
Rich farmers	30–50	16	17
Small landlords	50–100	10	20
Big landlords	Over 100	5	43

In other words, landlords, who form 15 per cent of the population, possess 63 per cent of the cultivated land, whereas the "poor peasants" (i.e., those owning less than 30 *mou*), who make up 69 per cent of the population, own only 20 per cent of the cultivated land.

Another estimate is that supplied by the Sun Yat-sen Institute of Nanking and Chungking.[20] (See the table on page 474.) This has the blessing of the orthodox opinion of the ruling Kuomintang. Here is a picture of 10 per cent of the farm population owning

53 per cent of the cultivated land, while the other 90 per cent possesses only 47 per cent of the land. These estimates are supported by government statistics on land concentration.

From August, 1934, to July, 1935, the National Land Commission (organized by the National Economic Council, the Ministry of the Interior, and the Ministry of Finance) made an investigation of 1,545 big-landlord families and 752,865 peasant families in 87 districts scattered throughout eleven provinces. The commissioners

Class of owners	Percentage of farm households	Percentage of cultivated land
Landlords...............................	3	26
Rich farmers............................	7	27
Middle-class farmers....................	22	25
Poor farmers and farm laborers..........	68	22

found the average size of lands owned by these two classes of families to be as follows: landlord family, 2,030 *mou;* peasant family, 15.8 *mou*. So a landlord owns, on the average, 128 times more land than a peasant! The findings of the Commission indicate also that real-estate possessions of landlords range from 300 to 20,000 *mou* per family.

Thus all sources agree, first, that China is not a country of small peasant proprietors owning more or less equal amounts of land, and second, that there is great concentration of landownership in a relatively small percentage of the population.[21] (See chap. xi, above.) Such landlords are frequently met with in the rich rice regions of the Yangtze and Pearl River valleys and in recently settled provinces in Manchuria and Inner Mongolia; in wheat regions of the northern China plain there is wider prevalence of independent small and medium owner-operators and less concentration of landownership. To many observers, foreign and native, the Communist movement in China is primarily a peasant revolt caused by dissatisfaction with the land system and hatred of landlords and tax collectors.[22] (See chap. vii, above.)

High rents are another feature of the tenancy problem. According to an investigation made in May, 1934, by the National Agricultural Research Bureau,[23] covering 879 counties (hsien) in 22 of the 28 provinces, rent per *mou* at modal rate for three types of renting systems, in Chinese dollars, was: cash rent, $3.60; crop rent, $4.20; and share rent, $4.60. Taking the average land value for the provinces investigated as Chinese $32.60 per *mou*, the annual interest realized by landowners for their investment was 11 per cent with cash rent, 13 per cent with crop rent, and 14 per cent with share rent. Such income for landlords was higher than the normal interest rate of 8 per cent a year paid for long-term deposits by banks in Shanghai, Peiping, and other cities. Additional advantages were safety of investment and the social prestige which comes from owning land.

In general, landlords prefer to have share rent since that yields the highest rate of return. In share rent the tenant divides with the landlord in specified proportions—generally half and half—the main crops raised on the rented land. In crop rent the tenant pays to his landlord a fixed amount of the crop raised, or sometimes its money equivalent. In cash rent the tenant pays a fixed sum of money per *mou*. From the investigation of 1934 it is found that percentage distribution of the three types of renting used on Chinese farms is as follows: cash rent, 21.2 per cent; crop rent, 50.7 per cent; and share rent, 28.1 per cent. According to Professor Buck, 25 per cent of tenant farmers pay cash rent; 51 per cent, crop rent; 22 per cent, share rent; and only 2 per cent are croppers—a system by which the tenant obtains a very small share of the crop because he supplies only labor.[24] Because of the light burden borne by tenants under the cash-rent system, several leading Chinese agricultural economists advocated, in 1936, the enactment of a law for its wider adoption in conjunction with government provision of liberal credit facilities to tenants.[25]

❖ ❖ ❖

Poor credit facilities and high interest rates are common in Chinese villages. Reports received in 1933 by the National Agricultural Research Bureau from 850 hsien in 22 provinces indicate that of the farm households investigated 52 per cent had to borrow money and 48 per cent had to borrow grain for food. The accompanying table shows the percentage of loans made at different interest rates. From this it is seen that less than 10 per cent of farm loans paid an annual interest of 10–20 per cent, 66.5 per cent of loans paid 20–40 per cent, and nearly 25 per cent of loans paid more than 40 per cent. This situation does not, however, tell the whole story. Interest rates for loans of grain are more exorbitant, averaging 7.1 per cent a month, or 85 per cent a year. Thus if one bushel of wheat is borrowed in February, two, or at least one and one-half, bushels must be paid back in June.[26]

Percentage of annual interest	Percentage of loans made
10–20	9.4
20–30	36.2
30–40	30.3
40–50	11.2
Over 50	12.9

Professor Buck found that interest rates in the rice regions of the Yangtze Valley and southwestern China averaged 2.3 per cent a month, or 28 per cent a year, whereas in the wheat region (northern and northwestern China) they averaged 3.2 per cent a month, or 38 per cent a year. The lower rate in the rice region is explained by the greater development of trade and communications within the Yangtze Valley. In the wheat region lower productivity and greater risks of farming because of uncertain crops are responsible for the higher rate.[27]

In an economic survey of 184 farms in Shentse hsien, Hopei, in 1931, by A. Kaiming Chiu and T. C. Han, it was found that 10.4 per cent of loans paid an annual interest of 12–24 per cent, 63.9 per cent paid 24 per cent, 16.6 per cent paid 24–36 per cent, and 9.1 per cent paid 36–57 per cent. A total of 259 loans amounting to Chinese $23,197 were contracted by 137 out of 184 farm households interviewed; that is, average indebtedness was Chinese $169 per family. About 51.8 per cent of loans were employed for productive purposes: buying seeds, fertilizers, farm implements, and materials for handicrafts and for supplementary enterprises. About 48.2 per cent of loans were used for consumption or unproductive purposes: ordinary living expenses, marriage and funeral expenditures, medical fees, and payment of old debts. Included under the second category was 2.9 per cent for educational expenses of children, which could not really be called unproductive.

The chief sources from which farmers obtained credit were personal and local, from relatives, friends, and wealthy neighbors. These accounted for 61.5 per cent of loans. The other single large source was the money shops or local native banks, which furnished 36.7 per cent of the credit. Rural credit coöperatives supplied only 1.8 per cent of loans.[28] The insignificant part played by credit coöperatives and modern banks (which usually charge lower rates of interest) in supplying rural credit is borne out by a survey conducted by the National Agricultural Research Bureau,[29] in 1933, of 2,268 rural communities in 22 provinces. Sources of farm credit as reported by these communities are as follows:

Source	Percentage of loans obtained
Merchants (mostly in county seat)	25.0
Landlords	24.2
Well-to-do farmers	18.4
Village stores	13.1
Pawnshops	8.8
Money shops or native banks	5.5
Coöperatives	2.6
Modern banks	2.4
Total	100.0

Farm layout in China is entirely different from that in the United States. Chinese farmhouses are, for the most part, in villages surrounded by cultivated fields. Isolated farmsteads with large tracts of land are rare in China. The typical Chinese farm is small and often consists of a group of scattered plots. The mean size of farms is 21 *mou,* or 3.2 acres,[30] but 61 per cent are smaller. The 1934 survey by the National Agricultural Research Bureau of 891 hsien scattered in 22 provinces reveals that 36 per cent of farms are under 10 *mou,* 25 per cent are between 10 and 20 *mou,* 14 per cent are between 20 and 30 *mou,* 17 per cent are between 30 and 50 *mou,* and 8 per cent are over 50 *mou.*[31]

The tiny scattered plots are usually not contiguous. Professor

Buck finds that there are, on the average, 5.6 parcels of land per farm. These often contain more than one field; so the average number of fields is 11.6 compared with 5.6 parcels per farm. The average size of a parcel is 0.94 acre and that of a field is 0.49 acre. The average distance of parcels from the farmstead is 0.4 of a mile and the average distance of the farthest parcels of land from the farmstead is 0.7 of a mile.[32] In the Shentse hsien survey the writer found that the average number of parcels was 6 per farm, and the average size of a parcel was 4.28 *mou,* or 0.64 acre, the smallest being 0.2 *mou* and the largest being 52 *mou,* or 7.9 acres. The average distance of all parcels from the farmhouse was 1.46 *li,* or half a mile, and the farthest parcel from the farmstead was about two miles.[33]

The two chief causes for fragmentation of land in China are the democratic inheritance system by which the owner's land is divided relatively equally among his sons, and the farmer's desire for diversity of crops, so that he often selects scattered plots suitable for different crops instead of buying one large plot. This motive also works in dividing inherited land. Thus if the property consists of three fields to be divided among three heirs, each often wants to get a third of each field. Such fragmentation results in a most uneconomical system of farm layout. The disadvantages are: (1) great amount of time consumed in carrying implements, fertilizers, seeds, and harvest between the farmstead and the several parcels, (2) limitation of the size of fields and, therefore, of the extent to which improved farm machinery may be used, (3) wasting of land in boundaries between different parcels, (4) difficulty in protecting crops in scattered plots from stray animals, thieves, and trespassers, and (5) difficulty in irrigating land because irrigation channels from private wells must extend for long distances past neighbors' fields.

Of all phases of Chinese education in the last thirty years, the least developed is primary education in rural districts. In Professor Buck's study of a cross section of Chinese rural population, including 46,358 males and 40,690 females seven or more years old, scattered in 119 localities in 16 provinces, "only 30 per cent of the males, and 1 per cent of the females, had attended school long enough to learn to read a common letter. The schooling of the few who did receive some education was, for the most part, extremely brief. Males who received some education attended school an average of four years, and females an average of three years."[34] In a survey of the more prosperous and progressive rural section of Chekiang (je-jiang) province, the sericultural regions in Wuhsing hsien, in 1935, the China Institute of Economic and Statistical Research, under the direction of Dr. D. K. Lieu, lists the following findings with respect to rural education: of the 924 families investigated, only 271, or about 29 per cent, had members who had received some education. Among 4,613 persons interviewed, only 413, or about 9 per cent, were literate. The percentage of adult males who had received schooling was much higher than that of adult females: 15 per cent for the former and 1 per cent for the latter. Only 10 per cent of the children were attending schools.[35]

◇   ◇   ◇

Before Japan's invasion of Manchuria in 1931, attempts at rural reforms were undertaken, for the most part, by private organizations, such as the China International Famine Relief Commission, mass education centers like that at Tinghsien (ding-sien) under the direction of Dr. James Yen (see chap. xxix, above), and rural improvement extension works of several colleges in neighboring villages. Active government work in rural reconstruction did not begin until 1933, when the National Economic Council and the Rural Rehabilitation Commission, both of the Executive Yüan, formally came into being, and the National Agricultural Research Bureau of the Ministry of Industries (organized in 1931) began its work seriously. The chief events responsible for the participation of the central government in rural rehabilitation were the Japanese invasion of Manchuria, the Communist uprising in central China, and the Yangtze flood of 1931.

Conspicuous achievements in hydraulic engineering (dredging operations, dikes, irrigation canals, and wells), motor highways, and public health were accomplished by the National Economic Council before the beginning of the Fifth Sino-Japanese War in 1937. Construction of levees and sea walls and dredging operations were carried on largely in the Yangtze and Huai Ho valleys to prevent floods and to reclaim land from the river. Irrigation canals were built in the northwest and irrigation wells were dug in the northern provinces, especially in Hopei. During two years' operation, 1933–1935, the National Economic Council spent about Chinese $6,000,000 for such works in ten provinces. The land reclaimed for cultivation amounted to more than half a million *mou,* or 100,000 acres, in Shensi alone.[36]

Strenuous efforts in road building by the National Economic Council brought the mileage of motor highways from 66,000 kilometers in 1931 to over 100,000 kilometers in 1937, linking practically all important trading centers and provincial capitals in a closely woven network. In addition, several tens of thousands of kilometers were projected or under construction. Besides automobile roads, Chinese government railways also increased mileage. The Canton-Hankow line was completed and opened to traffic in September, 1936. A junction was effected in the spring of 1937 between the Peiping-Hankow and Tientsin-Pukou railways. Work had started on the Chungking-Chengtu, the Hunan-Kueichow (guei-jou), and the Hunan-Kuangsi railways before the shots were fired at the Marco Polo Bridge.[37]

The work of the Rural Rehabilitation Commission of the Executive Yüan consisted mainly of investigating rural conditions and planning for their improvement. In and after 1933 it made a series of agricultural surveys in the provinces of Kiangsu, Chekiang, Shensi, Honan, Kuangsi, and Yünnan, and published several studies on marketing of farm products, rural taxation, farm credit, and underground water problems.

The technical aspects of agricultural improvement were undertaken by the National Agricultural Research Bureau[38] after 1933. As a result of its research and extension work in plant and animal breeding, soil and fertilizer improvement, control of insects and disease, and veterinary medicine, the production of field and forest crops and animal products showed a decided increase in 1937. Thus, figures for fourteen provinces of Unoccupied China showed a percentage increase in production of six winter crops over the average for the five preceding years: wheat, 17 per cent; barley, 5 per cent; field peas, 0.3 per cent; broad beans, 5 per cent; rapeseed, 4 per cent; and oats, 3 per cent. For cotton the cultivation of improved seeds increased from 570,000 *mou* in 1934 to 2,676,025 *mou* in 1936, which made China almost self-sufficient in raw cotton. The increase in wood-oil production may be seen in the following figures of its export,[30] mainly to the United States, in the accompanying table.

The improvement of sericulture was undertaken jointly by the National Agricultural Research Bureau and the National Economic Council, which set up a Sericulture Commission in 1934, with Dr. Benito Mari from the League of Nations as a member. A three-year plan calling for an expenditure of Chinese $1,500,000 each year for the improvement of the silk industry in Kiangsu,

Year	Quantity (quintals)	Value (Chinese dollars)
1934	652,836	$26,216,683
1935	738,865	41,582,879
1936	867,383	73,378,654
1937	1,029,789	89,845,563

Chekiang, Shantung, Szechuan, and Kuangtung was embarked upon in 1935. By 1937 the Chinese silk industry was beginning to recover its lost business in domestic and foreign markets.[40]

◇ ◇ ◇

As China's agrarian ills arise mainly from collusion between corrupt officials and greedy landlords, certain of the reforms started by the National government were directed against these two obstacles.[41] On the political side the government has made strenuous efforts to improve local administration by introducing and encouraging the new hsien (county) system.

The first step in dealing with the problem of landlordism was the enactment of a land law in 1930 (revised in 1936 and 1942). This aims to enable tillers of the soil to become owners of land and to reduce rent by legal enforcement. Some of the chief provisions of the law are as follows:

(1) The tenant has the right to extend the term of contract indefinitely unless the landlord takes back the land for his own operation at the expiration of the contract; (2) the tenant is free to make any improvement on the land and will be compensated for it by the landlord; (3) the tenant cannot be evicted unless his payment of rent is two years in arrears or he has not operated the land for an

entire year without proper reason; (4) the tenant shall have pre-emption to the land he rents if his landlord wants to sell it; (5) if the landlord is absent from the locality where his land is situated, the tenant may proceed to own the land, under certain legal conditions, after operating it for ten years; (6) land rent shall not be more than 37.5 per cent of the value of the produce from the land; (7) farmers shall have the use of uncultivated public land, but they are not allowed to own it; and (8) the rate of taxation on improved farm land shall be 1 per cent of its value, that on unimproved land shall be 1.5–10 per cent of its value.[42]

The movement for a 25 per cent reduction of land rent originated in 1926 in Kuangtung, and spread to Hunan, Kiangsu, and Chekiang in 1927 and to Hupeh in 1929. It arose from the grievance of tenants that the usual rent amounting to 50 per cent of the principal crop was too high. After the reduction (25 per cent of 50 per cent) the maximum rent payable is 37.5 per cent of the main crop. But the enforcement of this article of the land law was not remarkably successful. Even in Chekiang, where reduction of rent was seriously enforced for several years, results were not encouraging. In counties where efficient organizations were established to settle rent disputes the law was operative; elsewhere, tenants continued to pay high rents.

Reform of the land tax was undertaken by the National Financial Conference called by the finance minister in May, 1934. Decisions reached therein were: first, that the basic land tax should be reduced in proportion to the actual value of land by the abolition, reduction, or limitation of surcharges according to different local conditions, and second, that land registration should be carried out in all provinces before a complete land survey was undertaken. Accordingly, a set of thirty-five regulations was prepared by the Ministry of Finance and promulgated by the Executive Yüan. Like the provision for reduction of rent in the land law, this administrative decree for reform of the land tax was carried out with varying degrees of success in the provinces as the central government extended its authority.

A notable achievement in rural reconstruction prior to 1937 was the development of the coöperative credit movement. The first urban coöperative credit society was started in 1919 by Professor

Hsieh Hsi-chou of Futan (fu-dan) University, Shanghai, who later organized the Chinese Coöperative Union and published the *Chinese Coöperative Monthly*. Coöperative credit societies in rural districts were started by the China International Famine Relief Commission about 1923 in the province of Chihli—since 1928, Hopei—whence they were extended to other northern provinces and later to the central provinces, which were affected by the Yangtze flood of 1931. Meanwhile other organizations evinced an active interest in rural credit coöperatives. Beginning in Hopei with eight societies and a membership of 256, the movement spread to sixteen provinces and three municipalities and numbered 26,224 coöperatives and 1,004,402 members by the end of 1935; each society averaged 38 members. Loans made by these coöperatives in 1935 amounted to Chinese $9,956,674, an average of $10 to each member.

Classified according to their function, 59 per cent of the 26,224 coöperatives were credit societies, 9 per cent were marketing societies, 9 per cent were production societies, 4 per cent were utility societies, 3 per cent were supply societies (including purchasing and consumer societies), and 16 per cent were integrated societies having multiple functions of furnishing credit, marketing, purchasing, production, or utility. Of the 1,004,402 members, 42 per cent belonged to credit societies, 12 per cent to marketing societies, 11 per cent to production societies, 7 per cent to utility societies, 7 per cent to supply societies, and 21 per cent to integrated societies. Classifying the multiple-purpose societies with the credit societies, credit coöperatives in China account for 75 per cent of all coöperatives and 63 per cent of the total membership.

As for the agencies responsible for organizing these coöperatives, the percentage distribution was as follows: 51 per cent were organized under the hsien government, 27 per cent under the hsien coöperative organizing office, 7 per cent under the China International Famine Relief Commission, 4 per cent under the Provincial Coöperative Committee, and 11 per cent under other institutions (colleges, banks, civic bodies). Of coöperatives, 19 per cent were financed by the Hsien Farmers Loan Office or Hsien Farmers Banks, 17 per cent by provincial coöperative committees or coöperative unions, 16 per cent by the China International Famine Relief Commission, 13 per cent by the Farmers Bank of China, 12 per cent by the Provincial Farmers Banks, 7 per cent by the Bank of China, 4 per cent by the Shanghai Commercial and Savings Bank, and 12 per cent by other financial institutions.[43]

Because of the rapid growth of coöperative societies and the numerous laws concerning them passed by various provincial governments after 1928, the Ministry of Industries initiated, in 1931, the first national law on coöperatives, known as the "Provisional Regulations Governing Rural Coöperative Societies." After three years' trial this law was replaced by the Coöperative Societies Act of 1934, which was put into force on September 1, 1935. Administration of agricultural coöperatives was decidedly improved by the establishment, in September, 1935, of a central supervisory organ, the Department of Coöperatives, in the Ministry of Industries.

◇   ◇   ◇

After midsummer of 1937, rural reconstruction achieved even more remarkable results than in prewar years. Generalissimo Chiang, realizing the necessity for a strong agricultural base against, *inter alia,* the Japanese invader, mobilized government departments for the improvement of agriculture in general and for maximum food production in particular. A Ministry of Agriculture and Forestry was inaugurated on July 1, 1940, and under it all agricultural improvement programs were centralized.[44]

The principal means employed to improve wartime agriculture were: (1) increase of crop acreage by improving irrigation, reclaiming waste land, and planting more winter crops, (2) introduction of scientific farming methods, (3) promotion of agricultural coöperation, (4) extension of large amounts of rural credits, (5) reform of local government and extension of rural education, (6) reform of the land-tax system, and (7) a program to reduce abusive landlordism and enable tenants to become owners. These measures had been started before the outbreak of war; now they were intensified and put into execution in a more rational way.

The following statistics on these seven phases of agricultural progress after 1937 cover chiefly the fifteen provinces of Unoccupied China: Szechuan, Yünnan, Kueichow, Kuangsi, Kuangtung, Hunan, Hupeh, Kiangsi, Chekiang, Fukien, Ningsia, Chinghai, Kansu, Shensi, and Honan. Sinkiang (sin-jiang), or Chinese Turkestan, and Sikang were also under the control of the central government, but figures from those provinces are few and more than ordinarily irregular.

From 1937 to 1941, about 2,165,000 *mou* of arid land were brought under cultivation because of new hydraulic construction. In 1941–1942, 258 irrigation projects, at a total cost of Chinese $137,246,806, were constructed. By July, 1942, Nationalist China was using about 580,000,000 *mou* of cultivated land to produce 1,500,000,000 piculs of cereals. About 68.5 per cent of this land was planted to cereals. This made the total cultivated area about 846,000,000 *mou*.[45] Prewar China had 657,612,000 *mou* in the same fifteen provinces. In addition, crop acreage was being increased by double cropping, that is, the planting of rice and other cereals in summer and the planting of wheat or beans on the same piece of land in winter. According to the findings of the National Agricultural Research Bureau, total winter-crop acreage before 1938 in the fifteen provinces mentioned was only three-fourths of the total summer-crop area.

Year	Planted area* (*mou*)	Increase over 1931–1937 average	
		Amount (*mou*)	Percentage
Average for 1931–1937..	269,524,000	....	...
1938.................	270,139,000	615,000	0.2
1939.................	276,677,000	7,153,000	2.7
1940.................	288,669,000	19,145,000	7.1
1941.................	300,299,000	30,775,000	11.4

* Winter crops planted are wheat, rapeseed, barley, oats, peas, and broad beans.

Acreage for food crops was further extended by drastic reduction of poppy-growing areas, which had been estimated in 1934 at close to one million acres. The vigorous opium-suppression campaigns conducted by Generalissimo Chiang had reportedly decreased this, by 1938, to slightly more than two thousand acres. Moreover, the raising of glutinous rice for making wine was persistently discouraged. Limitation was also imposed in various provinces upon tobacco acreage.

Food production was increased, not only by extension of crop acreage, but also by greater crop yield per unit of land. The miracles accomplished by scientific farming in other countries were repeated in China in this period of direst need. By the end of 1942 no less than 120 kinds of improved rice seeds were producing 20 per cent more rice than the old-type seed. Crop reports received by the University of Nanking at Chengtu in 1939 showed that in five Szechuan counties the production of No. 2905 wheat selection was 29.3 per cent higher than that of local strains. Improved corn and potato seeds, too, were widely used in Szechuan, Hunan, Yünnan, and Shensi. On the average, improved potato seeds produced from 100 to 250 catties per *mou* more than ordinary varieties. American improved cotton seeds were used in both the Yangtze and Yellow River valleys. In Szechuan province alone the acreage planted to such seeds rose from 1,500 acres in 1937 to 87,000 in 1940. In Unoccupied China as a whole, cotton acreage was advanced by one-fifth and crops by one-half from 1938 to 1940.

The National Animal Husbandry Research Bureau exerted every effort in extending crossbreeding to horses and other labor animals through artificial fertilization. Its mobile epizoötic prevention corps traveled widely. With the help of three American veterinary doctors, the Northwest Epizoötic Prevention Bureau manufactured serums and vaccines for use in Shensi, Kansu, Ningsia, and Chinghai. The Northwest Sheep's Wool Improvement Bureau conducted tests on crossbreeding of sheep and goats and sought better methods of fur and leather treatment. In 1942 the Bureau imported 150 New Zealand sheep via India to Lanchow for crossbreeding purposes. Better veterinary practices resulted, in 1939–1940, in an increase of 50,000 head of work cattle and 400,000 sheep in Shensi, Kansu, and Ningsia. Plans were made for increasing the sheep herd in northwestern China from 15,000,000 to 20,000,000 within five years.

Measures for controlling insects and diseases were employed on 6,454,638 *mou* of grain crops. They helped to reduce crop damage by about 21 per cent in 1941.

Bone-powder factories were established in Szechuan and in the northwestern provinces for the manufacture of fertilizers. About 3,960 piculs of fertilizers were produced annually. In 1941, with the help of an American fertilizer expert, Mr. G. F. Winfield, the

China Fertilizer Corporation was organized. The scheme took the form of a garbage-disposal plant in the city of Chungking. In full operation the plant can turn out 15 to 20 tons of fertilizer daily. Various types of fertilizers were applied to 2,768,841 *mou* of crop land in eleven provinces in 1941. Their use was estimated to have increased production by 1,361,077 piculs.

Technical workers from the Ministry of Agriculture and Forestry taught farmers how to use water-power cotton gins and improved "seven-seven" looms, which were distributed free or at a nominal price. With the help of new tools, farmers are able to increase production by 50 to 100 per cent.

⬦ ⬦ ⬦

Rural coöperatives got a good start before 1937. Later the government emphasized nation-wide development of various types of coöperatives. In May, 1939, the National Coöperative Administration was established to encourage and supervise coöperative enterprises, sponsor coöperative experiments, and train coöperative personnel. In February, 1941, a national coöperative supply and selling depot, with a capital of Chinese $5,000,000, was established in Chungking by the National Coöperative Administration. Agricultural products from other provinces were bought and carried by government purchasing agents to the depot to be sold at low prices. To the end of 1940 a total of 146,297 rural coöperative societies, with a membership of 7,582,107, were registered with the administration.

When Sino-Japanese hostilities broke out in 1937, the extension of rural credits was undertaken by the Agricultural Credit Administration. In October, 1940, the work of rural financing was transferred to the joint control board of the four government banks. Farm loans extended in 1941 by these banks amounted to Chinese $498,561,000. Total loans outstanding at the end of 1941 reached Chinese $465,306,000, a 50 per cent increase over 1940. These loans were spread over 948 hsien in 19 provinces and benefited approximately 6,000,000 farmers who were members of over 100,000 rural coöperatives.[46]

The Agricultural Credit Administration and the four government banks extended loans to farmers through three types of rural

financial organizations: rural credit coöperatives, rural coöperative banks, and granaries. The joint board of the four government
banks granted loans to rural credit coöperatives at a monthly interest rate of 1 per cent; the coöperatives, in turn, charged individual
farmers an interest of 1.2 per cent a month. Loans might be repaid
in installments ranging from one to ten years. Credits were given
only to coöperatives or other soundly organized farmers' associations. The last two types of rural financial institutions were started
by the Agricultural Credit Administration. Rural coöperative
banks, numbering some 400 in Chungking-controlled China, extended loans on personal credit, whereas granaries made loans
only on crops as security, undertaking at the same time to market
agricultural produce for farmers. When the four government
banks took over the work of rural financing from the Agricultural
Credit Administration, they gradually came to use rural coöperative banks as intermediaries. Government banks made more and
more loans to rural coöperative banks and also subscribed to a
major portion of their capital. Rural coöperatives, in turn, dealt
with coöperative banks through which farm loans were made.

In addition to granting loans, rural coöperative banks operated
rural remittance and savings offices in villages, managed granaries,
and began to finance mortgages. Most of them were hsien (county)
coöperative banks. Szechuan, Kiangsi, Chekiang, and Fukien each
had a coöperative bank and Chungking opened a municipal coöperative bank. The combined capital of these banks amounted, in
1944, to nearly Chinese $60,000,000, of which three-fourths was
provided by the four government banks. In addition to these four
banks, other organizations, such as provincial banks and administrative organs for the coöperative movement, gave financial assistance to rural coöperative banks. The objective was to provide each
hsien—of which there are 1,950 in all China—with one coöperative
bank and to enable farmers eventually to take over the shares
owned by government banks.

Loans extended by these four banks in 1941 fell into four major
classes, distributed as follows: agricultural production, 92.9 per
cent; irrigation, 6.1 per cent; agricultural extension, 0.8 per cent;
and land reclamation, 0.2 per cent.[47] After July 1, 1942, the Farmers
Bank of China, with its 180 branches and sub-branches, assisted by

350 hsien and municipal coöperative banks, was entrusted solely with rural financing activities. Its capital was increased from Chinese $20,000,000 to $60,000,000.

In 1941 the Ministry of Education initiated a five-year program for popular education in rural districts. The aim was to have at least one "people's school" for every three *pao* (each *pao* has 36–225 households) and a "nucleus" school for every *hsiang*, or *chen* (village or township consisting of 6–15 *pao*). By June, 1943, there were 27,655 *chen*, or *hsiang*, nucleus schools and 194,646 *pao* people's schools in non-Communist and non-Japanese-controlled China. It was estimated that about 65 per cent of children of school age (six to fifteen) and more than 30 per cent of illiterate adults had been benefited by the program.[48]

◇ ◇ ◇

The land-tax reform was another achievement in the speeding up of agricultural production. Reference has been made to the decision in 1934 to reform the land tax by a land survey and registration and by reduction of surcharges. Between 1934 and 1937, 239 counties in 13 provinces were said to have completed the land survey. The resurvey was resumed during the first four years of the renewed struggle with Nippon; it was carried forward in two steps. In 1941 the land tax was transferred from the provinces back to the central government, to which was returned 50 per cent of the tax in cash by the national treasury; payment of the tax was ordered to be made in kind (i.e., in rice or wheat). In 1942 a National Land Administration was created directly under the Executive Yüan to complete the land survey and registration throughout the country in order to start collection of taxes on revised land values.

At first the tax rate was set at 2 *tou* (22 lb.) of rice, wheat, or other cereals for each tax dollar. By this means the value of the tax was revised upward in proportion to the rise in wheat or rice prices, whereas the tax rate remained the same. By the spring of 1942 land-tax collections totaled 20,000,000 piculs. The estimated quotas for several provinces were exceeded by collections. In view of the excellent performance of this measure, quotas for 1942 were revised upward. The quantity of grain to be collected for each tax dollar was not changed, but tax rates were revised on the basis of revised land values resulting from the new land survey.

The primary purpose of the establishment of the National Land Administration was the realization of Sun Yat-sen's policy of equalization of landownership. To attack the problem of landlordism the author of the *San Min Chu I* had advocated two methods: collection of the land tax on the value assessment made by landowners themselves and the right of the government to purchase land at the valuation declared by the owners. After land values had been fixed, all increases in future land values should revert to the community, that is, such increments in value should be offset by increased taxes. In 1942 the land law was revised with a view to attaining this objective. The reform aimed at reassessment of the value of the land. The land tax, 1 to 2 per cent according to locality, was based on the reassessed value. Increments in land value are also to be taxed, but in the beginning the tax will be a minor portion of the increased value. To avoid too large variations the law provides that assessments declared by landowners shall not be 10 per cent more or less than the valuation made by the Land Finance Department (created in 1941) of the Farmers Bank of China.

In order to realize Dr. Sun's principle that those who till the land shall be its owners, the land law empowers the government to buy land from owners and sell it to tenant farmers by paying the owners partly in cash and partly in land bonds. Land bonds amounting to Chinese $100,000,000, secured on government-owned lands and mines, were issued in 1942 by the Land Finance Department,[49] which was started with a capital of Chinese $10,000,000. This department of the Farmers Bank will eventually be enlarged into an independent national land credit bank with branches in every one of China's 1,950 hsien. Land bonds will enable the government to purchase land for promoting public enterprises or for reselling to tenant farmers, to make resurveys of land and new registration of owners, and to assist in farm improvements.[50]

The law allows tenant farmers to make payments in installments when purchasing land from the government. It further provides that the tenant enjoys priority in buying land whenever the owner wants to sell it. One other fundamental provision of the revised land law is limitation of rent to 10 per cent of assessed land value.

Rent, if collected in kind by the landlord, is not to exceed 37.5 per cent of the proceeds.[51] When carried out, this reform will be revolutionary in its effects upon agriculture and industry alike. To landlords it will be a great reduction from the customary fifty-fifty division of farm products.

A statute limitation of rent to 10 per cent of assessed land value will drive much capital into industry and commerce, where there is no legal limitation on amount of profits. Industrialization is the best means for farm relief in China.[52] By it, some believe that the chief problems of Chinese agricultural economy—pressure of population upon limited land resources and scientific and technical backwardness of farming methods—will be solved simultaneously. If the percentage of population engaged in farming pursuits can be reduced from 80 to 60 or 55 per cent of the country's total population, land vacated by those who go into industry can be redistributed among the remaining smaller farming population. This will result in a general increase in size of farms.

As farms increase in size and as industrialization produces more agricultural implements and electrical power in rural districts, farm machinery can be economically introduced. With opportunities for employment in factories, the surplus farming population will not compete for the land. Parcellization of land can be stopped; at the time of inheritance one son can buy his father's land from his brothers who may wish to leave the farm to enter industry.

This assumes, of course, that methods are put into practice to arrest the rapid population growth; otherwise the vacated land will soon be swallowed by new mouths. Therefore a rational industrialization program, which aims also at modernization of Chinese farms, and an intelligent population policy[53] are necessary instruments for the reconstruction of Chinese agriculture. For the first, *China's Destiny,* a book sponsored by Generalissimo Chiang, supplies a sound blueprint. For the second, the emergence of an unsentimental public opinion is necessary, since there is little hope of improving the standard of living of China's farmers until the size of farms is enlarged and the produce of farms per unit of labor as well as per unit of land is increased. Industrialization in the sense of application of science to agriculture as well as to industry seems to be the only way to achieve this objective.

CHAPTER XXXIII

International Trade

BY LI CHOH-MING

CHINA HAS PAID A HIGH PRICE for its economic transformation during the past century. Hand in hand with foreign trade came political institutions and practices which have hampered its development. In any evaluation of the influence of trade upon the country's economic development, recognition must be made of the struggle of foreign Powers for spheres of control and the abuses inherent in the interwoven Treaty Port and extraterritorial systems.

Although international trade as a crucially potent force did not come into being until the latter half of the nineteenth century, this does not mean that earlier commercial relations did not affect Chinese economy. In ancient times caravan trade developed—even reaching the Mediterranean before the Christian era. Later there was sea-borne trade. Both grew through the centuries by carrying the products of Chinese craftsmen and industries, particularly silk fabrics and porcelain, to distant markets in exchange for dyestuffs, precious stones, metals, and such commodities as sea food and tropical produce.

By the beginning of the nineteenth century, trade had brought into China enormous quantities of silver, thereby making it possible for that non-silver-producing country to have a convenient and more or less unified medium of exchange for development of domestic or interregional commerce. Many agricultural products, such as cotton, corn, and tobacco, were introduced from abroad and later became staple crops for large areas. The chief drawback of this early commerce was the import of opium, which not only drained the stock of silver after the 1830's but encouraged extensive domestic poppy cultivation, to the impairment of the people's health.

It is noteworthy that early trade took place neither as a result of economic pressure from overdeveloped Chinese industries searching for outside markets nor from lack of raw materials or necessities of life that must be obtained from abroad. Although Chinese merchants went abroad, trade was carried on mainly by foreign merchants in China, who imported luxury goods in exchange for such commodities as tea and silk. The nature of these activities very considerably influenced the attitude of the imperial government. Trading had long been regarded as a favor granted to foreigners from countries so poorly endowed by nature as to compel their merchants to travel to the land of abundance for the products necessary to maintain the livelihood of their people. For this reason, as well as to facilitate government supervision, foreign trade was confined to a few ports and handled by the imperial merchants or, as in Canton, by a monopolistic organization known as the Co-hong. The First Anglo-Chinese War (1839–1842) was fought by Great Britain primarily to break down the restrictive system, to obtain an unfettered right to trade in the country, and to be treated as a sovereign state equal in dignity to China.

◇ ◇ ◇

After 1842, trade took on new life in the Treaty Ports, where both native and foreign merchants transacted business in concessions or settlements under the general protection of extraterritorial rights. By 1894 the number of Treaty Ports had increased from five to twenty-one. Reaching wider markets, trade gained momentum in combating the traditional economic system of the country, but its effects did not permeate deeply.

Gradually the Treaty Ports grew into large commercial cities. Until its opening for foreign residence in 1843, Shanghai was but a third-rate walled city of small commercial importance; it took no more than a decade, however, to supersede Canton as the chief port. Foreign bottoms arrived in increasing tonnage and were employed even in coastal trade. Official efforts began to provide aids to navigation without which commerce could never have expanded as it did. The administration of the Customs was placed (*ca.* 1854–

1863) in foreign hands. Postal services on Western models were subsequently introduced. Emigration, which later figured significantly in China's balance of international payments in the form of remittances, entered a new phase. From 1847 to 1862 the export of contract or indentured labor was estimated at 150,000, with free emigration twice as large.

Many factors operated to bring China closer to world economy. As a result of implementation of the Tientsin treaties of 1858, which opened the principal ports of the Yangtze River to foreign merchants, trade reached the whole of that rich and densely populated valley, and ocean ships sailed from Western ports directly to Hankow. The opening of the Suez Canal, in November, 1869, shortened the distance between East and West and gave impetus to steam navigation in China. Only three years later the Chinese established the China Merchants Steam Navigation Company, which engaged in the coastal trade. An incidental but important result was that coal mines were developed to supply the coastal steamers with fuel. Another event which brought China closer to world economy was the completion of the submarine telegraph in June, 1871. By putting Shanghai in direct communication with London, the use of the cable lowered the risk of loss and tended to reorganize trade on a basis of regular shipments for full or partial commissions. Modern methods of trade financing were introduced with the establishment in Hongkong of the Chartered Bank of China, India, and Australia in 1853 and of the Hongkong and Shanghai Banking Corporation in 1864.

But trade had yet to beget industry. It was only when manufactured goods were imported in large quantities at prices low enough to reach the general public—which broke down old habits of consumption and created new demands—that industry could be profitably developed. The luxurious character of early imports is to be explained chiefly by the high cost of transport, which necessitated trading in expensive goods of small bulk. Thus the opening of the Suez Canal, which immediately led to an appreciable reduction in freight rates, must be considered a turning point in China's trade. But foreign traders had still to learn the need for creating demand, and large consignments of table knives and forks, tuning forks, and so on, were recklessly sent to China on speculation.

Since for unnumbered centuries the Middle Kingdom had been self-sufficient in manufactured goods, the resistance of its economy to new habits was great. For example, the native handicraft industry in cotton goods at first held out against British machine manufacturing. Whereas in recent decades China has been a market for Western textile products, all cotton goods moved in the opposite direction until well into the nineteenth century. Products of Chinese craftsmanship were better than those of the looms of Lancaster, and "nankeens" were fashionable even in England. For many years, machine-made piece goods could not compete in China either in price or in quality. As late as 1841 the value of raw cotton imported for Chinese handicrafts was second only to that of opium and constituted one-fifth of commodity imports.

It was only in the 1880's, with the mechanical refinement of processes of cotton weaving in the West and cheap production of cotton yarn in the factories of India, that import of cotton goods into China began to exceed that of any other item. Cotton goods occupied 8.5 per cent of total commodities in a normal year before the First Anglo-Chinese War, but the percentage increased to 29.2 in 1882 and to 40 in 1891. Cotton handicrafts disintegrated in regions reached by imported cotton goods. With the superiority of the mechanical process thus proved in the production of such a necessity as cloth, it is obvious that the cotton industry would be the first to develop within China.

Introduction of other imports now regarded as daily necessities took a longer period of time. Kerosene, which was to become a product generally used by rural families, was at first frowned upon by officials on the grounds of its great inflammability and was not accepted widely because of its unsuitability for the old-fashioned lamp. As late as the early 'eighties the import of matches, needles, and window glass catered only to a special or luxury demand.

Persistence of old consumption habits was, however, only one aspect of the general resistance to change. The first railroad was built between Shanghai and Woosung in 1875, but it had to be dismantled in the following year partly because of the superstitions of the people. The failure of a factory to produce bean cakes and bean oil in Newchwang is typical of many attempts to erect factories in this period. On foreign advice, a modern mill was set up in 1867 with machinery ordered from England. Work commenced, but the machinery soon had to be discarded, not only because the employees opposed it for fear of eventual unemployment, but also because the machinery did not press out the oil as effectively as did manual labor.

Creation of new consumption habits, breakdown of social prejudices, and readjustment of machinery to meet the problems peculiar to Chinese production were not accomplished quickly. Whatever slight effect trade had produced upon Chinese industry was evidenced by increase of imports of dyes and metals; the latter expanded from 1.2 per cent of total imports in 1841 to 5.4 per cent in 1891.

The effect on agriculture was farther-reaching, and large markets developed for various Chinese agricultural products. Tea and silk predominated on the export list, but whereas in 1842 tea contributed 71 per cent to the total export trade and silk 20.5 per cent, leaving only 8.5 per cent for all other items, in 1891 the percentages for tea and silk were 30.7 and 30, respectively, and other items, consisting of many agricultural products heretofore unknown to the world markets, had increased to 32.7 per cent. Raw cotton was required for new factories in Japan; straw braid made in Shantung was needed abroad; and beans and bean cake, hides and skins, vegetable oils, seeds, and other commodities were beginning to be exported in quantities. The total volume of trade had increased from Chinese $60,000,000 in 1844 to $366,000,000 in 1891, with corresponding increase from $40,000,000 to $209,000,000 in imports and from $20,000,000 to $157,000,000 in exports.

<>   <>   <>

Industrial development would have taken much longer if it had had to await the breakdown of conservatism. The rapid rise of Japan as an industrial power, particularly after the Sino-Japanese War of 1894–1895, convinced many Chinese of the necessity of a reoriented economy. But prejudices still prevailed and economic development would have been much slower if foreign merchants had not begun to bring in investments as well as commerce.

The subsidiary treaty of commerce signed at Peking by China with Japan on July 21, 1896, granted to Japanese—and hence, by

application of the most-favored-nation clause, to other foreigners—
the privilege of erecting and operating factories and workshops
with power-driven machinery in the Treaty Ports. The Inland
Navigation Regulations of 1898 permitted foreign ships to ply and
trade in inland waters between Treaty Ports. From 1894 to 1915,
twenty-nine more ports, including several in Manchuria, were
opened to foreign trade. This brought to fifty the number of Treaty
Ports. In 1900, foreign investments in China totaled United States
$750,000,000; this figure, according to Professor C. F. Remer,
doubled during the First World War and doubled once more by
the time of the Japanese occupation of Manchuria in September,
1931.

The first factories were cotton mills and steam filatures started
by foreigners. Impressed by superiority of mechanical methods of
production, the Chinese followed suit and established modern
factories. It has been estimated that there were 832,300 spindles
and 2,100 looms at work in the new machine cotton industry on the
eve of the Revolution of 1911–1912. Flour mills, oil mills, glass
works, soap and candle factories, and cigarette and match factories
were developed, together with shipbuilding and engineering works,
paper mills, printing works, and electric-light plants. But all this
development was confined to the Treaty Ports and, more often than
not, was under foreign control and management.

Chinese banks organized in the Western manner also appeared,
and large department stores were opened by overseas Chinese who
returned with capital and modern methods of merchandising.

The effect of trade on agriculture may be seen in the development of exports. The opening of Manchuria to trade made possible
the first trial shipment of soybeans to London in 1906. This product
rose in three years to represent more than one-eighth the value of
all exports from China. Foreign demand for Chinese seed oils had
augmented their prices so steadily as to drive the peasants to the
cheaper, although imported, kerosene for illuminating purposes.[1]
Export of eggs and egg products also began to show significantly
in trade returns.

Not until 1929 did industrial development receive protection
from a favorable tariff. The conventional 5 per cent, which applied

---

[1] For notes to chapter xxxiii see page 545.

equally to imports and exports, had been reduced through price changes to an effective tariff schedule of a mere 3 per cent. In spite of lack of preferential treatment, industry after the Revolution of 1911–1912 received favorable impetus from two factors. The First World War cut China off from many imports and thus encouraged development of domestic industries. This was followed by years of the falling gold price of silver, which caused the ratio of import to export prices to move against China and therefore served not only as a protection to Chinese industry but also as an inducement to the influx of foreign capital.

The result was a boom in the import of machinery of all kinds, railway equipment, and electric apparatus in the years immediately following the end of the war. More power-driven factories were erected than at any previous time. A program of road building was undertaken by the central government, and the import of motor vehicles swelled rapidly. Modernization spread over many parts of the country; electric-light plants and waterworks were installed even in small towns. At this time the initiative for modernization passed from the hands of foreign traders and entrepreneurs to the Chinese.

Economic development is clearly reflected in the changing character of foreign trade. Although cotton goods had headed the list of imports in 1891, accounting for 40 per cent of China's total imports, their relative importance steadily declined to 30.5 per cent in 1911, 23 per cent in 1921, 8.4 per cent in 1931, and 2.3 per cent in 1937. The establishment of native and foreign mills inside the country had made this possible and had led also to an increase in exports of textile products from China from a mere 2 per cent of total exports to more than 8 per cent from 1921 to 1931. Growth of the textile industry resulted, for a long period, in an enormous import of raw cotton, which by 1931 accounted for 12.5 per cent of total imports. The government, however, fostered a program to improve and expand domestic cultivation of cotton. The result was immediately registered in the dwindling importation of this commodity; it amounted to only 1.7 per cent of total imports in 1937.

Imports of such commodities as flour, sugar, matches, and cigarettes had also declined as a result of domestic industrial development, whereas importation of machinery, metals, dyes, and the like increased. Metal imports swelled from 4.5 per cent of total imports in 1914 to 13.8 per cent in 1937; imports of machinery and machines varied from 0.25 per cent in 1902 to 9.9 per cent in 1921 and 6.8 per cent in 1937. In 1937, large imports of other metal manufactures and chemicals took place, representing 8.8 per cent and 6.4 per cent of total imports, respectively.

In export trade, new products emerged to play leading roles. Silk and tea, which accounted for 91.5 per cent of China's exports in 1841 and 34.8 per cent in 1911, amounted to no more than 11.7 per cent in 1937. On the other hand, beans and bean cake, though only 3 per cent of total exports in 1896, rose to first place in 1931, with a share of more than 21 per cent. When Japanese occupation of Manchuria deprived China of the source of beans and bean products, tung oil became the leading export. In 1931 all vegetable oils accounted for 5.7 per cent of total exports; in 1937 tung oil alone contributed 10.7 per cent. Eggs and egg products advanced from 0.7 per cent of total exports in 1904 and 1 per cent in 1911 to 4 per cent in 1931 and 6.3 per cent in 1937. Hides and skins were other important items; their relative importance in export trade increased slowly from 3.4 per cent of total exports in 1896 to 6.4 per cent in 1937. Finally, the development of mining made it possible to increase the export of mineral ores from 1.6 per cent of total exports in 1904 and 3 per cent in 1931 to 12.2 per cent in 1937.

Economic development after 1918 may best be seen through analysis of the composition of China's foreign trade according to commodity groups. Such an analysis was made by the writer to cover the period 1913–1931. Beginning in 1934 the Chinese Customs published trade statistics by economic groups. Inevitable differences in classification do not prevent the combined use of these two reports to indicate general trends. (See table overleaf.)

Economic development in the period 1914–1931 was toward growth of industry. The position of finished manufactures in both imports and exports declined, whereas the relative decline of semimanufactures in total imports was greater than their relative increase in total exports, and the share of raw materials advanced more considerably in imports than it declined in exports. The share of crude foodstuffs increased appreciably in both import and export trade, but there was a definite decline in position of manufactured foodstuffs in imports, with a simultaneous, although slight, improvement in position of the same group in exports.

The temporary loss of Manchuria, the chief source of soybeans and bean products, produced an important change in the character of exports after 1931, reducing in particular the share of crude foodstuffs. But agricultural production, especially of cotton, stead-

CHINA'S TRADE BY ECONOMIC GROUPS, 1913–1937

Year	Crude foodstuffs	Manufactured foodstuffs	Raw materials	Semimanufactures	Finished manufactures
IMPORTS					
1913..............	1.4	17.2	11.9	22.5	47.2
1921..............	5.6	12.6	9.3	18.4	54.1
1926..............	10.8	14.1	14.7	13.6	46.8
1931..............	11.2	9.7	19.3	14.6	45.2
1934..............	21.7		13.8	21.3	43.2
1937..............	13.9		8.2	22.8	55.1
EXPORTS					
1913..............	18.9	14.1	42.6	9.9	14.5
1921..............	22.8	10.0	36.0	8.9	22.3
1926..............	25.3	13.2	36.2	10.2	15.1
1931..............	30.2	12.9	29.9	12.4	14.5
1934..............	28.2		33.0	18.6	20.2
1937..............	21.4		37.7	24.7	16.2

ily improved in China south of the Wall, and mining was stepped up rapidly. The result was that, up to 1937, foodstuffs declined in importance in both imports and exports, whereas raw materials declined in imports but increased in exports. The relative position of semimanufactures improved in both imports and exports. Finished manufactures, especially machinery, increased in imports in relation to other groups, but declined in exports.

The change in China's international economic position in the last hundred years may be summarized in the estimates made by various authors of its balance of international payments for certain years. (See the table opposite.)

With the introduction of steamships, the building of the Suez Canal, and the opening of additional ports, China's foreign trade expanded. The effect of this upon the whole economy was first seen in the introduction of commodities of general demand, a process that was slow in breaking down old consumption habits. Under the

BALANCE OF CHINA'S INTERNATIONAL PAYMENTS, 1841–1935
(In millions of Chinese dollars)

	1841 (Sargent)	1903 (Morse)	1930 (Remer)	1935 (Bank of China)
Current outpayments:				
Merchandise imports	25*	492	1,965	1,129
Specie imports	..	58	101	.....
Service of foreign loans	..	69	111	108
Chinese expenditures abroad	..	7	13	55
Remittance of foreign enterprises and other profits	..	35	227	55
Total	25	661	2,417	1,347
Current inpayments:				
Merchandise exports	13.3	374	1,476	662
Specie exports	11.2	51	48	357
Foreign expenditures in China	0.5	81	218	150
Overseas remittances	....	114	316	260
Total	25.0	620	2,058	1,429
Capital inpayments:				
New foreign investments in China	....	42	202	140
Unaccounted for	....	−1	−157	222

* Including treasure imports.

system of extraterritoriality and Treaty Ports, however, trade brought with it foreign investments which soon led to development of banking, communications, modern business methods, industry, and mining. Industrial growth accelerated under the impetus of the First World War and later of silver depreciation; in 1929 it received the added benefit of tariff protection.

As many products now found increasing demand from the industrialized cities at home or from abroad, commercialization of agriculture could not fail to develop from trade and industrial expansion. In spite of exploitation on the part of middlemen—a class newly emerged and having special significance for commercial development—the income and hence the standard of living of peasants producing such products was raised.

Foreign trade became the largest single source of income of the national treasury; it contributed 53 per cent of the total revenue in 1937. The material prosperity brought to China through foreign trade may be seen from the growing surplus of imports over exports since the 1880's, running to as much as one billion Chinese dollars in 1931, paid for mainly by foreign borrowing and investments on the one hand, and emigrant remittances on the other.

But this development of trade brought about a crisis in the erstwhile self-sufficient economy. After fruitless struggle, many handicraft industries failed and brought unemployment to an army of artisans who had been working on a full-time basis, and also to peasants and their families who had been working on a part-time basis. This was true particularly of hand spinning and in large measure of weaving as well. Since the 1880's the products of these industries had given way to machine-made yarn and cloth wherever these could be purchased. So far as goods of general demand are concerned, it has been proved again and again that handicraft industry cannot meet competition from factory manufactures. With income of many rural districts reduced and with many unemployed, readjustment of the economy was painful.

The force that brought suffering to artisans and peasants, however, eventually made possible the development of new handicraft industries for domestic and world markets, as well as commercialization of crops. Hairnets, braid, bristles, lace, and embroidery are a few of the many products which gave handicraft industries new life by reason of growing demand in foreign markets. But the character of these industries has changed. They have come to be controlled by merchants or factories that supply raw materials or look after the markets. On the whole, the artisan is no longer the owner of the product, but is a worker for an industrial or commercial concern.

Commercialization of crops was an almost inevitable result of increasing demand communicated to peasants by middlemen or factories. Factories were in a position to exploit peasants by manipulating prices and by charging sizable commissions. The peasants, who formerly were self-sufficient, were now compelled to face the new experience of sharing the vicissitudes of fortune, that is, the demand fluctuations in domestic and foreign markets. Finally, the growth of commercial capital, as a result of developments in the economy as a whole, even had the effect of depriving many peasants of ownership of land in favor of absentee owners.

While all this may be regarded as the price a country must pay for economic transformation, the fact that the change was effected by forces outside instead of within the country resulted in unbalanced economic development. Practically all foreign investments, with the exception of railways and mining, were confined to Treaty Ports, where they were given protection by governing councils consisting of foreign residents not subject to Chinese law—and, in case of need, by foreign arms. Under these circumstances foreign investments took the form of establishments directly managed and owned by foreigners; financing institutions, foreign trading concerns, and a labor force trained and developed by foreign enterprise grew in the ports where concessions and settlements were located. Ocean shipping brought raw materials to these ports at a much lower transportation cost than that of the same commodities obtained from the interior of the country. Consequently, these advantages encouraged Chinese private capital to seek safety and employment in the port cities. For these reasons, in the main, Shanghai became the commercial, financial, and industrial center of China.

That this development was unhealthy is shown by the fact that, although the Treaty Ports and their immediate vicinity developed rapidly, the rest of the country lagged farther and farther behind. Rural districts were depleted of funds, whereas there was a glut of capital in the Treaty Ports. Notoriously high rates of interest for peasants were, in some measure, an outcome of this movement of capital.

The food problem illustrates even more pointedly the unbalanced economic development. China had long been basically self-sufficient in food. But the introduction of industry to the ports attracted large numbers of peasants to the cities and even rendered food production less profitable than that of crops for world markets.

One of the results was that the traditional balance between town and village economy was upset and food imports to cities had to be increased. Had the rest of the country kept pace with the industrialization of the cities, agriculture might have become more commercialized. But this did not occur, and China in recent decades has had to import increasing quantities of foodstuffs from abroad. That this need not have happened was amply proved after 1937, when the enemy's blockade did not result in widespread food deficiency except in regions suffering from drought.

Finally, the fact that many raw materials, including food, which could have been supplied at least as cheaply inside the country, have been imported from abroad because of lower cost of transportation is another illustration of the unbalanced development of national economy. On the basis of distribution of natural resources, the location of many industries would have been quite different had internal transportation been properly developed. The Japanese occupation of the chief manufacturing and commercial centers in 1937–1938, and the driving of the people westward into largely undeveloped areas, made clear the dangers of concentration of economic development.

Under these circumstances even trade itself, expanding from Chinese $60,000,000 in 1842 to $1,791,000,000 in 1937, did not develop in a healthy manner. Upward of 80 per cent of prewar trade was handled by foreign firms located in Treaty Ports, mostly in Shanghai. These firms were much more interested in selling their own wares to "400,000,000 customers" than in expanding foreign markets for Chinese products. It is true, nevertheless, that foreign firms were often the first to introduce Chinese products abroad, many of which gradually loomed large in China's export trade. But it almost always happened that no sooner did production in other countries begin to compete with that of China than the Chinese product receded from the market without much struggle. The story of China's teas and silks affords a good illustration of this.

The reason is not far to seek. To survive in the highly competitive world market requires the utmost effort and planning by the exporter, as well as close coöperation with the producers at home. Yet the Chinese paid little attention to this matter, and foreign firms handling the bulk of the trade properly considered it beyond their concern. This goes far to explain why, in the last hundred years, China's exports have been lopsided.

Another contributory result of this commercial development was that terms of international exchange moved against China, though these items were affected principally by the continuous fall of the gold price of silver. In comparison with the period before 1905, China bartered each year less and less imported goods for its total exports up to 1935 and, in addition, had to pay many times more for them in money value. Moreover, for an *equal* money value of imports China paid increasing amounts of exported goods after the 1870's.   ◇   ◇   ◇

Limited as have been its benefits, foreign trade has shown the way in which the economy of China should be reorganized. Events of the war years, 1937–1945, thoroughly convinced both leaders and people of the immediate necessity of developing natural resources by modern scientific methods. History has also brought home the important lesson that balanced economic development can come about only when change is engendered by forces within the country. The inescapable conclusion is that there must be a national plan which aims at coördinated and simultaneous development of transportation, industry, mining, agriculture, handicrafts, finance, and commerce. Along with this, the interests of society must be safeguarded by encouraging full play of private initiative in all fields other than a few to be operated as government enterprises. And that is the plan of the government with regard to postwar reconstruction—a reconstruction which will, it is hoped, be unlike the industrialization of Japan, where the will of the leaders was imposed on society, with the result that industry and commerce were developed for the benefit of the few at the expense of the welfare of the people as a whole.

This program will require huge amounts of capital for which China will have to look abroad, since the low standard of living within the country makes accumulation of capital very slow. Thus foreign trade will be the channel through which foreign capital will flow as the active and accelerating force in Chinese economic reconstruction. The old era in which foreign trade operated as the powerful initiative force of eccentric modernization has come to an end. A new era begins with the influence of trade on China's economic development managed and guided by the National government in accordance with a plan. The resultant balanced development of the country is expected to raise the standard of living of the people and thereby open to the world new sources of wealth and expanding markets.

Part Six

RETROSPECT
AND PROSPECT

CHAPTER XXXIV

China among the Nations

BY DAVID NELSON ROWE

AT THE SAN FRANCISCO CONFERENCE in 1945 China was one of the four Powers sponsoring basic plans for international organization. This fact constituted more than an indication of the essential unity of China's peace aims with those of Britain, the Soviet Union, and the United States. Its real significance was as a symbol of China's new position in world politics. This position is strikingly different from that which China held in 1918 at the end of the First World War. It may therefore be illuminating to go back a few years and consider briefly the course of events through which the country has passed.

When the First World War began, the military phases of the revolution which had overthrown the Manchu dynasty were less than three years old. The Revolution of 1911–1912 had been preceded by three-quarters of a century of increasing internal and international weakness. During that time the international position of the Middle Kingdom had deteriorated steadily with the decline of its standing as a military power. Internal weaknesses, combined with a succession of defeats by foreign adversaries, had, by the end of the nineteenth century, brought the Manchu-Chinese Empire to a condition in which it was no longer able to determine its own fate.

The Treaty Powers supplemented their often collaborative military actions by coöperative political policies. From the outset, by insertion of "most-favored-nation" clauses in their treaties with China, improvement by any Power of its relationship with China was made a stake of all other Powers.

This was a feasible device only under certain conditions. It was bound to fail in its basic objective—preservation of equal privileges for all foreign interests in China—as soon as those privileges combined with other factors to weaken China to the point where total collapse seemed imminent. When, at the end of the nineteenth century, this situation appeared to have developed, coöperation of the Powers with respect to China gave way to a policy of staking out areas for exclusive colonial possession in the near future.

In 1899 an attempt was made to reverse the trend and return to the previous policy of international trade without special privileges or exclusive areas of economic domination for the Powers in China: the United States fostered a return to these practices under the open-door policy. This was a reflection of its own interests and was based on the oldest traditions in American international practice, derived from the Revolutionary War, which had been to an appreciable degree a struggle against "colonial exclusiveness" in trade.[1] With respect to China, it was based firmly on the interest of Great Britain in preventing colonial fragmentation. This would allow Britain to maintain to the fullest that primacy in the China trade which was the result of superiority in industrial development and commercial experience.

Thus in its practical effect the open-door policy would have constituted an important support to the interest of Britain in the arena of European power politics. The Power chiefly to suffer from its acceptance would have been Russia, which, by advances in Manchuria and Korea, was becoming the chief threat to commercial interests based on equality of opportunity throughout the Manchu-Chinese Empire.

That no self-denying ordinance could at this time resolve the clash of power politics over China was demonstrated by the Russo-Japanese War of 1904–1905, which was fought to a great extent on Chinese soil. Military weakness rendered Peking a nullity in the power complex. Russia and Japan merely demonstrated anew the relationship between foreign imperialism in China and the operations of Western power politics. Japan's technique then, as later, was to utilize the facts of the European balance of power to implement its own long-term plans for imperialistic expansion.

When, in August, 1917, China entered upon direct participation

---

[1] For notes to chapter xxxiv see page 545.

in the First World War, domestic disunity and other weaknesses prevented strong action. Japan was plotting the total conquest of the country, as had been made evident in the attempt to succeed Germany in Shantung and to impose on President Yüan Shih-k'ai the notorious Twenty-one Demands of 1915. These, if carried into effect, would have turned China into a colonial appendage of the Japanese Empire. They were a logical extension of the policy toward the nations of continental Asia enunciated by Japanese statesmen as early as 1887 and they constituted a major step in attempting to carry out this policy.

At the Washington Conference of 1921–1922 a final attempt was made to forestall all efforts to deprive China of sovereignty or territorial integrity. By agreement of the Powers, China was to have the opportunity to further its internal revolution in the hope that it might emerge with the strength necessary for self-defense.

This agreement was embodied in treaties. It was, even more than the open-door notes, an attempt to guarantee voluntary self-denial by the Power most interested. This is true because the agreement to keep hands off China was accompanied by agreements for limitation of naval armaments and prevention of the construction of naval bases in the China-Japan area by the Powers most interested in seeing that the agreements were observed.

By limiting their naval armaments the Powers could attempt to guarantee that their territorial possessions would be secure from attack by each other. But they could not guarantee that their interests in third countries would be secure from attack merely by mutual agreement unless that agreement were rooted firmly in the interests of all assenting Powers. That this did not hold for Japan becomes clear from elementary study of Japanese history since 1868. Motivations for continental imperialism were not diminished in force by the facts of international power politics.

The Western idea of causing the Nipponese to bind themselves by paper agreements to maintain a course contrary to their interests, as they had always seen them, is based on failure to understand Japanese political psychology. Orthodox Japanese political theory states clearly the concept that law is inferior to persons. In domestic politics this means the rule of an oligarchic aristocracy with practical, though not theoretical, absence of constitutionalism. In international politics it means, even more than for other states, the dominance of unilateralism and the practical weakness of treaties as legal limitations on the pursuit of basic national interests.

Between 1922 and the invasion of Manchuria in September, 1931, international developments in the field of military power were largely favorable to Japan. The United States and Great Britain were victims of a desire for disarmament; the United States failed even to keep its navy up to the strength allowed in the treaties. Japan, on the other hand, pushed naval construction to the limit.

In China the Kuomintang Nationalist government had come to power in 1927–1928. The years between that date and the Japanese attack in Manchuria brought progress in political consolidation and internal development. Even more so did the years up to 1937, when the Japanese renewed attack in northern China. China's resistance was not alone founded on domestic elements of political and military-strategic strength: its success was predicated on a judgment by Generalissimo Chiang Kai-shek of the probable course of world events.[2] (See chap. x, above.) Unless Japan's aggression should produce an alignment of Powers on China's side, the Chinese strategy of defensive warfare and retreat would fail. Final victory required a counteroffensive, and this China could never support on its own military resources. Eviction of the Japanese could be accomplished only by much help from allies.

Before Japan renewed the attack against China in 1937, the alliances for the war were taking shape. When the Anti-Comintern Pact became the Berlin-Tokyo Axis in 1936, China and the Soviet Union were automatically forced together. An almost immediate sequel was the formation of a united front of Nationalists and Communists in China. When, in July, 1937, Japan renewed war on China, the Soviet Union became the chief supplier of arms and military personnel to Chiang Kai-shek's forces. This help was kept up in considerable volume until the Soviet Union became involved in war with Japan's Axis partner. Even thereafter some items were sent in, and the long supply routes from Russian Turkestan carried rather large quantities of lend-lease materials from the United States.

If the Berlin-Tokyo Axis was aimed at the U.S.S.R., it was aimed also at Great Britain and the United States. These Powers were

slower to recognize its threat than was the U.S.S.R. But the resultant temporizing treatment of Japan was also a logical outcome of
the absence in the China-Japan area of any substantial elements
of their military strength. In this they differed from the U.S.S.R.,
whose power to defend interests in the Far East had been borne in
on the Japanese during numerous armed encounters on the Manchurian and Mongolian borders.

The eventual Anglo-American attitude of increasing opposition
to Japan's aims in China and southeastern Asia outran the efforts
of the American and British governments to strengthen themselves
militarily in these regions. As Japan recognized the likelihood of
the eventual use of force to thwart it, the best chance lay in joining
battle before the Westerners could prepare a defense in Asia. The
raid on Pearl Harbor was a stroke at the only element of Anglo-
American power which at that time, unless first crippled, could be
transported to the Orient and, if based partially on Singapore,
could threaten Japanese progress southward. The soundness of
this strategy could be impeached only by those having a better appreciation than had the Japanese of the probable psychological
reaction and the possibilities of over-all military mobilization in
the United States.

But whereas the Japanese underestimated these factors, most
Chinese, in December, 1941, tended to overestimate the military
strength of the United States. The writer, at that time in Chungking, found many Chinese reluctant to recognize the existing condition of unpreparedness in the United States. Chinese hopes of
a quick defeat of Japan, once Britain and America were involved,
had been fostered by overzealous friends from those countries,
some of whom had predicted easy victory within six months. The
jubilation in Unoccupied China at the acquisition of allies in the
war was soon quenched by the succession of Allied losses to Japan.
That these actually weakened the ability of China to resist made
the disillusionment even more severe. The evil results of this complex of frustration on both sides for a time clouded relations between the Allies in the Far Eastern war.

Despite these events and occasional disagreements over strategy,
China's eventual victory was guaranteed by the development of
rivalries of other Powers in the Far East. It is erroneous to say that

Nippon's drive into southeastern Asia was caused by stalemate in China. But it would be equally wrong to suppose that the drive would have come when it did except for two reasons strongly related to that stalemate: these were the embargo on oil to Japan which made it necessary to seize the sources of supply in the Dutch possessions, and increasing American aid to China which made it necessary for Japan to seize Hongkong and Burma, accessible points of ingress to that country. For both these causes of southward advance Japan could thank the stalemate in China. And this does not overlook the probable Japanese estimate that the situation in Europe made unlikely a strong defense by Britain and the Netherlands of their possessions in southeastern Asia.

Japanese policy toward China before and after 1931 was motivated chiefly by desire to prevent the unification and modernization of China before these could advance sufficiently to make permanent control impossible. That Japan failed in this strategy surprised at least its military leaders. But China's resistance also astonished its friends—so much so that some of them made the mistake of assuming that China's strength in the postwar period would be sufficient to allow it to stand virtually alone as the defender of the peace in eastern Asia.

China's presence at San Francisco as one of the "Big Four" should effectively have countered any feeling that it might stand alone in eastern Asia. Apparently the days are past when China can be considered fair game for self-seeking Powers. The restoration—in which Great Britain and the United States participated in 1943—of full internal sovereignty by abolition of extraterritoriality and return of foreign concessions marks the end of the old period of imperialistic exploitation.

On the other hand, China's resistance in the war against Japan and its share in Japan's defeat cannot be taken as proof of military self-sufficiency. In the modern world, military potential is compounded not only of geography, man power, food supply, and political relationships but of primary industrial capacity for producing large quantities of the heavy machinery of war. In the latter, particularly, China's modernization is only beginning. It may be true that Japan's defeat has removed the chief threat to China's security. But if history teaches anything, one of its lessons is that a large political unit in which there is a high degree of power vacuum constitutes a standing invitation to aggression. For the past century China's military weakness has made it the victim of a series of wars. This lesson is not lost on China's leaders. They now insist that their first task is the building of real military power in modern China.

But if China is to become strong its strength must be based on thorough modernization. More and more must unity be fostered, and fostered on the basis of modern transportation and communication. Economically, these two factors will make possible the exploitation of natural resources, the development of industry, and a consequent and accompanying improvement in the standard of economic livelihood of the Chinese people. This will make possible, also, a general rise in the level of education, with all it implies in political consciousness and technical advance.

A mere statement of the problems gives an impression of the task confronting China. But its immensity can be realized only when the wide scope of these problems is considered. Thoroughgoing modernization must cover an area of subcontinental proportions. It must permeate a population of perhaps 450,000,000, which will probably increase at least as rapidly as the new industry can provide a rise in production. Also, this modernization must be achieved by a people whose general poverty makes difficult the accumulation of capital resources and who possess within their national boundaries only moderate amounts of basic resources.

With a maximum of effort, carefully planned and guided, the obstacles to China's modernization can be overcome. The question of vital importance, however, is how quickly they can be overcome, and how rapidly the country can achieve actual modernization. Speed is vital to military preparedness. To demonstrate this, one has only to consider the past twenty-five years of Soviet history. The successful resistance of the U.S.S.R. to Nazi aggression required the strictest mobilization of every ounce of the strength built up during the past quarter of a century of total effort and the greatest possible material help from the United States and Great Britain—and this in a country where the ratio of over-all resources to population is much more favorable than it is in China. The development of war potential in the Soviet Union was rapid, but it is unlikely that any of its leaders would claim that it was unnecessarily so.

In China, as elsewhere, the price of rapid development of war potential must be the development of mechanisms for total control. It will probably be necessary also to emphasize heavy industry at the expense of consumer goods. But for China a rise in general economic level is a necessity, even if it be considered only as it relates to increasing the efficiency of military man power. This cannot be accomplished without undertaking economic development of a well-balanced type and avoiding overemphasis on heavy industry.

At this point China's modernization becomes primarily a matter of international concern. The question is: Will the peace provide sufficient guaranties of security for China to allow modernization to proceed normally and with only a moderate emphasis on preparation for military defense?

Upon the answer depends the future of China, for it will determine the course of the nation's social and economic revolution during the next century. The course the revolution takes is of vital importance to world peace. A channeling of the people's energies for the next generation, or longer, into all-out development of military strength must have evil consequences for China and for the world. For, although total militarization might help to guarantee the country against attack, it could be brought about only at the expense of solving internal problems. China is unlikely to pile up armaments sufficient to bring on war because of that alone. But unless present problems of social disintegration and decay are solved, the Chinese government—like governments of other countries on occasion—is likely to resort to external aggression to divert attention from internal stresses.

The history of Japan since 1868 demonstrates that to build modern industry on a foundation of feudal agrarian society leads to social and psychological anomalies. Yet this type of superficial modernization is a natural response to the demand for rapid development of military power in a completely backward society. This is true for two reasons: first, the preservation of feudal authoritarianism in social relations facilitates rapid mobilization of all resources by the state and prevents the development of obstacles to mobilization in the shape of demands for greater share by individuals in the outcomes of industrial production; and second, the preservation of feudal authoritarianism in social relations guarantees monopolis-

tic political control, thereby inhibiting democratic control over
the employment of state military power. Moreover, monopolistic
political control guides toward a release in war of psychological
tensions caused by the coincidence of feudalism and modernity.

That these things helped lead Japan to imperialistic aggression
is well recognized. It is not so often realized that China today is
faced with the possible development of the same phenomena. It is
exceedingly probable that an attempt to modernize China predominantly in terms of military power will lead to a similar result.

The influence on Nippon of nineteenth-century world imperialism must not be forgotten. If China's security in the postwar
generation is made to appear dependent solely, or even mainly, on
the development of its own military resources, the Far East—and
most of the world—may again suffer the consequences of a country's
internal social development.

China emerged in 1945 from war with Japan in a state of relative
military weakness. The best way to guarantee its postwar security
is to have that security effectively provided by its partners, Great
Britain, the U.S.S.R., and the United States of America. Their
efforts to do so, however, should not in the future rely on treaties
such as those eventuating from the Washington Conference of 1921–
1922, in which the most probable aggressor, Japan, gave worthless
promises of self-denial. Peace in the Far East can be founded only
on sound measures of military preparedness in the region by those
nations which have the military power at their disposal.

This means that Great Britain, the Soviet Union, and the United
States must jointly and by mutual agreement undertake responsible
functions in the forestalling, by military action, of aggression by
Japan in the Pacific. There are those who assert that such measures
will be unnecessary by reason of Japan's reduction from the rank
of a Power. They should be reminded that Japan began its development as a world menace from a position of no apparent consequence in the third quarter of the nineteenth century. What was
done once may well be tried again. It should be noted also that postwar Nippon may remain potentially the most highly organized of
Far Eastern states, with the great resource of social integration to
make up for possible lack of physical resources.

The chief problem of the postwar Far East is the preservation and strengthening of unity between the four Powers. It is no detraction from this unity to recognize the difference between China and the other three Powers with respect to their functions and responsibilities in the postwar world. Differences in function cannot disturb the great fact of collaboration of the four Powers on a basis of full political equality. Achievement of complete independence and political equality for China is one great result of the war. This achievement can guarantee to China a full recognition of vital interests in the postwar community of nations and can assure it a useful function in the development of world-wide international coöperation.

NOTES AND
REFERENCES

Notes and References

NOTES TO CHAPTER I

Molding Forces

[1] Harold E. Gorst, *China* (London, 1899), p. 171.

[2] Le P. Etienne Zi (Siu), S.J., *Pratique des examens littéraires en Chine* (Shanghai, 1894).

[3] See Appendix A, "Animals in the Writing of Shang," and Appendix B, "Agriculture in the Shang Pictographs," by Harry E. Gibson, in Arthur de Carle Sowerby, *Nature in Chinese Art* (New York, 1940).

[4] To use a personal example, my own "milk" name was Shih-t'ou (shzh-tou), Stone, chosen for me because no other child of my mother had survived infancy; my parents selected a name suggesting strength. My "book" name became Yü-shan, Jade Mountain. The character *yü*, jade, was the first character in the "book" names of all my first cousins, male and female; the character *shan*, mountain, was chosen by my parents for the same reason that they chose Shih-t'ou for my "milk" name.

NOTES TO CHAPTER II

Dominant Ideas

The original of this paper was presented in Boston, on April 8, 1942, at the centennial meeting of the American Oriental Society. Reprinted from *Journal of the American Oriental Society*, Vol. 62, No. 4 (1942), pp. 293–299, with emendations by the editor of this volume.

[1] This does not mean that there have not been periods of intense religious activity in Chinese history; throughout some five hundred years, from the fourth through the eighth centuries, many of China's best minds turned to Buddhism. Nor does it mean that the Chinese masses have been free from superstitious beliefs; China is one of the richest storehouses in the world for the folklorist. (See chap. xiv.) Nevertheless, religion as such has been taken more lightly in China than in most other countries. It is significant that Confucianism, despite periods of eclipse, has for the last eight hundred years succeeded in retaining its dominance at the expense of both Buddhism and religious Taoism.

[2] Analects, XI, 11.

[3] On this point, which has not been clearly stated before, see Derk Bodde, "The Chinese View of Immortality: Its Expression by Chu Hsi and Its Relationship to Buddhist Thought," in *Review of Religion*, Vol. 6, No. 4 (May, 1942), pp. 369–

383. See also Hu Shih, Harvard Ingersoll Lecture, 1945, to be published in the Harvard Divinity School *Bulletin*, 1946. It must be remembered that this view was expressed only by a sophisticated minority. The great majority in China, as elsewhere, held a contrary opinion.

[4] This contradicts the denial of personal immortality, discussed above. But see the preceding note.

[5] This, like all sweeping statements, is not absolutely true. Hints of a mythology can be found in early Chinese literature, but they have, in large measure, been obliterated through euhemerization. See Henri Maspero, "Les Légendes mythologiques dans le Chou King," in *Journal Asiatique*, 214 (1924), 1–100.

[6] Maspero, *La Chine antique* (Paris, 1927), pp. 176–179, 182–183.

[7] Derk Bodde, "The Attitude toward Science and Scientific Method in Ancient China," in *T'ien Hsia Monthly*, Vol. 2, No. 2 (February, 1936), pp. 139–160; Fung Yu-lan, "Why China Has No Science," in *International Journal of Ethics*, Vol. 32, No. 3 (April, 1922), pp. 237–263.

[8] For a table showing a few of these correspondences see Alfred Forke, *The World-Conception of the Chinese* (London, 1925), pp. 240–241.

[9] Bodde, "Types of Chinese Categorical Thinking," in *Journal of the American Oriental Society*, Vol. 59, No. 2 (1939), pp. 200–219.

[10] Charles S. Gardner, *Chinese Traditional Historiography* (Cambridge, Harvard University Press, 1938).

[11] Not everyone held this belief. The Confucian, Hsün Tzŭ (*ca.* 298–*ca.* 238, or 340–245 B.C.), for example, proclaimed that man's nature is essentially evil. Yet he maintained that man can be taught goodness. His school, moreover, was eventually rejected in favor of that of Mencius (372–289, or 390–305 B.C.), who was the chief proponent of the doctrine of the goodness of human nature. See Homer H. Dubs, *The Works of Hsüntze* (London, 1928); also Fung Yu-lan, *A History of Chinese Philosophy* (trans. by Derk Bodde; Peiping and London, 1937–).

[12] Voltaire, *Œuvres complètes* (Gotha, 1785), XXXVIII, 492; quoted in Adolf Reichwein, *China and Europe* (trans. from the German by J. C. Powell; New York, 1925), p. 89. Voltaire was unaware of certain abuses in the Chinese governmental system. One of these has been the ever-present tendency for arable land to gravitate into the hands of a comparatively small landowning class—a class largely made up of those same scholar-officials who governed the country and who, because of their contempt for trade, usually preferred to invest their money in land rather than in commercial enterprises. The result has been increasing economic burden upon the peasants, leading finally to revolt, overthrow of the dynasty or central government, and redistribution of land. Though many ingenious governmental measures have been instituted to check this cycle, they have never been permanently successful. Today one of the most important problems confronting the Kuomintang National government is the age-old question of the distribution of land. See chaps. vii and xi, below.

[13] *Hao t'ieh pu ta ting*
Hao jên pu tang ping.

Chinese soldiers—certain ones, at least—have come at last to be regarded as something more than parasites on society and agents of destruction.

[14] *Mêng Tzŭ*, VIIa, 4.

[15] Translation by Fung Yu-lan, *Chuang Tzŭ* (Shanghai, 1933), chap. 2, p. 56.

[16] Translation by James Legge, *Sacred Books of the East* (ed. by F. Max Müller; Oxford, 1885), XXVIII, 300–301.

NOTES TO CHAPTER III
SOME REVELATIONS OF RECENT EXCAVATIONS

[1] Academia Sinica, *Preliminary Reports of Excavations at Anyang* (Peiping, 1929–1933), Parts I–IV; see also H. G. Creel, *The Birth of China* (New York and London, 1936).

[2] See, for example, Kenneth Scott Latourette, *The Chinese: Their History and Culture* (New York, 1934, 2 vols.; 2d rev. ed., 1942, 2 vols. in 1), I, 65–66, 85.

[3] William Charles White, *Tombs of Old Lo-yang* (Shanghai, 1934).

[4] C. G. Seligman and H. C. Beck, "Far Eastern Glass," in *Bulletin of the Museum of Far Eastern Antiquities* (Stockholm), No. 10 (1938).

[5] J. G. Andersson, "The Goldsmith in Ancient China," *ibid.*, No. 7 (1935).

[6] See, for example, Sir Aurel Stein, *Serindia* (London, 1921), *Innermost Asia* (London, 1928), and *On Central-Asian Tracks* (London, 1933).

[7] A. D. Brankston, *Early Ming Wares of Ching Tê Chên* (Peiping, 1938); R. L. Hobson, *The Potter's Art* (London, 1935), pp. 45–71.

NOTES TO CHAPTER IV
ANTIQUITY: TO THE FALL OF SHANG (*ca.* 1028 B.C.)

[1] J. G. Andersson, *Children of the Yellow Earth* (London, 1934), *passim*.

[2] *Far Eastern Quarterly*, Vol. II, No. 1 (November, 1942), pp. 58–65.

[3] *Nature*, November 20, 1926; see also "Fossil Man in China," Geological Survey of China (Peiping), *Geological Memoirs*, Series A, No. 11 (1933).

[4] *Bulletin of the Geological Society of China*, Vol. XIX, No. 1 (March, 1939), pp. 88–89.

[5] *Ibid.*, Vol. XI, No. 2 (December, 1931), pp. 147–154.

[6] New York *Times*, October 1, 1933.

[7] "The Mandibles of *Sinanthropus Pekinensis*," in *Paleontologia Sinica*, Series D, Vol. VII (1936), fasc. 3.

[8] P. Teilhard de Chardin and F. Licent, in *Bulletin of the Geological Society of China*, Vol. III, No. 1 (March, 1924), pp. 45–50; Shigeyasu Tokunaga and Nobuo Naora, *Report of the First Scientific Expedition to Manchukuo*, June–October, 1933; V. V. Ponosov, *Report of XVIth International Geological Congress* (Washington, D.C., 1933); Aleš Hrdlička, in *Science*, September 29, 1939, pp. 296–298; Franz Weidenreich and W. C. Pei, in *Peking Natural History Bulletin*, Vol. XIII, No. 3 (March, 1939), pp. 161–180.

[9] *Geographical Review*, Vol. XXXI, No. 2 (April, 1941), pp. 343–345.

[10] *Natural History*, 35 (April, 1935), 356; and *American Antiquity*, 2 (April, 1937), 267–272.

[11] K. A. Wittfogel, "The Society of Prehistoric China," in *Studies in Philosophy and Social Science*, pp. 138–186 [formerly *Zeitschrift für Sozialforschung*, VIII (1939), 161–164].

[12] Carl W. Bishop, *Smithsonian Explorations* (1934), p. 46. See also a monograph on this subject by G. D. Wu, *Prehistoric Pottery in China* (1938); J. G. Andersson, "Prehistory of the Chinese," in *Bulletin of the Museum of Far Eastern Antiquities* (hereafter abbreviated *BMFEA*), No. 15 (1943), and "The Site of Chu Chia Chai," in *BMFEA*, No. 17 (1945).

[13] *Sino-Swedish Expedition*, Vol. VII, No. 1 (1939), pp. 23–26.

[14] *Antiquity*, Vol. VII, No. 28 (December, 1933), p. 402.

[15] *Paleontologia Sinica*, Series D, Vol. I (1925), fasc. 3. See also *Pal. Sin.*, Series C, Vol. XII, No. 1 (1936), p. 19.

[16] This paragraph is based mainly on the report of Mr. Liang Ssŭ-yung, in *Quarterly Bulletin of Chinese Bibliography*, N.S., Vol. I, No. 3 (September, 1940), pp. 251–262. Mr. Liang has taken a leading part in uncovering this stage of Chinese civilization. See also *BMFEA*, No. 15 (1943), and Wu, *op. cit.* Andersson, who does not follow the traditional dating of ancient Chinese periods, favors placing the black pottery stage around the eighteenth century before our era.

[17] Tung Tso-pin, in the fortieth anniversary volume of National Peking University (dated 1938, published in Kunming, 1940). This reference is owed to Dr. Roswell S. Britton of New York University. See also B. Karlgren, *BMFEA*, No. 17 (1945), pp. 114–121.

[18] A. F. Albright, *From the Stone Age to Christianity* (Baltimore, 1940), pp. 40–43.

[19] Sir P. Yetts, *An-yang: A Retrospect* (China Society, London, 1942), p. 22.

[20] H. E. Gibson, in *Journal of the North China Branch of the Royal Asiatic Society*, LXIX (1938), 13. In the excellent study by P. Teilhard de Chardin and C. C. Young, "On the Mammalian Remains from the Archeological Site of Anyang," in *Pal. Sin.*, Series C, Vol. XII, No. 1 (1936), it is surprising to learn that virtually no bones of the horse have been discovered *in situ*. The divination literature, however, makes it clear that the Shang people sacrificed the horse.

[21] *Geographical Review*, Vol. XXX, No. 1 (January, 1940), pp. 110–133.

[22] Yetts, *op. cit.*, p. 25: "Local tradition says that long ago copper and tin, as well as other metals, were mined some 40 *li* north-west of Anyang city..." P. Teilhard de Chardin and C. C. Young, *op. cit.*, p. 56, state that the discovery of ingots of tin and an enormous quantity of *Lamprotula* shells—which were used by Shang craftsmen for their mother-of-pearl—prove the existence of an extensive trade between An-yang and southern China.

[23] Helen Chapin, *Leaves from a Western Garden*, I, 2, 36.

[24] *Journal of the American Oriental Society*, Vol. 61, No. 3 (September, 1941), p. 130.

[25] H. G. Creel, *The Birth of China* (New York and London, 1936), and *Studies in Early Chinese Culture*, First Series (Baltimore, 1937).

NOTES TO CHAPTER VI

FROM THE FALL OF CHOU TO THE FALL OF T'ANG (*ca.* 221 B.C–A.D. 906)

[1] *Les Mémoires historiques de Se-Ma-Ts'ien* (translated and annotated by Edouard Chavannes; Paris, 1895–1905), V, 1–2.

[2] The provincial names used in this chapter are modern.

[3] J. J. L. Duyvendak (trans.), *The Book of Lord Shang* (London, 1928).

[4] Ssŭ-ma Ch'ien, *Shih Chi* (Tung-wên ed., 1884), 6:11.

[5] Ch'ien Mu, *Kuo-shih Ta-kang* (Outline History of China) (Chungking, 1944), I, 79–82. Consult also Derk Bodde, *China's First Unifier* (Leiden, 1938).

[6] Hu Shih, "Wang Mang, the Socialist Emperor of Nineteen Centuries Ago," in *Journal of the North China Branch of the Royal Asiatic Society*, LIX (1928), 218–230. Liang Ch'i-ch'ao, also, considered Wang Mang one of China's six greatest statesmen.

[7] Homer H. Dubs, "Wang Mang and His Economic Reforms," in *T'oung Pao*, 35, 222. K'ang Yu-wei charged Wang Mang with forging many Confucian classics in order to provide seemingly traditional support for his usurpation.

[8] Herbert A. Giles, *A Chinese Biographical Dictionary* (London and Shanghai, 1898), No. 2013.

[9] *Ibid.*, No. 645.

[10] Stories of this age have been popularized in the novel *San Kuo Chih Yen I; or, Romance of the Three Kingdoms* (trans. by C. H. Brewitt-Taylor; Shanghai, 1925, 1926), in 2 vols.

[11] Samuel Couling, "Tartar," article in *Encyclopaedia Sinica*, p. 549.

[12] *Sui Shu* (1884 ed.), 81, 5b.

[13] Tschen Yinkoh [Ch'en Yin-k'o], "On the Ancestors of T'ang T'ai-tsung," in *Bulletin of the Institute of History and Philology* (Academia Sinica, Peiping), Vol. III (1935), Part 1, pp. 39–48. Further notes by the author on this problem appear elsewhere in the same magazine.

[14] Ch'en Yin-k'o, *T'ang Tai Chêng-chih Shih Shu Lun Kao* (A Draft Critical Political History of the T'ang Dynasty) (Chungking, Commercial Press, 1943), Part A, p. 36.

[15] Giles, *op. cit.*, No. 1211.

[16] *Ibid.*, No. 1575.

[17] *Ibid.*, No. 847.

[18] Ibn Khordadben, "Le Livre des routes et des provinces," in *Journal Asiatique*, 1865, p. 292; J. T. Reinaud, *Relation des voyages*, Tome 1, p. cvi.

[19] Giles, *op. cit.*, No. 1155.

[20] *Ibid.*, No. 475.

NOTES TO CHAPTER VII

FROM THE FALL OF T'ANG TO THE FALL OF CH'ING (906–1912)

[1] But see L. Carrington Goodrich, *A Short History of the Chinese People* (New York and London, 1943), chap. vii; Florence Ayscough, *A Chinese Mirror* (London, Boston, and New York, 1925), chap. iv; Juliet Bredon, *Peking* (Shanghai,

1922); L. C. Arlington and William Lewisohn, *In Search of Old Peking* (Peking, 1935).

² For this and other figures of the seventeenth to the twentieth centuries, see *Eminent Chinese of the Ch'ing Period (1644–1912)* (ed. by Arthur W. Hummel; Washington, D.C., 1943, 1944), I, 491–493.

³ *Ibid.*, pp. 594–599.

⁴ *Ibid.*, under "Hsüan-yeh," pp. 327–331.

⁵ *Ibid.*, pp. 369–373.

⁶ *Ibid.*, pp. 361–367.

⁷ *Ibid.*, II, 751–756.

⁸ *Ibid.*, pp. 762–767.

⁹ *Ibid.*, I, 464–471.

NOTES TO CHAPTER VIII
CHINESE SOCIETY AND THE DYNASTIES OF CONQUEST

¹ K. A. Wittfogel and C. S. Feng, *History of Chinese Society: Liao* (American Philosophical Society, Philadelphia, 1945), General Introduction.

² Sun Yat-sen, "The True Solution of the Chinese Question," in *Supplement to Sun Chung-shan, Collected Works* (Shanghai, 1928), II, 6.

³ Ralph Linton, "Nativist Movements," in *American Anthropologist,* 45 (1943), 237.

⁴ R. Redfield, R. Linton, and M. J. Herskovits, "A Memorandum for the Study of Acculturation," in *American Anthropologist,* 38 (1936), 149–152.

⁵ Wittfogel and Feng, *op. cit., passim.*

⁶ The argument in the following sections is based on data collected by the Chinese History Project, Columbia University, from 1936 to 1943. The Chin material was prepared by Mr. Fêng Chia-shêng.

⁷ Herbert A. Giles, *A Chinese Biographical Dictionary* (London and Shanghai, 1898), No. 6.

⁸ *Ibid,* No. 2127.

⁹ *Ibid.,* No. 2126.

¹⁰ *Ibid.,* No. 2128.

¹¹ *Ibid.,* No. 1012.

¹² Owen Lattimore, *Manchuria, Cradle of Conflict* (New York, 1932), p. 45.

¹³ *Eminent Chinese of the Ch'ing Period (1644–1912)* (ed. by Arthur W. Hummel; Washington, D.C., 1943, 1944), I, 662–663.

¹⁴ *Ibid.,* under "Fu-lung-an," by Fang Chao-ying.

¹⁵ Giles, *China and the Manchus* (London, 1912), p. 118.

¹⁶ In 1747 the emperor prefaced a new version of the Manchu religious code, emphasizing his attachment to the tribal tradition. Besides the Chinese, there is also a French translation by Ch. de Harlez, in *Mémoires couronnés et autres mémoires publiés par l'Académie Royale des Sciences, des Lettres, et des Beaux-Arts de Belgique* (Brussels, 1887), Vol. 40.

¹⁷ S. M. Shirokogoroff, *Social Organization of the Manchus* (Shanghai, 1924), p. 2.

¹⁸ Wittfogel and Feng, *op. cit.,* chap. xv.

NOTES TO CHAPTER IX
THE REPUBLIC: PHASE OF WAR-LORDISM (1911–1928)

[1] *Eminent Chinese of the Ch'ing Period (1644–1912)* (ed. by Arthur W. Hummel; Washington, D.C., 1943, 1944), I, 594–599.

[2] *Ibid.*, pp. 361–367.

[3] *Ibid.*, under "T'an Ssŭ-t'ung," II, 702–705.

[4] *Ibid.*, under "Tsai-t'ien," pp. 731–734.

[5] *Ibid.*, under "Hsiao-ch'in Hsien Huang-hou," I, 295–300.

[6] H. F. MacNair, *China in Revolution* (Chicago, 1931), p. 32.

[7] Hummel, *op. cit.*, under "Yüan Chia-san," II, 950–954.

[8] *Ibid.*, under "Tsai-t'ien," p. 733.

[9] MacNair, *op. cit.*, pp. 34–35.

[10] *China Yearbook, 1924* (ed. by H. G. W. Woodhead), p. 863.

[11] MacNair, *op. cit.*, pp. 98–99.

[12] One of Chiang's sons, who at this time was studying in Moscow, remained in Russia for several years after the rupture of Kuomintang-Communist ties. On returning to China he served in his father's government with distinction.

[13] For accounts of Pi Yün Ssŭ consult Juliet Bredon, *Peking* (Shanghai, 1922), pp. 294–300; also L. C. Arlington and William Lewisohn, *In Search of Old Peking* (Peking, 1935), pp. 298–299.

NOTES TO CHAPTER X
THE REPUBLIC: PHASE OF RESURGENCE (1928–1946)

[1] The political schema underlying this presentation has been outlined by Paul M. A. Linebarger in three related studies: *The Political Doctrines of Sun Yat-sen: An Exposition of the San Min Chu I* (Baltimore, 1937), *Government in Republican China* (New York, 1938), and *The China of Chiang K'ai-shek: A Political Study* (Boston, 1941). For the long background of Chinese ideology, account must be taken of H. F. MacNair's *The Real Conflict between China and Japan* (Chicago, 1938); and of Lin Mousheng's two pioneer surveys: *Antistatism: Essay in Its Psychiatric and Cultural Analysis* (Washington, D.C., 1939), and *Men and Ideas: An Informal History of Chinese Political Thought* (New York, 1942).

[2] The "First" World War was not, in reality, that of 1914–1918, but the one often designated as the Second Hundred Years' War, between England and France (1688–1815).—EDITOR'S NOTE.

[3] C. C. Wu, "Economic Reconstruction and Planning: Wartime and Post-war," in H. F. MacNair (ed.), *Voices from Unoccupied China* (Chicago, 1944), chap. vi.

NOTES TO CHAPTER XI
THE SOCIAL REVOLUTION

[1] Michael Lindsay, "The North China Front," in *Amerasia*, Vol. VIII, No. 7 (March 31, 1944), pp. 99–110; and No. 8 (April 14, 1944), pp. 117–125.

[2] See New York *Times*, Vol. XCIII, No. 31 (Saturday, June 3, 1944), for the first

report of "A party of foreign correspondents proceeding to the Chinese Communist areas—the first such visit in five years,"—months after they had requested to be allowed to make such inspection.

³ See Agnes Smedley, *Battle Hymn of China* (1943), Book V, concerning medical work.

⁴ Passages from this document may be found in *Asia and the Americas,* Vol. XLIV, No. 5 (May, 1944), pp. 207–208.

⁵ "Real Democracy for China," *ibid.,* No. 7 (July, 1944), pp. 293–297; Sun Fo, *China Looks Forward* (New York, 1944), pp. 105–117.

⁶ The following courses are among those given by army training schools: Principles and Tactics of the National United Front; History of the Chinese Revolution (1839–1944); History of China's Relations with Japan: History of China's Relations with Western Powers; The Three People's Principles; Social Science [Marxist theory]; Theories and Practices of Fascism; The History of Human Progress; The Japanese Language; Natural Science; Hygiene; First Aid; Methods of Mass Organization; Propaganda Work among the Enemy and among Puppet Armies; Espionage and Propaganda of the Enemy; Counterespionage.

⁷ New York *Times,* November 27, December 4, 11, and 15, 1945, and January 3, 10, and February 1, 1946.

NOTES TO CHAPTER XII

INTERNATIONAL RELATIONS: THE TWENTIETH CENTURY

¹ Sino-Japanese wars had been fought in the seventh, thirteenth, and sixteenth centuries.

² H. F. MacNair, *The Real Conflict between China and Japan* (Chicago, 1938), p. 16 *et passim.*

³ Charles Roger Hicks, *Japan's Entry into the War, 1914* (Reno, Nev., 1944), 8 pp.; H. B. Morse and H. F. MacNair, *Far Eastern International Relations* (Boston, 1931), p. 572.

⁴ Morse and MacNair, *ibid.,* p. 566.

⁵ For the list see J. V. A. MacMurray, *Treaties and Agreements with and Concerning China* (Oxford, 1921), in 2 vols.

⁶ Kurt Bloch in a personal letter to Harley F. MacNair, transmitted to the present writer on March 1, 1943.

⁷ Eleanor Lattimore, "Behind the Sinkiang Incident," in *Far Eastern Survey,* Vol. XIII, No. 9 (May 3, 1944), pp. 78–81.

⁸ In *China's Military Potential and the Enforcement of Peace* (Yale Institute of International Studies, New Haven, September 1, 1943, for private circulation), Professor David Nelson Rowe argues that China does not possess the industrial resources or equipment adequate to make it a determining military power in the Far East. See also Professor Rowe's *China among the Powers* (New York, 1945).

⁹ The texts as broadcast by the Moscow radio on August 26, 1945, are to be found in "Jap Surrender in China," in *China at War* (special issue), September–October, 1945.

NOTES TO CHAPTER XIII
CHINESE THOUGHT

[1] Confucius remained the idol of millions of people even as late as my boyhood days. I remember that before I went to Shanghai for modern schooling I had my own Confucian shrine made from a paper box.

[2] The conception that a scholar's burden is heavy and his journey long is one of the most important traditions in Chinese intellectual history. I remember my first experience in reading the ninth chapter of St. Matthew, where Jesus, seeing the crowds coming toward him, was moved with compassion upon them and said, "The harvest truly is plenteous, but the laborers are few." When I first read that passage, tears came to my eyes and I thought of this sentence in the Analects of Confucius, "The scholar's burden is heavy and his journey long."

[3] Herbert A. Giles, *A Chinese Biographical Dictionary* (London and Shanghai, 1898), No. 632.

[4] *Ibid.*, No. 535.

[5] *Ibid.*, No. 2134; see also H. R. Williamson, *Wang An Shih* (London, 1935–1937), in 2 vols.

[6] Giles, *op. cit.*, No. 446.

NOTES TO CHAPTER XIV
FOLK RELIGION

[1] Marcel Granet, *La Religion des Chinois* (Paris, 1922), p. 27.

[2] Dwight Condo Baker, *T'ai Shan* (Shanghai, 1925); Florence Ayscough, "T'ai Shan: The Great Mountain," pp. 341–376, and "Cult of the Spiritual Magistrates of City Walls and Moats," pp. 377–420, in *A Chinese Mirror* (Boston, 1925); Edouard Chavannes, *Le T'ai Chan: Essai de monographie d'un culte chinois. Appendice: Le Dieu du sol dans la Chine antique* (Paris, 1910); G. E. Hubbard, "The Pilgrims of Taishan," in *China Journal of Science and Arts*, Vol. III, No. 6 (June, 1925), pp. 322–330 (with illustrations from photographs taken by Mrs. William Calhoun).

[3] Eduard Erkes, "Idols in Pre-Buddhist China," in *Artibus Asiae*, No. 1 (1928), pp. 5–12.

[4] For examples see Wang Chi-chen (trans.), *Traditional Chinese Tales* (New York, 1944), and E. D. Edwards (trans.), *Chinese Prose Literature of the T'ang Period, A.D. 618–906* (London, 1937, 1938), in 2 vols.

NOTES TO CHAPTER XVI
NEO-CONFUCIANISM

[1] Material for this chapter was drawn in large measure from the author's essay, "Philosophies of China," in *Twentieth Century Philosophy* (ed. by D. D. Runes; New York, Philosophical Library, 1943). For explanation of the term Neo-Confucianism see Chan Wing-tsit, "The Story of Chinese Philosophy," in *Philosophy: East and West* (ed. by Charles A. Moore; Princeton, 1944), note 214.

[2] *Ch'êng-shih I-shu* (Posthumous Writings of the Brothers Ch'êng [Hao and I]), chap. xiii. See also Herbert A. Giles, *A Chinese Biographical Dictionary* (London and Shanghai, 1898), Nos. 278, 279, 280.

[3] Chang Hêng-chu (1025–1077), *Chêng Mêng*, chap. vii.

[4] Chu Hsi, *Yü Lei* (Sayings Arranged by Topics), chap. cxxvi.

[5] *Ch'êng-shih I-shu*, chaps. i, xiv, xv, xviii.

[6] *Ibid.*, chap. xvii.

[7] Or relativity, according to Th. Stcherbatsky (Shcherbatskoï). See his *The Conception of Buddhist Nirvana* (Leningrad, 1927).

[8] Chou Lien-hsi (1017–1073), *T'ai-chi T'u-shuo* (Explanation of the Diagram of the Great Ultimate), *I T'ung-shu* (Explanation of the Book of Changes).

[9] *Ibid.*

[10] *Ch'êng-shih I-shu*, chaps. ii, xviii.

[11] *Yü Lei*, chap. cxiv.

[12] *Ch'êng-shih I-shu*, chap. vii.

[13] *Ibid.*, chaps. xv, ii.

[14] Chu Hsi, *Chu-tzŭ Ch'üan-shu* (Complete Works), chap. xlviii.

[15] *Yü Lei*, chap. cxxvi.

[16] *Ch'êng-shih I-shu*, chap. xviii.

[17] The brothers Ch'êng, *Wai-shu* (Supplementary Works), chap. vii.

[18] *Chêng Mêng*.

[19] *Ibid.*

[20] *Ch'êng-shih I-shu*, chap. xi.

[21] *Yü Lei*, chap. iii.

[22] Wang Yang-ming, *Ch'üan-shu* (Complete Works), Book I; *The Philosophy of Wang Yang-ming* (trans. by F. G. Henke; Chicago, 1916), Book I, p. 50; Book III, p. 156; Book XXVI, p. 210. See also Giles, *op. cit.*, No. 2224, and reference to Wang Shou-jên, in *Eminent Chinese of the Ch'ing Period (1644–1912)* (ed. by Arthur W. Hummel; Washington, D.C., 1943, 1944), II, 1026.

[23] *Jih-chih Lu*, I. See also Hummel, *op. cit.*, I, 421–426.

[24] *Wên-chi* (Collected Works), "Letter to a Friend about Learning."

[25] *Chêng-mêng Chu* (Commentary on *Chêng Mêng*).

[26] *Wên-chi*, "Letter to Friends," No. 2.

[27] *Mêng Tzŭ Tzŭ-i Su-chêng* (Commentary on the Works of Mencius), Part II, No. 17; see also *Eminent Chinese of the Ch'ing Period*, II, 695–700; I, 45–46.

[28] *Yüan Shan* (An Inquiry into Goodness), I.

[29] *Mêng Tzŭ*, Part II, No. 40.

[30] *Tu-i Hsi-tzŭ Lun-hsin* (On the Discussions of Human Nature in Appendix I of the Book of Changes).

[31] *Yüan Shan*, I.

[32] *Tu-i Hsi-tzŭ Lun-hsin*.

[33] *Mêng Tzŭ*, Part II, No. 10.

[34] *Ibid.*, Part I, No. 3.

[35] *T'ai-t'ung Shu* (Book of the Great Commonwealth); see also Lin Mousheng, *Men and Ideas* (New York, 1942).

[36] *Li-yün Chu* (Commentary on chapter ix of the Book of Changes).

[37] *Ibid.*

[38] Hu Shih, *The Chinese Renaissance* (Chicago, 1934), p. 45.

[39] Be it noted that this is not the place for an analysis of the works of West-erners and Western-trained Chinese from the seventeenth century to the present day, although they have contributed greatly to modern transformations in Chinese thought and institutions. But see, in part, chaps. xix and xxviii, below.—EDITOR'S NOTE.

[40] *Eminent Chinese of the Ch'ing Period*, II, 702–705.

[41] *Ibid.*, I, 351–354.

NOTES TO CHAPTER XVII

TAOISM

[1] Usually called the Yellow Emperor, but mistakenly, since the title of emperor was invented only in 221 B.C.

[2] Herbert A. Giles, *A Chinese Biographical Dictionary* (London and Shanghai, 1898), No. 1537.

[3] *Ibid.*, Nos. 293, 693, 1328, 1675, 2188, 2544, 2548.

[4] *Ibid.*, No. 1062.

[5] Comment on *Chuang Tzŭ*, 4:29a, in chap. xi.

[6] *Ibid.*, 5:25a, in chap. xiii.

[7] *Ibid.*, 4:11b, in chap. ix.

[8] Y. L. Fung, *Chuang Tzŭ*, pp. 154–155.

[9] Giles, *op. cit.*, No. 807.

[10] *Ibid.*, No. 978.

[11] *Ibid.*, No. 1269.

[12] *Ibid.*, No. 1300.

[13] T. L. Davis, "Primitive Science," in *Journal of Chemical Education*, 12 (1935), 3–10; also "Pictorial Representations of Alchemical Theory," in *Isis*, 28 (1938), 73–86.

[14] Giles, *op. cit.*, No. 112.

NOTES TO CHAPTER XVIII

BUDDHISM

[1] In the Chinese language are such volumes as: Lü Chen, *A Guide to the Study of Buddhism* (Shanghai, 1926); Tsiang Wei-chiao, *A History of Buddhism in China* (Shanghai, 1929), in 3 vols.; and Huang Ch'an-hua, *Main Ideas of the Buddhist Sects* (Shanghai, 1934), in 2 vols. In English there are the following: Shao-chang Lee, *Popular Buddhism in China* (Shanghai, 1939); and the recent brief interpretation by Y. C. Yang, *China's Religious Heritage* (New York, 1943).

[2] Expressed in Hu Shih's lecture on "Chinese Culture before and after Indianization," at the Harvard Tercentenary Conference. See abstract in *Nature*, 139 (1937), 333.

[3] Translated by S. Beal, *A Catena of Buddhist Scriptures from the Chinese* (London, 1871), pp. 191–203; and by Leo Wieger, *History of the Religious Beliefs and Philosophical Opinions in China* (Hsien-hsien, China, 1927), pp. 345–350.

[4] Bunyiu Nanjio, *Catalogue of the Chinese Buddhist Tripitaka* (Oxford, 1883), pp. 381–385.

[5] Three thousand, according to tradition. *Ibid.*, p. 407.

[6] I here interpret the meaning of *ch'êng fu* literally, "to become Buddha" or "to attain Buddhahood." *

[7] Chandra Bagchi, *Le Canon bouddhique en Chine* (Paris, 1927, 1938), in 2 vols.; Nanjio, *op. cit.*, where 1,662 titles are listed; Herbert A. Giles, *A Chinese Biographical Dictionary* (London and Shanghai, 1898), Nos. 526, 801, 897.

[8] Sir Charles [N. E.] Eliot, *Hinduism and Buddhism* (London, 1921), Vol. III, chap. 43.

[9] J. J. M. de Groot, *Sectarianism and Religious Persecution in China* (Amsterdam, 1903, 1904), I, 59–69.

[10] Eliot, *op. cit.*, pp. 265–267; Giles, *op. cit.*, Nos. 632, 446.

[11] Eliot, *op. cit.*, pp. 275–279.

[12] Karl L. Reichelt, *Truth and Tradition in Chinese Buddhism* (Shanghai, 1927–1934), pp. 36–38.

[13] *Ibid.*, chap. v; also Shao-chang Lee, *Popular Buddhism in China* (Shanghai, 1939), pp. 10–20.

[14] J. Prip-Møller, *Chinese Buddhist Monasteries* (London and Copenhagen, 1937), pp. 304–320.

[15] C[aroline] C[ouling], "Buddhist Schools," in *Encyclopaedia Sinica* (ed. by Samuel Couling; Shanghai, 1917), pp. 73–75; Reichelt, *op. cit.*, pp. 42–45. Mrs. Couling makes the following very illuminating comment (p. 74): ". . . it was among the Chinese, who are supposed to be above all things a practical people, rather than among the people of India that Contemplative Buddhism was mainly developed, and it is at this day [*ca.* 1917] the prevailing form." [H.F.M.]

[16] Reichelt, *op. cit.*, pp. 304–305.

[17] See James B. Pratt, *The Pilgrimage of Buddhism* (New York, 1928), pp. 338 ff., for Tai-hsü's "Statement to Asiatic Buddhists."

[18] On T'ai-hsü's plans for reform consult Y. Y. Tsu, "Trends of Thought and Religion in China," in *The New Orient* (Chicago, 1933), II, 321 ff.; and F. R. Millican, "T'ai-hsü and Modern Buddhism," in *The Chinese Recorder* (Shanghai, 1923), pp. 326–332. On later activities, see Pratt, *op. cit.*, chap. xix, and *China Christian Year Book, 1936–37* (Shanghai), pp. 101–104.

[19] T'ai-hsü, *Lectures on Buddhism* (Paris, 1928), p. 24.

[20] *Ibid.*, pp. 47 f., 50, 62–64, 66, 75 f., *et passim*.

[21] Y. Y. Tsu, *op. cit.*, II, 323.

[22] T'ai-hsü, *op. cit.*, pp. 25 ff.

[23] Giles, *op. cit.*, No. 801.

[24] For a translation of one text of this literature see C. H. Hamilton, *Wei Shih Er Shih Lun; or, The Treatise in Twenty Stanzas on Representation-Only* (American Oriental Society, New Haven, 1938)

[25] In *Wên-hua-chien-shê* (Cultural Reconstruction) (Shanghai), III, No. 1 (October, 1936), pp. 102–111.

[26] See note 2, above.

[27] *Yenching Journal of Chinese Studies* (Peking), No. 22 (December, 1937).

[28] See his "Wei-shih-hsin-chieh," *ibid.*, No. 23 (June, 1938).

[29] For brief notices of war activities see *World Christianity, a Digest*, Fourth Quarter (1938), pp. 54–55; also *China Christian Year Book, 1936–37* (Shanghai), pp. 108–109, and *1938–39*, pp. 149–151.

[30] H. G. Q. Wales, "Buddhism as a Propaganda Instrument," with a commentary by Lin Yutang, in *Free World*, V (May, 1943), 428–432.

[31] Reichelt, *op. cit.* (Introduction, 4th ed., 1934, p. 5), observes: "One hears occasionally that Buddhism in the Far East is a decadent religion. This is not the case. On the contrary, a noticeable advance can be traced in recent years." [H.F.M.]

[32] Reported in *Time*, Vol. XLI, No. 24 (June 14, 1943).

NOTES TO CHAPTER XX

TRENDS IN CONTEMPORARY PHILOSOPHY

Most of the material in this chapter is reprinted from the author's essay, "Philosophies of China," in *Twentieth Century Philosophy* (ed. by D. D. Runes; New York, Philosophical Library, 1943).

[1] K'ang Yu-wei, *The Book of the Great Commonwealth* (in Chinese; 1884, not published until 1915). See also "T'an Ssŭ-t'ung," pp. 702–705, and page references to K'ang, p. 1008, in *Eminent Chinese of the Ch'ing Period (1644–1912)* (ed. by Arthur W. Hummel; Washington, D.C., 1943, 1944), II.

[2] T'an Ssŭ-t'ung, *The Philosophy of Jên* (in Chinese; 1896), Introduction. See also Hummel, as cited above, and II, 861.

[3] By Yen Fu (1853–1921), celebrated translator, who first introduced Western philosophy. See Hummel, *op. cit.*, II, 643.

[4] *The Youth* (in Chinese), Vol. VI, No. 4 (1919), pp. 342–358.

[5] Works by William James translated include: *Pragmatism, Talks to Teachers on Psychology: and to Students on Some of Life's Ideals, Psychology*, and *Introduction to Philosophy*. Chinese versions of works by John Dewey include: *Reconstruction in Philosophy, How We Think, Democracy and Education*.

[6] See Hu Shih's chapter, in *Living Philosophies* (New York, Simon and Schuster, 1931), pp. 255, 259, 261–262; also his *Recent Essays*, First Series (in Chinese; Shanghai, Commercial Press, 1935), pp. 630, 632, 636, 641. Consult also L. Forster, *The New Culture in China* (London, 1936), chap. xix; and K. J. Saunders, *Whither Asia* (New York, 1933), chap. ii.

[7] *Chung Yung* (The Golden Mean), chap. xx.

[8] *The Youth*, II (1916).

[9] Li Ta-chao, "My Views on Marxism," in *The Youth*, Vol. VI, No. 5 (1919), pp. 521–537, and No. 6, pp. 612–624.

[10] In the periodical, *Young China* (in Chinese; 1919).

[11] H. A. E. Driesch, *The Problem of Individuality*, has been translated into Chinese.

[12] Chang Chün-mai, *Controversy over Life-View* (in Chinese; Shanghai, T'ai-tung Publishing Co., 1923), I, 1–13. 3 vols.

[13] *Ibid.*, p. 17.

[14] The major works of Professor Chang are: *Epistemology, Moral Philosophy, Essays on Modern Philosophy* (all in Chinese; Shanghai, Commercial Press).

[15] See the article in *Essays in Honor of Mr. Chang Chü-shêng's Seventieth Birthday* (in Chinese; ed. by Hu Shih *et al.*; Shanghai, Commercial Press, 1937), pp. 95–137.

[16] Few of their works are translated, however. These include Eucken, *The Meaning and Value of Life*, and Hocking, *Types of Philosophy*.

[17] This school is called Avataṅsaka in Sanskrit, Hua-yen in Chinese, and Kegon in Japanese, all meaning "wreath." See also *Eminent Chinese of the Ch'ing Period*, II, 703.

[18] Various names of the mystical school are Mantra, Mi-tsung (mystery school), Chên-yen, and Shingon, all meaning "true word."

[19] Founded by Asaṅga (*ca.* A.D. 410–500) and his brother Vasubandhu (*ca.* A.D. 420–500) in India, developed in China by Hsüan-tsang (A.D. 596–644) and his pupil K'uei-chi (A.D. 632–682); called Vijñaptimātratā and Vijñanavāda in Sanskrit, Fa-hsiang (dharma-character) and Wei-shih (ideation-only) in Chinese, Hossō in Japanese, and idealism, mere-ideation, or representation-only in English. For source material see Vasubandhu, *Wei Shih Er Shih Lun; or, The Treatise in Twenty Stanzas on Representation-Only* (trans. by C. H. Hamilton; American Oriental Society, New Haven, 1938); S. Lévi, *Matériaux pour l'étude du système vijñaptimātra* (Paris, Librairie Ancienne Honoré Champion, 1932); *Vijñaptimātratāsiddhi: La Siddhi de Hiuen-Tsang* (trans. by Louis de La Vallée Poussin; Paris, Guethner, 1928, 1929), in 2 vols. For critical studies see A. B. Keith, *Buddhist Philosophy in India and Ceylon* (Oxford, 1923), chap. xiv; E. J. Thomas, *The History of Buddhist Thought* (New York, 1933), chap. xviii.

[20] *Vijñaptimātratāsiddhi*, chap. vii.

[21] To mention two outstanding ones, Wang Ch'uan-shan (1619–1693) and Chang Ping-lin (1868–1936).

[22] Chief works by Ou-yang: *Talks on the Mere-Ideation Doctrine*, and *Lectures on the Mere-Ideation Philosophy* (Institute of the Inner Learning, Nanking, n.d.). The chief treatises of T'ai-hsü have been collected in *The Mere-Ideation Philosophy of the Dharma-Character School* (Shanghai, Commercial Press, 1938), in 2 vols. All in Chinese.

[23] English translations by Timothy Richard and Yang Wên-hui, *The Awakening of Faith in the Mahāyāna Doctrine* (1894); and by D. T. Suzuki, *Asvaghosha's Discourse on the Awakening of Faith in the Mahāyāna* (Chicago, 1900).

[24] T'ai-hsü, *op. cit.*, I, 3.

[25] *Ibid.*, pp. 62–73.

[26] Hsiung Shih-li, "An Essay on the New Mere-Ideation Philosophy, I: The Object-Domains."

[27] Liang Sou-ming, *The Civilization and Philosophy of the East and the West* (in Chinese; Shanghai, Commercial Press, 1927). The English translation is still in process. For a summary see *Contemporary China*, August 9, 1943.

[28] Liang Sou-ming, *op. cit.*, pp. 121, 127, 171, 211.

[29] Fung Yu-lan, *A History of Chinese Philosophy* (Shanghai, Commercial Press, Part I, 1930; Part II, 1933).

[30] Fung Yu-lan, *The New Rational Philosophy* (Shanghai, Commercial Press, 1939), 312 pp. Chapter headings are: Reason and the Great Ultimate, The Vital Principle (*Ch'i*) and the Two Modes, The Way (*Tao*) and the Way of Heaven, The Nature and the Mind, Morality and the Way of Man, Tendencies and History, Truth, Art, Past and Future Existences, and The Sage.

NOTES TO CHAPTER XXI
CALLIGRAPHY, POETRY, AND PAINTING

Text, in part (ed. by H. F. MacNair), of a lecture given in February, 1930, before the Verein der Freunde Asiatischer Kunst und Kultur in Wien. *Wiener Beiträge zur Kunst- und Kulturgeschichte Asïens* (Krystall Verlag, Vienna, 1931), Band VI. Sincere thanks are due to Mr. Wang Chi-chen for information regarding the "fish-basket" Kuan-yin. The translations from the Chinese are original; several poems are taken from *Tu Fu: The Autobiography of a Chinese Poet, A.D. 712–759* (Boston, 1929), Vol. I, and *Fir-Flower Tablets, Poems Translated from the Chinese* (London, 1921). For a somewhat similar handling of this subject by the same writer, with numerous illustrations, see "Chinese Painting," in *The Mentor*, Vol. 6, No. 20, Serial No. 168 (December 2, 1918).

[1] *Mémoires concernant les Chinois par les missionnaires de Pékin* (Paris; 15 vols., 1776–1791), Vol. II, Plate I facing p. 151. See also Florence Ayscough, *A Chinese Mirror: Being Reflections of the Reality behind Appearance* (Boston, 1925), p. 261; and David Nelson Rowe, "The T'ai Chi Symbol in Japanese War Propaganda," in *Public Opinion Quarterly*, Winter, 1941, pp. 532–547.

[2] Thomas F. Carter, *The Invention of Printing in China and Its Spread Westward* (New York, 1925), p. 2.

[3] Herbert A. Giles, *A Chinese Biographical Dictionary* (London and Shanghai, 1898), Nos. 503 (Ch'ü Yüan), 263 (Chêng Chan-yin), 585 (Fu Hsi), 1991 (Ts'ang Chieh).

[4] *Ibid.*, No. 1741.

[5] *Das älteste Dokument ... T'ien-Wen ... die "Himmelsfragen" des K'üh Yüan* (trans. by August Conrady; ed. by Eduard Erkes; Leipzig, 1931).

[6] Edouard Chavannes, *Mission archéologique dans la Chine septentrionale* (L'Ecôle Française d'Extrême-Orient, 1909–1915).

[7] Carter, *op. cit.*, p. 3. See also Giles, *op. cit.*, No. 1977.

[8] Giles, *ibid.*, No. 989, also No. 1432.

[9] *Ibid.*, No. 2174.

[10] Arthur Waley, *An Introduction to the Study of Chinese Painting* (London, 1923), Plate XI.

[11] *Chinesische Kunst. Zweihundert Hauptwerke der Ausstellung der Gesellschaft für ostasiatische Kunst* . . . (ed. by Otto Kümmel; Berlin, 1929), Plate LXIX.

[12] *Ibid.*, Plate LXXIX.

[13] Giles, *op. cit.*, No. 1712.

[14] Chavannes, *op. cit.*, Plate 172.

[15] Giles, *op. cit.*, No. 494.

[16] *Ibid.*, No. 2058.

[17] *Masterpieces Selected from the Fine Arts of the Far East* (ed. by Shiichi Tajima; Tokyo, Shimbi Shoin, 1913), Plate XCVI.

[18] Giles, *op. cit.*, No. 14.

[19] Ernst Grosse, *Die ostasiatische Tuschmalerei* (Berlin, 1923), Plates 121 and 105.

[20] *Masterpieces Selected from the Fine Arts of the Far East*, Plate LXXXIV.

[21] *Ibid.*, Plate XCV.

[22] *Tu Shih Ching Ch'uan*, Vol. 13. For the rest of the translation of this poem see Florence Ayscough, *Travels of a Chinese Poet: Tu Fu, Guest of Rivers and Lakes, A.D. 759–770* (London and New York, 1934), II, 215–217.

[23] Otto Kümmel, *Die Kunst ostasiens* (Berlin, 1922), Plate 143.

[24] Florence Ayscough, *Fir-Flower Tablets, Poems Translated from the Chinese* (Boston, 1921), pp. xciii–xciv, 151–172. See also *Florence Ayscough and Amy Lowell: Correspondence of a Friendship* (ed. by H. F. MacNair; Chicago, 1946), *passim.*

[25] *Fir-Flower Tablets*, p. 160.

[26] *Masterpieces Selected from the Fine Arts of the Far East*, Plate XLIX.

[27] Chavannes, *op. cit.*, Plate 89. A rubbing from this monument may be seen in the Florence Ayscough and Harley Farnsworth MacNair Collection in the Art Institute of Chicago.

[28] *Masterpieces Selected from the Fine Arts of the Far East*, Plate XLV

[29] Giles, *op. cit.*, No. 2241.

[30] *Ibid.*, No. 1181.

[31] *Ibid.*, No. 2058.

[32] *Ibid.*, No. 266.

NOTES TO CHAPTER XXII

ART

[1] See examples in Chiang Yee, *Chinese Calligraphy* (London, 1938); see also Lucy Driscoll and Kenji Toda, *Chinese Calligraphy* (Chicago, 1935).

[2] See, for example, the Bahr Collection in the Chicago Museum of Natural History.

[3] It is to be noted, however, that glass was made by the Chinese as early as about the fifth century B.C. See C. G. Seligman, "The Roman Orient and the Far East," in *Antiquity*, XI (March, 1937); and L. Carrington Goodrich, *A Short History of the Chinese People* (New York and London, 1943), p. 27.

[4] Arthur de Carle Sowerby, *Nature in Chinese Art* (New York, 1940).

China," in H. F. MacNair (ed.), *Voices from Unoccupied China*, the 1943 annual volume of the Harris Memorial Foundation, University of Chicago (Chicago, 1944). See also the important account, by Gunther Stein, "A People Goes to School," chap. xxvii, in *The Challenge of Red China* (New York, 1945), of educational efforts made during the past decade in Communist-controlled China. [The foregoing notes have been supplied by the editor.]

NOTES TO CHAPTER XXX

CHINA'S EXAMINATION SYSTEM AND THE WEST

[1] Gaspar da Cruz, *Tractado em que contam muito por estenso as cousas da China* (Evora, 1569). See also Richarde Eden, *The History of Travayle in the West and East Indies, and Other Countreys . . .* (London, 1577), pp. 239–240.

[2] Samuel Purchas, *Hakluytus Posthumus* (old ed., 1599; new ed., Glasgow, 1905–1907, in 20 vols.), II, 569–580.

[3] Nicolas Trigault, *Du Voyage de la Chine* (Lyons, 1616), pp. 50–72.

[4] Robert Burton, *The Anatomy of Melancholy* (1st ed., London, 1621; later ed., 1893).

[5] "Essai sur les mœurs," in *Œuvres complètes de Voltaire*, XIII, 162.

[6] Pierre Martino's work, *L'Orient dans la littérature française* (Paris, 1906), is reviewed by Brunetière in *Revue des Deux Mondes* (1906), pp. 35, 699, *et seq.* The same review is included in *Etudes critiques sur l'histoire de la littérature française*, Tome 8 (1907), pp. 196–199.

[7] William Leonard Schwartz, *The Imaginative Interpretation of the Far East in Modern French Literature, 1800–1925* (Paris, 1927), p. 2; Mary G. Mason, *Western Concepts of China and the Chinese, 1840–1876* (New York, 1939), p. 170; Henri Bernard's article, "Etudes sur l'humanisme chrétien en Chine à la fin de la dynastie des Ming," in *Nankai Social and Economic Quarterly*, Vol. 9, No. 1 (April, 1936), pp. 109–110.

[8] *Gentleman's Magazine*, III (March, 1733), 112.

[9] Eustace Budgell, *A Letter to Cleomenes, King of Sparta* (London, 1731), pp. 91–98.

[10] John Nichols, *Illustrations of the Literary History of the Eighteenth Century* (London, 1817–18??), I, 197.

[11] Sir George Staunton, *An Authentic Account of an Embassy from the King of Great Britain . . . Emperor of China* (London, 1797), II, 153, 294–335.

[12] George T. Staunton, *Miscellaneous Notices Relating to China* (London, 1847), II, 81.

[13] Robert Morrison, *A Dictionary of the Chinese Language* (Macao, 1815–1823), pp. 757–782.

[14] Charles Gutzlaff, *A Sketch of Chinese History* (London, 1834), I, 46.

[15] Gutzlaff, *China Opened* (London, 1838), II, 346.

[16] W. H. Medhurst, *China: Its State and Prospects* (London, 1838), p. 151.

[17] The part played by Meadows has long been of interest; in a letter to the editor of this volume from Florence Ayscough, dated July 3, 1929, are the following queries: "The point that I have never solved and one which is important is

---

[5] Herbert A. Giles, *A Chinese Biographical Dictionary* (London and Shanghai, 1898), Nos. 1204, 2349, 2241, and other sketches for other artists mentioned; John C. Ferguson, *Chinese Painting* (Chicago, 1927).

[6] *Eminent Chinese of the Ch'ing Period (1644–1912)* (ed. by Arthur W. Hummel; Washington, D.C., 1943, 1944), II, 787–789.

[7] Several of Jên Po-nien's paintings are in the Florence Ayscough and Harley Farnsworth MacNair Collection in the Art Institute of Chicago.

NOTES TO CHAPTER XXIII

ARCHITECTURE

[1] D. G. Mirams, *A Brief History of Chinese Architecture* (Shanghai, Hongkong, Singapore, 1940); Osvald Sirén, "Chinese Architecture," in *Encyclopaedia Britannica* (14th ed.), Vol. 5, pp. 556–565 (esp. the bibliography, p. 565); Carroll B. Malone, *History of the Peking Summer Palaces under the Ch'ing Dynasty* (Urbana, Ill., 1934); see also comments of L. Carrington Goodrich in *A Short History of the Chinese People* (New York and London, 1943), on *Ying Tsao Fa-shih*, the basic work on Chinese architecture, by Li Chieh (d. 1100).

[2] Florence Ayscough, "The Grass Hut by the Yellow Reach," chap. i, pp. 23–99, and "The Symbolism of the Forbidden City," chap. iv, pp. 257–340, in *A Chinese Mirror* (Boston, 1925).

[3] Exquisitely carved models—done at Zikawei, near Shanghai—of some of the most famous pagodas may be seen in the Chicago Museum of Natural History.

[4] Florence Ayscough, "The Chinese Idea of a Garden," chap. iii, pp. 213–256, *op. cit.*; Dorothy Graham, *Chinese Gardens* (New York, 1938); Florence Lee Powell, *In the Chinese Garden* (New York, 1943).

[5] James Whitall, *Chinese Lyrics from the Book of Jade Translated from the French of Judith Gautier* (London, n.d.), p. 36.

[6] Daniel Sheets Dye, *A Grammar of Chinese Lattice* (Cambridge, Mass., 1937), in 2 vols.; Eleanor von Erdberg, *Chinese Influence on European Garden Structures* (Cambridge, Mass., 1936).

[7] H. F. MacNair, "Low Library," in *St. John's, 1879–1919* (Shanghai, 1919).

NOTES TO CHAPTER XXIV

DRAMA

[1] Herbert A. Giles, *A Chinese Biographical Dictionary* (London and Shanghai, 1898), No. 787.

[2] *Ibid.*, No. 1750.

[3] *Ibid.*, No. 1720.

[4] *Ibid.*, No. 2070.

[5] *Ibid.*, No. 1239.

[6] *Ibid.*, No. 1172.

[7] *Ibid.*, No. 1654.

NOTES TO CHAPTER XXV

TRADITIONAL LITERATURE: NATURE AND LIMITATIONS

[1] Herbert A. Giles, *A Chinese Biographical Dictionary* (London and Shanghai, 1898), Nos. 70 and 1775.

[2] *Ibid.*, No. 2008.

[3] *Ibid.*, No. 1892.

[4] *Ibid.*, No. 1750.

[5] *Ibid.*, No. 293.

[6] *Ibid.*, No. 2058.

[7] *Ibid.*, No. 1654.

[8] *Ibid.*, No. 1181.

[9] *The Book of Songs* (trans. by Arthur Waley; London, 1937).

[10] *Traditional Chinese Tales* (trans. by Wang Chi-chen; New York, 1944); E. D. Edwards (trans.), *Chinese Prose Literature of the T'ang Period, A.D. 618–906* (London, 1937, 1938), in 2 vols.

[11] *San Kuo Chih Yen I; or, Romance of the Three Kingdoms* (trans. by C. H. Brewitt-Taylor; Shanghai, 1925, 1926), in 2 vols.

[12] *Shui Hu Chuan* (Story of the Liangshan Bandits), translated by Pearl S. Buck under the title, *All Men Are Brothers* (New York, 1933), in 2 vols.

[13] *The Golden Lotus: A Translation, from the Chinese Original, of the Novel Chin P'ing Mei* (trans. by Clement Egerton; London, 1939), in 4 vols. See also an abridged translation, *Chin P'ing Mei: The Adventurous History of Hsi Men and His Six Wives*, with an Introduction by Arthur Waley (New York, 1940), in 2 vols.

[14] *Monkey*, by Wu Ch'êng-ên (trans. from the Chinese by Arthur Waley; New York, 1943).

[15] *Eminent Chinese of the Ch'ing Period (1644–1912)* (ed. by Arthur W. Hummel; Washington, D.C., 1943, 1944), I, 164–166.

[16] *Ibid.*, II, 628–630.

[17] *Ibid.*, pp. 866–867.

[18] *Ibid.*, pp. 737–739; Ts'ao Chan, *Hung-lou Mêng* (Dream of the Red Chamber) (translated in part and adapted by Wang Chi-chen; New York, 1929).

[19] For examples see *Contemporary Chinese Stories* (trans. by Wang Chi-chen; New York, 1944); *Living China: Modern Chinese Short Stories . . . With an Essay on Modern Chinese Literature by Nym Wales* (comp. and ed. by Edgar Snow; New York, 1937); T'ien Chün, *Village in August* (New York, 1942); *The True Story of Ah Q by Lu-hsün, Translated into English by George Kin Leung* (Shanghai, 1926).

NOTES TO CHAPTER XXVII

LETTERS AND ARTS IN THE WAR YEARS

For considerable information in this chapter I am indebted to Mr. Chu Fu-sung's "Wartime Chinese Literature," in *China: After Seven Years of War* (New York, Macmillan, 1945); Miss Yang Kang's "China's Wartime Literature,"

in *Asia and the Americas*, July, 1945; Mr. Ch'êng Ch'i-yü's "T[...] Always Been Poets," *ibid.*, April, 1944; Dr. Hu Shih's "A Hi[...] Chinese Painting," *ibid.*, May, 1941; Mr. H. P. Lazarus' "Lusin[...] ern," in *The Nation*, October 4, 1941; Mrs. Ch'ên Mêng-chia; [...] of the Department of Oriental Languages, University of Chic[...] many Chinese writers and artists to be represented in my forthc[...] of English translations of recent Chinese plays, short storie[...] poetry, with paintings, woodcuts, and music, under the ausp[...] American Institute of Cultural Relations.—D. L. PHELPS.

NOTES TO CHAPTER XXVIII

CHINA: A FRONTIER IN AMERICAN LITERATURE [...]

[1] See, for example, *The Journals of Major Samuel Shaw: The[...] Consul at Canton* (Boston, 1847). In 1786 Major Shaw establishe[...] first American trading house in China. Captain Richard Jeffry [...] of the *Caroline*" was kept in 1799 during a fur-trading voyage [...] the northwest coast of America and return (ed. by H. F. Mac[...] *Northwest Quarterly*, January, 1938, pp. 61–84, and April, 193[...] See also Captain R. J. Cleveland, *A Narrative of Voyages and Co[...] prises* (Boston, 1850); and Charles W. King, *The Claims of Japa[...] upon Christendom, Exhibited in Notes of Voyages Made in 183[...] in the Ship Morrison.*

[2] Note also the magnificent biographical dictionary edited by [...] Hummel, *Eminent Chinese of the Ch'ing Period (1644–1912)* (Wa[...] 1943, 1944), in 2 vols., so frequently cited in this volume.

NOTES TO CHAPTER XXIX

MODERN EDUCATION

[1] *Eminent Chinese of the Ch'ing Period (1644–1912)* (ed. by Art[...] mel, Washington, D.C., 1943, 1944), I, 402–405.

[2] *Ibid.*, II, 731–734.

[3] *Ibid.*, I, 295–300.

[4] *Ibid.*, pp. 27–32.

[5] *Ibid.*, II, 871.

[6] The figures here given are in Chinese currency, the value of [...] smaller than that of the United States, and is constantly fluctuatin[...]

[7] Pearl S. Buck, *Tell the People—Mass Education in China* (Ne[...]

[8] T. H. White, "*Life* Looks at China," *Life*, Vol. XVI, No. 18 ([...] pp. 99–110, esp. p. 104.

[9] As well as of one-party government and attempts at "though[...] wartime China.

[10] For a brief analysis by a Chinese scholar of the educational [...] Unoccupied China since 1937, see Chin Yueh-lin, "Education in C[...]

this: how much did Meadows have to do with the founding of the English Civil Service Exams.? ... how much did his urging have to do with it? ... Is there any connection and what is it? Meadows thought that he had accomplished something in this line." [H. F. M.]

[18] Herman Finer, *The British Civil Service* (London, 1937), p. 38.

[19] *Chinese Repository*, July, 1835, pp. 127–128.

[20] J. F. Davis, *The Chinese: A General Description of the Empire of China* (London, 1840), p. 209.

[21] The titles and excerpts of these works are presented in a much longer article by the present writer in *Harvard Journal of Asiatic Studies*, Vol. 7, No. 4 (1943).

NOTES TO CHAPTER XXXI
ECONOMIC DEVELOPMENT

[1] From Pan Ku, *Ch'ien Han Shu* (History of the Earlier Han Dynasty), Book 24; quotation translated by C. C. Wu.

[2] Ssŭ-ma Ch'ien, *Shih Chi* (Historical Record), Book 29. Translated by Ch'ao-ting Chi for his *Key Economic Areas in Chinese History as Revealed in the Development of Public Works for Water-Control* (London, 1936), pp. 75–76.

[3] Quoted in Ellsworth Huntington, *The Character of Races* (New York and London, 1924), p. 154.

[4] See also W. H. Mallory, *China—Land of Famine* (New York, 1926); and H. F. MacNair, *With the White Cross in China* (Peking, 1939).—EDITOR'S NOTE.

[5] This phenomenon is portrayed fictionally by Pearl Buck in *The Good Earth*.—EDITOR'S NOTE.

[6] Of value, in connection with this subject, is Fung Yu-lan's essay, "Why China Has No Science—An Interpretation of the History and Consequences of Chinese Philosophy," in *International Journal of Ethics*, Vol. XXXII, No. 3 (April, 1922), pp. 237–263.—EDITOR'S NOTE.

[7] See also the author's "Economic Reconstruction and Planning: Wartime and Post-war," in H. F. MacNair (ed.), *Voices from Unoccupied China* (Chicago, 1944).

NOTES TO CHAPTER XXXII
AGRICULTURE

[1] Chinese Government Directorate of Statistics, *Statistical Monthly (T'ung-chi Yüeh-pao)* (Nanking), No. 3 (January–February, 1932); or C. C. Chang, *An Estimate of China's Farms and Crops* (Chinese and English; Nanking, 1932); Boris P. Torgasheff, "Town Population, China," in *China Critic* (Shanghai), III (1930), 317–322.

[2] The area figures are taken from *The New Atlas of China* (Shanghai, Shun Pao, 1934), p. 162, compiled by China's three outstanding geologists: V. K. Ting, W. H. Wong, and S. Y. Tsêng. The population figure of 450,000,000 for all China is the best working figure. It is accepted by the International Institute of Agriculture, the International Statistical Institute, and the Economic Section of the

League of Nations. For a detailed table of various estimates of China's population see Chang Hsiao-mei and others, *Chinese-Foreign Economic Yearbook* (in Chinese; 3d issue, Hongkong and Chungking, World Book Co., 1941), p. 46; or George B. Cressey, *China's Geographic Foundations* (New York, McGraw-Hill Book Co., 1934), pp. 18–19. Figures on arable land, total area, and population for Western countries are taken from Institut International d'Agriculture, *Annuaire International de Statistique Agricole* (Rome, 1932–1933), pp. 2–159.

[3] *Chinese Economic Yearbook* (in Chinese; Nanking, 1934), p. B 24. The section on geography was written by Dr. Wong according to information from Professor Chang Chi-yun of Chekiang University.

[4] W. H. Wong, "The Distribution of Population and Land Utilization in China," in *Independent Review (Tu-li P'ing-lun)* (Peiping), Nos. 3–4 (June 5 and 12, 1932). An English summary of this article under the same title was published by the China Institute of Pacific Relations (Shanghai, 1933). See also "Colonization Possibilities of Northwest China," in *Pacific Affairs*, December, 1935. James Thorp, an American soil scientist, supports Dr. Wong's conclusions and thinks his estimate for northwestern China is extremely generous.

[5] John Lossing Buck, *Land Utilization in China* (University of Chicago Press, 1937), chap. vi.

[6] The National Agricultural Research Bureau gives percentage of cultivated land to total area as 13.2. See *China Handbook* (New York, Macmillan, 1943), p. 547. This is very near to what I have estimated in this chapter, written before the *Handbook* came off the press. F. V. Field (ed.), in *Economic Handbook of the Pacific Area* (New York, Doubleday, Doran, 1934), p. 63, gives a table of percentage of cultivated land to total area as estimated by different authorities.

[7] For an account of phases of this famine, the importance of transportation, and methods used in administering relief, see H. F. MacNair, *With the White Cross in China* (Peking, 1939); see also W. H. Mallory, *China—Land of Famine* (New York, 1926).—EDITOR'S NOTE.

[8] K. Y. Cheng, "Floods and Rainfall along the Yangtze Valley during the Period 1911–1932," in *Science* (in Chinese; Shanghai), Vol. 18, No. 10 (October, 1934).

[9] University of Nanking, Department of Agricultural Economics, *The 1931 Flood: A Survey* (Nanking, 1932); China, National Flood Relief Commission, *Report for 1931–1932* (Shanghai, 1933).

[10] National Agricultural Research Bureau, *Crop Reports*, Vol. IV, No. 8 (August, 1936), p. 232.

[11] The study of freight rates for rice and wheat by the National Tariff Commission is quoted by Hsu Yin, "China Cannot Forever Import Food," in *National Reconstruction Forum Newsletter No. 11* (in Chinese; published by the China Institute, New York City), September, 1943.

[12] The subject of China's land tax has been exhaustively treated in the following Chinese works: Sun Tso-ch'i, *Chung-kuo T'ien-fu Wên-t'i* (The Problem of China's Land Tax) (Shanghai, New Life Publishing Co., 1935), 472 pp.; Lin Shih-jên, *Chung-kuo T'ien-fu Wên-t'i* (The Problem of China's Land Tax)

(Shanghai, Commercial Press, 1935), 347 pp.; *Journal of Land Economics* (in Chinese; Nanking), Vol. IV, Nos. 2–3 (January, 1936), special number on Chinese land taxation; National Central University, Department of Economics, *T'ien-fu Fu Chia Shui Tiao Ch'a* (A Survey of Surcharges on the Land Tax) (Shanghai, Commercial Press, 1935).

[13] National Agricultural Research Bureau, special publication No. 1, as quoted in C. C. Chang, "Rural Economy," in *Chinese Year Book 1935–36*, p. 841.

[14] Buck, *op. cit.*, p. 326.

[15] Sun Yat-sen Institute for the Advancement of Culture and Education, *Chung-kuo Liang-shih Wên-t'i* (China's Food Problem) (Nanking and Chungking, Cheng Chung Book Co., 1940), pp. 70–74.

[16] Hsia I-shan, *Ch'ing Tai T'ung-shih* (History of the Ch'ing Dynasty) (Shanghai, Commercial Press, 1928), II, 440–442.

[17] Buck, *op. cit.*, pp. 192–194.

[18] *Crop Reports*, Vol. III, No. 4 (April, 1935), pp. 88–89.

[19] Hsieh Nung-shan, *Chung-kuo Nung Min Chan Chêng Chih Shih Ti Yen Chiu* (A Study of Agrarian Movements or Farmers' Revolts in Chinese History) (Shanghai, 1935), p. 492.

[20] Sun Yat-sen Institute, *op. cit.*, pp. 55–57.

[21] "Land Ownership and Its Concentration in China," in *Agrarian China: Selected Source Materials from Chinese Authors* (trans. and comp. by Research Staff, Institute of Pacific Relations; University of Chicago Press, 1938); Chen Han-seng, *The Present Agrarian Problem in China* (China Institute of Pacific Relations, Shanghai, 1933), 32 pp. Also reproduced in abridged form in *Problems of the Pacific* (Chicago, 1933), pp. 271–298.

[22] Edgar Snow, *Red Star over China* (New York, 1938, 1944); Fei Hsiao-tung, *Peasant Life in China* (London, 1939), esp. chap. xvi, "Agrarian Problems in China," pp. 282–286.

[23] *Crop Reports*, Vol. III, No. 6 (June, 1935); Vol. IV, No. 4 (April, 1935).

[24] Buck, *op. cit.*, p. 198.

[25] Sun Yat-sen Institute, *Chung-kuo Ti-tsu Wên-t'i T'ao-lun-chi* (A Symposium on Renting Systems and Rents in China) (Shanghai, Commercial Press, 1927), 95 pp.

[26] *Crop Reports*, Vol. II, No. 4 (April, 1934).

[27] Buck, *op. cit.*, pp. 462–463.

[28] A. K. Chiu and T. C. Han, *An Economic Survey of 184 Farms in Shentse County, Hopei Province* (Peiping Institute of Social Research, 1936), the publication of which was interrupted by the war. A Chinese version of the same survey was published in *Quarterly Review of Social Sciences* (Peiping), Vol. V, No. 2 (June, 1934).

[29] *Crop Reports*, Vol. II, No. 4 (April, 1934).

[30] C. C. Chang, *An Estimate of China's Farms and Crops* (Nanking, 1932), p. 14.

[31] *Crop Reports*, Vol. III, No. 4 (April, 1935), pp. 85–87.

[32] Buck, *op. cit.*, pp. 184–185.

[33] *Quarterly Review of Social Sciences*, Vol. V, No. 2 (June, 1934), pp. 223–224.

[34] Buck, *op. cit.*, pp. 373–375.

[35] China Institute of Economic and Statistical Research, Shanghai and Chungking, *A Study of the Rural Economy of Wuking* (Chekiang, 1939), pp. 22–23.

[36] Chin Feng, "The National Economic Council," in *Chinese Year Book, 1935–36*, pp. 294–326; Li Hsieh, "Hydraulic Engineering Works," in *Chinese Year Book, 1935–36*, pp. 987–1009.

[37] Chin Feng, "War Economy," in *Chinese Year Book, 1938–39*, pp. 462–482. For more recent studies of railway development in China see Chang Kia-ngau, *China's Struggle for Railroad Development* (New York, 1943).

[38] Hsieh Chia-sheng, "The National Development of Agricultural Science in China," in *Chinese Year Book, 1935–36*, pp. 722–768. See also National Agricultural Research Bureau, *Report* for 1937 and for 1938. For more recent development of technical aspects of Chinese agriculture see *China Handbook*, pp. 546–629.

[39] Chin Feng, "War Economy," in *Chinese Year Book, 1938–39*, pp. 471–474.

[40] *Chinese Year Book, 1935–36*, pp. 156, 324–326; see also *China Handbook*, pp. 99–108.

[41] But see chap. xi, above, and Gunther Stein, *The Challenge of Red China* (New York, 1945).—EDITOR'S NOTE.

[42] China, Legislative Yüan, *The Land Law* (in Chinese; Shanghai, Min-chih Book Co., 1930), 98 pp. The English translation of the provisions is by C. C. Chang, in *Chinese Year Book, 1935–36*, pp. 843–844.

[43] *Crop Reports*, Vol. VI, No. 2 (February, 1936), pp. 35–37.

[44] This was the first time the Kuomintang National government attempted to improve agriculture through a properly organized and administered ministry. In the first two years of its existence at Nanking it had had a token and ineffective Ministry of Agriculture and Mines which was abolished in 1930.

[45] Chinese Ministry of Information, *China after Five Years of War* (Chinese News Service, New York, 1942), pp. 122, 124, 129, 155, 158. Other data on crop and animal production are derived from the same source. For more recent data see *China Handbook*, pp. 550–589. For improvement of animal production see R. W. Phillips, R. G. Johnson, and R. T. Moyer, *The Livestock of China* (Washington, D.C., 1945).

[46] The discussion in this chapter is limited to coöperatives active in agriculture. For information on industrial coöperatives and the work of Rewi Alley and his colleagues consult George Hogg, *I See a New China* (Boston, 1944).—EDITOR'S NOTE.

[47] For a thorough discussion of China's banking and finance see Frank M. Tamagna, *Banking and Finance in China* (New York, 1942); see also *China at War* (Chinese News Service, New York), Vol. X, No. 2 (February, 1943), p. 28.

[48] *Contemporary China* (Chinese News Service, New York), Vol. I, No. 20 (February 23, 1942); Tuan-sheng Chien, "Wartime Local Government in China," in *Pacific Affairs*, Vol. XVI, No. 4 (December, 1943); Y. Y. Hsu, "The Pao-chia System in China," in *Far Eastern Survey*, Vol. XII, No. 24 (December 8, 1943); see also *China at War*, Vol. X, No. 6 (June, 1943), pp. 40–42. For the subject of

mass education in China see Pearl S. Buck, *Tell the People—Mass Education in China* (New York, 1945).

[49] *China at War*, Vol. X, No. 6 (June, 1943), p. 26.

[50] "Realizing Sun Yat-sen's Land Policy," *ibid.*, Vol. IX, No. 2 (February, 1942), pp. 40–42.

[51] "Towards Equal Land Ownership," *ibid.*, No. 7 (July, 1942), pp. 25–26.

[52] C. C. Wu, "Economic Reconstruction and Planning: Wartime and Post-war," in H. F. MacNair (ed.), *Voices from Unoccupied China* (Chicago, 1944), pp. 65–80.

[53] *Ibid.*, pp. xxvi–xxxv, and xlviii–xlix.

NOTES TO CHAPTER XXXIII
INTERNATIONAL TRADE

In preparing this chapter the writer was aided by discussion with Dr. T. F. Tsiang. For possible errors and for all interpretations the writer alone is responsible.

[1] For a fictional study of this development see Alice Tisdale Hobart, *Oil for the Lamps of China* (Indianapolis, 1933).—EDITOR'S NOTE.

NOTES TO CHAPTER XXXIV
CHINA AMONG THE NATIONS

[1] See the unpublished doctoral dissertation by the writer, entitled "A Comparative Analysis of the Historical Background of the Monroe Doctrine and the Open Door Policy in the Far East" (University of Chicago, 1935), pp. 9–12.

[2] See David Nelson Rowe, *China among the Powers* (New York, 1945), chap. i, for a detailed analysis of political and military strategy.

A SELECTED
BIBLIOGRAPHY

A Selected Bibliography

BY CHAN WING-TSIT AND OTHERS

THE FOLLOWING WORKS have been selected and arranged by topics for readers who desire to continue their study of China.*

For topical or historical surveys of **Chinese culture** see: (1) Kenneth Scott Latourette, *The Chinese: Their History and Culture* (New York, 1934, 2 vols.; 3d rev. ed., 1946, 2 vols. in 1); (2) O. Franke, *Geschichte des chinesischen Reiches* (Berlin and Leipzig, 1930, 1936, 1937), in 3 vols.; (3) C. P. Fitzgerald, *China: A Short Cultural History* (New York, 1938); (4) L. Carrington Goodrich, *A Short History of the Chinese People* (New York and London, 1943), emphasizing cultural developments and cultural contacts with other peoples; (5) Sophia H. Chen ZEN (ed.), *Symposium on Chinese Culture* (Shanghai, 1931); (6) Samuel Wells Williams, *The Middle Kingdom* . . . (New York, 1848; rev. eds., 1883, 1901), in 2 vols.; (7) Edward Thomas Williams, *China Yesterday and Today* (1923; 5th ed., New York, 1932); (8) Marcel Granet, *Chinese Civilization* (trans. by K. E. Innes and M. R. Brailsford; London, 1930).

The author of **chap. i** (Molding Forces) recommends for further reading: (9) Florence Ayscough, *Chinese Women, Yesterday and To-day* (Boston, 1937); (10) Harold E. Gorst, *China* (London, 1899); (11) LIN Yutang, *My Country and My People* (New York, 1935); (12) LIN Yutang, *The Importance of Living* (New York, 1937); (13) W. A. P. Martin, *The Lore of Cathay* . . . (New York, 1901); (14) Arthur Henderson Smith, *Proverbs and Common Sayings from the Chinese* (Shanghai, 1902); (15) Henry H. Hart (comp. and trans.), *Seven Hundred Chinese Proverbs* (Stanford University, Calif., 1937); also No. 1, above, and Nos. 108, 166, 248, 249, 252, 270, below.

The author of **chap. iii** (Some Revelations of Recent Excavations) has included the following references: (16) Academia Sinica, *Preliminary Reports of Excavations at Anyang* (Peiping, 1929–1933), Parts I–IV; (17) William Charles White, *Tombs of Old Lo-yang* (Shanghai, 1934); (18) C. G. Seligman and H. C. Beck, "Far Eastern Glass," in *Bulletin of the Museum of Far Eastern Antiquities* (Stockholm), No. 10 (1938); (19) C. G. Seligman, "The Roman Orient and the Far East," in *Antiquity*, XI (March, 1937); (20) Sir Aurel Stein, *Serindia* (London, 1921); (21) Sir Aurel Stein, *Innermost Asia* (London, 1928); (22) Sir Aurel Stein, *On Central-Asian Tracks* (London, 1933); (23) A. D. Brankston, *Early Ming Wares of Ching Tê Chên* (Peiping, 1938); (24) R. L. Hobson, *The Potter's Art* (London, 1935). See also: (25) Sir Percival Yetts, *An-yang: A Retrospect* (China

---

* Surnames of Chinese authors are in capitals and small capitals.

Society, London, 1942); (26) G. D. Wu, *Prehistoric Pottery in China* (Washington, D.C., 1939).

For general history (chaps. vi–xii) the following may also be consulted: (27) Kenneth Scott Latourette, *A Short History of the Far East* (New York, 1946); (28) Li Ung Bing, *Outlines of Chinese History* (Shanghai, 1914); (29) G. Nye Steiger, *A History of the Far East* (Boston, 1936); (30) René Grousset, *Histoire de l'Extrême-Orient* (Paris, 1929), in 2 vols.; (31) René Grousset, *The Civilizations of the East: China* (trans. by Catherine Alison Phillips; London, 1931, New York, 1941), in 4 vols.; (32) Richard Wilhelm, *A Short History of Chinese Civilization* (trans. by Joan Joshua; New York, 1929).

For ancient and early history in particular see: (33) Edouard Chavannes (trans.), *Les Mémoires historiques de Se-Ma-Ts'ien* (Paris, 1895–1905), in 5 vols.; (34) Homer H. Dubs (trans.), *The History of the Former Han Dynasty, by Pan Ku* (Baltimore, 1938, 1944), in 2 vols.; (35) H. G. Creel, *The Birth of China: A Study of the Formative Period of Chinese Civilization* (New York and London, 1936); (36) H. G. Creel, *Studies in Early Chinese Culture,* First Series (Baltimore, 1937); (37) Henri Maspero, *La Chine antique* (Paris, 1927); (38) Friedrich Hirth, *The Ancient History of China to the End of the Chóu Dynasty* (New York, 1908, 1923); (39) Derk Bodde, *China's First Unifier: A Study of the Ch'in Dynasty as Seen in the Life of Li Ssŭ (280?–208 B.C.)* (Leiden, 1938); (40) Esson M. Gale (trans.), *Discourses on Salt and Iron: A Debate on State Control of Commerce and Industry in Ancient China, Chapters I–XIX Translated from the Chinese of Huan K'uan with Introduction and Notes* (Leiden, 1931); (41) Peter A. Boodberg and T. C. Lin (trans.), "Discourses on Salt and Iron," in *Journal of the North China Branch of the Royal Asiatic Society,* LXV (1934), 73–110; also No. 174, below.

Studies on specific problems or persons of Chinese history include: (42) J. G. Andersson, *Children of the Yellow Earth: Studies in Prehistoric China* (trans. by E. Classen; London, 1934); (43) J. G. Andersson, *Preliminary Reports on Archaeological Research in Kansu* ... (Peking, 1925); (44) Berthold Laufer, *Jade: A Study in Chinese Archaeology and Religion* (Chicago, 1912); (45) Ch'ao-ting Chi, *Key Economic Areas in Chinese History as Revealed in the Development of Public Works for Water-Control* (London and New York, 1936); (46) Li Chi, *The Formation of the Chinese People: An Anthropological Enquiry* (Cambridge, Mass., 1928); (47) Arthur W. Hummel (trans.), *The Autobiography of a Chinese Historian* [Ku Chieh-kang]: *Being the Preface to a Symposium on Ancient Chinese History (Ku Shih Pien)* (Leiden, 1931); (48) Marcel Granet, *Festivals and Songs of Ancient China* (New York, 1932); (49) Nancy Lee Swann, *Pan Chao: The Foremost Woman Scholar of China, First Century A.D.* (New York, 1932); (50) John K. Shryock (trans. and ed.), *The Study of Human Abilities: The Jên Wu Chih of Liu Shao* (New Haven, 1937); (51) Woodbridge Bingham, *The Founding of the T'ang Dynasty* ... (Baltimore, 1941); (52) H. R. Williamson, *Wang An Shih ... a Chinese Statesman and Educationalist of the Sung Dynasty* (London, 1935–1937), in 2 vols.; (53) Colonel Henry Yule, *The Book of Ser Marco Polo* (3d ed., London, 1921), in 2 vols.; (54) Marco Polo, *The Descriptions of the World* (trans. and ed. by A. C. Moule and Paul Pelliot; London, 1938), in 2 vols.; (55) Sir Edmund

T. Backhouse and J. O. P. Bland, *Annals and Memoirs of the Court of Peking from the Sixteenth to the Twentieth Century* (Boston, 1914); (56) L. Carrington Goodrich, *The Literary Inquisition of Ch'ien-Lung* (Baltimore, 1935); (57) Franz Michael, *The Origin of Manchu Rule in China* . . . (Baltimore, 1942); (58) TÊNG Ssŭ-yü, *Chang Hsi and the Treaty of Nanking, 1842* (Chicago, 1944); (59) William James Hail, *Tseng Kuo-fan and the Taiping Rebellion* (New Haven, 1927); (60) Meribeth E. Cameron, *The Reform Movement in China, 1898–1912* (Stanford University, Calif., 1931); (61) Arthur W. Hummel (ed.), *Eminent Chinese of the Ch'ing Period (1644–1912)* (Washington, D.C., 1943, 1944), in 2 vols.

Cultural relations between China and Persia and the West are reviewed in: (62) Berthold Laufer, *Sino-Iranica: Chinese Contributions to the History of Civilization in Ancient Iran* . . . (Chicago, 1919); (63) Friedrich Hirth, *China and the Roman Orient: Researches into Their Ancient and Mediaeval Relations as Represented in Old Chinese Records* (Shanghai, 1885); (64) Frederick J. Teggart, *Rome and China: A Study of Correlations in Historical Events* (Berkeley, 1939); (65) Thomas F. Carter, *The Invention of Printing in China and Its Spread Westward* (New York, 1925; 2d ed., 1931); (66) G. F. Hudson, *Europe and China: A Survey of Their Relations from the Earliest Times to 1800* (London, 1931); (67) Adolf Reichwein, *China and Europe: Intellectual and Artistic Contacts in the Eighteenth Century* (trans. by J. C. Powell; New York, 1925); (68) George H. Danton, *The Culture Contacts of the United States and China* . . . *1784–1844* (New York, 1931); (69) Arthur E. Christy (ed.), *The Asian Legacy and American Life* (New York, 1945); (70) Derk Bodde, *China's Gifts to the West* (Washington, D.C., 1942).

For China's **international relations** see: (71) William Woodville Rockhill, *China's Intercourse with Korea from the Fifteenth Century to 1895* (London, 1905); (72) Harley Farnsworth MacNair, *Modern Chinese History, Selected Readings* . . . (Shanghai, 1923); (73) Hosea Ballou Morse, *The International Relations of the Chinese Empire* (London, 1910–1918), in 3 vols.; (74) Hosea Ballou Morse and Harley Farnsworth MacNair, *Far Eastern International Relations* (rev. ed., Boston and New York, 1931); (75) Kenneth Scott Latourette, *The History of Early Relations between the United States and China, 1784–1844* (New Haven, 1917); (76) T. A. Bisson, *America's Far Eastern Policy* (New York, 1945); (77) Tyler Dennett, *Americans in Eastern Asia: A Critical Study of the Policy of the United States with Reference to China, Japan, and Korea in the Nineteenth Century* (New York, 1922); (78) Knight Biggerstaff, *The Far East and the United States* (Ithaca, N.Y., 1943).

The author of **chap. xii** (International Relations: The Twentieth Century) recommends for further reading: Nos. 29, 74, 76–77, above, and No. 100, below; (79) Payson J. Treat, *The Far East* . . . (New York, 1935); (80) Paul Hibbert Clyde, *A History of the Modern and Contemporary Far East* . . . (New York, 1937); (81) Robert T. Pollard, *China's Foreign Relations, 1917–1931* (New York, 1933); (82) Harold S. Quigley, *Chinese Politics and Foreign Powers* (New York, 1927); (83) Harold S. Quigley, *Far Eastern War, 1937–1941* (Boston, 1942); (84) Westel W. Willoughby, *Foreign Rights and Interests in China* (rev. ed., Baltimore, 1927), in

2 vols.; (85) Westel W. Willoughby, *China at the Conference: A Report* (Baltimore, 1922); (86) Westel W. Willoughby, *The Sino-Japanese Controversy and the League of Nations* (Baltimore, 1935); (87) A. Whitney Griswold, *The Far Eastern Policy of the United States* (New York, 1938); (88) Stanley K. Hornbeck, *Principles of American Policy in Relation to the Far East* (Washington, D.C., 1934); (89) Thomas Edward La Fargue, *China and the World War* (Stanford University, Calif., 1937); (90) Leo Pasvolsky, *Russia in the Far East* (New York, 1932); (91) Ernest Batson Price, *The Russo-Japanese Treaties of 1907–1916 Concerning Manchuria and Mongolia* (Baltimore, 1933); (92) Victor A. Yakhontoff, *Russia and the Soviet Union in the Far East* (New York, 1931); (93) Victor A. Yakhontoff, *USSR Foreign Policy* (New York, 1945); (94) Robert J. Kerner, *The Urge to the Sea: The Course of Russian History* (Berkeley, 1942); (95) Robert J. Kerner, "Russian Policy in the Far East," in *Yale Review*, Vol. XXXV, No. 1 (Autumn, 1945), pp. 119–138; (96) Robert J. Kerner, "Russian Naval Aims," in *Foreign Affairs*, Vol. XXIV, No. 2 (January, 1946), pp. 290–299; (97) Harriet L. Moore, *Soviet Far Eastern Policy, 1931–1945* (Princeton, 1945); (98) Stanley K. Hornbeck, *Contemporary Politics in the Far East* (New York, 1916); (99) Stanley K. Hornbeck, *China Today: Political* (Boston, 1927); (100) Stanley K. Hornbeck, *The United States and the Far East: Certain Fundamentals of Policy* (Boston, 1942); (101) C. Walter Young, *Japanese Jurisdiction in the South Manchuria Railway Areas* (Baltimore, 1931); (102) Sir Harold Parlett, *A Brief Account of Diplomatic Events in Manchuria* (London, 1929); (103) Henry L. Stimson, *The Far Eastern Crisis: Recollections and Observations* (New York, 1936); (104) William C. Johnstone, *The United States and Japan's New Order* (New York, 1941). See also: (105) Sir John T. Pratt, *War and Politics in China* (London, 1943), esp. chap. xiii and appendix.

Further information on the history and government of **twentieth-century China (chaps. ix–xi)** may be obtained in: (106) Harold M. Vinacke, *A History of the Far East in Modern Times* (rev. ed., New York, 1942); (107) Arthur N. Holcombe, *The Chinese Revolution...* (Cambridge, Mass., 1930); (108) Harley Farnsworth MacNair, *China in Revolution: An Analysis of Politics and Militarism under the Republic* (Chicago, 1931); (109) T'ANG Leang-Li, *The Inner History of the Chinese Revolution* (New York, 1930); (110) SUN Yat-sen, *San Min Chu I: The Three Principles of the People* (trans. by Frank W. Price; 1924; Shanghai, 1927); (111) Leonard Shihlien Hsü, *Sun Yat-sen, His Political and Social Ideals: A Source Book* (Los Angeles, 1933); (112) [Mrs.] Lyon Sharman, *Sun Yat-sen, His Life and Its Meaning: A Critical Biography* (New York, 1934); (113) Paul M. A. Linebarger, *The Political Doctrines of Sun Yat-sen: An Exposition of the San Min Chu I* (Baltimore, 1937); (114) Paul M. A. Linebarger, *Government in Republican China* (New York, 1938); (115) Paul M. A. Linebarger, *The China of Chiang K'ai-shek: A Political Study* (Boston, 1941). See also John B. Powell, *My Twenty-five Years in China* (New York, 1946).

For material on Chinese **geography** see: (116) George B. Cressey, *China's Geographic Foundations: A Survey of the Land and Its People* (New York, 1934); (117) George B. Cressey, *Asia's Lands and Peoples...* (New York, 1944); (118)

Owen Lattimore, *Manchuria, Cradle of Conflict* (rev. ed., New York, 1935); (119) Andrew J. Grajdanzev, *Formosa Today* (New York, 1942); (120) Martin R. Norins, *Gateway to Asia: Sinkiang . . .* (New York, 1944); (121) Albert Herrmann, *Historical and Commercial Atlas of China* (Cambridge, Mass., 1935); (122) China, Directorate General of Posts, *Postal Atlas* (4th ed., Nanking, 1936); (123) V. K. TING, W. H. WONG, and S. Y. TSÊNG, *The New Atlas of China* (Shanghai, 1934).

The story of China's **recent social and intellectual movements** (chap. xi) is partly told in: (124) HU Shih, *The Chinese Renaissance* (Chicago, 1934); (125) Tsi Chang WANG, *The Youth Movement in China* (New York, 1927); (126) William HUNG (ed.), *As It Looks to Young China . . .* (New York, 1932); (127) T'ANG Leang-Li, *Reconstruction in China: A Record of Progress and Achievement in Facts and Figures* (Shanghai, 1935); (128) T'ANG Leang-Li, *The New Social Order in China* (Shanghai, 1936). For communism see: (129) Edgar Snow, *Red Star over China* (New York, 1938, 1944); (130) Agnes Smedley, *Battle Hymn of China* (New York, 1943); (131) Gunther Stein, *The Challenge of Red China* (New York, 1945); (132) LIN Yutang, *The Vigil of a Nation* (New York, 1945). For twentieth-century Chinese thought see Nos. 240–243, below; for economic movements, Nos. 354–368.

See the following for accounts of **religion** as practiced by the masses: (133) Y. C. YANG, *China's Religious Heritage* (New York, 1943); (134) W. J. Clennell, *The Historical Development of Religion in China* (1917; 2d ed., London, 1926); (135) W. E. Soothill, *The Three Religions of China . . .* (1923; 3d ed., London, 1929); (136) J. J. M. de Groot, *The Religious System of China . . .* (Leiden, 1892–1910), in 6 vols.; Nos. 137, 139, 140, below. For references on Confucianism, Taoism, Buddhism, Christianity, and Islam see Nos. 166–175, 184–239, below.

The author of chap. xiv (Folk Religion) and the editor refer the reader to the following: (137) Marcel Granet, *La Religion des Chinois* (Paris, 1922); No. 35, above; (138) Eduard Erkes, "Idols in Pre-Buddhist China," in *Artibus Asiae*, No. 1 (1928), pp. 5–12; (139) John K. Shryock, *The Temples of Anking and Their Cults: A Study of Modern Chinese Religion* (Paris, 1931); (140) Henri Doré, *Recherches sur les superstitions en Chine* (Shanghai, 1913–1938), in 18 vols. (Vols. I–X available in English); (141) Lewis Hodous, *Folkways in China* (London, 1929), for descriptions of seasonal festivals; (142) Florence Ayscough, "Cult of the Spiritual Magistrates of City Walls and Moats," in *A Chinese Mirror: Being Reflections of the Reality behind Appearance* (Boston, 1925); (143) Clarence Burton Day, *Chinese Peasant Cults: A Study of Chinese Paper Gods* (Shanghai, 1940); (144) Clifford H. Plopper, *Chinese Religion Seen through the Proverb* (Shanghai, 1926); (145) Ta CHEN, *Emigrant Communities in South China* (New York, 1940), for the effect of emigration on religion; (146) John C. De Korne, *The Fellowship of Goodness* (mimeographed; Grand Rapids, Mich., 1934), for a study of a modern secret sect.

A complete history of Chinese **philosophy** in English has yet to be written. For surveys in the German language the reader is referred to: (147) Alfred Forke, *Geschichte der altern chinesischen Philosophie* (Hamburg, 1927); (148) Alfred Forke, *Geschichte der mittelalterlichen chinesischen Philosophie* (Hamburg, 1934); (149) Alfred Forke, *Geschichte der neuren chinesischen Philosophie* (Hamburg, 1938). A bird's-eye view of Chinese philosophy may be obtained in: Hu Shih, "Religion and Philosophy in Chinese History," in No. 5, above, pp. 31–58; (150) CHAN Wing-tsit, "The Story of Chinese Philosophy," in *Philosophy: East and West* (ed. by Charles A. Moore; Princeton, 1944), chap. iii. For special studies see: (151) Alfred Forke, *The World-Conception of the Chinese: Their Astronomical, Cosmological and Physico-philosophical Speculations* (London, 1925); (152) Frank Rawlinson, *Chinese Ethical Ideals* (Peiping, 1934); (153) LIN Mousheng, *Men and Ideas: An Informal History of Chinese Political Thought* (New York, 1942).

On ancient Chinese philosophy see, *inter alia*: (154) Hu Shih, *The Development of the Logical Method in Ancient China* (1922; Shanghai, 1928); (155) FUNG Yu-lan, *A History of Chinese Philosophy: The Period of the Philosophers (from the Beginnings to about 100 B.C.)* (trans. by Derk Bodde; Peiping, 1937–); (156) E. R. Hughes (ed. and trans.), *Chinese Philosophy in Classical Times* (London, 1942); (157) Arthur Waley, *Three Ways of Thought in Ancient China* (London, 1939); (158) LIANG Ch'i-ch'ao, *History of Chinese Political Thought during the Early Tsin* [pre-Ch'in] *Period* (trans. by L. T. CHEN; London, 1930); (159) Wu Kuo-cheng, *Ancient Chinese Political Theories* (Shanghai, 1928); (160) LUNG Chien-fu, *The Evolution of Chinese Social Thought* (Los Angeles, 1941).

For source materials on **Confucianism** and **Taoism** see Nos. 160–163, 170, 171, 174, 178–185, below. Note: (161) James Legge (trans.), *The Yi King* [Book of Changes] (Oxford, 1882); (162) Yi-Pao MEI (trans.), *The Ethical and Political Works of Motse* (London, 1929); (163) A. Forke (trans.), "The Chinese Sophists," in *Journal of the North China Branch of the Royal Asiatic Society*, XXXVI (1901–1902), 1–85; (164) W. K. LIAO (trans.), *The Complete Works of Han Fei Tzŭ ... A Classic of Chinese Legalism* (London, 1939). For descriptions of Chinese philosophical terms see: (165) articles by CHAN Wing-tsit, in *The Dictionary of Philosophy* (ed. by D. D. Runes; New York, 1942).

Basic reading materials on ancient **Confucianism (chap. xv)** are: (166) James Legge (trans.), *The Chinese Classics ...* (2d ed., Oxford, 1893–1895), in 5 vols.; (167) Arthur Waley (trans.), *The Analects of Confucius* (London, 1938); (168) Homer H. Dubs (trans.), *The Works of Hsüntze* (London, 1928); (169) LIN Yutang (trans. and ed.), *The Wisdom of Confucius* (New York, 1938). For Mencius see Nos. 166 and 169, above. For systematic studies of ancient Confucianism see: Nos. 147, 150–160, above; (170) Leonard Shihlien Hsü, *The Political Philosophy of Confucianism ...* (New York, 1932); (171) Homer H. Dubs, *Hsüntze, the Moulder of Ancient Confucianism* (London, 1927); (172) Andrew Chih-Yi CHENG, *Hsüntzŭ's Theory of Human Nature and Its Influence on Chinese Thought* (Peiping, 1928).

The development of Confucianism in medieval times is related in: (173) Hu Shih, "The Establishment of Confucianism as a State Religion during the Han Dynasty," in *Journal of the North China Branch of the Royal Asiatic Society*, LX (1929), 20–41; (174) John K. Shryock, *The Origin and Development of the State Cult of Confucius* (New York, 1932); No. 156, above; (175) Reginald F. Johnston, *Confucianism and Modern China* (London, 1934).

Even relatively complete accounts of **Neo-Confucianism (chap. xvi)** are lacking. Brief summaries are contained in Nos. 149 and 150, above. Comprehensive presentations of specific phases may be found in: (176) J. P. Bruce, *Chu Hsi and His Masters: An Introduction to Chu Hsi and the Sung School of Chinese Philosophy* (London, 1923); (177) J. P. Bruce (trans.), *The Philosophy of Human Nature, by Chu Hsi* (London, 1922); (178) FUNG Yu-lan, "The Philosophy of Chu Hsi" (trans. by Derk Bodde), in *Harvard Journal of Asiatic Studies,* Vol. VII, No. 1 (1942), pp. 1–51; (179) Siu-chi HUANG, *Lu Hsiang-shan, a Twelfth-Century Chinese Idealist Philosopher* (New Haven, 1944); (180) Frederick G. Henke (trans.), *The Philosophy of Wang Yang-ming (A.D. 1473–1529)* (Chicago, 1916); (181) WANG Tch'ang-tche, *La Philosophie morale de Wang Yang-ming* (Shanghai, 1936); (182) P. C. Hsu, *Ethical Realism in Neo-Confucian Thought* (Peiping, 1933); (183) FUNG Yu-lan, "The Rise of Neo-Confucianism and Its Borrowings from Buddhism and Taoism" (trans. by Derk Bodde), in *Harvard Journal of Asiatic Studies,* Vol. VII, No. 2 (1942), pp. 89–125.

Source materials on **Taoism (chap. xvii)** include: (184) Paul Carus (trans.), *The Canon of Reason and Virtue . . . Being Lao-Tze's Tao-teh-king* (rev. ed., Chicago, 1927); (185) Arthur Waley (trans.), *The Way and Its Power: A Study of the Tao Tê Ching and Its Place in Chinese Thought* (London, 1935); (186) FUNG Yu-lan (trans.), *Chuang Tzŭ, a New Selected Translation* [chaps. i–vii] *with an Exposition of the Philosophy of Kuo Hsiang* (Shanghai, 1931); (187) Herbert A. Giles (trans.), *Chuang Tzŭ: Mystic, Moralist and Social Reformer* (rev. ed., Shanghai, 1926); No. 157, above; (188) Evan Morgan (trans.), *Tao, the Great Luminant: Essays from Huai Nan Tzŭ* (London, 1935); (189) Lionel Giles (trans.), *Taoist Teachings from the Book of Lieh Tzŭ* (London, 1912); (190) Anton Forke (trans.), *Yang Chu's Garden of Pleasure* (London, 1912); (191) Tenney L. Davis and CH'ÊN Kuo-fu (trans.), "The Inner Chapters of Pao-p'u-tzŭ," in *Proceedings of the American Academy of Arts and Sciences,* LXXIV (1941), 297–325. For studies of Taoist philosophy see Nos. 147–160, above. For discussions on Taoist religion and alchemy see: Nos. 133–145, above; (192) Obed Simon Johnson, *A Study of Chinese Alchemy* (Shanghai, 1928). For Taoist religious teachings see: (193) D. T. Suzuki and Paul Carus (trans.), *T'ai-Shang Kan-Ying P'ien: Treatise of the Exalted One on Response and Retribution* (Chicago, 1906); (194) D. T. Suzuki and Paul Carus (trans.), *Yin Chih Wên: The Tract of the Quiet Way* (Chicago, 1906); (195) Richard Wilhelm (trans.), *The Secret of the Golden Flower* (trans. into English by Cary F. Baynes; London, 1931); (196) Tenney L. Davis and CHAO Yun-ts'ung (trans.), "Wu Chên P'ien: Essay on the Understanding of the Truth," in *Proceedings of the American Academy of Arts and Sciences,* LXXIII (1939), 97–117. For descriptions of Chinese religious terms see: (197) articles by CHAN Wing-tsit in *An Encyclopedia of Religion* (ed. by Vergilius Ferm; New York, 1945).

Some fundamental ideas of **Buddhism (chap. xviii)** may be obtained from the following: (198) Henry Clarke Warren, *Buddhism in Translations* (1896; Cambridge, Mass., 1922); (199) F. Max Müller (ed.), *Sacred Books of the East,* XLIX (1894); (200) D. T. Suzuki (trans.), *Asvaghosha's Discourse on the Awakening of*

Faith in the Mahāyāna (Chicago, 1900); (201) Hendrik Kern (trans.), *Saddharma Puṇḍarīka; or, The Lotus of the True Law* (1884; 2d ed., Oxford, 1909); or (202) the abridged version by W. E. Soothill, *The Lotus of the Wonderful Law* . . . (Oxford, 1930); (203) Clarence Herbert Hamilton (trans.), *Wei Shih Er Shih Lun; or, The Treatise in Twenty Stanzas on Representation-Only* (New Haven, 1938); (204) Louis de La Vallée Poussin (trans.), *Vijñaptimātratāsiddhi: La Siddhi de Hiuen-Tsang* (Paris, 1928, 1929), in 2 vols.; (205) Th. Stcherbatsky (Shcherbatskoï), *The Conception of Buddhist Nirvana* (Leningrad, 1927); (206) Max Walleser (trans.), *Die mittlere Lehre des Nagarjuna* (Heidelberg, 1912); (207) D. T. Suzuki (trans.), *The Lankavatara Sutra* (London, 1932); (208) D. T. Suzuki, *Manual of Zen Buddhism* (Tokyo, 1935).

A reading guide is to be found in: (209) Clarence Herbert Hamilton, *Buddhism in India, Ceylon, China and Japan: A Reading Guide* (Chicago, 1931).

The life of the Buddha is studied in: (210) Herman Oldenburg, *Buddha: His Life, His Doctrine, His Order* (trans. by William Hoey; London, 1928); (211) Edward J. Thomas, *The Life of Buddha as Legend and History* (2d ed., London, 1930); (212) Caroline A. F. Rhys Davids, *Gotama the Man* (London, 1928).

Material on Buddhist philosophy as developed in China is lacking. For Indian background see: (213) A. B. Keith, *Buddhist Philosophy in India and Ceylon* (Oxford, 1923); (214) Edward J. Thomas, *The History of Buddhist Thought* (New York, 1933); (215) Th. Stcherbatsky, *The Central Conception of Buddhism and the Meaning of the Word "Dharma"* (London, 1923); (216) D. T. Suzuki, *Studies in the Lankavatara Sutra* (London, 1930). For development in Zen see: (217–220) D. T. Suzuki, *Essays in Zen Buddhism,* in four series (London, 1927, 1933, 1934, 1938).

Comprehensive accounts of the Buddhist religion in China are given in: (221) Karl L. Reichelt, *Truth and Tradition in Chinese Buddhism* (trans. by Kathrina Van Wagenen Bugge; rev. ed., Shanghai, 1934); (222) Sir Charles [N. E.] Eliot, *Hinduism and Buddhism, an Historical Sketch* (London, 1921), in 3 vols.; (223) Lewis Hodous, *Buddhism and Buddhists in China* (New York, 1924); (224) James B. Pratt, *The Pilgrimage of Buddhism and a Buddhist Pilgrimage* (New York, 1928). See also: (225) Alice Getty, *The Gods of Northern Buddhism: Their History, Iconography, and Evolution through the Northern Buddhist Countries* (1914; 2d ed., Oxford, 1928).

For Lamaism see: (226) Sir Charles Bell, *The Religion of Tibet* (Oxford, 1931); (227) L. Austine Waddell, *The Buddhism of Tibet, or Lamaism* (1895; 2d ed., London, 1934); (228) Albert Grünwedel, *Mythologie du Bouddhisme au Tibet et en Mongolie* . . . (Paris, 1900); (229) F. D. Lessing, *Yung Ho Kung, an Iconography of the Lamaist Cathedral in Peking, with Notes on Lamaist Mythology and Cult* (Stockholm, 1942), Vol. I.

For special topics consult: (230) Paul Demiéville (ed.), *Hôbôgirin: Dictionnaire encyclopédique du Bouddhisme d'après les sources chinoises et japonaises* (Tokyo, A-Chi, 1929; Paris, 1937); (231) W. E. Soothill and Lewis Hodous, *A Dictionary of Chinese Buddhist Terms* . . . (London, 1937).

Historical studies of **Christianity** in China (**chap. xix**) are presented in: (232)

Kenneth Scott Latourette, *A History of Christian Missions in China* (New York, 1929); (233) Kenneth Scott Latourette, *A History of the Expansion of Christianity* (New York, 1937–1944), in 6 vols.; *The Great Century in Northern Africa and Asia, A.D. 1800–A.D. 1914* (New York, 1944), Vol. VI; (234) A. C. Moule, *Christians in China before the Year 1550* (London, 1930); (235) A. C. Moule, *Nestorians in China: Some Corrections and Additions* (London, 1940); (236) Arnold H. Rowbotham, *Missionary and Mandarin: The Jesuits at the Court of China* (Berkeley, Calif., 1942). An appraisal is made in: (237) Lucius C. Porter, *China's Challenge to Christianity* (New York, 1924). See also No. 342, below.

Islam in China may be studied in: (238) Marshall Broomhall, *Islam in China, a Neglected Problem* (London, 1910); (239) D'Ollone *et al., Recherches sur les musulmans chinois* (Paris, 1911).

Some trends in **contemporary Chinese thought (chap. xx)** are traced in: Hu Shih, No. 124, above; (240) Homer H. Dubs, "Recent Chinese Philosophy," in *Journal of Philosophy*, Vol. XXXV, No. 13 (1938), pp. 345–355; (241) Han Yü-shan, "Some Tendencies of Contemporary Chinese Philosophy," *ibid.*, Vol. XXV, No. 19 (1928), pp. 505–513; (242) Tseng Yu-hao, *Modern Chinese Legal and Political Philosophy* (Shanghai, 1930); (243) Kyoson Tsuchida, *Contemporary Thought of Japan and China* (New York, 1927). See also Nos. 125–132, 153, above.

For an introduction to Chinese **art (chaps. xxi–xxii)** see: Lin Yutang, No. 11, above, section on Chinese artistic life; and Dagny Carter, *China Magnificent* (New York, 1935); (244) Roger Fry, "Chinese Art," in *Last Lectures by Roger Fry* (Cambridge, Eng., 1939); (245) Encyclopaedia Britannica, *The Romance of Chinese Art* (Garden City, N.Y., 1936), a collection of illustrated articles; (246) John C. Ferguson, *Survey of Chinese Art* (Shanghai, 1939); No. 31, above, an aesthetic approach.

Treatises on the art and spirit of Chinese **calligraphy (chap. xxi)** are: (247) Lucy Driscoll and Kenji Toda, *Chinese Calligraphy* (Chicago, 1935); (248) Chiang Yee, *Chinese Calligraphy: An Introduction to Its Aesthetics and Technique* (London, 1938). See also No. 11, above.

For interpretative studies of Chinese **painting (chaps. xxi–xxii)** the reader is referred to: (249) Laurence Binyon, *The Flight of the Dragon: An Essay on the Theory and Practice of Art in China and Japan, Based on Original Sources* (London, 1911); (250) Laurence Binyon, *The Spirit of Man in Asian Art* (Cambridge, Mass., 1935); (251) G. H. Edgell, Kojiro Tomita, A. K. Chiu, and R. P. Dart, "1500 Years of Chinese Painting," in *Art News* (New York), April 1, 1944; (252) Chiang Yee, *The Chinese Eye: An Interpretation of Chinese Painting* (London, 1937). What Chinese painters have thought of their art is recorded in: (253) Shio Sakanishi (trans.), *The Spirit of the Brush, Being the Outlook of Chinese Painters on Nature from Eastern Chin to Five Dynasties, A.D. 317–960* (London, 1939); (254) Kuo Hsi, *An Essay on Landscape Painting* (trans. by Shio Sakanishi; London, 1935); (255) Osvald Sirén, *The Chinese on the Art of Painting* (Peiping, 1936). For historical studies see: (256) Arthur Waley, *An Introduction to the Study of Chinese Painting* (London, 1923); (257) Laurence Binyon, *Painting in the Far East* . . . (rev. ed., London, 1923); (258) Osvald Sirén, *A History of Early*

Chinese Painting (London, 1933), in 2 vols.; (259) Osvald Sirén, *A History of Later Chinese Painting* (London, 1938), in 2 vols.; (260) Arthur de Carle Sowerby, *Nature in Chinese Art* (New York, 1940).

A general survey of Chinese **architecture (chap. xxiii)** is offered in: (261) D. G. Mirams, *A Brief History of Chinese Architecture* (Shanghai, Hongkong, and Singapore, 1940); (262) H. Killam Murphy, "An Architectural Renaissance in China," in *Asia*, XXVIII (1928), 468–475, 507–509. For advanced study the following are recommended: (263) Ernst von Boerschmann, *Chinesische Architektur* (Berlin, 1925), in 2 vols.; (264) Osvald Sirén, *A History of Early Chinese Art* (London, 1930), Vol. IV; (265) Osvald Sirén, *The Imperial Palaces of Peking* (London, 1926), in 3 vols.; (266) Osvald Sirén, *The Walls and Gates of Peking* (London, 1924); (267) Gustav Ecke and Paul Demiéville, *The Twin Pagodas of Zayton* . . . (Cambridge, Mass., 1935); (268) J. Prip-Møller, *Chinese Buddhist Monasteries: Their Plan and Its Function as a Setting for Buddhist Monastic Life* (London and Copenhagen, 1937); (269) Daniel Sheets Dye, *A Grammar of Chinese Lattice* (Cambridge, Mass., 1937), in 2 vols. For Chinese conception, styles, and designs of gardens see: Florence Ayscough, "The Chinese Idea of a Garden," in No. 142, above; (270) Dorothy Graham, *Chinese Gardens: Gardens of the Contemporary Scene* (New York, 1938). For photographs see: (271) Florence Lee Powell, *In the Chinese Garden* . . . (New York, 1943); (272) Henry INN, *Chinese Houses and Gardens* (ed. by S. C. LEE; Honolulu, 1924). Of interest also is: (273) Eleanor von Erdberg, *Chinese Influence on European Garden Structures* (Cambridge, Mass., 1936). For Chinese architectural designs and engineering see: (274) LI Ming-chung, *Ying-tsao Fa-shih* (1103; 2d ed., 1145, later reissued by the Commercial Press, Shanghai).

On Chinese **sculpture** consult: (275) Leigh Ashton, *An Introduction to the Study of Chinese Sculpture* (London, 1924); (276) Osvald Sirén, *Chinese Sculpture from the Fifth to the Fourteenth Century* (London, 1925), in 4 vols.; (277) Paul Pelliot, *Les Grottes de Touen-Houang* . . . (Paris, 1914–1924), in 6 vols.; (278) Alan Priest, *Chinese Sculpture in the Metropolitan Museum of Art* (New York (1944); (279) J. Hackin *et al.*, *Studies in Chinese Art and Some Indian Influence* (London, 1938); (280) C. Hentze, *Chinese Tomb Figures: A Study in the Beliefs and Folklore of Ancient China* (London, 1928); (281) Mary A. Mullikin and Anna M. Hotchkis, *Buddhist Sculpture at the Yun Kang Caves* (Peiping, 1935).

The following works on Chinese **drama (chap. xxiv)** are recommended: (282) "Drama," pp. 148–149, in *Encyclopaedia Sinica* (ed. by Samuel Couling; Shanghai, 1917); and No. 318 below, pp. 256–275, 325–328; (283) A. E. Zucker, *The Chinese Theatre* (Boston, 1925), for historical and literary aspects of the art; (284) Cecilia S. L. ZUNG, *Secrets of the Chinese Drama* . . . (London, 1937); and (285) L. C. Arlington, *The Chinese Drama, from the Earliest Times until Today* . . . (Shanghai, 1930), for stagecraft and music; (286) L. C. Arlington and Harold Acton, *Famous Chinese Plays* (Peiping, 1937), for synopsis; (287) S. I. HSIUNG (trans.), *The Romance of the Western Chamber (Hsi Hsiang Chi): A Chinese Play Written in the Thirteenth Century* (London, 1935; New York,

1936); (288) Vincenz Hundhausen (trans.), *Die Rückkehr der Seele* ... (Zurich, 1937); (289) S. I. Hsiung (trans.), *Lady Precious Stream: An Old Chinese Play Done into English According to Its Traditional Style* (1934; 2d ed., London, 1935); (290) Benjamin March, *Chinese Shadow-Figure Plays and Their Making* (Detroit, 1938); (291) Genevieve Wimsatt, *Chinese Shadow Shows* (Cambridge, Mass., 1936).

General accounts of Chinese **music** are given in: Y. R. Chao, "Music," in No. 5, above, pp. 82–96; (292) Chao Mei-Pa, *The Yellow Bell* ... (Baldwin, Md., 1934). Classical music is analyzed in: (293) John Hazedel Levis, *Foundations of Chinese Musical Art* (Peiping, 1936). For Chinese philosophy of music see: "The Classic of Music," in No. 169, above, pp. 251–272.

For the spirit of Chinese **poetry (chap. xxi)** see: (294) C. W. Luh, *On Chinese Poetry* (Peiping, 1935); (295) John C. Wu, "The Four Seasons of T'ang Poetry," in *T'ien Hsia Monthly,* VI (1938), 342–368, 453–474; VII (1938), 51–88, 357–401; VIII (1939), 155–176; IX (1939), 48–79. Among translations of Chinese poems are: (296) Arthur Waley (trans.), *The Book of Songs* (London, 1937); (297) Arthur Waley (trans.), *Translations from the Chinese* (New York, 1941); (298) Arthur Waley (trans.), *A Hundred and Seventy Chinese Poems* (1918; 2d ed., New York, 1936); (299) Arthur Waley (trans.), *More Translations from the Chinese* (New York, 1919); (300) Arthur Waley (trans.), *The Temple and Other Poems* (London, 1923); (301) Lim Boon Keng (trans.), *The Li Sao, an Elegy on Encountering Sorrows, by Chu Yuan* (Shanghai, 1929); (302) Florence Ayscough (trans.), *Tu Fu: The Autobiography of a Chinese Poet, A.D. 712–759* (London; Boston and New York, 1929), Vol. I; (303) Florence Ayscough (trans.), *Travels of a Chinese Poet: Tu Fu, Guest of Rivers and Lakes, A.D. 759–770* (London and New York, 1934), Vol. II; (304) S. Obata (trans.), *The Works of Li Po, the Chinese Poet* (New York, 1922); (305) Cyril D. Le Gros Clark (trans.), *The Prose Poetry of Su Tung-p'o* (Shanghai, 1935); (306) Herbert A. Giles (trans.), *Gems of Chinese Literature: Verse* (2d rev. ed., London, 1923); (307) L. Cranmer-Byng (trans.), *A Lute of Jade* ... (London, 1909); (308) L. Cranmer-Byng (trans.), *A Feast of Lanterns* (1916; London, 1924); (309) Witter Bynner and Kiang Kang-hu (trans.), *The Jade Mountain* ... (New York, 1929); (310) Ts'ai T'ing-kan (trans.), *Chinese Poems in English Rhymes* (Chicago, 1932); (311) Arthur E. Christy (trans.), *Images in Jade* ... (New York, 1929); (312) Florence Ayscough and Amy Lowell, *Fir-Flower Tablets, Poems Translated from the Chinese* (Boston, 1921); also (313) *Florence Ayscough and Amy Lowell: Correspondence of a Friendship* [dealing largely with *Fir-Flower Tablets*] (edited, with a preface, by Harley Farnsworth MacNair; Chicago, 1946); (314) W. J. B. Fletcher (trans.), *Gems of Chinese Verses* (Shanghai, 1918); (315) W. J. B. Fletcher (trans.), *More Gems of Chinese Verses* (Shanghai, 1919); (316) Clara M. Candlin (trans.), *The Herald Wind: Translations of Sung Dynasty Poems, Lyrics and Songs* [*tz'ǔ*] (London, 1933); (317) Harold Acton and Ch'en Shih Hsiang (trans.), *Modern Chinese Poetry* (London, 1936). See also No. 9, above.

The history of Chinese **literature (chaps. xxi, xxiv–xxviii)** is briefly narrated in: (318) Herbert A. Giles, *A History of Chinese Literature* (1901; New York,

1924); and more extensively in: (319) Wilhelm Grube, *Geschichte der chinesischen Litteratur* (Leipzig, 1902). See also: (320) A. Wylie, *Notes on Chinese Literature, with Introductory Remarks on the Progressive Advancement of the Art; and a List of Translations from the Chinese into Various European Languages* (1867; London, 1923).

For Chinese prose see: Nos. 156, 161–169, 176–177, 180, 184–190, above; and the following anthologies: (321) Hsu Sung-nien, *Anthologie de la littérature chinoise* (Paris, 1933); (322) Herbert A. Giles, *Gems of Chinese Literature: Prose* (2d rev. ed., London, 1923); (323) Lin Yutang (ed.), *The Wisdom of China and India* (New York, 1942); (324) E. D. Edwards (trans.), *Chinese Prose Literature of the T'ang Period, A.D. 618–906* (London, 1937, 1938), in 2 vols.; (325) Cyril D. Le Gros Clark (trans.), *Selections from the Works of Su Tung-p'o* (London, 1931); (326) Georges Margouliès, *Evolution de la prose artistique chinoise* (Munich, 1929).

For a discussion of the Chinese novel see: (327) Pearl S. Buck, *The Chinese Novel* ... (New York, 1939). Among translations of Chinese short stories and novels are: (328) Wang Chi-chen (trans.), *Traditional Chinese Tales,* and (329) *Contemporary Chinese Stories* (New York, 1944), in 2 vols.; (330) Pearl S. Buck (trans.), *All Men Are Brothers (Shui Hu Chuan)* (New York, 1933), in 2 vols.; (331) Wang Chi-chen (trans.), *Dream of the Red Chamber* (New York, 1929); (332) C. H. Brewitt-Taylor (trans.), *San Kuo Chih Yen I; or, Romance of the Three Kingdoms* (Shanghai, 1925, 1926), in 2 vols.; (333) Arthur Waley (trans.), *Monkey, by Wu Ch'êng-ên* (London, 1942; New York, 1943); (334) Herbert A. Giles (trans.), *Strange Stories from a Chinese Studio* (1916; New York, 1925); (335) Clement Egerton (trans.), *The Golden Lotus: A Translation, from the Chinese Original, of the Novel Chin P'ing Mei* (London, 1939), in 4 vols.; (336) Wang Chi-chen (trans.), *Ah Q and Others* (New York, 1941); (337) Edgar Snow (comp. and ed.), *Living China: Modern Chinese Short Stories* (London, 1936; New York, 1937); (338) T'ien Chün, *Village in August* (New York, 1942); (339) Lau Shaw, *Ricksha Boy* (trans. by Evan King; New York, 1945).

The author of **chap. xxix** (Modern Education) has listed these for further reference: (340) P.E.N. Club of Shanghai, *Education in China during the War* (Hongkong, n.d.); (341) Hubert Freyn, *Chinese Education in the War* (Shanghai, 1940); (342) William Ernest Hocking et al., *Re-thinking Missions, a Laymen's Inquiry after One Hundred Years* (New York, 1932); (343) Ping Wen Kuo, *The Chinese System of Public Education* (New York, 1915); (344) Paul Monroe, *China: A Nation in Evolution* (New York, 1927); (345) Cyrus H. Peake, *Nationalism and Education in Modern China* (New York, 1932); (346) C. H. Becker et al., *The Reorganization of Education in China* (Paris, 1932); (347) R. E. Speer, *"Re-thinking Missions" Examined* (New York, 1933); (348) W. T. Tao and C. P. Chen, *Education in China* (1924; Peking, 1925); (349) G. R. Twiss, *Science and Education in China* (Shanghai, 1925); (350) Dyke Van Putten, *Christian Higher Education in China* (unpublished doctoral dissertation, University of Chicago); (351) Le P. Etienne Zi (Siu), S.J., *Pratique des examens littéraires en Chine* (Shanghai, 1894); Nos. 411–414, below. See also: (352) Pearl S. Buck, *Tell* the *People—Mass Education in China* (New York, 1945); (353) Chinese Library Association, *Libraries in China* (Peiping, 1935).

For the various **economic aspects** of China (**chaps. xxxi–xxxiv**) see: (354) SUN Yat-sen, *The International Development of China* (1921; 2d ed., New York, 1929); (355) F. H. King, *Farmers of Forty Centuries; or, Permanent Agriculture in China, Korea and Japan* (Madison, Wis., 1911); (356) John Lossing Buck, *Land Utilization in China* ... (Chicago, 1937); (357) John Lossing Buck, *An Agricultural Survey of Szechuan Province* (New York, 1937); (358) CHEN Hanseng, *Landlord and Peasant in China: A Study of the Agrarian Crisis in South China* (New York, 1936); (359) *Agrarian China: Selected Source Materials from Chinese Authors* (trans. and comp. by Research Staff, Institute of Pacific Relations, Chicago, 1938); (360) Hsiao-tung FEI and Chih-i CHANG, *Earthbound China: A Study of Rural Economy in Yunnan* (Chicago, 1945); (361) R. H. Tawney, *Land and Labour in China* (New York, 1932); (362) CHANG Kia-ngau, *China's Struggle for Railroad Development* (New York, 1943); (363) Frank M. Tamagna, *Banking and Finance in China* (New York, 1942); (364) Ch'ao-ting CHI, *War-Time Economic Development in China* (New York, 1942); (365) Hubert Freyn, *Free China's New Deal* (New York, 1943); (366) H. D. FONG, *Post War Industrialization of China* (Washington, D.C., 1942); (367) Kuo-heng SHIH, *China Enters the Machine Age* ... (trans by Hsiao-tung FEI and Francis L. K. HSU; Cambridge, Mass., 1944); No. 389, below; (368) Nym Wales, *The Chinese Labor Movement* (New York, 1945).

For reference on Chinese **foreign trade** the author of **chap. xxxiii** (International Trade) recommends: (369) T. R. Barnister, "A History of the External Trade of China, 1834–81," Chinese Maritime Customs, *Decennial Reports, 1922–1931,* Vol. I; (370) T. R. Barnister, "Synopsis of the External Trade of China, 1882–1931," *ibid.*; (371) Chinese Maritime Customs, *The Trade of China* (annual and decennial reports since 1882); (372) LI Choh-ming, "An Analysis of the Recent Trends of China's Foreign Trade" (unpublished M.A. thesis, University of California, 1933); (373) LI Choh-ming, "China's International Trade Statistics: An Evaluation," in *Nankai Social and Economic Quarterly,* April, 1937; (374) LI Choh-ming, "Theory of International Trade under Silver Exchange," in *Quarterly Journal of Economics,* August, 1939; (375) C. F. Remer, *Foreign Investments in China* (New York, 1933); (376) A. J. Sargent, *Anglo-Chinese Commerce and Diplomacy* (Oxford, 1907); (377) C. S. SEE, *The Foreign Trade of China* (New York, 1919); (378) Chih TSANG, *China's Postwar Markets* (New York, 1945).

The following books bear on certain aspects of China in **war and peace** (**chaps. ix–xii, xxxiii**): (379) Generalissimo CHIANG Kai-shek, *Resistance and Reconstruction: Messages during China's Six Years of War, 1937–1943* (New York, 1943); (380) Sven Hedin, *Chiang Kai-shek, Marshal of China* (trans. by Bernard Norbelie; New York, 1940); (381) Harley Farnsworth MacNair, *The Real Conflict between China and Japan: An Analysis of Opposing Ideologies* (Chicago, 1938); (382) Chinese Ministry of Information, *China after Five Years of War* (New York, 1942); (383) Hollington K. TONG (ed.), *China: After Seven Years of War*

(New York, 1945); (384) Lawrence K. Rosinger, *China's Wartime Politics* (Princeton, 1944); (385) Harley Farnsworth MacNair (ed.), *Voices from Unoccupied China* (Chicago, 1944); (386) SUN Fo, *China Looks Forward* (New York, 1944); (387) S. R. CHOW, *Winning the Peace in the Pacific* . . . (New York, 1944); (388) Owen Lattimore, *Solution in Asia* (Boston, 1945); (389) David Nelson Rowe, *China among the Powers* (New York, 1945); (390) Nathaniel Peffer, *Basis for Peace in the Far East* (New York, 1942); (391) Institute of Pacific Relations, *Security in the Pacific* (New York, 1945).

Among **periodicals** dealing chiefly with the current scene are: (392) *Far Eastern Quarterly* (New York); (393) *Pacific Affairs* (New York); (394) *Far Eastern Survey* (New York); (395) *Asia and the Americas* (New York). The Chinese government publishes: (396) *China at War* (New York); (397) *Contemporary China* (New York). Dealing chiefly with China's history and culture are: (398) *T'ien Hsia Monthly* (Shanghai); (399) *China Journal* (Shanghai); (400) *Journal of the North China Branch of the Royal Asiatic Society* (Shanghai); (401) *Monumenta Serica* (Peiping); (402) *Journal of the American Oriental Society* (New Haven); (403) *Harvard Journal of Asiatic Studies* (Cambridge, Mass.); (404) *Journal Asiatique* (Paris); (405) *T'oung Pao, Archives concernant l'histoire, les langues, la géographie, l'éthnographie et les arts de l'Asie orientale* (Leiden); (406) *Bulletin de l'Ecóle Française d'Extrême-Orient* (Hanoï); (407) *Mitteilungen des Seminars für orientalische Sprachen an der Friederich-Wilhelms-Universität zu Berlin* (Berlin); (408) *Asia Major, a Journal Devoted to the Study of the Languages, Arts and Civilization of the Far East and Central Asia* (Leipzig). For earlier periods see: (409) *Chinese Repository* (Canton, 1832–1851); (410) *China Review; or, Notes and Queries on the Far East* (Hongkong, 1872–1901).

Yearbooks are: (411) *China Handbook* (New York, 1937–1943, 1945); (412) *Chinese Year Book* (ed. by KWEI Chung-shu; Shanghai, 1935–1939); (413) *China Yearbook* (ed. by H. G. W. Woodhead; Chicago, 1921–1939); (414) *China Christian Year Book* (Shanghai, 1919–1939).

For **bibliography** see: (415) Henri Cordier, *Bibliotheca Sinica* (Paris, 1904–1924); (416) Charles S. Gardner, *A Union List of Selected Western Books on China in American Libraries* (2d rev. ed., Washington, D.C., 1938); (417) Earl H. Pritchard, "Far Eastern Bibliography," in No. 392, above; (418) L. Carrington Goodrich and H. C. Fenn, *A Syllabus of the History of Chinese Civilization and Culture* (1929; 2d ed., New York, 1934); (419) Robert J. Kerner, *Northeastern Asia: A Selected Bibliography* (Contributions to the Bibliography of the Relations of China, Russia, and Japan, with Special Reference to Korea, Manchuria, Mongolia, and Eastern Siberia, in Oriental and European Languages) (Berkeley, 1939), in 2 vols.

INDEX

Index

Acknowledgment

The General Editor desires to record here his sincere appreciation of the splendid coöperation he has received from the staff of the University of California Press in the editing of the manuscript and the making of this book. In particular he is indebted to Mr. Harold A. Small, the Editor of the Press; to Miss Genevieve Rogers for editorial assistance in every part of the volume; and to Miss Ellen Gordon for accurate and painstaking typing and secretarial work.